OBLIGATIONS IN PRIVATE LAW

edited by

T. Brettel Dawson

Department of Law
Carleton University

CANADIAN LEGAL STUDIES SERIES

Captus Press

Canadian Legal Studies Series
Obligations in Private Law

Captus Press Inc.
Units 14 & 15
1600 Steeles Avenue West
Concord, ON
L4K 4M2
Telephone: (416) 736–5537
Fax: (416) 736–5793
Email: Info@captus.com
Internet: http://www.captus.com

Library and Archives Canada Cataloguing in Publication

Obligations in private law / edited by T. Brettel Dawson.

(Canadian legal studies series)
Includes bibliographical references.
ISBN 978-1-55322-252-1

1. Obligations (Law) — Canada 2. Contracts — Canada.
I. Dawson, B. (Brettel)   II. Series: Canadian legal studies series

KE474.C64O24 2012   346.7102   C2011-908356-6
KF807.2.O24 2012

Canada ⋮ *We acknowledge the financial support of the Government of Canada through the Canada Book Fund for our publishing activities.*

098765432
Printed and bound in Canada

Table of Contents

II
Contracts

III
Unjust Enrichment

IV
Conscience in Private Law

Dedication

Dedicated, as always, to Mary Angela, who nourishes mind and soul and body; and to the legions of students whose thoughtful interaction with me as I have taught in this area has enlivened and grounded the study.

Introduction and Preface

This edited collection of materials was developed for a course on Obligations in Private Law offered by the Department of Law at Carleton University to examine "the concepts employed by the law for creating and enforcing legal obligations between persons within society, including contract, tort, unjust enrichment and fiduciary obligation. Consideration is given to the role of persons and the role of the state in ordering private legal obligations." These subjects can (and do) form the basis for entire courses, which suggests that our treatment of them this book is selective and driven by a particular and limited focus. Also, we discuss the law of torts; we focus on negligence causing personal injury rather than the many other dimensions of tort liability. Our focus is on how tort law protects bodily integrity and navigates policy questions between individual autonomy and social responsibility. Is tort law a sentinel of safety? Within the consideration of contract law, material is focused on doctrines of formation, terms, and how they have changed in response to (i) changes in how markets function, (ii) the changing regulatory involvement of the state, and (iii) shifts in the role of the judiciary. The broadest contours of unjust enrichment (restitution) are addressed by comparing the approach of the courts to defective transactions in the market, on the one hand, and to resolving property disputes in the family in the absence of a formal legislative framework (such as that provided by marriage). A similar broad brush approach is taken to the law of fiduciary obligation, locating it within the thesis that the private law of obligations is concerned not only with markets but also with ensuring that we can rely on one another.

Some animating questions in the materials include the following: How and why does private law categorize certain fact patterns into distinct legal subjects? What interests does private law seek to protect and promote through the law of obligations? How do the contours of private law obligation reflect (changing) social and economic contexts and philosophical (theoretical) tenets? How do the courts navigate and balance policy considerations in responding to new situations? How do ideas of individual autonomy and choice in the common law interact with equitable concerns to protect people from abuses of power or the consequences of systemic inequality?

By the end of their study of these materials, readers should be able to (i) differentiate between the kinds (or branches) of obligations in private law; (ii) identify the essential principles of obligation in each branch, as derived from leading cases; (iii) explain how private law principles reflect social and economic objectives; (iv) link policy considerations and the normative vision of judges to legal outcomes; (v) contrast the approaches of the common law and equity, particularly in relation to defective transactions and broken relationships; and (vi) reconcile residual principles in private law (such as reliance, confidentiality and conscience) to the dominant principles of inviolability and exchange in the market.

The book has five main divisions. In the first, the Introduction, the taxonomy (or conceptual structure) of private law is introduced, together with a view of its main functions to systematize, develop and locate obligations in a social structure. The *Norberg* case, which involved an older medical doctor trading drugs for sexual favours from a younger, addicted patient, is used as an example of how law sifts through and organizes certain facts into distinct patterns from which obligation may (or may not) arise. The judges in that case took sharply divergent approaches to what kind of obligation (or breaches) were involved, with a resulting divergence in how the issues were stated and resolved. The three parts of the book that follow consider the classic division of the private law of obligations. They consider, in turn, the law of torts (obligations for harms to persons and property arising from actions that the law regards as negligent), the law of contract (relationships based on exchange of goods or services for value provided), and the law of unjust enrichment (where the law seeks to repair some defects in formal legal relationships to avoid market principles being subverted by windfalls, or self-help, or profits being made from wrongs). The final part of the book is organized around the concept of conscience in private law — a theme that has always been present in private law (through cross-cutting principles of reliance and confidentiality and long-standing prohibitions on undue influence), and that, arguably, is increasing in scope and importance. Our case studies address the estoppel, fiduciary duties and the law's dalliance with redressing inequality of bargaining power. The materials close with an invitation to use theory to gain a deeper appreciation of and perspective on the various values and concepts that are in play in the field of private law obligations.

This book has genetic links of its own to the earlier Carleton University Course, *Introduction to Private Law Relationships*, and to various collections to which I contributed for that course. The threads of many colleagues are evident in the intellectual interweaving of the concepts and sources in this collection.

Thanks as always to the impressive and indefatigable team at Captus Press, including Lily Chu, Pauline Lai and Randy Hoffman. My Teaching Assistants, including Eric Vallilee and Molly Stogran, also played an important research role.

Chelsea
November 2011

(a) Private Right and Public Interest[†]

Stephen Waddams

It is common for writers to relate legal concepts to each other in terms of such metaphors as maps and organisational or taxonomic schemes. Distinctions are drawn among contract, tort, and unjust enrichment, and between obligations and property, and, at a higher level of generality, between private rights and public policy. These distinctions are then commonly depicted as distinct areas on a map, or as separate classes, orders, genera, and species in a taxonomic scheme. Metaphors may illuminate a complex subject, but any metaphor, if pressed too far, is apt to distort. The ideas of mapping and taxonomy in law owe their attraction partly to their indeterminacy and variability. Mapping, as applied to law, is not a single metaphor, but multiple metaphors: the idea of a political map is not the same metaphor as the idea of a map of physical geography, and the idea of an urban map differs from the idea of a global map of seas and continents. Any set of ideas may claim its map, but different writers have used the word in different ways. Blackstone spoke of a map,[1] and his map (rights of persons, rights of things, private wrongs, public wrongs) was useful for his purpose but plainly did not seek to set out mutually exclusive categories. Many private law obligations might fall simultaneously into all of his first three books. Modern writers, by contrast, have often envisaged a map that separates obligations rather as a map of physical geography separates places (Ottawa is in Canada, and therefore not in Europe) or as a taxonomical scheme separates biological specimens (an animal is either an insect or a mammal, but cannot be both).

Some maps and taxonomic schemes claim, expressly or by implication, to be descriptive of the past. In that case the accuracy of the map or scheme can be assessed by historical evidence, as a geographical map may be compared with the terrain it depicts, or a taxonomic scheme may be tested by whether it includes all known specimens; in case of discrepancy, of course, it must be the map or scheme, not the terrain or collection of specimens, that is amended.

Actual assertions about the past should be tested and if they turn out to be false, should be contradicted. So, if it were asserted that every legal obligation has been derived from one only of three or four discrete concepts, this assertion could be contradicted by evidence that some legal obligations have been derived from the concurrent and cumulative operation of several concepts. It is true of many rules of private law that they have not been derived exclusively from a single concept. The law of vicarious liability cannot be derived entirely from the concept of fault, nor can the law of agency be derived entirely from the idea of consent, and so a map or scheme with fault, consent, and unjust enrichment as primary and mutually exclusive categories would not accurately describe the past. If it were sought to marginalise the non-conforming cases by suggesting that instances of vicarious liability and agency had been infrequent or of small importance, the criteria of frequency and importance should be demanded: if testable, the assertions should be tested by historical evidence, and if untestable, this should be pointed

---

† Michael Bryan, ed., *Private Law in Theory and Practice* (New York: Routledge Cavendish, 2007) chapter 1 at 2–5, 7–10, 16–17, 23. [Notes/references omitted.] Reproduced by permission of Taylor & Francis Books UK.

out. A statement that could not be falsified by historical evidence might be valid, but it would not be a statement about the past.

Alternatively a map or scheme might depict an ideal. A writer might propose that for reasons (for example) of ethics, utility, logic, elegance or of conformity with a philosophical or political system, or with another legal system (ancient or modern), every legal obligation *should be* derived from one only of three or four discrete concepts. This would be a quite different undertaking. It could not, of course, be refuted by historical evidence, but then neither could it be supported by such evidence. To vindicate such a proposal it would be necessary to identify the rules of existing law that would be altered by it, and to persuade the reader of the superior virtue of the value underlying the proposed scheme (ethics, utility, logic, elegance, etc.). If the rules in question were of long standing and answered to an instinctive sense of fairness or convenience this would be a difficult task — to abolish vicarious liability and the law of agency for the sake of elegance would imply a very high view of elegance as an unqualified and overriding human good — but if the argument succeeded, a persuasive case for reform would have been made out.

Each of these two approaches has been common in legal discourse, and each is valuable, but what is undesirable (I would suggest) is to run them together, using the proposed map or scheme to eliminate or marginalize inconsistent features of the past, and then using the past, so pruned, as evidence in support of the map or scheme. Such an approach tends to assume what is sought to be proved; it confuses description of the past with prescription for the future; it produces assertions about the past that cannot be falsified (or tested) because contradictory evidence is automatically marginalized; and it produces prescriptions for the future that cannot be evaluated because neither the extent to which the law is to be changed nor the underlying reason for making the change is made explicit.

The conclusion I would draw is not that maps and taxonomic schemes are useless, nor that better maps and schemes are needed, but that the metaphors of mapping and taxonomy should not be pressed too far. If we wish to understand Rouen Cathedral (to adopt Calabresi's well-known metaphor, 'one view of the cathedral')[2] we need more views or perspectives, not just a better ground plan, or a catalogue of building materials.

. . . .

The topic of our attention is the relation between principle and policy in private law. Peter Cane has observed that 'the word "policy" is one of the most under-analysed terms in the modern legal lexicon'.[5] I agree and would suggest that there is much uncertainty also in the meaning of the word 'principle'. There is never a single agreed principle that applies to a controversial legal question; principles may be stated and restated at an infinite number of levels of generality; often principles conflict with each other; any legal rule, as Hart pointed out, may be called a principle.[6] As with other legal ideas the meaning of the word varies according to what is contrasted: for example, 'principle and policy', 'principle and precedent', 'principle and authority', 'principle and pragmatism', 'principle and practice', 'principle and utility'. Commonly the word is used to signify a reason or rule framed at a higher level of generality than another: 'general principle' as opposed to a particular rule, instance, or application. Principles confidently asserted by one judge or writer may be equally confidently contradicted by others at another time or place, or by dissenting judges at the same time and place. 'In the law of England, certain principles are fundamental. One is that only a person who is a party to a contract can sue on it,' Lord Haldane asserted confidently in 1915.[7] But the law had been different 50 years earlier, and it has changed subsequently, in some jurisdictions by judicial development and in others by statute. On the same point Viscount Simonds said, in 1962, having quoted Lord Haldane's assertion, "The law is developed by the application of old principles to new circumstances. Therein lies its genius. Its reform by the abrogation of those principles is the task not of the courts of law but of Parliament."[8] But, in an uncodified system, it is always a matter of judgment whether a proposed change in the law is an application of an established principle or the creation of a new one. The results in particular cases depend entirely on the level of generality at which principles are framed. The denial of specific performance in a land sale contract, for example, has been called a 'principled approach'[9] on the premise that the principle is that specific performance is only available in sales of unique property. But if the principle were stated at a higher level of generality, for example that contracts should be observed, or that sales of land should normally be enforced, the opposite result would appear to be principled. Neil Duxbury has said, with reference to Pollock's attempt to discover the principles of contract law, that "jurists when they dedicate themselves seriously to determining principles of law, will almost inevitably discover instances where those principles are ambiguous, incoherent, insufficiently developed or even absent."[10] Commonly the word is used to mean a reason in support of a legal conclusion that the writer considers persuasive, legitimate, or satisfactory: conclusions that are approved are never called unprincipled. The holding that a racially discriminatory contract is unenforceable is clearly an instance where modern policy (against racial discrimination) has overridden a legal principle (enforceability of contracts), but no one who agrees with the policy would venture to describe the holding as 'unprincipled'.

. . . .

Many shades of opinion are to be found among judges and academics on the question of the relation between private law and public policy. Three main strands may be discerned. First is the view that the two are separate; legal rules are to be derived or deduced strictly from formal legal sources, the function of private law being not the creation of law in the public interest, but the declaration and application of pre-existing law for the prevention and correction of injustice between the individual parties to each dispute. Second, there is the view that when courts are called upon to create a new rule, or to modify an old one, or to extend it to a new situation, they address the question of whether the proposed rule would be, on balance, beneficial to the community; assessment of this question requires the weighing of the costs and benefits of the proposed rule as it will be applied in the future to parties other than the individual litigants in the current case. Third is the view that an element of judgment is frequently involved that includes broad social and political considerations. There are many intervening combinations and shades of opinion.

The three main views correspond broadly with what may, for sake of convenience, be epitomised as principle, utility, and policy. These have sometimes been presented as competing 'theories', of which the reader is impliedly invited to choose one and reject the other two. But from a historical standpoint they appear rather as complementary strands in a single rope, or different dimensions of a single phenomenon. They merge into each other, because, where a new legal problem presents itself for decision, it has not been possible to consider what would be a just rule for the particular parties without to some extent considering the consequences of the proposed rule in other cases. Principle and policy, though sometimes contrasted, have been in practice inseparable, for principles have been adopted to give effect to poli-

cies, and adherence to principle has been itself a policy. Holmes wrote that judges take into account 'what is expedient in the community concerned', adding that 'every important principle which is developed by litigation is in fact and at bottom the result of more or less definitely understood views of public policy'.[12] Emphasis has varied from time to time and from one jurisdiction to another, but elements of all three dimensions have been consistently present, sometimes on the lips of a single judge in different cases, or even in the same case.[13]

In the important eighteenth-century case of *Omychund v Barker*,[14] where the issue was the admissibility of the evidence of a witness who could not take the Christian form of oath, all three dimensions were evident. Counsel (William Murray, later Lord Mansfield), arguing in favour of admissibility, said that the question was 'whether upon principles of reason justice and convenience this witness ought to be admitted'.[15] His fellow counsel (Dudley Rider, also, like Murray, a future Chief Justice of the King's Bench) said that 'trade requires it [admission of the testimony]; policy requires it'. The Lord Chancellor (Hardwicke) relied both on the principle of justice between the parties and on the overt policy consideration that 'if we did not give this credence, courts abroad would not allow our determinations here to be valid'.[16] This was also the case in which Murray said, in urging judicial reform of the law, that the common law 'works itself pure'.[17] The remark has sometimes been quoted out of context to suggest that Murray favoured a purity of formal legal principle, but it is evident that 'purity' did not, in Murray's mind, nor in the Chancellor's, exclude considerations of utility and policy, and it certainly did not require that policy decisions should be left to parliament: Murray's argument was to precisely the opposite effect. All three dimensions (principle, utility, and policy) can derive support from historical evidence. But from this it necessarily follows also that historical evidence cannot support a claim of any one of them to be the *exclusive* explanation of private law.

. . . .

To these instances should be added the many cases where considerations of public policy have played an auxiliary role concurrently with considerations of property, contract, wrongdoing, and unjust enrichment. Together these examples show that judgment, in a broad sense, has played an important part, and sometimes a crucial part, in private law adjudication. On the basis of such evidence it was suggested, in the first half of the twentieth century, by the school of thought loosely known as[48] 'American legal realism'[49] that formal legal reasoning was often fictitious, and this line of thinking was taken up in the second half of the twentieth century, and given a powerful political edge, by the school known (again loosely) as 'critical legal studies', and also by writers who have shown that judgment on matters of social policy has often been influenced by disputable assumptions about race and gender. These lines of thinking have drawn attention to an important aspect of the relation between law and policy, and they support the conclusion that judgment on matters of social policy has often played a significant role in adjudication. Attempts to deny this, if they cannot be effectively supported by historical evidence, are likely to encourage a more radical scepticism than they seek to oppose. The conclusion that policy has played an important part, however, does not establish that it has been the *exclusive* explanation of private law, or that considerations of principle and utility have not also been important.

Closely related to these questions is the capacity of the law to change by judicial decision. This has important implications for the role of the judge and for the relevance, in judicial decision making, of public policy. Judges in civil litigation have had both an adjudicative and a rule-making function. As Joseph Jaconelli put it, 'the adjudicative process in developed legal systems may be said to possess both a private and a public aspect'.[50] Considerations of public policy have been to some degree inescapable, for the court, in making a new rule, has always, implicitly if not expressly, taken into account the probable costs and benefits to potential future litigants of the proposed change. Many judges have been reluctant openly to avow a rule-making function; hence the 'agreeable fiction',[51] or 'fairy tale'[52] that judges only declare and do not make the law. Some would doubt whether the fiction is agreeable, or the tale innocuous, but the judicial reluctance overtly to assume a law-making power has been strongly associated with perceptions of the proper constitutional role of judges and of the need for legal continuity. The relation between the declaratory and law-making functions is complex, for rules may be stated at many different levels of generality, and it is often impossible, even for the decision maker, to distinguish between the application of an existing rule and the making of a new one, for 'the application of existing law to new circumstances can never be clearly distinguished from the creation of a new rule of law'.[53] There may be good reasons for judges and for advocates to disclaim creativity, but legal his-torians, whose function is different from both, cannot always accept such disclaimers at face value.

It cannot be doubted that the courts, particularly at the appellate level, do change the law, and there are examples from all areas of private law. In 1998 Lord Golf said, 'we all know that in reality, in the common law as in equity, the law is the subject of development by the judges ... It is universally recognised that judicial development of the common law is inevitable'. It has often been said that the role of the court in changing the law has been 'interstitial' or 'incremental', but it is not very clear what this has meant in practice. ...

. . . .

The evidence, overall, establishes that judicial perceptions of public policy have often played an important (and sometimes a decisive) role in Anglo-American private law. It follows that considerations of formal legal logic and internal coherence have not been everything. But it does not follow that they have been nothing. The two most influential American judges of the twentieth century have stressed the simultaneous presence of formal and policy considerations. Holmes' statement that 'the life of the law has not been logic; it has been experience' has usually been quoted out of its context. Holmes' immediately preceding words were 'it is something to show that the consistency of a system requires a particular result, but it is not all'.[94] Cardozo spoke also of 'the demon of formalism [that] tempts the intellect with the lure of scientific order', but added:

> I do not mean, of course, that judges are commissioned to set aside existing rules at pleasure in favor of any other set of rules which they may hold to be expedient or wise. I mean that when they are called upon to say how far existing rules are to be extended or restricted, they must let the welfare of society fix the path, its direction and its distance.[95]

Cardozo's opinion, like Holmes', was that 'logical consistency does not cease to be a good because it is not the supreme good'.[96] Historical evidence supports these opinions: both principle and policy have, in the past, been influential in Anglo-American private law, and so closely interrelated as to be inseparable. Vicarious liability, for example, is seen to be good policy partly because, by internalising costs, it creates an incentive to avoid (at least some) injuries, but partly also because, as between the injured claimant and the enterprise, justice requires the cost of (at least some) injuries to be borne by the enterprise.

4

Neither of these reasons. standing alone, would be sufficient to justify the current rule of vicarious liability, and neither has been carried to its logical conclusion, but together they support a rule that is perceived to be sound in principle partly *because* it is perceived also as good policy, and vice versa.

(b) Unjust Enrichment, Quasi-Contract and Restitution: A Study in Organizing Legal Rules†

R.A. Samek

PRELIMINARIES

Legal Subjects and Branches of Law

There is an old parable about a group of blind men who are ushered into the presence of an elephant and asked to name the object with which they are confronted. One touches a foot of the elephant and claims that he is touching a mountain. Another touches its tail and claims that it must be a snake, and so on. I was reminded of this parable when I started thinking about the identity of the subject designated by the names unjust enrichment, quasi-contract and restitution. The position here, however, is different and more complicated than in the parable. There we know that the blind men are confronted by *one* object, and we also know that it is correctly named "elephant". Here, on the other hand, we are not dealing with a physical object which can be recognized as one unit and correctly named by almost everybody; we are dealing with an abstraction, namely, with an alleged legal subject or subjects. Hence, what is the legal subject, or what are the legal subjects, which are designated by the names unjust enrichment, quasi-contract and restitution, will depend on what we mean by a "legal subject" and on how we use these names. Although no lawyer will have any difficulty in giving *examples* of legal subjects, few will have considered what makes a particular legal subject a "legal subject", and there will be no general agreement about the use of the names unjust enrichment, quasi-contract and restitution.

The examples of legal subjects given by lawyers will be those which figure in the syllabi of law schools and in legal textbooks. We can learn from them an important lesson, namely, that by and large the names of legal subjects correspond to the names of branches of law. We may say, therefore, that legal subjects are concerned with branches of law. The relation between legal subjects and branches of law is illuminating up to a point, but the notion of a legal subject cannot be explicated with reference to the notion of a branch of law, unless we also explicate the latter. This cannot be done simply by reducing it to a collection of legal rules, for such a reduction fails to explain why some legal rules can figure in more than one branch of law, and how it comes about that a mere collection of legal rules can have the coherence and unity of a branch of law.

Branches of Law and Legal Conceptual Schemes

According to my model, it is the relevance of certain legal rules to a "legal conceptual scheme", and *vice versa*, which gives these rules the coherence and unity of a branch of law. The same legal rules may be relevant to more than one legal conceptual scheme, in which case they will figure in more than one branch of law. Although legal conceptual schemes appear to have grown up organically, they are in fact a loose agglomeration of first order models which are constructed and reconstructed through a process of trial and error by judges, and through a process of rationalisation by legal commentators. What makes such models "models of *a* legal conceptual scheme" are certain family resemblances between them which may but need not include a common legal key concept.[2] It is a necessary condition of a legal conceptual scheme that it be *used* by judges, but their verbal approval is not a sufficient condition of such a scheme, and their verbal disapproval is not necessarily fatal. The ade-

---

† (1969) 47:1 Can. Bar Rev. 1 at 2–4, 26–28. [Notes/references omitted.] Reproduced by permission of the author and the publisher.

quacy of a legal conceptual scheme should be judged mainly, as I have already suggested, by its relevance to the legal rules with reference to which it is constructed, by its simplicity and elegance, and by its legal and social fruitfulness.

The relation between legal rules and legal conceptual schemes is one of interdependence. Legal rules are dependent on legal conceptual schemes inasmuch as they are not separate self-contained units, but are related to other legal rules with reference to a legal conceptual scheme or schemes, however fragmentary and provisional these schemes may be. Legal conceptual schemes, on the other hand, are dependent on legal rules inasmuch as the former must be relevant to the latter and reflect any changes in them. A legal conceptual scheme is not a purely theoretical construct, but a construct with a certain empirical content and with a certain predictive power.

Legal Concepts

According to my model, legal concepts serve as *focal points* through which certain legal rules are linked to one or more legal conceptual schemes. Although ostensibly the same legal concept may link the same legal rule to several legal conceptual schemes, legal concepts and rules are "bent" by the way they are used in legal conceptual schemes. Usually a legal concept, or a cluster of legal concepts, link a number of legal rules to a certain part of a conceptual scheme, but sometimes a legal concept is so basic that it is regarded as *the key* to a whole legal conceptual scheme, though ostensibly the same legal concept may figure in a subsidiary capacity in other legal conceptual schemes. In the first case the name which designates the legal concept, or the cluster of legal concepts, may also designate a sub-branch of law and a topic of a legal subject. In the second case the name of the basic legal concept may designate a whole branch of law and a whole legal subject. No rigid line can be drawn between a single legal concept and a cluster of legal concepts, for the former may be split into sub-units and the latter consolidated into single units.

The Functions of Legal Conceptual Schemes

Legal conceptual schemes fulfil, I suggest, three main functions: a *systematising* function, a *developmental* function and a *social* function. These functions are all interdependent. Since legal rules are not static, and do not operate in a vacuum, they cannot

be systematised without taking into account their future development and social purposes. They cannot be developed without systematising them and taking into account their social purposes; and their social purposes cannot be achieved without systematising them and taking into account their future development. The capacity of serving these functions [is] broadly what I meant when I said that the adequacy of a first order model should be judged, *inter alia*, by its legal and social fruitfulness.

. . . .

UNJUST ENRICHMENT AND RESTITUTION

. . . .

THE TRIPARTITE DIVISION OF LAW

In bringing the above situations together under one heading, the reporters say that the Institute "*recognized the tripartite division of the law into contracts, torts and restitution, the division being made with reference to the purposes which each subject serves in protecting one of three fundamental interests*".[84]

The postulate of the law of contracts (or of undertakings) is that a person is entitled to receive what another has promised him or promised another for him. (The obligations from trusts are considered as falling within the contract field.) The interest of the promisee or beneficiary which is protected by the law is his reasonable expectation that a promise freely made will be performed. The interest of the promisee or beneficiary which is protected by the law is his reasonable expectation that a promise freely made will be performed. The law requires the promisor, if he fails to perform the promise, to place the other, as far as reasonably can be done, in as good a position as if the promise had been performed.

The law of torts is based on the premise that a person has a right not to be harmed by another, either with respect to his personality or with respect to his interests in things and other persons. The law protects this right by requiring a wrongdoer to give such compensation to the person harmed as will be substantially equivalent to the harm done. The accent is on wrong and harm.

> Besides these two postulates there is a third, sometimes overlapping the others, but different in its purpose. This third postulate, which underlies the rules assembled in the Restatement under the heading "Restitution", can be expressed thus: *A person has a right to have restored to him a benefit gained at his expense by*

another, if the retention of the benefit by the other would be unjust. The law protects this right by granting restitution of the benefit which otherwise would, in most cases, unjustly enrich the recipient.[85]

The basis of the tripartite division of law is presumably the *social* purpose which each division serves in protecting one of three fundamental social *interests*. But here we must surely wonder (1) why there are just these three divisions of law, (2) why there are just these three fundamental social interests, and (3) why there should be a one to one correspondence between divisions of law and fundamental social interests. The model, moreover, being static, makes no allowance for changes in the law and in the fundamental social interests protected by them. Thus according to the reporters, the social purpose of the law of torts is to protect a person's interest not to be harmed by another through that person's wrong or fault. Now we may say that this *was* its *key* social purpose at one stage of its development, but it is doubtful whether this is still true today. For instance, according to Fleming, the "law of torts ... is concerned with the allocation of losses incident to man's activities in a modern society".[86]

It is arguable that a similar shift from the protection of private interests to public policy has occurred in the law of contract, and that the "expectation interest" now takes second place to the policy objective of regulating transactions for the public good. But even in the heyday of the "expectation interest", it never had a monopoly. Thus Fuller, its great exponent, mentions three principal purposes in awarding contract damages: (1) Prevention of gain by the defaulting promisor at the expense of the promisee, that is, prevention of unjust enrichment. (2) To undo the harm which reliance on the defendant's promise has caused, that is, to put him in as good a position as he was in before the promise was made. (3) To give the promisee the value of the expectancy, that is, to put the plaintiff in as good a position as he would have occupied if the defendant had performed his promise. Fuller calls these three interests the "restitution interest", the "reliance interest" and the "expectation interest" respectively. They do not all, he says, present equal claims to judicial intervention:[87]

> ... ordinary standards of justice would regard the need for judicial intervention as decreasing in the order in which we have listed the three interests. The "restitution interest", involving a combination of unjust impoverishment with unjust gain, presents the strongest case for relief. If, following Aristotle, we regard the purpose of justice as the maintenance of an equilibrium of goods among members of society, the restitution interest presents twice as strong a claim to judicial intervention as the reliance interest, since if A not only causes B to lose one unit but appropriates that unit to himself, the resulting discrepancy between A and B is not one unit but two.[88]

(c) *Norberg v. Wynrib*[†]

Supreme Court of Canada

[La FOREST J.:]

This case concerns the civil liability of a doctor who gave drugs to a chemically dependent woman patient in exchange for sexual contact. ...

FACTS

In 1978, the appellant, then a modestly educated young woman in her late teens, began to experience severe headaches and pains in her jaw. She went to doctors and dentists but none of them could diagnose the cause of her excruciating pain. They prescribed various types of painkillers. However, the medication provided no relief. The headaches became worse. More and more medication was prescribed in increasing amounts and dosages. In addition to this medication, her sister, a drug addict, gave her Fiorinal, a painkiller drug. Finally in December 1978, a dentist diagnosed her difficulty as being related to an abscessed tooth. It was extracted and at last her pain was relieved.

---

† [1992] 2 S.C.R. 226.

But now the appellant had a new problem. She had a craving for painkillers. Her sister gave her more Fiorinal. In 1981, when she broke her ankle, she found a doctor who was willing to prescribe Fiorinal for her. She continued to obtain prescriptions from him until he retired. However, his replacement refused to give her more pills. She discussed the situation with her sister and in March 1982 she commenced to see Dr. Wynrib, an elderly medical practitioner in his seventies. She told him she was experiencing pain in the ankle she had broken in 1981 and asked for Fiorinal. He gave her the prescription. She kept going back to him using the ankle injury and other illnesses as a pretext for obtaining prescriptions. Her dependence on Fiorinal continued to increase as did her dependence on Dr. Wynrib. But the pretext could not continue. Later in 1982, Dr. Wynrib confronted the appellant. The appellant described this confrontation as follows:

> I had gone into his office one day and I asked him — I asked him for a prescription of Fiorinal, and I remember that he sat back in his chair and he pulled out like the medical file and he looked at me and he asked me come on, Laura, why is the real reason you're taking the Fiorinal. I told him because it's for my back or my ankle, whatever it was that I had been asking him for, and he said — no he said. And he looked again over my file. He said you can't be taking them for this long and not be addicted to them. Why is the real reason. And I denied it again. I said it's for the pain. And he told me that if I didn't admit to him that I was addicted to the Fiorinal that he wouldn't give me any more prescriptions. And I remember that I had started crying and I had denied [sic] to him, and he had told me to leave the office. And I wouldn't leave the office and finally I admitted to him that I was addicted to the Fiorinal.

Dr. Wynrib responded by giving the appellant another prescription.

After the appellant admitted to Dr. Wynrib that she was addicted to Fiorinal, she testified that he told her that "if I was good to him he would be good to me" and he made suggestions by pointing upstairs where he lived above his office. The appellant recognized this for what it was and sought her drugs elsewhere. She managed to secure Fiorinal through other doctors and by buying them off the street. Her tolerance and dependence grew. Eventually the other doctors reduced her supply. She was, as she put it, desperate. Near the end of 1983 she went back to Dr. Wynrib because she knew he would give her Fiorinal. She gave in to his demands.

Initially the sexual encounters took place in the back examination room of his office. He kissed her and fondled her breasts. In time, he required her to meet him upstairs in his bedroom where he kept a bottle of Fiorinal in his dresser drawer beside the bed. She managed to stall him for awhile by asking for the Fiorinal first and then leaving after she obtained it. But this device did not work long. Dr. Wynrib told her that he would not give her the Fiorinal until she complied with his demands. The pattern was that he would tell her to undress and put the bottle of Fiorinal by his bed for her to see. Both parties would lie on the bed. Dr. Wynrib would kiss the appellant, touch her and then get on top of her. He would go through the motions of intercourse. There was no penetration, however, because he could not sustain an erection. On at least one occasion, however, he penetrated her with his fingers. He would give her pills each time she visited him in his apartment. She then would go back to his office the next day and he would write out a prescription. When the encounters began, the appellant did not want to believe what was happening. She thought he would do it once and then stop. However, the appellant testified that these incidences of simulated intercourse occurred 10 or 12 times, up to the early part of 1985.

During this period, the appellant was obtaining Fiorinal from a number of other sources: other doctors, off the street and from her sister. In February 1985, she left her job. She became depressed and no longer had the money to buy the drugs she needed off the street. She told Dr. Wynrib that she needed help. Her evidence at trial was:

> A. . . . I remember telling him that I needed help, and he told me to just quit. He said just quit. I said I can't. The pills were on my mind all the time.
> Q. Did he direct you anywhere else apart from telling you to quit, giving you advice?
> A. No, no.

At some point in 1985, the appellant became the subject of a criminal investigation leading the RCMP to visit Dr. Wynrib in April 1985. After this visit, Dr. Wynrib told the appellant that he could no longer give her prescriptions in the office. However, he still gave her pills from the bottle in his dresser drawer when she visited him upstairs. Eventually, she was charged with the summary conviction offence of "double doctoring" under s. 3.1(1) of the *Narcotic Control Act*, R.S.C. 1970, c. N-1, as am. by S.C. 1985, c. 19, s. 198, i.e., obtaining narcotic prescription drugs from a doctor without disclosing particulars of prescriptions from other doctors. In July 1985, she went to a rehabilitation centre for drug addicts on her own initiative. She left the centre after one month and has not taken any drugs for non-medical reasons since. In September 1985, the appellant pleaded guilty to the offences for which she was charged and received an absolute discharge.

At trial, the respondent did not testify. However, the appellant admitted that Dr. Wynrib did not at any time use physical force. She also testified that he did things for her such as giving her money as well as coffee and cookies. She agreed that she "played" on the fact that he liked her and that she knew throughout the relationship that he was lonely.

. . . .

The Appeal to this Court

The appellant then appealed [dismissal of her claims] to this Court. In addition to the parties, the Women's Legal Education and Action Fund appeared as intervener. At trial and in the Court of Appeal, the appellant sought recovery on a number of grounds: sexual assault, negligence, breach of fiduciary duty, and breach of contract. ...

ASSAULT — THE NATURE OF CONSENT

The alleged sexual assault in this case falls under the tort of battery. A battery is the intentional infliction of unlawful force on another person. Consent, express or implied, is a defence to battery. Failure to resist or protest is an indication of consent "if a reasonable person who is aware of the consequences and capable of protest or resistance would voice his objection": see Fleming, *The Law of Torts* (7th ed. 1987), at pp. 72–73. However, the consent must be genuine; it must not be obtained by force or threat of force or be given under the influence of drugs. Consent may also be vitiated by fraud or deceit as to the nature of the defendant's conduct. The courts below considered these to be the only factors that would vitiate consent.

In my view, this approach to consent in this kind of case is too limited. ... The concept of consent as it operates in tort law is based on a presumption of individual autonomy and free will. It is presumed that the individual has freedom to consent or not to consent. This presumption, however, is untenable in certain circumstances. A position of relative weakness can, in some circumstances, interfere with the freedom of a person's will. Our notion of

consent must, therefore, be modified to appreciate the power relationship between the parties.

An assumption of individual autonomy and free will is not confined to tort law. It is also the underlying premise of contract law. The supposition of contract law is that two parties agree or consent to a particular course of action. However, contract law has evolved in such a way that it recognizes that contracting parties do not always have equality in their bargaining strength. The doctrines of duress, undue influence, and unconscionability have arisen to protect the vulnerable when they are in a relationship of unequal power. For reasons of public policy, the law will not always hold weaker parties to the bargains they make. Professor Klippert in his book *Unjust Enrichment* refers to the doctrines of duress, undue influence, and unconscionability as "justice factors". He lumps these together under the general term "coercion" and states, at p. 156, that "[i]n essence the common thread is an illegitimate use of power or unlawful pressure which vitiates a person's freedom of choice". In a situation where a plaintiff is induced to enter into an unconscionable transaction because of an inequitable disparity in bargaining strength, it cannot be said that the plaintiff's act is voluntary: see Klippert, *supra*, at p. 170.

. . . .

An unconscionable transaction arises in contract law where there is an overwhelming imbalance in the power relationship between the parties. In *Morrison v. Coast Finance Ltd.* (1965), 55 D.L.R. (2d) 710 (B.C.C.A.), at p. 713, Davey J.A. outlined the factors to be considered in a claim of unconscionability:

> ... a plea that a bargain is unconscionable invokes relief against an unfair advantage gained by an unconscientious use of power by a stronger party against a weaker. On such a claim the material ingredients are proof of inequality in the position of the parties arising out of the ignorance, need or distress of the weaker, which left him in the power of the stronger, and proof of substantial unfairness of the bargain obtained by the stronger. On proof of those circumstances, it creates a presumption of fraud which the stronger must repel by proving that the bargain was fair, just and reasonable....

. . . .

An inequality of bargaining power may arise in a number of ways. As Boyle and Percy, *Contracts: Cases and Commentaries* (4th ed. 1989), note, at pp. 637–38:

[A person] may be intellectually weaker by reason of a disease of the mind, economically weaker or simply situationally weaker because of temporary circumstances. Alternatively, the "weakness" may arise out of a special relationship in which trust and confidence has been reposed in the other party. The comparative weakness or special relationship is, in every case, a fact to be proven.

As the last sentence of this passage suggests, the circumstances of each case must be examined to determine if there is an overwhelming imbalance of power in the relationship between the parties.

. . . .

There has been some recognition in the lower courts that an unequal power relationship is a relevant consideration in cases of sexual misconduct. *W.(B.) v. Mellor*, [1989] B.C.J. No. 1393 (S.C.) (QL Systems), has some similarities with the present case. There the plaintiff sued for damages in contract and tort for unwelcome sexual conduct by her doctor extending over two years. At the time the doctor-patient relationship was established, the plaintiff was in a vulnerable state owing to matrimonial, financial and personal problems. The first sexual advance occurred when the plaintiff asked the doctor for medication to help her calm down. She testified that the doctor directed her into one of his examining rooms where he said he would give her medication. In the examining room, he kissed her and touched her breasts and lower body. She "stormed out of his office" on that occasion but continued to see the doctor. When asked why, she responded that she needed medication and counselling to help her cope. The intimacy between them progressed and eventually led to intercourse. She testified that she had considered changing doctors and that she had discussed this with the defendant. However, she was afraid that he would fix her file to make her appear mentally ill. McKenzie J. found for the plaintiff on the basis that the doctor was in breach of his fiduciary duty of care to his patient and that he breached his contract of professional services. In the course of his reasons, however, he had made the following remarks that show the effect of a power relationship on consent:

I find that he <u>dominated</u> her when she was in a vulnerable state wholly to satisfy his sexual desires and with no intention to carry the relationship beyond that.

. . . .

Viewed in human terms they both bear responsibility for this affair — he for initiating and perpetuating it and she for allowing him to perpetuate it. <u>But he has special responsibilities and obligations of care imposed upon him as a doctor.</u> He committed himself to an elevated duty of care upon entering the medical profession. This was spelled out for him in several ways and prominent among them was the Hippocratic Oath he swore.... [Emphasis added.]

. . . .

... Professor Coleman outlines a number of situations which she calls "power dependency" relationships: see Coleman, "Sex in Power Dependency Relationships: Taking Unfair Advantage of the 'Fair' Sex" (1988), 53 *Alb. L. Rev.* 95. Included in these relationships are parent-child, psychotherapist-patient, physician-patient, clergy-penitent, professor-student, attorney-client, and employer-employee. She asserts that "consent" to a sexual relationship in such relationships is inherently suspect. She notes, at p. 96:

The common element in power dependency relationships is an underlying personal or professional association which creates a significant power imbalance between the parties....

Exploitation occurs when the "powerful" person abuses the position of authority by inducing the "dependent" person into a sexual relationship, thereby causing harm.

While the existence of one of these special relationships is not necessarily determinative of an overwhelming power imbalance, it will, at least in the ordinary case, be required.

It must be noted that in the law of contracts proof of an unconscionable transaction involves a two-step process: (1) proof of inequality in the positions of the parties, and (2) proof of an improvident bargain. Similarly, a two-step process is involved in determining whether or not there has been legally effective consent to a sexual assault. The first step is undoubtedly proof of an inequality between the parties which, as already noted, will ordinarily occur within the context of a special "power dependency" relationship. The second step, I suggest, is proof of exploitation. A consideration of the type of relationship at issue may provide a strong indication of exploitation. Community standards of conduct may also be of some assistance. In *Harry v. Kreutziger* (1978), 9 B.C.L.R. 166 (C.A.), an unconscionable transaction case dealing with the sale of a commercial fishing boat for less than its value, Lambert J.A., at p. 177, approached the issue of unconscionability from a different angle:

... questions as to whether use of power was unconscionable, an advantage was unfair or very unfair, a consideration was grossly inadequate, or bargaining power was grievously impaired, to select words from both statements of principle, the *Morrison* case and the *Bundy* case, are really aspects of one single question. That single question is whether the transaction, seen as a whole, is sufficiently divergent from community standards of commercial morality that it should be rescinded.

If the type of sexual relationship at issue is one that is sufficiently divergent from community standards of conduct, this may alert the court to the possibility of exploitation.

APPLICATION TO THIS CASE

The trial judge held that the appellant's implied consent to the sexual activity was voluntary. Dr. Wynrib, he stated, exercised neither force nor threats of force and the appellant's capacity to consent was not impaired by her drug use. The Court of Appeal agreed that the appellant voluntarily engaged in the sexual encounters. However, it must be asked if the appellant was truly in a position to make a free choice. It seems clear to me that there was a marked inequality in the respective powers of the parties. The appellant was a young woman with limited education. More important, she was addicted to the heavy use of tranquilizers and painkillers. On this ground alone it can be said that there was an inequality in the position of the parties arising out of the appellant's need. The appellant's drug dependence diminished her ability to make a real choice. Although she did not wish to engage in sexual activity with Dr. Wynrib, her reluctance was overwhelmed by the driving force of her addiction and the unsettling prospect of a painful, unsupervised chemical withdrawal. ...

The appellant's vulnerability on the basis of need is also evident from the following report of Dr. Fleming of the Department of Psychiatry, Faculty of Medicine, University of British Columbia and entered as expert evidence:

> As she herself states, she wished to obtain a supply at any cost, and was willing to compromise her beliefs concerning appropriate behaviour in order to obtain supply. In the absence of dependence on and tolerance to Fiorinal it is my impression that Ms. Norberg would not have consented to have any social or sexual activity with Dr. Wynrib. On the basis of my clinical examination and the material provided it is my

belief that she did so in order to obtain a supply of medication.

On the other side of the equation was an elderly, male professional — the appellant's doctor. An unequal distribution of power is frequently a part of the doctor-patient relationship. As it is stated in *The Final Report of the Task Force on Sexual Abuse of Patients*, An Independent Task Force Commissioned by The College of Physicians and Surgeons of Ontario (November 25, 1991) (Chair: Marilou McPhedran), at p. 11:

> Patients seek the help of doctors when they are in a vulnerable state — when they are sick, when they are needy, when they are uncertain about what needs to be done.
>
> The unequal distribution of power in the physician-patient relationship makes opportunities for sexual exploitation more possible than in other relationships. This vulnerability gives physicians the power to exact sexual compliance. Physical force or weapons are not necessary because the physician's power comes from having the knowledge and being trusted by patients.

In this case, Dr. Wynrib knew that the appellant was vulnerable and driven by her compulsion for drugs. It is likely that he knew or at least strongly suspected that she was dependant upon Fiorinal before she admitted her addiction to him. It was he who ferreted out that she was addicted to drugs. As a doctor, the respondent knew how to assist the appellant medically and he knew (or should have known) that she could not "just quit" taking drugs without treatment. ...

The respondent's medical knowledge and knowledge of the appellant's addiction, combined with his authority to prescribe drugs, gave him power over her. It was he who suggested the sex-for-drugs arrangement.

. . . .

There is also a body of opinion which regards sexual contact in any doctor-patient relationship as exploitative. In the opinion of the Task Force on Sexual Abuse of Patients, *supra*, at p. 12:

> Due to the position of power the physician brings to the doctor-patient relationship, there are NO circumstances — NONE — in which sexual activity between a physician and a patient is acceptable. Sexual activity between a patient and a doctor ALWAYS represents sexual abuse, regardless of what rationalization or belief system the doctor chooses to use to excuse it. Doctors need to recognize that they have power and sta-

tus, and that there may be times when a patient will test the boundaries between them. It is ALWAYS the doctor's responsibility to know what is appropriate and never to cross the line into sexual activity.

Indeed, the Hippocratic Oath indicates that sexual contact between a doctor and his or her patient is fundamentally improper....

. . . .

To summarize, in my view, the defence of consent cannot succeed in the circumstances of this case. The appellant had a medical problem — an addiction to Fiorinal. Dr. Wynrib had knowledge of the problem. As a doctor, he had knowledge of the proper medical treatment, and knew she was motivated by her craving for drugs. Instead of fulfilling his professional responsibility to treat the appellant, he used his power and expertise to his own advantage and to her detriment. In my opinion, the unequal power between the parties and the exploitative nature of the relationship removed the possibility of the appellant's providing meaningful consent to the sexual contact.

EX TURPI CAUSA

In my opinion, the principle of *ex turpi causa non oritur actio* does not bar the appellant's recovery for damages. It is wise to recall the statement of Estey J. in *Canada Cement LaFarge Ltd. v. British Columbia Lightweight Aggregate Ltd.*, [1983] 1 S.C.R. 452, at p. 476, that "cases where a tort action has been defeated by the *ex turpi causa* maxim are exceedingly rare". In my view, this is not one of those "rare" cases. The respondent forced the sex-for-drugs transaction on the appellant by virtue of her weakness. He initiated the arrangement for his own sexual gratification and then impelled her to engage in it. She was unwilling to participate but did so because of her addiction to drugs. It was only because the respondent prolonged the appellant's chemical dependency that the illicit relationship was available to him. The respondent has been found liable in this appeal because he took advantage of the appellant's addiction. To apply the doctrine of *ex turpi causa* in this case would be to deny the appellant damages on the same basis that she succeeded in the tort action: because she acted out of her desperation for Fiorinal. Surely public policy would not countenance giving to the appellant with one hand and then taking away with the other.

. . . .

In sum, I do not believe that it is in the public interest to absolve a doctor of civil liability where he deliberately abuses his position of power and influence by suggesting and pursuing a sex-for-drugs arrangement with a self-admitted drug addict. Accordingly, the *ex turpi causa* maxim does not operate in the circumstances of this case to bar relief.

DAMAGES

The appellant asks for an award of damages which includes the following: (1) compensatory damages for wrongful supply of drugs and prolongation of addiction, (2) aggravated damages for the remorse, shame, damaged self-confidence and emotional harm caused by the continued supply of drugs and the sexual exploitation of the appellant, and (3) punitive damages for the respondent's breach of trust. The courts below were unwilling to award damages. ...

I begin by noting that the battery is actionable without proof of damage. Moreover, liability is not confined to foreseeable consequences. Aggravated damages may be awarded if the battery has occurred in humiliating or undignified circumstances. These damages are not awarded in addition to general damages. Rather, general damages are assessed "taking into account any aggravating features of the case and to that extent increasing the amount awarded": see *N. (J.L.) v. L. (A.M.)* (1988), 47 C.C.L.T. 65 (Man. Q.B.), at p. 71, *per* Lockwood J. These must be distinguished from punitive or exemplary damages. The latter are awarded to punish the defendant and to make an example of him or her in order to deter others from committing the same tort; see Linden, *Canadian Tort Law* (4th ed. 1988), at pp. 54–55. In *Vorvis v. Insurance Corporation of British Columbia*, [1989] 1 S.C.R. 1085, at pp. 1107–8, McIntyre J. thus set forth the circumstances where the defendant's conduct would merit punishment:

> ... punitive damages may only be awarded in respect of conduct which is of such nature as to be deserving of punishment because of its harsh, vindictive, reprehensible and malicious nature. I do not suggest that I have exhausted the adjectives which could describe the conduct capable of characterizing a punitive award, but in any case where such an award is made the conduct must be extreme in its nature and such that by any reasonable standard it is deserving of full condemnation and punishment.

Although aggravated damages will frequently cover conduct which could also be the subject of punitive damages, as I noted, the two types of damages are distinguishable; punitive damages are designed to punish whereas aggravated damages are designed to compensate. See *Vorvis*, at pp. 1098–99.

An award of damages should reflect the nature of the assault. In *R. v. McCraw*, [1991] 3 S.C.R. 72, this Court noted that a sexual assault results in a greater impact on the complainant than a non-sexual assault. Given that one can obtain considerable damages for an assault of a non-sexual nature, the appellant, in my opinion, is entitled to significant aggravated damages for the indignity of the coerced sexual assault. ...

General damages (including aggravated damages in some cases) have been awarded by the lower courts in a number of recent sexual assault cases. ...

In the present case, there were repeated sexual encounters over a substantial period of time with a person in a position of power. The respondent used his power as a doctor to take advantage of the fact that the appellant was addicted to drugs. There is some distinction between this case and the rape cases cited above in that the assault here was not physically violent. However, the respondent's conduct has caused the appellant humiliation and loss of dignity as is evident from her testimony. She testified at trial that she thinks about the events with Dr. Wynrib on a daily basis and that she has felt a great deal of shame. In fact, she felt that she did not deserve to have her son because of what she had done with Dr. Wynrib. In view of the circumstances, I would award general damages of $20,000.

In several of the sexual assault cases, punitive damages were not awarded because the defendant had been convicted. An award of punitive damages in such circumstances would have amounted to double punishment. ...

The question that must be asked is whether the conduct of Dr. Wynrib was such as to merit condemnation by the Court. It was not harsh, vindictive or malicious to use the terms cited in *Vorvis*, *supra*. However, it was reprehensible and it was of a type to offend the ordinary standards of decent conduct in the community. ...

An award of punitive damages is of importance to make it clear that this trend of underestimation cannot continue. Dr. Wynrib's use of power to gain sexual favours in the context of a doctor-patient relationship is conduct that is offensive and reprehensible. In all the circumstances, I would award an additional $10,000 in punitive damages.

DISPOSITION

I would allow the appeal and enter judgment for the plaintiff against the defendant. The plaintiff is entitled to aggravated damages in the amount of $20,000 and punitive damages in the amount of $10,000, the whole with costs throughout.

[SOPINKA J.:] - - -

I have had the advantage of reading the reasons of Justice La Forest. He disposes of this appeal on the basis of the battery claim. With respect, I cannot agree with his approach on the issue of consent. I am also of the view that this case is more appropriately resolved on the basis of the respondent's duty to treat the appellant arising out of the doctor-patient relationship.

. . . .

With respect to the doctor–patient relationship, as I have already stated, special relationships between the plaintiff and defendant should alert the trier of fact to the possibility that apparent consent is not genuine; however, the existence of a particular relationship is not determinative of the presence or absence of consent. The beneficiary of a fiduciary relationship can still consent to a transaction with the fiduciary but the court will subject such a consent to special scrutiny. There may well be cases in which a doctor, by virtue of his or her status, exercises such control or authority over a patient that the patient's submission will not be considered genuine consent. However, in my view, that cannot be said about this case. The appellant began and continued to participate in the sexual encounters in order to obtain drugs. She acknowledged that she played on the respondent's loneliness in order to continue obtaining prescriptions. While it is clear that the sexual contact was contrary to the appellant's wishes, in my view it cannot be said that it was without her consent. I therefore do not find any basis on which to set aside the conclusion of the courts below on the issue of consent.

This is sufficient, in my view, to dispose of the battery claim. ...

. . . .

I [also] do not find the contractual doctrine of unconscionability of assistance in attempting to answer the factual question of whether the appellant consented to sexual contact with the respondent. ... Furthermore, in my view, the facts of this case are more accurately reflected by acknowledging that the appellant consented to the sexual contact and by considering the respondent's conduct in light of his professional duty towards the appellant.

BREACH OF DUTY

This professional duty arises out of the relationship of doctor-patient which is essentially based on contract. Breach of the duty can be the subject of an action in either contract or negligence. While undoubtedly, as in the case of lawyer and client, this relationship in some of its aspects involves fiduciary duties, not all facets of the obligations are fiduciary in nature.

. . . .

The breach of duty alleged here is the obligation of a physician to treat the patient in accordance with standards in the profession. The trial judge found that there was a breach of this duty. ...

. . . .

The Court of Appeal agreed with this finding. ...

Locke J.A. [...] found that the respondent breached his duty as a physician. He concluded, however, that to the extent that the appellant relied on contract, it had been abandoned by mutual consent. ...

In my opinion, whether the appellant relies on contract or negligence, the duty to treat was not vacated by consent. In contract this would require the abandonment of the contractual relationship between the parties. The authorities reviewed by Locke J.A. show that this requires the mutual consent of the parties supported by consideration. I am satisfied that there was no such consent in this case.

While the parties may very well have had a relationship independent of the doctor-patient relationship, the latter relationship continued and was not abandoned. After the addiction was admitted to him in late 1982, the respondent's conduct was consistent with the continuation of a doctor and patient relationship. He ordered a series of x-rays to be taken of various parts of the appellant's body. He accepted these x-ray reports in August and November of 1984. He made gynaecological referrals for the appellant and in due course Dr. Gowd, a gynaecologist, reported to the respondent in this regard. The only conclusion to be drawn from the evidence is that the respondent continued to act as the appellant's general practitioner and the appellant continued to seek medical care from him in this capacity. Neither the parties nor the medical community had any reason to believe that the parties had mutually abandoned their contract. In fact, the conduct of both the appellant and the respondent reinforced the existence of their doctor and patient relationship.

Moreover, even if the contract was abandoned, that did not put an end to the duty. The respondent did not change his status as a physician; nor did the appellant change her status as one who was in need of and sought treatment. This relationship continued even if technically the contract between them was terminated by mutual consent. The duty is supportable independently of contract on the basis of this relationship. Duty arising out of relationship is, of course, the basis of the law of negligence.

. . . .

... While the appellant consented to the sexual encounters, she did not consent to the breach of duty that resulted in the continuation of her addiction and the sexual encounters. The fact that a patient acquiesces or agrees to a form of treatment does not absolve a physician from his or her duty if the treatment is not in accordance with medical standards. Otherwise, the patient would be required to know what the prescribed standard is. In the absence of a clear statement by the respondent to the appellant that he was no longer treating her as her physician and an unequivocal consent to the cessation of treatment, I conclude that the duty to treat the appellant continued until she attended at the rehabilitation centre on her own initiative and was treated.

. . . .

[McLACHLIN J. (for L'Heureux-Dubé J. and himself):]

I have had the advantage of reading the reasons of my colleagues Justice La Forest and Justice Sopinka. With respect, I do not find that the doctrines of tort or contract capture the essential nature of the wrong done to the plaintiff. Unquestionably, they do catch aspects of that wrong. But to look at the events which occurred over the course of the relationship between Dr. Wynrib and Ms. Norberg from the perspective of tort or contract is to view that relationship through lenses which distort more than they bring into focus. Only the principles applicable to fiduciary relationships and their breach encompass it in its totality. In my view, that doctrine is clearly applicable to the facts of this case on principles articulated by this Court in earlier cases. It alone encompasses the true relationship between the parties and the gravity of the wrong done by the defendant; accordingly, it should be applied.

. . . .

It is not disputed that Dr. Wynrib abused his duty to the plaintiff. He provided her with drugs he knew she should not have. He failed to advise her to enrol in an anti-addiction program, thereby prolonging her addiction. Instead, he took advantage of her addiction to obtain sexual favours from her over a period of more than two years.

The relationship of physician and patient can be conceptualized in a variety of ways. It can be viewed as a creature of contract, with the physician's failure to fulfil his or her obligations giving rise to an action for breach of contract. It undoubtedly gives rise to a duty of care, the breach of which constitutes the tort of negligence. In common with all members of society, the doctor owes the patient a duty not to touch him or her without his or her consent; if the doctor breaches this duty he or she will have committed the tort of battery. But perhaps the most fundamental characteristic of the doctor-patient relationship is its fiduciary nature. All the authorities agree that the relationship of physician to patient also falls into that special category of relationships which the law calls fiduciary.

. . . .

... I think it is readily apparent that the doctor-patient relationship shares the peculiar hallmark of the fiduciary relationship — trust, the trust of a person with inferior power that another person who has assumed superior power and responsibility will exercise that power for his or her good and only for his or her good and in his or her best interests. Recognizing the fiduciary nature of the doctor-patient relationship provides the law with an analytic model by which physicians can be held to the high standards of dealing with their patients which the trust accorded them requires. ...

The foundation and ambit of the fiduciary obligation are conceptually distinct from the foundation and ambit of contract and tort. Sometimes the doctrines may overlap in their application, but that does not destroy their conceptual and functional uniqueness. In negligence and contract the parties are taken to be independent and equal actors, concerned primarily with their own self-interest. Consequently, the law seeks a balance between enforcing obligations by awarding compensation when those obligations are breached, and preserving optimum freedom for those involved in the relationship in question. The essence of a fiduciary relationship, by contrast, is that one party exercises power on behalf of another and pledges himself or herself to act in the best interests of the other.

. . . .

The fiduciary relationship has trust, not self-interest, at its core, and when breach occurs, the balance favours the person wronged. The freedom of the fiduciary is limited by the obligation he or she has undertaken — an obligation which "betokens loyalty, good faith and avoidance of a conflict of duty and self-interest": *Canadian Aero Service Ltd. v. O'Malley*, [1974] S.C.R. 592, at p. 606. To cast a fiduciary relationship in terms of contract or tort (whether negligence or battery) is to diminish this obligation. If a fiduciary relationship is shown to exist, then the proper legal analysis is one based squarely on the full and fair consequences of a breach of that relationship.

. . . .

Wilson J. in *Frame v. Smith*, [1987] 2 S.C.R. 99, at p. 136, ... attributed the following characteristics to a fiduciary relationship: "(1) [t]he fiduciary has scope for the exercise of some discretion or power; (2) the fiduciary can unilaterally exercise that power or discretion so as to affect the beneficiary's legal or practical interests; (3) the beneficiary is peculiarly vulnerable to or at the mercy of the fiduciary holding the discretion or power."

Dr. Wynrib was in a position of power vis-à-vis the plaintiff; he had scope for the exercise of power and discretion with respect to her. He had the power to advise her, to treat her, to give her the drug or to refuse her the drug. He could unilaterally exercise that power or discretion in a way that affected her interests. And her status as a patient rendered her vulnerable and at his mercy, particularly in light of her addiction. So Wilson J.'s test appears to be met. All the classic characteristics of a fiduciary relationship were present. Dr. Wynrib and Ms. Norberg were on an unequal footing. He pledged himself — by the act of hanging out his shingle as a medical doctor and accepting her as his patient — to act in her best interests and not permit any conflict between his duty to act only in her best interests and his own interests — including his interest in sexual gratification — to arise. As a physician, he owed her the classic duties associated with a fiduciary relationship — the duties of "loyalty, good faith and avoidance of a conflict of duty and self-interest".

. . . .

The case at bar is not concerned with the protection of what has traditionally been regarded as a legal interest. It is, however, concerned with the protection of interests, both societal and personal, of the highest importance. Society has an abiding interest in ensuring that the power entrusted to physicians by us, both collectively and individually, not be used in corrupt ways ...

. . . .

... The recently issued *Final Report of the Task Force on Sexual Abuse of Patients*, commissioned by The College of Physicians and Surgeons of Ontario, makes highly instructive reading in this regard. In the words of the Task Force, at p. 79:

Patients seek the help of doctors when they are vulnerable — when the [*sic*] are sick, when they are needy, when they are uncertain about their physical or emotional health. The physician has the knowledge, the skills, and the expertise the patient needs to heal. The patient often suspends both judgement and personal power idealizing the doctor in order to feel secure. The physician, therefore, has more power than the patient, and this power can be used to invade sexual boundaries and to force sexual compliance. Physical force is not necessary.

Women, who can so easily be exploited by physicians for sexual purposes, may find themselves particularly vulnerable. That female patients are disproportionately the targets of sexual exploitation by physicians is borne out by the Task Force's report. Of the 303 reports they received of sexual exploitation at the hands of those in a position of trust (the vast majority of whom were physicians), 287 were by female patients, 16 by males: at p. 10. ...

. . . .

Why then have so many of the jurists who looked at this case declined to consider it as an example of breach of fiduciary duty? The trial judge, Oppal J. ((1988), 27 B.C.L.R. (2d) 240, at. p. 246), while finding in the end that the plaintiff was barred from recovering by her own illegal and immoral acts, clearly felt the relationship was one of trust, traditionally the hallmark of a fiduciary duty:

A relationship between a physician and a patient is one in which trust and confidence must be placed in the physician. Clearly, in the case at bar, the doctor breached a duty which was owed to his patient and, in the ordinary course of events, she should be entitled to damages.

The majority of the Court of Appeal ((1990), 44 B.C.L.R. (2d) 47), per McEachern C.J., addressed the question only in passing, stating at p. 52:

If the defendant breached a duty to the plaintiff in this case it was a breach of the duty which a physician owes to his patient to treat her professionally and, unless the breach relates to an improper disclosure of confidential information or something like that, it adds nothing to describe the breach as a fiduciary one.

The majority went on to find that there was no compensable breach of any duty owed by Dr. Wynrib to Ms. Norberg until after such time as Dr. Wynrib discovered her addiction, and that in any event the plaintiff's conduct barred her from recovering. Locke J.A., dissenting, would have allowed the plaintiff's claim in negligence. He held that recovery on the basis of breach of fiduciary duty was not available because Dr. Wynrib had revealed Ms. Norberg's affairs to no one and did not unduly influence her, effectively confining fiduciary obligations in the doctor-patient relationship to the duty of confidence and the duty to avoid undue influence, and construing "undue influence" in such a narrow fashion that the obvious influence which Dr. Wynrib exercised over Ms. Norberg was excluded from consideration.

In this Court, La Forest J. (at p. 000 [*sic*]) says with respect to the Court of Appeal's refusal to characterize the relationship between the parties as fiduciary simply that, "[s]ince I am dealing with the case on the basis of the assault claim, I need not consider this point." He goes on to treat the plaintiff's claim under the rubric of the tort of battery, using the equitable doctrine of unconscionable transactions to negate the defence of consent. As Sopinka J. notes, this approach is not without difficulty. First, the doctrine of unconscionable transactions has hitherto been confined to setting aside unconscionable contracts, not negating defences to tort actions. Second, where applicable, it serves not to negate the consent, but to set aside a consensual agreement on grounds of inequality of bargaining power and fairness: *Lloyds Bank Ltd. v. Bundy*, [1975] Q.B. 326 (C.A.), per Lord Denning M.R.

Having rejected, by reason of the plaintiff's consent, La Forest J.'s battery approach, Sopinka J. treats the matter simply as the contractual or tortious breach of the physician's duty to his patient. He recognizes that some aspects of the physician-patient relationship may be fiduciary, but finds no such duty relevant to the acts alleged by the plaintiff. He adopts the conclusion of McEachern C.J., at p. 52, that "unless the breach relates to an improper disclosure of confidential information or something like that, it adds nothing to describe the breach as a fiduciary one." The only applicable duty, according to Sopinka J. (at p. 000 [*sic*]) "is the obligation of a physician to treat the patient in accordance with standards in the profession".

I would summarize the situation as follows: the trial judge appears to have found a duty of trust and confidence and abuse thereof. None of the appellate judges who have written on the case offers a convincing demonstration of why it is wrong to characterize the relationship between Dr. Wynrib and Ms. Norberg as a fiduciary relationship; indeed none of the judgments seriously discusses the legal requirements for establishing the existence of a fiduciary duty or its breach, much less considers the facts in relation to those requirements. While the majority of the Court of Appeal and Sopinka J. suggest that the fiduciary duties to which Dr. Wynrib was subject go no further than his duties in tort or contract, they offer no basis for this suggestion in principle, policy or authority, appearing to rest their case on the assumption that the only additional duties which a fiduciary relationship could impose would be akin to the duty of confidence. This closed, commercial view of fiduciary obligations is neither defended nor reconciled with the authorities, including those of this Court. Nor can thorough consideration of the plaintiff's rights as the victim of a breach of fiduciary obligation be avoided, with respect, on the ground that it was not a live issue or argued; it has been a central issue since the trial judge found the relationship to be one of trust, it was alluded to by all the judgments below, and it was argued before us.

I proceed then to consider the matter on the footing that the essential elements of breach of a fiduciary relationship are made out. ...

But, it is said, there are a number of reasons why the doctrine of breach of fiduciary relationship cannot apply in this case. I turn then to these alleged conditions of defeasibility.

The first factor which is said to prevent application of the doctrine of breach of fiduciary duty is Ms. Norberg's conduct. Two terms have been used to raise this consideration to the status of a legal or equitable bar — the equitable maxim that he who comes into equity must come with clean hands and the tort doctrine of *ex turpi causa non oritur actio.*

For our purposes, one may think of the two respectively as the equitable and legal formulations of the same type of bar to recovery. The trial judge found that although Dr. Wynrib was under a trust obligation to Ms. Norberg, she was barred from claiming damages against him because of her "immoral" and "illegal" conduct. While he referred to the doctrine of *ex turpi*, there seems to be little doubt that in equity the appropriate term is "clean hands" and consequently that is the expression I will use.

The short answer to the arguments based on wrongful conduct of the plaintiff is that she did nothing wrong in the context of this relationship. She was not a sinner, but a sick person, suffering from an addiction which proved to be uncontrollable in the absence of a professional drug rehabilitation program. She went to Dr. Wynrib for relief from that condition. ...

We do not know when Dr. Wynrib first identified Ms. Norberg as a person suffering from drug addiction; we do know that he confronted her with his knowledge in the first year of their doctor-patient relationship. But whenever he became aware of the true nature of her medical condition, at that point only one form of relief was appropriate: Dr. Wynrib, if he were to discharge properly the trust relationship he had assumed, was obliged to refuse Ms. Norberg further drugs and to refer her for professional addiction treatment. He did neither, but instead took advantage of her sickness to obtain sexual favours in exchange for the drugs she craved. ...

The law might accuse Ms. Norberg of "double doctoring" and moralists might accuse her of licentiousness; but she did no wrong because not she but the doctor was responsible for this conduct. He had the power to cure her of her addiction, as her successful treatment after leaving his "care" demonstrated; instead he chose to use his power to keep her in her addicted state and to use her for his own sexual purposes.

It is difficult not to see the attempt to bar Ms. Norberg from obtaining redress for the wrong she has suffered through the application of the clean hands maxim as anything other than "blaming the victim". ...

· · · ·

This brings us to a second objection to treating this case on the basis of breach of fiduciary duty — that nothing that the law would not otherwise accord flows from categorizing the duty as fiduciary; in short, that the fiduciary obligation adds nothing, except perhaps a duty of confidence and non-disclosure, to an action in tort or contract. This appears to have been the view of the majority of the Court of Appeal below, per McEachern C.J. Sopinka J. adopts that same view. Neither authority nor principle is offered in support of this proposition.

What is really at issue here is the scope of the fiduciary obligation. The majority in the Court of Appeal and Sopinka J. would confine it to matters akin to the duty not to disclose confidential information ... But I do not think that narrow view of the scope of the fiduciary obligation is correct. ... The principles alluded to by Wilson J. in *Frame v. Smith* and applied by this Court in its earlier decision in *Guerin v. The Queen*, [1984] 2 S.C.R. 335, are principles of general application, translatable to different situations and the protection of different interests than those hitherto recognized. They are capable of protecting not only narrow legal and economic interests, but can also serve to defend fundamental human and personal interests, as recognized by Wilson J. in *Frame v. Smith*.

If we accept that the principles can apply in this case to protect the plaintiff's interest in receiving medical care free of exploitation at the hands of her physician, as I think we must, then the consequences are most significant. As we have just seen, the defences based on the alleged fault of the plaintiff, so pressing in tort, may carry little weight when raised against the beneficiary of a fiduciary relationship. This is because the fiduciary approach, unlike those based on tort or contract, is founded on the recognition of the power imbalance inherent in the relationship between fiduciary and beneficiary, and to giving redress where that power imbalance is abused. Another consequence that flows from considering the matter on the basis of breach of fiduciary obligation may be a more generous approach to remedies, as I will come to presently. Equity has always held trustees strictly accountable in a way the tort of negligence and contract have not. Foreseeability of loss is not a factor in equitable damages. Certain defences, such as mitigation, may not apply.

But the most significant consequence of applying the doctrine of fiduciary obligation to a person in the position of Dr. Wynrib is this. Tort and contract can provide a remedy for a physician's failure to provide adequate treatment. But only with considerable difficulty can they be bent to accommodate the wrong of a physician's abusing his or her position to obtain sexual favours from his or her patient. The law has never recognized consensual sexual relations as capable of giving rise to an obligation in tort or in contract. My colleagues, with respect, strain to conclude the contrary. La Forest J. does so by using

the contractual doctrine of relief from unconscionable transactions to negate the consent which the plaintiff, as found by the trial judge, undoubtedly gave. ... Sopinka J., at p. 000 [*sic*], finds himself tacking damages for the sexual encounters onto the breach of the duty to treat on the ground that "[t]he sexual acts were causally connected to the failure to treat and must form part of the damage suffered by the appellant". But can damages flow from acts the law finds lawful simply on the ground they are "connected" to damages for an actionable wrong? And what of the patient whose medical needs are fully met but who is sexually exploited? On Sopinka J.'s reasoning she has no cause of action. These examples underline the importance of treating the consequences of this relationship on the footing of what it is — a fiduciary relationship — rather than forcing it into the ill-fitting molds of contract and tort. Contrary to the conclusion of the court below, characterizing the duty as fiduciary <u>does</u> add something; indeed, without doing so the wrong done to the plaintiff can neither be fully comprehended in law nor adequately compensated in damages.

A third objection raised to viewing the relationship between Dr. Wynrib and Ms. Norberg as fiduciary is that it will open the floodgates to unfounded claims based on the abuse of real or perceived inequality of power ... The answer to this objection lies in defining the ambit of the fiduciary obligation in a way that encompasses meritorious claims while excluding those without merit. The prospect of the law's recognizing meritorious claims by the powerless and exploited against the powerful and exploitive should not alone serve as a reason for denying just claims. This Court has an honourable tradition of recognizing new claims of the disempowered against the exploitive: see, for example, *Pettkus v. Becker*, [1980] 2 S.C.R. 834 (constructive trust benefiting "common law" wife whose husband had been unjustly enriched); *Guerin, supra* (aboriginal people the beneficiaries of fiduciary relationship with the Crown, which consequently has obligations with respect to dealings with land subject to aboriginal title); and *R. v. Lavallee*, [1990] 1 S.C.R. 852 (expert evidence on the psychological effects of battered wife syndrome admissible for the purposes of establishing defence of self-defence).

The criteria for the imposition of a fiduciary duty already enunciated by this Court in cases such as *Frame, Lac Minerals and Guerin* provide a good starting point for the task of defining the general principles which determine whether such a relationship exists. As we have seen, an imbalance of power is not enough to establish a fiduciary relationship. It is a necessary but not sufficient condition. There must also be the potential for interference with a legal interest or a non-legal interest of "vital and substantial 'practical' interest." And I would add this. Inherent in the notion of fiduciary duty, inherent in the judgments of this Court in *Guerin* and *Canson*, is the requirement that the fiduciary have assumed or undertaken to "look after" the interest of the beneficiary. As I put it in *Canson* at p. 543, quoting from this Court's decision in *Canadian Aero Service Ltd. v. O'Malley*, *supra*, at p. 606, "[t]he freedom of the fiduciary is diminished by the nature of the obligation he or she has undertaken — an obligation which 'betokens loyalty, good faith and avoidance of a conflict of duty and self-interest'". It is not easy to bring relationships within this rubric. Generally people are deemed by the law to be motivated in their relationships by mutual self-interest. The duties of trust are special, confined to the exceptional case where one person assumes the power which would normally reside with the other and undertakes to exercise that power solely for the other's benefit. It is as though the fiduciary has taken the power which rightfully belongs to the beneficiary on the condition that the fiduciary exercise the power entrusted exclusively for the good of the beneficiary. ...

. . . .

I conclude that the wrong suffered by the plaintiff falls to be considered under the rubric of breach of fiduciary duty. The duty is established, as is the breach. The plaintiff is entitled to succeed against Dr. Wynrib and to recover the appropriate damages at equity.

I
TORTS

OVERVIEW

The study of tort law in this collection is focused on the law of negligence. This Part contains three chapters. The first considers the concept of duty of care, which was most famously articulated in the 1932 decision of *Donoghue v. Stevenson*. The emergence of a refined concept of proximity and an explicit role for policy considerations enunciated by the Canadian Supreme Court in *Cooper v. Hobart* is then considered: is negligence law in an expanding or contracting phase, and in response to what considerations? To what extent, and when, is the government liable in tort? In the following chapter additional contours of negligence liability are sketched in: the principle of reasonableness and the requirement of a causal connection between actions, breach of duty and harm. In the final readings in this chapter, Richard Abel and Allen Linden ask us to consider the strengths and limitations of the law of negligence in responding to harms to individuals from 'accidents' and to society from so-called mass torts. Two case studies round out this Part in the final chapter and apply the principles to two particular social problems. The first case study addresses how the law has responded to drinking and driving when a person is injured by a drunk driver leaving a bar or a private party. Why has the law decided that social hosts are, in general, not liable, while commercial hosts may be? What is the balance between individual accountability (and choice), on the one hand, and recognition of drunk driving as a systemic social harm? Where this first case study looks at 'private actors', the second case study turns to 'public actors' or agents of the state, in particular police officers. While there is no doubt that police officers can be liable in general terms for negligence, does that liability extend to harms caused when they make errors in investigating crimes? Do they owe a duty to victims of crime? Do they owe a duty to suspects they investigate? The views of judges have been sharply divided in this area.

LEARNING OBJECTIVES

At the conclusion of this Part, readers should be able to

- state the duty of care set out in *Donoghue v. Stevenson* (the 'glorious principle' of negligence law);
- outline the distinction introduced by the *Anns* case, and accepted in *Kamloops*, between operational and policy decisions made by government;
- state the test for proximity given in the *Cooper* case, and outline the two-step inquiry required in novel situations, and correctly state what policy considerations are to be taken into account and at what stage;
- define the reasonable person standard and the elements of causation in a claim for negligence;
- compare and contrast arguments about the efficacy and appropriateness of negligence liability in response to personal injury, differentiating between those who say it doesn't work well enough, those who say it works too well and harms business, and those who argue that it remains vibrant and relevant in a changing world;
- state the reasons for differing legal outcomes between commercial hosts who allow patrons to drive away drunk and hosts of private parties who allow guests to drive away drunk. Evaluate the arguments in favour and against liability in this situation for private hosts;
- identify and evaluate the arguments in favour and opposed to police liability for negligence when investigating crimes (whether to victims or suspects);
- observe and critique the operation of class, gender and race as systemic factors behind people's actions and how this may have flowed into policy considerations and legal responses.

LEARNING RESOURCES

Two engaging documentary films are useful supplements to the documents provided:

- *The Paisley Snail: Donoghue v Stevenson*, 1995
- *Hot Coffee: The Movie*, 2011.

The Glorious Principle and Its Proximity Gloss

(a) *Donoghue (or McAlister) v. Stevenson*†

U.K. House of Lords

[Lord ATKIN:]

My Lords, the sole question for determination in this case is legal: Do the averments made by the pursuer in her pleading, if true, disclose a cause of action? I need not restate the particular facts. The question is whether the manufacturer of an article of drink sold by him to a distributor, in circumstances which prevent the distributor or the ultimate purchaser or consumer from discovering by inspection any defect, is under any legal duty to the ultimate purchaser or consumer to take reasonable care that the article is free from defect likely to cause injury to health. I do not think a more important problem has occupied your Lordships in your judicial capacity: important both because of its bearing on public health and because of the practical test which it applies to the system of law under which it arises. ... The law of both [Scotland and England] appears to be that in order to support an action for damages for negligence the complainant has to show that he has been injured by the breach of a duty owed to him in the circumstances by the defendant to take reasonable care to avoid such injury. In the present case we are not concerned with the breach of the duty; if a duty exists, that would be a question of fact which is sufficiently averred and for present purposes must be assumed. We are solely concerned with the question whether, as a matter of law in the circumstances alleged, the defender owed any duty to the pursuer to take care.

It is remarkable how difficult it is to find in the English authorities statements of general application defining the relations between parties that give rise to the duty. The Courts are concerned with the particular relations which come before them in actual litigation, and it is sufficient to say whether the duty exists in those circumstances. The result is that the Courts have been engaged upon an elaborate classification of duties as they exist in respect of property, whether real or personal, with further divisions as to ownership, occupation or control, and distinctions based on the particular relations of the one side or the other, whether manufacturer, salesman or landlord, customer, tenant, stranger, and so on. In this way it can be ascertained at any time whether the law recognizes a duty, but only where the case can be referred to some particular species which has been examined and classified. And yet the duty which is common to all the cases where liability is established must logically be based upon some element common to the cases where it is found to exist. To seek a complete logical definition of the general principle is probably to go beyond the function of the judge, for the more general the definition the more likely it is to omit essentials or to introduce non-essentials. The attempt was made by Brett M.R. in *Heaven v. Pender* (11 Q.B.D. 503, 509.), in a definition to which I will later refer. As framed, it was demonstrably too wide, though it appears to me, if properly limited, to be capable of affording a valuable practical guide.

---

† [1932] AC 562.

At present I content myself with pointing out that in English law there must be, and is, some general conception of relations giving rise to a duty of care, of which the particular cases found in the books are but instances. The liability for negligence, whether you style it such or treat it as in other systems as a species of "culpa," is no doubt based upon a general public sentiment of moral wrongdoing for which the offender must pay. But acts or omissions which any moral code would censure cannot in a practical world be treated so as to give a right to every person injured by them to demand relief. In this way rules of law arise which limit the range of complainants and the extent of their remedy. The rule that you are to love your neighbour becomes in law, you must not injure your neighbour; and the lawyer's question, Who is my neighbour? receives a restricted reply. You must take reasonable care to avoid acts or omissions which you can reasonably foresee would be likely to injure your neighbour. Who, then, in law is my neighbour? The answer seems to be — persons who are so closely and directly affected by my act that I ought reasonably to have them in contemplation as being so affected when I am directing my mind to the acts or omissions which are called in question. This appears to me to be the doctrine of *Heaven v. Pender* (11 Q.B.D. 503, 509.), as laid down by Lord Esher (then Brett M.R.) when it is limited by the notion of proximity introduced by Lord Esher himself and A. L. Smith L.J. in *Le Lievre v. Gould* ([1893] 1 Q.B. 491, 497, 504), Lord Esher says:

> That case established that, under certain circumstances, one man may owe a duty to another, even though there is no contract between them. If one man is near to another, or is near to the property of another, a duty lies upon him not to do that which may cause a personal injury to that other, or may injure his property.

So A.L. Smith L.J.:

> The decision of *Heaven v. Pender* (11 Q.B.D. 503, 509.) was founded upon the principle, that a duty to take due care did arise when the person or property of one was in such proximity to the person or property of another that, if due care was not taken, damage might be done by the one to the other.

I think that this sufficiently states the truth if proximity be not confined to mere physical proximity, but be used, as I think it was intended, to extend to such close and direct relations that the act complained of directly affects a person whom the person alleged to be bound to take care would know would

be directly affected by his careless act. That this is the sense in which nearness or "proximity" was intended by Lord Esher is obvious from his own illustration in *Heaven v. Pender* (11 Q.B.D. 503, 510.) of the application of his doctrine to the sale of goods:

> This (i.e., the rule he has just formulated) includes the case of goods, etc., supplied to be used immediately by a particular person or persons, or one of a class of persons, where it would be obvious to the person supplying, if he thought, that the goods would in all probability be used at once by such persons before a reasonable opportunity for discovering any defect which might exist, and where the thing supplied would be of such a nature that a neglect of ordinary care or skill as to its condition or the manner of supplying it would probably cause danger to the person or property of the person for whose use it was supplied, and who was about to use it. It would exclude a case in which the goods are supplied under circumstances in which it would be a chance by whom they would be used or whether they would be used or not, or whether they would be used before there would probably be means of observing any defect, or where the goods would be of such a nature that a want of care or skill as to their condition or the manner of supplying them would not probably produce danger of injury to person or property.

I draw particular attention to the fact that Lord Esher emphasizes the necessity of goods having to be "used immediately" and "used at once before a reasonable opportunity of inspection." This is obviously to exclude the possibility of goods having their condition altered by lapse of time, and to call attention to the proximate relationship, which may be too remote where inspection even of the person using, certainly of an intermediate person, may reasonably be interposed. With this necessary qualification of proximate relationship as explained in *Le Lievre v. Gould* ([1893] 1 Q.B. 491.), I think the judgment of Lord Esher expresses the law of England; without the qualification, I think the majority of the Court in *Heaven v. Pender* (11 Q.B.D. 503.) were justified in thinking the principle was expressed in too general terms. There will no doubt arise cases where it will be difficult to determine whether the contemplated relationship is so close that the duty arises. But in the class of case now before the Court I cannot conceive any difficulty to arise. A manufacturer puts up an article of food in a container which he knows will be opened by the actual consumer. There can be no inspection by any purchaser and no reasonable preliminary inspection by the consumer. Negligently, in the course of preparation, he allows the contents to be mixed with poison. It is said that the law of England and Scotland is that the poisoned consumer has no remedy against the negligent manufacturer. If this were the result of the authorities, I should consider the result a grave defect in the law, and so contrary to principle that I should hesitate long before following any decision to that effect which had not the authority of this House. I would point out that, in the assumed state of the authorities, not only would the consumer have no remedy against the manufacturer, he would have none against anyone else, for in the circumstances alleged there would be no evidence of negligence against anyone other than the manufacturer; and, except in the case of a consumer who was also a purchaser, no contract and no warranty of fitness, and in the case of the purchase of a specific article under its patent or trade name, which might well be the case in the purchase of some articles of food or drink, no warranty protecting even the purchaser-consumer. There are other instances than of articles of food and drink where goods are sold intended to be used immediately by the consumer, such as many forms of goods sold for cleaning purposes, where the same liability must exist. The doctrine supported by the decision below would not only deny a remedy to the consumer who was injured by consuming bottled beer or chocolates poisoned by the negligence of the manufacturer, but also to the user of what should be a harmless proprietary medicine, an ointment, a soap, a cleaning fluid or cleaning powder. I confine myself to articles of common household use, where every one, including the manufacturer, knows that the articles will be used by other persons than the actual ultimate purchaser — namely, by members of his family and his servants, and in some cases his guests. I do not think so ill of our jurisprudence as to suppose that its principles are so remote from the ordinary needs of civilized society and the ordinary claims it makes upon its members as to deny a legal remedy where there is so obviously a social wrong.

It will be found, I think, on examination that there is no case in which the circumstances have been such as I have just suggested where the liability has been negatived. There are numerous cases, where the relations were much more remote, where the duty has been held not to exist. There are also dicta in such cases which go further than was necessary for the determination of the particular issues, which have caused the difficulty experienced by the Courts below. I venture to say that in the branch of the law which deals with civil wrongs, dependent in England at any rate entirely upon the application by judges of general principles also formulated by judges, it is of particular importance to guard against the danger of stating propositions of law in wider terms than is necessary, lest essential factors be omitted in the wider survey and the inherent adaptability of English law be unduly restricted. For this reason it is very necessary in considering reported cases in the law of torts that the actual decision alone should carry authority, proper weight, of course, being given to the dicta of the judges.

In my opinion several decided cases support the view that in such a case as the present the manufacturer owes a duty to the consumer to be careful. ...

[Note: Lord Atkin goes on to discuss several cases.]

It now becomes necessary to consider the cases which have been referred to in the Courts below as laying down the proposition that no duty to take care is owed to the consumer in such a case as this.

In *Dixon v. Bell* (5 M.S. 198.), the defendant had left a loaded gun at his lodgings and sent his servant, a mulatto girl aged about thirteen or fourteen, for the gun, asking the landlord to remove the priming and give it her. The landlord did remove the priming and gave it to the girl, who later levelled it at the plaintiff's small son, drew the trigger and injured the boy. The action was in case for negligently entrusting the young servant with the gun. The jury at the trial before Lord Ellenborough had returned a verdict for the plaintiff. A motion by Sir William Garrow (Attorney-General) for a new trial was dismissed by the Court, Lord Ellenborough and Bayley J., the former remarking that it was incumbent on the defendant, who by charging the gun had made it capable of doing mischief, to render it safe and innoxious.

... *Winterbottom v. Wright* (10 M.W. 109.) was a case decided on a demurrer. The plaintiff had demurred to two of the pleas, as to which there was no decision by the Court; but on the hearing of the plaintiff's demurrer the Court, in accordance with the practice of the day, were entitled to consider the whole record, including the declaration, and, coming to the conclusion that this declaration disclosed no cause of action, gave judgment for the defendant: see Sutton's Personal Actions at Common Law, p. 113. The advantage of the procedure is that we are in a position to know the precise issue at law which arose for determination. The declaration was in case, and alleged that the defendant had contracted with the Postmaster-General to provide the mail-coach to convey mails from Hartford to Holyhead and to keep the mails in safe condition; that Atkinson and others, with notice of the said contract, had contracted with the Postmaster-General to convey the road mail-coach from Hartford to Holyhead; and that the plaintiff, relying on the said first contract, hired himself to Atkinson to drive the mail-coach; but that the defendant so negligently conducted himself and so utterly disregarded his aforesaid contract that the defendant, having the means of knowing, and well knowing, all the aforesaid premises, the mail-coach, being in a dangerous condition, owing to certain latent defects and to no other cause, gave way, whereby the plaintiff was thrown from his seat and injured. It is to be observed that no negligence apart from breach of contract was alleged — in other words, no duty was alleged other than the duty arising out of the contract; it is not stated that the defendant knew, or ought to have known, of the latent defect. The argument of the defendant was that, on the face of the declaration, the wrong arose merely out of the breach of a contract, and that only a party to the contract could sue. The Court of Exchequer adopted that view, as clearly appears from the judgments of Alderson and Rolfe BB. There are dicta by Lord Abinger which are too wide as to an action of negligence being confined to cases of breach of a public duty. The actual decision appears to have been manifestly right; no duty to the plaintiff arose out of the contract; and the duty of the defendant under the contract with the Postmaster-General to put the coach in good repair could not have involved such direct relations with the servant of the persons whom the Postmaster-General employed to drive the coach as would give rise to a duty of care owed to such servant. ...

[Note: Lord Atkin considered several other cases before remarking:]

... With all respect, I think that the judgments in the case err by seeking to confine the law to rigid and exclusive categories, and by not giving sufficient attention to the general principle which governs the whole law of negligence in the duty owed to those who will be immediately injured by lack of care. ...

. . . .

It is always a satisfaction to an English lawyer to be able to test his application of fundamental principles of the common law by the development of the same doctrines by the lawyers of the Courts of the United States. In that country I find that the law appears to be well established in the sense in which I have indicated. The mouse had emerged from the ginger-beer bottle in the United States before it appeared in Scotland, but there it brought a liability upon the manufacturer. I must not in this long judgment do more than refer to the illuminating judgment of Cardozo J. in *MacPherson v. Buick Motor Co.* in the New York Court of Appeals (217 N.Y. 382.), in which he states the principles of the law as I should desire to state them, and reviews the authorities in other States than his own. Whether the principle he affirms would apply to the particular facts of that case in this country would be a question for consideration if the case arose. It might be that the course of business, by giving opportunities of examination to the immediate purchaser or otherwise, prevented the relation between manufacturer and the user of the car being so close as to create a duty. But the American decision would undoubtedly lead to a decision in favour of the pursuer in the present case.

My Lords, if your Lordships accept the view that this pleading discloses a relevant cause of action you will be affirming the proposition that by Scots and English law alike a manufacturer of products, which he sells in such a form as to show that he intends them to reach the ultimate consumer in the form in which they left him with no reasonable possibility of intermediate examination, and with the knowledge that the absence of reasonable care in the preparation or putting up of the products will result in an injury to the consumer's life or property, owes a duty to the consumer to take that reasonable care. It is a proposition which I venture to say no one in Scotland or England who was not a lawyer would for one moment doubt. It will be an advantage to make it clear that the law in this matter, as in most others, is in accordance with sound common sense. I think that this appeal should be allowed.

(b) *Kamloops v. Nielsen*†

Supreme Court of Canada

[WILSON J. (for Ritchie and Dickson JJ.):

This case raises the rather difficult question whether a municipality can be held liable for negligence in failing to prevent the construction of a house with defective foundations. It also raises a number of ancillary questions, such as whether such a liability, assuming it exists, extends to third party purchasers, what sort of damages are recoverable, and when the limitation period starts to run.

1. THE FACTS

Since the facts are of vital importance I set them out in some detail. Mr. Hughes, Jr. set out to build a house on a hillside for his father who was an Alderman in the City of Kamloops. To this end he submitted plans to the City's building inspector. The plans were approved, subject to the requirement that the footings were to be taken down to solid bearing, and a building permit was issued. Mr. Hughes did not take the footings down to solid bearing; instead he set the foundations on piles which were set into loose fill. He then requested an inspection of the foundations. When one of the City's building inspectors arrived to make his inspection on December 18, 1973 he realized that the foundations were not in accordance with the plans but he was unable to check whether they were adequate to support the building because the concrete had been poured. Accordingly, on his own initiative the building inspector followed up with two further inspections on December 23, 1973 and January 2, 1974 and sent a letter to Mr. Hughes on the latter date indicating that a stop work order had been placed on the site and would not be lifted until new plans had been submitted showing how the structural defects were going to be remedied. Mr. Hughes retained a firm of professional engineers to prepare the new plans and on receipt of their proposal the building inspector lifted the stop work order. Mr. Hughes, however, did not cooperate with the engineers on the required changes but continued with the construction of the house on the original plans.

The engineers, disavowing all liability, notified the building inspector.

On February 27, 1974 two building inspectors attended at the site. This was followed next day by a registered letter from the building inspector to Mr. Hughes telling him that the stop work order would remain in effect until he submitted a report from a structural engineer. Mr. Hughes ignored this communication and carried on with the building. Various further inspections were made by building inspectors who reported to their superior, the building inspector, that construction was continuing despite the stop work order.

On April 9, 1974 Mr. Hughes, Sr. and his wife purchased the property from their son. The City Solicitor wrote to them on April 22, 1974 advising them of the City's concern over the structural integrity of the building and that the stop work order which was currently in force would not be lifted until the City was provided with complete structural drawings from an engineer verifying the adequacy of the proposed construction. Mr. Backmeyer, Director of Planning for the City, became involved at this stage but no resolution to the problem was effected. The dialogue moved into the Council Chamber and Mr. Backmeyer testified that Mr. Hughes, Sr.'s plea to his fellow council members was that this was his retirement home and, since he was going to live in it, any problems that arose would be his and his alone. It was therefore no one's business but his and why was he being subjected to this kind of harassment?

At this point a strike of city employees broke out and the Director of Planning and the Building Division Administrator were left to run the Building Division by themselves until the strike ended sometime in July. No further inspections were made after the strike and no occupancy permit was ever issued. A plumbing permit was, however, issued in August 1974. The house was completed and the Hughes moved in February 1975. In December 1977 they sold the property to the present plaintiff who was told nothing of its chequered history. Before purchasing the house the plaintiff had taken a contractor with him to advise him on the cost of some

---

† [1984] 2 S.C.R. 2.

renovations and also to make a general inspection of the house. The contractor did not see anything to alert him to a potential problem with the foundations but he did not crawl under the house to examine them. Accordingly, the first the plaintiff knew of the defective foundations was when they were drawn to his attention in November 1978 by a plumber called to attend to a burst pipe. The plumber discovered the situation when he went into the four-foot crawl space under part of the house and saw that the foundations had subsided.

The plaintiff issued his writ in January 1979 alleging against his vendor: (1) fraudulent misrepresentation; (2) breach of contract; and (3) negligence in the construction of the house. He alleged negligence also against the City of Kamloops for failing to enforce the stop work order or alternatively for failing to condemn the building as unfit for habitation.

Andrews J. found both defendants liable and apportioned fault between them, 75 per cent against the Hughes and 25 per cent against the City. No appeal was taken by the Hughes. The City's appeal to the Court of Appeal of British Columbia was dismissed.

But for the issue of limitations which I will deal with later, the City's grounds of appeal to this Court were substantially the same as those presented to the Court of Appeal and rejected by it. The first was that no duty of care was owed by the City to the plaintiff and, absent such a duty, no liability in negligence could be incurred.

2. THE DUTY OF CARE

The leading English authority favouring the existence of a duty of care owed by the City to the plaintiff is the decision of the House of Lords in *Anns v. Merton London Borough Council, [1978]* A.C. 728. The facts, in brief, were that the Borough Council in February 1962 approved plans for the creation of a two-storey block of flats. The plans called for the foundations to be "3'0" or deeper to the approval of local authority". In fact the foundations were only two feet six inches deep. By February 1970 cracks had appeared in the walls of the flats and the floors had begun to slope. Two of the plaintiffs were original lessees; the others were assignees from original lessees. All claimed against the Borough for the negligence of the council surveyor in approving foundations that were inadequate.

The relevant English legislation was the *Public Health Act 1936*, s. 61 of which empowered Council to make by-laws to regulate the construction of

buildings. By-law 18(1)(b) provided that the foundations of every building should be taken down to such depth or be so designed as to safeguard the building against damage caused by swelling and shrinking of the subsoil. The builder was under a statutory duty to notify the local authority before covering up the foundations and the local authority had at that stage the right to inspect and to insist on any correction necessary to bring the work into conformity with the by-laws.

Lord Wilberforce pointed out that the local authority is a public body whose powers and duties are definable in terms of public rather than private law. However, in some circumstances the law could impose over and above, or perhaps alongside, these public law powers and duties a private law duty towards individuals enabling them to sue the authority for damages in a civil suit. The difficulty was to determine when such a private law duty could be imposed. The first step, Lord Wilberforce said, is to analyse the powers and duties of the authority to determine whether they require the authority to make "policy" decisions or "operational" decisions. He said at p. 754:

> Most, indeed probably all, statutes relating to public authorities or public bodies, contain in them a large area of policy. The courts call this "discretion" meaning that the decision is one for the authority or body to make, and not for the courts. Many statutes also prescribe or at least presuppose the practical execution of policy decisions: a convenient description of this is to say that in addition to the area of policy or discretion, there is an operational area. Although this distinction between the policy area and the operational area is convenient, and illuminating, it is probably a distinction of degree; many "operational" powers or duties have in them some element of "discretion." It can safely be said that the more "operational" a power or duty may be, the easier it is to superimpose upon it a common law duty of care.

His Lordship then adverted to the fact that frequently policy decisions are affected by budgetary considerations. It is for the local authority to decide what resources it should make available to carry out its role in supervising and controlling the activities of builders. For example, budgetary considerations may dictate how many inspectors should be hired for this purpose, what their qualifications should be, and how often inspections should be made. He approved the statement of du Parcq L.J. in *Kent v. East Suffolk Rivers Catchment Board*, [1940] 1 K.B. 319, at p. 338, that public authorities have to strike a balance between the claims of efficiency and thrift and whether they get the right balance can only be decided through the ballot box and not in the courts. He then dealt with the argument that where the local authority is under no duty to inspect but merely has a power to inspect, it can avoid liability for negligent inspection by simply deciding not to inspect at all. He pointed out that this overlooks the fact that local authorities are public bodies operating under statute with a clear responsibility for public health in their area. They must, therefore, make their discretionary decisions responsibly and for reasons that accord with the statutory purpose. They must at the very least give due consideration to the question whether they should inspect or not and, having decided to inspect, they must then be under a duty to exercise reasonable care in conducting that inspection.

Lord Wilberforce rejected the notion that a distinction was to be made in this context between statutory duties and statutory powers, the former giving rise to possible liability and the latter not. Such a distinction, he says, overlooks the fact that parallel with public law duties owed by local authorities there may co-exist private law duties to avoid causing damage to other persons in proximity to them. The trilogy of House of Lords cases — *Donoghue v. Stevenson*, [1932] A.C. 562, *Hedley Byrne & Co. v. Heller & Partners Ltd.*, [1964] A.C. 465, and *Home Office v. Dorset Yacht Co.*, [1970] A.C. 1004 — clearly established that in order to decide whether or not a private law duty of care existed, two questions must be asked:

(1) is there a sufficiently close relationship between the parties (the local authority and the person who has suffered the damage) so that, in the reasonable contemplation of the authority, carelessness on its part might cause damage to that person? If so,

(2) are there any considerations which ought to negative or limit (a) the scope of the duty and (b) the class of persons to whom it is owed or (c) the damages to which a breach of it may give rise?

These questions, Lord Wilberforce said, must be answered by an examination of the governing legislation.

Lord Wilberforce categorized the various types of legislation as follows:

(1) statutes conferring powers to interfere with the rights of individuals in which case an action in respect of damage caused by the exercise of such powers will generally not lie except in the case where the local authority has done what the legislature authorized but has done it negligently;

(2) statutes conferring powers but leaving the scale on which they are to be exercised to the discretion of the local authority. Here there will be an option to the local authority whether or not to do the thing authorized but, if it elects to do it and does it negligently, then the policy decision having been made, there is a duty at the operational level to use due care in giving effect to it.

Lord Wilberforce found that the defendant in *Anns* was under a private law duty to the plaintiff. It had to exercise a *bona fide* discretion as to whether to inspect the foundations or not and, if it decided to inspect them, to exercise reasonable skill and care in doing so. He concluded that the allegations of negligence were consistent with the Council or its inspector having acted outside any delegated discretion either as to the making of an inspection or as to the manner in which the inspection was made.

Following the path charted by Lord Wilberforce and directing myself to the governing legislation, s. 714 of the *Municipal Act of* British Columbia, R.S.B.C. 1960, c. 255, as amended, now R.S.B.C. 1979, c. 290, provides in part as follows:

> 714. The Council may, for the health, safety, and protection of persons and property, and subject to the *Health Act* and the *Fire Marshal Act* and the regulations made thereunder, by by-law
> (a) regulate the construction, alteration, repair, or demolition of buildings and structures;
> (b) require that, prior to any occupancy of a building or part thereof after construction, wrecking, or alteration of that building or part thereof, or any change in class of occupancy of any building or part thereof, an occupancy permit be obtained from the Council or the proper authorized official, which permit may be withheld until the building or part thereof complies with the health and safety requirements of the by-laws of the municipality or of any Statute.

It would appear from the use of the word "may" in s. 714 that the Council has a discretion under the statute whether to regulate the construction of buildings by by-laws or not. However, in fact Council decided to exercise its regulatory power and passed By-law No. 11-1. The By-law prohibited construction without a building permit, provided for a scheme of inspections at various stages of construction, prohibited occupancy without an occupancy permit and, perhaps most important, imposed on the building inspector the duty to enforce its provisions. It should be noted, however, that the By-law also imposed a duty on the owner of the building or his agent to give notice to the building inspector when the building reached the various stages at which inspection was called for under the By-law.

It seems to me that, applying the principle in *Anns*, it is fair to say that the City of Kamloops had a statutory power to regulate construction by by-law. It did not have to do so. It was in its discretion whether to do so or not. It was, in other words, a "policy" decision. However, not only did it make the policy decision in favour of regulating construction by by-law, it also imposed on the city's building inspector a duty to enforce the provisions of the By-law. This would be Lord Wilberforce's "operational" duty. Is the City not then in the position where in discharging its operational duty it must take care not to injure persons such as the plaintiff whose relationship to the City was sufficiently close that the City ought reasonably to have had him in contemplation?

3. THE ARGUMENT ON CAUSATION

Counsel for the City puts forward two main propositions which it says should insulate it against liability to the plaintiff. The first is that even if this Court were to adopt the principle in Arms and find that the City owed the plaintiff a private law duty of care, the plaintiff's damage was not caused by any fault of the City. The plaintiff's damage, it submits, was caused solely by the wilful disregard by the Hughes of the building by-law and the structural safety requirements imposed on them by the building inspector and their deceit in concealing their knowledge of the structural defects from the plaintiff when he bought the house. Reliance was placed on the House of Lords' decision in *East Suffolk Rivers Catchment Board v. Kent*, [1941] A.C. 74. Alternatively, the City argued, the plaintiff's damage was caused or contributed to by the plaintiff's own negligence in failing to make a proper inspection at the time of purchase. Counsel for the City submits that surely a careful examination of the foundations of a house built on a hillside would be a primary consideration in the mind of any competent contractor retained by a prospective purchaser to opine on the structural integrity of the house.

It seems to me that the learned trial judge was right in the way he dealt with the liability of the Hughes. He agreed that they played a major role in causing the plaintiff's damage and imposed a 75 per cent liability on them. He did not deal in his brief reasons for judgment with the defence of contribu-

tory negligence on the part of the plaintiff put forward by the City but it is implicit in the result he reached that he found none. The Court of Appeal in dealing with this issue said there was no evidence to show that, at the time the plaintiff had his contractor check out the house, the subsidence of the foundations had taken place or would have been apparent even if his contractor had entered the four-foot crawl space. It seems to me that this may not be completely accurate. There was some evidence that efforts had been made to shore up the foundations prior to the plaintiff's acquisition of the house. I prefer therefore to adopt the inference to be drawn from the trial judge's finding of no contributory negligence that the plaintiff had no obligation in the circumstances to crawl under the house to inspect the foundations.

I do not think the House of Lords' decision in *East Suffolk* helps the City on the causation issue. In that case the Catchment Board exercised its statutory power to repair a breach in a retaining wall when the river broke through it as a result of a flood. But the Board carried out its work so inefficiently that the flooding continued over an extensive period of time and did serious damage to the plaintiff's pasture land. The evidence disclosed that the breach could with reasonable skill have been repaired in fourteen days. The trial judge found for the plaintiff. If the defendant Board had done nothing, he concluded, it would have been free of liability. But having injected itself into the action it owed a duty to the plaintiff to use reasonable care. The Court of Appeal agreed with the trial judge that the defendant, having elected to exercise its powers, came under a duty to exercise them with a reasonable degree of skill and care. The House of Lords, however, (Lord Atkin dissenting) reversed the Court of Appeal, holding that the defendant Board was under no obligation to repair the wall or to complete the work after having started it. Viscount Simon and Lord Thankerton both found that the plaintiff's damage was caused by the flooding and not by the abortive efforts of the defendant to repair the gap in the wall. There was no evidence that any additional damage was caused as a result of its intervention.

Lord Wilberforce was not content to characterize *East Suffolk* simply as a case on causation. He thought rather that it revealed that in 1940 the concept of a general duty of care resting on public officials was not yet fully recognised and, indeed, that that recognition did not come until 1970 with the decision in *Home Office v. Dorset Yacht Co., supra.*

In my view, the *East Suffolk* case is clearly distinguishable from the present case. This is not the case of a power which the City decided to exercise but exercised in a negligent manner. This is the case of a duty owed by the City to the plaintiff, a person who met Lord Wilberforce's test of proximity in *Anns*. The City's responsibility as set out in the By-law was to vet the work of the builder and protect the plaintiff against the consequences of any negligence in the performance of it. In those circumstances it cannot, in my view, be argued that the City's breach of duty was not causative. The builder's negligence, it is true, was primary. He laid the defective foundations. But the City, whose duty it was to see that they were remedied, permitted the building to be constructed on top of them. The City's negligence in this case was its breach of duty in failing to protect the plaintiff against the builder's negligence.

In *Anns* Lord Wilberforce suggests that if *East Suffolk* were being decided today the Catchment Board, although free of liability if it decided to take no steps to stem the flood, might attract a liability if it decided to exercise its power and take steps but exercised its power negligently. It seems to me that this would follow from a finding that the Board had made a policy decision to exercise its power and acted negligently in carrying its policy decision into operation. A liability might then be incurred not only with respect to any fresh damage caused by its negligent intervention but also with respect to damage the flood would have caused regardless of its intervention provided that damage could and ought to have been mitigated by a non-negligent intervention.

I believe that if the courts below had found in this case that the City owed no private law duty of care to the plaintiff, they would have held the Hughes one hundred per cent liable. Their apportionment of liability therefore must stand or fall on the existence of such a duty.

[Note: Material on 4. Non-feasance and Misfeasance has been omitted.]

5. THE NATURE OF THE ALLEGED BREACH

Two important questions that must be answered in the present case are: (1) What was it that the building inspector failed to do in this case that is alleged to have contributed to the plaintiff's damage? and (2) Was he under a duty to do that thing? ...

Lambert J.A., speaking for the Court of Appeal, [(1981), 31 B.C.L.R. 311], found that the building inspector was under a public law duty to prevent the continuation of the construction of the build-

ing on structurally unsound foundations once he became aware that the foundations were structurally unsound. He was also under a public law duty to prevent the occupancy of the building by the Hughes or the plaintiff. He failed to discharge either of those public law duties. Lambert J.A. then went on to discuss the nature of the private law duty he was under. He said at p. 319:

> I turn now to the private law duty. The conduct of the building inspector in response to the public law duties involved decisions on alternative courses of conduct which were, in my opinion, operational in character. The building was a danger to the occupant of the house and to adjoining property owners. It may have been a danger to anyone in the house. Policy decisions could have confronted the city as to whether to prosecute or to seek an injunction. There may have been other policy choices. But a decision not to act at all, or a failure to decide to act, cannot be supported by any reasonable policy choice. That decision or failure was not "within the limits of a discretion bona fide exercised", using again the words of Lord Wilberforce. It was certainly open to the trial judge to reach that conclusion. Indeed, having regard to the evidence of Mr. Backmeyer, it was open to the trial judge to conclude that the decision not to act or the failure to decide to act, was influenced by the pressure exerted by Mr. Hughes Sr. in his capacity as alderman.
>
> I would follow the reasons of Lord Wilberforce in *Anns* in concluding that a private law duty was owed to Mr. Nielsen as the owner and occupier of the house at the time when the defective foundations first became apparent by causing actual subsidence and damage. [My emphasis.]

It seems to me that Lambert J.A. was correct in concluding that the courses of conduct open to the building inspector called for "operational" decisions. The essential question was what steps to take to enforce the provisions of the by-law in the circumstances that had arisen. He had a duty to enforce its provisions. He did not have a discretion whether to enforce them or not. He did, however, have a discretion as to how to go about it. This may, therefore, be the kind of situation envisaged by Lord Wilberforce when, after discussing the distinction between policy decisions and operational decisions, he added the rider [[1978] A.C. 728, at p. 754]:

> Although this distinction between the policy area and the operational area is convenient, and illuminating, it is probably a distinction of degree; many "operational" powers or duties have in

them some element of "discretion". It can safely be said that the more "operational" a power or duty may be, the easier it is to superimpose upon it a common law duty of care.

It may be, for example, that although the building inspector had a duty to enforce the by-law, the lengths to which he should go in doing so involved policy considerations. The making of inspections, the issuance of stop orders and the withholding of occupancy permits may be one thing; resort to litigation, if this became necessary, may be quite another. Must the City enforce infractions by legal proceedings or does there come a point at which economic considerations, for example, enter in? And if so, how do you measure the "operational" against the "policy" content of the decision in order to decide whether it is more "operational" than "policy" or vice versa? Clearly this is a matter of very fine distinctions.

Mr. Justice Lambert resolves this problem, as I apprehend the passage already quoted from his reasons, by concluding that the City could have made a policy decision either to prosecute or to seek an injunction. If it had taken either of those steps, it could not be faulted. Moreover, if it had considered taking either of those steps and decided against them, it could likewise not be faulted. But not to consider taking them at all was not open to it. In other words, as I read his reasons, his view was that the City at the very least had to give serious consideration to taking the steps toward enforcement that were open to it. If it decided against taking them, say on economic grounds, then that would be a legitimate policy decision within the operational context and the courts should not interfere with it. It would be a decision made, as Lord Wilberforce put it, within the limits of a discretion *bona fide* exercised.

There is no evidence to support the proposition that the City gave serious consideration to legal proceedings and decided against them on policy grounds. Rather the evidence gives rise to a strong inference that the City, with full knowledge that the work was progressing in violation of the by-law and that the house was being occupied without a permit, dropped the matter because one of its aldermen was involved. Having regard to the fact that we are here concerned with a statutory duty and that the plaintiff was clearly a person who should have been in the contemplation of the City as someone who might be injured by any breach of that duty, I think this is an appropriate case for the application of the principle in *Anns*. I do not think the appellant can take any comfort from the distinction between non-feasance and misfeasance where there is a duty to act or, at the very least, to make a conscious decision not to

act on policy grounds. In my view, inaction for no reason or inaction for an improper reason cannot be a policy decision taken in the *bona fide* exercise of discretion. Where the question whether the requisite action should be taken has not even been considered by the public authority, or at least has not been considered in good faith, it seems clear that for that very reason the authority has not acted with reasonable care. I conclude therefore that the conditions for liability of the City to the plaintiff have been met.

It is of interest to note in this connection that other courses were open to the City. It could have posted warning notices on the building and it could have condemned it. In fact, it did neither even although it knew that work was continuing despite the stop work order and that the house was being occupied without an occupancy permit. Indeed, it issued a plumbing permit in August 1974 before the Hughes moved in.

6.   THE "FLOODGATES" ARGUMENT

Before leaving the issue of the liability of public officials and moving on to the equally vexatious issue of recovery for pure economic loss, I should like to say a word or two about what has come to be known as the "floodgates" argument. The floodgates argument would discourage a finding of private law duties owed by public officials on the ground that such a finding would open the flood-gates and create an "open season" on municipalities. No doubt a similar type of concern was expressed about the vulnerability of manufacturers following the decision in *Donoghue v. Stevenson, supra*. While I think this is an argument which cannot be dismissed lightly, I believe that the decision in *Anns* contains its own built-in barriers against the flood. For example, the applicable legislation or the subordinate legislation enacted pursuant to it must impose a private law duty on the municipality or public official before the principle in *Anns* applies. Further, the principle will not apply to purely policy decisions made in the *bona fide* exercise of discretion. This is, in my view, an extremely important feature of the *Anns* principle because it prevents the courts from usurping the proper authority of elected representatives and their officials. At the same time, however, the principle ensures that in the operational area, *i.e.* in implementing their policy decisions, public officials will be exposed to the same liability as other people if they fail in discharging their duty to take reasonable care to avoid injury to their neighbours. The only area, in my view, which leaves scope for honest concern is that difficult area identified by Lord Wilberforce where the operational subsumes what might be called secondary policy considerations, *i.e.* policy considerations at the secondary level. This, I believe, is the area into which this case falls. This case, however, is more easily disposed of by virtue of the complete failure of the municipality to deal with the policy considerations. On the assumption that by and large municipalities and their officials discharge their responsibilities in a conscientious fashion, I believe that such a failure will be the exception rather than the rule and that the scope for application of the principle in *Anns* will be relatively narrow. I do not see it, as do some commentators, as potentially ruinous financially to municipalities. I do see it as a useful protection to the citizen whose ever-increasing reliance on public officials seems to be a feature of our age: see Linden, "Tort Law's Role in the Regulation and Control of the Abuse of Power", *Special Lectures of the Law Society of Upper Canada, 1979*, p. 67.

. . . .

I would dismiss the appeal with costs.

(c) *Cooper v. Hobart*†

Supreme Court of Canada

[McLACHLIN C.J. and MAJOR J.:]

[1] The present appeal revisits the *Anns* test (from *Anns v. Merton London Borough Council*, [1978] A.C. 728 (H.L.)) and, in particular, highlights and hones the role of policy concerns in determining the scope of liability for negligence. The appellant is an investor who alleges that the Registrar of Mortgage Brokers, a statutory regulator, is liable in negligence for failing to oversee the conduct of an investment company which the Registrar licensed. The question is whether the Registrar owes a private law duty of care to members of the investing public giving rise to liability in negligence for economic losses that the investors sustained. Such a duty of care is as yet unrecognized by Canadian courts. For the reasons that follow, we find that this is not a proper case in which to recognize a new duty of care. In the course of these reasons, we attempt to clarify the distinctive policy considerations which impact each stage of the *Anns* analysis.

I.   FACTS

[2] Eron Mortgage Corporation ("Eron") was registered as a mortgage broker under the *Mortgage Brokers Act*, R.S.B.C. 1996, c. 313 ("the Act"), from early 1993 until 1997. On October 3, 1997, the respondent, Robert J. Hobart, in his capacity as the Registrar under the Act, suspended Eron's mortgage broker's licence and issued a freeze order in respect of its assets.

[3] Eron acted as a mortgage broker for large syndicated loans. It arranged for numerous lenders (or investors) to pool their funds for the purpose of making a single loan to a borrower, which was typically a developer of commercial real estate. The syndicated loans were made in the name of Eron or one of its related companies, which held the security in trust for the investors.

[4] It is alleged that the funds provided by the investors were used by Eron for several unauthorized purposes, such as funding interest payments on other non-performing mortgages and paying for personal items for the benefit of the principals of Eron. It is currently estimated that $222 million is outstanding to the investors on these loans. Investors will likely realize only $40 million from the security taken from the loans, leaving a shortfall of $182 million.

[5] Soon after Eron's mortgage licence was suspended, it went out of business. The appellant Mary Francis Cooper ("Cooper"), one of over 3000 investors who advanced money to Eron, brought an action against the Registrar. The Statement of Claim alleged that the Registrar breached the duty of care that he allegedly owed to the appellant and other

† [2001] 3 S.C.R. 537, 2001 SCC 79.

investors. The appellant asserted that by August 28, 1996, the Registrar was aware of serious violations of the Act committed by Eron but that he failed to suspend Eron's mortgage broker's licence until October 3, 1997 and failed to notify investors that Eron was under investigation by the Registrar's office. According to the appellant, if the Registrar had taken steps to suspend or cancel Eron's mortgage broker's licence at an earlier date, the losses suffered by the investors would have been avoided or diminished.

[6] The appellant applied to have the action certified as a class proceeding under the *Class Proceedings Act*, R.S.B.C. 1996, c. 50. Pursuant to s. 4(1)(a), in order to certify an action as a class proceeding, a court must first determine whether the pleadings disclose a cause of action. The cause of action alleged in the Statement of Claim is negligence which requires, among other things, that a duty of care in tort law be owed by the Registrar to the appellant investor. Therefore, the question was whether the Registrar of Mortgage Brokers, a statutory regulator, owes a private law duty of care to members of the investing public for alleged negligence in failing to properly oversee the conduct of an investment company licensed by the regulator.

. . . .

III. ISSUE

[20] Does a statutory regulator owe a private law duty of care to members of the investing public for (alleged) negligence in failing to properly oversee the conduct of an investment company licensed by the regulator?

IV. ANALYSIS

[21] Canadian courts have not thus far recognized the duty of care that the appellants allege in this case. The question is therefore whether the law of negligence should be extended to reach this situation. While the particular extension sought is novel, the more general issue of how far the principles of liability for negligence should be extended is a familiar one, and one with which this Court and others have repeatedly grappled since Lord Atkin enunciated the negligence principle in *Donoghue v. Stevenson*, [1932] A.C. 562 (H.L.), almost 70 years ago. That case introduced the principle that a person could be held liable only for reasonably foreseeable harm. But it also anticipated that not all reasonably foreseeable harm might be caught. This posed the

issue with which courts still struggle today: to what situations does the law of negligence extend? This case, like so many of its predecessors, may thus be seen as but a gloss on the case of *Donoghue v. Stevenson*.

[22] In *Donoghue v. Stevenson* the House of Lords revolutionized the common law by replacing the old categories of tort recovery with a single comprehensive principle — the negligence principle. Henceforward, liability would lie for negligence in circumstances where a reasonable person would have viewed the harm as foreseeable. However, foreseeability alone was not enough; there must also be a close and direct relationship of proximity or neighbourhood.

[23] But what is proximity? For the most part, lawyers apply the law of negligence on the basis of categories as to which proximity has been recognized in the past. However, as Lord Atkin declared in *Donoghue v. Stevenson*, the categories of negligence are not closed. Where new cases arise, we must search elsewhere for assistance in determining whether, in addition to disclosing foreseeability, the circumstances disclose sufficient proximity to justify the imposition of liability for negligence.

[24] In *Anns*, *supra*, at pp. 751–52, the House of Lords, *per* Lord Wilberforce, said that a duty of care required a finding of proximity sufficient to create a *prima facie* duty of care, followed by consideration of whether there were any factors negativing that duty of care. This Court has repeatedly affirmed that approach as appropriate in the Canadian context.

[25] The importance of *Anns* lies in its recognition that policy considerations play an important role in determining proximity in new situations. Long before *Anns*, courts in Canada and elsewhere had recognized that the decision of how far to extend liability for negligence involved policy considerations. As H. Street put it in *The Law of Torts* (6th ed. 1976), at p. 108, citing a Canadian case, *Nova Mink Ltd. v. Trans-Canada Airlines*, [1951] 2 D.L.R. 241 (N.S.C.A.), at pp. 254–55:

> ... it cannot be too strongly stressed that the use of [the] test of foreseeability in order to determine whether there is a duty-relationship between the parties conceals the true judicial process — that test is in fact a conclusion embracing within it, and yet concealing the identity of, the several considerations of policy, and the balancing of interests which have led the court to decide that a duty is owed.

[26] The House of Lords in *Anns* for the first time expressly recognized the policy component in determining the extension of the negligence principle. However, it left doubt on the precise content of the first and second branches of the new formulation of the negligence principle. This gave rise to debate — debate which the submissions in this case revive. Was the first branch concerned with foreseeability only or foreseeability and proximity? If the latter, was there duplication between policy considerations relevant to proximity at the first stage and the second stage of the test?

[27] To some extent, these concerns are academic. Provided the proper balancing of the factors relevant to a duty of care are considered, it may not matter, so far as a particular case is concerned, at which "stage" it occurs. The underlying question is whether a duty of care should be imposed, taking into account all relevant factors disclosed by the circumstances. *Anns* did not purport to depart from the negligence test of *Donoghue v. Stevenson* but merely sought to elucidate it by explicitly recognizing its policy component.

[28] We continue in the view, repeatedly expressed by this Court, that the *Anns* two-stage test, properly understood, does not involve duplication because different types of policy considerations are involved at the two stages. In our view, *Anns* continues to provide a useful framework in which to approach the question of whether a duty of care should be imposed in a new situation.

[29] Nevertheless, it is important from the point of view of methodology and clarity in the law to be clear on what falls to be considered at each stage of the *Anns* test. In this connection, it is useful to consider the leading English case on that question. The Judicial Committee of the Privy Council held in *Yuen Kun Yeu v. Attorney-General of Hong Kong*, [1988] 1 A.C. 175, that to find a *prima facie* duty of care at the first stage of the test there must be reasonable foreseeability of the harm plus something more. As will be seen, we agree with this conclusion. The Privy Council went on to opine that *Anns'* second branch, negation for policy reasons, would seldom come into play. If this is read as a suggestion that policy is not important in determining whether the negligence principle should be extended to new situations, we would respectfully differ. As Street points out, the *Donoghue v. Stevenson* foreseeability-negligence test, no matter how it is phrased, conceals a balancing of interests. The quest for the right balance is in reality a quest for prudent policy. The dif-

ference in the two positions, if there is one, may turn on how one defines policy; the Privy Council in *Yuen Kun Yeu* appears to regard policy as confined to practical considerations dictating immunity despite a close relationship and foreseeability.

[30] In brief compass, we suggest that at this stage in the evolution of the law, both in Canada and abroad, the *Anns* analysis is best understood as follows. At the first stage of the *Anns* test, two questions arise: (1) was the harm that occurred the reasonably foreseeable consequence of the defendant's act? and (2) are there reasons, notwithstanding the proximity between the parties established in the first part of this test, that tort liability should not be recognized here? The proximity analysis involved at the first stage of the *Anns* test focuses on factors arising from the relationship between the plaintiff and the defendant. These factors include questions of policy, in the broad sense of that word. If foreseeability and proximity are established at the first stage, a *prima facie* duty of care arises. At the second stage of the *Anns* test, the question still remains whether there are residual policy considerations outside the relationship of the parties that may negative the imposition of a duty of care. It may be, as the Privy Council suggests in *Yuen Kun Yeu*, that such considerations will not often prevail. However, we think it useful expressly to ask, before imposing a new duty of care, whether despite foreseeability and proximity of relationship, there are other policy reasons why the duty should not be imposed.

[31] On the first branch of the *Anns* test, reasonable foreseeability of the harm must be supplemented by proximity. The question is what is meant by proximity. Two things may be said. The first is that "proximity" is generally used in the authorities to characterize the type of relationship in which a duty of care may arise. The second is that sufficiently proximate relationships are identified through the use of categories. The categories are not closed and new categories of negligence may be introduced. But generally, proximity is established by reference to these categories. This provides certainty to the law of negligence, while still permitting it to evolve to meet the needs of new circumstances.

[32] On the first point, it seems clear that the word "proximity" in connection with negligence has from the outset and throughout its history been used to describe the type of relationship in which a duty of care to guard against foreseeable negligence may be imposed. "Proximity" is the term used to describe

the "close and direct" relationship that Lord Atkin described as necessary to grounding a duty of care in *Donoghue v. Stevenson, supra,* at pp. 580–81:

> Who then, in law is my neighbour? The answer seems to be — persons who are so closely and directly affected by my act that I ought reasonably to have them in contemplation as being so affected when I am directing my mind to the acts or omissions which are called in question.
>
> ...
>
> I think that this sufficiently states the truth if proximity be not confined to mere physical proximity, but be used, as I think it was intended, to extend to such close and direct relations that the act complained of directly affects a person whom the person alleged to be bound to take care would know would be directly affected by his careless act. [Emphasis added.]

[33] As this Court stated in *Hercules Managements Ltd. v. Ernst & Young,* [1997] 2 S.C.R. 165, at para. 24, *per* La Forest J.:

> The label "proximity", as it was used by Lord Wilberforce in *Anns, supra,* was clearly intended to connote that the circumstances of the relationship inhering between the plaintiff and the defendant are of such a nature that the defendant may be said to be under an obligation to be mindful of the plaintiff's legitimate interests in conducting his or her affairs. [Emphasis added.]

[34] Defining the relationship may involve looking at expectations, representations, reliance, and the property or other interests involved. Essentially, these are factors that allow us to evaluate the closeness of the relationship between the plaintiff and the defendant and to determine whether it is just and fair having regard to that relationship to impose a duty of care in law upon the defendant.

[35] The factors which may satisfy the requirement of proximity are diverse and depend on the circumstances of the case. One searches in vain for a single unifying characteristic. As stated by McLachlin J. (as she then was) in *Canadian National Railway Co. v. Norsk Pacific Steamship Co.,* [1992] 1 S.C.R. 1021, at p. 1151: "[p]roximity may be usefully viewed, not so much as a test in itself, but as a broad concept which is capable of subsuming different categories of cases involving different factors" (cited with approval in *Hercules Managements, supra,* at para. 23). Lord Goff made the same point in *Davis v. Radcliffe,* [1990] 2 All E.R. 536 (P.C.), at p. 540:

> ... it is not desirable, at least in the present stage of development of the law, to attempt to state in broad general propositions the circumstances in which such proximity may or may not be held to exist. On the contrary, following the expression of opinion by Brennan J. in *Sutherland Shire Council v Heyman* (1985) 60 ALR 1 at 43–44, it is considered preferable that 'the law should develop categories of negligence incrementally and by analogy with established categories'.

[36] What then are the categories in which proximity has been recognized? First, of course, is the situation where the defendant's act foreseeably causes physical harm to the plaintiff or the plaintiff's property. This has been extended to nervous shock (see, for example, *Alcock v. Chief Constable of the South Yorkshire Police,* [1991] 4 All E.R. 907 (H.L.)). Yet other categories are liability for negligent misstatement: *Hedley Byrne & Co. v. Heller & Partners Ltd.,* [1963] 2 All E.R. 575 (H.L.), and misfeasance in public office. A duty to warn of the risk of danger has been recognized: *Rivtow Marine Ltd. v. Washington Iron Works,* [1974] S.C.R. 1189. Again, a municipality has been held to owe a duty to prospective purchasers of real estate to inspect housing developments without negligence: *Anns, supra; Kamloops, supra.* Similarly, governmental authorities who have undertaken a policy of road maintenance have been held to owe a duty of care to execute the maintenance in a non-negligent manner: *Just v. British Columbia,* [1989] 2 S.C.R. 1228, *Swinamer v. Nova Scotia (Attorney General),* [1994] 1 S.C.R. 445, etc. Relational economic loss (related to a contract's performance) may give rise to a tort duty of care in certain situations, as where the claimant has a possessory or proprietary interest in the property, the general average cases, and cases where the relationship between the claimant and the property owner constitutes a joint venture: *Norsk, supra; Bow Valley Husky (Bermuda) Ltd. v. Saint John Shipbuilding Ltd.,* [1997] 3 S.C.R. 1210. When a case falls within one of these situations or an analogous one and reasonable foreseeability is established, a *prima facie* duty of care may be posited.

[37] This brings us to the second stage of the *Anns* test. As the majority of this Court held in *Norsk,* at p. 1155, residual policy considerations fall to be considered here. These are not concerned with the relationship between the parties, but with the effect of recognizing a duty of care on other legal obligations, the legal system and society more generally. Does the law already provide a remedy? Would recognition of the duty of care create the spectre of unlimited liability to an unlimited class? Are there other reasons of broad policy that suggest that the

duty of care should not be recognized? Following this approach, this Court declined to find liability in *Hercules Managements, supra*, on the ground that to recognize a duty of care would raise the spectre of liability to an indeterminate class of people.

[38] It is at this second stage of the analysis that the distinction between government policy and execution of policy falls to be considered. It is established that government actors are not liable in negligence for policy decisions, but only operational decisions. The basis of this immunity is that policy is the prerogative of the elected Legislature. It is inappropriate for courts to impose liability for the consequences of a particular policy decision. On the other hand, a government actor may be liable in negligence for the manner in which it executes or carries out the policy. In our view, the exclusion of liability for policy decisions is properly regarded as an application of the second stage of the *Anns* test. The exclusion does not relate to the relationship between the parties. Apart from the legal characterization of the government duty as a matter of policy, plaintiffs can and do recover. The exclusion of liability is better viewed as an immunity imposed because of considerations outside the relationship for policy reasons — more precisely, because it is inappropriate for courts to second-guess elected legislators on policy matters. Similar considerations may arise where the decision in question is quasi-judicial (see *Edwards v. Law Society of Upper Canada*, [2001] 3 S.C.R. 562, 2001 SCC 80).

[39] The second step of *Anns* generally arises only in cases where the duty of care asserted does not fall within a recognized category of recovery. Where it does, we may be satisfied that there are no overriding policy considerations that would negative the duty of care. In this sense, we agree with the Privy Council in *Yuen Kun Yeu* that the second stage of *Anns* will seldom arise and that questions of liability will be determined primarily by reference to established and analogous categories of recovery. However, where a duty of care in a novel situation is alleged, as here, we believe it necessary to consider both steps of the *Anns* test as discussed above. This ensures that before a duty of care is imposed in a new situation, not only are foreseeability and relational proximity present, but there are no broader considerations that would make imposition of a duty of care unwise.

V. APPLICATION OF THE TEST

[40] The appellants submit that the Registrar of Mortgage Brokers owed them, as investors with a firm falling under the Registrar's administrative mandate, a duty of care giving rise to liability for negligence and damages for losses that they sustained. The investors allege that the Registrar should have acted earlier to suspend Eron or warn them of Eron's breaches of the Act's requirements, and that their losses are traceable to the Registrar's failure to act more promptly.

[41] The first question is whether the circumstances disclose reasonably foreseeable harm and proximity sufficient to establish a *prima facie* duty of care. The first inquiry at this stage is whether the case falls within or is analogous to a category of cases in which a duty of care has previously been recognized. The answer to this question is no.

[42] The next question is whether this is a situation in which a new duty of care should be recognized. It may be that the investors can show that it was reasonably foreseeable that the alleged negligence in failing to suspend Eron or issue warnings might result in financial loss to the plaintiffs. However, as discussed, mere foreseeability is not enough to establish a *prima facie* duty of care. The plaintiffs must also show proximity — that the Registrar was in a close and direct relationship to them making it just to impose a duty of care upon him toward the plaintiffs. In addition to showing foreseeability, the plaintiffs must point to factors arising from the circumstances of the relationship that impose a duty.

[43] In this case, the factors giving rise to proximity, if they exist, must arise from the statute under which the Registrar is appointed. That statute is the only source of his duties, private or public. Apart from that statute, he is in no different position than the ordinary man or woman on the street. If a duty to investors with regulated mortgage brokers is to be found, it must be in the statute.

[44] In this case, the statute does not impose a duty of care on the Registrar to investors with mortgage brokers regulated by the Act. The Registrar's duty is rather to the public as a whole. Indeed, a duty to individual investors would potentially conflict with the Registrar's overarching duty to the public.

[45] A brief review of the relevant powers and duties of the Registrar under the Act confirms this conclusion. Part 1 sets out the Registrar's regulatory powers with respect to the operation of mortgage brokers and submortgage brokers in British Colum-

bia. Specifically, s. 4 provides that the Registrar must grant registration or renewal of registration to an applicant if, in his opinion, the applicant is "suitable" for registration and the proposed registration is "not objectionable". He may also attach such conditions and restrictions to the registration as he considers necessary. Once registered, a mortgage broker must comply with s. 6 of the Regulations which mandates that registrants maintain proper books and records and file annual financial statements with the Registrar.

[46] Sections 5 and 6 of the Act cover the investigatory powers of the Registrar. Pursuant to s. 5, the Registrar may, and on receipt of a sworn complaint must, investigate any matter arising out of the Act or Regulations. In pursuit of this purpose, the Registrar may examine any records and documents of the person being investigated. He may summon witnesses and compel them to give evidence on oath or otherwise and to produce records, property, assets or things in the same manner as the court does for the trial of civil actions. Section 7 allows the Registrar to "freeze" funds or securities where he has made or is about to make a direction, decision, order or ruling suspending or cancelling the registration of a person under the Act. He may also apply to the court for an appointment of a receiver, or a receiver and manager, or trustee of the property of the person.

[47] Under s. 8, the Registrar may, after giving a person registered under the Act an opportunity to be heard, suspend or cancel any registration if, in his opinion, any of the following or other conditions apply: the person would be disentitled to registration if the person were an applicant under s. 4; the person is in breach of a condition of registration; the person is a party to a mortgage transaction which is harsh and unconscionable or otherwise inequitable; or the person has conducted or is conducting business in a manner that is otherwise prejudicial to the public interest. Section 14 prohibits a broker from making any false, misleading or deceptive statements in any advertisement, circular or similar material. Part 2 of the Act is directed towards the protection of borrowers, investors and lenders, mandating in part specific disclosure requirements by mortgage lenders and their agents. Section 8 of the Regulations provides that every direction, decision, order or ruling of the Registrar refusing registration, refusing to renew registration, suspending registration or cancelling registration shall be made in writing and shall be open to public inspection.

[48] Finally, s. 20 exempts the Registrar or any person acting under his authority from any action brought for anything done in the performance of duties under the Act or Regulations, or in pursuance or intended or supposed pursuance of the Act or Regulations, unless it was done in bad faith.

[49] The regulatory scheme governing mortgage brokers provides a general framework to ensure the efficient operation of the mortgage marketplace. The Registrar must balance a myriad of competing interests, ensuring that the public has access to capital through mortgage financing while at the same time instilling public confidence in the system by determining who is "suitable" and whose proposed registration as a broker is "not objectionable". All of the powers or tools conferred by the Act on the Registrar are necessary to undertake this delicate balancing. Even though to some degree the provisions of the Act serve to protect the interests of investors, the overall scheme of the Act mandates that the Registrar's duty of care is not owed to investors exclusively but to the public as a whole.

[50] Accordingly, we agree with the Court of Appeal *per* Newbury J.A.: even though the Registrar might reasonably have foreseen that losses to investors in Eron would result if he was careless in carrying out his duties under the Act, there was insufficient proximity between the Registrar and the investors to ground a *prima facie* duty of care. The statute cannot be construed to impose a duty of care on the Registrar specific to investments with mortgage brokers. Such a duty would no doubt come at the expense of other important interests, of efficiency and finally at the expense of public confidence in the system as a whole.

[51] Having found no proximity sufficient to found a duty of care owed by the Registrar to the investors, we need not proceed to the second branch of the *Anns* test and the question of whether there exist policy considerations apart from those considered in determining a relationship of proximity, which would negative a *prima facie* duty of care, had one been found. However, the matter having been fully argued, it may be useful to comment on those submissions.

[52] In our view, even if a *prima facie* duty of care had been established under the first branch of the *Anns* test, it would have been negated at the second stage for overriding policy reasons. The decision of whether to suspend a broker involves both policy and quasi-judicial elements. The decision requires the Registrar to balance the public and private inter-

ests. The Registrar is not simply carrying out a predetermined government policy, but deciding, as an agent of the executive branch of government, what that policy should be. Moreover, the decision is quasi-judicial. The Registrar must act fairly or judicially in removing a broker's licence. These requirements are inconsistent with a duty of care to investors. Such a duty would undermine these obligations, imposed by the Legislature on the Registrar. Thus even if a *prima facie* duty of care could be posited, it would be negated by other overriding policy considerations.

[53] The *prima facie* duty of care is also negated on the basis of the distinction between government policy and the execution of policy. As stated, the Registrar must make difficult discretionary decisions in the area of public policy, decisions which command deference. As Huddart J.A. (concurring in the result) found, the decisions made by the Registrar were made within the limits of the powers conferred upon him in the public interest.

[54] Further, the spectre of indeterminate liability would loom large if a duty of care was recognized as between the Registrar and investors in this case. The Act itself imposes no limit and the Registrar has no means of controlling the number of investors or the amount of money invested in the mortgage brokerage system.

[55] Finally, we must consider the impact of a duty of care on the taxpayers, who did not agree to assume the risk of private loss to persons in the situation of the investors. To impose a duty of care in these circumstances would be to effectively create an insurance scheme for investors at great cost to the taxpaying public. There is no indication that the Legislature intended that result.

[56] In the result the judgment of the British Columbia Court of Appeal is affirmed and the appeal is dismissed with costs.

(d) After *Cooper v Hobart*†

Honourable Mr. Justice A.M. Linden

The law of duty was dramatically transformed by the legendary *Donoghue v. Stevenson* case in 1932, outlining a "general conception of relations giving rise to a duty of care, of which the particular cases found in the books are but instances". The much celebrated "neighbour principle" was born in that case, to this effect:

> The rule that you are to love your neighbour becomes in law you must not injure your neighbour; and the lawyer's question, 'Who is my neighbour?' receives a restricted reply. You must take reasonable care to avoid acts or omissions which you can reasonably foresee would be likely to injure your neighbour. Who, then, in law, is my neighbour? The answer seems to be — persons who are so closely and directly affected by my act that I ought reasonably to have them in contemplation as being so affected when I am directing my mind to the acts or omissions which are called in question.

This principle led to much expansion of the negligence principle in the following decades, but certain areas remained immune from the call of *Donoghue v. Stevenson*. It was said that the principle "ought to apply unless there is some justification or valid explanation for its exclusion." A general principle, therefore, was recognized to the effect that reasonable foreseeability of harm to a neighbour created a duty, unless good policy reasons dictated otherwise. In the ensuing years, pursuant to this fundamental principle, negligence law grew to cover nervous shock, negligent representations, some pure economic losses, new areas of products liability and others, while nonfeasance, government liability and some pure economic losses were less influenced by the new principle.

This neighbour principle, which had been accepted by all for 45 years, was, for some unknown

† Excerpts from a speech given to the National Judicial Institute, Civil Law Seminars, on April 11, 2005. Reproduced with permission of the author.

reason, reformulated by Lord Wilberforce in the *Anns v. Merton* case (1977) as follows:

> ... the position has now been reached that in order to establish that a duty of care arises in a particular situation, it is not necessary to bring the facts of that situation within those of previous situations in which a duty of care has been held to exist. Rather the question has to be approached in two stages. First one has to ask whether, as between the alleged wrongdoer and the person who has suffered damage there is a sufficient relationship of proximity or neighbourhood such that, in the reasonable contemplation of the former, carelessness on his part may be likely to cause damage to the latter — in which case a *prime facie* duty of care arises. Secondly, if the first question is answered affirmatively, it is necessary to consider whether there are any considerations which ought to negative, or to reduce or limit the scope of the duty or the class of person to whom it is owed or the damages to which a breach of it may give rise: ...

This two step *prima facie* duty approach of *Anns* was embraced by the Supreme Court of Canada in *Kamloops v. Nielsen* and, even after the House of Lords retreated from *Anns* in *Murphy v. Brentwood*, the Supreme Court remained, with minor refinements, steadfastly faithful to *Anns*. This was the case until 2001 and the case of *Cooper v. Hobart*, a claim against an allegedly negligent governmental regulator of mortgage brokers. In *Cooper,* which case the Supreme Court described as a "gloss" on *Donoghue v. Stevenson*, the Court explained that it needed to "elucidate" the *Anns* approach, which, the Court said, had merely "elucidated *Donoghue v. Stevenson*". *Anns* was "still appropriate in the Canadian context", but the Court felt that there was "doubt" about the application of the *Anns* test and about which policy considerations were to be undertaken at which stage of the analysis. While the Court stated that the concerns are "academic" and that "it may not matter at which stage it occurs," it was "important from the point of view of methodology and clarity in the law to be clear on what falls to be considered at each stage of the *Anns* test." The Court reaffirmed that *Anns* continued to "provide a useful framework in which to approach the question of whether a duty of care should be imposed in a new situation."

.   .   .   .

In a significant later case, *Odhavji Estate v. Woodhouse,* a police regulator case, the Court[] further adjusted the new *Cooper* analysis of the *Anns*

test. Justice Iacobucci reminded us that it is well established in Canada that the existence of a tort duty is to be determined according to the two-step analysis first enunciated in *Anns v. Merton*. He opines that the neighbour principle of *Donoghue v. Stevenson*, while a "sacrosanct preamble" to the exercise, is not enough by itself; "something in addition to foreseeability" is needed, that is, a relationship of proximity. The "essential purpose of the inquiry", he writes, "is to evaluate the nature of that relationship in order to determine whether it is just and fair to impose a duty." He reiterates that the factors to consider in this inquiry include "the expectations of the parties, representations, reliance and the nature of the property or interest involved." He then reminds us of the second stage involving residual policy considerations that might negative or reduce the scope of the duty or the class of persons to whom it is owed.

In summarizing the analysis, Iacobucci J, perhaps cursorily, but maybe more honestly, modifies the so-called two-step *Anns* analysis by offering an adjustment of the adjustment in *Cooper,* listing three elements that must now be established by a plaintiff in a new duty situation:

> On the analysis above, this requires the Odhavji family to establish each of the following:
> (i)   that the harm complained of is a reasonably foreseeable consequence of the alleged breach;
> (ii) that there is sufficient proximity between the parties that it would not be unjust or unfair to impose a duty of care on the defendants; and
> (iii) that there exist no policy reasons to negate or otherwise restrict that duty.

A careful observer of these passages will notice that we have gradually moved from the simple neighbour test of *Donoghue v. Stevenson,* to the *prima facie* duty analysis of *Anns* involving the two step test, to the new *Cooper* analysis composed of a two-step test which includes a two-part first step, and ended up with a frankly recognized three-step test in *Woodhouse*. After having stoutly refused to follow the U.K. decisions in their retreat from *Anns*, the Supreme Court has now quietly succumbed and backed into a remarkably similar, though somewhat more sophisticated position. Incrementalism has replaced principle. Caution has supplanted creativity.

In the aftermath of *Cooper*, *Edwards* and *Woodhouse*, there is not more clarity, as had been hoped for, but less. Surprisingly these decisions, which were initially described as merely of academic importance, have precipitated nearly 150 reported cases struggling with the application of the new approach in virtually every kind of negligence case. An amazing burst of imaginative new attempts to expand duty has been countered by an equally amazing effort to restrain that expansion. It is no wonder that the Canadian Judiciary is having some difficulty with the new duty reasoning.

. . . .

The origin of this concept of proximity was the reformulation of *Donoghue v. Stevenson*, by Lord Wilberforce in *Anns*, who unwittingly unleashed the proximity concept, when he wrote that the issue was whether there was a "sufficient relationship of proximity or neighbourhood such that damage was reasonably foreseeable." Note, he wrote proximity or neighbourhood, not proximity and neighbourhood. As the British courts, later retreated from *Anns*, they rejected Wilberforce's *prima facie* duty idea but retained his new proximity idea, requiring both foreseeability and proximity[] (as well as justice, fairness and reasonableness) in order to create a duty. The so-called "imperial march" of tort law had to be halted. Until *Cooper*, Canadians refused to retreat and resisted the complex new approach used in the U.K., but in *Cooper* and later in *Woodhouse* the Supreme Court of Canada also decided to insist on proximity as well as reasonable foresight, in addition to the usual residual policy reasons. Now, our courts must undertake this proximity analysis, which is fraught with confusion, and decide whether it is just and fair to impose a duty, which is fraught with even more uncertainty. Regrettably, tort law is becoming very much like tax law in its complexity.

Many of the cases discussing proximity are government liability cases. The courts post *Cooper* have immunized most government agencies from negligence liability using this concept. The legislation is usually examined fully and then the court often concludes, paradoxically, that there is no proximity because there is only a public duty owed by the agency, not a private one, even though the agency is supposed to protect people. This is sad and disingenuous logic, used in the past in another context, for it is plain to everyone, as one judge, at least, remarked that a public and private duty may coexist easily. Nevertheless, there are several decisions after *Cooper* in which the failure by municipal, provincial and federal agencies have been held on this basis not subject to a civil law duty to enforce their by-laws, regulations or other laws.

Strangely, in these government cases, there already exist numerous protections for regulatory agencies. They are frequently immunized from tort liability by statute, unless they act in bad faith. Oddly, such legislation is often weighed as a mere factor by judges in the proximity analysis, instead of being treated as a conclusive bar to liability. Also, the *Just v. B.C.* reasoning has been available to shield from any negligence liability all policy decisions of government. In addition, some governmental agencies like legislative, judicial and political ones, have been entitled to immunity from negligence law. As one judge reminded us, rather ironically, that the current law is that "Government when it legislates, even wrongly, incompetently, stupidly, or misguidedly is not liable in damages". Nevertheless, this new *Cooper* analysis has been added to the already over-stocked arsenal of defensive weapons protecting governments from negligence law.

Consequently, negligence law is becoming an infrequent visitor in the halls of government, in spite of [Crown] liability statutes that stipulate that the Crown shall be liable in tort in the same way as if it were a person. This is somewhat inexplicable to me, since, at the same time, constitutional and administrative law review of government is expanding in its scope. Nevertheless, in the future, there will be many fewer successful claims against governments, but they will not be totally blocked always. One Judge bravely, perhaps overly optimistically, proclaimed that "*Cooper* does not stand for the universal proposition that a statutory regulator will never owe a duty of care to individual investors", at least in a case where individual complaints were made. Remember also that Justice Iacobucci himself in *Woodhouse* did not rule out the possibility of a civil action against the police regulatory agency if there is a "widespread problem of excessive force or racism". Thus, it appears that the negligence action against public authorities is not yet dead, but it is clearly on life-support.

As for non-governmental proximity cases, most of them deal with new kinds of economic losses, as should be the case. However, some of the Courts, before finding proximity, appear to be mistakenly insisting on formal legal relationships between the plaintiff and defendant, something that was resoundingly discarded in *Donoghue v. Stevenson*. Thus, it has been held that without a contract, a legal retainer, or an agency relationship there is no proximity and, hence, no duty. This is a worrisome trend in my view, completely at odds with the fundamental principle of *Donoghue*.

While in some of these proximity cases there may be good reason to deny a *prima facie* duty, in my view, the policy analysis relating to the relationship between the parties, dealing with expectations, reliance, representations and property interests, would have been better done along with the other residual policy analysis that must be done in stage three. If the connection between the parties is tenuous, or if it is a nonfeasance case, there are good policy reasons to deny a duty, despite reasonable foresight. If there is no reliance or representation, there is no reasonable foresight of harm and there need not be any duty imposed on that basis alone. If there is a contractual or other legal relation that may be interfered with by negligence law, the court might well deny the duty, in appropriate cases. But we must be careful not to return to the pre-*Donoghue* days and insist, before establishing a new duty, on privity or another particular relationship in addition to foresight. Nevertheless, the decision of the Supreme Court to split the policy analysis into two stages, although confusing and unhelpful, respectfully, must be respected, for now at least. Not the least of the problems is that it seems that the onus is on the plaintiff to overcome the first policy analysis in the proximity stage, but on the defendant with regard to the more general second stage policy analysis. While judges must, of course, abide by the teachings of the Supreme Court, because of the uncertainty, caution and restraint [are] in order here.

... It is in the third residual policy analysis stage that judges need most help because it is here that they have done most poorly in applying the *Cooper* test. With some notable exceptions, too often an amateurish one-line [statement] or a short [list] of possible negative effects [is] offered as policy analysis, even in the Supreme Court of Canada. This is not good enough! This cannot justify denying a new *prima facie* duty. If judges are going to engage in policy analysis in this area, [...] they must do so. They should do so professionally, by insisting on better material than they have had available to them so far.

Once taboo in legal discourse, policy analysis is [*de rigueur*] nowadays, in the Charter era. Once policy was an unruly horse, not to be ridden, but now it is bucking bronco that must be mounted, like it or not. This is actually one of Canadian tort law's major advances, reiterated in *Cooper*, that is, recognizing openly that our courts must engage in policy analysis as part of the duty decision. The British Courts still do not generally admit this, disguising their policy analysis in duty cases by asking instead the question, "is it just, fair and reasonable", which in reality invokes the same type of considerations as policy analysis.

We must remind ourselves that to decide that there should be no duty on the basis of policy considerations is a serious matter, blocking access to tort law by persons who may have been negligently harmed. To deny a duty, it is not <u>any</u> policy reason that is needed, but <u>good</u>, substantial, well-founded policy reasons. Idle musings and vague speculation [are] not enough. With respect, it is not acceptable, for example, to deny a duty on the basis of a policy reason, without any supporting data, by saying, for example, that insurance premiums may rise or that taxes may be increased. There should be some statistical assessment of the potential negative effects of a positive duty ruling, and this must then be balanced against the potential negative effect of denying compensation in these circumstances to one negligently harmed by the defendant. To say that the discretion of a government official may be interfered with by imposing a duty is not a sufficient reason to deny a duty, according to the *Just v. B.C.* analysis; it must be discretion about a policy decision. If the exercise of discretion is in relation to an operational matter, *Cooper* should not allow litigants to circumvent the earlier jurisprudence established in *Just*. Nor is it enough to say that indeterminate liability may flow from the creation of a new duty. This phrase merely repeats the old floodgates argument, dressed up in loftier language. Indeterminacy is a proper policy consideration which, properly founded, may be determinative occasionally, but certainly not invariably. Remember that this idea was brought into Canadian tort law by Justice LaForest in *Hercules* from Cardozo J. in *Ultramaries v. Touche*, who held that accountants owed no duty to third persons because of the risk of "liability for an indeterminate amount for an indeterminate time to an indeterminate class". This is a specific three-part test, not just a vague concern that, by creating a new duty, a lot of people may be held liable for violating it. To overcome a *prima facie* duty there should normally be some solid evidence forecasting the massive, uncontrolled numbers of law suits that threaten to drown not only this defendant but others similarly situated, and even then, there may still be offsetting reasons to allow a new *prima facie* duty to be born. Further, when alternative avenues of redress are said to exist as a policy reason to deny a new duty, these should be closely examined to see if they <u>really</u> exist, or merely whether they may potentially be available.

.   .   .   .

(d) After Cooper v Hobart

By now, it is obvious that I am not a big fan of *Cooper* and what it has unwittingly done to Canadian negligence law. Professor Klar and others forecasted that, not only would *Cooper* cause confusion, it would shrink tort law. He was right. For some, that is a good thing; for others, not so good. What is most vexing is that the Supreme Court did not expressly say that it was seeking to downsize tort law. The Supreme Court insisted that it was merely clarifying the law and that *Cooper* would have little effect on the decisions, being merely an academic exercise. It was wrong on both counts, largely because too many Canadian judges have been too easily enticed by counsel to engage in flawed *Cooper* analysis. I hope the Supreme Court will revisit *Cooper* soon....

3 Contours of Obligation in Negligence

(a) *Arland and Arland v. Taylor*†

Ontario Court of Appeal

[LAIDLAW J.A.:]

[4] The facts are short. On 15th January 1952, at about 8.25 a.m., the respondent was driving his motor car in a westerly direction on a highway about two miles west of the town of Uxbridge, and struck Robert Arland, aged about nine years, who was walking on the highway. The weather was foggy; the visibility was poor; the pavement was wet and, at the place of the accident, the respondent was driving on a down grade. The learned trial judge charged the jury properly that the onus of proof that the loss or damage sustained by the appellants did not arise through the negligence or improper conduct of the respondent, rested upon the respondent. He defined the meaning in law of negligence and referred the jury particularly to the plan (ex. 1) showing the highway for a distance east and west of the place where the infant appellant was struck, and also the profile of that section of the highway. He explained the manner of reading the plan and profile to determine the view available under normal conditions to a motorist travelling in a westerly direction before reaching the place of the accident. He directed the attention of the jury to the weather conditions and said, in part: "It is for you to say what the conditions were on this day. Some say it was misty, you could see some distance. One witness said that when patches of fog closed in he could not see 60 feet.... However, I am not going to try to decipher that evidence. Counsel dealt with it with you." Later in his charge he said: "Now there is nothing in the Act [The Highway Traffic Act, R.S.O. 1950, c. 167] deal-

ing with fog. I think the law has been well established in other cases that a driver who drives his car must drive having the vehicle under control, full control, within the limit of his visibility."

. . . .

[21] The second ground of appeal arises from the following passage, in particular, in the charge to the jury: "First of all you will consider his [the respondent's] negligence. I suggest that you put yourself in the driver's seat of his car. After you have determined the weather and the conditions that existed, ask yourself — 'Would I have done that? Was that reasonable for him to do? What precautions would I have taken that he did not? Would I have gone over that hill at the same speed that he did? Would I have reduced my speed?', especially if you decided that as he approached he could not have seen over that hill". I extract another passage of the charge in which the learned judge said: "... having put yourself in the driver's seat and asked yourself whether he satisfied you under the circumstances, then we go on to the next question...." The learned trial judge told the jury in more than one part of his charge then ten of them "set the standard of what is reasonable under a given set of circumstances".

[22] The learned trial judge was in error in those instructions to the jury, and this manner of leaving the case to the jury was the subject of disapproval in *Kralj v. Murray, supra*. The standard of care by which a jury is to judge the conduct of parties in a case of

---

† [1955] O.R. 131.

the kind under consideration is the care that would have been taken in the circumstances by "a reasonable and prudent man". I shall not attempt to formulate a comprehensive definition of "a reasonable man" of whom we speak so frequently in negligence cases. I simply say he is a mythical creature of the law whose conduct is the standard by which the Courts measure the conduct of all other persons and find it to be proper or improper in particular circumstances as they may exist from time to time. He is not an extraordinary or unusual creature; he is not superhuman; he is not required to display the highest skill of which anyone is capable; he is not a genius who can perform uncommon feats, nor is he possessed of unusual powers of foresight. He is a person of normal intelligence who makes prudence a guide to his conduct. He does nothing that a prudent man would not do and does not omit to do anything a prudent man would do. He acts in accord with general and approved practice. His conduct is guided by considerations which ordinarily regulate the conduct of human affairs. His conduct is the standard "adopted in the community by persons of ordinary intelligence and prudence." See *Blyth v. Birmingham Waterworks Co.* (1856), 11 Exch. 781, 156 E.R. 1047, and Mazengarb, Negligence on the Highway, 2nd ed. 1952, p. 15.

[23] In *Glasgow Corporation v. Muir et al.*, [1943] A.C. 448, [1943] 2 All E.R. 414, Lord Macmillan at p. 457 said: "The standard of foresight of the reasonable man is, in one sense, an impersonal test. It eliminates the personal equation and is independent of the idiosyncracies of the particular person whose conduct is in question. Some persons are by nature unduly timorous and imagine every path beset with lions. Others, of more robust temperament, fail to foresee or nonchalantly disregard even the most obvious dangers. The reasonable man is presumed to be free both from over-apprehension and from over-confidence, but there is a sense in which the standard of care of the reasonable man involves in its application a subjective element. It is still left the judge to decide what, in the circumstances of the particular case, the reasonable man would have had in contemplation, and what, accordingly, the party sought to be made liable ought to have foreseen.

Here there is room for diversity of view.... What to one judge may seem far-fetched may seem to another both natural and probable." In Mazengarb, op. cit., p. 18, the learned author says: "In fixing responsibility, the law has adopted an external standard of care. It realizes that care is a matter of degree, and therefore it has set a standard which is neither too high nor too low. It seeks safety without at the same time unduly hampering transport and transit. It does not require the highest degree of care of which mankind is capable."

[24] And I quote further from p. 20: "The legal standard of care always remains the same in the sense that it is what a reasonably prudent man would have done in like circumstances. But although this legal standard is fixed and immutable, the factual standard changes from time to time and from place to place."

[25] It will be plain from the statements I have quoted that it is improper for a juryman to judge the conduct of a person in given circumstances by considering, after the event, what he would or would not have done in the circumstances.

[26] In *Eyres v. Gillis & Warren Limited et al.*, 48 Man. R. 164 at 170, [1940] 3 W.W.R. 390, [1940] 4 D.L.R. 747, Trueman J.A., delivering the unanimous judgment of the Court of Appeal of Manitoba, referred to the definition of negligence as given by Baron Alderson in *Blyth v. Birmingham Waterworks Co.*, supra, and then said: "In determining the standard of duty so defined a Judge must not interpose himself, for, the accident having happened, his point of view may be warped by extraneous or subjective considerations, however much he may think he is free from bias. It is for this reason that a jury must not be instructed by the Judge or counsel to put themselves in the place of a defendant in a negligence action when called upon to pronounce upon his conduct."

. . . .

[28] My conclusion is that this appeal fails on all grounds and must accordingly be dismissed with costs.

(b) Negligence Law: The "Reasonable Person" Standard as an Example of Male Naming and the Implicit Male Norm†

Leslie Bender

That implicit male norms have been used to skew legal analysis can be seen in tort negligence law. To assess whether a defendant's conduct is negligent, and hence subject to liability, we ask whether the defendant has a duty to the plaintiff and whether she has met the legally required standard of conduct or care. "Standard of care" is a term of art in the law. It is alternatively described as the care required of a reasonably prudent person under the same or similar circumstances, or of a reasonable person of ordinary prudence, an ordinarily prudent man, or a man of average prudence. Prosser and Keeton explain the standard as some "blend of reason and caution." A "reasonable person" standard is an attempt to establish a universally applicable measure for conduct. This reasonable person is a hypothetical construct, not a real person, and is allegedly objective rather than subjective.

Not surprisingly, the standard was first articulated as a reasonable *man* or *man* of ordinary prudence. Recognizing the original standard's overt sexism, many courts and legal scholars now use a "reasonable person" standard. My concern with the "reasonable person" standard is twofold. Does converting a "reasonable man" to a "reasonable person" in an attempt to eradicate the term's sexism actually exorcise the sexism or instead embed it? My second concern is related. Should our standard of care focus on "reason and caution" or something else?

It was originally believed that the "reasonable man" standard was gender neutral. "Man" was used in the generic sense to mean person or human being. But man is not generic except to other men. Would men regard a "prudent woman" standard as an appropriate measure of their due care? As our social sensitivity to sexism developed, our legal institutions did the "gentlemanly" thing and substituted the neutral word "person" for "man." Because "reasonable man" was intended to be a universal term, the change to "reasonable person" was thought to continue the same universal standard without utilizing the gendered term "man." The language of

tort law protected itself from allegations of sexism, it did not change its content and character.

This "resolution" of the standard's sexism ignores several important feminist insights. The original phrase "reasonable man" failed its claim to represent an abstract, universal person. Even if such a creature could be imagined, the "reasonable man" standard was postulated by men, who, because they were the only people who wrote and argued the law, philosophy, and politics at that time, only theorized about themselves. When the standard was written into judicial opinions, treatises, and casebooks, it was written about and by men. The case law and treatises explaining the standard are full of examples explaining how the "reasonable man" is the "man on the Clapham Omnibus" or "the man who takes the magazines at home and in the evening pushes the lawn mower in his shirt sleeves." When the authors of such works said "reasonable man," they meant "male," "man" in a gendered sense. The legal world that generated the "reasonable man" was predominantly, if not wholly, male. What other connotations or meanings could the phrase have had? When it was converted to "reasonable person," it still meant "person who is reasonable by my standards" almost exclusively from the perspective of a male judge, lawyer, or law professor, or even a female lawyer trained to be "the same as" a male lawyer.

Changing the word without changing the underlying model does not work. Specifically addressing the "reasonable person" tort standard, Guido Calabresi challenges whether the "reasonable person" is in any way meant to include women or, for that matter, people of non-WASP beliefs or attitudes. Calabresi explains that use of a universal standard is intended to cause those who are "different" from that standard to adopt the dominant ideological stance. Like the notion of America as a melting pot, the reasonable person standard encourages conformism and the suppression of different voices.

Not only does "reasonable person" still mean "reasonable man" — "reason" and "reasonableness"

---

† This material is originally published in Leslie Bender, "A Lawyer's Primer on Feminist Theory and Tort" (1988) 38 Journal of Legal Education 3 at 20–25. [Notes omitted.] Reproduced with permission of the author and the publisher.

are gendered concepts as well. Gender distinctions have often been reinforced by dualistic attributions of reason and rationality to men, emotion and intuition (or instinct) to women. Much of Western philosophy is built on that distinction. Aristotle describes the female body as "a deformity, though one which occurs in the ordinary course of nature" and regards women as inferior beings whose reasoning capacity is defective. Immanuel Kant observes that women are devoid of characteristics necessary for moral action because they act on feelings, not reason. In his *Philosophy of Right*, Hegel explains:

> Women are capable of education, but they are not made for activities which demand a universal faculty such as the more advanced sciences, philosophy, and certain forms of artistic production. Women may have happy ideas, taste, and elegance, but they cannot attain to the ideal. The difference between men and women is like that between animals and plants. Men correspond to animals, while women correspond to plants because their development is more placid.... When women hold the helm of government, the state is at once in jeopardy, because women regulate their actions not by the demands of universality but by arbitrary inclinations and opinion.... The status of manhood, on the other hand, is attained only by the stress of thought and much technical exertion.

Schopenhauer writes that woman "is in every respect backward, lacking in reason and reflection ... a kind of middle step between the child and the man, who is the true human being.... In the last resort, women exist solely for the propagation of the race." We also see evidence of the attitude that woman is unfit for the life of the mind in the Supreme Court's decision in *Bradwell v. Illinois*. The medical community made similar pronouncements about the unfitness of women for intellectual

pursuits. These are but isolated examples of a continuous tendency in our Western culture to define "woman" by an absence of developed rationality or, at best, by an inferior capacity to reason. If we have been culturally and socially informed by a concept of "woman" that does not correlate with notions of reason or reasonableness, then how is the phrase "reasonable person" or the notion of "reasonableness" as a tort standard of conduct going to connote women's thinking, values, attitudes, or approaches to problem solving?

We would be hard pressed today to find many people who would openly assert that women cannot be reasonable. Today we are taught to consider women reasonable when they act as men would under the same circumstances, and unreasonable when they act more as they themselves or as other women act. If it is true that somewhere, at some subconscious level, we believe men's behavior is more reasonable and objective than women's, then changing the phrase "reasonable man" to "reasonable person" does not really change the hypothetical character against whom we measure the actors in torts problems. By appending the very term "reasonable," we attach connotations and characteristics of maleness to the standard of conduct. If we are wedded to the idea of an objective measure, would it not be better to measure the conduct of a tortfeasor by the care that would be taken by a "neighbor" or "social acquaintance" or "responsible person with conscious care and concern for another's safety"?

Perhaps we have gone astray in tort-law analysis because we use "reason" and caution as our standard of care, rather than focusing on care and concern. Further study of feminist theory may help to suggest how a feminist ethic can affect our understanding of standards of care in negligence law. But first one more aspect of the relationship between sex and gender needs exploration.

(c) *Palsgraf v. Long Island Railroad Co.*[†]

New York Court of Appeals

[CARDOZO, Ch. J. (Pound, Lehman and Kellogg JJ., concurring):]

Plaintiff was standing on a platform of defendant's railroad after buying a ticket to go to Rockaway

---

† 248 N.Y. 339, 162 N.E. 99 (N.Y. 1928), rev'g 222 A.D. 166 (N.Y. App. Div. 1927).

Beach. A train stopped at the station, bound for another place. Two men ran forward to catch it. One of the men reached the platform of the car without mishap, though the train was already moving. The other man, carrying a package, jumped aboard the car, but seemed unsteady as if about to fall. A guard on the car, who had held the door open, reached forward to help him in, and another guard on the platform pushed him from behind. In this act, the package was dislodged, and fell upon the rails. It was a package of small size, about fifteen inches long, and was covered by a newspaper. In fact it contained fireworks, but there was nothing in its appearance to give notice of its contents. The fireworks when they fell exploded. The shock of the explosion threw down some scales at the other end of the platform, many feet away. The scales struck the plaintiff, causing injuries for which she sues.

The conduct of the defendant's guard, if a wrong in its relation to the holder of the package, was not a wrong in its relation to the plaintiff, standing far away. Relatively to her it was not negligence at all. Nothing in the situation gave notice that the falling package had in it the potency of peril to persons thus removed. Negligence is not actionable unless it involves the invasion of a legally protected interest, the violation of a right. "Proof of negligence in the air, so to speak, will not do" (Pollock, Torts [11th ed.], p. 455; *Martin v. Herzog*, 228 N. Y. 164, 170; cf. Salmond, Torts [6th ed.], p. 24). "Negligence is the absence of care, according to the circumstances" (WILLES, J., in *Vaughan v. Taff Vale Ry. Co.*, 5 H. & N. 679, 688; 1 Beven, Negligence [4th ed.], 7; *Paul v. Consol. Fireworks Co.*, 212 N. Y. 117; *Adams v. Bullock*, 227 N. Y. 208, 211; *Parrott v. Wells-Fargo Co.*, 15 Wall. [U. S.] 524). The plaintiff as she stood upon the platform of the station might claim to be protected against intentional invasion of her bodily security. Such invasion is not charged. She might claim to be protected against unintentional invasion by conduct involving in the thought of reasonable men an unreasonable hazard that such invasion would ensue. These, from the point of view of the law, were the bounds of her immunity, with perhaps some rare exceptions, survivals for the most part of ancient forms of liability, where conduct is held to be at the peril of the actor *Sullivan v. Dunham*, 161 N. Y. 290). If no hazard was apparent to the eye of ordinary vigilance, an act innocent and harmless, at least to outward seeming, with reference to her, did not take to itself the quality of a tort because it happened to be a wrong, though apparently not one involving the risk of bodily insecurity, with reference to some one else. "In every instance,

before negligence can be predicated of a given act, back of the act must be sought and found a duty to the individual complaining, the observance of which would have averted or avoided the injury" (McSHERRY, C. J., in *W. Va. Central R. Co. v. State*, 96 Md. 652, 666; cf. *Norfolk & Western Ry. Co. v. Wood*, 99 Va. 156, 158, 159; *Hughes v. Boston & Maine R. R. Co.*, 71 N. H. 279, 284; *U. S. Express Co. v. Everest*, 72 Kan. 517; *Emry v. Roanoke Nav. Co.*, 111 N. C. 94, 95; *Vaughan v. Transit Dev. Co.*, 222 N. Y. 79; *Losee v. Clute*, 51 N. Y. 494; *DiCaprio v. N. Y. C. R. R. Co.*, 231 N. Y. 94; 1 Shearman & Redfield on Negligence, § 8, and cases cited; Cooley on Torts [3d ed.], p. 1411; Jaggard on Torts, vol. 2, p. 826; Wharton, Negligence, § 24; Bohlen, Studies in the Law of Torts, p. 601). "The ideas of negligence and duty are strictly correlative" (BOWEN, L. J., in *Thomas v. Quartermaine*, 18 Q. B. D. 685, 694). The plaintiff sues in her own right for a wrong personal to her, and not as the vicarious beneficiary of a breach of duty to another.

A different conclusion will involve us, and swiftly too, in a maze of contradictions. A guard stumbles over a package which has been left upon a platform. It seems to be a bundle of newspapers. It turns out to be a can of dynamite. To the eye of ordinary vigilance, the bundle is abandoned waste, which may be kicked or trod on with impunity. Is a passenger at the other end of the platform protected by the law against the unsuspected hazard concealed beneath the waste? If not, is the result to be any different, so far as the distant passenger is concerned, when the guard stumbles over a valise which a truckman or a porter has left upon the walk? The passenger far away, if the victim of a wrong at all, has a cause of action, not derivative, but original and primary. His claim to be protected against invasion of his bodily security is neither greater nor less because the act resulting in the invasion is a wrong to another far removed. In this case, the rights that are said to have been violated, the interests said to have been invaded, are not even of the same order. The man was not injured in his person nor even put in danger. The purpose of the act, as well as its effect, was to make his person safe. If there was a wrong to him at all, which may very well be doubted, it was a wrong to a property interest only, the safety of his package. Out of this wrong to property, which threatened injury to nothing else, there has passed, we are told, to the plaintiff by derivation or succession a right of action for the invasion of an interest of another order, the right to bodily security. The diversity of interests emphasizes the futility of the effort to build the plaintiff's right upon the basis of a wrong to some one else. The gain is one of emphasis, for a like result would follow if the interests were the same. Even then, the orbit of the danger as disclosed to the eye of reasonable vigilance would be the orbit of the duty. One who jostles one's neighbor in a crowd does not invade the rights of others standing at the outer fringe when the unintended contact casts a bomb upon the ground. The wrongdoer as to them is the man who carries the bomb, not the one who explodes it without suspicion of the danger. Life will have to be made over, and human nature transformed, before prevision so extravagant can be accepted as the norm of conduct, the customary standard to which behavior must conform.

The argument for the plaintiff is built upon the shifting meanings of such words as "wrong" and "wrongful," and shares their instability. What the plaintiff must show is "a wrong" to herself, i. e., a violation of her own right, and not merely a wrong to some one else, nor conduct "wrongful" because unsocial, but not "a wrong" to any one. We are told that one who drives at reckless speed through a crowded city street is guilty of a negligent act and, therefore, of a wrongful one irrespective of the consequences. Negligent the act is, and wrongful in the sense that it is unsocial, but wrongful and unsocial in relation to other travelers, only because the eye of vigilance perceives the risk of damage. If the same act were to be committed on a speedway or a race course, it would lose its wrongful quality. The risk reasonably to be perceived defines the duty to be obeyed, and risk imports relation; it is risk to another or to others within the range of apprehension (Seavey, Negligence, Subjective or Objective, 41 H. L. Rv. 6; *Boronkay v. Robinson & Carpenter*, 247 N. Y. 365). This does not mean, of course, that one who launches a destructive force is always relieved of liability if the force, though known to be destructive, pursues an unexpected path. "It was not necessary that the defendant should have had notice of the particular method in which an accident would occur, if the possibility of an accident was clear to the ordinarily prudent eye" (*Munsey v. Webb*, 231 U. S. 150, 156; *Condran v. Park & Tilford*, 213 N. Y. 341, 345; *Robert v. U. S. E. F. Corp.*, 240 N. Y. 474, 477). Some acts, such as shooting, are so imminently dangerous to any one who may come within reach of the missile, however unexpectedly, as to impose a duty of prevision not far from that of an insurer. Even today, and much oftener in earlier stages of the law, one acts sometimes at one's peril (Jeremiah Smith, Tort and Absolute Liability, 30 H. L. Rv. 328; Street, Foundations of Legal Liability, vol. 1, pp. 77,

78). Under this head, it may be, fall certain cases of what is known as transferred intent, an act willfully dangerous to A resulting by misadventure in injury to B (*Talmage v. Smith*, 101 Mich. 370, 374) These cases aside, wrong is defined in terms of the natural or probable, at least when unintentional (*Parrot v. Wells-Fargo Co. [The Nitro-Glycerine Case]*, 15 Wall. [U. S.] 524). The range of reasonable apprehension is at times a question for the court, and at times, if varying inferences are possible, a question for the jury. Here, by concession, there was nothing in the situation to suggest to the most cautious mind that the parcel wrapped in newspaper would spread wreckage through the station. If the guard had thrown it down knowingly and willfully, he would not have threatened the plaintiff's safety, so far as appearances could warn him. His conduct would not have involved, even then, an unreasonable probability of invasion of her bodily security. Liability can be no greater where the act is inadvertent.

Negligence, like risk, is thus a term of relation. Negligence in the abstract, apart from things related, is surely not a tort, if indeed it is understandable at all (BOWEN, L. J., in *Thomas v. Quartermaine*, 18 Q. B. D. 685, 694). Negligence is not a tort unless it results in the commission of a wrong, and the commission of a wrong imports the violation of a right, in this case, we are told, the right to be protected against interference with one's bodily security. But bodily security is protected, not against all forms of interference or aggression, but only against some. One who seeks redress at law does not make out a cause of action by showing without more that there has been damage to his person. If the harm was not willful, he must show that the act as to him had possibilities of danger so many and apparent as to entitle him to be protected against the doing of it though the harm was unintended. Affront to personality is still the keynote of the wrong. Confirmation of this view will be found in the history and development of the action on the case. Negligence as a basis of civil liability was unknown to mediaeval law (8 Holdsworth, History of English Law, p. 449; Street, Foundations of Legal Liability, vol. 1, pp. 189, 190). For damage to the person, the sole remedy was trespass, and trespass did not lie in the absence of aggression, and that direct and personal (Holdsworth, op. cit. p. 453; Street, op. cit. vol. 3, pp. 258, 260, vol. 1, pp. 71, 74.) Liability for other damage, as where a servant without orders from the master does or omits something to the damage of another, is a plant of later growth (Holdsworth, op. cit. 450, 457; Wigmore, Responsibility for Tortious Acts, vol. 3, Essays in Anglo-American Legal History, 520, 523, 526, 533). When it emerged out of the legal soil, it was thought of as a variant of trespass, an offshoot of the parent stock. This appears in the form of action, which was known as trespass on the case (Holdsworth, op. cit. p. 449; cf. *Scott v. Shepard*, 2 Wm. Black. 892; Green, Rationale of Proximate Cause, p. 19). The victim does not sue derivatively, or by right of subrogation, to vindicate an interest invaded in the person of another. Thus to view his cause of action is to ignore the fundamental difference between tort and crime (Holland, Jurisprudence [12th ed.], p. 328). He sues for breach of a duty owing to himself.

The law of causation, remote or proximate, is thus foreign to the case before us. The question of liability is always anterior to the question of the measure of the consequences that go with liability. If there is no tort to be redressed, there is no occasion to consider what damage might be recovered if there were a finding of a tort. We may assume, without deciding, that negligence, not at large or in the abstract, but in relation to the plaintiff, would entail liability for any and all consequences, however novel or extraordinary (*Bird v. St. Paul F. & M. Ins. Co.*, 224 N. Y. 47, 54; *Ehrgott v. Mayor*, etc., of N. Y., 96 N. Y. 264; *Smith v. London & S. W. Ry. Co.*, L. R. 6 C. P. 14; 1 Beven, Negligence, 106; Street, op. cit. vol. 1, p. 90; Green, Rationale of Proximate Cause, pp. 88, 118; cf. *Matter of Polemis*, L. R. 1921, 3 K. B. 560; 44 Law Quarterly Review, 142). There is room for argument that a distinction is to be drawn according to the diversity of interests invaded by the act, as where conduct negligent in that it threatens an insignificant invasion of an interest in property results in an [unforeseeable] invasion of an interest of another order, as, e. g., one of bodily security. Perhaps other distinctions may be necessary. We do not go into the question now. The consequences to be followed must first be rooted in a wrong. The judgment of the Appellate Division and that of the Trial Term should be reversed, and the complaint dismissed, with costs in all courts.

[ANDREWS, J. (dissenting, and joined by Crane and O'Brien JJ.):]

Assisting a passenger to board a train, the defendant's servant negligently knocked a package from his arms. It fell between the platform and the cars. Of its contents the servant knew and could know nothing. A violent explosion followed. The concussion broke some scales standing a considerable distance away. In falling they injured the plaintiff, an intending passenger.

Upon these facts may she recover the damages she has suffered in an action brought against the master? The result we shall reach depends upon our theory as to the nature of negligence. Is it a relative concept — the breach of some duty owing to a particular person or to particular persons? Or where there is an act which unreasonably threatens the safety of others, is the doer liable for all its proximate consequences, even where they result in injury to one who would generally be thought to be outside the radius of danger? This is not a mere dispute as to words. We might not believe that to the average mind the dropping of the bundle would seem to involve the probability of harm to the plaintiff standing many feet away whatever might be the case as to the owner or to one so near as to be likely to be struck by its fall. If, however, we adopt the second hypothesis we have to inquire only as to the relation between cause and effect. We deal in terms of proximate cause, not of negligence.

Negligence may be defined roughly as an act or omission which unreasonably does or may affect the rights of others, or which unreasonably fails to protect oneself from the dangers resulting from such acts. Here I confine myself to the first branch of the definition. Nor do I comment on the word "unreasonable." For present purposes it sufficiently describes that average of conduct that society requires of its members.

There must be both the act or the omission, and the right. It is the act itself, not the intent of the actor, that is important. (*Hover v. Barkhoof*, 44 N. Y. 113; *Mertz v. Connecticut Co.*, 217 N. Y. 475.) In criminal law both the intent and the result are to be considered. Intent again is material in tort actions, where punitive damages are sought, dependent on actual malice — not on merely reckless conduct. But here neither insanity nor infancy lessens responsibility. (*Williams v. Hays*, 143 N. Y. 442.)

As has been said, except in cases of contributory negligence, there must be rights which are or may be affected. Often though injury has occurred, no rights of him who suffers have been touched. A licensee or trespasser upon my land has no claim to affirmative care on my part that the land be made safe. (*Meiers v. Koch Brewery*, 229 N. Y. 10.) Where a railroad is required to fence its tracks against cattle, no man's rights are injured should he wander upon the road because such fence is absent. (*Di Caprio v. N. Y. C. R. R.*, 231 N. Y. 94.) An unborn child may not demand immunity from personal harm. (*Drobner v. Peters*, 232 N. Y. 220.)

But we are told that "there is no negligence unless there is in the particular case a legal duty to take care, and this duty must be one which is owed to the plaintiff himself and not merely to others." (Salmond Torts [6th ed.], 24.) This, I think too narrow a conception. Where there is the unreasonable act, and some right that may be affected there is negligence whether damage does or does not result. That is immaterial. Should we drive down Broadway at a reckless speed, we are negligent whether we strike an approaching car or miss it by an inch. The act itself is wrongful. It is a wrong not only to those who happen to be within the radius of danger but to all who might have been there — a wrong to the public at large. Such is the language of the street. Such the language of the courts when speaking of contributory negligence. Such again and again their language in speaking of the duty of some defendant and discussing proximate cause in cases where such a discussion is wholly irrelevant on any other theory. (*Perry v. Rochester Line Co.*, 219 N. Y. 60.) As was said by Mr. Justice HOLMES many years ago, "the measure of the defendant's duty in determining whether a wrong has been committed is one thing, the measure of liability when a wrong has been committed is another." (*Spade v. Lynn & Boston R. R. Co.*, 172 Mass. 488.) Due care is a duty imposed on each one of us to protect society from unnecessary danger, not to protect A, B or C alone.

It may well be that there is no such thing as negligence in the abstract. "Proof of negligence in the air, so to speak, will not do." In an empty world negligence would not exist. It does involve a relationship between man and his fellows. But not merely a relationship between man and those whom he might reasonably expect his act would injure. Rather, a relationship between him and those whom he does in fact injure. If his act has a tendency to harm some one, it harms him a mile away as surely as it does those on the scene. We now permit children to recover for the negligent killing of the father. It was never prevented on the theory that no duty was owing to them. A husband may be compensated for the loss of his wife's services. To say that the wrongdoer was negligent as to the husband as well as to the wife is merely an attempt to fit facts to theory. An insurance company paying a fire loss recovers its payment of the negligent incendiary. We speak of subrogation—of suing in the right of the insured. Behind the cloud of words is the fact they hide, that the act, wrongful as to the insured, has also injured the company. Even if it be true that the fault of father, wife or insured will prevent recovery, it is because we consider the original negligence not the proximate cause of the injury. (Pollock, Torts [12th ed.], 463.)

In the well-known *Polemis Case* (1921, 3 K. B. 560), SCRUTTON, L. J., said that the dropping of a plank was negligent for it might injure "workman or cargo or ship." Because of either possibility the owner of the vessel was to be made good for his loss. The act being wrongful the doer was liable for its proximate results. Criticized and explained as this statement may have been, I think it states the law as it should be and as it is. (*Smith v. London & South-western Ry. Co.*, [1870–71] 6 C. P. 14; *Anthony v. Slaid*, 52 Mass. 290; *Wood v. Penn. R. R. Co.*, 177 Penn. St. 306; *Trashansky v. Hershkovitz*, 239 N. Y. 452.)

The proposition is this. Every one owes to the world at large the duty of refraining from those acts that may unreasonably threaten the safety of others. Such an act occurs. Not only is he wronged to whom harm might reasonably be expected to result, but he also who is in fact injured, even if he be outside what would generally be thought the danger zone. There needs be duty due the one complaining but this is not a duty to a particular individual because as to him harm might be expected. Harm to some one being the natural result of the act, not only that one alone, but all those in fact injured may complain. We have never, I think, held otherwise. Indeed in the *Di Caprio* case we said that a breach of a general ordinance defining the degree of care to be exercised in one's calling is evidence of negligence as to every one. We did not limit this statement to those who might be expected to be exposed to danger. Unreasonable risk being taken, its consequences are not confined to those who might probably be hurt.

If this be so, we do not have a plaintiff suing by "derivation or succession." Her action is original and primary. Her claim is for a breach of duty to herself—not that she is subrogated to any right of action of the owner of the parcel or of a passenger standing at the scene of the explosion.

The right to recover damages rests on additional considerations. The plaintiff's rights must be injured, and this injury must be caused by the negligence. We build a dam, but are negligent as to its foundations. Breaking, it injures property down stream. We are not liable if all this happened because of some reason other than the insecure foundation. But when injuries do result from our unlawful act we are liable for the consequences. It does not matter that they are unusual, unexpected, unforeseen and unforeseeable. But there is one limitation. The damages must be so connected with the negligence that the latter may be said to be the proximate cause of the former.

These two words have never been given an inclusive definition. What is a cause in a legal sense, still more what is a proximate cause, depend in each case upon many considerations, as does the existence of negligence itself. Any philosophical doctrine of causation does not help us. A boy throws a stone into a pond. The ripples spread. The water level rises. The history of that pond is altered to all eternity. It will be altered by other causes also. Yet it will be forever the resultant of all causes combined. Each one will have an influence. How great only omniscience can say. You may speak of a chain, or if you please, a net. An analogy is of little aid. Each cause brings about future events. Without each the future would not be the same. Each is proximate in the sense it is essential. But that is not what we mean by the word. Nor on the other hand do we mean sole cause. There is no such thing.

Should analogy be thought helpful, however, I prefer that of a stream. The spring, starting on its journey, is joined by tributary after tributary. The river, reaching the ocean, comes from a hundred sources. No man may say whence any drop of water is derived. Yet for a time distinction may be possible. Into the clear creek, brown swamp water flows from the left. Later, from the right comes water stained by its clay bed. The three may remain for a space, sharply divided. But at last, inevitably no trace of separation remains. They are so commingled that all distinction is lost.

As we have said, we cannot trace the effect of an act to the end, if end there is. Again, however, we may trace it part of the way. A murder at Serajevo may be the necessary antecedent to an assassination in London twenty years hence. An overturned lantern may burn all Chicago. We may follow the fire from the shed to the last building. We rightly say the fire started by the lantern caused its destruction.

A cause, but not the proximate cause. What we do mean by the word "proximate" is, that because of convenience, of public policy, of a rough sense of justice, the law arbitrarily declines to trace a series of events beyond a certain point. This is not logic. It is practical politics. Take our rule as to fires. Sparks from my burning haystack set on fire my house and my neighbor's. I may recover from a negligent railroad. He may not. Yet the wrongful act as directly harmed the one as the other. We may regret that the line was drawn just where it was, but drawn somewhere it had to be. We said the act of the railroad was not the proximate cause of our neighbor's fire. Cause it surely was. The words we used were simply indicative of our notions of public policy.

Other courts think differently. But somewhere they reach the point where they cannot say the stream comes from any one source.

Take the illustration given in an unpublished manuscript by a distinguished and helpful writer on the law of torts. A chauffeur negligently collides with another car which is filled with dynamite, although he could not know it. An explosion follows. A, walking on the sidewalk nearby, is killed. B, sitting in a window of a building opposite, is cut by flying glass. C, likewise sitting in a window a block away, is similarly injured. And a further illustration. A nursemaid, ten blocks away, startled by the noise, involuntarily drops a baby from her arms to the walk. We are told that C may not recover while A may. As to B it is a question for court or jury. We will all agree that the baby might not. Because, we are again told, the chauffeur had no reason to believe his conduct involved any risk of injuring either C or the baby. As to them he was not negligent.

But the chauffeur, being negligent in risking the collision, his belief that the scope of the harm he might do would be limited is immaterial. His act unreasonably jeopardized the safety of any one who might be affected by it. C's injury and that of the baby were directly traceable to the collision. Without that, the injury would not have happened. C had the right to sit in his office, secure from such dangers. The baby was entitled to use the sidewalk with reasonable safety.

The true theory is, it seems to me, that the injury to C, if in truth he is to be denied recovery, and the injury to the baby is that their several injuries were not the proximate result of the negligence. And here not what the chauffeur had reason to believe would be the result of his conduct, but what the prudent would foresee, may have a bearing. May have some bearing, for the problem of proximate cause is not to be solved by any one consideration.

It is all a question of expediency. There are no fixed rules to govern our judgment. There are simply matters of which we may take account. We have in a somewhat different connection spoken of "the stream of events." We have asked whether that stream was deflected—whether it was forced into new and unexpected channels. (*Donnelly v. Piercy Contracting Co.*, 222 N. Y. 210). This is rather rhetoric than law. There is in truth little to guide us other than common sense.

There are some hints that may help us. The proximate cause, involved as it may be with many other causes, must be, at the least, something without which the event would not happen. The court must ask itself whether there was a natural and continuous sequence between cause and effect. Was the one a substantial factor in producing the other? Was there a direct connection between them, without too many intervening causes? Is the effect of cause on result not too [attenuated]? Is the cause likely, in the usual judgment of mankind, to produce the result? Or by the exercise of prudent foresight could the result be foreseen? Is the result too remote from the cause, and here we consider remoteness in time and space. *(Bird v. St. Paul F. & M. Ins. Co.,* 224 N. Y. 47, where we passed upon the construction of a contract — but something was also said on this subject.) Clearly we must so consider, for the greater the distance either in time or space, the more surely do other causes intervene to affect the result. When a lantern is overturned the firing of a shed is a fairly direct consequence. Many things contribute to the spread of the conflagration — the force of the wind, the direction and width of streets, the character of intervening structures, other factors. We draw an uncertain and wavering line, but draw it we must as best we can.

Once again, it is all a question of fair judgment, always keeping in mind the fact that we endeavor to make a rule in each case that will be practical and in keeping with the general understanding of mankind.

Here another question must be answered. In the case supposed it is said, and said correctly, that the chauffeur is liable for the direct effect of the explosion although he had no reason to suppose it would follow a collision. "The fact that the injury occurred in a different manner than that which might have been expected does not prevent the chauffeur's negligence from being in law the cause of the injury." But the natural results of a negligent act — the results which a prudent man would or should foresee — do have a bearing upon the decision as to proximate cause. We have said so repeatedly. What should be foreseen? No human foresight would suggest that a collision itself might injure one a block away. On the contrary, given an explosion, such a possibility might be reasonably expected. I think the direct connection, the foresight of which the courts speak, assumes prevision of the explosion, for the immediate results of which, at least, the chauffeur is responsible.

It may be said this is unjust. Why? In fairness he should make good every injury flowing from his negligence. Not because of tenderness toward him we say he need not answer for all that follows his wrong. We look back to the catastrophe, the fire kindled by the spark, or the explosion. We trace the consequences — not indefinitely, but to a certain point. And to aid us in fixing that point we ask what might ordinarily be expected to follow the fire or the explosion.

This last suggestion is the factor which must determine the case before us. The act upon which defendant's liability rests is knocking an apparently harmless package onto the platform. The act was negligent. For its proximate consequences the defendant is liable. If its contents were broken, to the owner; if it fell upon and crushed a passenger's foot, then to him. If it exploded and injured one in the immediate vicinity, to him also as to A in the illustration. Mrs. Palsgraf was standing some distance away. How far cannot be told from the record — apparently twenty-five or thirty feet. Perhaps less. Except for the explosion, she would not have been injured. We are told by the appellant in his brief "it cannot be denied that the explosion was the direct cause of the plaintiff's injuries." So it was a substantial factor in producing the result — there was here a natural and continuous sequence—direct connection. The only intervening cause was that instead of blowing her to the ground the concussion smashed the weighing machine which in turn fell upon her. There was no remoteness in time, little in space. And surely, given such an explosion as here it needed no great foresight to predict that the natural result would be to injure one on the platform at no greater distance from its scene than was the plaintiff. Just how no one might be able to predict. Whether by flying fragments, by broken glass, by wreckage of machines or structures no one could say. But injury in some form was most probable.

Under these circumstances I cannot say as a matter of law that the plaintiff's injuries were not the proximate result of the negligence. That is all we have before us. The court refused to so charge. No request was made to submit the matter to the jury as a question of fact, even would that have been proper upon the record before us.

The judgment appealed from should be affirmed, with costs.

(d)   Clarifying Causation in Tort[†]

Erik S. Knutsen

. . . .

I.   WHAT IS CAUSATION?

This article is concerned primarily with cause-in-fact — the third step in a standard negligence analysis in tort which links the defendant's breach of the applicable standard of care with the harm to the victim. A court only gets to the causation stage of the negligence analysis after the plaintiff has successfully proven that the defendant owed the plaintiff a duty of care and the defendant fell below the applicable standard of care. Causation links the defendant's breach of the requisite standard of care with the production of some harm to the plaintiff. Justice Sopinka aptly defined causation in tort as "an expression of the relationship that must be found to exist between the tortious act of the wrongdoer and the injury to the victim in order to justify compensation of the latter out of the pocket of the former."[7] The causation step in a negligence case is often the most contentious, most expensive step. It requires the most evidence, often in the form of expert evidence. And it is probably the most heated step in the analysis simply because, in order to arrive at the causation step, the plaintiff will have already had to prove that the defendant breached the standard of care. So the plaintiff will have already established fault. The causation step builds the connection between fault and harm.

II.   THE "BUT FOR" TEST IS THE DEFAULT TEST FOR CAUSATION

Despite what past case law may have appeared to suggest, the standard doctrinal test for causation in a negligence analysis remains the "but for" test.[8] And again, despite what past case law may have appeared to suggest, this test works for nearly all factual circumstances. The test requires that a fact-finder ask: "but for" the defendant's negligent behaviour, would the plaintiff have suffered some injury? The defendant's negligence only has to be "a" cause, not "the" sole cause, and there may be other tortious and non-tortious causes in the mix.[9] This simple test

often causes much confusion because two fundamental aspects of the test are misunderstood. They are misunderstood because it is forgotten that tort law is a fault-based system that relies on establishing a connection between responsibility for harm on the part of one party (the defendant) and the suffering of that harm on the part of another party (the plaintiff).[10] ...

The first misunderstood aspect of the "but for" test is the fact that the causal "trigger" (if it can be called such) is the defendant's breach of the standard of care. So, to put the test in more understandable and precise terms, it asks: "but for" the defendant's breach of the standard of care, would the plaintiff have suffered some injury? Clarifying this simple detail is fundamental to the operation of the test. The "but for" test is not about discovering what factor really caused the accident, in the real world. Nor is it about discovering what really happened factually to bring about the turn of events which resulted in injury. The only purpose the test serves is to determine the link between the at-fault conduct of the defendant and the plaintiff's alleged harm caused by that at-fault defendant.

. . . .

An example helps to clarify the basic concepts of "but for" causation. Imagine Lucy is in a motor vehicle collision with Ethel. Lucy and Ethel were each driving their own vehicles. Ethel did not stop at a "stop" sign because she was talking on a cell phone and accidentally drove into Lucy's vehicle. Lucy was injured. To recover from Ethel in tort, Lucy must establish that Ethel's breach of the applicable standard of care was a cause of her injuries. If Lucy was also intoxicated from alcohol at the time and had also forgotten to wear her prescription glasses she was legally required to wear to operate her vehicle, the causation question still remains the same: "but for" Ethel's breach of the standard of care of a reasonable driver, would Lucy have suffered some injury in the car accident? The "but for" test does not switch to some other inquiry about "what happened to make this mess?" Even though

---

† (2010) 33 Dalhousie L.J. 153. [Notes/references omitted.] Reproduced with permission of the author and the publisher.

there may be other causal factors at work, each operating to create an end result injury (i.e., the intoxication and the poor eyesight), the "but for" test remains steadfastly focused on the wrongful conduct of the at-fault tortfeasor. Is it Ethel's fault that resulted in some harm to Lucy?

The second often misunderstood element of the "but for" test is the fact that the injury in question must be the result of the defendant's conduct. This seems simple enough but, in a complex, multi-causal situation, can become confusing. The at-fault defendant is only being held responsible in tort law for the injury caused by her behaviour.[12] The defendant is not being held responsible for the fact that the accident merely happened. There is a significant difference between the "happening" of an event and the causing of an injury which is, in itself, just the result of a "happening." Tort law is only concerned with the result of the happening — the injury. In the example above, the question must be focused on whether or not, regardless of other potential causes of harm intermingled in the happening, Ethel's breach of the standard of care is "a" cause of "some" harm. Even if Lucy's drunkenness and her failure to wear her glasses also contributed to the end result injuries she suffered, if Lucy can prove that Ethel's breach of the standard of care resulted in "some" injury to Lucy, she has proven "but for" causation.[13] In this example, "but for" Ethel's at-fault behaviour, Lucy would not have been injured. This is so because the negligence system is only concerned with fault-based liability.

Time and again, the Supreme Court of Canada has re-affirmed that the "but for" test is the default test to apply when faced with determining causation.[14] Arguably, and despite much commentary to the contrary,[15] this test works for the vast majority of tort cases. There is typically no reason to reach for any novel doctrinal causation tool.[16] Indeed, the Supreme Court has said as much in *Hanke v. Resurfice* and again in *Fullowka*.[17] One primary reason this Court may have had to repeatedly remind the legal world that the bedrock test for causation is "but for" is simply because lower courts have often confused the utility of the test with the ease of operation of the alternative test for causation in Canada: the material contribution test. That test is reserved only for instances where the "but for" test is "unworkable."[18]

. . . .

III. THE MATERIAL CONTRIBUTION TEST: THE RARE EXCEPTION

. . . .

The material contribution test is the doctrinal test to use when "but for" causation is "unworkable."[21] The test is simple in operation, and there are two remarkably stringent pre-conditions to the application of the test.[22] First, it must be impossible for the plaintiff to prove causation under the "but for" test. This impossibility must be something beyond the plaintiff's control. The Supreme Court gives the notion of "current limits of scientific knowledge" as one reason for the impossibility. Another, implied from ... the *Cook v. Lewis (1951)*[23] example,[24] appears to be when it may be practically impossible to apply the "but for" test because of the particular facts of the happening (i.e., two hunters negligently shoot at once, but it is impossible to tell which one's birdshot strikes an incorrect target and injures someone). The plaintiff is unable to prove "but for" causation because of the inherent nature of the peculiar happening here, not because the plaintiff could obtain sufficient evidence in the circumstances but merely did not. The impossibility is thus beyond the plaintiff's control.[25]

The second pre-condition for the material contribution test is that the plaintiff must be able to prove that the defendant breached the standard of care, exposed the plaintiff to an unreasonable risk of injury, and the plaintiff must have suffered that type of injury.[26] Note that the pre-condition still requires a finding of fault on the part of the defendant — the defendant must have conducted herself below the accepted standard for that particular type of behaviour.

If both of these pre-conditions are met, a court can apply the material contribution test for causation. That test operates as follows: as long as the plaintiff can prove on a balance of probabilities that the defendant's breach of the standard of care materially contributed to the plaintiff's injury beyond the *de minimis* range, causation is proven.[27]

The point to emphasize is that the use of material contribution as a doctrinal test for causation is severely restricted and rare. "But for" will almost always work to answer the causation question about a particular case, and the answer depends upon the sufficiency of the evidence. The material contribution test has nothing to do with the number of potential causes, the complexity of the case, the number of parties, pre-existing conditions, crumbling or thin skulls, or anything other than the defendant's breach of the standard of care in relation to the plaintiff's resulting injury. But the problem with the material contribution test is that it usually works in favour of the plaintiff. One can almost always find causation against the defendant whose behaviour increased the risk of harm to the plaintiff. In essence, material contribution has the potential to create liability for breach of a standard of care plus risk creation.[28]

. . . .

IV. WHEN IS "BUT FOR" UNWORKABLE? CIRCULAR AND DEPENDENCY CAUSATION

1. Examples of "but for" unworkability

The Supreme Court in *Hanke* provides two examples of when "but for" is "unworkable" and it is therefore permissible to resort to the material contribution test. The first is the *Cook v. Lewis* "circular causation" situation, where it is impossible to tell which of two potential tortious sources caused the harm to the plaintiff. In *Cook v. Lewis*, two hunters simultaneously negligently shot at what they thought was a bird. Instead, one hunter's birdshot struck a third person. It was impossible to tell what shot came from which gun. Even modern forensic ballistic science would be hard-pressed to identify from which firearm the shot pellets came, assuming the same shot size was used by each hunter. Hence, there is a real limit to the scientific knowledge for uncovering causation. The "but for" test leads to an absurd result in this case, knowing at the very least that both hunters are at fault. One asks "but for the negligent shooting of hunter A, would the plaintiff have been injured?" The response is unknowable because of the actions of hunter B. One would respond "perhaps, because hunter B may have been the one whose shot struck the plaintiff." When one then returns the question about hunter B, one gets the same circular response: "but for the negligent shooting of hunter B, would the plaintiff have been injured?" One would respond "perhaps, because it may really have been hunter A whose shot struck the plaintiff."

The causal response is circular because the plaintiff knows that one of either hunter A or B was a cause of the harm, and one of either hunter A or B was not but, because causal analysis only accommodates focusing on one hunter at a time, the result is the unsatisfactory answer: "impossible to tell without knowing the answer for the other potential tortfeasor." Both hunters were at fault, and it is obvious one hunter's shot connected with the plaintiff and resulted in some harm. If not for both hunters acting negligently and shooting at once, the plaintiff would not be in such an impossible circular proof position. In a "one hunter" scenario, the answer is simple: liability for that hunter. But in the "two hunter" scenario where only one hunter's birdshot connects yet each is just as negligent as the other, it makes little sense for the causation answer of "impossible to tell" to lead to a finding of no liability when the victim was certainly shot by one of the two negligent hunters. The key to identifying a circular causation situation is that there is nothing the plaintiff can do to adduce evidence pointing more to one causal source than the other. The evidentiary frustration is one about identity of the causal source. It is not that there was merely not enough evidence adduced to prove identity. There must be no evidence available to prove identity because of the unique circumstances of the case. This evidentiary stalemate is not the fault of the plaintiff — proof is merely unobtainable due to how the accident happened.

. . . .

The second example in *Hanke* where the material contribution test is suitable to use involves a chain of multi-party actions, each depending on the other, in a situation of "dependency causation." The "but for" test may be impossible to prove when one must determine what a party would have done had the defendant not been negligent, and thus how that party's decision affects the plaintiff's resulting injury. The example the Court gives is *Walker v. York Finch Hospital*,[30] a case where it may have been impossible to prove "but for" causation.[31] In that case, it may have been impossible to prove that, but for the negligent screening of blood donors by the defendant blood collection service, a person with HIV-infected blood may not have donated the infected blood which eventually injured the plaintiff. The causal link between the at-fault defendant and the injured plaintiff is thus mediated by the action of a third party. This "dependency causation" necessarily relies on evidence of causation beyond the relationship between the at-fault defendant and the injured plaintiff, and is potentially very difficult to obtain.

An example of a third case ... which does pass the two pre-conditions to the material contribution test is the House of Lords case of *Fairchild v. Glenhaven Funeral Home*.[33] This is a case of circular causation, where the plaintiff ran up against an impossibility with the "but for" test because of multiple potential tortious causes and an inability to prove which of the tortious causes (all negligent defendants) was a cause of his injuries. The plaintiff worked at multiple asbestos operations over a period of time. He contracted mesothelioma. This disease can be caused by the inhaling of one single fibre of asbestos. The employers all breached the applicable standard of care in keeping unsafe work environments. The plaintiff could not prove "but for" one employer, he would not have suffered some injury. There were multiple negligent employers and it was impossible, based on current scientific limits, to prove at which employer he inhaled the asbestos fibre. Proof was beyond the plaintiff's control, but the plaintiff knew he inhaled the asbestos at one of the potential tortious employers. Again, because the causal analysis is structured to focus on one tortfeasor at a time, this scenario also leads to circular causation responses. The plaintiff, however, could prove breach of the standard of care, exposure to risk, and the fact that he contracted the very disease foreseeable by exposure to the ambit of such risk. Thus, in Canada, this type of case fits with the application of the material contribution test. In Britain, the House of Lords adopted a modified version of the test, holding that exposure to risk was sufficient proof of causation in this special case of mesothelioma.[34]

. . . .

CONCLUSION: CAUSATION CLARIFIED

In conclusion, the law of causation in Canada has often been decried as confusing. Despite the Supreme Court of Canada's economy of language in causation cases, the law can be seen as actually quite consistent and simple, as long as one keeps at the forefront the notion that the causation test is designed to assess liability for harm caused by fault-based behaviour. Most of the challenges in understanding the jurisprudence about causation come from confusing the message in the cases as directing a shift in the standard "but for" causation test. In fact, most cases are instead about evidentiary sufficiency in causation. The only instances where litigants are predictably able to step outside the standard "but for" test are in situations involving circular causation and dependency causation....

A brief concluding summary of the fundamental concepts of Canadian causation law may prove helpful:

(a) Negligence law is a fault-based inquiry requiring a link between breach of an applicable standard of care with some harm to an injured accident victim in order to trigger compensation for the victim;

(b) The default doctrinal test for causation in negligence is the "but for" test;

(c) The focus of the causal inquiry is on the defendant's breach of the standard of care as a potential cause for some injury to the plaintiff;

(d) Causation must be proven on a balance of probabilities;

(e) A plaintiff need only prove that a defendant's breach of the standard of care is "a" cause of her injuries;

(f) The material contribution test for causation is a rare and exceptional test, reserved only when the "but for" test fails;

(g) The "but for" test rarely fails, and currently only in situations involving circular causation and dependency causation:

　1. Circular causation involves factual situations where it is impossible for the plaintiff to prove which one of two or more possible tortious causes are the cause of the plaintiff's harm;

　2. Dependency causation involves factual situations where it is impossible for the plaintiff to prove if a third party would have taken some action in the face of a defendant's negligence and such third party's action would have facilitated harm to the plaintiff;

(h) If the "but for" test fails, the plaintiff must meet two pre-conditions to utilize the material contribution test for causation:

　1. It must be impossible for the plaintiff to prove causation (either due to circular or dependency causation); and,

　2. The plaintiff must be able to prove that the defendant breached the standard of care, exposed the plaintiff to an unreasonable risk of injury, and the plaintiff must have suffered that type of injury.

(i) The "robust and pragmatic" common sense approach to causation from *Snell v. Farrell* is an evidentiary sufficiency device that helps to solve evidentiary draws, providing the plaintiff has at least proffered "very little affirmative evidence" about causation;

(j) If the victim is overly susceptible to harm, and suffers greater than foreseeable harm as a result of the defendant's negligence, the defendant is liable for the entire harm, not for just harm that one might think foreseeable for a "normal," healthy person (thin-skull rule) — such a concept is triggered at the remoteness phase of the negligence analysis and not at the causation phase;

(k) A defendant is only liable for the extent of the plaintiff's injuries caused by the defendant's negligence (crumbling skull rule) — such a con-

cept is triggered at the damages phase of the negligence analysis and not at the causation phase.

. . . .

(e) Discussion Problem: The Careful Pedestrian and the Feckless Driver

A woman, Sally, who is a self-employed counsellor, heads out for a short walk to the local store. She walks along the sidewalk and, at an intersection, begins to cross the road. There are lights at this intersection and the 'walk' sign is on in her favour.

A car approaching the intersection has slowed down and seems about to stop. However, the driver, Martha, doesn't come to a stop but allows the car to continue slowly into the turn. The car strikes Sally. The driver is apologetic but doesn't think the accident is too serious. She admits to being distracted and inattentive but points out that she was going slowly enough for a pedestrian to get out of her way.

That said, the collision breaks Sally's ankle. It is a compound fracture that requires a pin to be inserted to set the fracture. It is a painful break and heals slowly and badly over the next months. Sally cannot work her usual hours.

About six months later, with the ankle still not fully healed, a scan shows that an aggressive cancer has taken hold in the bone of the ankle. Medical literature suggests that cancer can be triggered by the insertion of foreign bodies such as the pin used to set the ankle in susceptible individuals.

Sally receives excellent treatment for the cancer but nevertheless dies about six months later.

What do you think the 'law response' should be?

(f) A Critique of Torts[†]

Richard L. Abel

I. A VERY BRIEF HISTORY

Before the modern era, tort law was preoccupied with intentional wrongs; it still is in peripheral areas of the world relatively unaffected by industrialization, urbanization, capitalism, and the state. Accidents rarely caused serious injury because people did not control large amounts of energy.[2] In societies in which the means and relations of production did not generate great differences in wealth, status was differentiated by reputation, which was shaped significantly by intentional wrongs and the response they evoked.[3] Even misfortunes we now interpret as accidental — such as a snake bite, lightning bolt, or fatal disease — often were construed as intentional by reference to beliefs in witchcraft and sorcery or attributed to the wrath of ancestors or gods.[4] In the absence of a state, redress frequently depended on the victim's capacity to mobilize a support group, often based on kinship, residence, or age grade, whose members were likely to be outraged by intentional wrongs.

---

† This material is originally published in (1990) 37 UCLA L. Rev. 785 at 786–89, 791–94, 797–802, 806–831. [Notes/references omitted.]. Reproduced with permission of the author.

The social, economic, political, and cultural changes of the last few centuries inevitably transformed tort law. Technological development made it possible for inadvertence to inflict unimaginable misery. Individuals can trigger disaster when driving cars or starting fires (in office towers, hotels, or forests, for instance).[5] Collectivities, both public and private, can cause even worse damage through both discrete events (the Exxon oil spill, the Bhopal disaster) and ongoing activities (the manufacture and sale of asbestos, thalidomide, and cigarettes, and the dumping of nuclear waste). The concentration of private capital and political power, together with autocratic structures of control, have greatly augmented the potential effects of carelessness.

Mass migration and urbanization have produced a nation of strangers. Most people have little interest in inflicting intentional injuries; when they do, the goal is material gain rather than enhanced social status (which is lost by crime, except within deviant subcultures).[6] Similarly, victims of anonymous violence are more interested in compensation than personal revenge, but tort actions offer little redress because few criminals can pay damages. The world of status relationships has largely contracted to the family.[7] Violence and emotional abuse are endemic within that domain, but the state is reluctant to get involved because intervention would destroy intimacy; people disagree about behavioral standards, and those who wield power within the family — men and parents — strongly resist interference.

The same social structural changes that reduce the salience of intentional torts simultaneously increase the importance of negligent injuries. Strangers have less incentive to exercise care toward each other and greater difficulty in resolving conflict when injury occurs. The deepening divides of class and race aggravate both tendencies. Capitalism, technology, and the division of labor all have increased the social distance between those who make the "decision for accidents"[8] and their potential victims: consumers of goods, services, and environmental amenities (such as air and water), and workers. Tortious behavior has come to resemble modern warfare in the distance between tortfeasor and victim.

As the focus of tort law has shifted from intentional wrongs among intimates to unintentional injuries among strangers, its moral tone has changed as well. Although tort scholars disagree about the standard of care demanded by preindustrial tort law,[9] none would deny that nineteenth-century judges consciously adopted a highly moralistic rhetoric, allowing victims to recover only if they were free from fault and those they sued were morally culpable. In the last hundred years, these moral judgments have been subordinated to an equally explicit concern with compensation. Courts have awarded damages to victims who previously would have been barred from recovery: charitable hospital patients, social guests or trespassers on the land of another, guests in another's car, and those guilty of contributory negligence or assumption of risk. Similarly, courts have imposed liability without fault on those who caused injuries, simply because they were employers, manufacturers, or participants in abnormally dangerous activities.

The experience of injury also has changed fundamentally. Capitalism has created a proletariat that must sell its labor for wages in order to live. Lost earnings (past and future) are an essential element of compensatory damages because unemployment is tantamount to destitution. Those disabled by accident must purchase care from strangers because capitalism erodes the obligations of mutual support outside the nuclear family and increasingly compels both spouses to work.[10] As the medical profession has increased its own technical competence, it simultaneously has deskilled the laity. Medical expenses are another major component of tort damages because medical care now must be purchased from physicians or their subordinates at prices inflated by the state-created monopoly.

Capitalism and mass production have disseminated consumer goods among the general public. Most of these goods represent pure exchange value — bought rather than made and readily replaced (indeed, the newer the better). Consequently, property loss is another ingredient of tort damages. Finally, as explained more fully below, the commodity form has been extended from goods, labor, and care to all forms of human experience. Accordingly, courts grant tort damages for physical pain, disfigurement, loss of bodily function, fear, and damage to emotional relationships. The growing importance of damages for intangible injury reflects the value system of a postindustrial society that promises everyone a perfect life, unimpaired by accidents, and elevates leisure and consumption over work and production.

Social fragmentation has made it difficult for victims to mobilize group support for their claims, increasing their reliance on the state and on the commodified assistance they must buy from lawyers.[11] Both eagerly accept the responsibility. The state always has sought a central role in norm enforcement and conflict resolution, progressively asserting its monopoly over the use of force. Politicians and the media constantly reaffirm the centrality of these state functions by bombarding the public with calls for "law and order." Powerful state bureaucracies — courts, prosecutors, police, and prison officials — develop vested interests in processing crime. The victim becomes an embarrassing anachronism necessary to set the process in motion but inconvenient thereafter. Criminal prosecutions virtually supplant civil actions for intentional tort.

Private practitioners specializing in representing tort victims develop their own vested interests. The economic manifestation is the contingent fee — plaintiff's lawyers take a proportion of the victim's recovery, typically twenty-five to fifty percent. The political manifestation is the time and money devoted by the Association of Trial Lawyers of America and its state counterparts to advocating fault-based private law remedies.

. . . .

II. CRITIQUE

The purposes of tort law are to pass moral judgment on what has happened, respond to the victim's need for compensation, and encourage future safety. It does a poor job of all three.

A. Moral Judgment

Historically, moral judgment was the core of tort law. Few would deny that endangering or injuring another merits condemnation or that victims' wrongs deserve public recognition. Furthermore, those held liable experience tort damages as punishment. Yet tort liability is incoherent as a moral system.

It consistently violates the basic principle of proportionality between the wrongfulness of the defendant's conduct and the magnitude of the penalty imposed. Because punishment is a function of harm caused, it is either too severe or too lenient. It is too severe when momentary inadvertence results in catastrophic injury — for instance, a driver who takes his eyes off the road to tune the radio, causing an automobile accident that inflicts a lifetime of agony on one or more victims. It is too lenient when egregiously unsafe conduct happens to cause little or no injury, by chance or through the intervention of others — for instance, a negligently constructed and maintained office building consumed by fire in the middle of the night when it is empty. Courts deal with these inequities haphazardly: judges invoke doctrines of proximate cause and duty to curtail liability,[16] whereas triers of fact stretch notions of causation to extend liability.[17] But many injustices are not corrected, and the moral intuitions of judges and juries lack a principled basis.[18] Similar problems arise

when the law overvalues or undervalues victim misconduct; again courts make ad hoc accommodations, adjusting the standard of care to the victim's capacity (measured by age and physical or mental disability), making crude comparisons between the fault of the parties, or acknowledging environmental constraints on volition, such as an employer's domination of employees or the few choices enjoyed by poor people.

Notions of fault constructed when individuals were the significant actors and technology was simple are inadequate to assign responsibility today. Many torts, particularly the most serious, are caused by collectivities, both public and private. The doctrine of *respondeat superior* ensures victim compensation, but it also obviates the need to determine which employee was responsible.[19] Liability insurance pays most damages, but it also insulates the wrongdoer from moral judgment.[20] Many injuries are caused by the independent acts of several unrelated defendants among whom there is no principled basis for apportioning responsibility. Indeed, the very notion of individual responsibility is inconsistent with probabilistic theories of causation. But the imposition of liability on DES manufacturers whose products might have injured the plaintiffs seems to strain basic principles of fairness.[21]

Tort theory and practice violate the moral intuitions of lay-people. Survey research reveals that both victims and the general public believe that compensation ought to be divorced from fault.[22] On one hand, those injured deserve and need compensation regardless of their own behavior. On the other hand, compensation should be paid by those who can afford it most easily (because they are wealthy or can spread the burden) or who benefit from the activity that caused the injury (such as employers, manufacturers, or sellers). The attribution of fault becomes a mere rationalization for this more compelling ethical goal. Tortfeasors are even more averse to moral judgment. Most cases are settled rather than adjudicated, and settlements often explicitly deny any acknowledgment of fault. This contrasts sharply with many nonwestern societies in which the response to injury focuses on the causal actor's admission of guilt, apology, and plea for forgiveness.[23]

The moral incoherence of the tort system at the level of theory is reproduced at the level of practice in the proliferation of inconsistent standards of care. In preindustrial societies, liability was sometimes predicated on fault and sometimes imposed without fault; in yet other instances, fault went unpunished. Although nineteenth-century judges invoked fault to

61

constrict liability, even they did not embrace that principle wholeheartedly, as the persistence of strict liability for ultrahazardous activities shows. The last hundred years have seen continued tension between fault and nonfault principles. Nonfault recovery has expanded through workers' compensation, products liability, ultrahazardous activity, and no-fault automobile insurance. Some defenses have been restricted (such as assumption of risk or agreements not to sue), and others have been modified (comparative fault largely displaced contributory negligence). A few jurisdictions have created comprehensive compensation programs. Yet fault principles have reappeared within every nonfault scheme: worker intoxication or employer breach of safety regulations in workers' compensation; notions of the appropriateness of ultrahazardous activities; the requirement of a defect and comparative fault in products liability; criminal activity in comprehensive compensation programs.

The inconsistencies detailed above all reflect problems inherent in the dominant ethical framework —utilitarianism. When tort law expresses nonconsequentialist values, the results are even less satisfactory. The obligation to help another in danger is one of the most intractable issues in tort law. Our inability to find an acceptable position highlights the basic contradiction between egoism and altruism: we can neither embrace one of the extremes nor find any principled position between them.[24] We have just as much difficulty combining utilitarian and nonutilitarian ethics. We require informed consent before medical procedures out of respect for the patient's autonomy (a non-consequentialist perspective); but we impose liability only when the information withheld would have persuaded a reasonable person to reject the procedure, and we award damages in proportion to the physical injury caused by the procedure rather than to the violation of autonomy (both utilitarian perspectives).[25] Similar problems arise when we try to combine the utilitarian duty of reasonable care with non-utilitarian values, such as parents' right to raise their children or minority religious beliefs about illness and medicine.[26]

. . . .

B. Compensation

If moral judgment accounts for the origin of tort law, compensation is its contemporary preoccupation, at least among laypersons. Victims need money — often desperately — to replace lost earnings and pay medical expenses; they may want something more to allay their sense of outrage and ensure that the tortfeasor has been properly punished. Jurors are equally preoccupied with helping needy victims. Yet tort law is an unsatisfactory mechanism of compensation, both in its material consequences and as an ideology.

Tort law cannot compensate needy victims adequately because liability is a function of fault rather than need. A victim injured by someone not at fault will remain uncompensated. A victim at fault can never receive more than partial compensation. And even when the victim is found to be faultless and the defendant at fault, the consequences of liability depend on the material circumstances of the plaintiff and defendant. If the defendant lacks resources, a tort judgment is an empty remedy. If the parties have similar resources (or the victim is wealthier), shifting the financial burden from one to the other produces no social gain. Indeed, the goal is not to compensate the victim but to spread the financial burden among as many people as possible. But spreading turns on the happenstance that the tortfeasor either has insurance or is a large corporate entity whose liability will be shared by customers, shareholders, employees, or taxpayers.

Given the legal and financial obstacles to recovery, it is not surprising that relatively few victims succeed. The best empirical study, which examined English accident victims disabled for at least two weeks, found that only twelve percent recovered any tort damages.[34] Several American studies confirm that recovery is infrequent here as well.[35] Although lawyers are essential to successful claims, they are prohibited from initiating contact with accident victims.[36] Even the small fraction of victims who seek compensation recover only part of their damages because the vast bulk of claims is settled out of court.[37] Economic incentives persuade tortfeasors to overcompensate small claims (because of their nuisance value) and undercompensate large ones (because victims need immediate payment while the legal system allows defendants to delay for years). Many victims and their families are impoverished because of the inadequacy of other sources of compensation including loss insurance, sick pay, welfare, disability benefits, and pensions.[38]

Tort damages are not only inadequate as compensation, but also are unequal, thereby symbolizing, reproducing, and intensifying existing material inequalities. Because liberalism rejects status inequalities, tort law gradually has eliminated *de jure* distinctions between patients injured in charitable and profit-making hospitals, fee-paying passengers and gratuitous guests injured in automobile accidents, and business and social guests injured by landowner negligence.[39] Yet the legal celebration of formal equality obscures the persistence of real inequality.

First, some people are more likely than others to be victimized by tortfeasors who cannot or will not pay compensation. Crime victims, for instance, are disproportionately the poor, racial minorities, women, adolescents, and the elderly. Sovereign immunity often eliminates tortious liability for government, whose victims are likely to be charitable patients, criminal suspects, prison inmates, welfare recipients, military personnel, or veterans.[40]

Second, the process of making a claim is institutionalized differently in various settings. Automobile accidents are governed by reasonably clear behavioral rules — traffic laws. Witnesses often are available because accidents occur in public. Accidents create physical evidence such as skid marks and dents. Victims usually summon police, who make written reports. Finally, both parties are likely to be insured. Similarly, some compensation almost always is available for work accidents. Fellow workers both encourage victims to claim and act as witnesses. Trade unions provide assistance and legal representation. Class antagonisms create a sense of entitlement. When accidents occur elsewhere, however — at home, from consumer products, during leisure activities, for example — the claims process is much less institutionalized: no one may have witnessed the accidents; victims tend to blame themselves; and the potential defendant is not readily identifiable. In England, twenty-nine percent of road-accident victims and nineteen percent of work-accident victims recovered some damages, but only two percent of other victims, who represented eighty-six percent of those disabled for two weeks or more by accident, recovered.[41] Women, the young and old, and the unemployed are more likely to be in the last category.

Third, the measure of damages is inequitable. Tort damages are far more generous than workers' compensation payments, crime victim compensation schemes, or veterans' benefits for those disabled while in the military. Victims in the last three categories are more likely to be manual workers, poor individuals, or members of racial minorities. Tort damages deliberately reproduce the existing distribution of wealth and income. Those who question the legitimacy of that distribution will be troubled that the state uses its coercive power to recreate inequality. Furthermore, the cost of preserving privilege is borne by all those buying liability insurance, purchasing products and services, and paying taxes. For example, all insured car owners pay the cost of compensating the privileged few who drive a Rolls Royce or earn half a million dollars a year. They also pay the greater costs of the superior medical care consumed by victims from higher socioeconomic strata.

The privileged also recover more for their pain and suffering than the nonprivileged because nonpecuniary damages are calculated as a multiple of pecuniary damages — often twice as much. Finally, jurors may show more sympathy for those who have lost privilege than for those who never enjoyed it.[42]

Because these biases cumulate, tort law intensifies social inequality. Among English accident victims disabled for two weeks or more, men recovered tort damages almost twice as often as women, individuals between the ages of twenty-five and fifty-four recovered three times as often as those younger or older, the employed recovered more often than the unemployed, and housewives recovered less than a third as often as their proportion of the injured population would predict. The mean sick pay award to women was less than half that to men.[43]

. . . .

Tort damages are no more satisfactory on the level of ideology. Their fundamental justification is hopelessly incoherent — money cannot restore victims to their status quo before the accident.[51] Damages paid after prolonged delay are not the same as the wages lost or property destroyed years earlier even if the court adds prejudgment interest.[52] All goods are not fungible. Reimbursement for the cost of medical treatment is hardly the same as never being injured. Perhaps most telling, money is a poor equivalent for non-pecuniary loss. ...

. . . .

C. Safety

Moral judgment was the historical origin of tort law, and compensation is the preoccupation of laypersons today, but safety actually has the greatest claim on our attention. Many folk sayings capture this belief: safety first; better safe than sorry; an ounce of prevention is worth a pound of cure. Calabresi has restated it more formally, convincing most torts scholars that the reduction of accident costs must be our primary concern.[71] Indeed, were we unconcerned with safety, private law remedies would be hard to justify; criminal law expresses moral judgment more forcefully, and nofault schemes compensate victims more efficiently.

Although tort law is not the only means of fostering safety, each alternative has serious problems. The ideal mechanism would be self-interest: victims should control the risk to which they are exposed. But the extreme division of labor associated with technological development, mass production of consumer goods, and the separation of workers from ownership and control of the means of production under capitalism make this impossible. Nor can we rely on altruism to inspire a concern for safety in those with the power to inflict harm. Social distance, cultural difference, and class divisions undermine solicitude for others. In addition, profit seeking in a competitive market compels entrepreneurs to cut corners on safety.

Recognizing these limitations, we have created an elaborate regulatory apparatus that makes the state responsible for protecting the safety of workers, consumers, travelers, and those engaged in recreational activities. Yet the deficiencies of regulation are manifold and notorious.[72] Victims are not the sole concern of regulators, who are swayed by political exposure, bureaucratic convenience, good relations with the regulated, and outright corruption. Regulators are slow and legalistic. They generally have less information and expertise than those regulated. They lack sufficient resources to inspect, investigate, and prosecute. And both regulators and courts hesitate to impose severe penalties.[73]

Legal theorists representing very different political persuasions have responded to this predicament by making tort liability the central mechanism for promoting safety.[74] Although they disagree over whether liability ought to be strict or based on fault, they concur that the most efficient way to promote an optimum level of safety is to internalize accident costs by making tortfeasors liable for their consequences. At least since Learned Hand offered his famous formula more than forty years ago,[75] judges, lawyers, and legal scholars have argued that fear of liability will compel potential tortfeasors to engage in a cost-benefit analysis, taking just those safety precautions that cost less than the accidents they prevent. Yet the scientific facade of this economic formulation conceals a number of fundamental theoretical flaws and empirical problems.

First, although it is theoretically possible (if often difficult) to calculate the costs of safety precautions, it is theoretically impossible to calculate the benefits of accident avoidance. Economists cannot tell us the value of bodily integrity, emotional well-being, or life because these are not defined by the market.[76] The costs of accidents can only be determined collectively — after the fact by a judge or jury, or before by a legislature or regulatory agency. In each case, this is a political decision, not a finding of positive economics. Even those elements of damage that have market values — lost earnings and medical expenses — are extremely difficult to predict into the future.[77] Actuarial methods can only tell us how a

population will behave overall, not the outcome of an individual case. Thus a central element in the cost-benefit analysis is hopelessly indeterminate.

Second, tort liability necessarily translates unequal recoveries ... into unequal exposure to risk. An entrepreneur in a competitive market must spend less to protect those who are less likely to claim or who will recover lower damage awards — poor, unemployed, young, old, or inadequately educated individuals, racial minorities, noncitizens, and women.[78] Thus, cheap consumer products not only perform less well, but also are more dangerous;[79] low-paid workers suffer more frequent and more serious injuries and illnesses at work;[80] and the underprivileged are exposed to greater environmental pollution. Whether or not the Bhopal disaster was an "accident," it was no accident that its victims were among the poorest in the Third World.[81] Nor is it chance that toxic waste dumps are concentrated in black ghettoes in the United States.[82]

Third, the threat of tort liability can elicit the optimum level of safety only if the potential tortfeasor knows that the trier of fact will perform the cost-benefit analysis correctly. But that calculation is theoretically impossible. The trier of fact is asked to decide whether the defendant failed to take specific safety precautions that cost-effectively would have avoided the injury that actually occurred.[83] Yet cost-benefit analysis requires potential tortfeasors engaged in ongoing activities to evaluate all possible safety precautions for their contribution to reducing the costs of all accidents that may occur. Only a legal regime of true strict liability would place the decisional burden where it properly belongs — on potential tortfeasors to evaluate the safety of an activity in advance, rather than on the trier of fact to assign responsibility for an injury after the fact.[84]

Fourth, every tort system, whether based on fault or strict liability, must determine whether a particular defendant caused a particular plaintiff's injury. But both the natural and the social sciences describe causation in terms of probabilities. Therefore, we can only talk about the connection between populations of causes and effects. Consequently, judgments will hold tortfeasors liable for only some of the damages they cause and place the burden of compensating victims on only some of the causal actors.[85]

Fifth, safety sometimes must defer to the other two goals: moral judgment and compensation. Courts often invoke the highly malleable concepts of duty and proximate cause to curtail liability because the consequences seem disproportionate to the defendant's moral culpability.[86] Less often, they interpret negligence and causation broadly to impose liability because the defendant's behavior is particularly reprehensible.[87] Courts often look for the "deep pocket" defendant (large public or private entities or those likely to be insured) and then construct negligence and causation in order to rationalize the imposition of liability.[88] Less often, they refuse to find negligence or causation because the defendant seems less capable of bearing the burden than the plaintiff.[89]

. . . .

Finally, and perhaps most importantly, tort liability produces optimum safety only if all negligence victims recover all of their damages from all of those who caused their injuries. Yet we saw above that only a fraction of victims recover anything — just twelve percent of those disabled for at least two weeks in England (and doubtless even fewer of those who suffered less serious injuries). A rational entrepreneur must discount safety expenditures by the likelihood of being forced to pay damages — in England such an entrepreneur would make less than twelve percent of the optimum level of safety expenditures. If the market is perfectly competitive, as deterrence theory presupposes, it will drive out of business anyone who indulges in a higher level of safety. Nor are entrepreneurs equally likely to be sued: half of all federal products liability litigation between 1974 and 1986 was targeted at fewer than eighty companies; altogether, only nine percent of manufacturers were sued in 1986.[96]

Furthermore, the threat of damages encourages entrepreneurs to minimize liability, not accident costs.[97] It creates perverse incentives: to conceal information about danger, take actions that maximize success in litigation (such as defensive medicine), resist legitimate claims (especially those that may establish unfavorable precedents), use economic power to drive down claims, stall, and conclude settlements that limit publicity.[98] How else can we explain why Ford produced a Pinto with a gasoline tank it knew to be explosive,[99] Johns-Manville subjected its workers to asbestos for decades after it knew they were suffering lung damage and cancer,[100] McDonnell-Douglas produced and American Airlines flew a DC-10 they knew contained a faulty pylon and other design defects,[101] and tobacco companies continue to manufacture, promote, and sell cigarettes?[102] Studies of the deterrent effect of criminal sanctions demonstrate repeatedly that certainty is more important than severity.[103] Because full damages are rarely collected, tort liability encourages suboptimal safety.

Tort law fails as a deterrent even when evaluated by its own criteria. Economic theory argues that regulation ought to be unnecessary: contract can regulate risk more efficiently when the cost of transactions between the parties is low,[104] and the threat of tort liability should achieve optimum safety in the remaining cases. Yet even the most ardent advocate of *laissez-faire* economics would hesitate to eliminate all speed limits, end medical malpractice liability, or abolish the Food and Drug Administration. Furthermore, if deterrent theory worked perfectly, tort claims would disappear: fear of liability would ensure optimum safety, and unmeritorious lawsuits would not be brought. Nevertheless, conservatives loudly proclaim (and denounce) what they insist is a tort litigation explosion.[105]

Reliance on a private law mechanism like tort to promote safety has other unfortunate consequences. The focus on liability to the individual victim subverts collective efforts to control risk. Damages are paid only to individuals; group reparations and class actions rarely are available to those injured by the same polluter, manufacturer, common carrier, or employer.[106] Because liability arises only when an injury has occurred, tort law fails to address the underlying problem of risk. Under capitalism, private law, like private medicine, is obsessed with individual cure at the expense of collective prevention because capitalism creates a market for the former while opposing state involvement in the latter.[107] Money damages undermine the collective interest in safety both by conveying the false impression that they restore the victim to the status quo ante (so that greater safety is unnecessary) and by arousing jealousy of the suddenly wealthy victim, thereby diluting the sympathy and solidarity of others who are potential victims.

. . . .

III. PROPOSALS

Criticism can lead in two directions: concrete reforms capable of implementation within the existing political framework; and recognition that fully adequate solutions require a fundamental restructuring of society. This Part offers both responses, organized like the critique, although some issues overlap, and alternative responses to risk must reconcile tensions among the goals.

A. Moral Judgment

Tort law fails almost entirely to pass moral judgment on the infliction of risk and injury. Negligent behavior is a public as well as a private wrong because it endangers many people besides the victim. It therefore merits the public disapproval that only the state can express in order to reaffirm the norm of safety. Public prosecutors and administrative agencies must pursue safety offenders more vigorously. Actual and potential victims must organize to demand effective enforcement because both public prosecutors and administrative agencies respond to political pressure. Trade unions and consumer and environmental groups already do this; they deserve additional financial and legislative support from the state because of the substantial free rider problem.

The injured victim requires a different kind of moral response. First, this must recognize the victim's injury and sense of grievance; damages not only fail to do so, but also suggest that the victim has enjoyed a windfall. Second, the tortfeasor must acknowledge wrongdoing and apologize.

Finally, we must stop blaming victims. We do so now through legal doctrines like contributory negligence, comparative fault, assumption of risk, dangerous jobs, and agreements not to sue, as well as through economic theories that workers receive a "risk premium" or consumers "choose" to purchase dangerous products and services.[113] Liberalism fosters these misconceptions by locating all constraint within the state and portraying "private" behavior as free.[114] Actually, victims "choose" risk and injury within an environment of limited and grossly unequal economic resources, influenced by divergent cultural norms about their entitlement to safety and suffering from a profound sense of political powerlessness.[115] ...

B. Compensation

Accidents will happen even in utopia. The popular preoccupation with compensation accurately reflects the severe personal and social dislocations they can cause. Taking compensation seriously, however, will require a total restructuring of the legal mechanisms.[116]

First, compensation should respond to what happened rather than how it happened, to need rather than cause or fault. It should be available universally: to those suffering congenital disability and illness as well as injury; to those who cannot identify a culpable agent; and to those who have themselves to blame. After all, that is how we respond to the misfortunes of those we love. We must view compensation as a positive good to be encouraged if not required — like education or preventive medicine. It should not be seen as an undeserved benefit

extracted grudgingly from a reluctant bureaucracy or adversary.[117]

. . . .

... The trade-off between the quantum of damages awarded each victim and the number of victims benefited is not only logical, but also documented by historical experience. Workers' compensation, automobile no-fault insurance, Sweden's no-fault medical malpractice scheme, and New Zealand's comprehensive compensation program all have reduced benefits but served more victims.[122] Eliminating the adjudication of causation and fault and the calculation of past and future income and property loss, medical expenses, and intangible damages will reduce transaction costs enormously. It will obviate the need for lawyers, an original goal of workers' compensation.[123] And it will drastically reduce delay, which presently inflicts great hardship on victims, forcing them to accept inadequate settlements.[124]

. . . .

C. Safety

Although the reforms proposed above are valuable, safety must be our first priority. We want to prevent accidents, not just respond to them with moral condemnation and social support; the more we prevent, the less important those responses become. I offer two contradictory proposals: one could be pursued incrementally within the existing social framework, whereas the other would require a radical transformation.

The first proposal takes seriously the role of tort liability in deterring unsafe behavior. Many of the deficiencies criticized above can be ameliorated or eliminated. First, liability should be strict rather than based on fault. A strict liability regime encourages the tortfeasor to reduce accident costs rather than liability. It lodges responsibility for the "decision for accidents" in the experienced entrepreneur rather than the ignorant jury. It encourages research on safety. It internalizes in the price of the good or service the cost of all accidents, not just those caused by the defendant's fault, allowing the market mechanism of consumer choice to reduce the quantity of accident-causing behavior. And it reduces transaction costs by eliminating the hotly contested issue of fault (although it intensifies disputes about cause and increases the total number of claims).

Second, victim behavior should not bar or diminish recovery. Self-interest, the axiomatic foundation of economics, sufficiently discourages potential

66

victims from exposing themselves to risk; there is no evidence that the denial of compensation makes them safer.[128]

Third, damages should reflect all costs of the accident, however these ramify through chance circumstance, emotional attachment, or economic interdependence.[129] Doctrines of duty and proximate cause should not terminate liability. Proximate cause is both incoherent and unnecessary and should be eliminated altogether. Duty is just as incoherent and should be eliminated except insofar as it reflects the tension between egoism and altruism, which cannot be avoided in questions of affirmative obligations to help those at risk.

Fourth, claims should be actively encouraged—certainly by bar associations, possibly by individual lawyers.[130] As claimants pursue selfish interests, they simultaneously perform a public service. Furthermore, claiming is learned behavior.[131] And encouragement will have the greatest effect on those who have been least likely to claim.[132]

Many objections may be raised to this proposal. Some will maintain we cannot afford it: courts will be overburdened, prices inflated, and companies driven out of business. These are captious criticisms. Courts exist to hear valid claims—we do not close schools because there are too many students, libraries because there are too many readers, or roads because there are too many drivers. When police, prosecutors, and prisons are overextended by rising crime rates, we increase their budgets; we should be at least as generous when private individuals mobilize the law. If consumers purchase fewer goods or services when their prices reflect accident costs as well as labor and materials, we have simply moved closer to the efficient allocation of resources. If we want to subsidize goods or services, we can do so in ways that are fairer and more efficient than the denial of compensation to the random victim. In any case, liability costs contribute little to the prices of most goods and services.[133]

Others will raise the specter of fueling American "litigiousness" and increasing social conflict.[134] But Americans actually exhibit relatively low and fairly constant rates of civil litigation.[135] Social conflict could be reduced much more effectively if tortfeasors stopped causing so many injuries[136] and promptly acceded to claims when they were made.

Perhaps the most telling objection to this proposal is its inconsistency with my earlier endorsement of a no-fault compensation scheme. Politics is not logic, however, and I see no practical problems in pursuing both reforms simultaneously: encouraging a one hundred percent claims rate under a strict liabil-ity regime while gradually mobilizing support for public medical care and income maintenance. If forced to choose, I would sacrifice the former to achieve the latter: the unquestionable good of universal compensation outweighs the uncertain deterrent of tort liability, especially given its high administrative costs.[137]

But even a strict liability system with a one hundred percent claims rate (an empirical impossibility) remains seriously flawed. It reproduces inequality, since tortfeasors still find it cheaper to endanger the poor. It violates autonomy, since the state still evaluates the cost of accidents and the tortfeasor decides whether to inflict them. It also undermines community, since victims must claim as individuals. Fidelity to these three ideals in the confrontation with risk will require a commitment to democratic socialism.[138]

Human autonomy is the foundation of Kantian ethics. Contemporary tort law reflects this inspiration when it insists that those exposed to danger ought to be as autonomous as possible in the confrontation with risk. The doctrine of informed consent seeks to protect the autonomy of patients. Potential victims cannot "assume" the risk of negligence unless the decision is fully informed and voluntary; the difficulty of realizing these conditions in the workplace persuaded legislatures to abrogate the doctrine.[139] "Agreements" not to sue are unenforceable when the good or service is a necessity.[140] Warnings place consumers on notice only when they effectively communicate the danger.[141]

Autonomy in the encounter with risk in the workplace mandates worker ownership and control of the means of production. Only in producer cooperatives will those exposed to risk also profit from that exposure and have the power to make the cost-benefit analysis advocated by law and economics.[142]

Rawlsian theories of justice call for equality of benefits and burdens including risk.[143] This principle is reflected in daily life. Many countries, including our own, require universal military service (at least for men during wartime) in the belief that the threat of death or disability ought to be borne by all, however imperfectly that ideal is realized. None explicitly allows the wealthy to buy an exemption or substitute, as occurred during the nineteenth century.[144] State guarantees of a minimal level of medical care express a rudimentary notion of equal entitlement to well-being.[145] Americans are properly horrified when they read that Third World countries tolerate a market in bodily organs or that a physician proposed to create one here.[146]

Risk in the workplace can be equalized only by a substantial reduction in the division of labor through a rotation of tasks — headwork and hand-work, safe and dangerous. At the very least, every-one must be exposed periodically to the most dangerous jobs — only that experience will awaken self-interest in reducing risk and foster empathetic understanding of the dangers that fellow-workers encounter daily.[147]

Liberalism conceptualizes the encounter with risk as a matter of individual choice: where to work, how to travel, what to consume, how to spend one's leisure, where to live. But individuals choose within a framework constructed by others.[148] The most important decisions about risk — environmental pol-lution, the organization of work, the range of con-sumer goods — are made by collectivities (private enterprise and government). Consequently, those exposed to risk also must respond collectively. Together they can mobilize far more information than any individual could master. Collective decision-making also will compel individuals to reexamine their idiosyncratic risk preferences and aversions.

· · · ·

CONCLUSION

Contemporary tort law, not surprisingly, reflects the dominant traits of late-twentieth-century America: capitalist relations of production, individualism, extreme division of labor, and commodification. Some of the unfortunate consequences for the inci-dence and distribution of risk and injury could be ameliorated within the existing framework. The rhet-oric of "law and order" supports harsher and more certain penalties for those who endanger or injure others. Numerous countries have shown that social democracy is fully compatible with advanced capital-ism and political liberalism. Radicals could make common cause with free market enthusiasts to ensure that tort liability contributes to efficient resource allocation. But we can fully realize the widely shared values of autonomy, equality, and com-munity in the encounter with risk only by embracing democratic socialism: worker ownership and manage-ment, consumer cooperatives, equalization of benefits (resources) and burdens (risk), and a state suffi-ciently powerful to regulate environmental pollution.

(g)   The State of Canadian Tort Law[†]

Honourable Justice A.M. Linden

The Canadian judiciary ... [has done] its part in rationalizing and humanizing Canadian tort doc-trine [in the last 40 years]. Building on the classic and glorious neighbour principle of *Donoghue v. Stevenson,* that one must "take reasonable care to avoid acts or omissions which you can reasonably foresee would be likely to injure your neighbour," Canadian tort law was substantially overhauled and modernized consistently with that noble principle, which is as fresh, pure and sound today as it ever was. In my view, the results of these changes were neither pro-plaintiff nor pro-defendant; they were bal-anced and even-handed but, most importantly, they were logically, operationally and socially defensible.

For example, the reasonable man standard was dispatched to the dust bin, an early victim of the

women's liberation movement, to be replaced by the neutral reasonable person standard. Rescue Law was restated. The treatment by negligence law of a breach of statute was clarified — it was to be evi-dence of negligence, no more and no less. Evidence of compliance with statute was also to be treated as not conclusive evidence of reasonableness, but it was relevant to the issue. Custom was to be similarly handled — neither breach of custom nor compliance with custom were to be conclusive, but they were important factors to assess. The Supreme Court's trilogy of damage cases in 1978, applying a cap to non-pecuniary damages, *inter alia*, made the assess-ment of damages more scientific and economically based, long before the Americans ever thought of doing this to tame their runaway damage awards.

---

† Excerpts from a speech given to the National Judicial Institute, Civil Law Seminars, on June 11, 2008. Reproduced with permission of the author.

Punitive damages, which were always modest in Canada, and still are, were better explained so as to avoid the unjustifiably exorbitant awards given in the United States. The mysterious doctrine of *res ipsa loquitur* expired, ending decades of sterile debate signifying nothing. The law of causation was rethought, opened up, but is perhaps closing again. Medical malpractice liability was reconfigured, with informed consent properly situated in negligence law rather than battery law, to be judged by the reasonable patient standard, although some problems have lingered concerning the objective causation theory.

Other judicial reforms were instituted. Liability for governmental negligence was justly restated in *Just v. B.C.*, but the area kept percolating despite that. Rejecting the strict products liability revolution that swept the United States in the 60's, Canadian products liability law wisely continued to be governed by negligence law (except in NB and Sask.). The need for explicit warnings, however, was clarified. Economic losses were, after much uncertainty, finally reorganized and categorized intelligently along the lines suggested by Bruce Feldthusen's work. Negligent statement liability, born in *Hedley Byrne*, would expose communications to liability only if five specific requirements were present, but not otherwise. Relational economic losses were wisely limited to only a few exceptional situations. Even defamation law was adjusted, and clarified, without adopting the United States Constitutional partial immunity in relation to public figures. And vicarious liability law was finally rationalized with a sensible new test and using modern language, "employee" and "employer," replacing "servant" and "master." Mainly inspired by the neighbour principle, which I am still proud to support as a guiding light after all these eight decades, all of this was done gradually, incrementally if you will, in an undramatic, balanced, analytically sound way by many great tort judges, led by C.J. Laskin, C.J. Dickson, C.J. McLachlin, Bertha Wilson, Peter Cory, Gerald LaForest, John Sopinka, Frank Iacobucci, John Major and other skilled judges at all levels of courts.

The reasons of the judges in many of these cases are imbued with the typically Canadian spirit of caring for one's neighbours as well as fostering tort law's role as a "sentinel of safety." For example, Justice Bertha Wilson in *Kamloops v. Nielsen*, imposing liability on a municipality, rejected the floodgates argument that liability would be "ruinous financially to municipalities," explaining that tort liability is a "useful protection to the citizen whose ever-increasing reliance on public officials seems to be a feature of our age."

Justice Peter Cory in *Galaske v. O'Donnell*, a seat belt case, had this to say:

> if the fixing of liability on a driver to ensure that young passengers wear seat-belts saves one child from death or devastating injury, then all society will be benefited.

Mr. Justice Major also underscored the prophylactic aim of tort law in *Stewart v. Pettie*:

> "one of the primary purposes of negligence law is to enforce reasonable standards of Conduct so as to prevent the creation of unreasonable foreseeable risks. In this way tort law serves as a disincentive to risk-creating behaviour.

Add to this list Justice LaForest's view, as expressed in *Winnipeg Condo Corporation No. 36 v. Bird Construction Co.*:

> allowing recovery against contractors in tort for the cost of repair of dangerous defects thus serves an important preventative function by encouraging socially responsible behaviour.

Canadian judges, therefore, in the last third of the last century, invoked tort law to promote safety and responsibility in all kinds of risk-producing activities by all kinds of actors, seeing themselves as part of the apparatus of humane safety enforcement and caring for the victims of its failure.

At the turn of the century, Canadian tort law was a model for the common law world, even quoted and relied upon by the house of lords, that proud and heretofore largely insular body. Canadian tort law was even-handed, neither too generous nor too tough. Plaintiffs cheered some of the decisions like *Just, Galaske, Kamloops, Bazley* and *Ryan*, while defendants were overjoyed with others, like the damages trilogy, *Whiten, Hercules, Saskatchewan Wheat Pool* and *Bow Valley*. We Canadians — judges, legislators, lawyers, academics — had reason to be proud of the tort law we had created together in the last third of the 20th century.

Today

As the new century began to unfold, after three decades of steady, confident improvement, things began to change. The humane, rational and balanced Canadian tort law that was fashioned over three decades is now suffering from self-doubt and uncertainty. It is becoming more complex and less balanced. Tort law is now often as complex as tax law. It is getting meaner, tougher and less sensitive. It is no longer at the leading edge, no longer a model for the world to emulate.

It is hard to understand why this transformation is happening now. Some say that the UK retreat from *Anns* of the 1980's finally persuaded our Supreme Court to retreat after two decades of resisting the return to judicial colonialism. Many of the Supreme Court's true believers in tort law have moved on, to be replaced by more skeptical jurists. Others opine that it is in part a reaction to a tort reform movement in the United States, which is "unmaking tort law."

Because of unique conditions there, conditions that never existed and do not exist in Canada. There has also been a change in social attitudes with profits and bottom-line thinking mesmerizing our society. Hobbes has replaced Rousseau as our favourite philosopher.

The entertainment industry has been an accomplice in diminishing the respect for tort law and tort lawyers who are depicted as sleazy, unethical, alcoholic, and dishonest. The movie, *Fortune Cookie*, starring Walter Mathau, portrayed him as a dishonest ambulance chaser. *Liar Liar* was about a lawyer who was incapable of telling the truth. *The Rainmaker* and *The Sweet Hereafter* were about lawyers who solicited clients at hospitals, at their homes and at funerals. The musical, *Chicago*, although not dealing with a tort case, showed the trial lawyer as a magician spinning "razzle-dazzle." Jerry Seinfeld did a TV episode unfairly mocking the much-maligned McDonald's hot coffee case. TV's *Ally McBeal* and *Boston Legal*, although funny, did not enhance the reputation of lawyers. There are also books, mainly in the United States which disparage all lawyers, but tort lawyers in particular, such as John Grisham's, *The King of Torts*, Catherine Crier's, *The Case Against Lawyers* and Olson's *The Rule of Lawyers*. Do not forget Ison's *The Forensic Lottery* and Atiyah's *The Negligence Lottery*. One distinguished U.S. scholar has even written an entire book, *Lowering The Bar*, analyzing all the jokes ridiculing lawyers, which make people laugh at their [mercenariness], dishonesty, aggressiveness, and general repulsiveness. The media rarely portrays lawyers in a positive light these days, as it sometimes did in the past, with Atticus Finch, Perry Mason, Clarence Darrow, *L.A. Law*, and *The Defenders*.

The rethinking of Canadian tort law began after the House of Lords engaged in its unprecedented retreat from *Anns v. Merton*, during Prime Minister Thatcher's time in the 1980's. Initially, the Supreme Court Of Canada bravely refused to follow the British in their retreat, remaining true to *Donoghue v. Stevenson's* neighbour principle as elaborated in *Anns v. Merton*. However, a cold U.S. wind was generated by President Reagan's *Tort Policy Working Group* (1986) and the propaganda campaign of the American Tort Reform Association, which vigorously publicized the many excesses of the U.S. tort system, which did not exist in Canada. All of this infiltrated the Canadian psyche.

The main result of all this was a new analysis of duty by the Supreme Court which closely resembles the complex and super-cautious approach adopted by the House Of Lords in the 80's. It is, however, even more complicated in its execution, because it is more sophisticated in its treatment of policy. While insisting that *Donoghue v. Stevenson* and *Anns* were still the law, the Supreme Court unveiled a more elaborate version of the *Anns prima facie* duty approach in *Cooper v. Hobart*, where it inserted a new requirement to be considered, in addition to foreseeability, before creating a new tort duty — proximity.

... there may be some validity to Professor Klar's view about *Cooper*, that it was a "turning point" to a more "conservative," "pro-defendant" position, despite the court's denial of seeking to achieve this. Compare the caring spirit reflected in the late 20th century cases with the tougher, cribbed and confined views expressed in this new century. Like in the other areas of society, the business-oriented, bottom-line, more selfish attitude of concern for business, government and their insurers is emerging in the tort cases, replacing the earlier concern for victims and safety. The *Cooper* court, *in obiter*, worried about "efficiency" and "indeterminate liability" and did not want to "create an insurance scheme for investors at great cost to [taxpayers]." This concern for indeterminate liability and the danger of increased tax are repeatedly voiced in other cases at all levels of courts as part of the rationale for holding that there is no duty owed in the new factual circumstances of the case, something that was rarely expressed in the past. These new concerns about the financial cost of the application of tort principles used to be irrelevant considerations in days gone by, but no longer.

Sensitive and serious judges understand that new duties placed on governments and businesses may be onerous. It should not be done lightly. In one case contending for government liability for the West Nile disease, it was said by Justice Sharpe of the Ontario Court of Appeal, that liability would interfere with governments' decisions about "allocating scarce resources available to promote and protect the health of its citizens." The government, he opined, should be able to "focus their attention and resources without the fear or threat of lawsuits." This is a legitimate concern, one that, in particular cases, others might assess differently, but one that did not need the elaborate proximity analysis of *Cooper* to effectuate. The earlier *Just* analysis alone could as easily have led to the same result by treating the matter as a "policy" decision, and, hence, immune from negligence liability on that ground. The attitude of some judges, amazingly, is that governments, when they "legislate, even wrongly, incompetently, stupidly, or misguidedly," are not liable in damages. Fortunately we have administrative and constitutional law to protect us from these errors, but no longer tort law.

Despite the chilling effect of *Cooper*, I am happy to report that Canadian tort law has continued to manifest some vitality and imagination, at least in non-governmental cases. For example, the Supreme Court of Canada has held that a university owes a duty to its students not to report a student as a potential child molester without investigating carefully a student whose career was ruined by a professor's "speculation and conjecture," based on a disturbing paper she wrote, recovered tort damages because of the "broader relationships between professors and students" at the university, based in part on a contractual basis. Another case allowed an action to proceed against the manufacturer and the government on behalf of cattle farmers injured by contaminated feed that caused mad cow disease and the ensuing furor. It has been held that Canada Post could be liable for a "super-mailbox" which toppled over and caused loss to someone who crashed into it on the basis that it was too close to the highway. A school may be liable, in addition to a ski resort, for a snowboarding accident [that] severely injured a student. A mother can be liable for moving a chair in the kitchen, causing her daughter, who had climbed up on it to clean the cupboards, to fall. A husband driving his car while drinking coffee, who started to cough and lost control, causing an injury to his wife, is liable. A newspaper publisher can be liable for negligently failing to stop delivery of newspapers during a subscriber's holiday period, as instructed to do, which led to a break-in by criminals at a home that looked abandoned as a result of the pile of papers in front of it. A delay in shipping by air certain perishable drugs, without refrigeration, causing them to be ruined, can give rise to liability. There are other notable examples.

The state of Canadian tort law today is, therefore, tentative. The judicial confidence in its positive role in the last third of the 20th century has diminished, but it has not disappeared. The rapid growth period has largely ended, and has been replaced by a cautious stability period that evinces a skepticism toward tort law's role as a safety regulator and a caring compensator. Worries about the health of our economy abound and some fear that tort law may impede prosperity. While that may be so in the United States, where tort law's impact may have been dramatically different, that is more doubtful in Canada, where liability is less frequent, where damages are lower, and where civil juries are less common. The state of Canadian tort law, I can report at this time, is still relatively healthy but its future is by no means secure, as a substantial rethinking and restructuring is in process.

The Future

My dream, after half a century of tort study, is that we will soon emerge from this period of doubt and that we will see a resurgence of that excellence of analysis that produced the golden era of Canadian tort law in the last third of the 20th century. With the help of our superb judiciary, our dedicated bar, its organizations, and our responsible academic community, I foresee in the years ahead a new era of Canadian tort law, which will renew our pride in our unique, caring, balanced and efficient Canadian system, reflecting who we have been, who we are as a people, and who we want to become in this new century.

In addition to the *Cooper* duty questions, the state of Canadian tort law, as well as the rest of our society, indeed the world generally, is somewhat ambivalent these days after its period of robust health and assuredness in the last third of the century. We must regain our confidence in ourselves and in our Canadian tort law, for it endures as a respectable and useful body of law serving our society relatively well. Tort law compensates, deters, educates and provides psychological comfort to many. It reflects and reinforces our values of respect for the individual. It can act as an ombudsman focusing public attention on social problems, and as an empowerer of individuals wronged by the powerful forces in our society. Nevertheless, there remains much to be done to improve tort law, for there are still, I am sad to say, some warts on torts.

Let us continue to clarify, modernize, rationalize, humanize and render our tort system more efficient and just. Tort law must continue to be available to assist victims of wrongful conduct, both traditional and novel, to obtain compensation from those who should justly be made to pay it, and to deny it to those not justly entitled to it.

... let us remember that in many ways tort law is the radar of our society, providing an early detection system for emerging dangers. That will continue as long as tort law lives and tort lawyers breathe. In my view, tort lawyers represent not only their clients, but our society generally in its desire to promote safety, while being fair both to victims and defendants. In the U.S., fifty years of unsuccessful tobacco litigation has finally yielded some financial fruit to a few litigants and a major settlement, $246 billion dollars, reimbursing most state governments for their health care costs expended on sick and dying smokers. The unfairly maligned McDonald's Hot Coffee case and the US fast food obesity cases have led to McDonalds coffee that is not as scalding as it was before and more widespread use of trans-fat free cooking oil. The so-far unsuccessful actions in the U.S. on behalf of victims of copycat crimes against violent movies, TV, music and video games, whether they succeed or not, increase social pressure on the entertainment industry to mend its irresponsible ways. The shocking, all-too-prevalent sexual abuse law suits against churches, clergy, celebrities, enter-tainers and politicians may eventually help to teach potential transgressors that this conduct is totally unacceptable as well as financially costly in our society. Computers, new drugs and other new products and activities need the watchful eye of tort law to tame their capacity to cause harm.

. . . .

Lastly, I never cease to dream the impossible dream, as I have for decades, of a joint federal-provincial study on compensation for accidents and illness that would help coordinate all of our schemes, prevent overlaps, minimize conflicts, fill in gaps, and encourage uniformity in the provinces, where diversity is running rampant, especially in the no-fault auto insurance area. It will require a youthful and energetic team to undertake this herculean task, which is long overdue, but, in my view, more necessary now than ever.

Case Studies

A. Social Host Liability

(a) *Jordan House Ltd. v. Menow*†

Supreme Court of Canada

ISSUE

[LASKIN J.:]

This is a case of first instance. The principal issue is whether the operator of a hotel may be charged with a duty of care to a patron of the hotel beverage room who becomes intoxicated there, a duty to take reasonable care to safeguard him from the likely risk of personal injury if he is turned out of the hotel to make his way alone. If such a duty may be imposed, it falls to determine the nature or scope of the duty to the intoxicated patron. This determination must then be related to the present case by inquiring whether on its facts there has been a breach of the duty by the appellant hotel so as to engage its liability to the respondent plaintiff for personal injuries. I shall refer later in these reasons to another issue raised on behalf of the respondent Honsberger.

There are concurrent findings of fact in this case by the trial judge, Haines J., and by the Ontario Court of Appeal in favour of Menow, on the basis of which he was awarded damages against the appellant hotel and against the respondent Honsberger under an equal apportionment of fault among all three parties. Honsberger was the driver of a car which struck Menow as he was walking east near the centre line of Highway No. 8 after having been ejected from the hotel. Neither the quantum of damages nor the apportionment of fault is in issue in this appeal.

The hotel premises front on Highway No. 8, a much-travelled two-lane highway running east and west between Hamilton and Niagara Falls, Ontario. The road is asphalt, twenty-one feet wide, and, at the material time, January 18, 1968, the shoulders were icy, with snowbanks beyond them, and the pavement itself was wet although not slippery. Menow was employed by a fruit farmer and lived alone on his employer's farm which was on a side road about two and one-half miles east of the hotel. The direct route to his abode was along the highway and then north along the side road.

Menow was a frequent patron of the hotel's beverage room, where beer was served, and was well known to the owner-operator of the hotel, one Fernick. He was often there in the company of his employer and the latter's foreman, also well known to Fernick. Menow had a tendency to drink to excess and then to act recklessly, although ordinarily he was courteous and mannerly. The hotel management and the beverage room employees knew of his propensities, and, indeed, about a year before the events out of which this case arose he had been barred from the hotel for a period of time because he annoyed other customers, and thereafter the hotel's employees were instructed not to serve him unless he was accompanied by a responsible person.

On January 18, 1968, Menow, his employer and the foreman arrived at the hotel at about 5.15 p.m.

---

† [1974] S.C.R. 239. [Notes/references omitted.]

and drank beer. The employer and the foreman departed within a short time, leaving the plaintiff there alone. Fernick came on duty at about 7 p.m. and saw that the plaintiff was then sober. He was served with beer from time to time, and there is a finding that towards 10 p.m. Fernick was aware that Menow was drinking to excess and that he had become intoxicated, the hotel having sold beer to Menow past the point of visible or apparent intoxication. At about 10 p.m. or 10.15 p.m. Menow was seen wandering around to other tables in the beverage room and consequently was ejected from the hotel by employees thereof, Fernick then knowing that the plaintiff was unable to take care of himself by reason of intoxication and that he would have to go home, probably by foot, by way of a main highway.

No excessive force was used in turning Menow out of the hotel. The evidence shows that he was put out on a dark and rainy night and that he was wearing dark clothes not readily visible to motorists. It appears that Menow, when he was outside the hotel, was picked up by an unknown third person and taken part of the way home, being let out on Highway No. 8 at 13th Street. The ride had not been arranged by the hotel. It was while continuing in an easterly direction and, indeed, while walking beyond 11th Street, his turn-off point (because, according to his testimony, he was looking for a friend) that Menow was struck by the Honsberger vehicle. It is unnecessary to detail the circumstances attending the accident because Honsberger does not challenge in this Court the finding of negligence and the apportionment of one-third fault against him. It is enough to say that the accident occurred within half an hour after Menow was ejected from the hotel, and that he was staggering near the centre of the highway when he was hit by the Honsberger vehicle which was travelling east.

On the foregoing facts, Haines J. found that the hotel owed and was in breach of a common law duty of care to Menow. The duty of care was first put on two grounds, each related but in different ways, in the assessment of the duty and of its breach, to certain statutes. Adverting to s.53(3) of *The Liquor Licence Act*, R.S.O. 1960, c.218, and to s.81 of *The Liquor Control Act*, R.S.O. 1960, c.217, Haines J. held that in contravening those provisions the hotel was in breach of a common law duty to Menow not to serve him intoxicating drink when he was visibly intoxicated. He thus relied on these enactments as indicating a standard upon which a common law duty could be founded. Second, although in the view of the trial judge, s.53(4) and (6) of *The Liquor Licence*

Act imposes a duty on a licensed hotel operator to eject an intoxicated patron and empowers his forcible removal if he refuses to leave on request, he held that this authority is qualified by a duty not to subject that patron to danger of personal injury, foreseeable as a result of eviction. In the present case Haines J. found that the hotel was vicariously liable for the actions of its employees who were in breach of a common law duty of care not to eject Menow as they did when they knew or ought to have known that he would thereby be placed in a position of danger to his personal safety.

The trial judge took a third position in imposing liability on the hotel by holding that "the defendant's employees undertook affirmative action to remove the plaintiff from the premises. In so doing they assumed a duty of care to take reasonable precautions to ensure that his safety was not endangered as a result of their actions". I may say at once that I do not regard this assessment as adding anything to the first two grounds upon which Haines J. proceeded. The affirmative action of removal did not in itself result in any injury to the plaintiff, as might have been the case if excessive force had been used against him (which is not suggested in the present case) nor was it followed by any breach of duty raised by and resulting from the affirmative action *per se;* hence it can only be considered in the present case as wrapped up in the duty of care, if any, resting upon the hotel towards an intoxicated patron.

In its brief oral reasons supporting the judgment of Haines J., the Ontario Court of Appeal stated that "we place our dismissal of the appeal on the simple ground that so far as the hotel is concerned, there was a breach of the common law duty of care owed to the plaintiff in the circumstances of this case".

The following are the statutory provisions referred to by the trial judge in the course of his reasons relating to the hotel's liability to Menow:

Liquor Licence Act, R.S.O. 1960, c. 218:

s.53(3) No liquor shall be sold or supplied on or at any licensed premises to or for any person who is apparently in an intoxicated condition.

(4) No person holding a licence under this Act shall permit or suffer in the premises for which the licence is issued,

(b) any gambling, drunkenness or any riotous, quarrelsome, violent or disorderly conduct to take place.

(6) Any person holding a licence under this Act who has reasonable grounds to suspect from the conduct of any person who has come upon the premises in respect of which such licence is

issued that such person although not of notoriously bad character, is present for some improper purpose or is committing an offence against this Act or the regulations, may request such person to leave the licensed premises immediately and, unless the request is forthwith complied with, such person may be forcibly removed.

s.67 Where any person or his servant or agent sells liquor to or for a person whose condition is such that the consumption of liquor would apparently intoxicate him or increase his intoxication so that he would be in danger of causing injury to his person or injury or damage to the person or property of others, if the person to or for whom the liquor is sold while so intoxicated,

(*a*) commits suicide or meets death by accident, an action under *The Fatal Accidents Act* lies against the person who or whose servant or agent sold the liquor; or

(*b*) causes injury or damage to the person or property of another person, such other person is entitled to recover an amount to compensate him for his injury or damage from the person who or whose servant or agent sold the liquor.

Liquor Control Act, R.S.O. 1960, c. 217:

s.81 No person shall sell or supply liquor or permit liquor to be sold or supplied to any person under or apparently under the influence of liquor.

Section 67 of *The Liquor Licence Act* has no direct application to the facts of the present case, and the trial judge did not attempt to apply it even indirectly as pointing to a standard of care resting upon the hotel. Counsel for the appellant hotel urged, however, that the express provision for civil liability upon a breach of s.67 reflected a legislative policy precluding the founding of a cause of action upon breach of the other terms of *The Liquor Licence Act* (or of *The Liquor Control Act*) invoked by the trial judge. In my opinion, this is to mistake the use to which the trial judge put s.53(3) of *The Liquor Licence Act* and s.81 of *The Liquor Control Act*. I do not read his reasons as holding that the mere breach of those enactments and the fact that Menow suffered personal injury were enough to attach civil liability to the hotel. He regarded them rather as crystallizing a relevant fact situation which, because of its authoritative source, the Court was entitled to consider in determining, on common law principles, whether a duty of care should be raised in favour of Menow against the hotel.

. . . . .

I return to the main issue. The common law assesses liability for negligence on the basis of breach of a duty of care arising from a foreseeable and unreasonable risk of harm to one person created by the act or omission of another. This is the generality which exhibits the flexibility of the common law; but since liability is predicated upon fault, the guiding principle assumes a nexus or relationship between the injured person and the injuring person which makes it reasonable to conclude that the latter owes a duty to the former not to expose him to an unreasonable risk of harm. Moreover, in considering whether the risk of injury to which a person may be exposed is one that he should not reasonably have to run, it is relevant to relate the probability and the gravity of injury to the burden that would be imposed upon the prospective defendant in taking avoiding measures. *Bolton v. Stone*[2], in the House of Lords and *Lambert v. Lastoplex Chemicals Co. Ltd.*,[3] in this Court illustrate the relationship between the remoteness or likelihood of injury and the fixing of an obligation to take preventive measures according to the gravity thereof.

In the present case, it may be said from one point of view that Menow created a risk of injury to himself by excessive drinking on the night in question. If the hotel's only involvement was the supplying of the beer consumed by Menow, it would be difficult to support the imposition of common law liability upon it for injuries suffered by Menow after being shown the door of the hotel and after leaving the hotel. Other persons on the highway, seeing Menow in an intoxicated condition, would not, by reason of that fact alone, come under any legal duty to steer him to safety, although it might be expected that good Samaritan impulses would move them to offer help. They would, however, be under a legal duty, as motorists for example, to take reasonable care to avoid hitting him, a duty in which Honsberger failed in this case. The hotel, however, was not in the position of persons in general who see an intoxicated person who appears to be unable to control his steps. It was in an invitor-invitee relationship with Menow as one of its patrons, and it was aware, through its employees, of his intoxicated condition, a condition which, on the findings of the trial judge, it fed in violation of applicable liquor licence and liquor control legislation. There was a probable risk of personal injury to Menow if he was turned out of the hotel to proceed on foot on a much-travelled highway passing in front of the hotel.

There is, in my opinion, nothing unreasonable in calling upon the hotel in such circumstances to take care to see that Menow is not exposed to injury because of his intoxication. No inordinate burden would be placed upon it in obliging it to respond to Menow's need for protection. A call to the police or a call to his employer immediately come to mind as easily available preventive measures; or a taxi-cab could be summoned to take him home, or arrangements made to this end with another patron able and willing to do so. The evidence shows that the hotel had experience with or was sensitive to the occasional need to take care of intoxicated patrons. The operator had in other like instances provided rides. He also had spare rooms at the time into one of which Menow could have been put.

Given the relationship between Menow and the hotel, the hotel operator's knowledge of Menow's propensity to drink and his instruction to his employees not to serve him unless he was accompanied by a responsible person, the fact that Menow was served not only in breach of this instruction but as well in breach of statutory injunctions against serving a patron who was apparently in an intoxicated condition, and the fact that the hotel operator was aware that Menow was intoxicated, the proper conclusion is that the hotel came under a duty to Menow to see that he got home safely by taking him under its charge or putting him under the charge of a responsible person, or to see that he was not turned out alone until he was in a reasonably fit condition to look after himself. There was, in this case, a breach of this duty for which the hotel must respond according to the degree of fault found against it. The harm that ensued was that which was reasonably foreseeable by reason of what the hotel did (in turning Menow out) and failed to do (in not taking preventive measures).

The imposition of liability upon the hotel in the circumstances that I have recounted has roots in an earlier decision of this Court when related to the evolutionary principles stemming from *Donoghue v. Stevenson*,[4] which have become part of this Court's course of decision. The affinity of *Dunn v. Dominion Atlantic Railway Co.*[5] with the present case is sufficiently shown by the following three sentences from the reasons of Anglin J., who was one of the plurality of this Court which allowed the appeal of the administrator of the estate of a deceased passenger, killed by a passing train when put off at a closed and unlighted station in a drunken condition:

The right of removal of a disorderly passenger which is conferred on the conductor (under a railway bylaw) is not absolute. It must be exercised reasonably. He cannot under it justify putting a passenger off the train under such circumstances that, as a direct consequence, he is exposed to danger of losing his life or of serious personal injury.

I do not regard the *Dunn* case as turning on the fact that the defendant was a common carrier, any more than I regard it as relevant here whether or not the defendant hotel was under innkeeper's liability in respect of the operation of its beverage room.

The risk of harm to which Menow was exposed by the hotel was not abated to its exoneration by reason of the fortuitous circumstance that Menow obtained a ride part of the way home. The short period of time that elapsed between the time that he was removed from the hotel and the time of the accident is telling in this respect, as is the fact that the risk was not increased or changed in kind when he was dropped off at 13th Street. Counsel for the appellant did not argue on causation, but did contend that any duty that the hotel might have had evaporated because of voluntary assumption of risk. The argument is untenable, whether put on the basis of Menow's self-intoxication or on the basis of the situation that faced him when he was put out of the hotel. In his condition, as found by the trial judge, it is impossible to say that he both appreciated the risk of injury and impliedly agreed to bear the legal consequences. However, the trial judge did find Menow contributorily negligent in becoming intoxicated, adverting in this connection to s. 80(2) of *The Liquor Control Act* which enjoins any person against being in an intoxicated condition in a public place. This finding has not been attacked.

The result to which I would come here does not mean (to use the words of the trial judge) that I would impose "a duty on every tavern-owner to act as a watch dog for all patrons who enter his place of business and drink to excess". A great deal turns on the knowledge of the operator (or his employees) of the patron and his condition where the issue is liability in negligence for injuries suffered by the patron.

I would dismiss the appeal with costs.

(b) *Stewart v. Pettie*†

Supreme Court of Canada

[MAJOR J.:]

On December 8, 1985, Gillian Stewart, her husband Keith Stewart, her brother Stuart Pettie, and his wife Shelley Pettie went to the Stage West, a dinner theatre, in Edmonton for an evening of dinner and live theatre. Before the evening was finished tragedy had struck. After leaving Stage West at the conclusion of the evening a minor single vehicle accident left Gillian Stewart a quadriplegic. Among others, she sued Mayfield Investments Ltd. (Mayfield), the owner of Stage West[,] claiming contribution for her injuries. This appeal is to decide whether on the facts of this case the principles of commercial host liability, first established by this Court in *Jordan House Ltd. v. Menow*, [1974] S.C.R. 239, apply to impose liability on Mayfield.

I.   THE FACTS

Gillian Stewart and her sister-in-law, Shelley Pettie, were both employed by Dispensaries Limited. For its 1985 Christmas party, Dispensaries Limited paid the price of admission for its employees and their spouses and friends to attend a performance at Stage West, a dinner theatre operated in Edmonton by the appellant, Mayfield Investments Ltd., and located at the Mayfield Inn. The admission price included the dinner and performance, but did not include the cost of alcohol consumed.

The two sisters-in-law, with their husbands, went to the dinner theatre together in Stuart Pettie's car, with Stuart Pettie driving. They arrived at the dinner theatre around 6:00 p.m., and were seated by a hostess at a table which they selected from a group of tables which had been set aside for the approximately 60 people in the Dispensaries Limited group.

The dinner theatre was organized with a full buffet dinner to be followed at 7:45 p.m. by a three-act play. In addition, cocktail waitresses provided table service of alcohol. The Stewart and Pettie table was served by the same waitress all evening, and she kept a running total of all alcohol ordered, which she then presented at the end of the evening for payment. Waitresses would take drink orders during dinner and before the play started, and would also take drink orders during the two intermissions. No orders were taken while the play was in progress.

Stuart Pettie and Keith Stewart each ordered several drinks over the course of the evening, ordering the first drinks before dinner, and, in addition, ordering drinks after dinner but before Act I, and then during each of the two intermissions. Their wives, on the other hand, had no alcohol during the entire evening. They were present at the table during the entire course of the evening, while the drinks were ordered, served, and consumed. Gillian Stewart's testimony was clear that she knew, at least in general terms, the amount that Stuart Pettie had to drink during the evening.

Stuart Pettie was drinking "double" rum and cokes throughout the evening. The trial judge found that he drank five to seven of these drinks, or 10 to 14 ounces of liquor. The trial judge also found that despite the amount that he had to drink, Stuart Pettie exhibited no signs of intoxication. This appearance was deceiving, however, as he was intoxicated by the end of the evening.

The group left the dinner theatre around 11:00 p.m. Once out in the parking lot, they had a discussion amongst themselves about whether or not Stuart Pettie was fit to drive, given the fact that he had been drinking. Neither his wife, nor his sister (who acknowledged that she knew what her brother was like when he was drunk), had any concerns about letting Stuart Pettie drive. All four therefore got into the car and started home, with Stuart Pettie driving, Keith Stewart in the front passenger seat, and their spouses in the back seat.

That particular December night in Edmonton there was a frost which made the roads unusually slippery. The trial judge found that Pettie was driving slower than the speed limit (50 km/h in a 60 km/h zone), and also accepted the evidence of Gillian Stewart that he was driving properly, safely and cautiously in the circumstances. Despite his caution, Stuart Pettie suddenly lost momentary control of the vehicle. The car swerved to the right, hopped the curb, and struck a light pole and noise abate-

---

† [1995] 1 S.C.R. 131 at 135–38, 141–53.

ment wall which ran alongside the road. Three of the four persons in the vehicle suffered no serious injuries. Gillian Stewart, however, who was not wearing a seat belt, was thrown across the car, struck her head, and was rendered a quadriplegic.

The expert testimony at trial was that had she been wearing her seat belt (which was not required in Alberta in 1985) her injuries would have been prevented.

About an hour after the accident, Stuart Pettie registered blood alcohol readings of .190 and .200. The trial judge found that, while it is not clear what his blood alcohol reading would have been at the time of the accident, he was, without a doubt, intoxicated, and that his blood alcohol content would have been certainly over .1.

The Stewarts brought an action against Stuart Pettie, Mayfield, and the City of Edmonton. The action as against Stuart Pettie was settled, with Stuart Pettie admitting gross negligence (as was necessary under then-existing legislation covering gratuitous passengers). The action as against the City of Edmonton was settled prior to trial. The plaintiffs were unsuccessful at trial as against Mayfield Investments Ltd., but the trial judge awarded a provisional 10 percent against them in the event he was overturned on appeal. He also assessed 25 percent against Gillian Stewart for contributory negligence for failing to wear her seat belt. Finally, the trial judge found that Pettie's driving, while negligent, was not grossly negligent.

The Court of Appeal allowed the appeal and found that Mayfield was negligent. They did not, however, disturb the trial judge's apportionment, or his finding on the contributory negligence or gross negligence issues. Mayfield Investments Ltd. sought and was granted leave to appeal to this Court, and the Stewarts sought and were granted leave to cross-appeal the finding that Stuart Pettie was not grossly negligent in this driving.

. . . .

IV. ANALYSIS

1. Was Mayfield Investments Ltd. negligent in failing to take any steps to ensure that Stuart Pettie did not drive after leaving Stage West?

This Court has not previously considered a case involving the liability of a commercial host where the plaintiff was not the person who became inebriated in the defendant's establishment. In both *Jordan House Ltd. v. Menow, supra*, and *Crocker v. Sundance Northwest Resorts Ltd.*, it was the plaintiff who

became drunk and as a consequence was unable to look after himself.

. . . .

The present appeal is one in which a third party is claiming against the commercial host. This raises the question of whether the establishment owed any duty of care to that third party. If a duty of care is found to exist, then it is necessary to consider what standard of care was necessary and whether that standard was met.

Another consideration is whether there was a causal connection between the defendant's allegedly negligent conduct and the damage suffered by the plaintiff.

A. Duty of Care

The "modern" approach to determining the existence of a duty of care is that established by the House of Lords in *Anns v. Merton London Borough Council*, and adopted by this Court in City of *Kamloops v. Nielsen*. This test, as established by Wilson J. in *Kamloops*, paraphrasing *Anns* is:

(1) is there a sufficiently close relationship between the parties ... so that, in the reasonable contemplation of the authority, carelessness on its part might cause damage to that person? If so,

(2) are there any considerations which ought to negative or limit (a) the scope of the duty and (b) the class of persons to whom it is owed or (c) the damages to which a breach of it may give rise?

This approach has been approved in *Just v. British Columbia*, and *Hall v. Hebert*. The basis of the test is the historic case of *Donoghue v. Stevenson*, which established the "neighbour principle": that actors owe a duty of care to those whom they ought reasonably [to] have in contemplation as being at risk when they act.

In *Jordan House Ltd. v. Menow, supra*, it was established that a duty of care exists between alcohol-serving establishments and their patrons who become intoxicated, with the result that they were unable to look after themselves. The plaintiff, who was a well-known patron of that bar, became intoxicated and began annoying customers. He was ejected from the bar, even though the waiters and employees of the bar knew that, in order to get home, he would have to walk along a busy highway. While doing so, he was struck by a car. Laskin J. (as he then was) said that the bar owed a duty of care to

Menow not to place him in a situation where he was at risk of injury. He said (at pp. 247–48):

> If the hotel's only involvement was the supplying of the beer consumed by Menow, it would be difficult to support the imposition of common law liability upon it for injuries suffered by Menow after being shown the door of the hotel and after leaving the hotel.... The hotel, however, was not in the position of persons in general who see an intoxicated person who appears to be unable to control his steps. It was in an invitor-invitee relationship with Menow as one of its patrons, and it was aware, through its employees, of his intoxicated condition, a condition which, on the findings of the trial judge, it fed in violation of applicable liquor licence and liquor control legislation. There was a probable risk of personal injury to Menow if he was turned out of the hotel to proceed on foot on a much-travelled highway passing in front of the hotel.
>
> There is, in my opinion, nothing unreasonable in calling upon the hotel in such circumstances to take care to see that Menow is not exposed to injury because of his intoxication.

Laskin J. held that the hotel had breached the duty owed to Menow by turning him out of the hotel in circumstances in which they knew that he would have to walk along the highway. The risk to Menow that the hotel's actions created was foreseeable. The hotel was therefore found to be liable for one-third of Menow's injuries.

It is a logical step to move from finding that a duty of care is owed to patrons of the bar to finding that a duty is also owed to third parties who might reasonably be expected to come into contact with the patron, and to whom the patron may pose some risk. It is clear that a bar owes a duty of care to patrons, and as a result, may be required to prevent an intoxicated patron from driving where it is apparent that he intends to drive. Equally such a duty is owed, in that situation, to third parties who may be using the highways. In fact, it is the same problem which creates the risk to the third parties as creates the risk to the patron. If the patron drives while intoxicated and is involved in an accident, it is only chance which results in the patron being injured rather than a third party. The risk to third parties from the patron's intoxicated driving is real and foreseeable.

In this case, there was a sufficient degree of proximity between Mayfield Investments Ltd. and Gillian Stewart that a duty of care existed between them. The more difficult question is what was the standard of care and whether or not it was breached.

Before moving to the standard of care test, two points deserve comment. In so far as the existence of a duty of care is concerned it is irrelevant that Gillian Stewart was a passenger in the vehicle driven by the patron rather than the passenger or driver of another vehicle, other than for ancillary purposes such as contributory negligence. The duty of care arises because Gillian Stewart was a member of a class of persons who could be expected to be on the highway. It is this class of persons to whom the duty is owed.

On the second point, the respondents argue that Mayfield Investments Ltd. owed two duties of care to Gillian Stewart: first, not to serve Stuart Pettie past the point of intoxication, and second, having served him past the point of intoxication, to take positive steps to ensure that he did not drive a car. The respondents say that Mayfield breached both duties, and therefore should be liable to Gillian Stewart for her injuries.

I believe this argument confuses the existence of the duty of care with the standard of care required of Mayfield. The question of whether a duty of care exists is a question of the relationship between the parties, not a question of conduct. The question of what conduct is required to satisfy the duty is a question of the appropriate standard of care. The point is made by Fleming in his book *The Law of Torts* (8th ed. 1992), at pp. 105–6:

> The general standard of conduct required by law is a necessary complement of the legal concept of "duty". There is not only the question "Did the defendant owe a duty to be careful?" but also "What precisely was required of him to discharge it?" Indeed, it is not uncommon to encounter formulations of the standard of care in terms of "duty", as when it is asserted that a motorist is under a duty to keep a proper look-out or give a turn signal. But this method of expression is best avoided. In the first place, the duty issue is already sufficiently complex without fragmenting it further to cover an endless series of details of conduct. "Duty" is more appropriately reserved for the problem of whether the relation between the parties (like manufacturer and consumer or occupier and trespasser) warrants the imposition upon one of an obligation of care for the benefit of the other, and it is more convenient to deal with individual conduct in terms of the legal standard of what is required to meet that obligation. Secondly, it is apt to obscure the division of functions between judge and jury. It is for the court to determine the existence of a duty relationship and to lay down in general terms the standard of care by which to measure the defendant's conduct; it is

for the jury to translate the general into a particular standard suitable for the case in hand and to decide whether that standard has been attained.

There is no question that commercial vendors of alcohol owe a general duty of care to persons who can be expected to use the highways. To paraphrase Wilson J. in *City of Kamloops v. Nielsen*, it clearly ought to be in the reasonable contemplation of such people that carelessness on their part might cause injury to such third parties. It remains to determine what standard of care is necessary to discharge the duty.

B.   Standard of Care

Laskin J. said in *Jordan House Ltd. v. Menow*, *supra*, at p. 247, "The common law assesses liability for negligence on the basis of breach of a duty of care arising from a foreseeable and unreasonable risk of harm to one person created by the act or omission of another." The respondents argued, and the Court of Appeal agreed, that Mayfield was negligent because they (a) served Stuart Pettie past the point of intoxication, and (b) failed to take any steps to prevent harm from coming to himself or a third person once he was intoxicated.

I doubt that any liability can flow from the mere fact that Mayfield may have over-served Pettie. To hold that over-serving Pettie *per se* is negligent is to ignore the fact that injury to a class of persons must be foreseeable as a result of the impugned conduct. I fail to see how the mere fact that an individual is over-imbibing can lead, by itself, to any risk of harm to third parties. It is only if there is some foreseeable risk of harm to the patron or to a third party that Mayfield and others in their position will be required to take some action. This standard of care is the second "duty" identified by the respondents and the Court of Appeal.

It is true that applicable liquor control legislation in Alberta, and across the country, prohibits serving alcohol to persons who are apparently intoxicated. Counsel for the respondents pressed that point in argument. There are, however, two problems with this argument. The first is that it is not clear that there was any violation of liquor control legislation in this case, given the fact that Pettie was apparently not exhibiting any signs of intoxication. Moreover, even if it could be said that Mayfield was in violation of legislation, this fact alone does not ground liability: *The Queen in right of Canada v. Saskatchewan Wheat Pool*. Without a reasonably foreseeable risk of harm to him or a third party, the fact of

over-serving Pettie is an innocuous act. Therefore, liability on the part of Mayfield, if it is to be found, must be in their failure to take any affirmative action to prevent the reasonably foreseeable risk to Gillian Stewart.

Historically, the courts have been reluctant to impose liability for a failure by an individual to take some positive action. This reluctance has been tempered in recent years where the relationship between the parties is such that the imposition of such an obligation has been warranted. In those cases, there has been some "special relationship" between the parties warranting the imposition of a positive duty. *Jordan House Ltd. v. Menow*, *supra*, was such a case.

A similar positive obligation was found to exist in *Crocker v. Sundance Northwest Resorts Ltd.*, *supra*. The plaintiff entered a "tubing" competition put on by the defendant ski-hill. Before the race, the plaintiff became drunk in the ski-hill's bar, and by the time he was to race, was visibly intoxicated. The organizers of the race suggested that he not compete, but permitted him to do so nevertheless. As a result, he was thrown from his tube, and rendered a quadriplegic.

In finding liability on the part of the owner Sundance, Wilson J. noted that courts have increasingly required a duty to act where there is a "special relationship" between the parties. Canadian courts have been willing to expand the kinds of relationships to which a positive duty to act attaches. Wilson J. reviewed cases where the courts will require a positive action on the part of the defendant, and said at p. 1197:

> The common thread running through these cases is that one is under a duty not to place another person in a position where it is foreseeable that the person could suffer injury.

Wilson J. said that, given the fact that the activity was under Sundance's full control and was promoted by it for commercial gain, Sundance was under a positive obligation as the promoter of a dangerous sport to take all reasonable steps to prevent a visibly incapacitated person from participating. She concluded that these precautions were not taken.

It is apparent from Wilson J.'s reasoning that there are two questions to be answered. The first is whether the defendant was required, in the circumstances, to take any positive steps at all. If this is answered in the affirmative, the next question is whether the steps taken by the defendants were sufficient to discharge the burden placed on them.

There is no dispute that neither the appellant nor anyone on its behalf took any steps to ensure that Stuart Pettie did not drive. Mayfield suggested that they remained "vigilant" and maintained "careful observation" of Stuart Pettie, and that this should be sufficient. However, remaining "vigilant" is not the same as taking positive steps, and it is common ground that none of Mayfield's employees made inquires about whether Stuart Pettie intended to drive or suggested any alternative. Therefore, if Mayfield is to avoid liability, it will have to be on the basis that, on the facts of this case, Mayfield had no obligation to take any positive steps to ensure that Stuart Pettie did not drive.

. . . .

There is little difficulty with the proposition, supported by the above cases, that the necessary "special relationship" exists between vendors of alcohol and the motoring public. This is no more than a restatement of the fact, already mentioned, that a general duty of care exists between establishments in Mayfield's position and persons using the highways.

I do, however, have difficulty accepting the proposition that the mere existence of this "special relationship", without more, permits the imposition of a positive obligation to act. Every person who enters a bar or restaurant is in an invitor-invitee relationship with the establishment, and is therefore in a "special relationship" with that establishment. However, it does not make sense to suggest that, simply as a result of this relationship, a commercial host cannot consider other relevant factors in determining whether in the circumstances positive steps are necessary.

The existence of this "special relationship" will frequently warrant the imposition of a positive obligation to act, but the sine qua non of tortious liability remains the foreseeability of the risk. Where no risk is foreseeable as a result of the circumstances, no action will be required, despite the existence of a special relationship. The respondents argue that Mayfield should have taken positive action, even though Mayfield knew that the driver was with three other people, two of whom were sober, and it was reasonable to infer from all of the circumstances that the group was travelling together.

One of the primary purposes of negligence law is to enforce reasonable standards of conduct so as to prevent the creation of reasonably foreseeable risks. In this way, tort law serves as a disincentive to risk-creating behaviour. To impose liability even where the risk which materialized was not reasonably foreseeable is to lay a portion of the loss at the feet of a party who has, in the circumstances, acted reasonably. Tort law does not require the wisdom of Solomon. All it requires is that people act reasonably in the circumstances. The "reasonable person" of negligence law was described by Laidlaw J.A. in this way in *Arland v. Taylor*:

> He is not an extraordinary or unusual creature; he is not superhuman; he is not required to display the highest skill of which anyone is capable; he is not a genius who can perform uncommon feats, nor is he possessed of unusual powers of foresight. He is a person of normal intelligence who makes prudence a guide to his conduct. He does nothing that a prudent man would not do and does not omit to do anything a prudent man would do. He acts in accord with general and approved practice. His conduct is guided by considerations which ordinarily regulate the conduct of human affairs. His conduct is the standard "adopted in the community by persons of ordinary intelligence and prudence."

Obviously, the fact that tragedy has befallen Gillian Stewart cannot, in itself, lead to a finding of liability on the part of Mayfield. The question is whether, before 11:00 p.m. on December 8, 1985, the circumstances were such that a reasonably prudent establishment should have foreseen that Stuart Pettie would drive, and therefore should have taken steps to prevent this.

I agree with the Court of Appeal that Mayfield cannot escape liability simply because Stuart Pettie was apparently not exhibiting any visible signs of intoxication. The waitress kept a running tab, and knew that Pettie had consumed 10 to 14 ounces of alcohol over a five-hour period. On the basis of this knowledge alone, she either knew or should have known that Pettie was becoming intoxicated, and this is so whether or not he was exhibiting visible symptoms.

However, I disagree with the Court of Appeal that the presence of the two sober women at the table cannot act to relieve Mayfield of liability. Laskin J. in *Jordan House Ltd. v. Menow*, *supra*, made it clear that the hotel's duty to Menow in that case could have been discharged by making sure "that he got home safely by taking him under its charge or putting him under the charge of a responsible person ..." (p. 249, emphasis added). Had Pettie been alone and intoxicated, Mayfield could have discharged its duty as established in *Jordan House Ltd. v. Menow* by calling Pettie's wife or sister to take charge of him. How, then, can Mayfield be liable when Pettie was already in their charge, and they knew how much he had had to drink? While it is technically true that Stuart Pettie was not "put into" the care of his sober wife and sister, this is surely a matter of semantics. He was already in their care, and they knew how much he had to drink. It is not reasonable to suggest in these circumstances that Mayfield had to do more.

Mayfield would have known that the group arrived together, that they spent the evening together, and that they left together. In addition, they would have known that they were part of the Dispensaries Limited Company Christmas party, and that two sober adults were present at the table when the drinks were ordered and consumed. In the circumstances, it was reasonable for Mayfield to assume that the four people at the table were not travelling separately, and it was reasonable for Mayfield to assume that one of the two sober people who were at the table would either drive or find alternative transportation.

The trial judge was correct in concluding on these facts that it was not necessary for Mayfield to enquire who was driving or that it would have made any difference if they had. It was not reasonably foreseeable that Stuart Pettie would be driving when a sober wife and sister were present with full knowledge of the circumstances.

I agree that establishments which serve alcohol must either intervene in appropriate circumstances or

risk liability, and that this liability cannot be avoided where the establishment has intentionally structured the environment in such a way as to make it impossible to know whether intervention is necessary. Such was the situation in *Canada Trust Co. v. Porter*, *supra*, where the alcohol was served from behind a bar and it was impossible for the establishment either to monitor the amount consumed or to determine whether intervention was necessary. A similar situation arose in *Gouge v. Three Top Investment Holdings Inc.*, where the plaintiff attended a company Christmas party which had a "cash bar", overindulged, and then was involved in an accident. In such circumstances, it would not be open to the establishment to claim that they could not foresee the risk created when the inability to foresee the risk was the direct result of the way the serving environment was structured.

However that was not the situation here. Mayfield was aware of the circumstances in which Stuart Pettie was drinking. In the environment of the case at bar, it was not reasonable for them to intervene.

On the facts of this case I conclude that Mayfield Investments Ltd. did not breach the duty of care they owed to Gillian Stewart. On this basis I would allow the appeal.

(c)   *Childs v. Desormeaux*[†]

Supreme Court of Canada

[McLACHLIN C.J.:]

1.   INTRODUCTION

[1] A person hosts a party. Guests drink alcohol. An inebriated guest drives away and causes an accident in which another person is injured. Is the host liable to the person injured? I conclude that as a general rule, a social host does not owe a duty of care to a person injured by a guest who has consumed alcohol and that the courts below correctly dismissed the appellants' action.

2.   FACTS

[2] This case arises from a tragic car accident in Ottawa in the early hours of January 1, 1999. At 1:30 a.m., after leaving a party hosted by Dwight Courrier and Julie Zimmerman, Desmond Desormeaux drove his vehicle into oncoming traffic and collided head-on with a vehicle driven by Patricia Hadden. One of the passengers in Ms. Hadden's car was killed and three others seriously injured, including Zoe Childs, who was then a teenager. Ms. Childs' spine was severed and she has since been paralyzed from the waist down. Mr.

---

† [2006] 1 S.C.R. 643, 2006 SCC 18.

Desormeaux and the two passengers in his car were also injured.

[3] Mr. Desormeaux was impaired at the time of the accident. The trial judge found that he had probably consumed 12 beers at the party over two and a half hours, producing a blood-alcohol concentration of approximately 235 mg per 100 ml when he left the party and 225 mg per 100 ml at the time of the accident — concentrations well over the legal limit for driving of 80 mg per 100 ml. Mr. Desormeaux pleaded guilty to a series of criminal charges arising from these events and received a 10-year sentence.

[4] The party hosted by Dwight Courrier and Julie Zimmerman at their home was a "BYOB" (Bring Your Own Booze) event. The only alcohol served by the hosts was three-quarters of a bottle of champagne in small glasses at midnight. Mr. Desormeaux was known to his hosts to be a heavy drinker. The trial judge heard evidence that when Mr. Desormeaux walked to his car to leave, Mr. Courrier accompanied him and asked, "Are you okay, brother?" Mr. Desormeaux responded "No problem", got behind the wheel and drove away with two passengers.

[5] The trial judge found that a reasonable person in the position of Mr. Courrier and Ms. Zimmerman would have foreseen that Mr. Desormeaux might cause an accident and injure someone else. However, the *prima facie* duty of care this gave rise to was negatived, in his view, by policy considerations involving the social and legal consequences of imposing a duty of care on social hosts to third parties injured by their guests, government regulation of alcohol sale and use and the preferability of a legislative, rather than a judicial, solution. Accordingly, the trial judge dismissed the action ((2002), 217 D.L.R. (4th) 217).

[6] The Court of Appeal for Ontario dismissed Ms. Childs' appeal. In its view, the circumstances did not disclose even a *prima facie* duty of care. Unless social hosts are actively implicated in creating the risk that gives rise to the accident, they cannot be found liable. Here, the social hosts "did not assume control over the supply or service of alcohol, nor did they serve alcohol to [Mr.] Desormeaux when he was visibly impaired" ((2004), 71 O.R. (3d) 195, at para. 75). Unlike commercial hosts, they were under no statutory duty to monitor the consumption of alcohol or to control the premises where alcohol was served, nor did anyone rely on them to do so. The court, *per* Weiler J.A., concluded (at para. 75):

... I cannot accept the proposition that by merely supplying the venue of a BYOB party, a host assumes legal responsibility to third party users of the road for monitoring the alcohol consumed by guests, ... It would not be just and fair in the circumstances to impose a duty of care.

[7] Ms. Childs appeals to this Court and asks that we reverse the courts below and conclude that Mr. Courrier and Ms. Zimmerman, as social hosts of the party where Mr. Desormeaux was drinking, are liable for the injuries she suffered.

[8] The central legal issue raised by this appeal is whether social hosts who invite guests to an event where alcohol is served owe a legal duty of care to third parties who may be injured by intoxicated guests. It is clear that commercial hosts, like bars or clubs, may be under such a duty. This is the first time, however, that this Court has considered the duty owed by social hosts to plaintiffs like Ms. Childs.

3. ANALYSIS

3.1 The General Test for a Duty of Care

[9] Before the decision of the House of Lords in *Donoghue v. Stevenson*, [1932] A.C. 562, the law governing tort liability for wrongs to others was a complex of categories derived from cases decided over the centuries. In *Donoghue v. Stevenson*, the House of Lords replaced the category approach with a principled approach. It recognized the existence of a "general conception of relations giving rise to a duty of care, of which the particular cases found in the books are but instances" (p. 580, *per* Lord Atkin). The general concept of a duty owed to those whom one might injure proved both powerful and practical. However, it brought with it a question — a question we wrestle with to this day. How do we define the persons to whom the duty is owed?

[10] Lord Atkin recognized this problem in *Donoghue v. Stevenson*. He accepted that negligence is based on a "general public sentiment of moral wrongdoing for which the offender must pay", but distinguished legal duties from moral obligation: "... acts or omissions which any moral code would censure cannot in a practical world be treated so as to give a right to every person injured by them to demand relief" (p. 580). My legal duty, he said, extends to my "neighbour". Legal neighbourhood is "restricted" to "persons who are so closely and directly affected by my act that I ought reasonably to have them in contemplation as being so affected

83

when I am directing my mind to the acts or omissions which are called in question" (p. 580). This concept, sometimes referred to as proximity, remains the foundation of the modern law of negligence.

[11] In *Anns v. Merton London Borough Council*, [1978] A.C. 728 (H.L.), Lord Wilberforce proposed a two-part test for determining whether a duty of care arises. The first stage focuses on the relationship between the plaintiff and the defendant, and asks whether it is close or "proximate" enough to give rise to a duty of care (p. 742). The second stage asks whether there are countervailing policy considerations that negative the duty of care. The two-stage approach of *Anns* was adopted by this Court in *Kamloops (City of) v. Nielsen*, [1984] 2 S.C.R. 2, at pp. 10–11, and recast as follows:

(1) is there "a sufficiently close relationship between the parties" or "proximity" to justify imposition of a duty and, if so,

(2) are there policy considerations which ought to negative or limit the scope of the duty, the class of persons to whom it is owed or the damages to which breach may give rise?

[12] In *Odhavji Estate v. Woodhouse*, [2003] 3 S.C.R. 263, 2003 SCC 69, the Court affirmed the *Anns* test and spoke, *per* Iacobucci J., of three requirements: reasonable foreseeability; sufficient proximity; and the absence of overriding policy considerations which negate a *prima facie* duty established by foreseeability and proximity: para. 52. Some cases speak of foreseeability being an element of proximity where "proximity" is used in the sense of establishing a relationship sufficient to give rise to a duty of care: see, e.g., *Kamloops*. *Odhavji*, by contrast, sees foreseeability and proximity as separate elements at the first stage; "proximity" is here used in the narrower sense of features of the relationship other than foreseeability. There is no suggestion that *Odhavji* was intended to change the *Anns* test; rather, it merely clarified that proximity will not always be satisfied by reasonable foreseeability. What is clear is that at stage one, foreseeability and factors going to the relationship between the parties must be considered with a view to determining whether a *prima facie* duty of care arises. At stage two, the issue is whether this duty is negated by other, broader policy considerations.

[13] The plaintiff bears the ultimate legal burden of establishing a valid cause of action, and hence a duty of care: *Odhavji*. However, once the plaintiff establishes a *prima facie* duty of care, the evidentiary burden of showing countervailing policy considerations shifts to the defendant, following the general rule that the party asserting a point should be required to establish it.

[14] The courts in this case applied these general principles and concluded, for different reasons, that they did not give rise to a duty of care on social hosts of parties where alcohol is served, to members of the public who may be injured by an intoxicated guest's conduct. The trial judge found that the first stage of the test had been met, but that policy considerations at stage two negated a duty of care. The Court of Appeal, by contrast, found that the first stage of establishing a *prima facie* duty of care had not been met, making it unnecessary to go on to the second stage of the *Anns* test.

3.2 Is the Proposed Duty Novel?

[15] A preliminary point arises from a nuance on the *Anns* test developed in *Cooper v. Hobart*, [2001] 3 S.C.R. 537, 2001 SCC 79. The Court in *Cooper* introduced the idea that as the case law develops, categories of relationships giving rise to a duty of care may be recognized, making it unnecessary to go through the *Anns* analysis. The reference to categories simply captures the basic notion of precedent: where a case is like another case where a duty has been recognized, one may usually infer that sufficient proximity is present and that if the risk of injury was foreseeable, a *prima facie* duty of care will arise. On the other hand, if a case does not clearly fall within a relationship previously recognized as giving rise to a duty of care, it is necessary to carefully consider whether proximity is established. Following *Cooper*, the first issue raised in this case is whether claims against private hosts for alcohol-related injuries caused by a guest constitute a new category of claim. Like the courts below, I conclude that it does.

[16] Canadian law does not provide a clear answer to the question of whether people who host social events where alcohol is served owe a duty of care to third-party members of the public who may be harmed by guests who leave the event inebriated. The closest comparison is that of commercial alcohol providers, who have been held to owe a duty to third-party members of the public who are injured as a result of the drunken driving of a patron: *Stewart v. Pettie*, [1995] 1 S.C.R. 131. Although the action was dismissed on the facts, *Stewart* affirmed that a special relationship existed between taverns and the motoring public that could require the former to take positive steps to protect the latter.

[17] The situation of commercial hosts, however, differs from that of social hosts. As discussed, in determining whether a duty of care arises, the focus is on the nature of the relationship between the parties. Three differences in the plaintiff-defendant relationship suggest that the possibility of a duty of care on commercial hosts does not automatically translate into a duty of care for social hosts.

[18] First, commercial hosts enjoy an important advantage over social hosts in their capacity to monitor alcohol consumption. As a result, not only is monitoring relatively easy for a commercial host, but it is also expected by the host, patrons and members of the public. In fact, commercial hosts have a special incentive to monitor consumption because they are being paid for service. Patrons expect that the number of drinks they consume will be monitored, if only to ensure that they are asked to pay for them. Furthermore, regulators can require that servers undertake training to ensure that they understand the risks of over-service and the signs of intoxication (see, e.g., R.R.O. 1990, Reg. 719). This means that not only is monitoring inherently part of the commercial transaction, but that servers can generally be expected to possess special knowledge about intoxication.

[19] Second, the sale and consumption of alcohol is strictly regulated by legislatures, and the rules applying to commercial establishments suggest that they operate in a very different context than private-party hosts. This regulation is driven by public expectations and attitudes towards intoxicants, but also serves, in turn, to shape those expectations and attitudes. In Ontario, where these facts occurred, the production, sale and use of alcohol is regulated principally by the regimes established by the *Liquor Control Act*, R.S.O. 1990, c. L.18, and the *Liquor Licence Act*, R.S.O. 1990, c. L.19. The latter Act is wide-ranging and regulates how, where, by and to whom alcohol can be sold or supplied, where and by whom it can be consumed and where intoxication is permitted and where it is not.

[20] These regulations impose special responsibilities on those who would profit from the supply of alcohol. This is clear by the very existence of a licensing scheme, but also by special rules governing the service of alcohol and, as noted above, special training that may be required. Clearly, the sale of alcohol to the general public is understood as including attendant responsibilities to reduce the risk associated with that trade.

[21] The importance of this regulatory environment does not relate to the statutory requirements *per se*, but what they demonstrate about the nature of commercial alcohol sales and about the expectations of purveyors, patrons and the public. Selling alcohol is a carefully regulated industry. The dangers of over-consumption, or of consumption by young or otherwise vulnerable persons, means that its sale and service in commercial settings is controlled. It is not treated like an ordinary commodity sold in retail stores. The public expects that in addition to adherence to regulatory standards, those who sell alcohol to the general public take additional steps to reduce the associated risks. Furthermore, patrons are aware that these special responsibilities have very real and visible manifestations. The imposition of a "cut-off" at the bar is understood, and expected, as part of the institutionalization of these responsibilities. Similarly, in many establishments, "bouncers" both enforce admission and assist other members of the staff who might have to deal with patrons who may have become intoxicated. These features have no equivalent in the non-commercial context. A party host has neither an institutionalized method of monitoring alcohol consumption and enforcing limits, nor a set of expectations that would permit him or her to easily do so.

[22] Third, the contractual nature of the relationship between a tavern keeper serving alcohol and a patron consuming it is fundamentally different from the range of different social relationships that can characterize private parties in the non-commercial context. The appellants argue that there is "nothing inherently special" about profit making in the law of negligence. In the case of alcohol sales, however, it is clear that profit making is relevant. Unlike the host of a private party, commercial alcohol servers have an incentive not only to serve many drinks, but to serve too many. Over-consumption is more profitable than responsible consumption. The costs of over-consumption are borne by the drinker him or herself, taxpayers who collectively pay for the added strain on related public services and, sometimes tragically, third parties who may come into contact with intoxicated patrons on the roads. Yet the benefits of over-consumption go to the tavern keeper alone, who enjoys large profit margins from customers whose judgment becomes more impaired the more they consume. This perverse incentive supports the imposition of a duty to monitor alcohol consumption in the interests of the general public.

[23] The differences just discussed mean that the existence of a duty on the part of commercial pro-

viders of alcohol cannot be extended by simple analogy to the hosts of a private party. The duty proposed in this case is novel. We must therefore ask whether a duty of care is made out on the two-stage *Anns* test.

3.3 Stage One: A Prima Facie Duty?

[24] Applying the first stage of the *Anns* test requires, as noted above, an examination of the relationship between the parties to determine if it meets the requirement of sufficient proximity. The question is: What, if anything, links party hosts to third-party users of the highway?

[25] The law of negligence not only considers the plaintiff's loss, but explains why it is just and fair to impose the cost of that loss on the particular defendant before the court. The proximity requirement captures this two-sided face of negligence.

[26] I conclude that the necessary proximity has not been established and, consequently, that social hosts of parties where alcohol is served do not owe a duty of care to public users of highways. First, the injury to Ms. Childs was not reasonably foreseeable on the facts found by the trial judge. Second, even if foreseeability were established, no duty would arise because the wrong alleged is a failure to act or nonfeasance in circumstances where there was no positive duty to act.

3.3.1 Foreseeability

[27] Ms. Childs argues that the parties are linked by the foreseeability of physical harm due to the manner in which the party hosts exercised "control or influence over" the party at which Mr. Desormeaux was drinking.

[28] The question of foreseeability is complicated by ambiguity in the findings of the trial judge. The trial judge found that Mr. Desormeaux would be showing "obvious signs of impairment" (para. 73), but did not find that the hosts in the circumstances knew, or ought to have known, that Mr. Desormeaux was too drunk to drive. The risks of impaired driving, and their consequences for motorists and their passengers, are well known. However, if there is no finding that the hosts *knew*, or ought to have known, that the guest who was about to drive was impaired, how can it be said that they should have foreseen that allowing him to drive might result in injury to other motorists?

[29] Instead of finding that the hosts ought reasonably to have been aware that Mr. Desormeaux was

too drunk to drive, the trial judge based his finding that the hosts should have foreseen injury to motorists on the road on problematic reasoning. He noted that the hosts knew that Mr. Desormeaux had gotten drunk in the past and then driven. He inferred from this that they should have foreseen that unless Mr. Desormeaux's drinking at the party was monitored, he would become drunk, get into his car and drive onto the highway. The problem with this reasoning is that a history of alcohol consumption and impaired driving does not make impaired driving, and the consequent risk to other motorists, reasonably foreseeable. The inferential chain from drinking and driving in the past to reasonable foreseeability that this will happen again is too weak to support the legal conclusion of reasonable foreseeability — even in the case of commercial hosts, liability has not been extended by such a frail hypothesis.

[30] Ms. Childs points to the findings relating to the considerable amount of alcohol Mr. Desormeaux had consumed and his high blood-alcohol rating, coupled with the fact that Mr. Courrier accompanied Mr. Desormeaux to his car before he drove away, and asks us to make the finding of knowledge of inebriation that the trial judge failed to make. The problem here is the absence of any evidence that Mr. Desormeaux displayed signs of intoxication during this brief encounter. Given the absence of evidence that the hosts in this case in fact knew of Mr. Desormeaux's intoxication and the fact that the experienced trial judge himself declined to make such a finding, it would not be proper for us to change the factual basis of this case by supplementing the facts on this critical point. I conclude that the injury was not reasonably foreseeable on the facts established in this case.

3.3.2 Failure to Act: Nonfeasance Versus Misfeasance

[31] Foreseeability is not the only hurdle Ms. Childs' argument for a duty of care must surmount. "Foreseeability does not of itself, and automatically, lead to the conclusion that there is a duty of care": G. H. L. Fridman, *The Law of Torts in Canada* (2nd ed. 2002), at p. 320. Foreseeability without more *may* establish a duty of care. This is usually the case, for example, where an *overt act of the defendant* has *directly caused foreseeable physical harm* to the plaintiff: see *Cooper*. However, where the conduct alleged against the defendant is a *failure to act*, foreseeability alone may not establish a duty of care. In the absence of an overt act on the part of the defendant, the nature of the relationship must be exam-

ined to determine whether there is a nexus between the parties. Although there is no doubt that an omission may be negligent, as a general principle, the common law is a jealous guardian of individual autonomy. Duties to take positive action in the face of risk or danger are not free-standing. Generally, the mere fact that a person faces danger, or has become a danger to others, does not itself impose any kind of duty on those in a position to become involved.

[32] In this case, we are concerned not with an overt act of the social hosts, but with their alleged failure to act. The case put against them is that they should have interfered with the autonomy of Mr. Desormeaux by preventing him from drinking and driving. It follows that foreseeability alone would not establish a duty of care in this case.

[33] The appellants' argument that Mr. Courrier and Ms. Zimmerman committed positive acts that created, or contributed to, the risk cannot be sustained. It is argued that they *facilitated* the consumption of alcohol by organizing a social event where alcohol was consumed on their premises. But this is not an act that creates risk to users of public roads. The real complaint is that having organized the party, the hosts permitted their guest to drink and then take the wheel of an automobile.

[34] A positive duty of care may exist if foreseeability of harm is present *and* if other aspects of the relationship between the plaintiff and the defendant establish a special link or proximity. Three such situations have been identified by the courts. They function not as strict legal categories, but rather to elucidate factors that can lead to positive duties to act. These factors, or features of the relationship, bring parties who would otherwise be legal strangers into proximity and impose positive duties on defendants that would not otherwise exist.

[35] The first situation where courts have imposed a positive duty to act is where a defendant intentionally attracts and invites third parties to an inherent and obvious risk that he or she has created or controls: *Hendricks v. The Queen*, [1970] S.C.R. 237; *Horsley v. MacLaren*, [1972] S.C.R. 441; *Arnold v. Teno*, [1978] 2 S.C.R. 287; and *Crocker v. Sundance Northwest Resorts Ltd.*, [1988] 1 S.C.R. 1186. For example, it has been held that a boat captain owes a duty to take reasonable care to rescue a passenger who falls overboard (*Horsley*) and that the operator of a dangerous inner-tube sliding competition owes a duty to exclude people who cannot safely participate (*Crocker*). These cases turn on the defendant's causal relationship to the origin of the risk of injury faced by the plaintiff or on steps taken to invite others to subject themselves to a risk under the defendant's control. If the defendant creates a risky situation and invites others into it, failure to act thereafter does not immunize the defendant from the consequences of its acts. These cases are akin to the positive and *continuing* duty of manufacturers or transferors of goods to warn of inherently dangerous products or dangerous uses of safe products: *Lambert v. Lastoplex Chemicals Co.*, [1972] S.C.R. 569; *Hollis v. Dow Corning Corp.*, [1995] 4 S.C.R. 634.

[36] The second situation where a positive duty of care has been held to exist concerns paternalistic relationships of supervision and control, such as those of parent-child or teacher-student: *Dziwenka v. The Queen in right of Alberta*, [1972] S.C.R. 419; *Bain v. Board of Education (Calgary)* (1993), 146 A.R. 321 (Q.B.). The duty in these cases rests on the special vulnerability of the plaintiffs and the formal position of power of the defendants. The law recognizes that the autonomy of some persons may be permissibly violated or restricted, but, in turn, requires that those with power exercise it in light of special duties. In the words of Virtue J. in *Bain*, in the context of a teacher-student relationship, "[t]hat right of control carries with it a corresponding duty to take care for the safety of, and to properly supervise the student, whether he or she is a child, an adolescent or an adult" (para. 38).

[37] The third situation where a duty of care may include the need to take positive steps concerns defendants who either exercise a public function or engage in a commercial enterprise that includes implied responsibilities to the public at large: *Dunn v. Dominion Atlantic Railway Co.* (1920), 60 S.C.R. 310; *Jordan House Ltd. v. Menow*, [1974] S.C.R. 239; *Doe v. Metropolitan Toronto (Municipality) Commissioners of Police* (1998), 39 O.R. (3d) 487 (Gen. Div.). In these cases, the defendants offer a service to the general public that includes attendant responsibilities to act with special care to reduce risk. Where a defendant assumes a public role, or benefits from offering a service to the public at large, special duties arise. The duty of a commercial host who serves alcohol to guests to act to prevent foreseeable harm to third-party users of the highway falls into this category: *Stewart v. Pettie*.

[38] Running through all of these situations is the defendant's material implication in the creation of risk or his or her control of a risk to which others have been invited. The operator of a dangerous

sporting competition creates or enhances the risk by inviting and enabling people to participate in an inherently risky activity. It follows that the operator must take special steps to protect against the risk materializing. In the example of the parent or teacher who has assumed control of a vulnerable person, the vulnerability of the person and its subjection to the control of the defendant creates a situation where the latter has an enhanced responsibility to safeguard against risk. The public provider of services undertakes a public service, and must do so in a way that appropriately minimizes associated risks to the public.

[39] Also running through the examples is a concern for the autonomy of the persons affected by the positive action proposed. The law does not impose a duty to eliminate risk. It accepts that competent people have the right to engage in risky activities. Conversely, it permits third parties witnessing risk to decide not to become rescuers or otherwise intervene. It is only when these third parties have a special relationship to the person in danger or a material role in the creation or management of the risk that the law may impinge on autonomy. Thus, the operator of a risky sporting activity may be required to prevent a person who is unfit to perform a sport safely from participating or, when a risk materializes, to attempt a rescue. Similarly, the publican may be required to refuse to serve an inebriated patron who may drive, or a teacher be required to take positive action to protect a child who lacks the right or power to make decisions for itself. The autonomy of risk takers or putative rescuers is not absolutely protected, but, at common law, it is always respected.

[40] Finally, the theme of reasonable reliance unites examples in all three categories. A person who creates or invites others into a dangerous situation, like the high-risk sports operator, may reasonably expect that those taking up the invitation will rely on the operator to ensure that the risk is a reasonable one or to take appropriate rescue action if the risk materializes. Similarly, a teacher will understand that the child or the child's parents rely on the teacher to avoid and minimize risk. Finally, there is a reasonable expectation on the part of the public that a person providing public services, often under licence, will take reasonable precautions to reduce the risk of the activity, not merely to immediate clients, but to the general public.

[41] Does the situation of the social host who serves alcohol to guests fall within the three categories just

discussed or represent an appropriate extension of them having regard to the factors of risk-control and reasonable preservation of autonomy that animate them? I conclude that it does not.

[42] The first category concerns defendants who have created or invited others to participate in highly risky activities. Holding a house party where alcohol is served is not such an activity. Risks may ensue, to be sure, from what guests choose to do or not do at the party. But hosting a party is a far cry from inviting participation in a high-risk sport or taking people out on a boating party. A party where alcohol is served is a common occurrence, not one associated with unusual risks demanding special precautions. The second category of paternalistic relationships of supervision or control is equally inapplicable. Party hosts do not enjoy a paternalistic relationship with their guests, nor are their guests in a position of reduced autonomy that invites control. Finally, private social hosts are not acting in a public capacity and, hence, do not incur duties of a public nature.

[43] More broadly, do the themes that animate the cases imposing positive duties to act — risk enhancement and control, autonomy and reasonable reliance — suggest that the social hosts in this case owed a duty of care to third-party users of the highway, to take reasonable steps to prevent what happened? Again, the answer is that they do not.

[44] Holding a private party at which alcohol is served — the bare facts of this case — is insufficient to implicate the host in the creation of a risk sufficient to give rise to a duty of care to third parties who may be subsequently injured by the conduct of a guest. The host creates a place where people can meet, visit and imbibe alcohol, whether served on the premises or supplied by the guest. All this falls within accepted parameters of non-dangerous conduct. More is required to establish a danger or risk that requires positive action. It might be argued that a host who continues to serve alcohol to a visibly inebriated person knowing that he or she will be driving home has become implicated in the creation or enhancement of a risk sufficient to give rise to a *prima facie* duty of care to third parties, which would be subject to contrary policy considerations at the second stage of the *Anns* test. This position has been taken in some states in the U.S.A.: N.J. Stat. Ann. §§ 2A:15-5.5 to 2A:15-5.8 (West 2000). We need not decide that question here. Suffice it to say that hosting a party where alcohol is served, without more, does not suggest the creation or exacerbation of risk of the level required to impose a duty of care on

the host to members of the public who may be affected by a guest's conduct.

[45] Nor does the autonomy of the individual support the case for a duty to take action to protect highway users in the case at bar. As discussed, the implication of a duty of care depends on the relationships involved. The relationship between social host and guest at a house party is part of this equation. A person who accepts an invitation to attend a private party does not park his autonomy at the door. The guest remains responsible for his or her conduct. Short of active implication in the creation or enhancement of the risk, a host is entitled to respect the autonomy of a guest. The consumption of alcohol, and the assumption of the risks of impaired judgment, is in almost all cases a personal choice and an inherently personal activity. Absent the special considerations that may apply in the commercial context, when such a choice is made by an adult, there is no reason why others should be made to bear its costs. The conduct of a hostess who confiscated all guests' car keys and froze them in ice as people arrived at her party, releasing them only as she deemed appropriate, was cited to us as exemplary. This hostess was evidently prepared to make considerable incursions on the autonomy of her guests. The law of tort, however, has not yet gone so far.

[46] This brings us to the factor of reasonable reliance. There is no evidence that anyone relied on the hosts in this case to monitor guests' intake of alcohol or prevent intoxicated guests from driving. This represents an important distinction between the situation of a private host, as here, and a public host. The public host provides alcohol to members of the public, under a strict regulatory regime. It is reasonable to expect that the public provider will act to protect the public interest. There is public reliance that he will comply with the rules that prohibit serving too much alcohol to a patron and that if this should occur and the patron seeks to drive, that the public host will take reasonable steps to prevent the

person from driving. The same cannot be said of the private social host, who neither undertakes nor is expected to monitor the conduct of guests on behalf of the public.

[47] I conclude that hosting a party at which alcohol is served does not, without more, establish the degree of proximity required to give rise to a duty of care on the hosts to third-party highway users who may be injured by an intoxicated guest. The injury here was not shown to be foreseeable on the facts as found by the trial judge. Even if it had been, this is at best a case of nonfeasance. No duty to monitor guests' drinking or to prevent them from driving can be imposed having regard to the relevant cases and legal principles. A social host at a party where alcohol is served is not under a duty of care to members of the public who may be injured by a guest's actions, unless the host's conduct implicates him or her in the creation or exacerbation of the risk. On the facts of this case, I agree with the Court of Appeal, at para. 75, *per* Weiler J.A.:

> The person sought to be held liable must be implicated in the creation of the risk. ... The social hosts had no statutory duty to monitor the consumption of alcohol or to control the structure of the atmosphere in which alcohol was served. There is no evidence that anyone relied on them to do so. ... I cannot accept the proposition that by merely supplying the venue of a BYOB party, a host assumes legal responsibility to third party users of the road for monitoring the alcohol consumed by guests, ... It would not be just and fair in the circumstances to impose a duty of care.

[48] Having concluded that a *prima facie* duty of care has not been established, I find it unnecessary to consider whether any duty would be negated by policy considerations at the second stage of the *Anns* test.

4. CONCLUSION

[49] I would dismiss the appeal with costs.

(d) Supreme Court Couldn't Rule on Compassion in Party Host Case†

Michelle Mann

Considering throwing a party but worried about your liability for guests that drink and drive? Don't be, says the Supreme Court of Canada, unless you are actively implicated in your guest's destructive actions.

The court's recent ruling in Zoe Childs versus Desmond Desormeaux, considered by many lawyers to be the biggest tort case in 30 years, is, however, worth a read prior to hosting your next event.

Zoe Childs, who was 18 at the time of the accident, was left a paraplegic. (CBC)

Zoe Childs, a young woman rendered a paraplegic by a drunk driver, sued in negligence the people who held the house party at which the driver got drunk. The case is the first at the Supreme Court of Canada to raise the issue of whether those who host non-commercial, alcohol-related events owe a duty of care to those who suffer physical injury as a result of the impaired driving of one of their guests.

Canadian negligence law has already established a principle of commercial host liability. A bar owner can be held liable for serving excessive amounts of alcohol to someone who then drives and causes damage. However, in these circumstances the "host" is profiting from selling the alcohol, and subject to a strict regulatory regime.

With an estimated thousands of cases awaiting the outcome of this appeal, lawyers across the country were holding their collective breath.

A large exhale could be heard from those of us concerned with the responsibility of the individual for their actions.

In a unanimous and surprisingly short (by Supreme Court standards) judgment, the court stated unequivocally that "as a general rule a social host does not owe a duty of care to a person injured by a guest who has consumed alcohol."

Even if the hosts could have reasonably foreseen [Childs' injury,] the court said, under negligence law there was no positive duty to act and monitor guests' drinking or to prevent them from driving. Social host liability might only arise where the host's conduct implicates them in the exacerbation of the risk, for example, by continuing to serve alcohol to a visibly inebriated person knowing that they will be driving home.

Legally, this case was about the duty of care owed to others under negligence law, but practically it was also about deep pockets, with the injured victim pursuing compensation under the host's homeowners insurance. One certainly cannot blame Childs and her family for trying; I would go after anyone I could in her circumstances.

However, while she was an extremely sympathetic plaintiff, the court clearly knows that "bad facts make bad law." Ruling on the basis of compassion for her situation would have resulted in a dangerous precedent.

A judgment finding liability on behalf of the social hosts would have required that the bench divorce itself from reality. It is simply not possible to monitor guests that closely, though, of course, we might try, rooted in concern for our fellow citizens.

More importantly, there is a co-relation between our freedom to choose our course of action as individuals and personal responsibility for those choices.

Taken to the extreme, it has been hypothesized that a finding of social host liability in this case could ultimately have led to a drunk driver suing social hosts for not adequately supervising him or her.

The court clearly saw these implications, observing that: Short of active implication, a host is entitled to respect the autonomy of a guest. The consumption of alcohol, and the assumption of the risks of impaired judgment is in almost all cases a personal choice and an inherently personal activity.

The impact that these words of reason will have on numerous other "personal responsibility" type lawsuits currently working their way through the courts remains to be seen.

Take, for example, the tobacco-related class action lawsuits certified in Quebec in 2005. In the Blais case the representative plaintiff argues that the

---

† CBC News website, Viewpoint (May 5, 2006) <www.cbc.ca/news/viewpoint/vp_mann/20060505.html>. Reproduced with permission of the author.

tobacco companies denied the link between tobacco and cancer until the 1990s. Having lost a lung to cancer, he apparently still smoked about 40 cigarettes a day in 2005.

If tobacco companies have deliberately misled the public or withheld health information, they should be on the hook for resulting health related damages. But to what degree are manufacturers responsible for the period after which information about tobacco-related dangers was fully in the public domain?

Equally, gamblers suing governments over their casino-fuelled addictions and failed attempts by the obese to sue fast food companies in the U.S., speak to a trend in so-called "blaming lawsuits."

Childs does not bode well for these types of cases; as eloquently noted by the court: "The common law is a jealous guardian of individual autonomy."

Clearly, governments, corporations and individuals owe duties of care to others. Simultaneously, however, there is a co-relation between freedom of choice and personal responsibility for those choices; a corresponding price to be paid for abnegating our accountability.

(e) Before You Host a Party, Read This: Social Host Liability and the Decision in Childs v. Desormeaux[†]

Fiona Kelly

I. INTRODUCTION

At 1:30 am on New Year's Eve 1999, soon after leaving a 'bring your own booze' (BYOB) party hosted by Dwight Courrier and Julie Zimmerman ("the Hosts"), Desmond Desormeaux drove his uninsured car into oncoming traffic, colliding head-on with the vehicle Patricia Hadden was driving in the opposite direction. One of the passengers in Hadden's car was killed and three others were seriously injured, including Zoe Childs who was rendered paraplegic. While attending the party, Desormeaux had consumed approximately 12 beers in the space of about two-and-a-half hours. A blood sample taken from Desormeaux four hours after the accident showed that he had a blood-alcohol concentration of 183mg in 100ml of blood — approximately two-and-a-half times the legal limit. Desormeaux was known to the Hosts as a long-time heavy drinker and frequently slept over at their house when he had too much to drink. The Hosts also knew that Desormeaux had driven while drunk in the past. In fact, Desormeaux had been convicted of impaired driving in 1991 and 1994, and for driving while disqualified in 1996.[1] On the night of the accident, Courrier accompanied Desormeaux to his car and asked "Are you okay, brother?" Desormeaux responded "No problem", got behind the wheel, and drove away.

Recent cases in Canada dealing with the legal liability of social hosts for the harm caused to third parties by their (inebriated) guests have created an increasingly polemical public debate.[2] On one side of the debate are victims of drunk driving and advocacy organizations such as Mothers Against Drunk Driving (MADD)[3] who argue, both inside and outside of the courts, that social hosts who serve alcohol should bear legal liability for harm caused to third parties by their intoxicated guests.[4] They tend to draw little distinction between social hosts and commercial hosts (who may owe a legal duty to third parties)[5] on the basis that the risks associated with drunk driving remain the same whether the individual consumed alcohol at a private party or at a licensed establishment. They argue that drunk drivers are a hazard on our roads and we bear both individual and community responsibility for reducing the harm they cause.[6] The other side of the debate is presented by a far less cohesive constituency, largely made up of certain elements of the public press and the insurance industry.[7] They tend to view drunk driving as a matter of personal choice and argue that guests must remain

---

[†] (2006) 39 U.B.C. L. Rev. 371–388. [Notes/references omitted.] Reproduced with permission of the publisher.

responsible for their own conduct.[8] They also tend to reject the conflation of social and commercial hosts on the basis that commercial hosts serve alcohol in a legally regulated environment for the purpose of profit. They also point to the insurance implications of social host responsibility, arguing that homeowners' insurance premiums will rise if a duty of care is found to exist.

While the first case dealing with the liability of social hosts in Canada was decided in 1986,[9] the courts have offered little concrete guidance on the issue in the 20 years since. No court in Canada has been willing to find a social host liable, but several have suggested that if the requisite elements of responsibility are established, then liability might be imposed.[10] This has led some commentators to suggest that social host liability already exists in Canada, provided the requisite elements can be established.[11] However, the difficulty of establishing these elements, combined with the uncertainty of what is actually required, has led to ongoing confusion. Given the heated public debate and the lack of legal guidance on the issue, it was hoped that the Supreme Court of Canada decision in *Childs v. Desormeaux*[12] would provide a definitive response.

In dismissing Childs' case against the Hosts, the Supreme Court unanimously held that "[h]olding a private party at which alcohol is served ... is insufficient to implicate the host in the creation of a risk sufficient to give rise to a duty of care to third parties who may be subsequently injured by the conduct of a guest."[13] However, the Court went on to state that if the host somehow "implicates him or her[self] in the creation or exacerbation of the risk", perhaps by continuing to serve alcohol to a visibly impaired individual knowing that he or she will be driving home, then a duty may arise.[14] Because the facts in *Childs*[15] did not raise such a scenario, the Court did not go on to consider whether policy considerations might negative or limit the scope of such a duty. Thus, while the decision in *Childs* does offer some additional certainty in the law relating to social hosts, their actual responsibilities remain unclear.

In this Comment I will argue that while the decision in *Childs* is supported by the particular facts of the case, much of the underlying reasoning is problematic. I will focus my attention on three aspects of the decision. First, I will argue that the distinction the Court makes between commercial and social hosts is exaggerated, and that the differences that do exist should influence the standard of care required of social hosts rather than the existence of a duty. Second, I will argue that the suggestion in *Childs* that social host liability will impose an inordinate burden on social hosts is simply not true. There are few things that social hosts would be required to do that at least some hosts do not already do, and given that one of the purposes of liability is accident prevention, it is not too great a burden to require social hosts to take reasonable steps to prevent reasonably foreseeable risks arising out of the consumption of alcohol by their guests. Finally, I will argue that the assertion that social host liability will intrude on a guest's individual autonomy and personal choice, or diminish their individual responsibility, is deeply problematic. Such a claim invokes the decontextualized and individualized language of neo-liberalism[16] to deal with an issue that government and non-government organizations alike treat as involving both individual and community responsibility.[17]

II. THE DECISIONS: JUDICIAL RELUCTANCE TO RECOGNIZE SOCIAL HOST LIABILITY

Childs brought her initial claim in negligence against the driver, Desormeaux, and the Hosts. While the action against Desormeaux succeeded, the claim against the Hosts was dismissed by all three courts that heard the matter.[18] The reasons for dismissing the claim varied from court to court and are, for that reason, worthy of review.

The trial judge, Chadwick J., was alone in finding that the circumstances of the case gave rise to a duty of care.[19] He found that the injuries suffered by Childs were reasonably foreseeable and that the Hosts therefore "had a duty not to turn Desmond Desormeaux loose on the highway where he could cause injury or death to others."[20] Foreseeability was established on the basis that, although the Hosts did not know that Desmoreaux was intoxicated on the night in question, they knew he was an alcoholic and had a history of impaired driving. They were therefore under a positive duty to monitor his alcohol consumption and prevent him from driving. Chadwick J. went on to hold, however, that the duty of care owed by the Hosts to Childs was negatived by policy considerations. The judge felt that a finding of liability "would place an inordinate burden on all social hosts" because they would be obligated to inquire of their guests whether they had consumed alcohol before arriving and to monitor alcohol consumption during the event.[21] If the Hosts themselves were drinking, this could be an especially difficult task. Chadwick J. also argued that having to inquire as to a guest's state of intoxication, or having to refuse to continue to serve alcohol to a guest, may have a chilling effect on social relations.[22] For these policy reasons, Chadwick J. dismissed the claim and indicated that any future debate about social host liability should be left to the legislature.

In contrast to the trial decision, the Ontario Court of Appeal refused to find that social hosts owe third party road users a duty of care.[23] The Court held that unless social hosts are actively implicated in creating the risk that gives rise to the accident, no duty exists. The facts in *Childs*[24] indicate that the Hosts did not "assume control over the supply or service" of alcohol, nor did they serve alcohol to Desormeaux when he was visibly impaired.[25] In fact, they claim to have been unaware that he was impaired.[26] Given these facts, the Court held that it was impossible to argue that the Hosts were in any way implicated in the creation of the risk. The Court of Appeal also drew a distinction between commercial hosts, who are under a statutory duty to monitor and control the consumption of alcohol on their premises, and social hosts, who bear no such responsibility.[27] Refusing to extend the notion of commercial host liability to the private setting, the Court held that it could not "accept the proposition that by merely supplying the venue of a BYOB party, a host assumes legal responsibility to third party users of the road for monitoring the alcohol consumed by guests.... It would not be just and fair in the circumstances to impose a duty of care."[28] Having found that no duty exists, it was not necessary for the Court to consider policy implications in any great detail. However, the Court did make it clear that its judgment should not be interpreted as foreclosing social host liability to innocent third parties, particularly when it can be shown that a social host knew that an intoxicated guest was going to drive and did not nothing to protect third party users of the road.[29]

Childs appealed the decision of the Ontario Court of Appeal, setting the stage for the first Supreme Court pronouncement on the liability of social hosts in Canada. Relying largely on the same reasoning as the Court of Appeal, the Supreme Court dismissed the appeal, holding that the social host of a party where alcohol is being served is not under a duty of care to members of the public who may be injured by a guest's actions, unless the host's conduct implicates him or her in the creation or exacerbation of the risk.[30] The failure of the Court to find a duty rested on the lack of proximity between the party hosts and third parties and the absence of a reasonably foreseeable risk. The Court found that the Hosts did not know, and had no rea-

son to believe, that Desmoreaux was intoxicated. Unlike the trial judge, it was unwilling to infer from the amount of alcohol that Desmoreaux had consumed, or from his history of impaired driving, that the risk of injury to a third party was reasonably foreseeable. The Court held that even in the event that the risk had been reasonably foreseeable, no duty would arise because the alleged wrong was a failure to act in circumstances where there was no positive duty to act. Thus, the only situation in which a social host might be found liable would be where the host's conduct implicates him or her in the creation or exacerbation of the risk. Short of active implication, "a host is entitled to respect the autonomy of a guest."[31] Given the failure of the plaintiff to establish either foreseeability or proximity, it was not necessary for the court to consider whether any duty might be negated by policy considerations.[32]

III. ANALYSIS

Given the distinct facts of the case, the final outcome in Childs[33] appears to be well justified. This was not a situation where a host continued to serve alcohol to an intoxicated guest, or allowed an obviously impaired guest to get behind the wheel of a car. To the contrary, the Hosts in Childs served little alcohol at their party, and one of them actively inquired as to the defendant's ability to drive. While the Hosts were aware of the defendant's history of drunk driving, there was considerable evidence before the trial judge that he did not exhibit any signs of being intoxicated on the night of the party. The final result in *Childs* is therefore supported by the particular facts of the case. I will argue, however, that much of the underlying reasoning of the Court is problematic. My analysis will focus on three aspects of the decision: (i) whether the Court correctly determined the issue of whether social host liability is a new category of claim; (ii) whether social host liability would, as the Court suggests, impose an "inordinate burden" on social hosts; and (iii) whether the Court overstated the importance of respecting a guest's individual autonomy and personal choice in relation to their drinking habits.

A. Social Host Liability: An Extension of Commercial Host Liability?

Before determining whether the Hosts owed Childs a duty of care, it was necessary for the Supreme Court to determine whether a claim made against a social host for harm caused by a guest constituted a new category of claim. The need to make this determination stems from the Supreme Court decision in *Cooper v. Hobart*,[34] in which it was held that as case law develops, categories of relationships giving rise to a duty of care may be recognized, making it unnecessary to go through the two-stage duty test created in *Anns v. Merton London Borough Council*.[35] The assertion by the plaintiff in *Childs* was that claims made against social hosts are not a new category of claim but are rather an extension of the commercial host category. If this were the case, then all Childs would need to establish is: (a) that her case falls within a relationship previously recognized as giving rise to a duty of care, and (b) that the risk of injury was reasonably foreseeable. Rejecting this argument, the Supreme Court relied on three differences in the plaintiff-defendant relationship to distinguish between the liability of commercial hosts and the liability of social hosts.[36]

First, the court noted that commercial hosts have a greater capacity than social hosts to monitor their patrons' alcohol consumption. Not only must patrons pay for each drink they consume, thus bringing them under the watchful eye of the commercial host, but commercial servers are also required to undertake training to ensure that they understand the risks of over-service and the signs of intoxication. Second, the sale and consumption of alcohol in commercial establishments is strictly regulated by legislatures. These regulations impose special responsibilities on those who profit from the supply of alcohol. In contrast, social hosts have neither an institutionalized method of monitoring alcohol consumption and enforcing limits, nor a set of legislative expectations that would permit them to easily do so. Third, the contractual nature of the relationship between a bar owner serving alcohol and a patron consuming it is fundamentally different from the range of social relationships that can characterize private parties in the non-commercial context. In particular, the profit-making element of public establishments, by which bars benefit financially from over-consumption, supports the imposition of a special duty to monitor alcohol intake in the interests of the general public. Given these differences between the conditions under which commercial and social hosts serve alcohol, the Court concludes that the existence of a duty on the part of commercial hosts "cannot be extended by simple analogy to the Hosts of a private party."[37]

While each of the factors identified by the court might properly inform the standard of care imposed on a social host, it can be argued that none of them justify exclusion of a duty altogether.[38] There is no doubt that commercial hosts are more likely than social hosts to have the expertise needed to determine whether a patron is impaired. Many servers are in fact trained to identify the signs of intoxication, and some provinces mandate such training through statutory regimes. Commercial hosts are also in a better position to monitor a patron's alcohol consumption because each drink must be paid for. However, the fact that a commercial host is better placed than a social host to minimize a reasonably foreseeable risk does not change the nature of the risk itself. As Adjin-Tettey argues:

> Ultimately, a duty of care arises from provision of alcohol or more broadly the opportunity to consume alcohol, intoxication, and the foreseeability of risk of injury from the guest's intoxicated condition, such as knowledge (or likelihood) that the guest will soon drive. In such circumstances, a host has created or contributed to a foreseeable risk of injury and is obligated to take preventative steps to avoid the risk materializing.[39]

In fact, the Supreme Court in *Stewart v. Pettie* emphasized that recognition of a duty of care in commercial host cases is not because of the commercial nature of the relationship but the probable risk of injury to the patron or others in the particular circumstances.[40] In other words, as long as the risk is reasonably foreseeable — that is, that the duty is predicated on the knowledge of the host — a positive duty arises. In this regard, it can be argued that a social host is in no different a position than a commercial host. Where there is knowledge, it can be argued that both hosts have created or contributed to a reasonably foreseeable risk of injury, and both should be expected to take precautions to minimize that risk.

The logical conclusion flowing from *Stewart* is that it is at the stage of risk minimization — that is, the standard of care to be applied — rather than at the duty stage, that the differences between social and commercial hosts are most appropriately taken into account. Given their additional expertise, the economic benefit they derive from serving alcohol, and the statutory responsibilities that govern their activity, it is sensible to assume that commercial hosts might be expected to maintain a higher standard of conduct than a social host.[41] This might involve checking whether patrons are with a designated driver, calling a taxi, refusing to continue to serve alcohol, providing information regarding overnight accommodation, or calling the police.[42] Social hosts would also be required to take reasonable precautions when presented with a guest who is clearly intoxicated, such as checking that the guest has appropriate transport home or allowing him/her to stay overnight.[43] It is unlikely, however, that they would be expected to go to the same lengths as a commercial host to discharge their duty. They have none of the special skills and training, statutory obligations, or economic relationship that might require such a high standard of care.

If an innocent third party is injured by an intoxicated driver, the fact that the driver consumed the alcohol at a commercial venue and not a private home makes no difference to the victim. For the victim, the risk of harm is the same. As Richardson J. pointed out in *Coulter v. Superior* Court:

> [I]t is small comfort to the [victim of] ... an accident involving an intoxicated driver to learn that the driver received his drinks from a hospitable social host rather than by purchase at a bar.... The danger and risk to the potential victim on the highway is equally as great, regardless of the source of the liquor.[44]

In fact, approximately 80 percent of alcohol consumption in Canada occurs in homes and other private places, and night-time roadside surveys indicate that there are more impaired drivers on the roads coming from private homes than from licensed establishments.[45] There is thus no good reason to distinguish between the liability of commercial and social hosts in situations where there is a reasonably foreseeable risk of harm. In fact, to shield a social host from liability arising out of a reasonably foreseeable risk is a disincentive for accident prevention. As Adjin-Tettey argues, "[i]t weakens tort law's objectives of deterrence and education and creates a moral hazard."[46]

Recognizing that social hosts owe a duty of care to third parties will enable Canadian courts and/or legislatures to develop appropriate standards against which the behaviour of social hosts can be measured.[47] Such a decision will encourage socially responsible behaviour on the part of all hosts.

B. The "Inordinate Burden" of Social Host Liability?

The second problematic theme to emerge from the decision in *Childs*[48] is the Court's assertion that social host liability will place an inordinate burden on social hosts. The argument is that if social hosts are required to assess whether their guests are intoxicated, and take some action if they are, then they are being asked to bear too much responsibility. It is arguable, however, that if the duty imposed is carefully defined so that it arises only in a discrete set of circumstances, it is unlikely to be as inordinate as the court suggests.[49]

Drawing on the decision in *Dryden v. Campbell Estate*,[50] Adjin-Tettey proposes three discrete situations in which a duty on the part of a social host might be imposed:

1. where a guest exhibits visible signs of intoxication and there is a likelihood that the guest will pose a risk to herself or others;
2. where a guest, to the host's knowledge, consumes a significant amount of alcohol and a reasonable person might have reason, particularly in the absence of signs of sobriety, to suspect that s/he might be intoxicated; or
3. where a host has personal knowledge of the drinking habits of the guest and knows that the latter is intoxicated and will drive.[51]

Even in the event of one of these situations arising, liability would be predicated on the reasonable foreseeability of the risk of injury, the host's failure to take reasonable steps to prevent the risk from materializing, and evidence that the host's negligence caused or contributed to the injury. Thus, a social host will not be liable if they did not know that the guest would be driving,[52] if the guest appeared sober and had no history of impaired driving, or if the host made reasonable efforts to prevent an intoxicated guest from driving. The threshold for finding a social host liable would therefore be extremely high. Social hosts would not be asked to monitor every action of their guests or to impose limitations on guests who pose no reasonably foreseeable risk. As Adjin-Tettey points out, we cannot expect party hosts to be "human breathalyzer machines".[53] However, we can expect them to take reasonable steps when presented with an intoxicated guest who poses a reasonably foreseeable risk to others. This might involve calling a taxi, offering overnight accommodation, or arranging an alternative means of transport. In some more extreme situations, a social host might be required to request the guest's car keys or try to physically prevent the guest from driving. What is 'reasonable' in each case will depend on the facts of the case and what might be expected of the reasonable person in those circumstances.[54] While difficult to embark upon in a social setting where the intoxicated person might be a friend, boss, or family member, the actions being proposed are ones that at least some social hosts already undertake.[55] In the event that reasonable precautions are taken the social host will have fulfilled his or her duty. The law should expect no more than that.

If a duty on the part of social hosts were to be recognized, it would not involve them being asked to do anything that is unreasonable in the circumstances or that at least some of them do not already do. In fact, the Canadian campaign against drunk driving over the past few decades, supported and enacted by government and non-government organizations alike, has put the responsibilities of social hosts in the public eye. In many ways social host liability would ensure that the law caught up to practices that are already recommended and increasingly being followed.

C. Personal Autonomy and the Neo-liberal Private Party

The final issue to be dealt with is the Court's assertion that social host liability will intrude on a guest's personal autonomy and diminish their individual responsibility. These claims are summed up by the Court's statement that:

> A person who accepts an invitation to attend a private party does not park his autonomy at the door. The guest remains responsible for his or her conduct. Short of active implication in the creation or enhancement of the risk, a host is entitled to respect the autonomy of a guest. The consumption of alcohol, and the assumption of the risks of impaired judgment, is in almost all cases a personal choice and an inherently personal activity.[56]

Thus, in the absence of an "active implication" in the creation or enhancement of the risk, a host should not be required to make incursions on the autonomy of his or her guests. That the guest may pose a foreseeable risk to others appears irrelevant to the court, which seems intent on protecting the autonomy rights of individuals to drink irresponsibly without interference from their friends. The court's reasoning on this issue is cast in the individualized and decontextualized language of neo-liberalism that has become so central to Supreme Court jurisprudence in recent years.[57] The rhetoric of choice, autonomy, and personal responsibility, epitomized in such recent Supreme Court decisions as *Nova Scotia v. Walsh*[58] and *Gosselin v. Quebec*,[59] has reconstituted a broad range of social issues in highly individualized terms, both with respect to causes and solutions.[60] In this brave new world of individual choice, it does not seem incongruous for a court to speak of an inebriated guest's 'autonomy', or of an impaired driver's 'personal choice'. The reality, however, is that such an approach ignores both the social relationship the guest has with his or her host and the community responsibility we all have to protect third parties from the dangers of drunk drivers. A guest's 'autonomy' should not be understood as exempting a social host from taking reasonable precautions to prevent a foreseeable risk.

It is in fact ironic that the court uses the language of individual autonomy and personal choice to deal with an issue that is clearly treated by at least some government bodies as having both a personal and community component. For example, recognition of the safety-related responsibilities of party hosts is already part of the Liquor Control Board of Ontario's campaign against drunk driving. The Board distributes a pamphlet at its liquor outlets that provides tips on how to avoid problems when hosting a private party.[61] They include finding out how guests will be going home from the party, having a plan in place to deal with guests who drink too much, serving drinks yourself rather than having an open bar, being prepared to have guests stay overnight, and ceasing to serve alcohol a few hours before the party ends. The Liquor Control Board of Ontario obviously does not think that such actions detract from the autonomy of party guests or that they impose too inordinate a burden on hosts. In fact, it deems such host behaviour 'socially responsible'. That the court should have such a different view on this issue seems out of step with recommended community standards. The imposition of a duty on social hosts is both consistent with and supportive of a social goal — the reduction of drunk driving — that is widely accepted by society.[62]

By suggesting that the language of autonomy and personal choice is inappropriate in this context, I do not wish to imply that guests should not bear any personal responsibility for their behaviour. To the contrary, I would expect the guest to bear the lion's share of any damages awarded, and there is no suggestion that the courts would view this any differently. In fact, the trial judge in *Childs* distributed liability 85 percent in favour of Desmoreaux and 15 percent in favour of the Hosts.[63] Thus, we need not worry that social host liability will somehow diminish individual responsibility. Rather, social host liability will acknowledge the role of the entire community in alcohol-related accident prevention.

IV. A NOTE ON INSURANCE

While not explicitly mentioned by the Court, concerns about the economic implications of social host liability, and confusion as to how insurance policies might apply, arguably provide the underlying subtext of decisions such as *Childs*. Some cases from the United States have unequivocally asserted that the possibility of insurance coverage is a valid consideration when determining if social host liability should be imposed.[64] Similarly, the Court of Appeal in *Childs* indicated that the availability of insurance is relevant when considering how onerous a burden the imposition of liability on a social host might be.[65]

Even if the courts were unwilling to consider insurance issues, they are obviously a relevant consideration for policy makers and the legislature.

Many of the judges and academics writing on the issue of social host liability suggest that homeowners' insurance policies will play a significant role in the management of social host liability.[66] However, as Adjin-Tettey argues, homeowners' policies are not a particularly effective avenue for securing adequate compensation for victims of accidents and may be financially ruinous to the social host.[67] First, social hosts may not carry homeowners' or renters' insurance because, unlike car insurance, it is not compulsory. In such situations, the victim would have little chance of recovering the full amount and the host would likely lose everything. Second, the amount of insurance carried is highly variable and the individual's homeowners' policy might not cover omissions. This again might lead to an uneven ability to collect from social hosts. While these concerns are not without merit, they should not preclude the possibility of social host liability. In fact, there are a number of practical options available in the event of social host liability being imposed that would alleviate these insurance-related concerns. For example, the trial judge in *Childs* (Sup. Ct.), who ultimately concluded that the issue of social host liability was a matter for the legislature, suggested that if liability were to be legislatively imposed a new social host insurance scheme could be created.[68] Social hosts would then be required to obtain additional insurance coverage to cover foreseeable accidents caused by a driver who had been drinking at a private party. The trial judge also suggested that the government create a fund, perhaps paid for through alcohol related profits, to cover compensation where the insurance coverage is exhausted.[69] Certainty in relation to both of these schemes could be enhanced if legislatures were to strictly define the circumstances in which liability would be imposed.[70]

A second insurance-related concern expressed by those who oppose social host liability is that the homeowner/social host will be unable "to spread the cost" of liability.[71] This argument is usually made in contrast with commercial hosts who can spread the cost of insurance against liability among their customers. While concerns about the suitability of homeowners' insurance to deal with social host liability seem appropriate, the cost spreading argument appears to miss the purpose of tort law. The critical issue is not whether the homeowner can pass the cost on, but whether tort law should be used to spread the risk over a large segment of society through the device of insurance, rather than imposing the entire risk on the innocent victim of drunk driving. Homeowners' premiums will inevitably go up, but the homeowner's inability to pass that cost on to others is no more persuasive than that same argument would be in relation to automobile liability insurance or, for that matter, for homeowners' insurance as it currently exists.[72] It is therefore questionable whether insurance-related policy considerations should continue to be used to exclude the finding of a duty of care, especially given that "current public policy and opinion seem to favour zero-tolerance for drunk driving."[73]

V. CONCLUSION

In Canada, an average of 205,156 crashes are caused by impaired driving each year, resulting in 1,211 deaths, 74,181 injuries, and 45,174 damaged vehicles. In turn, this costs Canadians an average of $1.8 billion a year.[74] Impaired driving is also by far the single largest criminal cause of death in Canada.[75]

These statistics suggest that drunk driving is an issue that affects all Canadians and that we all have an interest in reducing its occurrence. The Supreme Court's suggestion that the risks associated with hosting a party where alcohol is served are "a far cry from inviting participation in a high-risk sport or taking people out on a boating party" is simply not true.[76] A private party at which alcohol is served is exactly the kind of social situation that produces alcohol-related accidents. Holding social hosts liable for failing to take reasonable precautions to prevent reasonably foreseeable risks should be one part of a larger community response to what is a devastating social problem.[77] The decision in *Childs*[78] seems to take a different approach. While it does not preclude social host responsibility in the 'right' circumstances, it makes it hard to imagine a situation in which the court would be comfortable in imposing liability. The court does refer to hosts who "actively implicate" themselves in the creation of the risk,[79] but its subsequent reasoning suggests that policy issues might still prevent a duty from being imposed. It is thus safe to say that we remain a long way from social host liability being the law of Canada.

(f)   E-link(s) and Further Reading

- Laura Wright, "A crusader finds contentment", *Ottawa Citizen*, December 28, 2009.

B. Police Investigations

(g)   *Hill v. Chief Constable of West Yorkshire*†

U.K. House of Lords

[LORD KEITH OF KINKEL:]

In 1975 a man named Peter Sutcliffe embarked upon a terrifying career of violent crime, centred in the metropolitan police area of West Yorkshire. All his victims were young or fairly young women. Between July 1975 and November 1980 he committed 13 murders and eight attempted murders upon such women, the *modus operandi* in each case being similar. Sutcliffe's last victim was a 20-year-old student called Jacqueline Hill, whom he murdered in Leeds on 17 November 1980. By chance, Sutcliffe was arrested in suspicious circumstances in Sheffield on 2 January 1981, and confessed to the series of murders and attempted murders following interrogation. On 22 May 1981, at the Central Criminal Court, Sutcliffe was convicted of *inter alia* the murder of Miss Hill.

Miss Hill's mother and sole personal representative now sues the Chief Constable of West Yorkshire, claiming on behalf of Miss Hill's estate damages on the ground of negligence, for *inter alia* loss of expectation of life and pain and suffering. The defendant is sued under section 48(1) of the Police Act 1964, enacting that the chief officer of police for any police area shall be liable in respect of torts committed by constables under his direction and control in the performance or purported performance of their functions. The plaintiff in her statement of claim sets out the 20 offences committed by Sutcliffe before the death of Miss Hill and avers that the circumstances of each of these were such that it was reasonable to infer that all were committed by the same man, and further that it was foreseeable that, if not apprehended, he would commit further offences of the same nature. The pleadings go on to allege that it was accordingly the duty of the defendant and all officers in his police force to use their best endeavours and exercise all reasonable care and skill to apprehend the perpetrator of the crimes and so protect members of the public who might otherwise be his future victims. A substantial number of matters are set out and relied upon as indicating that the West Yorkshire police force failed in that duty. It is unnecessary to set out these matters in detail. They amount broadly to allegations of failure to collate properly information in possession of the force pointing to Sutcliffe as a likely suspect, and of failing to give due weight to certain pieces of information while according excessive importance to others.

The defendant, without delivering defences, applied under R.S.C., Ord. 18, R.19 to have the statement of claim struck out as disclosing no reasonable cause of action. That application was granted by Sir Neil Lawson, sitting as a judge of the High court, on 19 December 1985. Upon appeal by the plaintiff the Court of Appeal [1988] Q.B. 60 (Fox and Glidewell L.JJ. and Sir Roualeyn Cumming-Bruce), on 19 February 1987, affirmed Sir Neil Lawson. The plaintiff now appeals, with leave given in the Court of Appeal, to your Lordship's House.

---

† [1987] UKHL 12 (28 April 1987).

In considering whether the statement of claim was rightly struck out it must be assumed that the averments of fact therein contained are true. In particular, it must be assumed that in the course of their investigations into the series of crimes committed by Sutcliffe the West Yorkshire police force made a number of mistakes which they would not have made if they had exercised a reasonable degree of care and skill such as would have been expected to be displayed in the circumstances by an ordinarily competent police force. It must also be assumed, though this is not specifically averred in the statement of claim, that had they exercised that degree of care and skill Sutcliffe would have been apprehended before the date upon which he murdered Miss Hill, with the result that that particular crime would not have been committed.

The question of law which is opened up by the case is whether the individual members of a police force, in the course of carrying out their functions of controlling and keeping down the incidence of crime, owe a duty of care to individual members of the public who may suffer injury to person or property through the activities of criminals, such as to result in liability in damages, on the ground of negligence, to anyone who suffers such injury by reason of breach of that duty.

There is no question that a police officer, like anyone else, may be liable in tort to a person who is injured as a direct result of his acts or omissions. So he may be liable in damages for assault, unlawful arrest, wrongful imprisonment and malicious prosecution, and also for negligence. Instances where liability for negligence has been established are *Knightly v. Johns* [1982] 1 W.L.R. 349 and *Rigby v. Chief Constable of Northamptonshire* [1985] 1 W.L.R. 1242. Further, a police officer may be guilty of a criminal offence if he wilfully fails to perform a duty which he is bound to perform by common law or by statute: *Reg. v. Dytham* [1979] Q.B. 722, where a constable was convicted of wilful neglect of duty because, being present at the scene of a violent assault resulting in the death of the victim, he had taken no steps to intervene.

By common law police officers owe to the general public a duty to enforce the criminal law: *Reg. v. Commissioner of Police of the Metropolis, Ex parte Blackburn [1968] 2 Q.B. 118.* That duty may be enforced by mandamus, at the instance of one having title to sue. But as that case shows, a chief officer of police has a wide discretion as to the manner in which the duty is discharged. It is for him to decide how available resources should be deployed, whether particular lines of inquiry should or should

not be followed and even whether or not certain crimes should be prosecuted. It is only if his decision upon such matters is such as no reasonable chief officer of police would arrive at that someone with an interest to do so may be in a position to have recourse to judicial review. So the common law, while laying upon chief officers of police an obligation to enforce the law, makes no specific requirements as to the manner in which the obligation is to be discharged. That is not a situation where there can readily be inferred an intention of the common law to create a duty towards individual members of the public.

Counsel for the appellant, however, sought to equiparate the situation to that which resulted in liability on the ground of negligence in *Anns v. Merton London Borough Council* [1978] A.C. 728. There the borough were under a duty, imposed by legislation, to supervise compliance with building bye-laws, in particular as regards the construction of foundations. It was held that though the borough had a discretion whether or not to carry out an inspection of foundations in any particular case, in order to check compliance, once a decision had been made to carry out an inspection the borough owed to future owners and occupiers of the building in question a common law duty to exercise reasonable care in the inspection. In the present case, so it was maintained, the respondent, having decided to investigate the Sutcliffe murders, owed to his potential future victims a duty to do so with reasonable care.

The foundation of the duty of care was said to be reasonable foreseeability of harm to potential future victims if Sutcliffe were not promptly apprehended. Lord Atkin's classic propositions in *Donoghue v. Stevenson* [1932] A.C. 562, 580 were prayed in aid, as was Lord Wilberforce's well-known two stage test of liability in negligence in *Anns* [1978] A.C. 728, 751, 752.

It has been said almost too frequently to require repetition that foreseeability of likely harm is not in itself a sufficient test of liability in negligence. Some further ingredient is invariably needed to establish the requisite proximity of relationship between plaintiff and defendant, and all the circumstances of the case must be carefully considered and analysed in order to ascertain whether such an ingredient is present. The nature of the ingredient will be found to vary in a number of different categories of decided cases. In the *Anns* case there was held to be sufficient proximity of relationship between the borough and future owners and occupiers of a particular building the foundations of which it was decided to inspect, and there was also a close relationship between the borough and the builder who had constructed the foundations.

In *Dorset Yacht Co. Ltd, v. Home Office* [1970] A.C. 1004, Lord Diplock said of Lord Atkin's proposition:

> Used as a guide to characteristics which will be found to exist in conduct and relationships which give rise to a legal duty of care this aphorism marks a milestone in the modern development of the law of negligence. But misused as a universal it is manifestly false.

Earlier at p. 1058, he had said:

> ... the judicial development of the law of negligence rightly proceeds by seeking first to identify the relevant characteristics that are common to the kinds of conduct and relationship between the parties which are involved in the case for decision and the kinds of conduct and relationships which have been held in previous decisions of the courts to give rise to a duty of care.

The *Dorset Yacht* case dealt with a situation where some Borstal boys, who, having record of previous escapes, were encamped on Brownsea Island under the supervision of prison officers and escaped in the night while their guardians slept, boarded a yacht moored nearby in order to make their way to the mainland and manoeuvred it so as to damage the plaintiffs' yacht. One of the features of the case was that the damage sustained by the plaintiffs was the direct consequence of a tortious act done with conscious volition by a third party responsible for his own acts, which was interposed between the allegedly negligent conduct of the prison officers and the damage suffered. The actual decision, which was on a preliminary point of law, was that a special relationship existed on the one hand between the prison officers and the Borstal boys who were in their custody, and on the other hand between the prison officers and the owners of yachts moored near the encampment. That the boys might seek to make use of a yacht in order to get away to the mainland and might damage it in the process was the very thing which the prison officers ought reasonably to have foreseen. The prison officers had brought the boys, of whose propensity to attempt escape they were aware, into the locality where the yachts were moored and so had created a potential situation of danger for the owners of those yachts. Accordingly liability was capable of being established on the facts.

However, the class of persons to whom a duty of care might be owed to prevent the escape of detainees was held to be limited. Lord Diplock said at pp. 1070–1071:

The risk of sustaining damage from the tortious acts of criminals is shared by the public at large. It has never been recognised at common law as giving rise to any cause of action against anyone but the criminal himself. It would seem arbitrary and therefore unjust to single out for the special privilege of being able to recover compensation from the authorities responsible for the prevention of crime a person whose property was damaged by the tortious act of a criminal merely because the damage to him happened to be caused by a criminal who had escaped from custody before completion of his sentence instead of by one who had been lawfully released or who had been put on probation or given a suspended sentence or who had never been previously apprehended at all. To give rise to a duty on the part of the custodian owed to a member of the public to take reasonable care to prevent a Borstal trainee from escaping from his custody before completion of the trainee's sentence there should be some relationship between the custodian and the person to whom the duty is owed which exposes that person to a particular risk of damage in consequence of that escape which is different in its incidence from the general risk of damage from criminal acts of others which he shares with all members of the public.

What distinguishes a Borstal trainee who has escaped from one who has been duly released from custody is his liability to recapture, and the distinctive added risk which is a reasonably foreseeable consequence of a failure to exercise due care in preventing him from escaping is the likelihood that in order to elude pursuit immediately upon the discovery of his absence the escaping trainee may steal or appropriate and damage property which is situated in the vicinity of the place of detention from which he has escaped.

So long as Parliament is content to leave the general risk of damage from criminal acts to lie where it falls without any remedy except against the criminal himself the courts would be exceeding their limited function in developing the common law to meet changing conditions if they were to recognise a duty of care to prevent criminals escaping from penal custody owed to a wider category of members of the public than those whose property was exposed to an exceptional added risk by the adoption of a custodial system for young offenders which increased the likelihood of their escape unless due care was taken by those responsible for their custody.

I should therefore hold that any duty of a Borstal officer to use reasonable care to prevent a Borstal trainee from escaping his custody was owed only to persons whom he could reasonably foresee had property situate in the vicinity of the place of detention of the detainee which the detainee was likely to steal or appropriate and damage in the course of eluding immediate pursuit and recapture. Whether or not any person fell within this category would depend upon the facts of the particular case including the previous criminal and escaping record of the individual trainee concerned and the nature of the place from which he escaped.

The *Dorset Yacht* case was concerned with the special characteristics or ingredients beyond reasonable foreseeability of likely harm which may result in civil liability for failure to control another man to prevent his doing harm to a third. The present case falls broadly into the same category. It is plain that vital characteristics which were present in the *Dorset Yacht* case and which led to the imposition of liability are here lacking. Sutcliffe was never in the custody of the police force. Miss Hill was one of a vast number of the female general public who might be at risk from his activities but was at no special distinctive risk in relation to them, unlike the owners of yachts moored off Brownsea Island in relation to the foreseeable conduct of the Borstal boys. It appears from the passage quoted from the speech of Lord Diplock in the *Dorset Yacht* case that in his view no liability would rest upon a prison authority, which carelessly allowed the escape of an habitual criminal, for damage which he subsequently caused, not in the course of attempting to make good his getaway to persons at special risk, but in further pursuance of his general criminal career to the person or property of members of the general public. The same rule must apply as regards failure to recapture the criminal before he had time to resume his career. In the case of an escaped criminal his identity and description are known. In the instant case the identity of the wanted criminal was at the material time unknown and it is not averred that any full or clear description of him was ever available. The alleged negligence of the police consists in a failure to discover his identity. But if there is no general duty of care owed to individual members of the public by the responsible authorities to prevent the escape of a known criminal or to recapture him, there cannot reasonably be imposed upon any police force a duty of care similarly owed to identify and apprehend an unknown one. Miss Hill cannot for this purpose be regarded as a person at special risk simply because she was young and female. Where the class of potential victims of a particular habitual criminal is a large one the precise size of it cannot in principle affect the issue. All householders are potential victims of an habitual burglar, and all females those of an habitual rapist. The conclusion must be that although there existed reasonable foreseeability of

likely harm to such as Miss Hill if Sutcliffe were not identified and apprehended, there is absent from the case any such ingredient or characteristic as led to the liability of the Home Office in the *Dorset Yacht* case. Nor is there present any additional characteristic such as might make up the deficiency. The circumstances of the case are therefore not capable of establishing a duty of care owed towards Miss Hill by the West Yorkshire Police.

That is sufficient for the disposal of the appeal. But in my opinion there is another reason why an action for damages in negligence should not lie against the police in circumstances such as those of the present case, and that is public policy. In *YuenKun Yeu v. Attorney General of Hong Kong* [1988] A.C. 175, 193, I expressed the view that the category of cases where the second stage of Lord Wilberforce's two stage test in *Anns v. Merton London Borough Council* [1978] A.C. 728, 752 might fall to be applied was a limited one, one example of that category being *Rondel v. Worsley* [1969] 1 A.C. 191. Application of that second stage is, however, capable of constituting a separate and independent ground for holding that the existence of liability in negligence should not be entertained. Potential existence of such liability may in many instances be in the general public interest, as tending towards the observance of a higher standard of care in the carrying on of various different types of activity. I do not, however, consider that this can be said of police activities. The general sense of public duty which motivates police forces is unlikely to be appreciably reinforced by the imposition of such liability so far as concerns their function in the investigation and suppression of crime. From time to time they make mistakes in the exercise of that function, but it is not to be doubted that they apply their best endeavours to the performance of it. In some instances the imposition of liability may lead to the exercise of a function being carried on in a detrimentally defensive frame of mind. The possibility of this happening in relation to the investigative operations of the police cannot be excluded. Further it would be reasonable to expect that if potential liability were to be imposed it would be not uncommon for actions to be raised against police forces on the ground that they had failed to catch some criminal as soon as they might have done, with the result that he went on to commit further crimes. While some such actions might involve allegations of a simple and straightforward type of failure — for example that a police officer negligently tripped and fell while pursuing a burglar — others would be likely to enter deeply into the general nature of a police investigation, as indeed the present action would seek to do. The manner of conduct of such an investigation must necessarily involve a variety of decisions to be made on matters of policy and discretion, for example as to which particular line of inquiry is most advantageously to be pursued and what is the most advantageous way to deploy the available resources. Many such decisions would not be regarded by the courts as appropriate to be called in question, yet elaborate investigation of the facts might be necessary to ascertain whether or not this was so. A great deal of police time, trouble and expense might be expected to have to be put into the preparation of the defence to the action and the attendance of witnesses at the trial. The result would be a significant diversion of police manpower and attention from their most important function, that of the suppression of crime. Closed investigations would require to be reopened and retraversed, not with the object of bringing any criminal to justice but to ascertain whether or not they had been competently conducted. I therefore consider that Glidewell L.J., in his judgment in the Court of Appeal in the present case [1988] Q.B. 60, 76, was right to take the view that the police were immune from an action of this kind on grounds similar to those which in *Rondel v. Worsley* [1969] 1 A.C. 191 were held to render a barrister immune from actions for negligence in his conduct of proceedings in court. My Lords, for these reasons I would dismiss the appeal.

[LORD TEMPLEMAN (concurring, with the following reasons:):]

The appellant, Mrs. Hill, is tormented with the unshakeable belief that her daughter would be alive today if the respondent the West Yorkshire police force had been more efficient. That belief is entitled to respect and understanding. Damages cannot compensate for the brutal extinction of a young life and Mrs. Hill proposes that any damages awarded shall be devoted to an appropriate charity. Damages awarded by the court would not be paid by any policeman found wanting in the performance of his duty but would be paid by the public. Mrs. Hill therefore brings these proceedings with the object of obtaining an investigation into the conduct of the West Yorkshire police force so that lives shall not be lost in the future by avoidable delay in the identification and arrest of a murderer.

The question for determination in this appeal is whether an action for damages is an appropriate vehicle for investigating the efficiency of a police force. The present action will be confined to narrow albeit perplexing questions, for example, whether, discounting hindsight, it should have been obvious to a senior police officer that Sutcliffe was a prime suspect, whether a senior police officer should not have been deceived by an evil hoaxer, whether an officer interviewing Sutcliffe should have been better briefed, and whether a report on Sutcliffe should have been given greater attention. The court would have to consider the conduct of each police officer, to decide whether the policeman failed to attain the standard of care of a hypothetical average policeman. The court would have to decide whether an inspector is to be condemned for failing to display the acumen of Sherlock Holmes and whether a constable is to be condemned for being as obtuse as Dr. Watson. The plaintiff will presumably seek evidence, for what it is worth, from retired police inspectors, who would be asked whether they would have been misled by the hoaxer, and whether they would have identified Sutcliffe at an earlier stage. At the end of the day the court might or might not find that there had been negligence by one or more members of the police force. But that finding would not help anybody or punish anybody.

It may be, and we all hope that the lessons of the Yorkshire Ripper case have been learned, that the methods of handling information and handling the press have been improved, and that co-operation between different police forces is now more highly organised. The present action would not serve any useful purpose in that regard. The present action could not consider whether the training of the West Yorkshire police force is sufficiently thorough, whether the selection of candidates for appointment or promotion is defective, whether rates of pay are sufficient to attract recruits of the required calibre, whether financial restrictions prevent the provision of modern equipment and facilities, or whether the Yorkshire police force is clever enough and if not, what can and ought to be done about it. The present action could only investigate whether an individual member of the police force conscientiously carrying out his duty was negligent when he was bemused by contradictory information or overlooked significant information or failed to draw inferences which later appeared to be obvious. That kind of investigation would not achieve the object which Mrs. Hill desires. The efficiency of a police force can only be investigated by an enquiry instituted by the national or local authorities which are responsible to the electorate for that efficiency.

Moreover, if this action lies, every citizen will be able to require the court to investigate the performance of every policeman. If the policeman concentrates on one crime, he may be accused of neglecting others. If the policeman does not arrest on suspicion a suspect with previous convictions, the police force may be held liable for subsequent crimes. The threat of litigation against a police force would not make a policeman more efficient. The necessity for defending proceedings, successfully or unsuccessfully, would distract the policeman from his duties.

This action is in my opinion misconceived and will do more harm than good. A policeman is a servant of the public and is liable to be dismissed for

incompetence. A police force serves the public and the elected representatives of the public must ensure that the public get the police force they deserve. It may be that the West Yorkshire police force was in 1980 in some respects better and in some respects worse than the public deserve. An action for damages for alleged acts of negligence by individual police officers in 1980 could not determine whether and in what respects the West Yorkshire police force can be improved in 1988. I would dismiss the appeal.

(h) *Doe v. Metropolitan Toronto (Municipality) Commissioners of Police*†

Ontario Court of Justice (Gen. Div.)

[MacFARLAND J.:]

Jane Doe was raped and otherwise sexually assaulted at knifepoint in her own bed in the early morning hours of August 24, 1986 by a stranger subsequently identified as Paul Douglas Callow. Ms. Doe then lived in a second-floor apartment at 88 Wellesley Street East, in the City of Toronto; her apartment had a balcony which was used by the rapist to gain access to her premises. At the time, Ms. Doe was the fifth known victim of Callow who would become known as "the balcony rapist".

Ms. Doe brings a suit against the Metropolitan Toronto Police Force (hereafter referred to as MTPF) on two bases; firstly she suggests that the MTPF conducted a negligent investigation in relation to the balcony rapist and failed to warn women whom they knew to be potential targets of Callow of the fact that they were at risk. She says, as the result of such conduct, Callow was not apprehended as early as he might otherwise have been and she was denied the opportunity, had she known the risk she faced, to take any specific measures to protect herself from attack. Secondly, she said that the MTPF being a public body having the statutory duty to protect the public from criminal activity, must exercise that duty in accordance with the Canadian Charter of Rights and Freedoms and may not act in

a way that is discriminatory because of gender. She says the police must act constitutionally, they did not do so in this case and as the result, her rights under ss. 15 and 7 of the Charter have been breached. She seeks damages against the MTPF under both heads of her claim.

. . . .

OVERVIEW

It is necessary when considering claims under s. 15 of the Charter that they be considered in relation to the larger social, political and legal context...

In this respect the plaintiff called Dr. Peter Jaffe, well experienced in the topic of male violence against women, to give evidence in relation to the social and political context in which the plaintiff's discrimination claim is made.

In his evidence Dr. Jaffe cited a number of surveys and studies which have concluded that a very large number of Canadian women have been sexually assaulted by Canadian men. This social phenomenon is not new and has been known for many years.

The evidence establishes beyond peradventure that among adults, the perpetrators of sexual violence are overwhelmingly male and the victims over-

---

† 39 O.R. (3d) 487 (Ontario Court (General Division).

whelmingly female. It is not disputed that this fact was known to the MTPF in 1986.

As Dr. Jaffe explained, sexual violence is a form of violence; it is an act of power and control rather than a sexual act. It has to do with the perpetrator's desire to terrorize, to dominate, to control, to humiliate; it is an act of hostility and aggression. Rape has nothing to do with sex, everything to do with anger and power.

It is accepted that one of the consequences of the pervasiveness of male sexual violence in our society is that most women fear sexual assault and in many ways govern their conduct because of that fear. In this way male sexual violence operates as a method of social control over women. For example, women are likely to avoid activities which they perceive may put them at risk of male sexual violence. They will, for example, avoid going out alone in the evening. As plaintiff's counsel put it in written submissions: "The sexual victimization of women is one of the ways that men create and perpetuate the power imbalance of the male-dominated gender hierarchy that characterizes our society."

It is also proved, on the evidence, that the majority of sexual assaults committed against women are not reported to police, a fact of which the MTPF was also aware in 1986. The evidence establishes, to my satisfaction, that a reason many sexual assault victims do not report to police is because they have concern about the attitudes of the police or courts to this type of incident and this fact has been recognized by the Supreme Court of Canada: see *R. v. Osolin*, [1993] 4 S.C.R. 595 at p. 628, 109 D.L.R. (4th) 478, where Madam Justice L'Heureux-Dubé said in part:

> One of the most powerful disincentives to reporting sexual assaults is women's fear of further victimization at the hands of the criminal justice system; as I discussed in *Seaboyer, supra*, at p. 650, almost half of unreported incidents may be traced to this perception on the part of sexual assault victims. With good reason, women have come to believe that their reports will not be taken seriously by police and that the trial process itself will be yet another experience of trauma.

For those women who do report the fact that they have been sexually assaulted, the police constitute their first contact with the criminal justice system. At this preliminary stage, the police can and do act as a filtering system for sexual assault cases. If, for example, an investigating officer determines that a particular complaint is "unfounded", it likely will not proceed further in the justice system. Studies exist which show that, generally, the "unfounded" rate for crimes of assault is lower than for crimes of sexual assault.

One of the reasons suggested for the higher "unfounded" rate in relation to sexual assaults is the widespread adherence among investigating police officers to rape mythology, that is, the belief in certain false assumptions, usually based in sexist stereotyping, about women who report being raped. The fact that these stereotypical beliefs are widely held in society is a factor to be considered in relation to the larger social and political context in which this aspect of the plaintiff's claim must be analyzed.

Dr. Jaffe in his evidence gave a number of examples of common rape myths:

- that women lie about being raped;
- that women are not reliable reporters of events;
- that women are prone to exaggerate;
- that women falsely report having been raped to get attention.

In general, in matters relating to rape and sexual assault women tend to report things which have no basis in fact. There exists the belief that the report is false, grossly exaggerated or is done for another purpose such as attention seeking, essentially that women either precipitated or falsely reported rapes. The literature documents in far more detail and provides more examples of commonly held rape myths involving the attribution of stereotypical characteristics to survivors of rape and other serious sexual assaults.

The existence of rape myths is not something new; their existence and widely held belief among members of society in general has been well-known at least since the early 1970s when rape trauma began to be studied in a serious way.

Certainly those persons engaged in the various fields of endeavour that would cause them to come into contact with survivors of sexual assault would have been aware of the Rape Trauma Syndrome and Rape Mythology from as early as the mid-1970s.

All of the investigative police personnel called to give evidence in this proceeding were aware of these matters in 1986 and earlier.

Every police officer who testified in this proceeding repeated the mantra that sexual assault was a very serious crime second only to homicide.

[Note: The judge went on to review reports prepared for the Toronto Police Force, including a 1975 Report of the Police Committee that indicated serious systemic problems in investigating allegations of rape, and a Task Force established in

1982 to respond to a spate of violence and rapes against women and children. This was known as the Godfrey Task Force. It too concluded that there was a need for better training of police officers with respect to violence against women. She continued:]

In September 1983 the MTPF responded to the preliminary report of the Task Force intending to specifically focus on the recommendations directed at the MTPF. They agreed with each and every one of the observations and recommendations noted above. The MTPF reported that a course outline and proposed syllabus had been developed for "Sexual Assault and Child Abuse Investigative Techniques" to deal with victims of sexual assault and their unique problems. The course would be a week long, would include guest lecturers from various professions dealing with sexual assault victims and would start in October of "this year" — i.e., October of 1983.

. . . .

Again the Task Force noted that historically sexual assaults have a low rate of reportage and the need for the co-ordination of sexual assault investigations on a Metro-wide basis.

. . . .

It would appear then from the written material emanating from the MTPF to the public that by March 1984, MTPF not only knew and understood the importance and the necessity of the training of all officers in relation to the investigation of sexual assaults,

- that officers be taught and understand the Rape Trauma Syndrome and Rape Mythology.

. . . .

The office of the Sexual Assault Co-ordinator was created in direct response to the recommendations of the Task Force on Public Violence against Women and Children — or the Godfrey Task Force as it became known. Its function in a very general sense was to look into the sexual abuse of adults generally, to catalogue and categorize all aspects of these crimes, to act as a liaison with other agencies both internal and external to the force and to train police officers. [Note: the officer appointed was Det. Sgt. Boyd.]

. . . .

In September 1986 Ms. Boyd authored a report which her immediate superior passed up the chain of command. That report clearly set out the problems the MTPF was still having as of that date. Ms. Boyd confirmed in her evidence that these problems were not new as of the date of this report — September 29, 1986 — but had been ongoing to her knowledge from early 1985. There was some effort made to address these problems by a training blitz over the summer of 1985 but the problems continued into 1986 and thereafter.

Detective Sgt. Boyd's report which Inspector Dennis of the Family and Youth Services sent on to Supt. Maywood of Investigation Services was a hard-hitting document. The problems were clearly stated and set out. Inspector Dennis remarked in his covering memorandum:

- this police force is not meeting the needs of sexual assault victims.
- the MTPF has committed to improving the method to which we respond to sex assault victims. Although the Police Force has agreed, the officers in the field are not meeting that commitment.
- the monitoring of these (sexual assault) investigations has revealed that there is less adherence to the procedures, less investigation into the occurrences, less resources being utilized and a lack of understanding and support being given to the victim.

He concludes the covering memorandum with the following:

> The object of this report is not to identify individual mistakes as it should be pointed out that the problems being discussed have been seen in every division in each district. (Emphasis added)

The author of the report made the following observations which are important I think in the context of this action:

> Victims' response to sexual assault is varied. When the victim becomes overly concerned with the control she now must regain in her life, she could be described as "over reactive" and at times "obstructive". Many trained sexual assault investigators can handle this situation. However, we are finding that certain "trained" officers are unable to deal with the victims' "response". This is reflected usually in a complaint from either the victim or hospital personnel in terms of the "treatment" the victim received from the police officer.

Certain victims' statements and synopsis as shown by the occurrence reports are not accurate and a proper analysis based on the information on the synopsis is not possible. The reasons for the inaccuracies are questionable.

"Trained" sexual assault investigators are ignoring important factors dealing with forensic evidence collection ... in many cases the Identification Bureau is not notified to attend.

The "supplementary reports" to an original sexual assault occurrence are not being submitted and we cannot determine if any follow-up at all by the investigating officer has taken place.

Victims of serious sexual assaults are not being "called back" by anyone involved with the investigation. The victim has then initiated a telephone call to the police unit concerned and in essence been "brushed off".

The victim has now become not only a victim of a criminal assault, but the victim of "our" poor investigative follow-up.

Occurrence Reports reflect the investigator's belief or disbelief of the victim's complaint.

In reported incidents, the investigator disbelieves the victim but cannot advise as to what investigation he has done in support or to refute the victim's story. This is reflected by noted discrepancies, cautions of public mischief and polygraph threats.

Occurrences can be cleared based on judgments of character and comments on victim's behaviour and not as established by investigation or lack of forensic evidence.

It is observed that although the Godfrey Task Force recommended the establishment of a Sexual Assault Co-ordinator and the training of specialized sexual assault co-ordinators — and although the Force responded to both recommendations the incidents, which are the subject of the report, demonstrate that "we have some trained field personnel that have done a poor job of not only investigating a criminal sexual assault but have also done a poor job of dealing with the victim!"

. . . . .

In spite of the problems noted in the 1975 MTPF's own report on rape, the recommendations of the Godfrey Task Force and the reports from the Sexual Assault Co-ordinator's office — the problems in relation to the investigation of sexual assault by the MTPF continued in 1985 and 1986. While public pronouncements were made to the effect that steps had been taken to implement the various recommen-

dations made, the reality was that the status quo remained unchanged. Whatever the changes were that may have been implemented they were clearly ineffective.

As Inspector Jean Boyd would note to Chief Marks in 1987:

> The bottom line is we are going to get roasted very soon if we don't get our act together. *Over three years have passed since the recommendations were tabled and we are not very much further ahead* except that Margo does a considerable amount of in-house and community speaking. WAVA has identified and it is accepted that more intensive training is required. (Emphasis added)

The Specific Investigation

[Note: the judge reviewed the investigations conducted with respect to the first four of Paul Callow's rape victims, noting a pattern of disbelieving the complainants for a range of reasons and with delayed or minimal follow-up. In some cases, police officers told the complainants they might be subject to public mischief complaints for making false allegations. Of course, in the course of events, all were established to have been raped by the same serial rapist following an identifiable pattern of conduct. The judge continued:]

Sergeant Cameron believes, through inquiries he made of the Sexual Assault Co-ordinator, Det. Sgt. Boyd, he learned of the P.A. occurrence and had spoken to her by on or about August 5, 1986.

As of August 3, 1986 Sgt. Cameron was assisted in the investigation by Det. Sgt. Derry who, in his own words, took charge of the paper side of the investigation.

I am persuaded on the evidence that Messrs. Cameron and Derry were aware by August 7, 1986 that P.A., B.K., R.P. and F.D. had most probably all been attacked by the same man. It is conclusively established that they had this knowledge by August 16, 1986 when Sgt. Cameron filed a supplementary occurrence report recording the fact.

The 52 C.I.B. office is an extremely busy one and was particularly so in the summer of 1986. The police officers assigned to that office had extremely heavy caseloads and almost overwhelming responsibilities. Sergeant Cameron and Det. Sgt. Derry were no exceptions.

In August of 1986 they were both necessarily spending a significant amount of their time preparing for the trial of a fraud investigation of which they had been in charge. A review of their memo books at the time details the substantial time commitment required by that case.

Between the "Two Toes" case (as the fraud case was known) their days off and vacation times — there was little time left, I find, available to be devoted to the detailed, plodding, necessary detective work involved in the investigation of this series of sexual assaults.

They and the MTPF knew in early August 1986 that there was most likely a serial rapist attacking women who lived alone in second- and third-floor apartments with climbable balconies in the Church/Wellesley area who would most certainly attack again.

Yet for all intents and purposes — prior to August 24, 1986 — only Sgts. Cameron and Derry were assigned to the investigation. Even when they were otherwise unavailable no one else was specifically assigned to take up this investigation on their behalf.

The contrast between this investigation and that conducted into the Annex Rapist earlier the same summer is extreme. In that case, a task force was created to conduct the investigation with a number of officers assisting Det. Sgt. Reilly and his partner, Glen Sinclair, who were in charge of that investigation. There was significant media coverage whereby in addition to the information contained in the majors, the MTPF gave interviews to the press detailing those occurrences.

In that case the area of the attacks was searched and the neighbourhoods canvassed. Those doing the canvass were not instructed not to reveal the fact that they were investigating sexual assaults.

As Det. Sgt. Reilly explained, they were desperate; they had nothing to go on and the violence of the attacks was escalating. The police feared the next victim may be killed. He felt a duty to protect the women living in this area who faced a very specific threat of attack by this predator. It would be not only inappropriate but neglectful were he simply to sit back at his desk and wait for a break.

As it turned out in that case, a tenant who moved into the premises vacated by Dawson Davidson (the Annex Rapist), found a wallet which he had apparently left behind. That tenant turned the wallet over to the landlord who contacted the secretary of the wallet's owner who in turn called police. The wallet belonged to one of Dawson Davidson's victims. This was the lucky break police needed and Davidson was arrested shortly later in Vancouver. The fact of Davidson's arrest was also publicized in local papers.

. . . .

I am satisfied that the only significant difference in the two investigations was the nature of the attacks themselves or as it has been characterized in submissions the "high level of violence" in the case of the Annex Rapist and the comparatively "low level of violence" in the case of the Balcony Rapist. The urgency that appeared to drive the investigation of the Annex Rapist was noticeably absent in the investigation of the Balcony Rapist to at least after August 29, 1986 and after Callow attacked his fifth known victim, the plaintiff, Jane Doe.

Jane Doe

Jane Doe lived at apartment 206, 88 Wellesley Street East when she was attacked in the early hours of August 24, 1986 by Paul Douglas Callow. As he had with other victims, Callow covered Ms. Doe's eyes with a pillow case, threatened her with the knife he had in his possession and spoke conversationally with her during the attack. He raped her and otherwise sexually assaulted her before leaving her apartment via the front door. Entrance to Ms. Doe's apartment had been gained by means of a balcony window which she had left slightly ajar for ventilation. For the duration of the attack Callow disguised his own appearance by covering his face.

. . . .

I accept that Sgt. Cameron told Ms. Doe that he believed she had been raped by a serial rapist and that four other women had been similarly attacked. While he may not have used the word "cyclical" I find it reasonable that he indicated there was a pattern of sorts to the attacks and accept that he likely indicated in Ms. Doe's case that the rapist had struck a day early. The R.P. and F.D. attacks (the third and fourth), had taken place on the 25th day of the month and Ms. Doe was attacked on the 24th day of the month. That the officers in charge of this investigation believed that the suspect was likely to attack around the 25th of the month is borne out by the arrangements later made for a stakeout of the area to be carried out five days before and after September 25, 1986. I accept that Ms. Doe was told all victims lived on second and third floors and entry had been via balconies.

Ms. Doe expressed shock that women in the neighbourhood had not been warned that a serial rapist was in their midst. Sergeant Cameron indicated, I find, that it was not the practice to issue warnings in such cases because women would become hysterical or panic (I do not see any real difference which word he used, the meaning is the same), the rapist would flee and the investigation would be compromised. Of course it was not true that it was not the policy of the MTPF to issue warnings in such cases because it had been done in the Dawson Davidson case — just months earlier and in the very same division.

When Ms. Doe indicated that if the police were not prepared to warn area women she would[, she] was told that if she did, she may be considered to be interfering in a police investigation and she could be charged for doing so.

. . . .

By memorandum dated August 27, 1986 Sgts. Cameron and Derry for the first time requested the assistance of other officers and this, for the purpose of conducting a canvass of local apartment buildings. They requested that all apartments on the first, second and third floors of each building be checked. The additional officers were to be instructed to tell tenants only that there had been a number of break and enters in the area and specifically instructed not to mention the sexual assaults. They were to note any single females living in the apartments canvassed.

Later in a memorandum dated September 7, 1986 Sgt. Derry indicated to Staff Sgt. Bukowski as follows:

> It is important that the officers check each apartment in order to establish the hair colour of the women and receive information from the people interviewed regarding prowlers etc.

On that same day Sgt. Cameron by memorandum detailed to Inspector Cowling, the officer in charge of 52 C.I.B. office, his request for manpower and equipment necessary for a stakeout to be carried out the five days before and after September 25, 1986. The operation is detailed as follows:

> The operation would run as follows:
>
> 1) Using the streets as boundaries each group of apartments would be covered by two, three or four men.
> 2) Each group of men would have at least one unmarked car at their disposal in the event there is an attack and they have to move quickly.
> 3) Vans would be used as stationary observation points within the area.
> 4) The uniform cars would stay just outside of their designated area and would be used to seal off the area around the location of any attack and stop all persons on foot or in vehicles. They will be assisted by some of the old clothes men.
> 5) The remainder of the old clothes men would then enter the area of attack and search on foot for any suspect that may be hiding.
> 6) The radio room would be advised in advance of this operation and would be required to assist in sealing off the area.
> 7) Sergeants Cameron and Derry would be present and take charge of the scene and direct the operation for those ten days.
> 8) Attached hereto is a map indicating the area of concern. Further recording will be made to the map upon completion of the canvassing detail.
>
> Respectfully submitted
> William Cameron Sgt. 2887
> Kim Derry Sgt. 3373

. . . .

Once again the staff sergeants were advised that the officers conducting the canvass were "not to mention anything about sexual assaults which have occurred in the area but to advise people contacted that this is a crime prevention program and that single women are victims of break and enters and theft". Officers were to obtain the names and addresses of single women and note their hair colour.

The stakeout proceeded as planned. Unmarked vehicles were used and those participating were informed the only time the cover would be broken was in the event they observed someone attempting to climb a balcony in which event the person was to be stopped. The stakeout did not produce any useful information except that for all the covertness of the operation, crime in the area of the stakeout was almost entirely eliminated for its duration. Obviously the criminal element was aware of the police presence.

It has been suggested that the women who occupied these apartments were being used as "bait". The police adamantly denied the suggestion which they say implies that they knew who would, and when an attack would occur, when in fact they had no idea who would, where, or even if an attack would occur. I can only conclude on the evidence that the police believed it to be a virtual certainty that there would be another attack and that it would be made against one of the women their canvass had identified as a potential target and in view of the fact that the last three victims had been attacked on the 24th or 25th of the month that the attack would likely take place during that general time period in

the month — the entire stakeout operation was premised on the assumption of these factors.

The police were there to wait and watch for an attack to occur. The women were given no warning and were thereby precluded from taking any steps to protect themselves against such an attack. Unbeknownst to them they were left completely vulnerable. When all of these circumstances are taken and considered together, it certainly suggests to me that the women were being used — without their knowledge or consent — as "bait" to attract a predator whose specific identity then was unknown to the police, but whose general and characteristic identity most certainly was.

The break in the investigation came when probation officer Debbie Alton contacted P.C. Gary Ellis of the 52 C.I.B. office to check a criminal record for her. Police Constable Ellis had arrested one, Paul Douglas Callow, on June 6, 1986 for assaulting his wife Jackie. Not being a "sexual" assault, the Sexual Assault Co-ordinator's office was not aware of this information. To me it is indicative that the MTPF as a whole did not understand the fundamental — that sexual assault is not about sex, it is about violence and anger against women. Had the force co-ordinated efforts to keep track of any and all acts of violence against women, they may have been aware of Callow's existence much sooner than they were. On September 24, 1986 Ms. Alton was preparing a pre-sentence report on Callow. Ms. Alton told P.C. Ellis that Callow had not been truthful with her about his previous criminal record and requested that he check it out for her. Callow's wife had told Ms. Alton that her husband had been convicted for rape in Vancouver which involved Callow "doing a break and enter then finding a woman sleeping and then raping her". According to the supplementary occurrence report prepared by P.C. Ellis, Callow's wife had indicated that her husband "has a sex problem (wants it all the time), booze problem and drug problem and he is still doing break and enters". Jackie Callow lived at 33 Maitland Street in the Church/Wellesley area and indicated her husband was in the area frequently and that she recently had problems with him.

Subsequent investigation would reveal that Paul Douglas Callow had, in May 1981, raped an elderly woman who resided in a fifth-floor apartment at 220 Wellesley Street East. The circumstances of that rape — for which Callow was arrested by the MTPF — were hauntingly similar to the *modus operandi* employed by him in the five rapes with which this action is concerned. Charges were not proceeded with in that case because of the age and health of the victim.

Police at the time felt reasonably confident however that Callow was responsible for that rape and noted that the *modus operandi* was similar to that used by Callow in the Vancouver rape in 1978 for which he was convicted and sentenced to four years imprisonment.

. . . .

Sergeants Cameron and Derry both indicated they did not want a media blitz alerting the public to this danger because they did not want their suspect to flee as Dawson Davidson had. The discussions, they say, which were ongoing in the 52 C.I.B. office where they worked, were to the effect that Dawson Davidson had left the jurisdiction because of the intense media coverage given to his criminal activity at the time. Additionally, they say the overwhelming and obvious police presence was a contributing factor in his departure.

For these reasons Derry and Cameron adopted the "low profile" approach[, with] next to no media coverage of the events, no community programs to specifically warn women in the area of the attacks and any additional police presence to be of a covert nature. This was also the reason that officers conducting the canvas were specifically told not to inform tenants about the sexual assaults. As Cameron and Derry said they believed their suspect lived in the neighbourhood and they could be knocking on his door during the canvass or the door of his wife or girlfriend; he would then be tipped off that a manhunt was under way and be likely to flee because of it.

. . . .

In any event Callow was soon after put under constant surveillance and arrested October 3, 1986. He ultimately confessed to having committed all five rapes. After the commencement of the preliminary inquiry he pled guilty and was sentenced in total to a period of incarceration of 20 years.

CONCLUSION

. . . .

Decision Not to Warn

As I have said, Sgts. Cameron and Derry determined that this investigation would be "low key" compared to the investigation conducted into the "Annex Rapist" and no warning would be given to the women they knew to be at risk for fear of displacing the rapist leaving him free to re-offend elsewhere undetected.

I am not persuaded that their professed reason for not warning women is the real reason no warning was issued.

Firstly, there is evidence that the Annex Rapist, Dawson Davidson, did not flee to Vancouver because of the media attention paid to his crimes and/or the obvious increased police presence in the neighbourhood. Indeed, much of the coverage occurred after Davidson had already left Toronto.

. . . .

There was, I find, no "policy" not to issue warnings to potential victims in these cases — clearly warnings had been given in the Dawson Davidson Annex Rapist investigation — warnings with which incidentally all defence expert witnesses agreed were appropriate in the circumstances.

I find that the real reason a warning was not given in the circumstances of this case was because Sgts. Cameron and Derry believed that women living in the area would become hysterical and panic and their investigation would thereby be jeopardized. In addition, they were not motivated by any sense of urgency because Callow's attacks were not seen as "violent" as Dawson Davidson's by comparison had been.

I am satisfied on the evidence that a meaningful warning could and should have been given to the women who were at particular risk. That warning could have been by way of a canvass of their apartments, by a media blitz — by holding widely publicized public meetings or any one or combination of these methods. Such warning should have alerted the particular women at risk, and advised them of suggested precautions they might take to protect themselves. The defence experts, with the exception of Mr. Piers, agreed that a warning could have been given without compromising the investigation on the facts of the case.

Even the experienced defence expert witnesses Det. Inspector Kevin Rossmo and former FBI special agent McCrary agreed that as Det. Inspector Rossmo said:

> The police have a responsibility to release a balanced volume of information to protect the community ... where that balance is will depend on the particular facts of the case.

In my view it has been conceded in this case clearly and unequivocally by the Chief of Police at the time, Jack Marks, that no warning was given in this case and one ought to have been. His public response to the proposals of the group known as Women against Violence against Women in the aftermath of this investigation presented to the Board of Commissioners of Police could not in my view be any clearer when he said:

> I would concede that for a variety of reasons unique to the Church/Wellesley investigation, no press release in the nature of a general warning was issued and [acknowledge] that one should have been. This is not only a matter for concern and regret, but action has already been taken to prevent a similar breakdown from occurring in the future. Specifically, the Sexual Assault Co-ordinator who monitors all of these offences has been directed to ensure that members of the public are informed about such matters which may affect their safety. These warnings will be directed toward all potential victims with special attention given to members of the public who have been identified as most at risk, e.g. as in the case at hand, women living in high-rise buildings in the downtown area would be targeted as a high risk group and requiring extra efforts to bring the potential risk to their attention.

I accept and agree entirely with these remarks.

. . . .

I am satisfied on Ms. Doe's evidence that if she had been aware a serial rapist was in her neighbourhood raping women whose apartments he accessed via their balconies she would have taken steps to protect herself and that most probably those steps would have prevented her from being raped.

Section 57 of the Police Act, R.S.O. 1980, c. 381 (the governing statute at the time these events occurred), provides:

> 57. ... members of police forces ... are charged with the duty of preserving the peace, preventing robberies and other crimes ...

The police are statutorily obligated to prevent crime and at common law they owe a duty to protect life and property. As Schroeder J.A. stated in *Schacht v. R.*, [1973] 1 O.R. 221 at pp. 231–32, 30 D.L.R. (3d) 641:

> The duties which I would lay upon them stem not only from the relevant statutes to which reference has been made, but from the common law, which recognizes the existence of a broad conventional or customary duty in the established constabulary as an arm of the State to protect the life, limb and property of the subject.

110

In my view, the police failed utterly in their duty to protect these women and the plaintiff in particular from the serial rapist the police knew to be in their midst by failing to warn so that they may have had the opportunity to take steps to protect themselves.

It is no answer for the police to say women are always at risk and as an urban adult living in downtown Toronto they have an obligation to look out for themselves. Women generally do, every day of their lives, conduct themselves and their lives in such a way as to avoid the general pervasive threat of male violence which exists in our society. Here police were aware of a specific threat or risk to a specific group of women and they did nothing to warn those women of the danger they were in, nor did they take any measures to protect them.

[Note: the judge also concluded on the evidence that the conduct of the police was discriminatory and compromised Jane Doe's security of the person contrary to the Canadian Charter of Rights. This evidentiary finding was later combined with a legal analysis of sections 15 (equality), s. 7 (security of the person) and s. 1 (reasonable limits), leading to a conclusion that damages were payable to Jane Doe for breach of her Charter rights by the actions of agents of the state (the police).]

Negligence

My task has been rendered less onerous by the very thorough analysis of Henry J. of the issues raised by the pleading in this case reported at (1989), 58 D.L.R. (4th) 396, 48 C.C.L.T. 105 (Ont. H.C.J.), when the matter came before him on a motion to strike out the statement of claim and the succinct reasons of Moldaver J. (as he then was) on behalf of the Divisional Court (1990), 74 O.R. (2d) 225, 72 D.L.R. (4th) 580, when the decision of Henry J. went to that court on appeal.

After citing s. 57 of the Police Act, and observing that by virtue thereof the police are charged with the duty of protecting the public from those who would commit or have committed crimes, Moldaver J. (as he then was) goes on at pp. 230–31 as follows:

> To establish a private law duty of care, foreseeability of risk must coexist with a special relationship of proximity. In the leading case of *Anns v. Merton (London Borough)*, [1978] A.C. 728, [1977] 2 All E.R. 492, 121 Sol. Jo. 377 (H.L.), Lord Wilberforce defined the requirements of this special relationship as follows at pp. 751–52 A.C.:

> > First one has to ask whether, as between the alleged wrongdoer and the person who has suffered damage there is a sufficient relationship of proximity or neighbourhood such that, in the reasonable contemplation of the former, carelessness on his part may be likely to cause damage to the latter — in which case a prima facie duty of care arises.

> This principle has been approved by the Supreme Court of Canada in *Kamloops (City) v. Nielsen*, [1984] 2 S.C.R. 2, 66 B.C.L.R. 273, 29 C.C.L.T. 97, 8 C.L.R. 1, 10 D.L.R. (4th) 641, 26 M.P.L.R. 81, 54 N.R. 1, [1984] 5 W.W.R. 1.

> Do the pleadings support a private law duty of care by the defendants in this case?

> The plaintiff alleges that the defendants knew of the existence of a serial rapist. It was eminently foreseeable that he would strike again and cause harm to yet another victim. The allegations therefore support foreseeability of risk.

> The plaintiff further alleges that by the time she was raped, the defendants knew or ought to have known that she had become part of a narrow and distinct group of potential victims, sufficient to support a special relationship of proximity. According to the allegations, the defendants knew:

> (1) that the rapist confined his attacks to the Church-Wellesley area of Toronto;
> (2) that the victims all resided in second or third floor apartments;
> (3) that entry in each case was gained through a balcony door; and
> (4) that the victims were all white, single and female.

> Accepting as I must the facts as pleaded, I agree with Henry J. that they do support the requisite knowledge on the part of the police sufficient to establish a private law duty of care. The harm was foreseeable and a special relationship of proximity existed.

> Do the pleadings support a breach of the private law duty of care?

> The law is clear that in certain circumstances, the police have a duty to warn citizens of foreseeable harm. See *Schact v. R.*, [1973] 1 O.R. 221, 30 D.L.R. (3d) 641 (C.A.), affd sub nom. *O'Rourke v. Schact*, [1976] 1 S.C.R. 53, 55 D.L.R. (3d) 96, 3 N.R. 453, and *Beutler v. Beutler; Adams v. Beutler* (1983), 26 C.C.L.T. 229 (Ont. H.C.J.). The obvious purpose of the warning is to protect the citizens.

> I would add to this by saying that in some circumstances where foreseeable harm and a special relationship of proximity exist, the police might reasonably conclude that a warning ought

not to be given. For example, it might be decided that a warning would cause general and unnecessary panic on the part of the public which could lead to greater harm.

It would, however, be improper to suggest that a legitimate decision not to warn would excuse a failure to protect. The duty to protect would still remain. It would simply have to be accomplished by other means.

In this case the plaintiff claims, inter alia, that the duty owed to her by the defendants required (1) that she be warned of the impending danger; or (2) in the absence of such a warning, that she be adequately protected. It is alleged that the police did neither.

Instead she claims they made a conscious decision to sacrifice her in order to apprehend the suspect. They decided to use her as "bait". They chose not to warn her due to a stereotypical belief that because she was a woman, she and others like her would become hysterical. This would have "scared off" the attacker, making his capture more difficult.

The evidence establishes that Det. Sgt. Cameron clearly had linked the four rapes which preceded Ms. Doe's by the early days of August in 1986 and he and Det. Sgt. Derry knew that the rapist would continue to attack women until he was stopped. They knew the rapist was attacking single white women living alone in second- and third-floor apartments with balconies in the Church/Wellesley area of the City of Toronto.

On the evidence I find the plaintiff has established a private law duty of care.

Detective Sgts. Derry and Cameron determined, in the context of their investigation, that no warning would be given to any women — let alone the specific target group they had identified and among the reasons given for deciding not to warn was their view that women would panic and compromise the investigation. Detective Sgt. Cameron gave this as a reason to Ms. Doe when he interviewed her following her rape and she asked why women had not been warned.

In spite of the knowledge that police had about this sexual rapist and their decision not to warn, they took no steps to protect Ms. Doe or any other women from this known danger. In my view, in the circumstances of this case, the police failed utterly in the duty of care they owed Ms. Doe.

The decision not to warn women was a decision made by Sgts. Cameron and Derry in the course of their investigation. It was made on the basis of "shop talk" they had overheard or been a part of, according to them, in relation to the Dawson

Davidson Annex Rapist investigation. What is apparent is that neither Sgts. Cameron nor Derry made any real effort to look into that investigation and determine whether in fact it had been the publicity that caused Dawson Davidson to flee.

Their decision was based largely on rumour and "shop talk" essentially within the 52 C.I.B. and they said they relied on it alone in making the very serious decision not to warn these women of the risk they faced. This they did in the face of the almost certain knowledge that the rapist would attack again and cause irreparable harm to his victim. In my view their decision in this respect was irresponsible and grossly negligent.

There is simply no evidence before this court which could be interpreted as suggesting that no warning should have been given in the circumstances of this case. The only persuasive expert opinion called by the defence, in fact, suggests that a suitable warning could have been and should have been given. While the defence experts were careful in giving their evidence when one looks at the totality of their evidence this conclusion is irresistible.

Sergeants Cameron and Derry made a decision not to warn women in the neighbourhood and did not do so. They took no steps to protect the women they knew to be at risk from an almost certain attack in result[;] they failed to take the reasonable care the law requires and denied the plaintiff the opportunity to take steps to protect herself to eliminate the danger and ensure that she would not be attacked.

In this respect they are liable to her in damages.

. . . .

Damages

Ms. Doe precisely detailed the events of the early morning hours of August 24, 1986 in her evidence. It was obvious to everyone that giving this evidence was a difficult and painful process for her. Her attacker was armed with a knife and had concealed his identity with a mask he had fashioned and wore. The attack was terrifying and she feared for her life.

Following her call to 911 a number of police officers arrived at her apartment and over the next hours she was obliged to repeat the details of her attack to a number of officers.

She was taken to hospital for forensic testing by ambulance — an intrusive and painful process.

This attack by a stranger in her own bed in her home has had a profound and lasting effect on Ms. Doe as she stated in her evidence:

> ... my life was shattered as a result of the rape, and I experienced it literally as being shattered for at least two to three years....

. . . .

Although Ms. Doe had suffered from depression prior to August 24, 1986, this condition was greatly exacerbated as the result of the rape.

On the evidence there can be no question but that the plaintiff suffered serious post-traumatic stress immediately following the rape and she continues to this day to exhibit symptoms which are consistent in post-traumatic stress disorder — at the time of trial some 11 years after her attack.

. . . .

Dr. Rosemary Barnes gave a most helpful explanation of why sexual assault is so traumatic for individuals who experience it:

> A. There are several aspects. The person is placed in a situation where they fear that they might die and where they're violated physically and emotionally in one of the most extreme ways.
>
> The level of the kind of threat to the individual psychologically and physically is the same as the kind of threat that a person who is assaulted would experience in a front-line kind of combat situation, and in some ways is worse in the sense that the soldier in a front-line combat situation entered into a certain kind of commitment and has been trained to carry out that commitment and is prepared as much as possible for what to expect.
>
> A person who has been sexually assaulted experiences the same kind of sense that their life might be over in that moment or in the next few moments, that they're — and their body has been profoundly violated and often that they feel psychologically humiliated.
>
> The sexual assaults are also different in that they often occur in circumstances where in contrast to being in combat where the person had expected to be safe, and that's certainly the case with Ms. Doe, that she was in her own home in bed in a situation where she expected — where she was safe and was completely, unexpectedly psychologically humiliated and physically violated in the most profound way, and thought in that moment that she would — that her life actually would be over, and that it's being faced with that kind of threat of being violated and deeply humiliated, that's the basis for the intense kinds

of psychological reactions that follow from sexual assault.

That Ms. Doe has been profoundly affected by the events of August 24, 1986 in every aspect of her life cannot be doubted on the evidence. That she continues to suffer, albeit not to the extent she did in the two years immediately following the rape, to this day is agreed by all experts.

. . . .

Rape is unlike any other sort of injury incurred by accident or neglect. Survivors of rape must bear social stigmatization which accident victims do not. Rape is not about sex; it is about anger, it is about power and it is about control. It is, in the words of Dr. Peter Jaffe, "an overwhelming life event". It is a form of violence intended to create terror, to dominate, to control and to humiliate. It is an act of hostility and aggression. Forced sexual intercourse is inherently violent and profoundly degrading.

As Mr. Justice Cory stated in *R. v. Osolin*, *supra*, at p. 669:

> It cannot be forgotten that a sexual assault is very different from other assaults. It is true that it, like all the other forms of assault, is an act of violence. Yet it is something more than a simple act of violence. Sexual assault is in the vast majority of cases gender based. It is an assault upon human dignity and constitutes a denial of any concept of equality for women.

It is not helpful to compare the assessments of damages in accidental injury cases nor to look to those cases for any sort of guidance in assessing damages for rape.

Ms. Doe's life has been affected by the events of August 24, 1986 in every respect, and while she has improved considerably in the 11 years since, she continues to experience [symptomatology] related to the rape. She will never be free of the terror and the indignity that Paul Douglas Callow brought into her life and left at the very core of her being. Her condition is chronic and the persuasive evidence suggests that this is likely to continue.

In my view, damage awards in the $40,000–50,000 range are reflective of neither the horrific nature of the violation nor of the overwhelming and all-encompassing consequences of it.

In my view, an appropriate general damage award for Ms. Doe in all the circumstances of this case is $175,000.

[The judge also awarded special damages for expenses and future costs.]

(i)   Tort Actions for Police Failures in Gendered Violence Cases†

Melanie Randall

3.   The Significance of the *Jane Doe* Decision

The *Jane Doe*[23] decision necessarily raises broader legal and policy implications surrounding imposition of civil liability on police as a mechanism for oversight of this public institution. Should the civil courts be retrospectively reviewing police criminal investigations with a view to whether or not they were conducted negligently? Of course they should.[24] And the Supreme Court of Canada has clearly acknowledged this in the recent decision of *Hill v. Hamilton-Wentworth Regional Police Services Board*.[25] In *Hill*, McLachlin C.J.C., writing for the majority, stipulated:

> police are not immune from liability under the Canadian law of negligence ... [and] their conduct during the course of an investigation should be measured against the standard of how a reasonable officer in like circumstances would have acted.[26]

The *Jane Doe* case is one which demonstrates the potential for an action in private law to be explicitly animated by larger public policy concerns. As such, the case demonstrates the utility of providing a private law remedy for a harm (the failure to protect) which, though perpetrated by an individual defendant — albeit an institutional one — is actually symptomatic of a wider and socially produced harm originating out of the structures of sexual inequality.

In fact, the plasticity of the public/private distinction becomes clear in this case because much of the evidence grounds both the private law and public law claims. This distinction is also engaged because the kind of contextual analysis both required and undertaken by the Court, examining the problem of rape and the history of police responses, engages larger issues which have both public and private dimensions. By straddling the public/private law divide and demonstrating the fluidity of this dichotomy, the *Jane Doe* case suggests that it can some-times be difficult to draw a bright line dividing public and private law.

The decision in *Jane Doe* stands as a legal judgment which moves the law of negligence forward by recognizing a somewhat novel claim. By confirming the existence of a private law duty owed by police to members of the public known to be at specific risk, the case integrates a social context analysis into negligence principles. Its integration of the sex discrimination and Charter analysis into the heart of the negligence analysis is, in fact, one of the decision's most striking and important features.

IV.   *M(B.) V. BRITISH COLUMBIA (ATTORNEY GENERAL)*: DUTIES, DOMESTIC VIOLENCE AND THE POLICE

In a recent case, *M.(B.) v. British Columbia (Attorney General)*,[27] which the Supreme Court disappointingly refused to hear, the British Columbia Court of Appeal denied a woman's claim against the police, in negligence, for their failure to investigate a complaint of domestic violence. The case is important, however, because both at trial, and at the appellate level, each and every judge found on the facts, that the police owed the plaintiffs a common law duty of care. Had the case been dismissed on the grounds that no private law duty of care was owed, this would have been a significant setback in Canadian tort law. It would have restricted the possibilities of expecting negligent public authorities to be held legally accountable for the harms they cause or contribute to, in relation to those members of the public they are empowered to serve and protect (a particularly salient mandate when the defendant is the police), and who are known to be at a specific risk of injury. While the case is certainly no major legal victory or milestone, the recognition of a private law duty on the facts, is a significant development.

---

† "Private Law, the State, and the Duty to Protect: Tort Actions for Police Failures in Gendered Violence Cases" in Sanda Rodgers, Rakhi Ruparela, and Louise Belanger-Hardy, eds., *Critical Torts* (Toronto: Butterworths, 2008) 343 at 352–70. [Notes/references omitted.] Reproduced with permission of LexisNexis Canada Inc.

Because a private law duty of care was found in an appellate level judgment to be owed by the police, the case advances and builds upon the finding from a lower court in *Jane Doe* about police duties in relation to violence against women. But on the facts of *M. (B.)*, both the trial level judge and the majority at the Court of Appeal found that the liability was negated by the lack of a sufficient causal connection between the breach of the duty and the violence which the plaintiffs ultimately suffered. While the duty analysis in *M. (B.)* is a positive development in the law of tort in Canada, the actual result of the case is disappointing, and is based both on shaky reasoning and a failure to apprehend the nature and dynamics of domestic violence.

1. The Facts of *M. (B.)* and the Foreseeable Risk of Harm (Which Should Have Been Known by the RCMP)

B.M. had separated from R.K., her estranged common law husband, at the time of the violent events which formed the subject of the civil action. R.K. had been violent to B.M. on a number of occasions prior to their separation, including one conviction for a serious assault with a weapon. On that occasion, and in relation to the only violent incident B.M. had reported to the police, she tried, as so many assaulted women do under pressure from violent male intimates, to have the charges against R.K. dropped. She also refused to testify at the criminal trial. Nevertheless, R.K. received a brief jail sentence (21 days) and a year's probation.

After their separation and because they had property matters to resolve, B.M. agreed to meet R.K. at a park where she felt it was safe to see him because it was "an open public place".[28] When R.K. became agitated during their discussion, B.M. got back into her vehicle and tried to leave, but R.K. tried to block her departure. She ultimately had to drive around R.K.'s truck which he manoeuvred to try to prevent her exit. He sped after her in chase, but B.M. was able to elude him.

Knowing his history of extreme violence, not only to her but before she met him, B.M. went to the police station to make a complaint about R.K.'s behaviour, to register her fear, and to seek police protection from him. However, the RCMP constable, who questioned her only briefly, decided that there were insufficient grounds to recommend a complaint under section 810 of the *Criminal Code* and declined to take any action in relation to the threat she reported. Instead he recommended to B.M. that she

see a lawyer to get a restraining order and suggested she stay in "public places". This advice was offered in spite of the fact that the constable had read B.M.'s statement, spoken with her directly and reviewed a copy of R.K.'s lengthy criminal record. Ironically, we see here a police officer, representing a public authority, telling a domestic violence victim that her best option was to seek a "private" remedy to deal with the complaint she tried to have the public authority take seriously.[29]

In B.M.'s case there was clear provincial domestic violence legislation. Specifically, the Ministry of the Attorney General for British Columbia had legislated policy, adopted by the RCMP, requiring an assertive and timely police response to domestic violence, including the mandatory enforcement of judicial protective orders. Decades of feminist intervention, community advocacy and law reform have sought to have the "private" issue of domestic violence translated into one of public responsibility and yet in this instance a police representative blithely ignored both the physical presence of and request for help from a fearful woman known to have been violently assaulted ("proven" beyond a reasonable doubt) in the face of the crystal clear directive of the provincial policy requiring prompt and effective police response.

A number of weeks later, R.K. arrived at B.M.'s property with a shotgun, smashed open her door, entered the house, shot and killed B.M.'s friend Hazel White, shot B.M.'s 12-year-old daughter in the shoulder, causing her injury and disability, and terrifying B.M. and her younger daughter. B.M. and her daughters managed to flee. R.K. then set fire to the house and killed himself.

In failing to take any action in relation to B.M.'s police complaint a number of weeks before the assault and murder, the police failed to grasp the dynamics of domestic violence and the particular risk faced by women who have recently separated from violent men. This is a period of time which is well documented and thoroughly researched in the domestic violence literature, demonstrating typical patterns of escalating domestic violence — including threats of suicide — and the fact that separation is the period of highest risk for further assault and/ or for spousal homicide or intimate homicide.[30]

But even more directly pertinent than this general knowledge about the high-risk period, the police knew that R.K. had an extensive history of criminal violence directed not only at B.M. but at others. This violence included convictions for manslaughter for a previous murder (of a girlfriend's boyfriend), several counts of sexual assault, forcible confinement, assault causing bodily harm, theft, and breaking and entering.[31] In fact, the trial judge described the assault B.M. reported to police and for which he was convicted, as "brutal".[32] Clearly, then, the police should have been well aware of the foreseeable risk of harm to B.M. (and others), that R.K. posed. Yet this risk was disregarded and she was left to fend for herself.

2. The Duty of Care Analysis in *M. (B.)*

In light of the larger failures of judicial reasoning in the trial judge and Court of Appeal's majority decision, the only positive development from the case is the recognition of the duty of care owed by the police and some of the powerful arguments advanced in the Court of Appeal's dissenting judgment explicating why the duty was owed.

Justice Donald, writing in dissent at the Court of Appeal, devotes the most sustained attention to the question of duty, and strongly asserts that the state has a duty to protect victims of domestic violence, a duty entrenched in policy. In his words, in analyzing the cause of action:

> Reference must be made to the policies laid down by the Ministry of the Attorney General and adopted by the RCMP in relation to domestic violence. They relate not only to the special proximity between police and complainants but they also give content to the duty of care and set the standard of care. The general duty of the police is to protect, but in the area of domestic violence the degree of protection is *heightened by government policy. The discretion whether to act on a complaint is very limited.*[33]

Justice Donald distinguished the facts of *M. (B.)* from *Hill v. Chief Constable of West Yorkshire*, a leading U.K. judgment in which a duty of care was not found to be owed by the police because the class of plaintiffs was too wide, and those at risk of harm from the offender were not, beyond all being female, a distinct and identifiable group. In Donald J.A.'s words:

> The facts in the instant case are quite different from *Hill* ... B.M. sought police assistance and had a direct engagement with an officer when she presented her complaint. She had a pressing need for protection as a potential victim of R.K.'s violence and the police should have recognized that. She cannot be said to fall into a large indeterminate class; to the contrary she was a person, in Lord Keith's words at 243 of *Hill. supra*, with a "special distinctive risk".[34]

In this way, then, in Donald J.A.'s analysis the foreseeability and proximity components of the duty analysis were clearly satisfied. Furthermore, there were no policy reasons to strike out the duty. To the contrary, government domestic violence policy directing proper police conduct strenuously reinforced its very existence and, further, imported specific content to the standard of care owed in relation to this duty.

In the majority decision Hall J.A. does not expressly undertake a duty analysis because he finds that the case is "more appropriately decided on a causation analysis".[35] However, a causation analysis presupposes the existence of a duty owed; otherwise undertaking the legal assessment of whether or not causation is met is gratuitous. This offers implicit support for the grounding of a duty, and, in any event, Hall J.A. does not at any point in the judgment strike out the finding of the trial judge that a duty is owed. Justice Smith also decides the case on causation, so the same points obtain in relation to his judgment. Furthermore, he finds that the trial judge, who did find the existence of a common law duty owed by the RCMP, "applied correct principles", and "made no error that would justify our intervention ... in his application of legal principle[s]".[36] In sum, then, the trial judge had no difficulty finding that a duty of care was owed by the police, the majority judgment at the Court of Appeal did not dispute this legal finding and, in dissent, Donald J.A. offered a sustained and persuasive analysis underwriting why it must be found to exist.

3. Causation and the Misapprehension of the Dynamics of Domestic Violence

The tort action failed at the British Columbia Court of Appeal on the issue of causation. Two of the three appellate judges supported the trial judge's finding that the temporal remove between the time of the RCMP's failure to investigate B.M.'s complaint and the date of R.K.'s homicidal shooting spree negated the finding of any factual causal connection.

In dissent, however, Donald J.A. approached the question of causation through a material contribution to the loss analysis, and found that the police breach of their duty and failure to meet the standard of care owed to B.M. added to the risk of the occurrence to a degree "above *de minimis*".[37] Justice Donald argued that the action should not be defeated because of an overly restrictive analysis of factual causation. He explained that:

> In the present matter, the general duty of care on the police to provide protection was height-

ened by government policy addressing the serious problem of domestic violence. The duty owed to potential victims of spousal abuse would be virtually unenforceable if claimants had to do more than show a material contribution of the risk because of the difficulty of proof to which I have referred. To insist upon strict proof would leave a right without a remedy.[38]

However, the "right" to police protection and the deprivation of a legal remedy in the face of its absence did not deter the Justices who formed the majority from denying the claim based on their approach to causation. Recognizing that the traditional "but for" test of causation is unworkable in some circumstances, either because of difficulties with regard to proof (such as in medical cases or complex multi-causal industrial diseases such as those resulting from asbestos exposure) Hall J.A. reviewed alternative causation analyses but found that none were applicable to the facts of B.M.'s case.

As Hall J.A. opined, the action in *M. (B.)* "involves a situation where the third party R.K. intentionally acted, causing harm to the plaintiff and her dependants".[39] Asserting that the trial judge's causation analysis was owed considerable deference because it was a "factual finding",[40] Hall J.A. found that R.K.'s violent break-in, shooting and murder occurred at a "considerable remove in time" from the report B.M. made to the police approximately six weeks earlier. Justice Hall then continued to sever the "what happened" on the date that R.K. killed B.M.'s friend, injured her daughter and terrorized her family, as if it were an isolated and separate event entirely disconnected from the well-documented pattern of domestic violence R.K. had demonstrated. As Hall J.A. constructed it:

> Notwithstanding the extant legal hazards and restraints that were applicable to R.K., he embarked on a course of violent conduct. This event seems to have been triggered by his anger over the proposed use to be made of the property.[41]

In this way Hall J.A. (mis)represents R.K.'s violence not as part of a continued campaign of harassment and intimidation typical of severe domestic violence but instead as a series of discrete and autonomous incidents, over which the police had no control. Simultaneously he seems to suggest that the "legal restraints" already imposed on the offender were useless, a suggestion conveniently in line with the judicial failure to believe that the police could and should — as they were directed to do by unambiguous government policy — have inter-

vened to investigate B.M.'s complaint, and escalate the legal constraints on the offender to put him on notice that there were forceful interventions to interrupt and contain his threatening behaviour. Justice Smith is even more explicit in characterizing R.K.'s murderous rampage as a "discrete traumatic event" and found that the police officer's inaction "did not materially contribute to the harm beyond *de minimis*".[42]

Perhaps most troubling was the majority judicial finding that the RCMP Constable's failure to investigate B.M.'s complaint against R.K. was unrelated to his "murderous rage".[43] This perceived disconnect between the negligent police failure to take any action in the face of a domestic violence victim's report of threatening behaviour by a known, very violent convicted offender, still legally bound by the terms of a section 810 *Criminal Code* order to "keep the peace", even when the police were "emphatically" statutorily bound to provide an "assertive and timely" response, speaks volumes about judicial failure to grasp the problem of domestic violence.

Particularly absent in these judicial analyses was any awareness of the escalated risk women face of further violence and/or of being killed in the immediate and short-term post-separation period. Both Smith and Hall JJ.A. described R.K.'s behaviour as erratic, unpredictable and out of control. Had Hall and Smith JJ.A. realized that perpetrators of intimate violence *typically* become easily enraged and prone to intensify their campaigns of intimate terrorization of the spouses who "dared" to leave them, they might not so easily have mischaracterized R.K.'s murderous rage as some kind of bizarre event disconnected from the already criminalized patterns of violence and control he had exhibited so often in the past, both distant and recent. Instead of being unpredictable, the tragic unfolding of events was rather textbook, and certainly predictable as an outcome not unlikely to occur.

Only Donald J.A., in dissent, seemed more sensitized to the risk of further violence R.K. posed. He commented that the "experienced trial judge predicted further violence and gave B.M. an assurance that the authorities would respond to any complaint if she was threatened again".[44] Further he pointed out that, "by not dealing with R.K.'s intimidation and threatening behaviour, the police failed to reduce the risk of more violence".[45]

At play in the case is the way in which dominant misperceptions about violence against women, and victim and perpetrator behaviour shaped not only the legal decision-making but also the police response. When she arrived at the police station to make a report and seek police enforcement of the section 810 *Criminal Code* order, the receptionist who first encountered her described B.M. as upset and frightened and noted that her hands "shook violently".[46] And yet, the police officer who interviewed her moments later and who refused to take action in response to B.M.'s complaint described her as "calm". This is a characterization he no doubt used to rationalize his inaction, but also one which perhaps led him to dismiss and discount her reports about the level of the threat the perpetrator posed. Clearly an assumption was operating about how a "real" victim should react in order to convey the level of threat and fear she experiences,[47] revealing yet another dangerous stereotype and the consequent radical minimization of the risk of domestic violence.

4. Significance of *M. (B.)*: Negligence, Accountability and Public Policy

Surprisingly, B.M.'s cause of action appears to have been pleaded strictly in private law terms, exclusively around a claim of negligence. Yet the facts seem to call out for a legal analysis which centrally foregrounds the constitutional issues also at stake, in particular the sex discrimination and equality issues implicated in the issue of domestic violence.[48] These include not only the discrimination analysis of a section 15 claim, but also the breach of section 7 rights to security of the person, all of which are implicated in state actors' failure to act effectively — *in the face of an explicit set of policies mandating them to do so* — to protect assaulted women. However, even only in private law terms, this case represents a failed opportunity to have common-law imposed state accountability for obvious police negligence, in the face of a clear and unambiguous government policy removing police discretion and directing them to investigate reports of domestic violence.

Although the outcome of *M. (B.)*[49] is troubling, there is no reason to suggest that future actions along these lines might not succeed. Given that the duty analysis seems relatively uncontentious (though even that cannot be guaranteed given that the Supreme Court of Canada declined to review the case), the greatest hurdles appear to lie in mounting a successful causation analysis. But this will perhaps be less onerous on different facts, which might, for example, involve a more specific breach of police duty, and with a more enlightened bench, both more attuned to the complexities of domestic violence and more committed to a more robust approach to issues of causation as well as to tort law's ability to be infused with social justice concerns.

Justice Donald, writing in dissent, noted that on the facts of *M. (B.)* and in the face of "emphatic" government policy requiring "an assertive and timely police response to domestic violence", the *"right to police protection in these circumstances is so strong and the need for teeth in the domestic violence policy so great* that the causal linkage must be found sufficient to ground liability".[50] As one commentator on the case astutely pointed out. "declining leave to appeal in the Mooney case, the Supreme Court of Canada passed over the opportunity to consider the issue of causation in the context of third-party perpetrators and professional protectors; but almost certainly — tragically — that opportunity will come again."[51]

V. THE LEGAL CONTOURS OF STATE ACCOUNTABILITY FOR FAILURE TO PROTECT[52]

Surprisingly, the common law has barely been used in Canada in order to impose liability on the police for the many cases of domestic violence and spousal homicide which involved police failures to enforce restraining orders or otherwise effectively intervene in the face of a known risk. But this does not mean that it will not or should not be in the future.

The risk of spousal homicide is one element of the problem of domestic violence. In Ontario, several high-profile Coroner's inquests have been called into the well-publicized deaths of Arlene May and Gillian Hadley.[53] Both of these women were killed at the hands of their male partners, and in each case, their stories starkly demonstrate the failure of state protection and concretize the kinds of system failures which should be legally actionable and which should, in some cases, attract liability. The juries in both inquests received submissions from a broad range of parties, including many that were explicitly informed by an equality rights and feminist perspective,[54] and in each case extensive lists of recommendations were advanced following the inquests.

In both cases, the murdered women had been subjected to ongoing and escalating abuse perpetrated by their male intimates, and they had repeatedly sought the intervention and protection of the police and the criminal justice system, for example, by reporting the assaults against them to the police and seeking protective orders. Despite seeking legal help, each woman ended up dead.

When Randy Iles killed his estranged spouse, Arlene May, he had a lengthy criminal history including convictions for indecent exposure, harassing phone calls, probation breaches, possession of stolen property and a weapons offence. At the time of the murder (and his suicide) there was one warrant for his arrest in a neighbouring jurisdiction, and another warrant for breaching his recognizance by contacting Arlene May in defiance of a court order not to do so. A condition of his bail terms was the surrender of his Firearms Acquisition Certificate, yet he was not actually compelled to relinquish it by anyone associated with the criminal justice system. As a result, while out on bail Iles was able to purchase the gun with which he killed his spouse.

Gillian Hadley was murdered by her estranged husband in her own house. Just moments before her death she had desperately handed her baby over to a neighbour, who had vainly tried to intervene in the standoff. This dramatic aspect of the story received considerable media attention. Less attention was paid, however, to the fact that at the time he perpetrated this murder, her killer was facing charges for criminal harassment and was also under court order to keep away from her.

While their experiences may seem extreme, what the tragic stories of Arlene May and Gillian Hadley illustrate is the more typical pattern of ongoing abuse and failed state interventions which characterize so many cases of intimate femicide. Furthermore, in direct contradiction to dominant myths about assaulted women's passivity, helplessness and/or complicity in the face of domestic violence, both of these deceased women's stories are filled with examples of their *repeated and persistent attempts to engage the criminal justice system* and use all legal remedies available to them to secure their own safety. The extensive and sweeping set of recommendations issued from each of these inquests (many of which were originally issued in the first report and then repeated in the second) languish largely unimplemented.

The even more recently released 2006 report of the Ontario Death Review Committee provides further documentation[55] that many intimate femicides are preventable with co-ordinated and skilled intervention. Based on a review of actual case files of women murdered by their intimates, these reports have identified common risk factors often present, and which could have allowed properly trained domestic violence professionals to have predicted and intervened to prevent a domestic homicide, had an effective system-wide response been in place.

The stories of failure to protect and failure to intervene which can be found in the Death Review reports, and in the lives and deaths of Arlene May and Gillian Hadley, provide clear examples of the kinds of tragedies which should give rise to justicia-

ble claims, not only constitutionally but at common law. It is not only spousal homicides which might give rise to these claims, though these are often the starkest examples. It is also the case that too often it is the most marginalized, vulnerable and socially unvalued women — poor, racialized, those who work in the sex trade — who suffer the greatest disregard from state agencies like the police. The systemic state failure in general, and police failure, in particular, to take seriously violence against Aboriginal women, including the now well-documented cases of multiple disappearances and murders of Aboriginal women, particularly in Vancouver and Edmonton, for example, is a problem crying out for legal consequences.

In Canada, research has documented the significantly higher rates of intimate violence, including child sexual abuse, sexual assault and domestic violence, experienced by Aboriginal women. Part of the imbrications of racism, colonialism and sexism, are the stories of murders and disappearances of Aboriginal women across Canada, which have not been treated with any serious, sustained or adequate police attention. The great number of Aboriginal women who "disappeared" from Vancouver's east side, whose disappearances and suspected murders were barely investigated by the police over the years, and who turned out to have been murdered by Robert Pickton is only the most recent example of police neglect.[56] The Native Women's Association of Canada's "Sisters in Spirit" campaign is dedicated to researching, documenting and remedying the alarmingly high rates of violence against Aboriginal women, and the systemic neglect of this social problem, dating back to the abduction and murder of Helen Betty Osborne in 1971.[57]

So systemic is the problem of the disappearance and sexualized murders of Aboriginal women in Canada that the issue has received international attention from Amnesty International, which published a report entitled, *Stolen Sisters: Discrimination and Violence Against Indigenous Women in Canada*.[58] The Amnesty International report begins its scathing expose of the neglect of crimes against Aboriginal women by reminding readers that an inquiry into the death of Helen Betty Osborne criticized the police for their sloppy and racist investigation, and for taking a decade and a half before one of the four men was brought to justice. Reviewing other instances of police disregard of sexual assaults, abductions and murders of indigenous women in Canada, the authors observe that, "in every instance,'" Canadian authorities should have done more to ensure the safety of these women and girls or to address the social and economic factors that helped put them in harm's way.[59]

These by now well-publicized examples of police neglect of crimes against Aboriginal women, and police and other system failures to protect in cases of spousal homicide and other cases of intimate violence, illustrate the ways in which too many women encounter massive gaps in criminal justice system responses — gaps, omissions and failure to protect which render them vulnerable to further harm, and deny them equal protection of and under the law. These gaps and failures must be made subject to legal scrutiny.

VI. PRIVATE LAW REMEDIES FOR PUBLIC HARMS: THE PUBLIC/ PRIVATE DISTINCTION, THE STATE AND THE ROLE OF LAW

Delineating where the "private" ends and the sphere of the public begins has proven to be a notoriously challenging exercise, and one which tort scholars have engaged from a variety of perspectives. Some argue that tort law is and ought to remain just that — a fundamentally private law adjudication of rights, conflicts and disputes between the particular parties involved, which should necessarily be disconnected from any broader social or policy implications or justice concerns, including equality concerns.[60] Others argue, to the contrary, that tort law can and should be concerned with its public dimensions and can and should be engaged with egalitarian goals. Tsachi Keren-Paz, for example, argues that tort law "can and should be used progressively as one mechanism in the ongoing struggle to achieve a more just and egalitarian society".[61]

In arguing that states should be subjected to private law tort claims (as well as other legal actions) for their failures to protect in cases of gendered violence, I am necessarily arguing for a view of tort law which sees private law as infused with public dimensions as well as for a view of tort law which, like Keren-Paz, sees it as a potential private law source of engagement with broader social justice issues. *Jane Doe*[62] was a legal action, for example, undertaken in private law but one that straddled the public/private legal divide. Given the complicated character of the divisions between public and private, the *Jane Doe* litigation and the *M. (B.)*[63] case, despite its underdeveloped legal analysis, illuminate how private legal actions can explicitly engage much wider public policy dimensions.

Critics have claimed that courts should not be engaged in a way that "interferes" with police work. But negligence and discrimination should not be insulated from legal liability by the policy-making role of public authorities. There is scarcely a private law question which does not have some public dimensions, and both *Jane Doe* and *M (B.)* illustrate the relationship between the public and the private in law in Canada.

The typical policy reasons public authority defendants often successfully advance for immunizing themselves from civil liability cannot obtain in cases such as these. I would go even further, however, and suggest that the policy arguments running through much of the case law[64] to protect government actors from owing a private law duty of care, or a constitutionally enforceable obligation, are tenuous at best, and provide far too wide a scope of protection from liability for state agencies. In fact, contrary to the view that policy should insulate state actors from private law liability, I would argue that there are more compelling policy arguments supporting the view that liability in tort should be imposed on the state (when the elements of the claim are made out). In other words, policy should support private law liability for the state, not insulate the state from it. Only a private law action potentially allows injured parties not only to have the symbolic legal recognition that their rights have been violated, but to have compensation awarded to restore them to the position they would have been in but for the state's negligent conduct toward them.

Given how difficult and overwhelmingly costly it is to mount a civil action, the vast majority of potential plaintiffs, even those with the worthiest claims, are more often than not effectively precluded from pursuing a legal remedy, demonstrating how overblown the "floodgates" concerns are, although courts are fond of identifying them. The access to justice issues plaguing the Canadian legal system have even been explicitly noted by the Chief Justice of the Supreme Court of Canada.[65] But beyond access to justice issues, while political processes allow for changes of government, only legal processes can specifically enable those directly harmed by government action or inaction, to seek a remedy against a public authority.

VII. CONCLUSION

In cases of violence against women, police inaction has proved deadly. A necessary function of the law here is to counteract the deeply rooted power of cultural framing devices, through liability, the ultimate social determination of wrongness.[66]

The trend towards refusing to recognize that public authorities such as the police can and should owe a private law duty of care and/or a constitutional obligation to citizens has been part and parcel of the larger protection of the state from private law liability. Given that one of the major legal remedies for a social problem such as violence against women is found in the state's commitment to protect those whose lives are at risk, state accountability for ensuring the adequacy of this protection may require legally imposed responsibility in the face of institutional carelessness or disregard, intransigence and denial of responsibility. It is also imperative that state accountability be imposed for failure to protect or for negligence related to other expressions of systemic discrimination.

The persistent absence of adequate legal protections for assaulted women in Canada poses a violation of a number of legally guaranteed rights, protected, in theory at least, both at common law and constitutionally. These rights must be justiciable and negligence is one important way to seek remedies for harms related to state failures. While constitutional rights protections are highly important they do not provide what private law does — that is compensation for the harms to the plaintiff caused by the negligent defendant, compensation which is the mechanism through which to attempt to put the plaintiff, as much as is possible, back in the position she would have been in, but for the defendant's negligence.

The concern that the imposition of civil liability on the police and other state agencies should be severely curtailed in order to keep the floodgates closed is problematic on many levels. This concern was raised after the release of the publicized *Jane Doe*[67] decision, and is an argument raised in virtually every case involving the police, or indeed, other public authorities. It is, however, a specious argument premised on faulty assumptions. There is no reason to presume that it will provoke uncontrolled pressure on the courts from eager litigants. Too many forces, including formidable access to justice barriers, conspire against this possibility. Even if it did, that is what the law is supposed to do — adjudicate and settle legal disputes and legal rights claims.

Along these lines, in contrast to the view that the "tort crisis" revolves around too many claims and too much liability — a particular concern for public authorities — it could be argued that there is not enough liability imposed upon negligent state agencies and that not enough claims are brought forward. Indeed, Richard Abel argues that the "real tort crisis is old, not new. It is a crisis of underclaiming rather than overclaiming".[68]

Tort law in general, and negligence in particular, provide legal remedies for harms or injuries caused by the careless conduct of those who owe us a duty to prevent foreseeable harms. When it is the state whose negligent conduct has caused or contributed to the harm, however, the scope of liability is often significantly restricted, for policy reasons which are, in the main, overly broad and sometimes completely untenable. Challenging these restrictions is part of the project of using law to move towards social justice and keeping tort law's potential dynamism alive and well.

Despite the difficulties that attach to tort actions, such actions are one way for citizens to force external public scrutiny of insular and self-protective institutions such as the police. Compensation for harms suffered is an important remedy available only through civil litigation. Where there is a duty owed to a plaintiff or class of plaintiffs, it is for the courts to determine liability and to establish the parameters of accountability within which institutions of the state must operate. Policy considerations should not form a legal shield behind which state agencies can be negligent or discriminate with impunity. We must continue to push the boundaries of the liberal state towards a state committed to substantive equality and positively bound to providing the conditions for its realization.

Tort law can and should play a role in the broader strategy of realizing substantive equality, and constitutional values can and sometimes should be drawn upon in developing negligence analyses intended to ground state accountability.[69] The Supreme Court of Canada has, in fact, expressly stipulated that tort law is to be developed and applied in accordance with Charter values.[70]

Subjecting state failures, inaction, and neglect both to constitutional and common law scrutiny, and pursuing test case litigation to establish positive duties flowing from the constitutional guarantee of equality as well as rights at common law, is a way of posing a direct legal challenge to the dominant construction of the liberal, minimalist, and non-interventionist state. As part of the legal arsenal available to undertake this challenge, tort law has a role to contribute, and this role needs insistently to be expanded.

(j) *Hill v. Hamilton-Wentworth Regional Police Services Board*†

Supreme Court of Canada

[McLACHLIN C.J. (for the majority of the Court):]

I. INTRODUCTION

[1] The police must investigate crime. That is their duty. In the vast majority of cases, they carry out this duty with diligence and care. Occasionally, however, mistakes are made. These mistakes may have drastic consequences. An innocent suspect may be investigated, arrested and imprisoned because of negligence in the course of a police investigation. This is what Jason George Hill, appellant in the case at bar, alleges happened to him.

[2] Can the police be held liable if their conduct during the course of an investigation falls below an acceptable standard and harm to a suspect results? If so, what standard should be used to assess the conduct of the police? More generally, is police conduct during the course of an investigation or arrest subject to scrutiny under the law of negligence at all, or should police be immune on public policy grounds from liability under the law of negligence? These are the questions at stake on this appeal.

[3] I conclude that police are not immune from liability under the Canadian law of negligence, that the police owe a duty of care in negligence to suspects being investigated, and that their conduct during the course of an investigation should be measured against the standard of how a reasonable officer in like circumstances would have acted. The tort of negligent investigation exists in Canada, and the trial court and Court of Appeal were correct to consider the appellant's action on this basis. The law of negligence does not demand a perfect investigation. It requires only that police conducting an investigation act reasonably. When police fail to meet the standard of reasonableness, they may be accountable through negligence law for harm resulting to a suspect.

II. FACTS AND PROCEDURAL HISTORY

[4] This case arises out of an unfortunate series of events which resulted in an innocent person being investigated by the police, arrested, tried, wrongfully convicted, and ultimately acquitted after spending more than 20 months in jail for a crime he did not commit.

[5] Ten robberies occurred in Hamilton between December 16, 1994 and January 23, 1995. The *modus operandi* in all of the robberies seemed essentially the same. Eyewitnesses provided similar descriptions of the suspect. The police, relying on similarities in the *modus operandi* and eyewitness descriptions, concluded early on in the investigation that the same person had committed all the robberies, and labelled the perpetrator "the plastic bag robber".

[6] The appellant, Jason George Hill, became a suspect in the course of the investigation of the "plastic bag" robberies. The police investigated. They released his photo to the media, and conducted a photo lineup consisting of the aboriginal suspect Hill and 11 similar-looking Caucasian foils. On January 27, 1995, the police arrested Hill and charged him with 10 counts of robbery. The evidence against him at that point included: a Crime Stoppers tip; identification by a police officer based on a surveillance photo; several eyewitness identifications (some tentative, others more solid); a potential sighting of Hill near the site of a robbery by a police officer; eyewitness evidence that the robber appeared to be aboriginal (which Hill was); and the belief of the police that a single person committed all 10 robberies.

[7] At the time of the arrest, the police were in possession of potentially exculpatory evidence, namely, an anonymous Crime Stoppers tip received on January 25, 1995 suggesting that two Hispanic men ("Frank" and "Pedro") were the perpetrators. As time passed, other exculpatory evidence surfaced. Two similar robberies occurred while Hill was in custody. The descriptions of the robber and the *modus*

---

† [2007] 3 S.C.R. 129, 2007 SCC 41.

operandi were similar to the original robberies, except for the presence of a threat of a gun in the last two robberies. The police received a second Crime Stoppers tip implicating "Frank", which indicated that "Frank" looked similar to Jason George Hill and that "Frank" was laughing because Hill was being held responsible for robberies that Frank had committed. The police detective investigating the last two robberies (Detective Millin) received information from another officer that a Frank Sotomayer could be the robber. He proceeded to gather evidence and information which tended to inculpate Sotomayer — that Sotomayer and Hill looked very much alike, that there was evidence tending to corroborate the credibility of the Crime Stoppers tip implicating "Frank", and that photos from the first robberies seemed to look more like Sotomayer than Hill. Information from this investigation of the later robberies was conveyed to the detective supervising the investigation of the earlier robberies (Detective Loft).

[8] Two of the charges against Hill were dropped in response to this new evidence, the police having concluded that Sotomayer, not Hill, had committed those robberies. However, the police did not drop all of the charges.

[9] Legal proceedings against Hill in relation to the remaining eight charges began. Two more charges were withdrawn by the Crown during the preliminary inquiry because a witness testified that Hill was not the person who robbed her. Five more charges were withdrawn by the Assistant Crown Attorney assigned to prosecute at trial. A single charge remained, and the Crown decided to proceed based on this charge, largely because two eyewitnesses, the bank tellers, remained steadfast in their identifications of Hill.

[10] Hill stood trial and was found guilty of robbery in March 1996. He successfully appealed the conviction based on errors of law made by the trial judge. On August 6, 1997, his appeal was allowed and a new trial was ordered. Hill was ultimately acquitted of all charges of robbery on December 20, 1999.

[11] To summarize, Hill first became involved in the investigation as a suspect in January of 1995 and remained involved in various aspects of the justice system as a suspect, an accused, and a convicted person, until December of 1999. Within this period, he was imprisoned for various periods totalling more than 20 months, although not continuously.

[12] Hill brought civil actions against the police (the Hamilton-Wentworth Regional Police Services Board

and a number of individual officers) and the Crown prosecutors involved in his preliminary inquiry and trial. The actions against some of the individual officers and all of the Crown prosecutors were discontinued before trial. The action against the remaining defendants was brought on the basis of negligence, malicious prosecution, and breach of rights protected by the *Canadian Charter of Rights and Freedoms*. This appeal is concerned with the negligence claim.

[13] Hill alleges that the police investigation was negligent in a number of ways. He attacks the identifications by the two bank tellers on the ground that they were interviewed together (not separately, as non-mandatory guidelines suggested), with a newspaper photo identifying Hill as the suspect on their desks, and particularly objects to the methods used to interview witnesses and administer a photo lineup. He also alleged that the police failed to adequately reinvestigate the robberies when new evidence emerged that cast doubt on his initial arrest.

. . . .

[18] Hill appeals [the decision of the lower courts] to this Court, contending that the majority of the Court of Appeal erred in finding that the police investigation leading to his arrest and prosecution was not negligent. The police cross-appeal, arguing that there is no tort of negligent investigation in Canadian law.

III.   ANALYSIS

The Tort of Negligent Investigation

1. Duty of Care

[19] The issue at this stage is whether the law recognizes a duty of care on an investigating police officer to a suspect in the course of investigation. This matter is not settled in Canada. Lower courts have divided and this Court has never considered the matter. We must therefore ask whether, as a matter of principle, a duty of care should be recognized in this situation.

[20] The test for determining whether a person owes a duty of care involves two questions: (1) Does the relationship between the plaintiff and the defendant disclose sufficient foreseeability and proximity to establish a *prima facie* duty of care; and (2) If so, are there any residual policy considerations which ought to negate or limit that duty of care? (See *Anns v. Merton London Borough Council*, [1978] A.C. 728 (H.L.), as affirmed and explained by this Court

in a number of cases [including] *Cooper v. Hobart*, [2001] 3 S.C.R. 537.

(A) DOES THE RELATIONSHIP ESTABLISH A PRIMA FACIE DUTY OF CARE?

[21] The purpose of the inquiry at this stage is to determine if there was a relationship between the parties that gave rise to a legal duty of care.

[22] The first element of such a relationship is foreseeability. In the foundational case of *Donoghue v. Stevenson*, [1932] A.C. 562 (H.L.), Lord Atkin stated:

> The rule that you are to love your neighbour becomes in law, you must not injure your neighbour; and the lawyer's question, Who is my neighbour? receives a restricted reply.... Who, then, in law is my neighbour? The answer seems to be — persons who are so closely and directly affected by my act that I ought reasonably to have them in contemplation as being so affected when I am directing my mind to the acts or omissions which are called in question. [Emphasis added; p. 580.]

Lord Atkin went on to state that each person "must take reasonable care to avoid acts or omissions which you can reasonably foresee would be likely to injure your neighbour" (p. 580). Thus the first question in determining whether a duty in negligence is owed is whether it was reasonably foreseeable that the actions of the alleged wrongdoer would cause harm to the victim.

[23] However, as acknowledged in *Donoghue* and affirmed by this Court in *Cooper*, foreseeability alone is not enough to establish the required relationship. To impose a duty of care "there must also be a close and direct relationship of proximity or neighbourhood": *Cooper*, at para. 22. The proximity inquiry asks whether the case discloses factors which show that the relationship between the plaintiff and the defendant was sufficiently close to give rise to a legal duty of care. The focus is on the relationship between alleged wrongdoer and victim: is the relationship one where the imposition of legal liability for the wrongdoer's actions is appropriate?

[24] Generally speaking, the proximity analysis involves examining the relationship at issue, considering factors such as expectations, representations, reliance and property or other interests involved: *Cooper*, at para. 34. Different relationships raise different considerations. "The factors which may satisfy the requirement of proximity are diverse and depend on the circumstances of the case. One searches in vain for a single unifying characteristic": *Cooper*, at para. 35. No single rule, factor or definitive list of factors can be applied in every case. "Proximity may be usefully viewed, not so much as a test in itself, but as a broad concept which is capable of subsuming different categories of cases involving different factors" (*Canadian National Railway Co. v. Norsk Pacific Steamship Co.*, [1992] 1 S.C.R. 1021, at p. 1151, cited in *Cooper*, at para. 35).

[25] Proximity may be seen as providing an umbrella covering types of relationships where a duty of care has been found by the courts. The vast number of negligence cases proceed on the basis of a type of relationship previously recognized as giving rise to a duty of care. The duty of care of the motorist to other users of the highway; the duty of care of the doctor to his patient; the duty of care of the solicitor to her client — these are but a few of the relationships where sufficient proximity to give rise to a *prima facie* duty of care is recognized, provided foreseeability is established. The categories of relationships characterized by sufficient proximity to attract legal liability are not closed, however. From time to time, claims are made that relationships hitherto unconsidered by courts support a duty of care giving rise to legal liability. When such cases arise, the courts must consider whether the claim for sufficient proximity is established. If it is, and the *prima facie* duty is not negated for policy reasons at the second stage of the *Anns* test, the new category will thereafter be recognized as capable of giving rise to a duty of care and legal liability. The result is a concept of liability for negligence which provides a large measure of certainty, through settled categories of liability — attracting relationships, while permitting expansion to meet new circumstances and evolving conceptions of justice.

[26] In this case, we are faced with a claim in negligence against persons in a type of relationship not hitherto considered by the law — the relationship between an investigating police officer and his suspect. We must therefore ask whether, on principles applied in previous cases, this relationship is marked by sufficient proximity to make the imposition of legal liability for negligence appropriate.

[27] Before moving on to the analysis of proximity in depth, it is worth pausing to state explicitly that this judgment is concerned only with a very particular relationship — the relationship between a police officer and a particularized suspect that he is investigating. There are particular considerations relevant to proximity and policy applicable to this relationship,

including: the reasonable expectations of a party being investigated by the police, the seriousness of the interests at stake for the suspect, the legal duties owed by police to suspects under their governing statutes and the *Charter* and the importance of balancing the need for police to be able to investigate effectively with the protection of the fundamental rights of a suspect or accused person. It might well be that both the considerations informing the analysis of both proximity and policy would be different in the context of other relationships involving the police, for example, the relationship between the police and a victim, or the relationship between a police chief and the family of a victim. This decision deals only with the relationship between the police and a suspect being investigated. If a new relationship is alleged to attract liability of the police in negligence in a future case, it will be necessary to engage in a fresh *Anns* analysis, sensitive to the different considerations which might obtain when police interact with persons other than suspects that they are investigating. Such an approach will also ensure that the law of tort is developed in a manner that is sensitive to the benefits of recognizing liability in novel situations where appropriate, but at the same time, sufficiently incremental and gradual to maintain a reasonable degree of certainty in the law. Further, I cannot accept the suggestion that cases dealing with the relationship between the police and victims or between a police chief and the family of a victim are determinative here, although aspects of the analysis in those cases may be applicable and informative in the case at bar. (See *Odhavji* and *Jane Doe v. Metropolitan Toronto (Municipality) Commissioners of Police* (1998), 160 D.L.R. (4th) 697 (Ont. Ct. (Gen. Div.)).) I note that *Jane Doe* is a lower court decision and that debate continues over the content and scope of the ratio in that case. I do not purport to resolve these disputes on this appeal. In fact, and with great respect to the Court of Appeal who relied to some extent on this case, I find the *Jane Doe* decision of little assistance in the case at bar.

[28] Having said this, I proceed to consider whether there is sufficient proximity between a police officer and a suspect that he or she is investigating to establish a *prima facie* duty of care.

[29] The most basic factor upon which the proximity analysis fixes is whether there is a relationship between the alleged wrongdoer and the victim, usually described by the words "close and direct". This factor is not concerned with how intimate the plaintiff and defendant were or with their physical proximity, so much as with whether the *actions* of the

alleged wrongdoer have a close or direct effect on the victim, such that the wrongdoer ought to have had the victim in mind as a person potentially harmed. A sufficiently close and direct connection between the actions of the wrongdoer and the victim may exist where there is a personal relationship between alleged wrongdoer and victim. However, it may also exist where there is no personal relationship between the victim and wrongdoer. In the words of Lord Atkin in *Donoghue*:

> [A] duty to take due care [arises] when the person or property of one was in such proximity to the person or property of another that, if due care was not taken, damage might be done by the one to the other. I think that this sufficiently states the truth if proximity be not confined to mere physical proximity, but be used, as I think it was intended, to extend to such close and direct relations that the act complained of directly affects a person whom the person alleged to be bound to take care would know would be directly affected by his careless act. [Emphasis added; p. 581.]

[30] While not necessarily determinative, the presence or absence of a personal relationship is an important factor to consider in the proximity analysis. However, depending on the case, it may be necessary to consider other factors which may bear on the question of whether the relationship between the defendant and plaintiff is capable in principle of supporting legal liability: *Cooper*, at para. 37.

. . . .

[32] In this appeal, we are concerned with the relationship between an investigating police officer and a suspect. The requirement of reasonable foreseeability is clearly made out and poses no barrier to finding a duty of care; clearly negligent police investigation of a suspect may cause harm to the suspect.

[33] Other factors relating to the relationship suggest sufficient proximity to support a cause of action. The relationship between the police and a suspect identified for investigation is personal, and is close and direct. We are not concerned with the universe of all potential suspects. The police had identified Hill as a particularized suspect at the relevant time and begun to investigate him. This created a close and direct relationship between the police and Hill. He was no longer merely one person in a pool of potential suspects. He had been singled out. The relationship is thus closer than in *Cooper* and *Edwards*. In those cases, the public officials were not acting in

relation to the claimant (as the police did here) but in relation to a third party (i.e. persons being regulated) who, at a further remove, interacted with the claimants.

[34] A final consideration bearing on the relationship is the interests it engages. In this case, personal representations and consequent reliance are absent. However, the targeted suspect has a critical personal interest in the conduct of the investigation. At stake are his freedom, his reputation and how he may spend a good portion of his life. These high interests support a finding of a proximate relationship giving rise to a duty of care.

. . . .

[36] The personal interest of the suspect in the conduct of the investigation is enhanced by a public interest. Recognizing an action for negligent police investigation may assist in responding to failures of the justice system, such as wrongful convictions or institutional racism. The unfortunate reality is that negligent policing has now been recognized as a significant contributing factor to wrongful convictions in Canada. While the vast majority of police officers perform their duties carefully and reasonably, the record shows that wrongful convictions traceable to faulty police investigations occur. Even one wrongful conviction is too many, and Canada has had more than one. Police conduct that is not malicious, not deliberate, but merely fails to comply with standards of reasonableness can be a significant cause of wrongful convictions. (See the Honourable Peter Cory, *The Inquiry Regarding Thomas Sophonow: The Investigation, Prosecution and Consideration of Entitlement to Compensation* (2001), at p. 10 ("Cory Report"); the Right Honourable Antonio Lamer, *The Lamer Commission of Inquiry into the Proceedings Pertaining to: Ronald Dalton, Gregory Parsons and Randy Druken: Report and Annexes* (2006), at p. 71; Federal/Provincial/Territorial Heads of Prosecutions Committee Working Group, *Report on the Prevention of Miscarriages of Justice* (2004); the Honourable Fred Kaufman, *The Commission on Proceedings Involving Guy Paul Morin: Report* (1998), at pp. 25–26, 30–31, 34–36, 1095–96, 1098–99, 1101 and 1124.)

[37] As Peter Cory points out, at pp. 101 and 103:

> [I]f the State commits significant errors in the course of the investigation and prosecution, it should accept the responsibility for the sad consequences....
>
> ...

> [S]ociety needs protection from both the deliberate and the careless acts of omission and commission which lead to wrongful conviction and prison.

[38] Finally, it is worth noting that a duty of care by police officers to suspects under investigation is consistent with the values and spirit underlying the *Charter*, with its emphasis on liberty and fair process. The tort duty asserted here would enhance those values, which supports the appropriateness of its recognition.

[39] These considerations lead me to conclude that an investigating police officer and a particular suspect are close and proximate such that a *prima facie* duty should be recognized. Viewed from the broader societal perspective, suspects may reasonably be expected to rely on the police to conduct their investigation in a competent, non-negligent manner. (See *Odhavji*, at para. 57.)

[40] It is argued that recognition of liability for negligent investigation would produce a conflict between the duty of care that a police officer owes to a suspect and the police's officer duty to the public to prevent crime, that negates the duty of care. I do not agree. First, it seems to me doubtful that recognizing a duty of care to suspects will place police officers under incompatible obligations. Second, on the test set forth in *Cooper* and subsequent cases, conflict or potential conflict does not in itself negate a *prima facie* duty of care; the conflict must be between the novel duty proposed and an "overarching public duty", and it must pose a real potential for negative policy consequences. Any potential conflict that could be established here would not meet these conditions.

[41] First, the argument that a duty to take reasonable care toward suspects conflicts with an overarching duty to investigate crime is tenuous. The officer's duty to the public is not to investigate in an unconstrained manner. It is a duty to investigate in accordance with the law. That law includes many elements. It includes the restrictions imposed by the *Charter* and the *Criminal Code*, R.S.C. 1985, c. C-46. Equally, it may include tort law. The duty of investigation in accordance with the law does not conflict with the presumed duty to take reasonable care toward the suspect. Indeed, the suspect is a member of the public. As such, the suspect shares the public's interest in diligent investigation in accordance with the law.

[42] My colleague Justice Charron suggests there is a conflict between the police officer's duty to investi-

gate crime, on the one hand, and the officer's duty to leave people alone. It may be that a citizen has an interest in or preference for being left alone. But I know of no authority for the proposition that an investigating police officer is under a duty to leave people alone. The proposed tort duty does not presuppose a duty to leave the citizen alone, but only a duty to investigate reasonably in accordance with the limits imposed by law.

[43] Second, even if a potential conflict could be posited, that would not automatically negate the *prima facie* duty of care. The principle established in *Cooper* and its progeny is more limited. A *prima facie* duty of care will be negated only when the conflict, considered together with other relevant policy considerations, gives rise to a real potential for negative policy consequences. This reflects the view that a duty of care in tort law should not be denied on speculative grounds.... Requiring police officers to take reasonable care toward suspects in the investigation of crimes may have positive policy ramifications. Reasonable care will reduce the risk of wrongful convictions and increase the probability that the guilty will be charged and convicted. By contrast, the potential for negative repercussions is dubious. Acting with reasonable care to suspects has not been shown to inhibit police investigation, as discussed more fully in connection with the argument on chilling effect.

[44] In a variant on this argument, it is submitted that in a world of limited resources, recognizing a duty of care on police investigating crimes to a suspect will require the police to choose between spending resources on investigating crime in the public interest and spending resources in a manner that an individual suspect might conceivably prefer. The answer to this argument is that the standard of care is based on what a reasonable police officer would do in similar circumstances. The fact that funds are not unlimited is one of the circumstances that must be considered. Another circumstance that must be considered, however, is that the effective and responsible investigation of crime is one of the basic duties of the state, which cannot be abdicated. A standard of care that takes these two considerations into account will recognize what can reasonably be accomplished within a responsible and realistic financial framework.

[45] I conclude that the relationship between a police officer and a particular suspect is close enough to support a *prima facie* duty of care.

(D) POLICY CONSIDERATIONS NEGATING THE PRIMA FACIE DUTY OF CARE

[46] The second stage of the *Anns* test asks whether there are broader policy reasons for declining to recognize a duty of care owed by the defendant to the plaintiff. Even though there is sufficient foreseeability and proximity of relationship to establish a *prima facie* duty of care, are there policy considerations which negate or limit that duty of care?

[47] In this case, negating conditions have not been established. No compelling reason has been advanced for negating a duty of care owed by police to particularized suspects being investigated. On the contrary, policy considerations support the recognition of a duty of care.

[48] The respondents and interveners representing the Attorneys General of Ontario and Canada and various police associations argue that the following policy considerations negate a duty of care: the "quasi-judicial" nature of police work; the potential for conflict between a duty of care in negligence and other duties owed by police; the need to recognize a significant amount of discretion present in police work; the need to maintain the standard of reasonable and probable grounds applicable to police conduct; the potential for a chilling effect on the investigation of crime; and the possibility of a flood of litigation against the police. In approaching these arguments, I proceed on the basis that policy concerns raised against imposing a duty of care must be more than speculative; a real potential for negative consequences must be apparent. Judged by this standard, none of these considerations provide a convincing reason for rejecting a duty of care on police to a suspect under investigation.

[The Chief Justice rejected arguments that police duties are by nature 'quasi-judicial and inherently discretionary. In her view the 'standard of care' assessment allows sufficient room for police to exercise appropriate discretion. The Chief Justice also rejected the view that the standard of care for negligence should be the same as for arrest. She preferred a 'flexible standard of care'. She also concluded that the finding of a duty of care would not have a chilling effect on policing and would not cause police officers to take an unduly defensive approach to investigations, stating:]

(iv) Chilling Effect

[56] ... In theory, it is conceivable that police might become more careful in conducting investigations if a

duty of care in tort is recognized. However, this is not necessarily a bad thing. The police officer must strike a reasonable balance between cautiousness and prudence on the one hand, and efficiency on the other. Files must be closed, life must move on, but care must also be taken. All of this is taken into account, not at the stage of determining whether police owe a duty of care to a particular suspect, but in determining what the standard of that care should be.

[57] The record does not support the conclusion that recognizing potential liability in tort significantly changes the behaviour of police. Indeed, some of the evidence suggests that tort liability has no adverse effect on the capacity of police to investigate crime. This supports the conclusion of the majority in the Court of Appeal below that the "'chilling effect' scenario" remains speculative and that concern about preventing a "chilling effect" on the investigation of crime is not (on the basis of present knowledge) a convincing policy rationale for negating a duty of care (para. 63)....

[58] The lack of [empirical] evidence of a chilling effect despite numerous studies is sufficient to dispose of the suggestion that recognition of a tort duty would motivate prudent officers not to proceed with investigations "except in cases where the evidence is overwhelming" (Charron J., at para. 152). This lack of evidence should not surprise us, given the nature of the tort. All the tort of negligent investigation requires is that the police act reasonably in the circumstances. It is reasonable for a police officer to investigate in the absence of overwhelming evidence — indeed evidence usually becomes overwhelming only by the process of investigation. Police officers can investigate on whatever basis and in whatever circumstances they choose, provided they act reasonably. The police need not let all but clearly impaired drivers go to avoid the risk of litigation, as my colleague suggests. They need only act reasonably. They may arrest or demand a breath sample if they have reasonable and probable grounds. And where such grounds are absent, they may have recourse to statutorily authorized roadside tests and screening.

[59] It should also be noted that many police officers (like other professionals) are indemnified from personal civil liability in the course of exercising their professional duties, reducing the prospect that their fear of civil liability will chill crime prevention.

(v) Flood of Litigation

[60] Recognizing sufficient proximity in the relationship between police and suspect to ground a duty of care does not open the door to indeterminate liability. Particularized suspects represent a limited category of potential claimants. The class of potential claimants is further limited by the requirement that the plaintiff establish compensable injury caused by a negligent investigation. Treatment rightfully imposed by the law does not constitute compensable injury. These considerations undermine the spectre of a glut of jailhouse lawsuits for negligent police investigation.

[61] The record provides no basis for concluding that there will be a flood of litigation against the police if a duty of care is recognized. As the Court of Appeal emphasized, the evidence from the Canadian experience seems to be to the contrary (majority reasons, at para. 64). Quebec and Ontario have both recognized police liability in negligence (or the civil law equivalent) for many years, and there is no evidence that the floodgates have opened and a large number of lawsuits against the police have resulted. (See the majority reasons in the Court of Appeal, at para. 64.) The best that can be said from the record is that recognizing a duty of care owed by police officers to particular suspects led to a relatively small number of lawsuits, the cost of which [is] unknown, with effects on the police that have not been measured. This is not enough to negate the *prima facie* duty of care established at the first stage of the *Anns* test.

(vi) The Risk that Guilty Persons Who Are Acquitted May Unjustly Recover in Tort

[62] My colleague Charron J. (at paras. 156 ff.) states that recognizing tort liability for negligent police investigation raises the possibility that persons who have been acquitted of the crime investigated and charged, but who are in fact guilty, may recover against an officer for negligent investigation. This, she suggests, would be unjust.

[63] This possibility of "injustice" — if indeed that is what it is — is present in any tort action. A person who recovers against her doctor for medical malpractice may, despite having proved illness in court, have in fact been malingering. Or, despite having convinced the judge on a balance of probabilities that the doctor's act caused her illness, it may be that the true source of the problem lay elsewhere. The legal system is not perfect. It does its best to arrive at the truth. But it cannot discount the possibility that a plaintiff who has established a cause of action may "factually", if we had means to find out, not have been entitled to recover. The possibility of error may be greater in some circumstances than others. How-

ever, I know of no case where this possibility has led to the conclusion that tort recovery for negligence should be denied.

[64] The answer to the ever-present possibility of erroneous awards of damages lies elsewhere, it seems to me. The first safeguard is the requirement that the plaintiff prove every element of his or her case. Any suspect suing the police bears the burden of showing that police negligence in the course of an investigation caused harm compensable at law. This means that the suspect must establish through evidence that the damage incurred, be it a conviction, imprisonment, prosecution or other compensable harm, would not have been suffered but for the police's negligent investigation. Evidence going to the factual guilt or innocence of the suspect, including the results of any criminal proceedings that may have occurred, may be relevant to this causation inquiry. It is not necessary to decide here whether an acquittal should be treated as conclusive proof of innocence in a subsequent civil trial. Existing authority is equivocal: *Toronto (City) v. C.U.P.E., Local 79*, [2003] 3 S.C.R. 77, 2003 SCC 63. (I note that in the United States, victims may recover damages against a defendant who has been acquitted in criminal proceedings: *Rufo v. Simpson*, 103 Cal.Rptr.2d 492 (Ct. App. 2001).) The second safeguard is the right of appeal. These safeguards, not the categorical denial of the right to sue in tort, are the law's response to the ever-present possibility of error in the legal process.

[65] I conclude that no compelling policy reason has been shown to negate the *prima facie* duty of care.

2. Standard of Care

[66] Two issues arise: What is the appropriate standard of care? and Was that standard met on the facts of this case?

(A) THE APPROPRIATE STANDARD OF CARE FOR THE TORT OF NEGLIGENT INVESTIGATION

[67] Both the trial judge and the Court of Appeal adopted the standard of the reasonable police officer in like circumstances as the standard that is generally appropriate in cases of alleged negligent investigation. I agree that this is the correct standard.

[68] A number of considerations support the conclusion that the standard of care is that of a reasonable police officer in all the circumstances. First, the standard of a reasonable police officer in all the circumstances provides a flexible overarching standard that covers all aspects of investigatory police work and appropriately reflects its realities. The particular conduct required is informed by the stage of the investigation and applicable legal considerations. At the outset of an investigation, the police may have little more than hearsay, suspicion and a hunch. What is required is that they act as a reasonable investigating officer would in those circumstances. Later, in laying charges, the standard is informed by the legal requirement of reasonable and probable grounds to believe the suspect is guilty; since the law requires such grounds, a police officer acting reasonably in the circumstances would insist on them. The reasonable officer standard entails no conflict between criminal standards (Charron J., at para. 175). Rather, it incorporates them, in the same way it incorporates an appropriate degree of judicial discretion, denies liability for minor errors or mistakes and rejects liability by hindsight. In all these ways, it reflects the realities of police work.

[69] Second, as mentioned, the general rule is that the standard of care in negligence is that of the reasonable person in similar circumstances. In cases of professional negligence, this rule is qualified by an additional principle: where the defendant has special skills and experience, the defendant must "live up to the standards possessed by persons of reasonable skill and experience in that calling". (See L. N. Klar, *Tort Law* (3rd ed. 2003), at p. 306.) These principles suggest the standard of the reasonable officer in like circumstances.

[70] Third, the common law factors relevant to determining the standard of care confirm the reasonable officer standard. These factors include: the likelihood of known or foreseeable harm, the gravity of harm, the burden or cost which would be incurred to prevent the injury, external indicators of reasonable conduct (including professional standards) and statutory standards. (See *Ryan v. Victoria (City)*, [1999] 1 S.C.R. 201; *R. v. Saskatchewan Wheat Pool*, [1983] 1 S.C.R. 205, at p. 227.) These factors suggest a standard of reasonableness, not something less onerous. There is a significant likelihood that police officers may cause harm to suspects if they investigate negligently. The gravity of the potential harm caused is serious. Suspects may be arrested or imprisoned, their livelihoods affected and their reputations irreparably damaged. The cost of preventing the injury, in comparison, is not undue. Police meet a standard of reasonableness by merely doing what a reasonable police officer would do in the same circumstances — by living up to accepted standards of professional conduct to the extent that it is reasonable to expect

in given circumstances. This seems neither unduly onerous nor overly costly. It must be supposed that professional standards require police to act professionally and carefully, not just to avoid gross negligence. The statutory standards imposed by the *Police Services Act*, R.S.O. 1990, c. P.15, although not definitive of the standard of care, are instructive (s. 1).

[71] Fourth, the nature and importance of police work reinforce a standard of the reasonable officer in similar circumstances. Police conduct has the capacity to seriously affect individuals by subjecting them to the full coercive power of the state and impacting on their repute and standing in the community. It follows that police officers should perform their duties reasonably. It has thus been recognized that police work demands that society (including the courts) impose and enforce high standards on police conduct (Cory Report, at p. 10). This supports a reasonableness standard, judged in the context of a similarly situated officer. A more lenient standard is inconsistent with the standards that society and the law rightfully demand of police in the performance of their crucially important work.

[72] Finally, authority supports the standard of the reasonable police officer similarly placed. The preponderance of case law dealing with professionals has applied the standard of the reasonably competent professional in like circumstances. (See Klar, at p. 349; see also the reasons of the trial judge at para. 63.) The Quebec Court of Appeal has twice stated that the standard is the ordinarily competent officer in like circumstances. (*Jauvin v. Procureur général du Québec*, [2004] R.R.A. 37, at para. 59, and *Lacombe v. André*, [2003] R.J.Q. 720, at para. 41).

[73] I conclude that the appropriate standard of care is the overarching standard of a reasonable police officer in similar circumstances. This standard should be applied in a manner that gives due recognition to the discretion inherent in police investigation. Like other professionals, police officers are entitled to exercise their discretion as they see fit, provided that they stay within the bounds of reasonableness. The standard of care is not breached because a police officer exercises his or her discretion in a manner other than that deemed optimal by the reviewing court. A number of choices may be open to a police officer investigating a crime, all of which may fall within the range of reasonableness. So long as discretion is exercised within this range, the standard of care is not breached. The standard is not perfection, or even the optimum, judged from the vantage of hindsight. It is that of a reasonable officer, judged in the circumstances prevailing at the time the decision was made — circumstances that may include urgency and deficiencies of information. The law of negligence does not require perfection of professionals; nor does it guarantee desired results (Klar, at p. 359). Rather, it accepts that police officers, like other professionals, may make minor errors or errors in judgment which cause unfortunate results, without breaching the standard of care. The law distinguishes between unreasonable mistakes breaching the standard of care and mere "errors in judgment" which any reasonable professional might have made and therefore, which do not breach the standard of care. (See *Lapointe v. Hôpital Le Gardeur*, [1992] 1 S.C.R. 351; *Folland v. Reardon* (2005), 74 O.R. (3d) 688 (C.A.); Klar, at p. 359.)

(B) APPLICATION OF THE STANDARD OF CARE TO THE FACTS — WAS THE POLICE CONDUCT IN THIS CASE NEGLIGENT?

[74] The defendant police officers owed a duty of care to Mr. Hill. That required them to meet the standard of a reasonable officer in similar circumstances. While the investigation that led to Mr. Hill's arrest and conviction was flawed, I conclude that it did not breach this standard, judged by the standards of the day.

[75] Hill alleges that Detective Loft, who was in charge of the investigation of the plastic bag robberies, conducted the investigation negligently, and that Officers McLaughlin, Stewart, Matthews and Hill acted negligently in aspects of the investigation assigned to them. On this basis, he argues that the Police Services Board is vicariously liable for the individual acts and omissions of its officers.

[76] The arrest itself is not impugned as negligent. Although there were problems in the case against Hill, it is accepted that the investigation, as it stood at the time the arrest was made, disclosed reasonable and probable grounds. It is the conduct of the police prior to and following the arrest that Hill criticizes. At the pre-arrest stage, Mr. Hill alleges: witness contamination as the result of publishing his photo (McLaughlin); failure to make proper records of events and interviews with witnesses (McLaughlin and Stewart); interviewing two witnesses together and with a photo of Hill on the desk (McLaughlin); and structural bias in the photo lineup in which Hill was identified (Hill and Loft). At the post-arrest stage, Hill charges that Detective Loft failed to reinvesti-

gate after evidence came to light that suggested the robber was not Hill, but a different man, Sotomayer. (It is also alleged that Detective Loft failed to communicate relevant facts to defence counsel. This has more to do with trial conduct than investigation, and I consider it no further.)

[77] We must consider the conduct of the investigating officers in the year 1995 in all of the circumstances, including the state of knowledge then prevailing. Police practices, like practices in other professions, advance as time passes and experience and understanding accumulate. Better practices that developed in the years after Hill's investigation are therefore not conclusive. By extension, the conclusion that certain police actions did not violate the standard of care in 1995 does not necessarily mean that the same or similar actions would meet the standard of care today or in the future. We must also avoid the counsel of perfection; the reasonable officer standard allows for minor mistakes and misjudgments. Finally, proper scope must be accorded to the discretion police officers properly exercise in conducting an investigation.

[78] Considered in this light, the first four complaints, while questionable, were not sufficiently serious on the record viewed as a whole to constitute a departure from the standard of a reasonable police officer in the circumstances. The publication of Hill's photo, the somewhat incomplete record of witness interviews, the fact that two witnesses were interviewed together and the failure to blind-test the photos put to witnesses are not good police practices, judged by today's standards. But the evidence does not establish that a reasonable officer in 1995 would not have followed similar practices in similar circumstances. Nor is it clear that if these incidents had not occurred, Hill would not have been charged and convicted. It follows that the individual officers involved in these incidents cannot be held liable to Hill in negligence.

[79] This brings us to the photo lineup. The photo array consisted of one aboriginal suspect, Hill, and eleven Caucasian foils. However, a number of the subjects had similar features and colouring, so that Hill did not in fact stand out as the only aboriginal.

[80] The first question is whether this photo lineup met the standard of a reasonable officer investigating an offence in 1995. The trial judge accepted expert evidence that there were "no rules" and "a great deal of variance in practice right up to the present time" in relation to photo lineups (paras. 66 and 70). These findings of fact have not been challenged. It

follows that on the evidence adduced, it cannot be concluded that the photo lineup was unreasonable, judged by 1995 standards. This said, the practice followed was not ideal. A reasonable officer today might be expected to avoid lineups using foils of a different race than the suspect, to avoid both the perception of injustice and the real possibility of unfairness to suspects who are members of minority groups — concerns underlined by growing awareness of persisting problems with institutional bias against minorities in the criminal justice system, including aboriginal persons like Mr. Hill. (See Royal Commission on Aboriginal Peoples, *Bridging the Cultural Divide: A Report on Aboriginal People and Criminal Justice in Canada* (1996).)

[81] In any event, it was established that the lineup's racial composition did not lead to unfairness. A racially skewed lineup is structurally biased only "if you can tell that the one person is non-Caucasian" and "assuming the suspect is the one that's standing out" (majority reasons in the Court of Appeal, at para. 105). Although the suspects were classified as being of a different race by the police's computer system, at least some of them appeared to have similar skin tones and similar facial features to Hill. On this evidence, the trial judge concluded that the lineup was not in fact structurally biased. Any risk that Hill might have been unfairly chosen over the 11 foils in the photo lineup did not arise from structural bias relating to the racial makeup of the lineup but rather from the fact that Hill happened to look like the individual who actually perpetrated the robberies, Frank Sotomayer.

[82] It remains to consider Mr. Hill's complaint that the police negligently failed to reinvestigate when new information suggesting he was not the robber came to light after his arrest and incarceration. This complaint must be considered in the context of the investigation as a whole. The police took the view from the beginning that the 10 robberies were the work of a single person, branded the plastic bag robber. They maintained this view and arrested Hill despite a series of tips implicating two men, "Pedro" and "Frank". Other weaknesses in the pre-charge case against Hill were the failure of a search of Hill's home to turn up evidence, and the fact that at the time of his arrest Hill had a long goatee of several weeks' growth, while the eyewitnesses to the crime described the robber as a clean-shaven man. While the police may have had reasonable and probable grounds for charging Hill, there were problems with their case.

[83] After Hill was charged and taken into custody, the robberies continued. Another officer, Detective Millin, was put in charge of the investigation of these charges. Sotomayer emerged as a suspect. Millin went into Hill's file and became concerned that Sotomayer, not Hill, may have committed at least some of the earlier robberies. He met with Detective Loft and discussed with him the fact that in the photographic record, the perpetrator of the December 16 robbery resembled Sotomayer more than Hill. As a result, on March 7 the charges against Hill relating to that robbery were withdrawn and Sotomayer was charged instead. Detective Millin met with Detective Loft again on April 4 and 6 to express concerns that Sotomayer and not Hill was the plastic bag bandit on the other charges. Detective Loft told Detective Millin that he would attempt to have the trial of the charges against Hill put over to permit further investigation. He never did so. The matter remained in the hands of the Crown prosecutors and no further investigation was done. Eventually, the Crown withdrew all the charges, except one, on which Hill was convicted. Detective Loft did not intervene to prevent that charge going forward. Nor did he check the alibi that Hill supplied. Had Detective Loft conducted further investigation, it is likely the case against Hill would have collapsed. Had he re-interviewed the eyewitnesses, for example, and shown them Sotomayer's photo, it is probable that matters would have turned out otherwise; when the witnesses were eventually shown the photo of Sotomayer, they recanted their identification of Hill as the robber.

[84] When new information emerges that could be relevant to the suspect's innocence, reasonable police conduct may require the file to be reopened and the matter reinvestigated. Depending on the nature of the evidence which later emerges, the requirements imposed by the duty to reinvestigate on the police may vary. In some cases, merely examining the evidence and determining that it is not worth acting on may be enough. In others, it may be reasonable to expect the police to do more in response to newly emerging evidence. Reasonable prudence may require them to re-examine their prior theories of the case, to test the credibility of new evidence and to engage in further investigation provoked by the new evidence. At the same time, police investigations are not never-ending processes extending indefinitely past the point of arrest. Police officers acting reasonably may at some point close their case against a suspect and move on to other matters. The question is always what the reasonable officer in like cir-

cumstances would have done to fulfil the duty to reinvestigate and to respond to the new evidence that emerged.

. . . .

4. Causal Connection

[93] Recovery for negligence requires a causal connection between the breach of the standard of care and the compensable damage suffered. Negligent police investigation may cause or contribute to wrongful conviction and imprisonment, fulfilling the legal requirement of causal connection on a balance of probabilities. The starting point is the usual "but for" test. If, on a balance of probabilities, the compensable damage would not have occurred but for the negligence on the part of the police, then the causation requirement is met.

[94] Cases of negligent investigation often will involve multiple causes. Where the injury would not have been suffered "but for" the negligent police investigation the causation requirement will be met even if other causes contributed to the injury as well. On the other hand, if the contributions of others to the injury are so significant that the same damage would have been sustained even if the police had investigated responsibly, causation will not be established. It follows that the police will not necessarily be absolved of responsibility just because another person, such as a prosecutor, lawyer or judge, may have contributed to a wrongful conviction causing compensable damage.

. . . .

IV. CONCLUSION

[105] I would dismiss Hill's appeal with costs. The Court of Appeal was correct to conclude that the police conduct impugned on this appeal met the standard of care and, therefore, was not negligent.

[106] I would also dismiss the cross-appeal. The Court of Appeal rightly concluded that the tort of negligent investigation is available in Canadian law.

[CHARRON J. (dissenting on the cross-appeal, for Bastarache and Rothstein JJ.):]

1. OVERVIEW

[107] The dictum that it is better for ten guilty persons to escape than for one innocent person to go to jail has long been a cornerstone of our criminal justice system (W. Blackstone, *Commentaries on the*

Laws of England (1769), Book IV, c. 27, at p. 352). Consequently, many safeguards have been created within that system to protect against wrongful convictions. Despite the presence of such safeguards, however, miscarriages of justice do occur. When an innocent person is convicted of a crime that he or she did not commit, it is undeniable that justice has failed in the most fundamental sense.

[108] Mr. Hill submits that he is one such victim of the criminal justice system. Of the 10 robbery charges laid against him, 9 were withdrawn by the Crown. Mr. Hill was convicted on the remaining charge but, following a successful appeal, was retried and ultimately acquitted of the offence. Mr. Hill claims that he has sustained significant damages because of substandard policing during the course of the criminal investigation leading to and following the charges laid against him. He therefore brings this action in negligence.

[109] While Mr. Hill acknowledges that his cause of action is novel, he nonetheless submits that the tort system can act as an effective deterrent against, and fairly allocate the costs arising from, negligent investigative practices. Consequently, he urges this Court to bring "[t]he law of negligence ... to bear on the problem of wrongful convictions" by recognizing a new tort of negligent investigation designed to compensate the wrongfully convicted who have suffered damages as a result of a substandard police investigation (appellant's factum, at para. 71).

. . . .

[111] The Crown argues further that, for important public policy reasons, tort liability should be limited to instances where the police seriously abuse or misuse their public powers, not where they are merely negligent in the discharge of their duties. According to the Crown, the imposition of a duty of care in negligence would not only subsume existing torts such as false arrest, false imprisonment, malicious prosecution, and misfeasance in public office, but would upset the careful balance between society's need for effective law enforcement and an individual's right to liberty.

[112] The novel question before this Court is therefore whether the new tort of negligent investigation should be recognized by Canadian law. I have concluded that it should not. A private duty of care owed by the police to suspects would necessarily conflict with the investigating officer's overarching public duty to investigate crime and apprehend offenders. The ramifications from this factor alone defeat the claim that there is a relationship of proximity between the parties sufficient to give rise to a *prima facie* duty of care. In addition, because the recognition of this new tort would have significant consequences for other legal obligations, and would detrimentally affect the legal system, and society more generally, it is my view that even if a *prima facie* duty of care were found to exist, that duty should be negatived on residual policy grounds.

[113] Therefore, for the reasons that follow, I would allow the Crown's cross-appeal and find that the tort of negligent investigation is not a remedy available at common law. In light of this conclusion, I find that the action was properly dismissed by the courts below and I would therefore dismiss Mr. Hill's appeal.

2. ANALYSIS

2.1 Elements of the Tort Action

[114] Mr. Hill claims that the defendants — who for simplicity I will refer to collectively as "investigating officers" — committed the tort of negligent investigation and that he is entitled to damages. In order to succeed in his claim, Mr. Hill must establish the following elements: (1) that the investigating officers owed him a duty of care; (2) that the investigating officers failed to meet the standard of care appropriate in the circumstances; (3) that he suffered a compensable loss or injury; and (4) that the loss or injury was caused by the investigating officers' negligent act or omission. While the most contentious elements of the proposed tort of negligent investigation are the duty and standard of care, the proposed new tort gives rise to difficult issues in respect of all four elements of the action. I will touch on each element in what follows, focussing principally on the duty of care.

2.2 The *Anns* Test

[115] Police officers have multiple duties. There is no question that one of them is the duty to investigate crime. This duty exists at common law and, in Ontario, is embodied in s. 42 of the *Police Services Act*, R.S.O. 1990, c. P.15, which describes the general duties of a police officer. Although "investigating crime" is not specifically listed, several of the listed duties are related to, or form part of, the police investigation into crime. Section 42(1) reads as follows:

42. — (1) The duties of a police officer include,

(a) <u>preserving the peace</u>;

(b) <u>preventing crimes</u> and other offences and providing assistance and encouragement to other persons in their prevention;

(c) assisting victims of crime;

(d) <u>apprehending criminals</u> and other offenders and others who may lawfully be taken into custody;

(e) laying charges and participating in prosecutions;

(f) executing warrants that are to be executed by police officers and performing related duties;

(g) performing the lawful duties that the chief of police assigns;

(h) in the case of a municipal police force and in the case of an agreement under section 10 (agreement for provision of police services by O.P.P.), enforcing municipal by-laws;

(i) completing the prescribed training.

. . . .

[116] There is no dispute that a police officer owes an overarching duty to the public to investigate crime. The question that occupies us here is whether this overarching public duty translates into a private duty owed to individual members of that public who fall in a particular class, namely suspects under investigation. This question calls for the application of what is commonly called the *Anns* test (in reference to the House of Lords decision in *Anns v. Merton London Borough Council*, [1978] A.C. 728), as refined by this Court in *Cooper v. Hobart*, [2001] 3 S.C.R. 537, 2001 SCC 79; *Edwards v. Law Society of Upper Canada*, [2001] 3 S.C.R. 562, 2001 SCC 80; *Odhavji Estate v. Woodhouse*, [2003] 3 S.C.R. 263, 2003 SCC 69, and *Childs v. Desormeaux*, [2006] 1 S.C.R. 643, 2006 SCC 18.

. . . .

2.3 Foreseeability

[118] The requirement of reasonable foreseeability poses no barrier to finding a duty of care in this case. A police investigator can readily foresee that a targeted suspect is among those persons who could be harmed as a result of the negligent conduct of the investigation. To be sure, when a targeted suspect is in fact the perpetrator of the offence under investigation, the public rather than the suspect may be the actual victim of a substandard investigation. Nonetheless, on the strict question of foreseeability, it is clear that this part of the test is made out.

2.4 Proximity

2.4.1 The Search For Analogous Categories

. . . .

[120] U.K. authorities holding that no duty of care is owed by the police to individual members of the public in the context of the investigation of crime are: *Hill v. Chief Constable of West Yorkshire*, [1988] 2 All E.R. 238 (H.L.), at pp. 243–44; ... See also *Calveley v. Chief Constable of the Merseyside Police*, [1989] 1 All E.R. 1025 (H.L.), at pp. 1030–32, in support of the proposition that the police do not owe a duty of care in the context of an internal police investigation and disciplinary proceeding against police officers.

[121] Australian authorities holding that no duty of care is owed to suspects in the context of a police investigation are *Emanuele v. Hedley* (1997), 137 F.L.R. 339 (A.C.T.S.C.). ...

[122] For American authorities supporting the proposition that police do not owe a duty of care to suspects, see *Gregoire v. Biddle*, 177 F.2d 579 (2d Cir. 1949). ...

. . . .

[124] In *Beckstead*, the Court of Appeal for Ontario confirmed a trial decision holding that a duty of care was owed by the investigating officer to the suspect under investigation ((1997), 37 O.R. (3d) 62 (p. 63)). Notably, however, neither the trial judge nor the panel of the Court of Appeal in that case carried out the *Anns* analysis to determine whether a duty of care in respect of this new category should be found to exist. This lack of any prior authority to support such a holding and the lack of any principled analysis in *Beckstead* prompted the Chief Justice of Ontario to create a five-judge panel for the hearing of this case to determine whether *Beckstead* was correctly decided (Court of Appeal judgment, at para. 2).

[125] In support of his conclusion that *Beckstead* was correctly decided, MacPherson J.A., writing for a unanimous court on this issue, relied in part on the existence of a duty of care in an analogous category, stating that "the duty of care exists in Ontario with respect to both suspects (*Beckstead*) <u>and victims</u> (*Jane Doe*)" (para. 65 (emphasis added)). He then concluded that he could "see no principled basis for distinguishing the two categories" (para. 65).

[126] The question whether the relationship between the investigating officer and the victim or potential victim of crime can give rise to a private duty of care has never been considered by this Court and we are not deciding this issue on this appeal. However, given the reliance placed by the Court of Appeal on *Jane Doe v. Metropolitan Toronto (Municipality) Commissioners of Police* (1998), 160 D.L.R. (4th) 697 (Ont. Ct. (Gen. Div.)), it is necessary to examine the import of the finding in that case to determine whether the Court of Appeal was correct in concluding that a general duty of care exists with respect to victims and that the categories of victim and suspect are indistinguishable.

[127] First, it is important to properly circumscribe the decision in *Jane Doe*. In order to do so, it may be helpful to briefly review the facts and the findings of the court in that case. From December 1985 to August 1986, a series of sexual assaults took place in Toronto. The sexual assaults shared certain characteristics: each took place in the same downtown Toronto neighbourhood; all the female victims lived in second or third floor apartments; each apartment contained an exterior balcony; and entry to the women's apartments had been effected via the balconies.

[128] After the fourth incident, but prior to the sexual assault of Jane Doe, the Metropolitan Toronto Police Force ("MTPF") had grounds to believe that a single individual was responsible for the sexual assaults. However, while anticipating that additional assaults were likely to occur, the MTPF deliberately refrained from informing potential victims of the specific risk to them on the grounds that doing so would cause the offender to flee. The trial judge, MacFarland J. (as she then was), found that the circumstances of the case suggested that "the women were being used — without their knowledge or consent — as 'bait' to attract a predator whose specific identity then was unknown to the police, but whose general and characteristic identity most certainly was" (p. 725).

[129] According to MacFarland J., the MTPF's decision not to inform members of the public who had been identified as being at risk was grossly negligent. Importantly, however, MacFarland J. took care to delineate the scope of the duty thus breached. She was "satisfied on the evidence that a meaningful warning could and should have been given to the women who were at <u>particular risk</u>" (p. 730 (emphasis added)). MacFarland J. went on to find that "the police failed utterly in their duty to protect <u>these</u>

<u>women</u> and <u>the plaintiff in particular</u> from the serial rapist the police knew to be in their midst by failing to warn so that they may have had the opportunity to take steps to protect themselves" (p. 732 (emphasis added)). MacFarland J. concluded that "[h]ere police were aware of a <u>specific threat or risk</u> to a <u>specific group of women</u> and they did nothing to warn <u>those women</u> of the danger they were in, nor did they take any measures to protect <u>them</u>" (p. 732 (emphasis added)).

[130] Hence, the trial judge in *Jane Doe* held that where the police are aware of a *specific* threat to a *specific* group of individuals, the police have a duty to inform those individuals of the specific threat in question so that they may take steps to protect themselves from harm. As Moldaver J. (as he then was) said, speaking for the Divisional Court in confirming that the action could proceed to trial, "[w]hile the police owe certain duties to the public at large, they cannot be expected to owe a private law duty of care to every member of society who might be at risk": *Jane Doe v. Metropolitan Toronto (Municipality) Commissioners of Police* (1990), 72 D.L.R. (4th) 580, at p. 584. Hence, *Jane Doe* cannot be read to stand for the wide proposition that the police owe a *general* duty of care to *all potential* victims of crime. Such an interpretation would ignore the fact that there must be more than mere foreseeability of harm before a duty of care will arise; there must also be sufficient proximity between the parties and the absence of policy considerations negating the existence of any *prima facie* duty of care.

[131] Without further qualification, therefore, I find myself unable to endorse MacPherson J.A.'s broad conclusion in this case that "the duty of care exists in Ontario with respect to ... victims" (para. 65). I also respectfully disagree with his assertion that there is no principled basis on which to distinguish between the two categories. To the contrary, there is crucial distinction between victim and suspect. The distinction resides in the fact that the public interest in having police officers investigate crime for the purpose of apprehending offenders and a potential victim's interest in being protected from the offenders are generally reconcilable. In contrast, the police officer's duty to investigate crime and apprehend offenders is diametrically opposed to the interests of the person under investigation. This is because the suspect's interest, regardless of whether that suspect is the actual perpetrator of the crime, is *always* to be left alone by the state. In other words, the suspect's interest is *always* at odds with the public interest in the context of a criminal investigation. I will explain.

[132] That a perpetrator's interest is at odds with the public interest in having him investigated and apprehended is too obvious to require explanation. It is important in this context to appreciate, however, that the interests of the suspect who is factually innocent of any criminal involvement is also at odds with the fulfilment of the officer's public duty to investigate crime. In my respectful view, it would be naive to simply assume that the innocent suspect's interest is not at odds on the ground that such a person will always be exonerated as a result of the investigation, if the police perform their duty in a competent manner. There is a significant gap between the "reasonable and probable grounds" standard upon which the initiation of the criminal process is based and the ultimate standard of proof beyond a reasonable doubt upon which a conviction is grounded. There is, moreover, a significant public interest in maintaining the long-established lower standard for the initiation of process. The result of this is that a criminal investigation, even of the most stellar quality, may well result in the targeting of the factually innocent. Further, even in those cases where the innocent suspect is exonerated as a result of the investigation, he or she will inevitably have suffered some harm as a result of the process that led to his exoneration: her reputation may be tarnished, or she may have suffered economic loss. This is why I say that *all* suspects, whether they have in fact committed the offence or not, stand to lose from being targeted by the police. It is *always* in the suspect's personal interest to be left alone by the state.

[133] Therefore, victims and suspects are not analogous categories.

.   .   .   .

[135] Because this case does not fall either directly or by analogy within a category of cases in which a duty of care has previously been recognized, it is necessary to turn to the proximity inquiry under the *Anns* test to determine whether the relationship between an investigating officer and a suspect under investigation is sufficiently close to give rise to a *prima facie* duty of care.

2.4.2 *The Interests Engaged by the Relationship Between the Investigator and the Investigated*

[136] As explained by my colleague (at paras. 26–30), the question at this stage of the inquiry is whether the relationship between the investigating officer and the suspect is such as "to make the

imposition of legal liability for negligence appropriate". Proximity is closely connected to the notion of foreseeability: the relationship must be sufficiently close and direct that the defendant *ought* to have had the plaintiff in mind as a person who could potentially be harmed by his or her conduct. But proximity is not exhausted by foreseeability. In addition, other factors that may bear on the question of whether the relationship between the defendant and the plaintiff is capable of supporting legal liability must be considered (*Cooper*, at para. 37). Such factors may include expectations, representations, reliance and the nature of the interests that characterize the relationship (*Cooper*, at para. 34). However, no definitive list of factors is possible and the list will vary depending on the circumstances of the case (*Cooper*, at para. 35).

[137] There is no question that the relationship between police officer and suspect is sufficiently close and direct that the investigating officer ought to have the targeted suspect in mind as a person potentially harmed by his actions. As I have noted, however, other factors engaged by the relationship must also be considered in order to reach a conclusion regarding proximity. In my view, none of these further factors, either jointly or severally, is sufficient to give rise to the required proximate relationship.

[138] McLachlin C.J. identifies the expectations of the parties and the interests engaged by the relationship as relevant factors giving rise to a relationship of proximity. In respect of the first factor, my colleague states: "Viewed from the broader societal perspective, suspects may reasonably be expected to rely on the police to conduct their investigation in a competent, non-negligent manner" (para. 39). From a logical standpoint, I take no issue with this proposition. Since society undoubtedly relies on police officers to perform their public duty to investigate crime and apprehend criminals in a competent, non-negligent manner, the suspect, as a member of that society, may reasonably be said to share that expectation. The critical factor, however, and one which, in my view, strongly militates *against* the recognition of a duty of care is the second one, the interests engaged by the relationship.

[139] McLachlin C.J. describes the high interests at stake for the targeted suspect. As she states, the suspect "has a critical personal interest in the conduct of the investigation. At stake are his freedom, his reputation and how he may spend a good portion of his life" (para. 34). In addition, as the Statement of Claim in this case reveals, the targeted suspect's

financial interests are also engaged. Mr. Hill claims loss of wages, decreased future income earning ability and numerous out-of-pocket expenses. My colleague concludes that "[t]hese high interests support a finding of a proximate relationship giving rise to a duty of care" (para. 34). With respect, however, the suspect's interests are not the only interests engaged by the relationship. As aptly stated in *Childs v. Desormeaux*:

> The law of negligence not only considers the plaintiff's loss, but explains why it is just and fair to impose the cost of that loss on the particular defendant before the court. The proximity requirement captures this two-sided face of negligence. [para. 25]

In other words, in assessing the proximity of the relationship between plaintiff and defendant, we must pay attention not only to the plaintiff's interests; we must also pay attention to those of the defendant, in this case the investigating officers. This requires us to consider their role in the enforcement of the criminal law.

[140] The enforcement of the criminal law is one of the most important aspects of the maintenance of law and order in a free society. Police officers are the main actors who have been entrusted to fulfill this important function. Often, this requires police officers to make decisions that might adversely affect the rights and interests of citizens. As the Canadian Association of Chiefs of Police notes in its factum:

> While there is a superficial similarity between liability in negligence for police officers and liability in negligence for other professionals, there is also a fundamental distinction. Other professionals have a private law duty to act in the best interests of their clients. Police officers however are public office holders, and have a public duty to act in the best interests of society as a whole. This public interest is not synonymous with the interests of private citizens in a police investigation. As stated in *Odhavji Estate* [at para. 28], "[i]n a democracy, public officers must retain the authority to make decisions that, where appropriate, are adverse to the interests of certain citizens". [para. 22]

The importance of maintaining the police officer's authority to make decisions in the public interest that are adverse to certain citizens is underscored in the case of suspects. As I explained earlier, because society's interest in having the police investigate crime and apprehend criminals inevitably collides with the suspect's interest to be left alone by the state, the imposition of a private duty of care would of necessity give rise to conflicting duties. I am not suggesting, as stated by the Chief Justice (at para. 42), that the police have "a duty to leave people alone". I am saying that it is always in the *interest* of individual members of society to be left alone rather than to be investigated by the police. This is because the individual, whether innocent or not, always stands to lose from being targeted by the police. Therefore, the imposition on the police of a legal duty to take reasonable care not to harm the individual inevitably pulls the police away from targeting that individual as a suspect. In such circumstances, it is neither just nor fair to the individual police officers, nor in the interest of society generally, to impose on police officers a duty that brings in its wake a set of conflicting duties.

[141] By way of example, we need only consider the — unfortunately not uncommon — occurrence of the suspected impaired driver. If in acting to combat impaired driving the police were duty-bound to take into account not only the public interest but also the suspect's interests, in all but the most obvious cases of impairment, the officer might well be advised to simply let the suspect go rather than risk harming the suspect by initiating a criminal law process that may not result in a conviction. By letting the suspect go, the officer would also avoid the risk of time-consuming legal entanglements and potential civil liability. This cautionary approach may seem even more advisable to the officer if the suspect in question is a person of stature and means who may personally stand to lose more from being "wrongfully" dragged into the criminal justice system.

[142] I do not mean to suggest that if a duty of care towards suspects is recognized, police officers will become "so apprehensive, easily dissuaded from doing their duty and intent on preserving public funds from costly claims" that they will be incapable of carrying out their assigned duties (*Dorset Yacht Co. v. Home Office*, [1970] A.C. 1004 (H.L.), at p. 1033, *per* Lord Reid). Like Lord Reid, in my view, the police are made of sterner stuff. Rather, my point is that the overly cautious approach that may result from the imposition of conflicting duties would seriously undermine *society's interest* in having the police investigate crime and apprehend offenders. Mr. Hill purports to answer this argument by denying that the police officer would be faced with such concerns because, he argues, the officer could always safely stand behind the reasonable and probable grounds standard. I will have more to say about the reasonable and probable grounds standard below. For the moment, however, let me simply say that I am dubious that a police officer, who has spent time in

impaired driving court and who has witnessed countless legal debates about whether the arresting officer had the requisite reasonable and probable grounds to believe the suspect had been driving while impaired, would regard this standard as a sufficient safety net. Therefore, I am not persuaded that the potential ramifications of imposing on police these conflicting duties can be so easily answered by an appeal to the reasonable and probable grounds standard.

. . . .

[147] This opposition of interests has been recognized by courts in other countries as a sufficient reason not to impose a duty of care. The imposition of a duty of care in negligence owed to suspects has been held to be inconsistent with a police officer's duty to fully investigate the conduct in question. For example, Australian courts have reasoned that to impose a duty of care in negligence to a person whose conduct is under investigation would conflict with and constrain the proper performance of the police officers' duty to fully investigate the conduct in question: see *Tame v. New South Wales*, at paras. 231 and 298–99; *Gruber v. Backhouse*, at paras. 29–30 and 35–39. Similarly, in England, the House of Lords has refused to extend the duty of care on the basis of a conflict with the "fearless and efficient discharge by police officers of their vitally important public duty of investigating crime": *Calveley v. Chief Constable of the Merseyside Police*, at p. 1030; see also *Hill v. Chief Constable of West Yorkshire*, at pp. 240–41; *Brooks v. Commissioner of Police of the Metropolis*, at para. 30.

[148] To sum up: in my view, although in the present case there is foreseeability of harm, there remains a lack of proximity. Consequently, I would conclude on the ground of lack of proximity alone that the relationship between the investigating officer and the suspect does not give rise to a *prima facie* duty of care. However, even if some degree of proximity were found, and even if this degree of proximity were held to be sufficient to give rise to a *prima facie* duty of care, it is my position that a consideration of additional policy considerations would militate against the recognition of such a duty. This takes us to the second stage of the *Anns* test.

2.5 Residual Policy Considerations

2.5.1 Potential Impact on the Exercise of Police Discretion

[149] It is at the second stage of the *Anns* test that so-called residual policy considerations fall to be con-

sidered. At this stage we are "not concerned with the relationship between the parties, but with the effect of recognizing a duty of care on other legal obligations, the legal system and society more generally" (*Cooper*, at para. 37; see also *Edwards*, at para. 10). I begin my analysis of the residual policy considerations with the question of police discretion since discussion of this factor is more closely related to the issue of conflicting duties we have just discussed. McLachlin C.J. finds that the discretion inherent in police work fails to provide a convincing reason to negate the proposed duty of care because, in her view, it is a factor to be "taken into account in formulating the *standard* of care, not whether a duty of care arises" (para. 51 (emphasis in original)). I disagree. The concern about police discretion in this context is not whether courts will be able to properly distinguish between mere errors of judgment and negligent acts. Police discretion is a significant factor because the police have the discretionary power not to investigate further or engage the criminal process despite the existence of reasonable and probable grounds to believe that an offence has been committed. A concern therefore arises from the fact that, should this Court recognize a private duty of care owed to the suspect under investigation, this power could be exercised, not to advance the public interest as it should be, but out of a fear of civil liability.

[150] The police discretionary power has been recognized by this Court as "an essential feature of the criminal justice system": *R. v. Beare*, [1988] 2 S.C.R. 387, at p. 410. As stated by La Forest J. in that case: "A system that attempted to eliminate discretion would be unworkably complex and rigid." Equally important, however, is the need to properly circumscribe this power so that it be exercised solely in the *public interest*. ...

[151] At first blush, it may be thought that the imposition of a private duty of care to the suspect and the consequent potential for civil liability should give rise to no concern about the improper exercise of police discretion. Just as a decision based on favouritism, or on cultural, social or racial stereotypes, cannot constitute a proper exercise of police discretion, so would a police officer be precluded from deciding not to engage the criminal law process simply to avoid potential civil liability. Again, however, I am not persuaded that we can so easily disregard the potential legal and societal ramifications of imposing on police such a duty.

[152] If this Court accepts Mr. Hill's argument, the investigating officer will be *legally bound*, not only to

fulfill his or her public duty to enforce the law, but also to take care not to harm the suspect by conduct that may ultimately be found to fall below the relevant standard of care. The law should not impose a duty unless it expects that it will be fulfilled. Of course, the surest way of avoiding harm to the suspect is for the officer to decide to not issue process and not engage the criminal law; in other words, in order to reconcile the conflicting duties imposed by law, the police officer may well choose to avoid any risk of harm to the suspect by the exercise of "police discretion". Since there is a significant gap between the "reasonable and probable grounds" standard to issue process and the "beyond a reasonable doubt" standard to convict, the prudent officer who tries to reconcile his public duty to enforce the law and his private duty not to harm the innocent suspect may be well advised not to issue process except in cases where the evidence is overwhelming. How then would we distinguish between a proper exercise of discretion based on a police officer's desire to fulfill his legal duty of care to the suspect and an improper one based on the selfish desire to avoid potential civil liability?

[153] There is significant public interest in maintaining the long-standing reasonable and probable grounds standard so as to ensure a robust and efficient enforcement of the law. Once this standard is met, it is left to others within the criminal justice system, namely the Crown prosecutor, the preliminary hearing justice, and the ultimate finder of fact, to delve more deeply into the legal and factual merits of a case. As this Court has recognized in *R. v. Storrey*, [1990] 1 S.C.R. 241, at pp. 249–50, the reasonable and probable grounds standard achieves a reasonable balance between the individual's right to liberty and the need for society to be protected from crime. In my view, because the imposition of a private duty of care as suggested in this case could only impede the police officers' ability to perform their public duties fearlessly and with despatch, it would detrimentally upset this delicate balance.

2.5.2 Identifying the Wrongfully Convicted for the Purpose of Compensation

[154] As stated earlier, Mr. Hill urges this Court to bring "[t]he law of negligence ... to bear on the problem of wrongful convictions" by recognizing a new tort of negligent investigation. McLachlin C.J. accepts his plea and, in fact, relies on the need to compensate the wrongfully convicted as an important factor in support of finding a duty of care (paras. 36–37). It is noteworthy that the proposed tort would also provide recourse to targeted suspects who, short of being convicted, suffer a loss or injury as a result of a negligent investigation. Indeed, from the plaintiff's viewpoint, it makes little sense to limit the right of action to cases of wrongful conviction. In the context of an action for negligent investigation, the difference between a negligent investigative process that results in a conviction and one that is terminated at an earlier point would seem to go only to the question of the quantum of damages.

[155] Mr. Hill relies on his ultimate acquittal in support of his claim that the losses he suffered as a result of being subjected to the criminal justice system should be compensable at law. The Crown disputes the notion that this is a case about providing a remedy for the wrongfully convicted, and states the following (factum, at para. 6):

> This case is not about preventing wrongful convictions. Wrongfully convicted persons would constitute only a tiny sub-set of the class who would be in a position to sue for negligent investigation (the largest sub-set being those who are acquitted at trial or against whom charges are dropped before trial). Even amongst the wrongfully convicted, few would be able to establish that negligent police investigation caused their conviction.

[156] No one is disputing the validity of Mr. Hill's acquittal. However, the distinction between an acquittal and a finding of innocence must be considered in assessing the potential ramifications of recognizing a tort of negligent investigation. The difficulty arises from the fact that our criminal justice system is not focussed on identifying the innocent. The verdict in a criminal case is guilty or not guilty. A verdict of not guilty is not a factual finding of innocence; neither is an order on appeal overturning a conviction. A verdict of not guilty encompasses a broad range of circumstances, from factual innocence to proof just short of beyond a reasonable doubt. That reality about our criminal justice system raises difficult questions of public policy when it comes time to consider the issue of compensation. Should compensation be reserved to those accused who are factually innocent of the crime with which they were charged or convicted? If so, how should factual innocence be determined? The question whether *any* inquiry should be made into the "true" status of the acquitted person is itself rather controversial. The controversy, in a nutshell, can be described as follows.

[157] On the one hand, a compelling argument can be made that a not guilty verdict should be consid-

ered as a determination of innocence for all purposes, including compensation. Under this first approach, all persons charged with a criminal offence who are ultimately found not guilty could fall in the category of potential plaintiffs. The most powerful argument in support of this approach is that any qualification of the verdict of acquittal would in effect introduce the third verdict of "not proven" which has not been accepted in our criminal justice system. The introduction of such a "Scotch verdict" would create a lingering cloud over those persons who have been found not guilty or in respect of whom the criminal process was terminated but whose innocence has not been conclusively ascertained. Professor H. A. Kaiser, in the context of discussing possible statutory compensation schemes, explains the rationale for having a more inclusive compensatory approach in his article "Wrongful Conviction and Imprisonment: Towards an End to the Compensatory Obstacle Course" (1989), 9 *Windsor Y.B. Access Just.* 96, as follows (at p. 139):

> It is argued that persons who have been wrongfully convicted and imprisoned are *ipso facto* victims of a miscarriage of justice and should be entitled to be compensated. To maintain otherwise introduces the third verdict of "not proved" or "still culpable" under the guise of a compensatory scheme, supposedly requiring higher threshold standards than are necessary for a mere acquittal. As Professor MacKinnon forcefully maintains [in his article "Costs and Compensation for the Innocent Accused" (1988), 67 *Can. Bar Rev.* 489, at pp. 497–98]:
>
> > ... one who is acquitted or discharged is innocent in the eyes of the law and the sights of the rest of us should not be set any lower.... There is a powerful social interest in seeing acquitted persons do no worse than to be restored to the lives they had before they were prosecuted.

[158] On the other hand, an equally compelling argument can be made that any compensation regime that is not limited to the "factually innocent" is unacceptable because it would provide the persons who have in fact committed the offence, but whose guilt could not be proven, with a possible means of profiting from the commission of their crime. Under the federal-provincial *Guidelines: Compensation for Wrongfully Convicted and Imprisoned Persons* (agreed to and adopted by federal and provincial justice ministers in March 1988), a clear distinction is made between a finding of not guilty and a finding of innocence for the purpose of compensation. The fol-

lowing was added to the listed prerequisites for eligibility for compensation:

> As compensation should only be granted to those persons who did not commit the crime for which they were convicted, (as opposed to persons who are found not guilty) a further criteria would require:
> (a) If a pardon is granted under Section 683 [of the *Criminal Code*], a statement on the face of the pardon based on an investigation, that the individual did not commit the offence; or
> (b) If a reference is made by the Minister of Justice under Section 617(b), a statement by the Appellate Court, in response to a question asked by the Minister of Justice pursuant to Section 617(c), to the effect that the person did not commit the offence. [Emphasis added.]

[159] The Chief Justice alludes to this concern when she stresses, at para. 64, that any suspect suing the police "bears the burden of showing that police negligence in the course of an investigation caused harm compensable at law" and that "[e]vidence going to the factual guilt or innocence of the suspect, including the results of any criminal proceedings that may have occurred, may be relevant to this causation inquiry." My colleague takes the position, however, that "[i]t is not necessary to decide here whether an acquittal should be treated as conclusive proof of innocence in a subsequent civil trial" (para. 64). While it is perhaps not necessary in order to dispose of this appeal to decide whether an acquittal should be treated as conclusive proof of innocence, it will certainly be necessary to do so in the next tort action where the plaintiff succeeds in proving negligence in the conduct of a police investigation. These are precisely the sorts of ramifications that must be considered at the second stage of the *Anns* test. The question I ask, therefore, is the following: how are we to distinguish between treatment that is "rightfully imposed by the law" and treatment that is "wrongful" for the purpose of compensation? If we adopt the first approach described earlier, namely that an acquittal should be regarded as the equivalent of a finding of innocence for the purpose of compensation, this could have wide-ranging ramifications. For example, every suspect, who is charged with an offence but who is not convicted because the criminal justice system has worked the way it should, would become a potential plaintiff if he can show that the police conducted a substandard investigation. This result would follow regardless of whether the suspect has in fact committed the crime or not.

[160] The issue is most pertinent in the context of a proposed right of action where, as here, the alleged wrong is the conduct of a substandard police investigation. On the one hand, there is no question that negligent police investigation may contribute to the wrongful conviction of a person who did not commit the crime. Negligent mishandling of physical evidence may lead to erroneous forensic results. Careless or incomplete investigations may fail to yield evidence that would have exonerated the accused or raised a reasonable doubt about his guilt. On the other hand, a negligent investigation will often be the effective cause of an acquittal — as indeed it should be in the criminal context. Numerous evidentiary and procedural safeguards are built in the criminal trial process to guard against wrongful convictions. Hence, evidence may be excluded or disregarded because improper investigative techniques were used in obtaining it. Or, a substandard investigation may yield insufficient evidence to support a conviction, even though the evidence may have been out there to be found.

[161] It is a principle of fundamental justice that the accused in a criminal trial be given the benefit of any reasonable doubt. Therefore, from a criminal law perspective, there is no question that an acquittal must be regarded as tantamount to a finding of innocence. However, in the context of a tort action, we must come to terms with the reality that the person who committed the offence may well stand to *benefit* rather than lose from a botched-up investigation. The true victim in such cases is not the suspect but the public at large. Should the successful accused who actually committed the offence be entitled to use the acquittal brought about by the negligent conduct of police investigators as a basis to claim compensation? A simple example may assist in understanding how this difficulty may easily arise and why it cannot simply be resolved by a careful tailoring of the appropriate standard of care.

. . . .

2.5.3 Competing Policy Concerns Not Resolved by Defining the Standard of Care

[168] The Court of Appeal was of the opinion that the policy concerns weighing against imposing a duty of care could be addressed by a "carefully tailored" standard of care (para. 70). The court went on however to simply adopt the standard of "the reasonable police officer in like circumstances" as the appropriate standard, adding: "In an arrest and prosecution

context, the standard becomes more specific and is directly linked to statutory and common law duties, namely did the police have reasonable and probable grounds to believe that the plaintiff had committed a crime?" (para. 83). McLachlin C.J. agrees that this is the correct standard (para. 67).

[169] With respect, I fail to see how the ordinary negligence standard, even if linked to the reasonable and probable grounds standard, can reconcile the conflicting standards at play. In my view, the usual negligence standard cannot easily co-exist with governing criminal standards. By way of illustration, I will refer, first, to the hypothetical fact situation I have just discussed and, second, to the analysis in the courts below in this case.

. . . .

[172] ... it is instructive to consider how the negligence analysis played out in the courts below in this case. While all five members of the panel in the Court of Appeal for Ontario agreed on the standard to be applied, the court was divided on the application of that standard on the facts before them. Of particular relevance to the point I am making is how the criminal standard for initiating process all but gets lost in the negligence analysis. I will explain.

[173] ... Mr. Hill's claim is based on alleged deficiencies in police identification techniques. In turn, he submits that these deficiencies led to his misidentification by witnesses, his wrongful arrest, and his conviction for the January 23, 1995 robbery. In particular, he alleges that the police failed to follow their own internal guidelines with respect to the presentation of photo lineups to witnesses and that the photo lineup of eleven Caucasians and one aboriginal person was structurally biased against him. In determining whether there was a breach of standard in this case, it therefore became incumbent upon the court to inquire whether the police, in using these identification techniques, met the "reasonable police officer in the same circumstances" standard. While all justices below proceeded with that analysis, they were divided on the result. The trial judge found that there was no breach of the standard ((2003), 66 O.R. (3d) 746), and this finding was upheld by three of the five justices in the Court of Appeal. The two dissenting justices were of the opinion that the identification techniques used by the police fell below this standard.

[174] However, despite the Court of Appeal expressly acknowledging that, in an arrest and prosecution context, the ordinary negligence standard must

be linked to the reasonable and probable grounds standard, none of the judges below considered the criminal standard for initiating process in their analysis. In other words, beyond inquiring into the identification techniques used by the police, none of the judges asked themselves whether the charges were nonetheless laid on the basis of reasonable and probable grounds. The latter standard, of course, is the one by which the police are governed in the conduct of their criminal investigation and, it is important to stress, it is in the public interest that it be maintained as the operative standard. As this Court has observed in *Storrey*, at pp. 249–50:

> The importance of this requirement [that police have reasonable grounds in order to affect an arrest] to citizens of a democracy is self-evident. Yet society also needs protection from crime. This need requires that there be a reasonable balance achieved between the individual's right to liberty and the need for society to be protected from crime. Thus the police need not establish more than reasonable and probable grounds for an arrest.

[175] Therefore, if the civil standard for liability is to be "carefully tailored" so as to complement and not conflict with governing criminal standards, the presence of reasonable and probable grounds for laying the charge must constitute a bar to any civil liability. It cannot be sufficient for the plaintiff to show that identification techniques used by the police were substandard. Rather, it must be established that the identification process was so flawed that it *destroyed* the reasonable and probable grounds for laying the charge. It is only when this standard is met that the plaintiff can be said to have suffered, as McLachlin C.J. puts it "compensable damage that would not have occurred but for the police's negligent conduct" (para. 92).

. . . .

[180] As evidenced by the above, the private nature of the tort action necessarily narrows the focus of the criminal investigation to the individual rights of the parties and, in the process, it is almost inevitable that courts lose sight of the broader public interests at stake. In short, tort law simply does not fit. In his article, Professor Kaiser aptly notes the following at p. 112:

> ... as Professor[s] Cohen and Smith have argued [in their article "Entitlement and the Body Politic: Rethinking Negligence in Public Law" (1986), 64 *Can. Bar Rev.* 1], private law in general and torts in particular are singularly ill-suited to deal with issues which fundamentally concern the nature of the state and the relationship of the individual to the state and the law:
>
> > ... the legislatures and courts, in developing rules of public conduct and responsibility premised on private law tort concepts, have failed to consider a wide range of factors which should be recognized in articulating the relationship of the private individual and the state.... [p. 5]
>
> > ... rights against the state are qualitatively different from rights against individuals. [p. 12]

. . . .

3. CONCLUSION

[187] For these reasons, I conclude, as have other courts of common law jurisdictions, that the common law tort of negligent investigation should not be recognized in Canada. The recognition that the civil tort system is not the appropriate vehicle to provide compensation for the wrongfully convicted should not be viewed as undermining the importance of achieving that important goal. However, how this goal is to be achieved is a complex issue that has been discussed in the context of a number of inquiries and governmental studies.... It may be that compensation for the wrongfully convicted is a matter better left for the legislators in the context of a comprehensive statutory scheme. It is certainly not a matter that should be left to the vagaries of the proposed tort action.

[188] I would allow the Crown's cross-appeal and dismiss Mr. Hill's appeal.

(k) "Denying Justice": Does the Tort of Negligent Investigation Go Far Enough?[†]

Rakhi Ruparelia

Jason George Hill, an Aboriginal man,[1] was investigated, tried, convicted and imprisoned for 20 months for a burglary he did not commit. The investigation that was launched against him was fraught with errors, including questionable witness interview techniques, a problematic photo lineup that included Mr Hill and 11 Caucasian foils, and exculpatory evidence that was ignored. Should suspects like Mr Hill have recourse to the private law for losses suffered as a result of negligent investigation? If so, were the police in this particular case negligent?

Canadian law has been in a state of flux as to when a private law action in negligence can be brought against the police. Lower courts in Canada have been divided on the issue. In *Beckstead v Ottawa (City)* (1997) 37 OR (3d) 62 (*Beckstead*), the Ontario Court of Appeal affirmed that police owe to suspects a common law duty of care; however, this holding was challenged by the Hamilton–Wentworth Police in Mr Hill's case. The Supreme Court of Canada resolved this dispute in *Hill v Hamilton–Wentworth Regional Police Services Board* (2007) 285 DLR (4th) 620 holding that the tort of negligent investigation should be recognised.

Although this case should be heralded as an important victory for the protection of citizens against unreasonable actions of the state, the decision leaves much to be desired. First, given the prevalence of wrongful convictions resulting from substandard police practices, it is deeply disturbing that there was a dissenting judgment on the issue of whether a tort of negligent investigation should be established. Secondly, although the majority decision recognised that the police owe a duty of care to suspects, the analysis surrounding the standard of care essentially ensures that negligence will rarely be found. In determining that the police did not breach the standard of care expected of reasonable police officers in these particular circumstances, the court has set an impossibly high standard for plaintiffs to prove police negligence, and one that mirrors the requirements of pre-existing torts such as malicious

prosecution and false arrest, torts generally considered inadequate. Moreover, an analysis of the role of systemic racism in the wrongful conviction of Mr Hill was noticeably absent. Ultimately, the Canadian justice system has distinguished itself in the common law world by recognising a tort of negligent investigation; however, the change may be more symbolic than real if the threshold for proving a breach of duty is set too high. This obstacle has particularly troubling implications for members of Aboriginal and racialised[2] communities who are disproportionately targeted and harmed by the criminal justice system.

. . . .

SUPREME COURT OF CANADA

Duty of care

In *Hill v Hamilton–Wentworth Regional Police Services Board* (2007) 285 DLR (4th) 620 McLachlin CJ, writing for the majority,[3] stated that the tort of negligent investigation in relation to police practices should be recognised in Canada. Applying the first stage of the *Anns* test,[4] the majority held that a prima facie duty of care was established. It is reasonably foreseeable that a negligent investigation of a suspect may cause harm to the suspect. Moreover, the relationship between a police officer and suspect is personal, and close and direct, thereby satisfying the requirement of sufficient proximity. The majority noted that recognising a duty of care owed by police to suspects under investigation is consistent with the values and spirit underlying the Canadian Charter of Rights and Freedoms. Furthermore, conditions were not established that would negate or limit the prima facie duty of care under the second stage of *Anns*.

On behalf of three dissenting justices,[5] Charron J agreed that reasonable foreseeability was easily established. However, she found no prima facie duty of care given that policy reasons, in her view, barred the finding of proximity. According to the dissent, a duty of care owed by police officers to suspects

[†] Extracts from (2008) 16 Tort L. Rev. 48 at 48, 50–55. [Notes/references omitted.] For further information or to purchase the full article, please visit <www.thomsonreuters.com.au/journalstalk>. Reproduced with permission.

would be incompatible with the police's "overarching public duty". She was also concerned that recognising a duty of care would have a chilling effect on policing, causing police officers to be more cautious in their investigations. Because no duty of care was recognised by the dissent, there was no determination of whether the standard had been breached in this case.

Standard of care

According to the majority, any legitimate policy concerns in recognising a duty of care can be addressed through a carefully articulated standard of care. The standard of care is that of a reasonable police officer in all the circumstances, and the particular conduct required is informed by the stage of the investigation and applicable legal considerations (at [68]). As such, the conduct of a reasonable police officer is informed by criminal law standards. The standard is not perfection and is not to be judged from the vantage of hindsight. Instead, it is judged in the circumstances that prevailed at the time the decision was made (at [73]).

In light of this standard, the court found that the conduct of the investigating officers did not breach the standard of care in 1995. The investigation, including the photo lineup, did not constitute a departure from the standard of a reasonable officer in the circumstances. As a result, there was no negligent investigation on these facts.

ANALYSIS

Although this decision is being celebrated as a groundbreaking decision in the law of torts, it is disconcerting that, in this day and age, there would be any debate as to whether the police should be granted immunity from civil liability in negligence. As the majority remarked (at [36]):

> The unfortunate reality is that negligent policing has now been recognized as a significant contributing factor to wrongful convictions in Canada ... Police conduct that is not malicious, not deliberate, but merely fails to comply with standards of reasonableness can be a significant cause of wrongful convictions.

Given this knowledge, it is even more worrisome that a dissenting opinion was written in this case at all. Knowing what we do about the serious and harmful consequences of poor police practice, it is difficult to see how immunity could be reasonably supported, particularly on the basis of policy, as the

dissenting opinion suggested. The dissenting justices essentially rejected the notion that police must act reasonably in their investigations and instead pointed to existing remedies as the solution. However, as the majority noted (at [35], footnotes omitted, emphasis added):

> On this point, I note that the existing remedies for wrongful prosecution and conviction are incomplete and may leave a victim of negligent police investigation without legal recourse. The torts of false arrest, false imprisonment and malicious prosecution do not provide an adequate remedy for negligent acts ... As the Court of Appeal pointed out, an important category of police conduct with the potential to seriously affect the lives of suspects will go unremedied if a duty of care is not recognized. This category includes "very poor performance of important police duties" and other "non-malicious category of police misconduct". To deny a remedy in tort is, quite literally, to deny justice.

Despite this important recognition by the majority of the Supreme Court, and a very thoughtful and persuasive analysis of why a duty of care is owed by police to suspects, the discussion surrounding the application of the standard of care is, at closer inspection, disheartening. The majority was very forgiving in judging the reasonableness of police conduct in 1995. Although the majority treated the events leading to Mr Hill's wrongful conviction as if they had occurred in another era, in reality 1995 was not that long ago.

Ultimately, the court believed that the publication of Mr Hill's photo, the interviewing of two witnesses together, and the incomplete record of witness interviews were not good police practices evaluated by today's standards, but were not unreasonable, judged against the practices of reasonable police officers in similar circumstances in 1995 (at [78]). Similarly, the majority determined that the photo lineup was not unreasonable judged by 1995 standards. It is difficult to evaluate on what basis the majority formed these conclusions; however, what is clear is that little was expected of police officers in 1995.

Wrongful convictions

Interestingly, the majority suggests that in 1995, "awareness of the danger of wrongful convictions was less acute than it is today" (at [88]). This observation leads to the conclusion that police practices were not as sensitive to the issues of wrongful convictions and institutional bias as they are today. However, numerous cases of wrongful convictions had already been well publicised by the time the events leading to Mr Hill's conviction had taken place.[6] Of particular relevance to this case is the role of faulty eyewitness evidence. Faulty eyewitness evidence led to the initial convictions of David Milgaard, Thomas Sophonow and Guy Paul Morin,[7] cases that received extensive attention as wrongful convictions in the 1990s.

These warnings were not limited to academic commentary. The Association in Defence of the Wrongfully Convicted (AIDWYC) was founded in 1993 in response to the wrongful conviction of Guy Paul Morin in 1992, and raised public awareness about this issue. The public was further educated by the CTV and CBC television networks, which exposed the issue of wrongful convictions beginning in the late 1980s.[8] The Globe and Mail newspaper published an article on 21 January 1995, which outlined the problems generated by eyewitness reporting and cited an American study that found that half of the wrongful conviction cases reviewed were due to eyewitness errors.[9] Ironically, this article appeared in the Globe and Mail during the same period in which Mr Hill was being investigated.

Systemic racism

It is impossible to have a meaningful discussion of the risk of wrongful convictions without recognising the role that systemic racism plays in targeting and prosecuting Aboriginal and racialised peoples. As the Royal Commission on the Donald Marshall, Jr, Prosecution noted:[10]

> Donald Marshall, Jr's status as a Native contributed to the miscarriage of justice that has plagued him since 1971. We believe that certain persons within the system would have been more rigorous in their duties, more careful, or more conscious of fairness if Marshall had been white.

The majority opinion of the Supreme Court remarked that a reasonable officer today might be expected to avoid lineups using foils of a different race than the suspect, to avoid unfairness to suspects who are members of minority groups as well as the perception of injustice (at [80]). The majority further noted (at [80]) that these concerns were "underlined by growing awareness of persisting problems with institutional bias against minorities in the criminal justice system, including aboriginal persons like Mr Hill". To support this claim of the "growing awareness" of such problems, the majority (ironically) cited the Royal Commission on Aboriginal Peoples' report from 1996.

Even more information was known in the mid-1990s that the Supreme Court did not acknowledge. In 1989, the Royal Commission on the Donald Marshall, Jr, Prosecution published its report which explored in significant detail the impact of systemic racism on Blacks and Aboriginals in the Nova Scotia criminal justice system.[11] The monumental study by the Commission on Systemic Racism in the Ontario Criminal Justice System was published in 1995, the same year the incidents in question occurred. The report exposed the insidious and systemic nature of racism in the criminal justice system. This Commission was established in 1992 in response to an already "growing awareness" of the extent and impact of racism at all levels of the criminal justice process. A large portion of the report was devoted to policing.[12] Similarly, in 1991, the Report of the Aboriginal Justice Inquiry of Manitoba emphasised the importance of clear and consistent police practices to address systemic racism.[13]

Ultimately, a discussion of systemic discrimination was woefully absent in the Supreme Court's decisions. The only mention of racism was in the abstract, when the majority opinion acknowledged that the tort of negligent investigation would be one way in which to address the problem of "institutional racism" (at [36]). There was no recognition of the role that systemic racism played in this investigation and how it tainted the entire process. Systemic racism, however, was at the core of the negligent investigation alleged. Mr Hill was targeted as a suspect because he was Aboriginal. Although many eyewitnesses described the robber in other ways, the police became convinced that the suspect was Aboriginal, and that the Aboriginal person in question was Mr Hill. The reasons for fixating on an Aboriginal suspect are not entirely clear from the decision; however, police officers are not immune from stereotypes that associate Aboriginality with crime.

In any event, cross-race eyewitness identification has been challenged as unreliable, given the dangers of misidentification documented over the past decades. As Tanovich noted, "[c]ross-racial identifications are now recognized as a leading cause of wrongful convictions".[14] The Manitoba Aboriginal Justice Inquiry questioned the value in describing suspects by race at all, when a description of the suspect's skin colouring would suffice.[15] As the Inquiry noted, "[to] advise police officers that a suspect in an offence is a native is a licence to commit racism. That should not be condoned."[16] Understood as a social construct rather than a biological one, race makes little sense as a physical descriptor.[17]

Although the majority believed that the police were not guilty of "tunnel vision" in their investigation of Mr Hill, it is difficult to explain for what other reason the police did not explore potentially exculpatory evidence.

Particularly troubling is the analysis of the photo lineup. The majority of the Supreme Court held that a photo lineup comprised of the suspect as the sole Aboriginal man among 11 white foils, though "not ideal", was not unreasonable in 1995. Moreover, in this case, the lineup did not lead to unfairness. Citing the majority reasons of the Ontario Court of Appeal, McLachlin CJ noted that a racially skewed lineup is structurally biased only "if you can tell that one person is non-Caucasian" and "assuming the suspect is the one that's standing out" (at [81]). In her view, Mr Hill did not stand out because a number of the subjects had similar features and colouring (at [79]).

This reasoning is problematic for a number of reasons. First of all, who assesses whether the suspect and the foils have "similar features and colouring"? Should white police officers be entrusted with the determination of who looks alike? Should the (primarily) white judiciary? The majority of the Supreme Court essentially articulated the standard of care from the dominant white perspective. In other words, did the white people in the lineup look, through white eyes, sufficiently like Mr Hill? Given that racialised people are often interchangeable through the dominant white gaze — hence the varying descriptions of the robber as Hispanic, "North American Indian", Asian and Aboriginal — it is not sufficient to articulate the standard of care in terms of whether "you" can tell that one person stands out in a lineup based on her or his race. Imagine the opposite situation. If a suspect was the sole white man in a lineup of light-skinned racialised and Aboriginal people, this practice would likely be seen as outrageous and clearly unfair. It is too risky to defer to the police and judiciary for these types of assessments.

Secondly, the majority opinion paid little attention to the perception of injustice that arises from a racially skewed lineup, which was a disservice to the carefully articulated reasons of the dissenting opinion of the Court of Appeal. Although the majority noted that a reasonable officer today "might be" expected to avoid lineups using foils of a different race than the suspect for this reason, it did not go far enough in setting the standard for even today's officers. The majority decision left open the possibility that under certain circumstances, this practice could be acceptable. Under no circumstances should this practice be condoned. As Feldman and LaForme JJA observed

in the dissenting opinion of the Court of Appeal (*Hill v Hamilton–Wentworth Regional Police Services Board* (2005) 76 OR (3d) 481 at [154]), the perception of fairness is particularly important in Canada where Aboriginal justice is concerned. As the Supreme Court of Canada has itself noted in other cases, widespread bias against Aboriginal peoples has translated into systemic discrimination in the criminal justice system.[18] The dissenting opinion of the Court of Appeal held (at [156]) that a lineup such as the one used in Mr Hill's case was "prima facie potentially structurally biased with obvious potential for unfairness".

At a minimum, the Supreme Court should have recognised, unequivocally, that this lineup was unacceptable by today's standards. However, the court should have also found that this lineup was unreasonable by the standards of 1995. The descriptions of the suspect were wide-ranging in terms of race, but most witnesses identified the suspect as someone who was not Caucasian. Detective Loft, the detective in charge of the investigation, released a composite that identified the suspect as having a "dark complexion" based on the descriptions he had gathered. And yet, Mr Hill was placed in a lineup with Caucasian foils.

The majority reasons of both the Court of Appeal and the Supreme Court suggested that regardless of whether the photo lineup had fallen below the standard of care in these circumstances, it was not connected to the charge for which Mr Hill was eventually convicted, but rather to one of the charges that had been dropped.[19] In other words, there was no causal relationship between the lineup in question and Mr Hill's wrongful conviction. As the dissenting opinion of the Court of Appeal pointed out, however, this lineup was also shown to a number of other witnesses to the robberies and contributed to Detective Loft's fixation on Mr Hill as the "plastic bag robber". This fixation also played a role in Detective Loft's decision not to explore potentially exculpatory evidence.

Individual stages of the investigation cannot be distinguished in the way attempted by the majority opinions. Separating the individual events in the investigation against Mr Hill facilitates a non-racist interpretation of each event and each exercise of discretion; however, when the investigation is viewed as a whole, it is difficult to discount the role that systemic racism played in the course of events, including the use of a structurally biased photo lineup and Detective Loft's tunnel vision in pursuing Mr Hill as the sole suspect. As Anderson and Anderson note, "[i]t is no longer acceptable to suggest that wrongful conviction resulting from police activities is simply the result of numerous bizarre elements coincidentally corning together".[20]

Ultimately, with the exception of the dissenting opinion of the Court of Appeal, the trial and appellate courts reflected a discomfort with recognising the role of race and racism in this case. The trial judge seemed uncomfortable even identifying the foils as Caucasian.[21] The analysis by the courts was decontextualised, and minimised the consideration of race, even though it was an issue that clearly warranted discussion. The courts lost sight of the fact that (yet another) Aboriginal man was wrongfully imprisoned due to a shoddy police investigation that was fuelled by racist practices. Rather than focusing on the injustice of the investigation, which produced a result that could have been prevented with simple precautionary measures, the Supreme Court minimised the gravity of the negligence by referring to the events leading to the wrongful incarceration as "unfortunate" (at [4]) and "questionable" (at [78]). The photo lineup was "not ideal" (at [80]) and the investigation was "flawed" (at [74]). Though "unfortunate", "questionable", "not ideal" and "flawed" enough to lead to the wrongful conviction of Mr Hill, the conduct of the police met the standard of a reasonable police officer in like circumstances. The majority opinion of the Supreme Court attempted to sanitise the events leading to the wrongful conviction of Mr Hill in order to avoid an uncomfortable recognition of [racism]. If there had been an explicit recognition of systemic racism in this analysis, perhaps it would have been more difficult to maintain that the investigation had been reasonably conducted.

Even in the context of 1995 police practices, it is troubling to label the conduct of the police officers as reasonable. First, as discussed above, it is not fair to suggest that little was known about the danger of wrongful convictions at that time. Even if this were an accurate evaluation of the state of knowledge in the mid-1990s, it is problematic to defer to a standard of racist police practices. Such practices should be viewed as inherently unreasonable. Otherwise, we risk the perverse outcome of recognising reasonableness in institutional racism because that in fact is the standard practice. The reasonable police officer in like circumstances does not engage in racist police practices. When the majority of the Supreme Court determined that a photo lineup with the suspect as the only racialised man was reasonable in 1995, but speculated that it might not be the case anymore, was the court implying there was a time when racism was reasonable? Given the grave consequences of systemic racism in the criminal jus-

tice system, recognised both in 1995 and today, the courts should assume a more proactive role in articulating the appropriate standard of care expected of police officers, rather than deferring to practices that have been widely criticised as harmful to racialised peoples.

The majority's deference to police practice was also evident in its response to the concern that the new tort will have a chilling effect on policing. The majority emphasised that it was not the role of the courts to second-guess the difficult decisions that police officers are required to make, as long as their discretion is exercised reasonably. Overall, the court permitted the police officers in this case a wide scope of discretion. The majority opinion encountered more difficulty in evaluating the allegations against Detective Loft, the detective in charge of the investigation, who did not ask the Crown to postpone the case to permit reinvestigation when potentially exculpatory evidence was made known to him. Nonetheless, the majority claimed (at [88]) that it was not a case of tunnel vision or blinding oneself to the facts, and excused the detective's exclusive focus on Mr Hill as falling into the "difficult area of the exercise of discretion". Once again, the court was able to interpret the troubling actions of the police in a way that evaded the acknowledgment of racism.

Of course, police officers, like other actors in the criminal justice system, require adequate discretion to do their work effectively. However, in a system that is tainted by systemic racism at every level, courts need to curtail some of this discretion, not defer to it when it is exercised in discriminatory ways. The majority opinion noted that "hearsay, suspicion and a hunch" might be enough of a basis from which to proceed at the outset of an investigation, as long as the police officer acts as a reasonable investigating officer would in those circumstances (at [68]). How courts will assess the reasonableness of "hunches" and "suspicions" in determining whether the standard of care was breached remains to be seen. Police officers' "hunches" are informed by their personal attitudes and prejudices, and have often resulted in the targeting of Aboriginal and racialised peoples as suspects. In *R v Simpson* (1993) 79 CCC (3d) 482 at 502 (Ont CA), Doherty JA warned against relying on "hunches":

> Such subjective based assessments can too easily mask discriminatory conduct based on such irrelevant factors as the detainee's sex, colour, age, ethnic origin or sexual orientation. Equally, without objective criteria detentions could be based on mere speculation. A guess which proves accurate becomes in hindsight a "hunch".

There have been strong warnings against giving the police too much discretion, which, consciously or unconsciously, has often been exercised to the disadvantage of Aboriginal and racialised communities.[22]

CONCLUSION

The Supreme Court of Canada made history on 4 October 2007, when it recognised the tort of negligent investigation. In principle, this recognition was an important step. However, the court's venture into this new territory was hesitant. The court set the standard for police conduct so low that it will likely be only in rare cases that a breach will be found. Even the lawyer for the Hamilton–Wentworth Police stated that although it was disappointing that police could be sued for simple negligence, the Supreme Court set such a high standard that it will be difficult for plaintiffs to prove their case.[23]

Most significantly, the court lost an important opportunity to show how tort of negligent investigation can be used to combat systemic racism against Aboriginal people like Mr Hill and members of other racialised communities. Despite the fact that the majority acknowledged the potential of this tort to address institutional bias, the Supreme Court demonstrated that application to particular cases will pose an obstacle for plaintiffs who fall victim to negligent policing. Justice was denied to Mr Hill. If the court seeks to fill in the gap left by torts such as false imprisonment and malicious prosecution,[24] the threshold for finding a breach of the standard of care will need to be relaxed in future cases to ensure that a remedy is available for non-malicious categories of poor police investigation.

If the criminal justice system, and the police in particular, are to earn the trust of Aboriginal and racialised communities, the police must be held responsible for their conduct. As LaForme JA, the first Aboriginal person to be appointed to an appellate court in Canadian history and co-author of the insightful dissenting opinion of the Ontario Court of Appeal in this case, observed extrajudicially:

> Police, perhaps even more than others, must accept the accuracy and depth of the attitudes and views Aboriginal people have with respect to the discrimination they experience, and demonstrate to them that they no longer need to be distrustful of the police.[25]

If the police are truly held accountable for their actions, not only in theory, public confidence in the system will be advanced.

II

Contracts

OVERVIEW

This Part contains three chapters. The first is concerned with the nature of contractual and exchange obligation. It opens with the infamous case of *Peevyhouse v. Garland Coal*, where a large coal company breached an agreement with a farming couple that it would fully restore their farmland after strip mining operations were completed. The court awarded a very small sum in damages based on value by which the land was diminished rather than the cost of restoring the land (which remains, to this day, in a damaged state). What is a contract? How absolute are its undertakings? What influences the outcome in contract disputes? Thereafter, the chapter outlines the elements of classical contract law developed in the 19th century as the industrial and urban market emerged. It advances the proposition that classical contract law reflected certain philosophical values — such as individualism, freedom of contract, a *laissez faire* approach to market regulation — the legacies of which remain today in a much altered economic context. We explore two dynamics: first, how judges have continued to evolve the principles of contract using contrasting values such as reciprocity, price, role solidarity and relational integrity; and second, how business people have avoided coming into courts with contractual disputes. Why might they want to "keep the lawyers out of it"?

The following two chapters consider several contract law questions that have vexed judges over the years: first, when can a contract be said to have been 'formed' and thus come into effect? We examine both a family situation and a major commercial dispute. Second, what terms excluding liability for defective products or services delivered will be upheld by courts, and why? Does the fact that someone signed a written contract make the difference? Does it matter if the parties are in equal or unequal positions? In this section we compare and contrast cases from the 19th century and more recent cases. Third, what happens if circumstances change after a contract has been entered into? Is a later promise that adjusts the amount to be paid binding? Why or why not? What constitutes legal and practical consideration (or exchange value)? Again, we contrast older and newer cases.

LEARNING OBJECTIVES

At the conclusion of this Part, readers should be able to

- outline the values and theories of 19th century philosophers and economists, and trace how these found their way into doctrines and principles of classical contract law;
- outline the contours of classical contract law, and state how they have been modified in 'neo-classical contract law';
- identify significant shifts in the market, in regulation, in government engagement in the market, and in the way in which judges perceive their roles in contract law disputes and their impact on the development of contract law;
- explain why business people tend to avoid taking contractual disputes to court as shown in the empirical work of Macaulay and others, and analyse whether this results from dissonance between contract law rules and business realities;
- outline the usual requirements for a valid contract in relation to agreement (formation through offer and acceptance), intention to create a legal relationship, and consideration;
- define an 'exclusion clause', and compare and contrast how older and newer cases have responded to attempts to limit contractual obligation;
- explain the doctrine of consideration, and outline when judges have upheld (or not upheld) purported agreement to 'new prices' after a contract has been formed;
- state the components of relational contract law as proposed by Ian MacNeil, and assess whether they explain some of the changes in contract law in the 20th and 21st centuries.

LEARNING RESOURCES

Professor Judith Maute of the University of Oklahoma has undertaken a comprehensive study of the *Peevyhouse* case. You can learn more through

- Judith L. Maute "Peevyhouse v. Garland Coal & Mining Co. Revisited: The Ballad of Willie and Lucille" (1995) 89 Nw. U.L. Rev. 1341 (Available on Quicklaw)
- By Podcast <http://itunes.apple.com/us/podcast/law-talk-legal-scholarship/id263510985>: Episode #12 — Maute on the Ballad of Willie and Lucille (Released October 2, 2008).
- Judith Maute, "The Unearthed Facts of *Peevyhouse v Garland Coal and Mining Co*", in Douglas G. Baird, ed., *Contracts Stories* (New York: Foundation Press, 2007) at 265–303.

5

The Emergence of Contract Law: Exchange and the Market

(a) *Peevyhouse v. Garland Coal & Mining Co.*[†]

Supreme Court of Oklahoma

[JACKSON, J. (Welch, Davison, Halley, and Johnson, JJ., concurring):]

In the trial court, plaintiffs Willie and Lucille Peevyhouse sued the defendant, Garland Coal and Mining Company, for damages for breach of contract. Judgment was for plaintiffs in an amount considerably less than was sued for. Plaintiffs appeal and defendant cross-appeals.

In the briefs on appeal, the parties present their argument and contentions under several propositions; however, they all stem from the basic question of whether the trial court properly instructed the jury on the measure of damages.

Briefly stated, the facts are as follows: plaintiffs owned a farm containing coal deposits, and in November, 1954, leased the premises to defendant for a period of five years for coal mining purposes. A "strip-mining" operation was contemplated in which the coal would be taken from pits on the surface of the ground, instead of from underground mine shafts. In addition to the usual covenants found in a coal mining lease, defendant specifically agreed to perform certain restorative and remedial work at the end of the lease period. It is unnecessary to set out the details of the work to be done, other than to say that it would involve the moving of many thousands of cubic yards of dirt, at a cost estimated by expert witnesses at about $29,000.00. However, plaintiffs sued for only $25,000.00.

During the trial, it was stipulated that all covenants and agreements in the lease contract had been fully carried out by both parties, except the remedial work mentioned above; defendant conceded that this work had not been done.

Plaintiffs introduced expert testimony as to the amount and nature of the work to be done, and its estimated cost. Over plaintiffs' objections, defendant thereafter introduced expert testimony as to the "diminution in value" of plaintiffs' farm resulting from the failure of defendant to render performance as agreed in the contract — that is, the difference between the present value of the farm, and what its value would have been if defendant had done what it agreed to do.

At the conclusion of the trial, the court instructed the jury that it must return a verdict for plaintiffs, and left the amount of damages for jury determination. On the measure of damages, the court instructed the jury that it might consider the cost of performance of the work defendant agreed to do, "together with all of the evidence offered on behalf of either party".

It thus appears that the jury was at liberty to consider the "diminution in value" of plaintiffs' farm as well as the cost of "repair work" in determining the amount of damages.

It returned a verdict for plaintiffs for $5000.00 — only a fraction of the "cost of performance", *but more than the total value of the farm even after the remedial work is done.*

On appeal, the issue is sharply drawn. Plaintiffs contend that the true measure of damages in this case is what it will cost plaintiffs to obtain perfor-

[†] 382 P.2d 109 (Oka. 1962).

mance of the work that was not done because of defendant's default. Defendant argues that the measure of damages is the cost of performance "limited, however, to the total difference in the market value before and after the work was performed".

It appears that this precise question has not heretofore been presented to this court. In *Ardizonne v. Archer*, 72 Okl. 70, 178 P. 263, this court held that the measure of damages for breach of a contract to drill an oil well was the reasonable cost of drilling the well, but here a slightly different factual situation exists. The drilling of an oil well will yield valuable geological information, even if no oil or gas is found, and of course if the well is a producer, the value of the premises increases. In the case before us, it is argued by defendant with some force that the performance of the remedial work defendant agreed to do will add at the most only a few hundred dollars to the value of plaintiffs' farm, and that the damages should be limited to that amount because that is all plaintiffs have lost.

Plaintiffs rely on *Groves v. John Wunder Co.*, 205 Minn. 163, 286 N.W. 235, 123 A.L.R. 502. In that case, the Minnesota court, in a substantially similar situation, adopted the "cost of performance" rule as opposed to the "value" rule. The result was to authorize a jury to give plaintiff damages in the amount of $60,000, where the real estate concerned would have been worth only $12,160, even if the work contracted for had been done.

It may be observed that *Groves v. John Wunder Co.*, *supra*, is the only case which has come to our attention in which the cost of performance rule has been followed under circumstances where the cost of performance greatly exceeded the diminution in value resulting from the breach of contract. Incidentally, it appears that this case was decided by a plurality rather than a majority of the members of the court.

Defendant relies principally upon *Sandy Valley & E.R. Co., v. Hughes*, 175 Ky. 320, 194 S.W. 344; *Bigham v. Wabash-Pittsburg Terminal Ry. Co.*, 223 Pa. 106, 72 A. 318; and *Sweeney v. Lewis Const. Co.*, 66 Wash. 490, 119 P. 1108. These were all cases in which, under similar circumstances, the appellate courts followed the "value" rule instead of the "cost of performance" rule. Plaintiff points out that in the earliest of these cases (*Bigham*) the court cites as authority on the measure of damages an earlier Pennsylvania *tort* case, and that the other two cases follow the first, with no explanation as to why a measure of damages ordinarily followed in cases sounding in tort should be used in contract cases. Nevertheless, it is of some significance that three out

of four appellate courts have followed the diminution in value rule under circumstances where, as here, the cost of performance greatly exceeds the diminution in value.

The explanation may be found in the fact that the situations presented are artificial ones. It is highly unlikely that the ordinary property owner would agree to pay $29,000 (or its equivalent) for the construction of "improvements" upon his property that would increase its value only about ($300) three hundred dollars. The result is that we are called upon to apply principles of law theoretically based upon reason and reality to a situation which is basically unreasonable and unrealistic.

In *Groves v. John Wunder Co.*, *supra*, in arriving at its conclusions, the Minnesota court apparently considered the contract involved to be analogous to a building and construction contract, and cited authority for the proposition that the cost of performance or completion of the building as contracted is ordinarily the measure of damages in actions for damages for the breach of such a contract.

In an annotation following the Minnesota case beginning at 123 A.L.R. 515, the annotator places the three cases relied on by defendant (*Sandy Valley*, *Bigham* and *Sweeney*) under the classification of cases involving "grading and excavation contracts".

We do not think either analogy is strictly applicable to the case now before us. The primary purpose of the lease contract between plaintiffs and defendant was neither "building and construction" nor "grading and excavation". It was merely to accomplish the economical recovery and marketing of coal from the premises, to the profit of all parties. The special provisions of the lease contract pertaining to remedial work were incidental to the main object involved.

Even in the case of contracts that are unquestionably building and construction contracts, the authorities are not in agreement as to the factors to be considered in determining whether the cost of performance rule or the value rule should be applied. The American Law Institute's Restatement of the Law, Contracts, Volume 1, Sections 346(1)(a)(i) and (ii) submits the proposition that the cost of performance is the proper measure of damages "if this is possible and does not involve *unreasonable economic waste*"; and that the diminution in value caused by the breach is the proper measure "if construction and completion in accordance with the contract would involve *unreasonable economic waste*". (Emphasis supplied.) In an explanatory comment immediately following the text, the Restatement makes it clear that the "economic waste" referred to consists of the destruction of a substantially completed building or other structure. Of course no such destruction is involved in the case now before us.

On the other hand, in McCormick, Damages, Section 168, it is said with regard to building and construction contracts that "... in cases where the defect is one that can be repaired or cured without *undue expense*" the cost of performance is the proper measure of damages, but where "... the defect in material or construction is one that cannot be remedied without *an expenditure for reconstruction disproportionate to the end to be attained*" (emphasis supplied) the value rule should be followed. The same idea was expressed in *Jacob & Youngs, Inc. v. Kent*, 230 N.Y. 239, 129 N.E. 889, 23 A.L.R. 1429, as follows:

> The owner is entitled to the money which will permit him to complete, unless the cost of completion is grossly and unfairly out of proportion to the good to be attained. When that is true, the measure is the difference in value.

It thus appears that the prime consideration in the Restatement was "economic waste"; and that the prime consideration in McCormick, Damages, and in *Jacob & Youngs, Inc. v. Kent, supra*, was the relationship between the expense involved and the "end to be attained" — in other words, the "relative economic benefit".

In view of the unrealistic fact situation in the instant case, and certain Oklahoma statutes to be hereinafter noted, we are of the opinion that the "relative economic benefit" is a proper consideration here. This is in accord with the recent case of *Mann v. Clowser*, 190 Va. 887, 59 S.E.2d 78, where, in applying the cost rule, the Virginia court specifically noted that "... the defects are remediable from a practical standpoint and the costs *are not grossly disproportionate to the results to be obtained*" (Emphasis supplied).

23 O.S. 1961 §§ 96 and 97 provide as follows:

> "§ 96. ... Notwithstanding the provisions of this chapter, no person can recover a greater amount in damages for the breach of an obligation, than he would have gained by the full performance thereof on both sides. ...
>
> "§ 97. ... Damages must, in all cases, be reasonable, and where an obligation of any kind appears to create a right to unconscionable and grossly oppressive damages, contrary to substantial justice no more than reasonable damages can be recovered."

Although it is true that the above sections of the statute are applied most often in tort cases, they are by their own terms, and the decisions of this court, also applicable in actions for damages for breach of contract. It would seem that they are peculiarly applicable here where, under the "cost of performance" rule, plaintiffs might recover an amount about nine times the total value of their farm. Such would seem to be "unconscionable and grossly oppressive damages, contrary to substantial justice" within the meaning of the statute. Also, it can hardly be denied that if plaintiffs here are permitted to recover under the "cost of performance" rule, they will receive a greater benefit from the breach than could be gained from full performance, contrary to the provisions of Sec. 96.

An analogy may be drawn between the cited sections, and the provisions of 15 O.S. 1961 §§ 214 and 215. These sections tend to render void any provisions of a contract which attempt to fix the amount of stipulated damages to be paid in case of a breach, except where it is impracticable or extremely difficult to determine the actual damages. This results in spite of the agreement of the parties, and the obvious and well known rationale is that insofar as they exceed the actual damages suffered, the stipulated damages amount to a penalty or forfeiture which the law does not favor.

23 O.S. 1961 §§ 96 and 97 have the same effect in the case now before us. *In spite of the agreement of the parties*, these sections limit the damages recoverable to a reasonable amount not "contrary to substantial justice"; they prevent plaintiffs from recovering a "greater amount in damages for the breach of an obligation" than they would have "gained by the full performance thereof".

We therefore hold that where, in a coal mining lease, lessee agrees to perform certain remedial work on the premises concerned at the end of the lease period, and thereafter the contract is fully performed by both parties except that the remedial work is not done, the measure of damages in an action by lessor against lessee for damages for breach of contract is ordinarily the reasonable cost of performance of the work; however, where the contract provision breached was merely incidental to the main purpose in view, and where the economic benefit which would result to lessor by full performance of the work is grossly disproportionate to the cost of performance, the damages which lessor may recover are limited to the diminution in value resulting to the premises because of the non-performance.

We believe the above holding is in conformity with the intention of the Legislature as expressed in the statutes mentioned, and in harmony with the better-reasoned cases from the other jurisdictions where analogous fact situations have been considered. It should be noted that the rule as stated does not interfere with the property owner's right to "do what he will with his own" *Chamberlain v. Parker*, 45 N.Y. 569), or his right, if he chooses, to contract for "improvements" which will actually have the effect of reducing his property's value. Where such result is in fact contemplated by the parties, and is a main or principal purpose of those contracting, it would seem that the measure of damages for breach would ordinarily be the cost of performance.

The above holding disposes of all of the arguments raised by the parties on appeal.

Under the most liberal view of the evidence herein, the diminution in value resulting to the premises because of non-performance of the remedial work was $300.00. After a careful search of the record, we have found no evidence of a higher figure, and plaintiffs do not argue in their briefs that a greater diminution in value was sustained. It thus appears that the judgment was clearly excessive, and that the amount for which judgment should have been rendered is definitely and satisfactorily shown by the record.

We are asked by each party to modify the judgment in accordance with the respective theories advanced, and it is conceded that we have authority to do so. 12 O.S. 1961 § 952; *Busboom v. Smith*, 199 Okl. 688, 191 P.2d 198; *Stumpf v. Stumpf*, 173 Okl. 1, 46 P.2d 315.

We are of the opinion that the judgment of the trial court for plaintiffs should be, and it is hereby, modified and reduced to the sum of $300.00, and as so modified it is affirmed.

[Williams, C.J., Blackbird, V.C.J., and Irwin and Berry, JJ., dissent. IRWIN, J.:]
By the specific provisions in the coal mining lease under consideration, the defendant agreed as follows:

> ... 7b Lessee agrees to make fills in the pits dug on said premises on the property line in such manner that fences can be placed thereon and access had to opposite sides of the pits.
>
> c Lessee agrees to smooth off the top of the spoil banks on the above premises.
>
> 7d Lessee agrees to leave the creek crossing the above premises in such a condition that it will not interfere with the crossings to be made in pits as set out in 7b.
>
> ...
>
> 7f Lessee further agrees to leave no shale or dirt on the high wall of said pits. ...

Following the expiration of the lease, plaintiffs made demand upon defendant that it carry out the provisions of the contract and to perform those covenants contained therein.

Defendant admits that it failed to perform its obligations that it agreed and [contracted] to perform under the lease contract and there is nothing in the record which indicates that defendant could not perform its obligations. Therefore, in my opinion defendant's breach of the contract was wilful and not in good faith.

Although the contract speaks for itself, there were several negotiations between the plaintiffs and defendant before the contract was executed. Defendant admitted in the trial of the action, that plaintiffs insisted that the above provisions be included in the contract and that they would not agree to the coal mining lease unless the above provisions were included.

In consideration for the lease contract, plaintiffs were to receive a certain amount as royalty for the coal produced and marketed and in addition thereto their land was to be restored as provided in the contract.

Defendant received as consideration for the contract, its proportionate share of the coal produced and marketed and in addition thereto, the *right to use* plaintiffs' land in the furtherance of its mining operations.

The cost for performing the contract in question could have been reasonably approximated when the contract was negotiated and executed and there are no conditions now existing which could not have been reasonably anticipated by the parties. Therefore, defendant had knowledge, when it prevailed upon the plaintiffs to execute the lease, that the cost of performance might be disproportionate to the value or benefits received by plaintiff for the performance.

Defendant has received its benefits under the contract and now urges, in substance, that plaintiffs' measure of damages for its failure to perform should be the economic value of performance to the plaintiffs and not the cost of performance.

If a peculiar set of facts should exist where the above rule should be applied as the proper measure of damages, (and in my judgment those facts do not exist in the instant case) before such rule should be applied, consideration should be given to the benefits received or contracted for by the party who asserts the application of the rule.

Defendant did not have the right to mine plaintiffs' coal or to use plaintiffs' property for its mining operations without the consent of plaintiffs. Defendant had knowledge of the benefits that it would receive under the contract and the approximate cost of performing the contract. With this knowledge, it must be presumed that defendant thought that it would be to its economic advantage to enter into the contract with plaintiffs and that it would reap benefits from the contract, or it would have not entered into the contract.

Therefore, if the value of the performance of a contract should be considered in determining the measure of damages for breach of a contract, the value of the benefits received under the contract by a party who breaches a contract should also be considered. However, in my judgment, to give consideration to either in the instant action, completely rescinds and holds for naught the solemnity of the contract before us and makes an entirely new contract for the parties.

In *Goble v. Bell Oil & Gas Co.*, 97 Okl. 261, 223 P. 371, we held:

> Even though the contract contains harsh and burdensome terms which the court does not in all respects approve, it is the province of the parties in relation to lawful subject matter to fix their rights and obligations, and the court will give the contract effect according to its expressed provisions, unless it be shown by competent evidence proof that the written agreement as executed is the result of fraud, mistake, or accident.

In *Cities Services Oil Co. v. Geolograph Co. Inc.*, 208 Okl. 179, 254 P.2d 775, we said:

> While we do not agree that the contract as presently written is an onerous one, we think the short answer is that the folly or wisdom of a contract is not for the court to pass on.

In *Great Western Oil & Gas Company v. Mitchell*, Okl., 326 P.2d 794, we held:

> The law will not make a better contract for parties than they themselves have seen fit to enter into, or alter it for the benefit of one party and to the detriment of the others; the judicial function of a court of law is to enforce a contract as it is written.

I am mindful of Title 23 O.S. 1961 § 96, which provides that no person can recover a greater amount in damages for the breach of an obligation than he could have gained by the full performance thereof on both sides, except in cases not applicable herein. However, in my judgment, the above statutory provision is not applicable here.

In my judgment, we should follow the case of *Groves v. John Wunder Company*, 205 Minn. 163, 286 N.W. 235, 123 A.L.R. 502, which defendant agrees "that the fact situation is apparently similar to the one in the case at bar", and where the Supreme Court of Minnesota held:

> The owner's or employer's damages for such a breach (i.e. breach hypothesized in 2d syllabus) are to be measured, not in respect to the value of the land to be improved, but by the reasonable cost of doing that which the contractor promised to do and which he left undone.

The hypothesized breach referred to states that where the contractor's breach of a contract is wilful, that is, in bad faith, he is not entitled to any benefit of the equitable doctrine of substantial performance.

In the instant action defendant has made no attempt to even substantially perform. The contract in question is not immoral, is not tainted with fraud, and was not entered into through mistake or accident and is not contrary to public policy. It is clear and unambiguous and the parties understood the terms thereof, and the approximate cost of fulfilling the obligations could have been approximately ascertained. There are no conditions existing now which could not have been reasonably anticipated when the contract was negotiated and executed. The defendant could have performed the contract if it desired. It has accepted and reaped the benefits of its contract and now urges that plaintiff's benefits under the contract be denied. If plaintiffs' benefits are denied, such benefits would inure to the direct benefit of the defendant.

Therefore, in my opinion, the plaintiffs were entitled to specific performance of the contract and since defendant has failed to perform, the proper measure of damages should be the cost of performance. Any other measure of damage would be holding for naught the express provisions of the contract; would be taking from the plaintiff the benefits of the contract and placing those benefits in defendant which has failed to perform its obligations; would be granting benefits to defendant without a resulting obligation; and would be completely rescinding the solemn obligation of the contract for the benefit of the defendant to the detriment of the plaintiffs by making an entirely new contract for the parties.

I therefore respectfully dissent to the opinion promulgated by a majority of my associates.

(b) Traditional Contract Law: An Interplay of Classical and Neo-Classical Rules†

T. Brettel Dawson

INTRODUCTION: CONTRACTS AND THE PURPOSES OF CONTRACT LAW

The preceding chapter advanced the proposition that the common law functions through an interplay between classical and neo-classical doctrines, so long as the basic rules are appropriate to the behaviours. In this Part, the proposition is explored in relation to the dynamic in contract law.

This chapter is organised around three areas which seem most pertinent to a subsequent discussion of estoppel. These are the formation, construction and termination of contracts.

There are several definitions of contract and of the appropriate model of contract law, but all connect contract law to the facilitation of beneficial economic activity. Further,

> any contract law system necessarily must implement certain norms. It must permit and encourage participation in exchange, promote reciprocity, reinforce role patterns appropriate to particular kinds of exchange relations, provide limited freedom for the exercise of choice, effectuate planning, and harmonize the internal and external matrixes of particular contracts.

In classical theory, a contract is defined as "a promise or a set of promises which the law will enforce" to facilitate the economic activity of 'trade and commerce'. This is still the dominant model of contract in so far as it "compels all other modes of (contractual) thought to define themselves negatively by contrast to it."

The task classical contract law sets is to determine which promises should be enforced and to act as a mechanism by which they may be enforced. This model of contract law is said to protect the expectation interest of the parties, through providing appropriate sanctions against the breach of contractual promises. In classical theory, it is the law which is the primary focus of enquiry and determination of obligation, in preference to the activity of the parties.

Economic theorists of contract law describe the objective of this classical model of contract law as being to create incentives for value-maximisation through the exchange of commodities from less valuable to more valuable uses. In this formulation it is readily apparent that contract law is not neutral but has an ideological function to uphold a political vision of property entitlement and distribution which has been translated into contract rules. In the words of Hugh Collins, classical contract law consisted of "a rigorous set of doctrines by which its particular vision of the just market order could be effected."

THE PARADIGM OF CLASSICAL CONTRACT LAW

The matrix of classical contract law is tightly interwoven. The language conventions, method, values and exemplars of contract law combine to produce distinct doctrines by which contracts may be identifiably formed, construed, limited, enforced and terminated. It gives meaning to the concept of 'contract', provides a mechanism by which 'contracts' operate in connection with the legal system and thereby implements a set of value presuppositions and creates a self-replicating model. As can be expected, this model is not static but must develop when its limits appear to be too tightly drawn.

Contract Formation

In the classical model, the formation of contracts was connected to two key concepts. The first was voluntary agreement or bargain, and the second was compliance with required formalities. The agreement aspect of contract formation required request for and consent to undertakings, expressed through an exchange of promises. This took the form of a specific offer by one party and exact acceptance of its terms by the other. The parties must have intended their interaction to create legal relations, have had the capacity to enter into the transaction concerned and the resulting contractual transaction could bind

---

† This material is originally published in *Estoppel and Obligation* (Osgoode Hall Law School, 1987). [Edited.]

and benefit only the promising parties. This was the "congruent will" theory of classical theory.

In keeping with the general commitment of mid-nineteenth century jurisprudence to rationalise and make legal study scientific, the classicists of contract sought to create a body of contract law which was universal in formulation and application. Thus, an objective test of the congruence of the 'wills' was developed. What a reasonable person would take to be the terms of the offer and acceptance, translated the parties' agreement. It was necessary also, that all the terms of the agreement between the parties be certain or be capable of being rendered certain. The result was a species of 'private legislation' between the parties to the contract.

Promises were enforceable if contained in deeds or supported by 'consideration', which was defined as the reciprocal exchange of value amounting to detriment to the promisee or benefit to the promisor. The giving of a promise in return for another promise could constitute consideration. No enquiry was to be made as to the adequacy of consideration. The market order was expected to dictate and control the prices of promises. Consideration marked out those promises which would be enforceable and constituted evidence of the seriousness of the promising and of the intention to be bound to the exchange. Thus, donative or gratuitous promises were not enforceable; variation of existing contracts was enforceable only if supported by consideration; and obligation was considered to arise from execution of the 'contract' rather than its performance.

Compliance with formalities was also necessary for the formation of a valid and enforceable contract. This was particularly the case where contracts were required to be in writing as provided by the *Statute of Frauds* or its modern equivalents. Similarly, if registration of the contract was required, failure to do so would avoid the contract.

Several themes emerge from this outline. Contracts were conceived as discrete events between unconnected individuals concerned with self-interested maximisation of their wealth and without responsiveness to general social policy. Contracts were idealised as being 'tailor-made' by the parties to express their needs, entered into voluntarily and effectuating their specific and detailed consent. Contractual terms were a presentation of future acts into present terms and commitments. A contract was a crystallised event. Further, contracts became 'reified' as being something which one could be either 'out of' or 'in', and something which was either 'off' or 'on'.

In this way individual parties and their circumstances were abstracted and decontextualised; the subject matter of the contract was commodified; and the sources by which its substantive content could be established were limited:

> formal communication (e.g., writings) controls informal communication (e.g., oral statements): linguistic communication controls non linguistic communication; and communicated circumstances ... control noncommunicated circumstances (e.g., status)

Thus, contract law was a process of identifying and giving signified meaning to contracts. It also expressed underlying value commitments to the autonomy of parties to contract freely, with limited intervention by the State, and a related acceptance that the market order would produce equality and reciprocity in exchange relations.

One problem with the neatness and logic of this pattern of contract formation, was that the parties did not always act with the perfection ascribed to them by this model.

They could overlook classical requirements and rely upon each other's performance without an explicit exchange of promises. They could choose to simply outline their undertakings subject to later elaboration. If they were in long term agreements of e.g., service or supply they might not be able to or may not wish to pre-define the terms of their interaction. Equally, parties could balance their exchange through considerations external to the particular transaction (e.g., a good price on the next deal), informally adjust their contracts during performance or they could also accept performance which differed from contractual specifications and so forth.

At this point, application of the classical model without modification would harm the exchange agreed upon rather than facilitating it. In these situations, norms providing scope for flexibility and preservation of the relationship in situations of conflict may be more relevant than the confines of the presentation of classical contract. Further, if one of the parties was at a disadvantage in the transaction, it could not operate to her or his benefit if enforced and to do so would run contrary to laissez-faire acceptance that the market order would produce just results.

Some intervention would seem to be mandated to support the paradigm and to deal with such situations, as application of the classical model in such circumstances would appear to have unsatisfactorily narrow results.

By way of expansion, to make the promise theory of contract work, a wide meaning must be given to 'promise' thus begging the question of why promises are to be binding in contract law; similarly consideration has been argued to comprehend concepts of reciprocal benefit, acts of reasonable reliance and effectuation of voluntary conduct between individuals. Reiter, for example, has proposed that 'academic formulations' of consideration be abandoned in favour of functional judicial definitions which allow enforcement:

> in the absence of sufficiently good reason not to enforce a promise. What is a sufficiently good reason must be determined in light of interests and policy factors present, relevant and valued differently in various fact situations. Consideration ... represents an evolving notion of the types of situation in which the absence-of-good-reason-not-to-enforce has been found.

In the area of exceptions to the model, the common law developed concepts of duress and *non est factum* which negated consent. Doctrines of frustration, impossibility and even mistake, developed in situations where adjustment was necessary between the parties. Beyond this internal movement, equity also played an important role. Doctrines such as undue influence, inequality of bargaining power, and even the possibility of a general rule against unconscionability, are examples of this. Similarly, rectification of documents in equity could relieve a party from terms which did not express the agreement of the parties. Such options were developed to assist in situations where adjustment was necessary between the parties, but was not permitted by the rigid model of the classical law. Estoppel in the common law courts also mitigated the rigours of consideration and other rules for the formation of contractual agreement.

These are all examples of neo-classical extension of, or exception to the paradigm to deal with situations where the classical model was considered to be inappropriate. A question remains as to their relationship with the basic model of contract law. Muir asserts that the modifying doctrines do not "tinker with contract law itself, because where equity operated to give effect to non-enforceable promises or agreements, the resultant liability was 'non-contractual'. Even so, their existence must be seen as redefining the limits of the classical model of contracting.

The classical model remains the basic conceptual framework. It may not be the only or the best framework to resolve the basic issues raised. MacNeil has argued that this neo-classical system

> may be seen as an effort to escape partially from such rigorous presentation, but since its overall structure is essentially the same as the classical

system it may often be ill-designed to raise and deal with the (basic issues) .... Nevertheless, the present neo-classical system permits a great deal of flexibility and gap-filling.

In the area of contract formation, there is a clear dynamic between the classical model and neo-classical responses to it. The outline of classical law, although still able to be discerned, has been blurred by the accretion of neo-classical extensions and exceptions which attempt to resolve basic issues facing the paradigm. A similar process is present in other contractual areas.

Construction of Contracts

The process of interpreting a validly formed contract most closely resembled the creation and implementation of a common language and meaning of contracting. The object of all construction of the terms of a contract was to discover the intention of the parties to the agreement. They were presumed to have meant what they put into their contract terms, and only the meaning of the words used could be considered.

The process of determining their meaning was, again, said to be an 'objective' one. Words were to be construed "according to their strict and primary acceptation," or "their plain, ordinary and popular sense" unless this would lead to absurdity or inconsistency. The purpose was to resolve any possible ambiguity and to produce the 'one right interpretation' of the terms.

A central assumption, and one which was supported by the requirement that the terms of the contract be certain at its formation, was that the crystallised contract contained all the terms which were to regulate the relationship of the parties. In particular, extrinsic evidence was limited by two well known rules.

The first rule was the parol evidence rule which stipulated that where there is a written document, "verbal evidence is not allowed to be given ... so as to add to or subtract from, or in any manner vary or qualify the written contract." Thus, matters discussed in prior negotiations or prior drafts of written agreements could not be considered by a judge in construing a contract. The second rule precluded evidence of the subsequent acts of parties to assist in the interpretation of the original 'contract'. The English rule was that "it is not legitimate to use as an aid in the construction of the contract anything which the parties said or did after it was made." This precluded giving an ambulatory interpretation to contracts and strictly limited the scope of adjustment to them. It reinforced the static notion of contract as a crystallised and reified entity. It certainly confirmed the objective test of meaning insofar as the parties are not able to interpret their contracts themselves, at least at the point of litigation.

Again, a body of neo-classical response has developed in this area of contract construction. The right of parties to form their agreements as a species of 'private legislation' has been eroded by a steady increase in the implication of terms into contracts through judicial and legislative action. A ready example is the legislation relating to the sale of goods, where fitness for purpose, compliance with description and merchantable quality are terms implied into every contract covered by such legislation. Such legislation was, in turn, a codification of prior judicial development. There may be implied conditions, warranties or innominate terms, implied terms to ensure business efficacy or reasonable performance of explicit or other implied obligations, and to take reasonable care in projections of contractual return.

Whilst Muir asserts that this process is little more than "limited exceptions" to the law of contract to give effect to the intentions of the parties, it can be seen also as the introduction of a tension between discrete individual autonomy as private legislators and paternalist ideals or collective standards of conduct.

In the context of the parties' relationship, and by way of extension to the basic parol evidence rule, courts can and do go to great lengths to locate ambiguity in the written terms and thus allow recourse to extrinsic evidence from the factual background known to the parties at the time of contracting, to 'clarify' the terms. The rule is also circumvented by a series of refinements, referred to in *Chitty on Contracts* as "either exceptions to the general rule or simply ... cases falling outside of the general rule." These include the admissibility of evidence which shows that there is in fact no contract, that consideration indicated in the contract was not in fact rendered, that the true legal relationship of the parties differed from that indicated on the face of the contract, or that it was not the whole agreement between the parties.

Such expansive statement of the rule was also limited by the refusal to allow evidence of subsequent conduct to interpret a contract or to modify the original agreement. Judges insist that they are simply determining the original terms of the contract. *Chitty* concludes that "subsequent actions are therefore inadmissible except as evidence of a new agreement or as the basis of an estoppel". However, in this, there is a statement of the second step of neo-classical development: the creation of exceptions.

For example, some Canadian cases suggest that where parties have accepted a particular meaning of an ambiguous term, and have undertaken an intentional course of conduct with reference to this meaning, evidence of these actions will be admitted to resolve the ambiguity. A limit to this is that difficulty in interpretation is said not to in itself create ambiguity. In turn, this appears to be a somewhat artificial distinction which seems more designed to conceal the expansion than to assist clarity.

Estoppel is also conceptualised as an exception to this rule.

An underlying value in these rules of construction is to secure certainty and allow effective planning for discrete transactions. It is assumed that contracting actors value flexibility less than certainty. In the context of on-going commercial relations, the assumption is highly questionable. It is also quite artificial in conventionally adjusted domestic relations.

Nevertheless, Lord Bridge expressed the ideal of certainty thus:

(although it) may never be fully attainable ... we shall certainly never even approximate to it unless we strive to follow clear and consistent principles and steadfastly refuse to be blown off course by the supposed merits of individual cases.

In this he was simply echoing the decision in *The Laconia*, where it was held that certainty is of primary importance in all *commercial* transactions. The rationale for this was urged fifty years ago by Atkin L.J. in *Re Wait*, when he commented that the extension of equitable principles into the sale of goods area would fundamentally affect the security of business transactions and introduce a 'disastrous innovation' into well-settled commercial relations. Recently, in *The Scrap Trade*, Goff L.J., as he then was, rejected a plea to relieve against forfeiture under a time charter for late payment of hire. He held that the form of contract in issue was well-established in the trade and that to circumvent it would "constitute an undesirable fetter on the exercise by the parties of their contractual rights."

In this way, models of discrete contracting continue to dominate classical and even neo-classical thinking. The tension between certainty and flexibility is a good example of the classical/neo-classical dynamic and of the limits beyond which neither will go.

Termination and Remedies

The classical contract, being based on the model of discrete transactions, needed to be highly planned and as fully presentiated as possible. Presentiation in contract is a concept developed by Ian MacNeil and defined as:

> to presentiate: 'to make or render present in place or time; to cause to be perceived or realised as present' .... Presentation is thus a recognition that the course of the future has for many purposes been brought effectively into the present.

This was reflected, as has already been outlined, in a requirement of certainty of terms. Such contracts were considered to be self-contained and of fixed purpose and duration. It followed that they would terminate by performance or breach. There was little concern with preserving relations between the parties, as this was not conceptualised as necessary, or as a problem to be solved: the only relation that the parties had was contained in the terms of the contract.

A breach of the contract could be conceptualised as damaging the expectation interest of the 'innocent party' or depriving her or him of the value sought to be obtained by entering into the transaction. Satisfaction of the expectation interest extended beyond preventing the party in breach from unjustly enriching themselves at the expense of the innocent party, (restitution interest) or simply giving recompense for expenses incurred in reliance on due performance of the agreement (reliance interest). It aimed to put the party who was not in breach in the same position as she would have been in had the contract been performed.

Often, however, the remedy given by the courts extended only to the reliance interest. This was first discussed by Fuller and Perdue in their influential article in 1936:

> the cases discussed, show ... that the contractual reliance interest receives a much wider (though often covert) recognition in the decisions than it does in the text books.

Arguably, the rule providing that the innocent party mitigate her losses from the breach also limited the award of expectation damages by containing damages within the scope of reasonable reliance and commercial efficacy. Certainly, estoppel remedies were considered to be directed only to reliance and not to the satisfaction of contractual expectation. The protection of expectations was the sole province of the classical law of contract.

Despite the practical diversity of contractual interests judicially protected, the range of remedies available in classical contract law was quite limited unless recourse was to be had to the wide range of remedies available in equity. In equity, a court could give relief in the form of a trust, a lien, an injunction and so forth. However, in contract the primary remedy was limited to the award of damages. In unique circumstances, specific performance might be awarded. Consistently with this, estoppel remedies were explained and marginalised, as being either as non-contractual or as supporting a reliance interest, rather than as giving non-classical remedies for breach of expectations.

SUMMARY

The preceding sections have outlined the paradigm of classical contract law. The basic structure is consistent with the model of common law developed in the first part of the thesis. The analysis has traced the lines which define and limit the scope of contractual obligation in legal theory. It has provided one way to understand the interaction of contractual principles *per se*, and in relation to the extensions and exceptions to the classical rules.

A model of contract as a discrete economic exchange between autonomous and unrelated individual contractors who accept the justice of exchange inherent in the 'free' market, produced a contract law which assumed individual tailoring of contracts and emphasised transactionalism, presentation, and decontextualisation. This classical static could not be maintained without modification when contracts in fact deviated from this model. A neo-classical response accommodated such changes and allowed conceptual modification of the classical contract law paradigm.

Some of these neo-classical doctrines have been discussed in this chapter in outlining the contract law dynamic which thereby arose and currently exists. Fundamental problems have been noted with even this process of reconceptualisation of contracts and contract law. The issue appears to be that the paradigm is being asked to solve problems for which it was not designed.

The issues that arise from this are how far classical contract doctrines can be stretched to satisfy the needs of contractors; whether this process clarifies or obscures legal principles; and at what point a shift in norms would lead to a shift in contracting model.

(c)   Contract Law in Perspective†

Linda Mulcahy

General Principles: The Nature and Content of Contract Law

In a society where the exchange of goods and services is central to its economic order, as in a developing capitalist society based on free enterprise, a means of supporting the process of exchange of goods and services needs to be found. It is in this context that the foundations of modern contract law were established, and contract became the juristic mechanism for the distribution and utilisation of the goods and services. By the third quarter of the nineteenth century, British society had experienced accelerating industrialisation generated by scientific innovation, economic entrepreneurship, more widespread access to capital and increasingly geographically mobile labour. This gave rise to an unprecedented boom in trade, both at home and in expanding markets overseas. This boom was accompanied by an extensive development of those areas of the law which are designed to facilitate and regulate business relationships. In particular, there was a considerable expansion of contract, commercial and company law.

The general principles of contract law are still, for the most part, of a judge-made character, and many of them emanate from the time of the industrial revolution and the 'classical' period of contract law which accompanied it. The theoretical assumptions underpinning the classical model were heavily influenced by prevailing economic theories of the nineteenth century, which treated contracting parties as economic units assumed to have equal bargaining strength and endowed with complete freedom of decision. Indeed, the key theme underpinning contract law during this period was the idea of *freedom of contract*. It is highly significant that, in this model of contract, the judges saw their role as a minimalist one. The purpose of the law was not to control the terms on which parties might contract, nor would it readily give relief if agreed terms turned out to be harsh or unfair to one party.

Since that time, the principles associated with managed rather than free markets have also taken a

hold in this area of law and we have seen a decline in influence of the idea of freedom of contract. In part, this has come about as a result of social change. In the twenty-first century it is no longer the individual entrepreneur but the government or large multi-national enterprises that are primarily concerned with the allocation of resources in the British economy. These facts of modern economic life have served to emphasise the myth of equality of bargaining power, presumed to exist between contracting parties in the classical era. But, then again, as we shall see, many modern commentators have argued that the notion of freedom of contract was never an adequate social tool through which to understand the market.

.   .   .   .

THE RISE AND FALL OF FREEDOM OF CONTRACT

Introduction

The law of contract cannot be fully understood without reference to the history of ideas which underpin it. It will become apparent in the course of this book that this branch of the law has undergone several important transformations in the last few decades. Reading cases and statutes will lead to familiarisation with the detail of such changes, but it is unlikely to allow you to gain a full appreciation of how it was possible for them to come about and the wider political context which made transformation acceptable to influential stakeholders. In a book of this kind, it is almost impossible to do justice to the rich spectrum of ideas which have been reflected in debates between academics, politicians and the wider community of users of contract law. Instead, the aim of this chapter and the next is to sketch out some key ideas which have influenced the ways in which we look at contracts. Of particular relevance here is the question of the extent to which the state, in the guise of the legislature and the judiciary, should interfere with contracts made by consenting parties

---

† Linda Mulcahy, *Contract Law in Perspective*, 5th ed. (London and New York: Routledge-Cavendish, 2008) at pp. 5, 25–34, 37–42. [Notes/references omitted.] Reproduced by permission of Taylor & Francis Books UK.

in order to redress imbalances of power between them.

Even the briefest perusal of the newspapers will demonstrate that the issues which lie at the heart of this debate reflect a much wider controversy about the role of the modern-state. The issue remains a contentious one which has troubled successive governments and debate has become particularly intense since the setting up of the welfare state. The political imperatives of the Conservative party under Margaret Thatcher and their emphasis on the 'rolling back of the state', debate about the 'third way', the growth of the regulatory state and visions of socialism in post-communist states, all hinge on the same critical issue of what constitute the appropriate boundaries between public and private or individual autonomy and central regulation. When you come to argue your first case in front of the country's premier Court of Appeal, a sound knowledge of the intricacies of former precedents and 'black letter' law will serve you well. But it is unlikely that your arguments will stimulate the judges you stand before unless you can provide justification for why the law should make a departure from what has gone before. The aim of the remainder of this chapter is to start you on a journey in which you reflect on these more abstract ideas about contractual relationships.

Legal and Other Views of Contract

The early legal history of contract is extensive, complex and not entirely free from controversy. Medieval law was primarily concerned with crime and land. From an early stage It recognised formal agreements which were written and 'understood' but slowly began to recognise claims arising out of informal, oral transactions as well. Of particular significance is the common law's recognition by the sixteenth century of claims involving four key elements. These were: reliance by the claimant on an undertaking given by the defendant; faulty performance, or non-performance of the undertaking by the defendant; loss to the claimant; and compensation in the form of damages. Later, the language of the courts began to link the idea of undertaking with that of promise. At that time the moral force of, and duty to keep, promises was very strong.

Nevertheless, the law stopped short of declaring that all promises were binding. Starting from an inquiry into the reasons why a promise was given, the doctrine of consideration came to set limits to promissory liability. It eventually did so by requiring that some form of *exchange* took place. This allowed

contracts to be distinguished from gifts or gratuitous promises made out of kindness rather than as part of a deal. The types of bargain recognised by the doctrine of consideration included the exchange of money for a service or the exchange of one possession for another. But it was also accepted that promises could be exchanged to form binding contracts as long as there was a connection between them. So if Ethelred offered to pay Edwina three cows for a stable of manure and she accepted, then it can be seen that their promises to give up the cows and transfer manure are related to each other and form a bargain. Edwina's promise would only have been made if Ethelred had made his. Thus, even before the onset of the industrial and commercial revolutions, contract law had developed considerably. It contained basic, interconnecting concepts such as undertaking, promise, expectations, bargain in the sense of commercial exchange, reliance, loss and compensation.

By the nineteenth century, the concept of contract came to be discussed more broadly by philosophers, political scientists, economists and sociologists, and became an important topic of debate. Contract came to be seen as the key to wealth and happiness in the emerging market society. 'Freedom of contract' became a prime ethical, political, economic and legal goal. Brownsword (2006) describes the model as involving freedom for everyone to make an agreement on whatever terms they chose to; and sanctity of contract or the expectation that the courts will enforce the terms that the parties have freely made. Justice was said to require that each individual be at liberty to make free use of their natural powers in bargains, exchanges and promises as long as they did not interfere with the rights of others. Not only were such ideas considered a laudable goal in their own right but were also seen as the key to the economic success of society. One of the most important aspects of this debate was that the individual was considered to be best placed to know what their needs were and should be allowed to make whatever contracts on whatever terms they thought appropriate.

Giving people the utmost liberty to contract was seen as both morally appropriate but as also having a clear economic rationale. Adam Smith's work proved to be particularly influential in the context of discussions about the latter. In the *Wealth of Nations*, published in 1776, Smith analysed exchange in terms of people's 'natural propensity' to 'truck, barter and exchange'. In his view it was this inclination which naturally gave rise to contract, trade and the division of labour. His wide-ranging arguments sought to show how the individual's self-interested pursuit of optimum gain and happiness was both regulated by, and harnessed to, the general good, by the economist's law of demand and supply. His thesis was that by trading with others individuals not only got what they wanted but gave others what they desired. The magical ingredient converting individual acquisitiveness into universal good was labelled the 'invisible hand' by Smith. In his view, the individual neither intends to promote the public interest, nor knows how much they are promoting it. Instead, they intend only their own gain.

As a result of these theories, Smith advocated minimum regulation of the economy, and therefore of contracts, by the state. However, he did see it as a prime function of the law to uphold and enforce contracts made by freely consenting adults. He stressed that promises were not binding as a consequence of some inherent quality but rather because of the expectations they created in the market and which should not be disappointed. So, for instance, a builder might make a contract with a railway owner to build a row of houses for his employees close to the train station. Unable to do all the work himself, the builder enters into a contract of employment with a bricklayer and a carpenter. They in turn make contracts to buy bricks and timber. Unable to supply the carpenter instantly with the particular type of wood they need, the [builder] orders some from a [forester] in Scotland. It very soon becomes clear that each contract is part of a network of commercial relationships which rely on each other. When the courts intervene to protect contracts, they lend a certain amount of certainty to an otherwise unpredictable market. In *The Concept of Law* (1961), Hart argued that

> where altruism is not unlimited, a standing procedure providing for such self-binding operations is required in order to create a minimum form of confidence in the future behaviour of others, and to ensure the predictability necessary for cooperation.

A number of commentators have shown an interest in why the individual came to play such an important role in the philosophical works of this era. Maine (Cocks, 2004) attempted to explain the reasons for this shift in his work on the movement of progressive societies from status to contract. In this he distinguished two theoretical 'ideal' types of society. The first was essentially a pre-industrial society in which power and relationships were based on the status you 'enjoyed'. These included kinship, marriage, neighbourhood and other close, continuing relationships. In such societies individuals were limited in what they could [choose] to do by the role they played. So, for instance, a tenant farmer might have unavoidable obligations to the local Lord imposed on him. The second type of society identified by Maine was one in which the individual becomes the central figure and their associations are predominantly motivated by reason and economic gain rather than association. Drawing on these ideas, Tennies (2003) talked of a similar drift from social union to an essential 'separation' of individuals in an industrial society. For him, the latter was merely an artificial construction of an aggregate of human beings in which rationality and calculation were the lynchpins.

The proliferation of the rational, impersonal relationship in the economic models of the eighteenth and nineteenth [centuries] was also examined by Weber (1992) who *also drew* a distinction between what he called 'status' and 'purposive' contracts. The first 'more primitive' type involved the creation of continuing 'total' social and legal relationships, such as those between husband and wife, or landowner and serf. By way of contrast, the archetypal purposive contract was 'the money contract'. In his terms this was specific, quantitatively delimited, qualityless, abstract, economically conditioned and usually achieved some specific, generally economic, performance or result. In his view, what distinguishes such contractual relationships from status relationships is the fact that the reciprocal rights and obligations are limited to those specified in the contract. The purposive market exchange contract created only a tenuous and temporary association while the exchange takes place. Because these impersonal associations were incapable of inspiring the high trust of the kind seen in status contracts, Weber (1992) argued that it was necessary to establish a legal machinery, which, while not raising levels of trust, did at least provide a greater required measure of economic certainty.

The Relationship between the Courts and the Market

The perceived role of the courts in this scheme of things can be summed up by reference to the words of Sir George Jessel:

> ... if there is one thing which more than another public policy requires it is that [people] of full age and competent understanding shall have the utmost liberty of contracting, and that their contracts when entered into freely and voluntarily shall be held sacred and shall be enforced by Courts of Justice. Therefore you have this para-

mount public policy to consider — that you are not lightly to interfere with this freedom of contract.

It is significant that, in the early part of the nineteenth century, the judiciary shifted its thinking towards recognition of both executed *and* executory contracts. In contrast to the executed contract in which exchange is immediate, executory contracts involve the exchange of promises about future conduct. The importance of the courts' recognition of executory contracts was that it allowed the business community to plan ahead. So, for example, if Sunil knows that he can rely on the courts to enforce Linda's promise to pay him £20,000 for 500 mobile phones from last year's stock, he can enter into negotiations with manufacturers of this year's latest mobile phones to supply him with 200 phones for his showroom, confident that they will have funds to pay for the consignment. Moreover, now that the manufacturer has a firm order, it can enter into discussions with different suppliers about the purchase of parts. And so the contract chain goes on without any material object having yet changed hands. In this example, the parties are able to enjoy the confidence and predictability that Hart (1961) talks about. With clear recognition that promises bind future performance, contract showed obvious potential to aid complex planning and risk allocation.

Two further developments in contract law, following fuller recognition of the executory contract, must be mentioned. It has long been accepted by the judiciary that an action for breach of an executory contract can be brought if one of the promisors fails to do what they promised to do. In other words, a party liable on an executory contract is liable not for what they have done but for what they have *not* yet done. As Professor [Atiyah] (1979) has explained each contractor must be liable because of his intention, his will, his promise. At the same time, in the early nineteenth century, wide acceptance of the idea of liability based on promises allowed a general theory of contract law to emerge which distinguished it from other areas of law. Academics and judges began to use the idea of promise and freely given consent as the basis of contract law, and contract was no longer merely regarded as an adjunct of the law of property.

The vision of contractual relations which emerged at this time has come to be known as the 'classical' model and we shall use this shorthand throughout the book for the theory of obligations explained above. The approach was clearly designed to serve a free market or *laissez-faire* economy and to act as a framework within which the free play of competitive forces could operate. As we proceed to examine substantive elements of contract law in this book, we will time and again be reminded of the legacy of nineteenth-century thinking and its continuing impact on the law today. For this reason the key features of the 'classical' model as it emerged from around 1800 onwards are summarised in Box 3.1.

The Changing Nature of Contract

Approaches to contracts have changed significantly since the heyday of the classical period. But change has taken the form of adjustments to the 'classical' model rather than a grand scale reformulation of the law. The main thrust of modern critiques of contract law is that a new model which moves more firmly away from the classical paradigm is now required. These are themes to which we shall return in the next chapter. In the remainder of this one, we describe how the classical model has adjusted to the changed circumstances of the modern world.

As we have seen, enthusiasm for freedom of contract went hand-in-hand with support for the operation of a free market. But assumptions under-

---

BOX 3.1: PRESUMPTIONS OF THE CLASSICAL MODEL

- Contracting parties were possessed of equal bargaining power.
- Contracting parties were self-motivated and self-assertive.
- A party was bound not so much because they had made a promise as because they had made a *bargain*.
- Agreement was based on consent and free choice and it is for the parties rather than the courts to determine what is fair.
- Contractual obligations were self-imposed and imbalances of power largely irrelevant.
- Lack of true consent would very rarely justify the setting aside of a contract on the grounds of such things as fraud, misrepresentation or fundamental mistake.
- Each party must perform, or pay damages for their failure to perform.

pinning the free market approach could be seen to be erroneous since sellers and buyers are rarely on an equal footing. This means that contracts simply reflect power, or lack of it. Responding to the challenge raised by such arguments, Weber (1992) cut straight through the simplistic abstractions of earlier legal and economic thinking on the subject of freedom of contract. In his view, markets for goods and services might be more plentiful and factors of production more mobile than in preindustrial societies, but this did not in itself result in more 'real' freedom. He argued that the exact extent to which the total amount of 'freedom' within a given legal community is actually increased depends entirely on the economic order and more specifically on property distribution.

Weber's argument was that, as they developed, free markets threw up new economic groups with powerful market interests based on capital and entrepreneurship. As was becoming clear to most people, it was the power relations in society, rather than economic and legal abstractions, which determined the operation of markets and the degree of real freedom in those markets. To his mind contractual 'freedom' provided the opportunity to use property ownership in the market without legal restraints as a means for the achievement of power over others. Weber illustrated his analysis by means of the contract of employment in which the employer was commonly the more powerful party and could offer jobs on a 'take it or leave it' basis. Given the more pressing economic needs of the worker, it was possible for employers to impose their terms on employees. Weber (1992) is not only pointing to the difference between formal and real freedom, but indicating how formal freedom protects and exacerbates inequality.

Durkheim (1964) was also keen to unravel the implications of the prevalent individualist, self-interested view of contract and the idea that contract could be regarded as a microcosm of society or a model for rational human relations. He argued that, within the contractual bond, the element of self-interest inevitably created an inherent contradiction. In his view, while contracting parties needed each other each sought to obtain what they needed at the lowest price, and to acquire the most rights possible in return for the fewest obligations. In contrast to many of his contemporaries, he was concerned to undermine the prevailing vision of contract as an essentially individualistic and utilitarian act rather than a social one. He suggested that unregulated self-interest would not enable the mechanism of contract to serve as a model for what he termed

'organic solidarity' in society. He would not accept that a society splintered by increasing division of labour could achieve 'solidarity' through the pursuit of economic self-interest within a loose framework of *laissez-faire*. He argued instead that, in economic exchange, the different agents remain remote from each other. In his view, interest is the least constant of all things in the world. Whilst today it might be in my interest to unite with you, tomorrow the same reason may make me your enemy.

It was necessary, in Durkheim's opinion, to place contract in a context wider than that of party autonomy and individual will. For him, the true focal point was not individuals but society, which should provide a framework of norms and laws able to promote social justice. Most significantly, in his view, social regulation of contract required clear recognition of unequal bargaining power. He turned to the example of the employee, and asked what the poor worker could do against the rich and powerful employer, and suggested that there was a palpable and cruel irony in assimilating these two forces which are so manifestly unequal. For this reason, he asserted that society and the law must no longer passively uphold unjust contracts which are antisocial as the agreement of parties cannot render just a clause which in itself is unjust.

Power in the Modern Marketplace

A series of transformations in British society has served to reinforce the arguments made by scholars such as Weber and Durkheim. These include an increasing concentration of power in the marketplace, the growth of the welfare state and changes in judicial attitudes. These have fuelled a transformation of the law of contract and, in the remainder of this section, we shall consider each in turn.

The concentration of power in the market

Commentators have observed that competitive capitalism inevitably tended towards monopoly. These developments clearly dilute key concepts such as choice and consent in contract and undermine the importance of pre-contractual negotiations. The legal result of this has been the mass-produced standard form of contract presented on 'take-it-or-leave-it' terms by those who are powerful in the market. The allocation of resources in the British economy no longer centres on the free market contracts of 'small enterprisers' but on the operations of massive multinational corporate groups and governmental agencies. A variety of factors have contributed to this movement in Britain. Some, such as cartelisation schemes designed to combat the worst effects of economic depression, the nationalisation of basic industries and the creation of a 'public sector' of the economy have come about as a direct result of government policies. Others, such as the growth of trade associations, encouragement of mergers in the private sector, the development of mass production and the tendency for large companies to take over small ones have been fuelled by the business community.

Contract specialists frequently draw attention to the need to regulate business activity where an organisation has become so powerful that it can dictate terms to anyone with whom it contracts. It is sometimes easy to forget that government contracts made on behalf of us all with public money also pose a significant threat to those concerned about inequality of bargaining power. The twentieth century witnessed a dramatic increase in the state's involvement in contract as a party with the setting up of the welfare state. The most obvious development was that the state has emerged as a *provider* of services such as health-care, social security, education, motorways and defence. This means that they are required to increase contractual activity because of the need to buy in construction and engineering works, technical services and hardware and vast quantities of other supplies and materials from independent contractors. It is in this area of public sector activity that contract has been the subject of major transformation. One of the legal corollaries of this development was a vast increase of government *procurement* contracts where government departments or other public authorities are on one side and a [private] party is on the other. In this context, rules of contract that draw on the notion of discrete and private exchanges between parties of roughly the same bargaining strength begin to look obsolete.

In principle, the general law of contract applies to government procurement contracts. There is no special branch of 'government contract law' in this country, no legislative code as for consumer credit or fair trading, and administrative law is largely irrelevant in this context. In fact, the complaint has been made that *no* adequate law has been evolved on public contracts. Any question of the 'adequacy' of the private law rules of contract is also largely redundant. This is a field dominated by standard form contractual documents, prepared on behalf of the government authority involved and rarely negotiated. Disputes that arise are hidden from the public gaze as they are very rarely settled in the courts. It would seem then that the government contract is an instrument of a power relationship which only vaguely resembles the consensual agreement extolled by Maine and Adam Smith. In Turpin's (1979) view:

> the classical law of contract, which was formulated by 19th-century judges was 'a law of the market' .... This law in general did not, and does not, make provision for the peculiar circumstances of government procurement, the unique relationship between the government and its principal contractors, or the specific issues of the public interest that arise in government contracting. p. 251

Government procurement contracts are, in broad terms, an expression of economic and social policies, and the contractor is the instrument whereby services and functions are executed. However, government expenditure of taxpayers' money on goods and services raises questions of public accountability. Although the relationship between the government and its major suppliers used to be described as a partnership with 'fair and reasonable prices' at its base, the current economic climate and concern about the government being ill-served by the private sector have led to changes. In particular, the rules of the European Union have led to more competitive tendering and a more 'free-market' approach to procurement. Hard bargaining, best value for money and the attainment of contract targets are now the order of the day.

Where standard form contracts are the outcome of co-operative planning on the part of all interests, fairness and impartiality are more likely to dominate the transactions based on them. But, in practice, the presence of government power and resources will tend to tilt the balance of bargaining power. As Turpin (1989) suggests:

> the general law of contract has only a subsidiary or contingent application to government contracts .... Although an awareness of the rules of the law of contract influences in these ways the departments engaged in the contracting process, government procurement is a notable instance of those sectors in which, in the words of a distinguished scholar [Julius Stone], 'the coercions of law are ... only in the background'. (p. 165)

It is clear, even from this brief survey, that government-procurement [contracts] are a rather special area, having only vague links with the general principles of contract law. From procurement policy to 'administrative' remedies, the contracting process is directed from somewhere along the corridors of power. In the absence of litigation or forms of public hearing other than occasional references in *Hansard*, fears of misuse of the system remain.

The regulatory state

Concerns about the concentration of commercial power in the hands of relatively few corporations have led the government to set up a number of regulatory body to ensure that consumers are protected in the marketplace, at least as far as basic utilities are concerned. The Competition Commission, set up in 1999 to replace the Monopolies and Mergers Commission, was established to ensure that healthy competition took place between companies. Box 3.2 lists a number of other regulatory organisations with responsibility to oversee activity in the commercial sector. It is important to note that concern about competition must go beyond our own jurisdiction. Increasing worries about the effects of globalisation of markets have largely focused on the ability of a relatively small number of global business interests to dominate markets across the globe. Some of these are thought to have economic power that is at least equivalent to some modern states.

The proliferation of publicly funded regulatory bodies makes clear that the state has also become a regulator of contracts. Many of the interests of consumers as regards prices, terms and quality of supply are provided for by statute-based regulatory agencies and not by the law of contract. For example, the Financial Services Authority was set up by the government to regulate most financial services markets, exchanges and firms. It sets the standards that they must meet and can take action against firms if they fail to meet the required standards. A key focus of its work is to help retail consumers achieve a fair deal. Whether or not these arrangements satisfy the need to balance value for money with the public interest continues to be hotly contested in the political area. Collins (2002) has argued that:

> The real substance of the issue of the scope of contracts in this context should turn on whether the statutes regulating public utilities provide adequate alternative means of redress for consumers, so that the exclusion of contractual rights is the price paid for the advantages of the statutory scheme for complaints.

Regulation has also increased through the proliferation of statutorily imposed standards across society. The use of contract as an instrument of governmental social and economic policy in this way has led to many contracts becoming institutionalised. This development can be seen in consumer-protection policy, in landlord-and-tenant legislation and in measures to be found in statutes concerning sexual discrimination, disability discrimination and racial discrimination. So for instance, it is unlawful for an employer to discriminate against someone in the terms of [their] employment or the conditions [they] work under because of their age, gender, race, disability, religion and belief or sexual orientation. In this context, terms and conditions cover aspects of the employment contract such as hours of work, dress codes, the physical conditions of the workplace, holidays and flexi-time. Box 3.3 lists the key legislation in this field.

Changes in judicial approaches

It will become clear throughout this book that changes in political ideology, in social and economic

---

BOX 3.2: EXAMPLES OF UK REGULATORS

- Office of Fair Trading (OFT):
  http://www.oft.gov.uk/default.htm
- Office of Communications (OFCOM):
  http://www.ofcom.org.uk
- Financial Services Authority:
  http://www.fsa.gov.uk
- Securities and Futures Authority:
  http://www.fsa.gov.uk/Pages/accessibility/index.shtml
- Takeover panel:
  http://www.thetakeoverpanel.org.uk
- Civil Aviation Authority (CAA):
  http://www.caa.co.uk
- Office of Rail Regulation:
  http://www.rail-reg.gov.uk
- Office of Gas and Electricity Markets (OFGEM):
  http://www.ofgem.gov.uk/ofgem/index.jsp
- Office for the Regulation of Electricity and Gas (OFREG):
  http://ofreg.nics.gov.uk
- Office of Water Services (OFWAT):
  http://www.ofwat.gov.uk/

**BOX 3.3:
LEGISLATION GOVERNING
THE CONTRACT OF EMPLOYMENT**

- Equal Pay Act 1970
- Sex Discrimination Act 1975
- Race Relations Act 1976
- Disability Discrimination Act 1995
- Human Rights Act 1998
- Race Relations (Amendment) Act 2000
- Civil Partnership Act 2004
- Disability Discrimination Act 2005
- Equality Act 2006

conditions and, bit by bit, in the law itself, have moved the judicial focus away from freedom and sanctity of contract, voluntary agreement and the 'classical' model generally. This has involved more than a change in judicial approaches, it has involved a change in ideas about the appropriate role of the judiciary. There has been a discernible shift away from strict rules towards less certain notions of 'fairness', reasonableness' and 'judicial discretion'.

Of particular value in understanding these fundamental issues is the analysis of judicial decision-making put forward by Adams and Brownsword (2007) in their book *Understanding Contract Law*. They argue that the common law increasingly displays signs of the *tensions* created by two *competing* judicial philosophies. These are a formalist approach, which focuses on rules, and a *realist*, result-orientated approach. Out of a number of possible stances along the continuum between these two positions, a judge may be seen as a strict adherent to the 'paper rules' (a [textual] formalist) at the expense of justice or commercial convenience. Alternatively, he or she may be a 'strong realist', even an iconoclast, like Lord Denning, for whom precedent is no bar to achieving the right result. As you read the chapters that follow, it would be useful for you to keep these different approaches in mind as you will see some excellent examples of both.

Adams and Brownsword (2007) argue that these different approaches to legal method actually reflect the broader political ideologies discussed above. The market philosophy sees the function of the law of contract as the facilitation of competitive exchange, which demands clear contractual ground rules, transactional security and the accommodation of commercial practice. At its most extreme, market individualism encompasses the notion of 'freedom of contract' and 'sanctity of contract'. This accords the parties the maximum licence in setting their own terms, and the ability to hold parties to their freely made bargains however bad a bargain it happens to be. They compare this to a trend in judicial reasoning towards consumer-welfarism, which stands for:

> reasonableness and fairness in contracting. More concretely, this is reflected in a policy of consumer protection and a pot-pourri of specific principles. For example, consumer-welfarism holds that contracting parties should not mislead one another, that they should act in good faith, that a strong party should not exploit the weakness of another's bargaining position, that no party should profit from his own wrong or be unjustly enriched, that remedies should be proportionate to the breach, that contracting parties who are at fault should not be able to dodge

> their responsibilities, and so on. Crucially, consumer-welfarism subscribes to the paternalistic principle that contractors who enter into bad bargains may be relieved from their obligations where justice so requires. (p. 39)

It should be readily apparent that, in line with political and economic developments, 'consumer-welfarism' has been a key driving force behind contract decision-making over the last 50 years or so. The trend has been such that some commentators have argued that the protection offered to some categories of contractor, most notably 'consumers' is such that the legislature and judiciary have recreated the status contract.

. . . .

FROM FORMALISM TO REALISM: CONTEMPORARY CRITIQUES OF CONTRACT LAW

Introduction

In the last chapter we visited classical contract theory and considered the various Challenges to it, with particular emphasis on those posed by the regulation state and welfarism. The response of many members of the judiciary and the legislature has been to try to adjust the classical model so that it better suits the goals of social policy and the marketplace of today. So, for instance, the judiciary has seen fit to provide greater protection for certain categories of people, most notably [consumers], in order to mitigate the inequalities of the market place and social life. Later chapters in this book, such as those on implied terms, consideration and unfair terms, will sketch out some of the detail of how some sense of balance has been achieved during this 'neo-classical' period. What has emerged is a mixture of approaches in which market individualism still competes for attention with the more modern notion of consumer welfarism. However, the classical, albeit in a modified form, continues to have much influence on how lawyers approach contracts. In the minds of many contemporary academics in the field, this is an unsatisfactory development. A number have suggested that we have only tinkered with the classical model when what is needed is a rethinking of the principles which should underpin this field of law. A growing number of scholars have argued that the very relevance and legitimacy of the assumptions underpinning the classical model are in crisis.

In this chapter we seek to look at some contemporary critiques of contract which encourage us to look at contractual relationships in different ways.

The strength of these various theories, and the reason why they have so much resonance in a book of this kind, is their attention to how contract is used and operates in everyday life. Commentators have expressed concern that the study and practice of law may become too narrowly based and tend to divorce itself from the general culture of which we are all a part.

Rather than seeing the function of law as being to *declare* how contracts ought to be, many of the approaches we will examine are based on the premise that law should *reflect* what constitutes ethical and workable commercial practice. The shift is described here as being from formalism to realism. The new breed of authors whose work is considered owe much to a socio-legal or realist tradition of scholarship, which takes as its starting point the need to understand how the law is received by the community it seeks to regulate.

Socio-legal Approaches to Contract Law

The socio-legal movement in law was in large part a reaction against traditional approaches to studying law, which tended to focus on the importance of the rules at the expense of studying their impact. Legal formalism, with its emphasis on how things *ought* to be, tended to encourage the spurious idea that law is in some way autonomous, an end in itself, rather than a means to social order. By way of contrast, socio-legal scholars have sought to put law firmly in its social, political and economic contexts. They look for relationships between law, legal systems and the wider society; and ask questions about the functions and effects of legal rules.

Socio-legal scholars have argued that there should be a connection between law and the standards of everyday life if law is to retain its legitimacy. According to this school of thought, the standards by which individuals and groups *actually* govern their relations consist only partly of the law to be found in statutes and judicial decisions. In other words, the centre of gravity lies not in legislation nor in judicial decision, but in society itself. It is argued that 'living law', or the rules and norms that people in the commercial sector use to govern their contracts, may be more advanced than doctrine developed by the courts because of an ability to develop quickly in response to problems in the marketplace. In her study of the cotton industry, Bernstein (2001) has argued convincingly that a 'private legal system operates to create and maintain successful co-operative contracting relationships. She has argued:

The stability of this and other cooperative-based commercial systems may also be due, in whole or in part, to the fact that social norms of honour, particularly when reinforced through group activity and a basic human desire to think of one's self as *trustworthy*, are more powerful motivators of transactional behaviour than economic models of behaviour typically assume. (p. 1774)

The development of standards within industries has also been encouraged by lack of access to the courts, as contract litigation is commonly regarded as a last resort. Moreover, profits earned from relationships maintained through goodwill and the compromise of differences often outweigh damages awarded against a company that now trades elsewhere. It could be argued then, that the business community has, for reasons of perceived convenience, efficiency and cost, been virtually impelled to develop its own customs, practices and techniques designed to avoid or mitigate business or 'legal' risk and loss.

The judiciary has not been insensitive to the need for the law to remain relevant to practice. For example, in the seventeenth century, in order to remedy weaknesses in the common law of the time, the judges began to incorporate into it what was known as the 'law merchant'. This was a body of relatively sophisticated rules and techniques developed for use in agreements between merchants, or in particular trades or centres of business. But the question of whether it is the law that should be sensitive to practice, or everyday practice of contracts that should be mindful of formal law, remains controversial. It is an issue that poses serious questions about the role of law and the judiciary, since for some there seems to be a growing remoteness from commercial realities on the part of the law.

It would seem that, to a large extent, business has withdrawn from contract law because of its expense, the time it takes to litigate and the irrelevance of formal to everyday notions of obligation. This is particularly the case as far as dispute resolution is concerned. The business community has come to place much greater reliance on bilateral negotiation, commercial mediation and arbitration in preference to the courts, which in turn means that the raw material from which judicial precedents are set is depleted. Some observers have gone further and suggested that the classical model would no longer be recognised in the modern world of commercial contracts. These arguments suggest that we should go beyond the material contained in most textbooks on the subject because of their propensity to focus only on the issue of what the formal law is. In short, we need to move from a position in which law is taken to be synonymous with commerce to a position where the most logical question to pose is of whether commercial exchange needs law.

Non-contractual Relations in Business

In the latter half of the last century, a number of important empirical studies of the use of contract law on a day-to-day basis were undertaken which provided fertile ground for reconsideration of the relevance of classical and neo-classical models. These studies are important because they have prompted the emergence of new theories about the role of contract that help us to visualise alternatives to the traditional models. The most obvious starting point for a discussion of the lived world of contract is the work of Stewart Macaulay who was the first legal researcher to explore in a systematic way the use that the business community made of contracts. He started with the assumption that contracts had the *potential* to serve two key functions. The first of these is the rational planning of transactions with careful provision for as many future contingencies as can be foreseen. The second is the existence, or use of, legal sanctions to induce performance or compensate for non-performance. In his seminal work, Macaulay (1963) saw planning as involving such things as the definition of performances, the effect of defective performances and the legally binding nature, or otherwise, of the agreement. His expectations about the role that contract might play in exchanges would have been familiar to classical scholars who focused considerable attention on planning and dispute resolution. What proved innovative about his work was the response of manufacturers and lawyers to his questions about the actual use to which the contract was put.

Somewhat surprisingly, Macaulay (1963) found that business people were not very concerned about planning their transactions in detail in advance. In a later study, Beale and Dugdale (1975) found that business people in the engineering industry considered it expensive to plan in detail. This was especially the case where a dispute or loss seemed unlikely. Lengthy negotiations resulting in detailed planned contractual documents took place only where high-risk, complex, expensive items, such as aircraft, were involved. Indeed, Macaulay (1963) found that detailed negotiations at the beginning of a relationship have even been found to be a sign of *mistrust*. It would seem that it is good relations and profit margins rather than legal rights and duties which are uppermost in the minds of commercial

contractors when they make contracts. In Macaulay's 1963 study, most respondents discussed what constituted performance for the purposes of the contract and the effect of certain things happening during performance. But less than half negotiated the consequences of non-performance and even less gave thought to the type of legal sanctions that would apply in such situations.

Macaulay (1963) found evidence of two widely accepted norms of business practice which bound the parties and business community in ways not anticipated by the classical model with its heavy emphasis on individualism and self-interest. First, an adherence to the principle that commitments should be honoured in almost all situations and a strong feeling that one should not 'welsh' on a deal. Second, that one ought to produce a good product and stand behind it. Neither of these motivations was as altruistic as might at first appear to be the case. Firmly behind these norms was a sure knowledge of the commercial value of trouble-free, continuing relationships with good customers.

It is clear from the burgeoning empirical literature on the day-to-day use of contract that, contrary to the classical model's assumption about the importance of certainty, flexibility is highly valued within the business community. Performance of contractual obligations often takes a significant amount of time. So, for instance the supply of aircraft parts to the Royal Air Force might involve a contractual relationship spanning years. Similarly, an architect might be employed to design a building and supervise its construction over a three-year period or longer. During this time, ideas, technology, world politics and fashions are likely to alter. Changes in market conditions and costs mean that adjustments to contracts are common, expected and necessary. The country's entry into war at short notice might mean, for instance, that more aircraft parts need to be produced or that the price of imported components increases rapidly. Similarly, the design of a civic theatre may have to be reconsidered when the builders find a site of archaeological interest when digging the foundations.

Empirical studies have discovered a number of instances in which one party sought an adjustment once an agreement had been made. In law, such unilateral proposals to vary an existing agreement require a new agreement to be negotiated and a new type of exchange to take place to seal the bargain. But in the business world, such adjustments, and even withdrawals from the contract, were in many instances allowed by the other party 'without dispute' or renegotiation. Cancellation was not always cause for an action for breach but, like bad debts, a recognised risk that could be budgeted for. One lawyer in Macaulay's study (1963) commented that there is a widespread attitude within the business community that one can back out of any deal within vague limits. Campbell and Harris (1993) have argued that, when the parties realise that there is a lack of fit between the real deal and the contract, they expect, and are commonly able to renegotiate on an extra-legal negotiating basis.

Even when such adjustments to the working agreement do not occur, there are limits to what those drafting a formal paper deal can predict or have time to express in words. This means that, when a judge or lawyer looks for the plain meaning of the original contract, it is often the case that it does not reflect what the parties want to achieve. As a result, it has been argued that traditional forms of analysing contracts are inadequate because they fail to understand the importance of ongoing alterations to long-term commercial contracts and the *implicit dimensions* of contracts. That is not to say that traditional doctrines have ignored the need for flexibility. It will be seen from the chapters that follow that even the most traditional of lawyers anticipate the need for such things as variation of contracts and interpretation of agreements in the context of a previous course of dealing or trade custom. But the emphasis of the classical model is on treating contracts as disembedded associations between individuals motivated only by financial gain in the short or medium term. For some, this is an inadequate response to contractual realities in the marketplace. Campbell and Collins (2003) have argued that judicial reasoning has developed only a weak capacity to incorporate these dimensions into its analysis of contract. In their words:

> If the law seeks to protect and enforce contractual agreements, the recognition that it has a partial and incomplete understanding of those agreements suggest that it fails in many instances to achieve its goals by enforcing not the agreement of the parties in all its relevant dimensions but a truncated perception of that agreement... misunderstandings of this practice create the risk that legal regulation will either fail adequately to support the practice when required or misdirect its controls so that they are ineffective.

A succession of empirical studies have found that the use of litigation in the business community is rare and many research participants have argued that they would *actively avoid* introducing lawyers into a dispute because they did not understand the give and take of business. In fact, it seems that the

parties to contracts frequently disregard the contract or legal sanctions available in negotiating a dispute. Lewis (1982) has suggested that this is because legal remedies are seen as inflexible, destructive, impractical, unfair, not reflecting commercial practice and difficult to enforce. As Macaulay (2003) has argued more recently:

> Business people do know that there are such things as actions for breach of contract. They also know that their reputation with their trading partner is valuable, and they do not knowingly do things that would damage it without a good reason. Most of the time, I would guess, avoiding breach of contract litigation is not something that business people spend much time thinking about. Insofar as this is true, the style of contract analysis used by judges will not matter much to people who are not law professors.

Socio-legal researchers have also discovered that it is not just that law is marginalised but that other normative frameworks are used to replace it. Studies suggest that widespread use is made of non-legal sanctions such as complaints, replacement procedures, negotiated settlements and blacklisting and that the effectiveness of these measures renders recourse to the courts unnecessary. Underpinning these various informal sanctions is an economic need to stay on good terms with those parties [...] whom business people were likely to want to contract with again. This finding alone provides a stark contrast to the classical model of contract which envisages a 'discrete' one-off exchange between strangers.

However, the failure of legal doctrine to reflect how contracts work in an everyday context and the fact that the courts may rarely be used by some sectors of the business community should not necessarily lead us to the conclusion that the law completely lacks legitimacy. It is possible that law plays a more indirect role in the contractual sphere than has been suggested so far. Other authors have argued that, while business people honour informal norms and sanctions while a contractual relationship is progressing well, when it breaks up they may well want recourse to the sort of 'end-game' rules that appear in formal written agreements. Moreover, although they may not use the courts, that is not to say that formal doctrine, favourable precedents and the threat of legal enforcement of contractual obligations are not used as bargaining tools in the process of negotiating an out-of-court settlement or compliance with a demand. In this way, it may be that formal doctrine continues to have a radiating effect or symbolic power not anticipated by some empirical studies. Even where disputes do not arise, the law may play some part in fostering confidence. If litigation is not thought about on a day-to-day basis, it may nonetheless constitute a vague symbolic threat which serves to encourage reliability. The question which remains is whether we want the law of contract to be more than this.

(d) Non-contractual Relations in Business: A Preliminary Study†

Stewart Macaulay

Preliminary findings indicate that businessmen often fail to plan exchange relationships completely, and seldom use legal sanctions to adjust these relationships or to settle disputes. Planning and legal sanctions are often unnecessary and may have undesirable consequences. Transactions are planned and legal sanctions are used when the gains are thought to outweigh the costs. The power to decide whether the gains from using contract outweigh the costs will be held by individuals having different occupational roles. The occupational role influences the decision that is made.

What good is contract law? who uses it? when and how? Complete answers would require an investigation of almost every type of transaction between individuals and organizations. In this report, research has been confined to exchanges between businesses, and primarily to manufacturers.[1] Furthermore, this report will be limited to a presentation of the findings concerning when contract is and is not used and to a tentative explanation of these findings.[2]

This research is only the first phase in a scientific study.[3] The primary research technique involved interviewing 68 businessmen and lawyers representing 43 companies and six law firms. The interviews ranged from a 30-minute brush-off where not all questions could be asked of a busy and uninterested sales manager to a six-hour discussion with the general counsel of a large corporation. Detailed notes of the interviews were taken and a complete report of each interview was dictated, usually no later than the evening after the interview. All but two of the companies had plants in Wisconsin; 17 were manufacturers of machinery but none made such items as food products, scientific instruments, textiles or petroleum products. Thus the likelihood of error because of sampling bias may be considerable.[4]

However, to a great extent, existing knowledge has been inadequate to permit more rigorous procedures — as yet one cannot formulate many precise questions to be asked a systematically selected sample of "right people." Much time has been spent fishing for relevant questions or answers, or both.

Reciprocity, exchange or contract has long been of interest to sociologists, economists and lawyers. Yet each discipline has an incomplete view of this kind of conduct. This study represents the effort of a law teacher to draw on sociological ideas and empirical investigation. It stresses, among other things, the functions and dysfunctions of using contract to solve exchange problems and the influence of occupational roles on how one assesses whether the benefits of using contract outweigh the costs.

To discuss when contract is and is not used, the term "contract" must be specified. This term will be used here to refer to devices for conducting exchanges. Contract is not treated as synonymous with an exchange itself, which may or may not be characterized as contractual. Nor is contract used to refer to a writing recording an agreement. Contract, as I use the term here, involves two distinct elements: (a) Rational planning of the transaction with careful provision for as many future contingencies as can be foreseen, and (b) the existence or use of actual or potential legal sanctions to induce performance of the exchange or to compensate for non-performance.

These devices for conducting exchanges may be used or may exist in greater or lesser degree, so that transactions can be described relatively as involving a more contractual or a less contractual manner (a) of creating an exchange relationship or (b) of

† This material is originally published in (1983) 28:1 *American Sociological Review* 55 at 55–67. [Notes/references omitted.]

solving problems arising during the course of such a relationship.

TENTATIVE FINDINGS

It is difficult to generalize about the use and nonuse of contract by manufacturing industry. However, a number of observations can be made with reasonable accuracy at this time. The use and nonuse of contract in creating exchange relations and in dispute settling will be taken up in turn.

The creation of exchange relationships. In creating exchange relationships, businessmen may plan to a greater or lesser degree in relation to several types of issues. Before reporting the findings as to practices in creating such relationships, it is necessary to describe what one can plan about in a bargain and the degrees of planning which are possible.

People negotiating a contract can make plans concerning several types of issues: (1) They can plan what each is to do or refrain from doing; e.g., S might agree to deliver ten 1963 Studebaker four-door sedan automobiles to B on a certain date in exchange for a specified amount of money. (2) They can plan what effect certain contingencies are to have on their duties; e.g., what is to happen to S and B's obligations if S cannot deliver the cars because of a strike at the Studebaker factory? (3) They can plan what is to happen if either of them fails to perform; e.g., what is to happen if S delivers nine of the cars two weeks late? (4) They can plan their agreement so that it is a legally enforceable contract — that is, so that a legal sanction would be available to provide compensation for injury suffered by B as a result of S's failure to deliver the cars on time.

As to each of these issues, there may be a different degree of planning by the parties. (1) They may carefully and explicitly plan; e.g., S may agree to deliver ten 1963 Studebaker four-door sedans which have six cylinder engines, automatic transmissions and other specified items of optional equipment and which will perform to a specified standard for a certain time. (2) They may have a mutual but tacit understanding about an issue; e.g., although the subject was never mentioned in their negotiations, both S and B may assume that B may cancel his order for the cars before they are delivered if B's taxi-cab business is so curtailed that B can no longer use ten additional cabs. (3) They may have two inconsistent unexpressed assumptions about an issue; e.g., S may assume that if any of the cabs fails to perform to the specified standard for a certain time, all S must do is repair or replace it. B may assume

S must also compensate B for the profits B would have made if the cab had been in operation. (4) They may never have thought of the issue; e.g., neither S nor B planned their agreement so that it would be a legally enforceable contract. Of course, the first and fourth degrees of planning listed are the extreme cases and the second and third are intermediate points. Clearly other intermediate points are possible; e.g., S and B neglect to specify whether the cabs should have automatic or conventional transmissions. Their planning is not as careful and explicit as that in the example previously given.

. . . .

Most larger companies, and many smaller ones, attempt to plan carefully and completely. Important transactions not in the ordinary course of business are handled by a detailed contract....

More routine transactions commonly are handled by what can be called standardized planning. A firm will have a set of terms and conditions for purchases, sales, or both printed on the business documents used in these exchanges. Thus the things to be sold and the price may be planned particularly for each transaction, but standard provisions will further elaborate the performances and cover the other subjects of planning. Typically, these terms and conditions are lengthy and printed in small type on the back of the forms....

In larger firms such "boiler plate" provisions are drafted by the house counsel or the firm's outside lawyer. In smaller firms such provisions may be drafted by the industry trade association, may be copied from a competitor, or may be found on forms purchased from a printer. In any event, salesmen and purchasing agents, the operating personnel, typically are unaware of what is said in the fine print on the back of the forms they use. Yet often the normal business patterns will give effect to this standardized planning. For example, purchasing agents may have to use a purchase order form so that all transactions receive a number under the firm's accounting system. Thus, the required accounting record will carry the necessary planning of the exchange relationship printed on its reverse side. If the seller does not object to this planning and accepts the order, the buyer's "fine print" will control. If the seller does object, differences can be settled by negotiation.

This type of standardized planning is very common. Requests for copies of the business documents used in buying and selling were sent to approximately 6,000 manufacturing firms which do business in Wisconsin. Approximately 1,200 replies were received and 850 companies used some type of standardized planning. With only a few exceptions, the firms that did not reply and the 350 that indicated they did not use standardized planning were very small manufacturers such as local bakeries, soft drink bottlers and sausage makers.

While businessmen can and often do carefully and completely plan, it is clear that not all exchanges are neatly rationalized. Although most businessmen think that a clear description of both the seller's and buyer's performances is obvious common sense, they do not always live up to this ideal. The house counsel and the purchasing agent of a medium size manufacturer of automobile parts reported that several times their engineers had committed the company to buy expensive machines without adequate specifications. The engineers had drawn careful specifications as to the type of machine and how it was to be made but had neglected to require that the machine produce specified results. An attorney and an auditor both stated that most contract disputes arise because of ambiguity in the specifications.

Businessmen often prefer to rely on "a man's word" in a brief letter, a handshake, or "common honesty and decency" — even when the transaction involves exposure to serious risks. Seven lawyers from law firms with business practices were interviewed. Five thought that businessmen often entered contracts with only a minimal degree of advance planning. They complained that businessmen desire to "keep it simple and avoid red tape" even where large amounts of money and significant risks are involved. One stated that he was "sick of being told, 'We can trust old Max,' when the problem is not one of honesty but one of reaching an agreement that both sides understand." Another said that businessmen when bargaining often talk only in pleasant generalities, think they have a contract, but fail to reach agreement on any of the hard, unpleasant questions until forced to do so by a lawyer. Two outside lawyers had different views. One thought that large firms usually planned important exchanges, although he conceded that occasionally matters might be left in a fairly vague state. The other dissenter represents a large utility that commonly buys heavy equipment and buildings. The supplier's employees come on the utility's property to install the equipment or construct the buildings, and they may be injured while there. The utility has been sued by such employees so often that it carefully plans purchases with the assistance of a lawyer so that suppliers take this burden.

Moreover, standardized planning can break down. In the example of such planning previously given, it was assumed that the purchasing agent would use his company's form with its 24 paragraphs printed on the back and that the seller would accept this or object to any provisions he did not like. However, the seller may fail to read the buyer's 24 paragraphs of fine print and may accept the buyer's order on the seller's own acknowledgment-of-order form. Typically this form will have ten to 50 paragraphs favoring the seller, and these provisions are likely to be different from or inconsistent with the buyer's provisions. The seller's acknowledgment form may be received by the buyer and checked by a clerk. She will read the *face* of the acknowledgment but not the fine print on the back of it because she has neither the time nor ability to analyze the small print on the 100 to 500 forms she must review each day. The face of the acknowledgment — where the goods and the price are specified — is likely to correspond with the face of the purchase order. If it does, the two forms are filed away. At this point, both buyer and seller are likely to assume they have planned an exchange and made a contract. Yet they have done neither, as they are in disagreement about all that appears on the back of their forms. This practice is common enough to have a name. Law teachers call it "the battle of the forms."

Ten of the 12 purchasing agents interviewed said that frequently the provisions on the back of their purchase order and those on the back of a supplier's acknowledgment would differ or be inconsistent. Yet they would assume that the purchase was complete without further action unless one of the supplier's provisions was really objectionable. Moreover, only occasionally would they bother to read the fine print on the back of suppliers' forms. On the other hand, one purchasing agent insists that agreement be reached on the fine print provisions, but he represents the utility whose lawyer reported that it exercises great care in planning. The other purchasing agent who said that his company did not face a battle of the forms problem, works for a division of one of the largest manufacturing corporations in the United States. Yet the company may have such a problem without recognizing it. The purchasing agent regularly sends a supplier both a purchase order and another form which the supplier is asked to sign and return. The second form states that the supplier accepts the buyer's terms and conditions. The company has sufficient bargaining power to force suppliers to sign and return the form, and the purchasing agent must show one of his firm's auditors such a signed form for every purchase order issued. Yet suppliers frequently return this buyer's form *plus* their own acknowledgment form which has conflicting provisions. The purchasing agent throws away the supplier's form and files his own. Of course, in such a case the supplier has not acquiesced to the buyer's provisions. There is no agreement and no contract.

Sixteen sales managers were asked about the battle of the forms. Nine said that frequently no agreement was reached on which set of fine print was to govern, while seven said that there was no problem. Four of the seven worked for companies whose major customers are the large automobile companies or the large manufacturers of paper products. These customers demand that their terms and conditions govern any purchase, are careful generally to see that suppliers acquiesce, and have the bargaining power to have their way. The other three of the seven sales managers who have no battle of the forms problem, work for manufacturers of special industrial machines. Their firms are careful to reach complete agreement with their customers. Two of these men stressed that they could take no chances because such a large part of their firm's capital is tied up in making any one machine. The other sales manager had been influenced by a law suit against one of his competitors for over a half million dollars. The suit was brought by a customer when the competitor had been unable to deliver a machine and put it in operation on time. The sales manager interviewed said his firm could not guarantee that its machines would work perfectly by a specified time because they are designed to fit the customer's requirements, which may present difficult engineering problems. As a result, contracts are carefully negotiated.

. . . .

It is likely that businessmen pay more attention to describing the performances in an exchange than to planning for contingencies or defective performances or to obtaining legal enforceability of their contracts. Even when a purchase order and acknowledgment have conflicting provisions printed on the back, almost always the buyer and seller will be in agreement on what is to be sold and how much is to be paid for it. The lawyers who said businessmen often commit their firms to significant exchanges too casually, stated that the performances would be defined in the brief letter or telephone call; the lawyers objected that nothing else would be covered. Moreover, it is likely that businessmen are least concerned about planning their transactions so that they are legally enforceable contracts.[5] For example, in Wisconsin requirements contracts — contracts to supply a firm's requirements of an item rather than a definite quantity — probably are not legally enforceable. Seven people interviewed reported that their firms regularly used requirements contracts in dealings in Wisconsin. None thought that the lack of legal sanction made any difference. Three of these people were house counsel who knew the Wisconsin law before being interviewed. Another example of a lack of desire for legal sanctions is found in the relationship between automobile manufacturers and their suppliers of parts. The manufacturers draft a carefully planned agreement, but one which is so designed that the supplier will have only minimal, if any, legal rights against the manufacturers. The standard contract used by manufacturers of paper to sell to magazine publishers has a pricing clause which is probably sufficiently vague to make the contract legally unenforceable. The house counsel of one of the largest paper producers said that everyone in the industry is aware of this because of a leading New York case concerning the contract, but that no one cares. Finally, it seems likely that planning for contingencies and defective performances are in-between cases — more likely to occur than planning for a legal sanction, but less likely than a description of performance.

Thus one can conclude that (1) many business exchanges reflect a high degree of planning about the four categories: description, contingencies, defective performances and legal sanction — but (2) many, if not most, exchanges reflect no planning, or only a minimal amount of it, especially concerning legal sanctions and the effect of defective performances. As a result, the opportunity for good faith disputes during the life of the exchange relationship often is present.

The adjustment of exchange relationships and the settling of disputes. While a significant amount of creating business exchanges is done on a fairly noncontractual basis, the creation of exchanges usually is far more contractual than the adjustment of such relationships and the settlement of disputes. Exchanges are adjusted when the obligations of one or both parties are modified by agreement during the life of the relationship. For example, the buyer may be allowed to cancel all or part of the goods he has ordered because he no longer needs them; the seller may be paid more than the contract price by the buyer because of unusual changed circumstances. Dispute settlement involves determining whether or not a party has performed as agreed and, if he has not, doing something about it. For example, a court may have to interpret the meaning of a contract, determine what the alleged defaulting party has done and determine what, if any, remedy the aggrieved party is entitled to. Or one party may assert that the other is in default, refuse to proceed with performing the contract and refuse to deal ever again with the alleged defaulter. If the alleged defaulter, who in fact may not be in default, takes no action, the dispute is then "settled."

Business exchanges in non-speculative areas are usually adjusted without dispute.

Under the law of contracts, if B orders 1,000 widgets from S at $1.00 each, B must take all 1,000 widgets or be in breach of contract and liable to pay S his expenses up to the time of the breach plus his lost anticipated profit. Yet all ten of the purchasing agents asked about cancellation of orders once placed indicated that they expected to be able to cancel orders freely subject to only an obligation to pay for the seller's major expenses such as scrapped steel.[6] All 17 sales personnel asked reported that they often had to accept cancellation. One said, "You can't ask a man to eat paper [the firm's product] when he has no use for it." A lawyer with many large industrial clients said,

> Often businessmen do not feel they have "a contract" — rather they have "an order." They speak of "cancelling the order" rather than "breaching our contract." When I began practice I referred to order cancellations as breaches of contract, but my clients objected since they do not think of cancellation as wrong. Most clients, in heavy industry at least, believe that there is a right to cancel as part of the buyer-seller relationship. There is a widespread attitude that one can back out of any deal within some very vague limits. Lawyers are often surprised by this attitude.

Disputes are frequently settled without reference to the contract or potential or actual legal sanctions. There is a hesitancy to speak of legal rights or to threaten to sue in these negotiations. Even where the parties have a detailed and carefully planned agreement which indicates what is to happen if, say, the seller fails to deliver on time, often they will never refer to the agreement but will negotiate a solution when the problem arises apparently as if there had never been any original contract. One purchasing agent expressed a common business attitude when he said,

> if something comes up, you get the other man on the telephone and deal with the problem. You don't read legalistic contract clauses at each other if you ever want to do business again. One doesn't run to lawyers if he wants to stay in business because one must behave decently.

Or as one businessman put it, "You can settle any dispute if you keep the lawyers and accountants out of it. They just do not understand the give-and-take needed in business." All of the house counsel interviewed indicated that they are called into the dispute settlement process only after the businessmen have failed to settle matters in their own way. Two indicated that after being called in house counsel at first will only advise the purchasing agent, sales manager or other official involved; not even the house counsel's letterhead is used on communications with the other side until all hope for a peaceful resolution is gone.

Law suits for breach of contract appear to be rare. Only five of the 12 purchasing agents had ever been involved in even a negotiation concerning a contract dispute where both sides were represented by lawyers; only two of ten sales managers had ever gone this far. None had been involved in a case that went through trial. A law firm with more than 40 lawyers and a large commercial practice handles in a year only about six trials concerned with contract problems. Less than 10 per cent of the time of this office is devoted to any type of work related to contracts disputes. Corporations big enough to do business in more than one state tend to sue and be sued in the federal courts. Yet only 2,779 out of 58,293 civil actions filed in the United States District Courts in fiscal year 1961 involved private contracts.[7] During the same period only 3,447 of the 61,138 civil cases filed in the principal trial courts of New York State involved private contracts.[8] The same picture emerges from a review of appellate cases.[9] Mentschikoff has suggested that commercial cases are not brought to the courts either in periods of business prosperity (because buyers unjustifiably reject goods only when prices drop and they can get similar goods elsewhere at less than the contract price) or in periods of deep depression (because people are unable to come to court or have insufficient assets to satisfy any judgment that might be obtained). Apparently, she adds, it is necessary to have "a kind of middle-sized depression" to bring large numbers of commercial cases to the courts. However, there is little evidence that in even "a kind of middle-sized depression" today's businessmen would use the courts to settle disputes.[10]

At times relatively contractual methods are used to make adjustments in ongoing transactions and to settle disputes. Demands of one side which are deemed unreasonable by the other occasionally are blocked by reference to the terms of the agreement between the parties. The legal position of the parties can influence negotiations even though legal rights or litigation are never mentioned in their discussions; it makes a difference if one is demanding what both concede to be a right or begging for a favor. Now and then a firm may threaten to turn matters over to its attorneys, threaten to sue, commence a suit or even litigate and carry an appeal to the highest court which will hear the matter. Thus, legal sanctions, while not an everyday affair, are not unknown in business.

One can conclude that while detailed planning and legal sanctions play a significant role in some exchanges between businesses, in many business exchanges their role is small.

TENTATIVE EXPLANATIONS

Two questions need to be answered: (A) How can business successfully operate exchange relationships with relatively so little attention to detailed planning or to legal sanctions, and (B) Why does business ever use contract in light of its success without it?

Why are relatively non-contractual practices so common? In most situations contract is not needed. Often its functions are served by other devices. Most problems are avoided without resort to detailed planning or legal sanctions because usually there is little room for honest misunderstandings or good faith differences of opinion about the nature and quality of a seller's performance. Although the parties fail to cover all foreseeable contingencies, they will exercise care to see that both understand the primary obligation on each side. Either products are standardized with an accepted description or specifications are written calling for production to certain tolerances or results. Those who write and read specifications are experienced professionals who will know the customs of their industry and those of the industries with which they deal. Consequently, these customs can fill gaps in the express agreements of the parties. Finally, most products can be tested to see if they are what was ordered; typically in manufacturing industry we are not dealing with questions of taste or judgment where people can differ in good faith.

When defaults occur they are not likely to be disastrous because of techniques of risk avoidance or risk spreading. One can deal with firms of good reputation or he may be able to get some form of security to guarantee performance. One can insure against many breaches of contract where the risks justify the costs. Sellers set up reserves for bad debts on their books and can sell some of their accounts receivable. Buyers can place orders with two or more suppliers of the same item so that a default by one will not stop the buyer's assembly lines.

Moreover, contract and contract law are often thought unnecessary because there are many effective non-legal sanctions. Two norms are widely accepted. (1) Commitments are to be honored in almost all situations; one does not welsh on a deal. (2) One ought to produce a good product and stand behind it. Then, too, business units are organized to perform commitments, and internal sanctions will induce performance. For example, sales personnel must face angry customers when there has been a late or defective performance. The salesmen do not enjoy this and will put pressure on the production personnel responsible for the default. If the production personnel default too often, they will be fired. At all levels of the two business units personal relationships across the boundaries of the two organizations exert pressures for conformity to expectations. Salesmen often know purchasing agents well. The same two individuals occupying these roles may have dealt with each other from five to 25 years. Each has something to give the other. Salesmen have gossip about competitors, shortages and price increases to give purchasing agents who treat them well. Salesmen take purchasing agents to dinner, and they give purchasing agents Christmas gifts hoping to improve the chances of making sale. The buyer's engineering staff may work with the seller's engineering staff to solve problems jointly. The seller's engineers may render great assistance, and the buyer's engineers may desire to return the favor by drafting specifications which only the seller can meet. The top executives of the two firms may know each other. They may sit together on government or trade committees. They may know each other socially and even belong to the same country club. The interrelationships may be more formal. Sellers may hold stock in corporations which are important customers; buyers may hold stock in important suppliers. Both buyer and seller may share common directors on their boards. They may share a common financial institution which has financed both units.

The final type of non-legal sanction is the most obvious. Both business units involved in the exchange desire to continue successfully in business and will avoid conduct which might interfere with attaining this goal. One is concerned with both the reaction of the other party in the particular exchange and with his own general business reputation. Obviously, the buyer gains sanctions insofar as the seller wants the particular exchange to be completed. Buyers can withhold part or all of their payments until sellers have performed to their satisfaction. If a seller has a great deal of money tied up in his performance which he must recover quickly, he will go a long way to please the buyer in order to be paid. Moreover, buyers who are dissatisfied may cancel and cause sellers to lose the cost of what they have done up to cancellation. Furthermore, sellers hope for repeat for orders, and one gets few of these from unhappy customers. Some industrial buyers go so far as to formalize this sanction by issuing "report cards" rating the performance of each supplier. The supplier rating goes to the top management of the seller organization, and these men can apply internal sanctions to salesmen, production supervisors or product designers if there are too many "D's" or "F's" on the report card....

Not only do the particular business units in a given exchange want to deal with each other again, they also want to deal with other business units in the future. And the way one behaves in a particular transaction, or a series of transactions, will color his general business reputation. Blacklisting can be formal or informal. Buyers who fail to pay their bills on time risk a bad report in credit rating services such as Dun and Bradstreet. Sellers who do not satisfy their customers become the subject of discussion in the gossip exchanged by purchasing agents and salesmen, at meetings of purchasing agents' associations and trade associations, or even at country clubs or social gatherings where members of top management meet. The American male's habit of debating the merits of new cars carries over to industrial items. Obviously, a poor reputation does not help a firm make sales and may force it to offer great price discounts or added services to remain in business. Furthermore, the habits of unusually demanding buyers become known, and they tend to get no more than they can coerce out of suppliers who choose to deal with them. Thus often contract is not needed as there are alternatives.

Not only are contract and contract law not needed in many situations, their use may have, or may be thought to have, undesirable consequences. Detailed negotiated contracts can get in the way of creating good exchange relationships between business units. If one side insists on a detailed plan, there will be delay while letters are exchanged as the parties try to agree on what should happen if a remote and unlikely contingency occurs.

In some cases they may not be able to agree at all on such matters and as a result a sale may be lost to the seller and the buyer may have to search elsewhere for an acceptable supplier. Many businessmen would react by thinking that had no one raised the series of remote and unlikely contingencies all this wasted effort could have been avoided.

Even where agreement can be reached at the negotiation stage, carefully planned arrangements may create undesirable exchange relationships between business units. Some businessmen object that in such a carefully worked out relationship one gets performance only to the letter of the contract. Such planning indicates a lack of trust and blunts the demands of friendship, turning a cooperative venture into an antagonistic horse trade. Yet the greater danger perceived by some businessmen is that one would have to perform his side of the bargain to its letter and thus lose what is called "flexibility." Businessmen may welcome a measure of vagueness in the obligations they assume so that they may negotiate matters in light of the actual circumstances.

Adjustment of exchange relationships and dispute settlement by litigation or the threat of it also has many costs. The gain anticipated from using this form of coercion often fails to outweigh these costs, which are both monetary and non-monetary.... Clearly actual litigation is even more costly than making threats. Lawyers demand substantial fees from larger business units.... Moreover, there will be the cost of diverting top management, engineers, and others in the organization from their normal activities. The firm may lose many days work from several key people. The non-monetary costs may be large too. A breach of contract law suit may settle a particular dispute, but such an action often results in a "divorce" ending the "marriage" between the two businesses, since a contract action is likely to carry charges with at least overtones of bad faith....

Why do relatively contractual practices ever exist? Although contract is not needed and actually may have negative consequences, businessmen do make some carefully planned contracts, negotiate settlements influenced by their legal rights and commence and defend some breach of contract law suits or arbitration proceedings. In view of the findings and explanation presented to this point, one may ask why. Exchanges are carefully planned when it is thought that planning and a potential legal sanction will have more advantages than disadvantages. Such a judgment may be reached when contract planning serves the internal needs of an organization involved in a business exchange. For example, a fairly detailed contract can serve as a communication device within a large corporation. While the corporation's sales manager and house counsel may work out all the provisions with the customer, its production manger will have to make the product. He must be told what to do and how to handle at least the most obvious contingencies. Moreover, the sales manager may want to remove certain issues from future negotiation by his subordinates. If he puts the matter in the written contract, he may be able to keep his salesmen from making concessions to the customer without first consulting the sales manager. Then the sales manager may be aided in his battles with his firm's financial or engineering departments if the contract calls for certain practices which the sales manager advocates but which the other departments resist. Now the corporation is obligated to a customer to do what the sales manager wants to do; how can the financial or engineering departments insist on anything else?

Also one tends to find a judgment that the gains of contract outweigh the costs where there is a likelihood that significant problems will arise....

An "irrational" factor may exert some influence on the decision to use legal sanctions. The man who controls a firm may feel that he or his organization has been made to appear foolish or has been the victim of fraud or bad faith. The law suit may be seen as a vehicle "to get even" although the potential gains, as viewed by an objective observer, are outweighed by the potential costs.

The decision whether or not to use contract — whether the gain exceeds the costs — will be made by the person within the business unit with the power to make it, and it tends to make a difference who he is....

The power to decide that a more contractual method of creating relationships and settling disputes shall be used will be held by different people at different times in different organizations. In most firms the sales department and the purchasing department have a great deal of power to resist contractual procedures or to ignore them if they are formally adopted and to handle disputes their own way. Yet in larger organizations the treasurer and the controller have increasing power to demand both systems and compliance. Occasionally, the house counsel must arbitrate the conflicting positions of these departments; in giving "legal advice" he may make the business judgment necessary regarding the use of contract. At times he may ask for an opinion from an outside law firm to reinforce his own position with the outside firm's prestige.

Obviously, there are other significant variables which influence the degree that contract is used. One is the relative bargaining power or skill of the two business units. Even if the controller of a small supplier succeeds within the firm and creates a contractual system of dealing, there will be no contract if the firm's large customer prefers not to be bound to anything. Firms that supply General Motors deal as General Motors wants to do business, for the most part. Yet bargaining power is not size or share of the market alone. Even a General Motors may need a particular supplier, at least temporarily. Furthermore, bargaining power may shift as an exchange relationship is first created and then continues. Even a giant firm can find itself bound to a small supplier once production of an essential item begins for there may not be time to turn to another supplier. Also, all of the factors discussed in this paper can be viewed as *components* of bargaining power-for example, the personal relationship between the presidents of the buyer and the seller firms may give a sales manager great power over a purchasing agent who has been instructed to give the seller "every consideration." Another variable relevant to the use of contract is the influence of third parties. The federal government, or a lender of money, may insist that a contract be made in a particular transaction or may influence the decision to assert one's legal rights under a contract.

Contract, then, often plays an important role in business, but other factors are significant. To understand the functions of contract the whole system of conducting exchanges must be explored fully.

A. Formation

(a)   *Carlill v. Carbolic Smoke Ball Co.*†

England and Wales Court of Appeal

The defendants, who were the proprietors and vendors of a medical preparation called "The Carbolic Smoke Ball," inserted in the Pall Ma. Gazette of November 13, 1891, and in other newspapers, the following advertisement:

£100 reward will be paid by the Carbolic Smoke Ball Company to any person who contracts the increasing epidemic influenza, colds or any disease caused by taking cold, after having used the ball three times daily for two weeks according to the printed directions supplied with each ball.

£1000 is deposited with the Alliance Bank, Regent Street shewing our sincerity in the matter.

During the last epidemic of influenza many thousand carbolic smoke balls were sold as preventives against the disease, and in no ascertained case was the disease contracted by those using the carbolic smoke ball.

One carbolic smoke ball will last a family several months, making it the cheapest remedy in the world at the price, 10s., post free. The ball can be refilled at a cost of 5s. Address, Carbolic Smoke Ball. Company, 27, Princes Street, Hanover Square, London.

The plaintiff, a lady, on the faith of this advertisement, bought one of the balls at a chemist's and used it as directed, three times a daily from November 20, 1891, to January 17, 1892, when she was attacked by influenza. Hawkins, J., held that she was entitled to recover the £100. The defendants appealed.

---

†   [1893] 1 Q.B. 256. (Appeal from a decision of HAWKINS, J., [1892].)

[LINDLEY, L.J.:]

. . . .

... We are dealing with an express promise to pay £100 in certain events. Read the advertisement how you will, and twist it about as you will, here is a distinct promise expressed in language which is perfectly unmistakable:

> £100 reward will be paid by the Carbolic Smoke Ball Company to any person who contracts the influenza after having used the ball three times daily for two weeks according to the printed directions supplied with each ball.

We must first consider whether this was intended to be a promise to all, or whether it was a mere puff which meant nothing. Was it a mere puff? My answer to that question is "No," and I base my answer upon this passage:

> £1000 is deposited with the Alliance Bank, shewing our sincerity in the matter.

Now, for what was that money deposited or that statement made except to negative the suggestion that this was a mere puff and meant nothing at all? The deposit is called in aid by the advertiser as proof of his sincerity in the matter, that is, the sincerity of his promise to pay this £100 in the event which he has specified. I say this for the purpose of giving point to the observation that we are not inferring a promise; there is the promise, as plain as words can make it.

Then it is contended that it is not binding. In the first place, it is said that it is not made with anybody in particular. Now that point is common to the words of this advertisement and to the words of all other advertisements offering rewards. They are offers to anybody who performs the conditions named in the advertisement, and anybody who does perform the conditions accepts the offer. In point of law this advertisement is an offer to pay £100 to anybody who will perform these conditions, and the performance of the conditions, is the acceptance of the offer. That rests upon a string of authorities, the earliest of which is *Williams v. Carwardine*, 4 Barn. & Adol. 621, which has been followed by many other decisions upon advertisements offering rewards.

. . . . .

It appears to me, therefore, that the defendants must perform their promise, and, if they have been so unwary as to expose themselves to a great many actions, so much the worse for them.

[BOWEN, L.J.:]

I am of the same opinion. ...

. . . .

Then it was said that there was no notification of the acceptance of the contract. One cannot doubt that, as an ordinary rule of law, an acceptance of an offer made ought to be notified to the person who makes the offer, in order that the two minds may come together. Unless this is done the two minds may be apart, and there is not that consensus which is necessary according to the English law — I say nothing about the laws of other countries — to make a contract. But there is this clear gloss to be made upon that doctrine, that is notification of acceptance is required for the benefit of the person who makes the offer, the person who makes the offer may dispense with notice to himself if he thinks it desirable to do so, and I suppose there can be no doubt that where a person in an offer made by him to another person, expressly or impliedly intimates a particular mode of acceptance as sufficient to make the bargain binding, it is only necessary for the other person to whom such offer is made to follow the indicated method of acceptance; and if the person making the offer, expressly or impliedly intimates in his offer that it will be sufficient to act on the proposal without communicating acceptance of it to himself, performance of the condition is a sufficient acceptance without notification.

. . . .

Now, if that is the law, how are we to find out whether the person who makes the offer does intimate that notification of acceptance will not be necessary in order to constitute a binding bargain? In many cases you look to the offer itself. In many cases you extract from the character of the transaction that notification is not required, and in the advertisement cases it seems to follow as an inference to be drawn from the transaction itself that a person is not to notify his acceptance of the offer before he performs the condition, but that if he performs the condition notification is dispensed with. It seems to me that from the point of view of common sense no other idea could be entertained. If I advertise to the world that my dog is lost, and that anybody who brings the dog to a particular place will be paid some money, are all the police or other persons whose business it is to find lost dogs to be expected to sit down and write a note saying that they have accepted my proposal? Why, of course, they at once look after the dog, and as soon as they find the dog they have performed the condition. The essence of the transaction is that the dog should be found, and it is not necessary under such circumstances, as it seems to me, that in order to make the contract binding there should be any notification of acceptance. It follows from the nature of the thing that the performance of the condition is sufficient acceptance without the notification of it, and a person

who makes an offer in an advertisement of that kind makes an offer which must be read by the light of the common sense reflection. He does, therefore, in his offer impliedly indicate that he does not require notification of the acceptance of the offer.

. . . .

Appeal dismissed.

(b) *Balfour v. Balfour*†

U.K. Court of Appeal

[WARRINGTON L.J.:]

The wife in this case sues her husband for money which she claims to be due to her from her husband as an agreed allowance of £30 a month, the wife agreeing to support herself throughout without calling upon her husband for any maintenance and support. The wife therefore sets out to prove a binding legal contract between herself and her husband, that the husband shall in consideration of a promise by the wife pay her the sum of £30 a month.

The learned judge in the court below has found in these terms:

> It seems to me on these letters that there was a definite bargain between the husband and the wife under which, while the husband was in India and in a sufficient position and the wife was in England living separate from him, she should be paid a definite sum of £30 a month, and that agreement was made when the husband returned to Ceylon, and was re-affirmed on at least two occasions after unhappy differences had shown themselves, at any rate on the part of the husband, and when it was probable that their separation might last for some time.

Then he proceeded, having found that there was this definite agreement.... But, having found on the facts that there was such an agreement, he proceeded to show that agreement could be supported as a legal contract because there was sufficient consideration in the promise made by the wife.

We have now to determine whether there was in the first place a contract in the legal sense between the husband and the wife under which the husband was bound to pay this £30 a month. There really is no dispute about the facts. The parties were married in August 1900. The husband had a post under the Government of Ceylon as director of irrigation, and after the marriage they went to Ceylon and lived there together until the year 1915, except that for a short time in 1906 they together paid a visit to this country, and in 1908 the wife came home to this country in order to submit to an operation. In November 1915, the wife came to this country [with the husband, who was on leave;] they came together intending to return. They remained in England until August 1916, when the husband's leave had expired and he had to return. The wife, however, on the doctor's advice, was to remain in England. On 8 August 1916, the husband was about to sail, and it is on that day that it is alleged that the agreement sued upon was made by parol between the husband and wife. The wife gave evidence of what took place, and I think that I cannot do better than refer to the learned judge's note for the account of what she said took place. She said:

> In August 1916, my husband's leave was up. I was suffering from rheumatoid arthritis. My doctor advised my staying in England for some months, and not to go out till Nov 4. I booked a passage for next sailing day in September. On Aug 8 my husband sailed. He gave me a cheque

† [1918–19] All ER Rep 860.

from Aug 8 to Aug 31 for £24, and promised to give me £30 per month till I joined him in Ceylon.

There were certain letters read as to which I shall have to say a word or two presently, and then the wife said later on:

My husband and I wrote the figure together on Aug. 8 and £34 was shown. Afterwards he said £30.

That means that the husband jotted down on a bit of paper certain figures which showed that the ordinary monthly expenses of the wife, at least, that is what I infer the sheet of paper showed, would amount to £22 a month, and then they added a round sum of £12 which brought it up to £34, but, after some discussion, the amount was taken to be the round sum of £30. In cross-examination the wife said that they had not agreed to live apart until subsequent differences arose between them, and that in August 1916, such agreement as might be made by a couple living in amity was made, the husband assessing the wife's needs and saying that he would send £30 per month. That is really all the evidence as to what took place between the parties. The agreement, if made at all, was a parol agreement made on 8 August 1916. The letters which have been referred to really throw no light at all upon the legal position between the parties....

Those being the facts, what is really the position? We have to say whether on these facts there is a legal contract between these parties. In other words, we have to decide whether what took place between the parties was in the nature of a legal contract, or whether it was merely an arrangement made between the husband and the wife of the same nature as a domestic arrangement which may be made every day between any ordinary husband and wife who are living together in friendly intercourse.

[ATKIN L.J.:]

The defence to this action on the alleged contract is that the husband says he entered into no contract with his wife, and for the determination of that it is necessary to remember that there are agreements between parties which do not result in contracts within the meaning of that term in our law. The ordinary example is where two parties agree to take a walk together, or where there is an offer and an acceptance of hospitality. Nobody would suggest in ordinary circumstances that those agreements result in what we know as a contract, and one of the most usual forms of agreement which does not constitute

a contract appears to me to be the arrangements which are made between husband and wife. It is quite common, and it is the natural and inevitable result of the relationship of husband and wife, that the two spouses should make agreements between themselves, agreements such as are in dispute in this action, agreements for allowances by which the husband agrees that he will pay to his wife a certain sum of money per week or per month or per year to cover either her own expenses or the necessary expenses of the household and of the children, and in which the wife promises either expressly or impliedly to apply the allowances for the purpose for which it is given.

To my mind those agreements, or many of them, do not result in contracts at all, and they do not result in contracts even though there may be what as between other parties would constitute consideration for the agreement. The consideration, as we know, may consist either in some right, interest, profit, or benefit accruing to one party, or some forbearance, detriment, loss, or responsibility given, suffered, or undertaken by the other. This is a well-known definition, and it constantly happens, I think, that such arrangements made between husband and wife are arrangements in which there are mutual promises, or in which there is consideration in form within the definition that I have mentioned. Nevertheless they are not contracts, and they are not contracts because the parties did not intend that they should be attended by legal consequences. It would be the worst possible example to hold that agreements such as this resulted in legal obligations which could be enforced in the courts. It would mean that when a husband made his wife a promise to give her an allowance of 30s or £2 per week, whatever he could afford to give her for the maintenance of the household and children, and she promised so to apply it, not only could she sue him for his failure in any week to supply the allowance, but he could sue her for non-performance of the obligation, express or implied, which she had undertaken upon her part. The small courts of this country would have to be multiplied one hundredfold if these arrangements did result in fact in legal obligations. They are not sued upon, and the reason that they are not sued upon is not because the parties are reluctant to enforce their legal rights when the agreement is broken, but they are not sued upon because the parties in the inception of the arrangement never intended that they should be sued upon. Agreements such as these, as I say, are outside the realm of contracts altogether. The common law does not regulate the form of agreements between spouses. Their promises are not sealed with seals and sealing wax. The consideration that really obtains for them is that natural love and affection which counts for so little in these cold courts.... In respect of these promises each house is a domain into which the King's writ does not seek to run, and to which his officers do not seek to be admitted.

The only question in the present case is whether or not this promise was of such a class.... For the reasons given by my brethren it appears to me to be plain. I think it is plainly established that the promise here was not intended by either party to be attended by legal consequences. I think the onus was upon the wife, and that the wife has not established any contract. The parties were living together, the wife intending to return to Ceylon. The suggestion is that she bound herself to accept, as he bound himself to pay £30 per month under all circumstances, and that she bound herself to be satisfied with that

sum under all circumstances, and, although she was in ill-health and in this country, that out of that sum she undertook to defray the whole of the medical expenses that might fall upon her whatever might be the development of her illness, and in whatever expenses it might involve her. To my mind neither party contemplated such a result. I think that the parol evidence upon which the contract turns does not establish a contract. I think that the written evidence, the letters to which alone, oddly enough, the learned judge in the court below in his judgment refers, do not evidence such a contract, or apply, as they should be applied, to the oral evidence which was given by the wife which is not in dispute. For these reasons I think that the judgment of the learned judge in the court below was wrong, and that this appeal should be allowed.

Appeal allowed.

(c)   Contract Law in Perspective[†]

Linda Mulcahy

THE MOMENT OF RESPONSIBILITY: KEY CONCEPTS IN DETERMINING WHETHER AGREEMENT HAS BEEN REACHED

Introduction

In the last chapter, we looked at the expectation that a contract is only formed when there is a valid offer which is met with an acceptance of that offer. Collins (2003) refers to this marrying of offer and acceptance as the 'moment of responsibility'. The main focus of case law in this area has been on finding a way of determining when it is appropriate to attach legal liability to statements or the conduct of the negotiating parties. It was made clear in the last chapter that the idea that there are rules which allow us to identify an 'offer' and 'acceptance' is an artificial one. Despite the tendency to aspire to clear, if somewhat illogical, rules, in practice it is often difficult for the judiciary to separate the two concepts

of offer and acceptance out. Negotiations leading up to a contract are often messier than some textbooks would have us think. In this chapter we will turn to some of the key concepts that have been used by the judiciary in an attempt to organise cases according to a coherent set of principles. In the chapter that follows we will turn to look at some of the difficulties which have arisen in using traditional concepts of offer and acceptance in the complex world of business.

If the courts are disposed towards a formalistic approach, it is important for students to understand the method of analysing negotiations in this way. An examination of the various things that occur in the pre-contractual stage requires an understanding of a range of terms such as invitation to treat, unilateral and bi-lateral offers, counter offers and revocation that have been used to distinguish the various activities which are akin to an offer or acceptance but do not quite fulfil the relevant criteria. It is to these various terms that we now turn. A major issue

---

† Linda Mulcahy, *Contract Law in Perspective*, 5th ed. (London and New York: Routledge-Cavendish, 2008) at 55–66. [Notes/references omitted.] Reproduced by permission of Taylor & Francis Books UK.

underpinning many of the judgments we will be considering is the courts' reluctance to bind the parties to a contract at an unexpectedly early stage.

Offers, Invitations to Treat and Advertisements

As was made clear in the last chapter, an offer has traditionally been defined by the courts as an expression of a willingness to enter into a binding contract[, which] was manifested by words or conduct. In determining whether something constitutes an offer, the courts place considerable emphasis on certainty and completeness. In other words, the offer must be clear enough for the person accepting it to understand the key matters on which the parties are in agreement. These commonly include issues such as price, quantity, the timing and manner of performance. There must also be an indication that the person making the offer intends to be bound as soon as the offer is accepted.

As a general proposition, offers must be distinguished from other statements made at a pre-contractual stage known as 'invitations to treat'. This is an old-fashioned expression which describes attempts by one party to encourage the other to enter into negotiations with them or make them an offer. Most people come across several examples of invitations to treat each day without being aware of this term of art used by lawyers to describe them. Each time you pass a shop which declares that it has the 'lowest prices in town' or an advertising board which declares that a certain airline offers 'lower prices than all its competitors' you are being tempted, or invited, to approach them with a view to buying a product or service from them. But few would expect the claims made to be substantiated. They are part of the 'puff' or sales technique used to encourage customers to enter a shop or access a website. But, as one moves on to look at other inducements and more specific wording, it becomes clear that there are fine lines to be drawn between what should be taken seriously and what should not.

A number of problems have arisen over whether the display of goods in a shop window or on the shelves in a shop with prices attached amounts to an offer. It could easily be argued that the display could amount to an offer if the price is clear and the goods can be clearly seen and inspected. However, as early as the mid-nineteenth century in the case of shop displays, the courts took a different view, which was endorsed in the supermarket case of *Pharmaceutical Society of Great Britain v Boots Cash Chemists (Southern) Ltd* (1953) in which the terms on which a

shop was prepared to sell displayed items appeared very clear. In this landmark case in which the focus was on the mechanics of buying and selling in one of the first self-service stores, a Boots customer selected goods from the shelves and presented them at the cash desk where she paid the price. Some of the goods were required by the Pharmacy and Poisons Act 1933 to be sold only under the supervision of a registered pharmacist and a pharmacist was present at the cash desk for this purpose. Boots were alleged to have infringed the Act because the contract had been formed before the woman presented the goods at the cash desk. The Pharmaceutical Society argued that the sale took place when the customer put the goods into her wire basket, so accepting the offer constituted by their display on the shelves. If this were so, certain medicines and poisons were being 'sold' without supervision contrary to the Act. However, the Court of Appeal disagreed and ruled that the sale took place at the cash desk. They argued that display of the goods did not mean that they were on offer. Instead, they argued that an offer to buy was made by the customer at the cash desk subject to supervision and possible refusal. In their view, the display of goods was merely an 'invitation to treat'.

This decision really rests on a policy choice which supported commercial innovation and convenience rather than on orthodox analysis of contract formation. The same issue usually arises in the context of criminal statutes where the *Boots* ruling has led to difficulties; (see, for instance, *Pilgram v Rice-Smith* 1977). In *Fisher v Bell* (1961) a case involving the alleged offence of 'offering for sale' a flick-knife contrary to the Restriction of Offensive Weapons Act 1959, the court was asked to analyse the law in relation to priced goods in a shop window. Although the statute was clearly intended to cover the situation, it was held that the display was merely an invitation and that no offence had been committed because an offer had not been made.

It has been argued that the law would be better served to regard displays or advertisements as offers subject to the condition, sometimes found in advertisements, that stocks remain available, as this position would better reflect the expectations of the public and business community. Parties may of course indicate that their statements do not constitute offers. Estate agents often do this by including a form of words on printed details of properties, such as the statement that: 'These particulars do not form, nor constitute any part of, an offer, or a contract, for sale'. However, the courts are not well disposed to this approach. Even where an advertisement in the 'For Sale' columns of a newspaper contains specific wording, a court would almost certainly, on the basis of the 'limited stocks' argument, regard the advertisement as an invitation to treat. This was 'business sense' according to Lord Parker in *Partridge v Crittenden* (1968), another statutory offence case in which the defendant inserted a notice in a periodical named *Cage and Aviary Birds* stating 'Bramblefinch cocks, bramblefinch hens, 25s each'. If the advertisement had been construed as an offer and demand had exceeded the defendant's supply, he could have faced any number of actions for breach of contract, as well as being guilty of an offence under the Protection of Birds Act 1954.

The issue of identifying whether a statement in an advertisement was *specific enough* to be construed as an offer which was intended to be binding was also addressed by the Court of Appeal in the famous case of *Carlill v Carbolic Smoke Ball Co* (1893). The case concerned a slightly different type of contract from the ones discussed so far, which have revolved around the bilateral negotiations in which two parties swap other of offers and acceptances. In contracts termed 'unilateral', the person making the offer waives the requirement that notification of acceptance be communicated to them. Instead, they can simply require that the contract can be accepted by any person who hears about the offer [and] doing something in a prescribed way. This means that acceptance can take place without the person making the offer even being aware that a contract has been formed. This may sound illogical but it is important to remember that the requirement of notification of acceptance is there to protect the person making the offer. It is for them to choose whether they wish to waive this right. An example of a contract formed in this way is a poster advertising that there will be a reward of £500 for anyone who returns a missing car to its owner at a specified address. The offer is accepted when a person performs the act of returning the car. A failure to provide the reward to someone who had done all that was requested of them would constitute a breach of contract.

In considering cases involving unilateral offers, the courts have been keen to stress that the offer must be sufficiently certain and much consideration has been given to the issue of what constitutes a valid offer. As a result, these cases are of significance to cases involving both unilateral and bilateral contracts. In the much cited *Carlill* case, the Carbolic Smoke Ball Company produced a medical preparation called the Carbolic Smoke Ball. They inserted an advertisement in the *Pall Mall Gazette* in which they offered to pay £100 to anyone who caught influ-

enza after having used the Smoke Ball in a specified manner and for a specified period of time. They also stated that they had deposited £1,000 with the Alliance Bank as a sign of their good faith in making these payments should anyone fall ill. On the strength of the advertisement, Mrs Carlill bought a smoke ball from a chemist, used it as prescribed, but nevertheless caught influenza. It was held that there was a contract between the parties and that the claimant could recover £100.

Much discussion in the case centred on the specificity of the wording of the advertisement. Bowen LJ stated that the advertisement in question 'was intended to be understood by the public as an offer to be acted upon' and Lindley LJ said: 'Read this how you will ... here is a distinct promise, expressed in language which IS perfectly unmistakeable, that £100 will be paid by the Carbolic Smoke Ball Co to any person who contracts influenza after having used the ball three times daily, and so on'. In finding that the company's advertisement was to be construed as an offer, the court rejected the claim that it was 'a mere puff' or a vague and non-actionable invitation to treat. The offer therefore constituted an express promise to pay £100 to any party who fulfilled its terms. When Mrs Carlill used the smoke ball as prescribed, she should be regarded as accepting the company's offer. The fact that communication of acceptance was not required was inferred from the wording of the offer and the nature of the transaction. The offer was seen as a serious one, showing an intention to create legal relations and therefore imposing a legally enforceable obligation on the company. Many commentators view the case as one which challenges the traditional conceptualisation of offer but it is clear that policy issues also underlie the court's ruling, decided as it was in an age of 'quack' medical preparations produced by rogues who did not deserve to succeed in the courts.

Counter Offers

The point has already been made that, in trying to determine whether agreement has been reached, the judiciary place considerable emphasis on certainty and completeness. They look for a firm offer and a firm acceptance of that particular offer. In other words, acceptance is expected to correspond *exactly* to the terms of the offer, like a mirror image. The search for agreement is often complicated by the fact that, in the run up to the 'moment of responsibility', negotiating parties will often become involved in drawn out discussions and exchanges in

---

BOX 6.1
JOSIE AND HANNIE'S NEGOTIATIONS

Email 1: Hi Josie, Just writing to find out whether you are still trying to get rid of those four tickets for the The Klaxons concert next week. Hannie

Email 2: Dear Hannie, Yes I am but need a quick deal. I have two left for the Sunday performance at 9pm. I would like to get about £30 for them. Josie

Email 3: Hi Josie, Great! Consider it done. Is that £30 per ticket or in total? I am happy to pay £30 per ticket for the chance to see them. The tickets sold out within half an hour of going on sale. Hannie

Email 4: Dear Hannie, £30 cash per ticket. I am off to a festival on tomorrow so you would need to drop by and pick them up before then. Please email back immediately. Josie

Email 5: Hi Josie, No problem. I will come whether round now. We don't have any cash on Josie and us — will you take a cheque? Hannie

Email 6: Dear Hannie, Sorry I don't want a cheque. I have an unauthorised overdraft and the Bank will take the money to pay it off. Any chance you could stop off at a cash point on the way round? I will be in until 9pm.

Email 7: Hi Josie. Will do. See you about 8pm. Hannie

---

which each makes requests for further information or clarification. This is made clear in Box 6.1 in which an email exchange between Hannie and Josie relating to the sale of some concert tickets is reproduced.

When trying to determine whether and when a contract between Hannie has taken place, it is important to make clear that, if a response to an offer differs from the offeror's terms, it is not taken as being an acceptance. Instead it is labelled a counter offer. These types of offer are viewed as rejections of the original offer and bring them to an end. This means that negotiators can not be selective about the parts of an offer they choose to accept. Moreover, once an effective acceptance has come about, the person who made the offer can no longer withdraw it because the acceptance binds them to what they have offered and turns the terms of the offer into the terms of a contract. It follows that

acceptance does not take place when the person to whom the offer is made rejects the offer, accepts it subject to certain qualifications or claims to be accepting an offer which is different from the one made.

These points are well illustrated in the case of *Hyde v Wrench* (1840) in which Wrench offered to sell his farm to Hyde for £1,000. Hyde said in reply that he would give £950 for it. Wrench turned down this proposal. Later Hyde wrote that he was prepared to pay £1,000 after all. This communication was ignored and Hyde sued to enforce an alleged sale at £1,000. It was held that no contract existed. Hyde had rejected Wrench's original offer by his counteroffer of £950 and he was unable to revive it by changing his mind and tendering a purported acceptance. The latter was considered to be nothing more than a new offer which Wrench was entitled to refuse.

The rigid application of this rule can cause difficulties where the intention of the offeree is clear but they introduce an additional element to the negotiations which has the effect of nullifying their 'acceptance'. In *Northland Airliners Ltd v Dennis Ferranti Meters Ltd* (1970), the sellers, a company in North Wales, negotiated with the buyers, a Canadian company, for the sale of an amphibian aircraft. The sellers sent the following telegram: 'Confirming sale to you Grummond Mallard aircraft .... Please remit £5,000'. The buyers replied: 'This is to confirm your cable and my purchase Grummond Mallard aircraft terms set out your cable ... £5,000 sterling forwarded your bank to be held in trust for your account pending delivery .... Please confirm delivery to be made thirty days within this date'. The sellers did not reply but sold the aircraft to a third party at a higher price. The Court of Appeal held that there was no contract between the claimant and defendant. The buyers' reply introduced two new terms, one as to payment and the other as to delivery, and the sellers were not bound to reply to this counter offer. Applying this analysis to the email exchange between Josie and Hannie, one reading would be that a sufficiently clear offer does not appear to emerge until email 4, email 5 constitutes a counter offer, email 6 a reiteration of the original offer and email 7 an acceptance on the exact terms offered.

However, case law suggests that an inquiry as to *whether* the offeror might modify his terms does not necessarily amount to a counter offer. In *Stevenson, Jacques & Co v McLean* (1880), it was held that Stevenson could still accept McLean's offer of a certain quantity of iron 'at 40s nett *cash* per ton', even though he had telegraphed to Mclean requesting details of possible credit terms. Bearing in mind that, as was known, Stevenson was buying for resale in an unsettled market, his words were 'nothing specific by way of [counter] offer or rejection, but a mere inquiry which should have been answered'. The case makes clear that the dividing line between a request for additional information and a counter offer is a fine one. Viewed in this way, email 5 in the exchange between Josie and Hannie could be construed as a mere request for additional information rather than a counter offer.

Communication of the Acceptance

The general 'rule' is that acceptance does not create a contract until it is communicated to the person making the offer. Mental acceptance or mere acquiescence, without more, is not sufficient. This is the case even where the person making the offer waives the need for communication by indicating that acceptance by silence will suffice see *Felthouse v Bindley* (1862). The requirement is that the person accepting the offer must say or do something which indicates to the person making the offer that they accept the terms. It follows that the courts have not been prepared to find acceptance of an offer where there have been faults in the method of communication, which mean that a message has not been received. Examples might include instances when a mobile phone line goes dead and acceptance is not communicated, an acceptance is not heard because of background music in a club or in cases where the fax machine of the person trying to accept the offer breaks down and fails to deliver a message. In each of these situations the application of the general rule would require the courts to find that no contract had been formed.

There are several explanations for this general rule. First, the requirement reflects the fact that the law expects both parties to be clear about the agreement they are entering into before it imposes legal obligations on them. The courts have also been concerned that the parties should know the exact moment that an offer has been accepted. If acceptance was able to occur without the person making the offer being told, then only one party would know that legal obligations had been created. Being clear about the exact moment when they are bound to each other also allows each of the parties to enter into further deals with others on the strength of the first. So, for instance, in the example of Josie and Hannie given above, Josie might agree to buy some CDs from a friend on the basis that Hannie will be honouring her contract for the sale of the concert

tickets later that day. Finally, on an evidential note, it could be extremely difficult to prove acceptance if the person accepting the contract was under no obligation to communicate it.

An established exception to the general rule that the offeror must receive notification of an acceptance developed in the guise of the 'postal rule' and has troubled generations of law students. The exception emerged in an era in which the post was a very popular and relatively fast form of communication, but the principal established continues to have some relevance today. The postal rules allows that, where the person accepting the offer sends their acceptance by post, the offer is regarded as accepted as soon as the letter of acceptance is put in a postbox rather than when it is received. The authority for this proposition comes from the judgment in *Adams v Lindsell* (1818). The rule shifts the burden of risk from the person accepting the offer to the person who made the offer, because the latter is bound by a contract before they are aware of the fact of its existence. In considering the rule, it is important to stress that it can easily be avoided. It is always open to the person making the offer to specify how an offer should be accepted, as Josie does in email 4 in the Box 6.1. In coming to their judgment, the court in *Adams* appears to have decided that a person making an offer who is prepared to accept the risks inherent in using the postal system should also bear the risk of an acceptance getting lost or there being a delay. It would seem that the person making an offer would be well advised to *exclude* the postal rule by the terms of their offer and insist that they will only be bound on actual receipt of a posted acceptance. In affirming the rule in *Adams*, Bramwell LJ in the Court of Appeal in *Household Fire Insurance Co v Grant* (1879), advised that the prudent offeror should stipulate that: 'Your answer by post is only to bind if it reaches me'.

More recently, in *Holwell Securities Ltd v Hughes* (1974), an offer to sell a house was made in the form of an option stated 'to be exercisable by *notice* in writing to the Intending Vendor at any time within six months hereof ...'. Such a notice, properly addressed, was posted within the time limit allowed but was never delivered. It was held that there was no contract as the terms of the option, on their true construction, required acceptance to be actually communicated. In their judgments, Lord Justices Russell and Lawton placed emphasis on the definition of 'notice' as a means of making something known, and if not known, then it follows that it can not constitute notice. The court went so far as to suppose that there *was no single or universal rule* determining the effect of a posted acceptance, and that the postal rule 'probably does not operate if its application would produce manifest inconvenience and absurdity'. It would seem then that the question is one of interpretation on a particular set of facts, practical considerations and convenience rather than deductions from a general rule.

Electronic Communication

It is clear from the discussion above that for many years the courts were troubled with relatively simple communication problems involving instantaneous oral negotiations or more time-consuming postal communications. As the number of large-scale corporations participating in global markets has increased and the means of communication become ever more speedy, new questions about the point at which a contract has formed have arisen. Since the founding principles relating to receipt of acceptance were discussed in the nineteenth century, new methods of communicating, such as telex, fax, email and other web-based exchanges, have come into being. Unfortunately, the case law in this area lags seriously behind technological developments. Nonetheless, we are able to gain insight into the principles that govern such exchanges in a set of cases decided in the later part of the last century.

In *Entores Ltd v Miles Far East Corporation* (1955), the Court of Appeal was asked to consider the impact of new technologies on formation of contracts. Rather than following the postal rule, they argued that, where such communications were instantaneous acceptance took place when it was received rather than where it was sent. The exception highlighted by Lord Denning was where the person making the offer did not receive the message through no fault of their own. The problems of delayed receipt when using electronic transactions was considered by the Court of Appeal in *The Brimnes* (1975). It was held that communication by telex was effective when it appeared on the recipient's machine, even though the message was not read until the next working day. This was because it had been received during office hours and it was reasonable for the person sending the acceptance to assume that someone would look at it during that time.

However, in the case of *Brinkibon Ltd v Stahag Stahl* (1983), the House of Lords gave a qualified endorsement of *Entores*, warning that its 'rule' could not be applied universally in view of the many variants in the use of telex. The court argued that, although telex was an instantaneous form of communication, receipt was not always instantaneous. For example, a message could be sent out of office hours with the intention that it would be read at a later time or there could be some undiscovered fault with a machine. Rather than impose a fixed rule, the court opined that the position should be resolved by reference to the parties' intentions, sound business practice and by a judgment as to where the risk should lie. It would seem from this that the communication should take effect at the time when the acceptor could reasonably have expected it to be read. By analogy electronic mail, sent to an electronic 'postbox' that will only be checked once or twice a day, could be said to have been 'communicated' once the normal time for checking has passed. A similar approach might need to be used in relation to messages left on a telephone answering system in that they should only be regarded as having been communicated once a reasonable time for the offeror to have heard it the message has elapsed.

If this line is taken, it is clearly to the advantage of the person making the acceptance because it allows an acceptance to be treated as effective when the person who made the offer remains unaware of it because of their failure to check incoming messages within a reasonable lime. These problems sit rather uncomfortably with traditional approaches to the identification of agreement. Rather, they provide an example of Collins, 2003 claim that what the courts are often concerned with, and should be concerned with, is not the mechanics of offer and acceptance but a consideration of the point at which it is reasonable for the parties to assume a contract has come into being.

Communicating by email

There is some debate as to whether the established rules governing instantaneous and postal communications are adequate for modern-day use. In particular, there has been some disagreement between scholars as to whether existing categories cover communications by email. As these now outnumber paper communications and are the preferred way for many in business to communicate with clients, the point is worth serious consideration. One of the problems posed by emails is whether receipt occurs when the email is downloaded onto a server, when it appears on the recipient's computer or when the email is actually read by the recipient. Another new issue which arises in this context is that an email address may consist of a name or number followed by the name of the service provider, but not indicate the physical location of the sender or the recipient. This leaves open the associated difficulty of *where* the acceptance becomes binding.

Some have argued that the postal rule should apply to acceptances made by email, as technically they are not transmitted 'instantaneously' and differ from other forms of communication discussed above in that the information is broken down and sent in 'packets' through different routes. On the other hand, emails often go astray. This means that the sender cannot be sure that their message has been transmitted successfully *and* this renders it unreasonable for them to rely on the communication having been received. Even if the sender asks for a delivery receipt, that receipt simply confirms that the message has been delivered to a mailbox, but not to the offeror. But it has been argued that an email with a delivery receipt is more like recorded delivery post than an instantaneous communication. As a result it could be argued that it should properly be subject to the postal rule.

Others have suggested that the usual receipt rule should apply because the sender is ultimately in a position to know if the email has or has not been sent. It follows from the reasoning in *The Brimnes* that, viewed in this way, the acceptance should become binding when it reaches the offeror's business premises or the place of their internet service provider during normal office hours. Article 11 of the E-Commerce Directive provides some guidance in respect of non-business-to-business contracting by requiring that electronic orders and acknowledgements will be taken to be received when the addressee can access them. This would seem to suggest that the downloading of the message from the server would constitute receipt. However, the directive does not clearly explain the legal position of electronic offer and acceptance, or even define when a contract is concluded. The result is that the law remains uncertain.

Click-wrap contracts

More recently, still new dilemmas about the formation of contract have been posed by the expansion of e-commerce. People have been making contracts through the agency of machines for some time. Every time you put your car through an automatic car wash, you make a contract through the medium of a machine. But using machines takes on new characteristics where the web is concerned. Since the web now hosts the fastest growing marketplace in the world, it is a pressing issue for contract lawyers to ensure that doctrine develops to support such exchanges. For a start, the web allows the making of more specific and customised contracts than is possible with a fizzy drinks machine. It allows you to place an order for a particular book from a host of different agents, with the option of gift wrapping and different methods of delivery. The web also allows people to make contracts across jurisdictions and continents with more ease than was previously possible.

To date, most commentators have attempted to apply traditional reasoning to web-based contracts by looking for invitations to treat offers and acceptances in the same way as lawyers have done for decades. Analogies with exchanges in a real marketplace are often facilitated by the design of websites. Many allow you to 'browse' through their products in the same way you might in a shop, provide you with a 'virtual shopping basket' and, once browsing is complete, instruct you to proceed to a 'virtual checkout'. These 'click-wrap' contracts are negotiated by the seller displaying their terms and conditions, and the buyer clicking on buttons to evidence their satisfaction with the choices made. Goods displayed on the virtual shelves of a website can by analogy be treated as an invitation to treat in the same way as the goods on the shelves in the *Boots* case. Once the purchase indicates what they are interested in buying, the supplier's programme checks the availability of the item. If it is in stock, the purchasers make offers by entering their credit card details and clicking on a button to confirm their choices.

However, while we tend to think of the web as akin to an instantaneous form of communication, it is not akin to the average transaction in a high-street store. This new technology actually gives consumers more time to ponder the terms and conditions prescribed by the seller in the comfort of their own home or office. It also allows closer inspection of detailed terms and conditions than is usually feasible. Many websites do not allow a buyer to proceed to the stage where they can order a product or service unless the purchaser indicates that they have pulled up, looked at and understood the company's terms of business. Some also allow the buyer to proceed along the 'negotiation' process in a number of clear-cut stages in which they are given several opportunities to reconsider their position and choices. Concern that these characteristics render the transaction somewhat different from those cases discussed so far is reflected in the fact that there are a growing number of regulations that focus specifically on electronic contracts.

It has been argued that these transactions are more akin to instantaneous telephone Conversations, as it will be immediately obvious to one of the parties if the other becomes disconnected. Accordingly, the sender of a message in a click-wrap contract is in a position to know whether the message has been transmitted successfully almost as soon as it has been sent. This would seem to make the receipt rule more relevant than the postal rule. The Consumer Protection (Distance Selling) Regulations 2000 provide some protection for the consumer by requiring that certain information be provided before the contract is concluded. This includes the identity of the supplier, the price, arrangements for the delivery and supply of goods or services and information on cancellation rights. This information must be provided to the consumer in another durable medium, which is 'available and accessible' prior to delivery.

Concluding Remarks

In this chapter we have looked at some of the key concepts underpinning the [courts'] treatment of offer and acceptance. It can be seen from the various cases surveyed that it is far from an easy task to determine when and where a contract has been formed. Recent cases on new forms of communication create new challenges to doctrines which were developed with very different market places in mind. In the chapter that follows, we will turn to look at another set of problems which question the concepts underpinning doctrine and their relevance to the business community.

(d) *Gendis Inc. v. Richardson Oil & Gas Ltd.*†

Manitoba Court of Appeal

[MONNIN J.A.:]

[1] The issue in this appeal is whether or not the trial judge was in error in finding that the parties had negotiated a valid contract for the sale of shares in a privately held company.

[2] A detailed account of the facts of this case can be found in the reasons of the trial judge reported at [1999] M.J. No. 504. I only provide in these reasons a summary of what I consider to be relevant to deal with the issues raised in this appeal.

[3] Since January 1, 1989, the appellant (Richardson) and the respondent (Gendis) had each held 50 per cent of the shares in Tundra Oil and Gas Ltd. (Tundra), a privately held company.

[4] On January 28, 1998, Albert Cohen, the chair of Gendis's board of directors, approached George Richardson, the managing director of James Richardson & Sons, Limited, the parent company of Richardson, for the purpose of selling the Gendis shares in Tundra to Richardson. Albert Cohen and George Richardson were not only two sophisticated businessmen who headed big business enterprises based in Winnipeg but who, in the words of George Richardson, had a "very cordial, very — business and social relationship, and nothing but the best."

[5] Albert Cohen and George Richardson met twice during the months of January and February 1998 and exchanged telephone calls in an attempt to reach an agreement. Following a meeting on February 12, 1998 Albert Cohen decided that the CEO of Gendis, Allan MacKenzie, should continue the negotiations on behalf of Gendis.

[6] Allan MacKenzie and George Richardson met on February 12, 1998 and again on February 26, 1998. During the course of the February 12 meeting, George Richardson suggested to Allan MacKenzie that the purchase and sale of the shares could be structured in a way that Gendis's proceeds of sale could be sheltered from tax consequences (the concept is known as safe income). This would permit Gendis to derive a greater net benefit from the transaction and would also permit Richardson to pay a reduced amount for the shares in question. Allan MacKenzie declined this arrangement, indicating to George Richardson that Gendis did not need to shelter income as it already carried sufficient tax losses on its books.

[7] Time also became of the essence as George Richardson wanted the deal concluded prior to the next meeting of the board of directors of Tundra scheduled for February 26, 1998. Prior to that meet-

† 2000 MBCA 33, 148 Man.R. (2d) 19.

ing, Allan MacKenzie and George Richardson met again. The two men agreed that Richardson would purchase the shares of Gendis for $39 million, plus two incentive payments of up to $1 million each if oil prices averaged $27 in the last six months of 1999 and $28 in the last six months of 2000. Upon reaching this agreement George Richardson told Allan MacKenzie that "we have a deal" and the two men then shook hands. Both businessmen further agreed that Gendis would provide Richardson with a written document to confirm and detail the transaction that they had agreed upon on that day.

[8] On the Monday following this meeting Allan MacKenzie sent to Richardson a document that, in his words, purported to structure the agreement reached. The document included three clauses which Richardson maintains changed the agreement that had been reached and which justified Richardson's refusal to complete the deal. The clauses in question were:

3. The Purchaser and the Vendor agree that they shall cause Tundra to pay a cash dividend on Closing on its common shares in such amount that the portion of the dividend to which the Vendor is entitled in respect of the fifty (50%) percent of the common shares which the Vendor owns (hereinafter the "Vendor Owned Shares") is equal to the safe income on hand (hereinafter the "Safe Income") attributable to the Vendor Owned Shares immediately before the payment of the dividend, as that concept is understood for the purposes of subsection 55(2) of the Income Tax Act (Canada).

Further, the Purchaser agrees to make available to the Vendor the financial statements and income tax returns of Tundra for all years up and including the taxation year in which the Closing takes place in order that the Vendor has available to it all information necessary to make a designation under paragraph 55(5)(f) of the Income Tax Act (Canada) if the Vendor, in its sole discretion, so decides to do in its income tax return.

6. In the event that the price of West Texas Intermediate Oil ("WTI") averages no less than $Cdn. 27.00 per barrel between July 1, 1999 and December 31, 1999, the Purchaser shall pay ONE MILLION DOLLARS ($1,000,000.00) to the Vendor on or before January 4, 2000 AND/OR in the event that the price of WTI averages no less than $Cdn. 28.00 per barrel between July 1, 2000 and December 31, 2000, the Purchaser shall pay

ONE MILLION DOLLARS ($1,000,000.00) to the Vendor on or before January 5, 2001.

9. This Agreement shall be open for acceptance by the Purchaser until 5:00 P.M., March 6, 1998 acceptance to be by proper execution hereof by the Purchaser and delivering same to the Vendor on or before said time and date, failing which this Agreement may be declared null and void at the sole option of the Vendor, at any time thereafter.

[9] Richardson replied by letter dated March 3, 1998 signed by George Richardson. The letter reads in part:

Over the last while we have been engaged in ongoing discussions respecting a possible purchase of Gendis Inc.'s interest in Tundra. Given our long association and the possibility of completing a fast and clean transaction, we were prepared to entertain the possibility of paying a premium over what we believe a third party would pay for your interest in Tundra. Notwithstanding our entertaining a premium price, our negotiations have been somewhat protracted due to a continually moving target. The Offer once again moved the target. Given our entertaining the possibility of paying a premium price, it was our understanding that the benefit of "safe income" should reduce the premium (i.e., the price). We were advised that Gendis would not realize any benefit from safe income and, as a result, that no adjustment to the price was possible for this matter. Accordingly, safe income was taken off the table yet the Offer provides for a safe income strip. Further, we have discussed the price escalation in relation to Tundra's realized price. The Offer uses West Texas Intermediate Oil as the benchmark which currently is in excess of $2 greater than Tundra's realized prices and which bears no direct relationship to Tundra's future operating performance.

Given the above, we have concluded that the purchase price for your interest in Tundra should be determined in accordance with the procedures set out in the Memorandum of Unanimous Shareholders Agreement made as of the 1st day of November, 1989 between ROGL (formerly Pioneer Energy Resources Limited), Gendis Inc. and Tundra (the "Agreement").

This will advise that ROGL does not accept the above-referenced offer. In addition, if any of our prior discussions could or might be construed as an offer by us to you, same is hereby revoked. ...

In the event that you receive an offer for your shares of Tundra that you desire to accept, we will evaluate whether to exercise our right of first refusal provided for by Section 4.1 of the Agreement. Alternatively, if you desire to make an offer in accordance with Section 5.1 of the Agreement, we would be happy to review same and provide you with our response within the thirty day period provided for in the Agreement.

[10] On March 4, 1998 Gendis forwarded another document to Richardson which Albert Cohen described in his covering letter as "a revised and simplified offer to sell." In addition he wrote:

> note that our offer makes no mention of the "safe income" to assist our tax position. However, the opportunity is there and should you wish to accommodate it we are prepared to share with you our tax saving on a 50/50 basis.

[11] This offer did not contain a safe-income clause nor did it contain any reference to the incentive payments. This offer was again refused. Shortly thereafter this lawsuit was initiated by Gendis seeking a declaration that the parties had entered into a valid agreement and also seeking damages for the breach.

[12] Following a trial the trial judge arrived at the following findings on the import of the safe-income clause at paras. 18–23:

> Mr. Richardson is correct in recalling that Mr. MacKenzie did not want to discuss the question of tax savings as suggested by Mr. Richardson because he realized that Mr. Richardson wanted the plaintiff to accept a lower price for the shares than what Mr. Cohen considered a fair value. Mr. MacKenzie's explanation for his reaction to Mr. Richardson's suggestion was that it would result in Richardson paying part of the purchase price with money that the plaintiff was entitled to in its own right. The tax savings to the plaintiff from a "safe-income strip" was available to the plaintiff on the sale of its shares to the defendant without any cost to the defendant. The court heard evidence from three tax experts, who all agreed that the safe-income clause in paragraphs 3 and 4 of the written agreement would not cost the purchaser a nickel. They all agreed that it was a neutral clause insofar as this purchase and sale was concerned.
>
> In my opinion, what happened in this case was that Mr. Richardson, on his own volition, kept increasing the cash component of the price from $36 million to $39 million. He indicated on numerous occasions in his evidence that that was because he wanted to be generous to his friend Mr. Cohen, with whom he had had a good relationship for many years. It was Mr. Richardson who "moved the goal posts" during the negotiations, not because Mr. MacKenzie objected to Mr. Richardson's using the plaintiff's safe-income to purchase the shares at a lower price. Mr. Richardson voluntarily increased the cash component of the price, in my opinion, not only to be generous and kind to Mr. Cohen, but also for the purpose of obtaining total control of Tundra. The evidence clearly indicates that the defendant was planning a tax benefit before closing the purchase of the shares, because for this purpose it required the co-operation of the plaintiff. This co-operation was granted by Mr. Cohen in delaying the closing date.
>
> Since the safe-income paragraphs in the written agreement would not cost the defendant a nickel, it is difficult to understand the reaction of Mr. Richardson when, without any cost or detriment to the defendant/purchaser, he based his rejection of the agreement on something that would be of benefit to his old friend.
>
> ...
>
> Although the safe-income clause in paragraphs 3 and 4 of the written agreement were not part of the agreement made orally between the plaintiff and the defendant as agreed to between Mr. Cohen, Mr. MacKenzie and Mr. Richardson, that does not provide a legal basis for refusing to close the agreement. However, these safe-income provisions were not, and are not, a term of the oral agreement entered into by Mr. Richardson on behalf of the defendant.

[13] On the issue of the validity of the agreement itself the trial judge reached the following conclusions at paras. 27–29:

> The authorities generally show circumstances where essential terms had not been agreed upon or where the oral agreement was on condition that a formal document would be prepared and signed. I conclude that all of the cases cited can be distinguished on the facts. I am satisfied, based on Mr. Richardson's evidence, that the written document to be prepared by the plaintiff was not a prerequisite to the contract being consummated. The written document was only for the purpose of identifying the terms of the agreement made between the parties on February 26 and 27, 1998.
>
> The general principle of law with regard to finding whether the parties have entered into a binding contract is discussed by Lord Maugham in the case of *G. Scammell & Nephew Ltd. v. Ouston et al.*, [1941] A.C. 251 at p. 255:
>
>> In order to constitute a valid contract the parties must so express themselves that their meaning can be determined with a reasonable degree of certainty. It is plain that unless this can be done it would be impossible to hold that the contracting parties had the same intention; in other words the consensus ad idem would be a matter of mere conjecture. This general rule, however

applies somewhat differently in different cases. In commercial documents connected with dealings in a trade with which the parties are perfectly familiar the court is very willing, if satisfied that the parties thought that they made a binding contract, to imply terms and in particular terms as to the method of carrying out the contract. ...

In my opinion, the circumstances of this case are such that the above principle is applicable to the contract entered into by the parties in this trial.

I find that the contract (agreement) entered into by Mr. Richardson for the plaintiff's shares in Tundra identifies the parties and the price of $39 million in cash plus the incentive clause as set forth in the written agreement. The closing date requested by Mr. Richardson was two to three weeks after February 27, 1998, namely, any date between March 20 and March 31, 1998. The court will supply the closing date as March 31, 1998.

[14] On this appeal Richardson argues that the trial judge erred in finding that the agreement reached by George Richardson with Allan MacKenzie on February 26, 1998 was a valid and binding final agreement. Richardson argues that the understanding arrived at on February 26, 1998 could not be binding as it was to be followed up by a written agreement, which written agreement, as the facts demonstrate, was never executed. Furthermore, Richardson argues that Gendis, by including clauses 3, 6 and 9 in the agreement, was still in the process of negotiating the terms of the contract and therefore the parties never reached an agreement.

[15] Richardson attaches particular importance to clause 3 in the initial written agreement to support its position. It argues that by including the safe-income clause Gendis was attempting to negotiate or obtain a term more favourable than what was originally agreed upon.

[16] To this argument Gendis responds that the writing submitted to Richardson was a document intended to structure the agreement reached by Allan MacKenzie and George Richardson, and that all of the essential terms of that agreement had been negotiated and finalized on February 26, 1998. Gendis further argues that since this also happens to be the finding of the trial judge, Richardson's appeal should be dismissed.

[17] In his argument counsel on behalf of Richardson relied primarily on three decisions to support the position being advanced. All of those cases deal with the essential elements required in a contract and the effect of writings subsequent to negotiations.

[18] *Bawitko Investments Ltd. v. Kernels Popcorn Ltd.* (1991), 79 D.L.R. (4th) 97, is a decision of the Ontario Court of Appeal. Robins J.A. wrote at pp. 103–4:

As a matter of normal business practice, parties planning to make a formal written document the expression of their agreement, necessarily discuss and negotiate the proposed terms of the agreement before they enter into it. They frequently agree upon all of the terms to be incorporated into the intended written document before it is prepared. Their agreement may be expressed orally or by way of memorandum, by exchange of correspondence, or other informal writings. The parties may "contract to make a contract", that is to say, they may bind themselves to execute at a future date a formal written agreement containing specific terms and conditions. When they agree on all of the essential provisions to be incorporated in a formal document with the intention that their agreement shall thereupon become binding, they will have fulfilled all the requisites for the formation of a contract. The fact that a formal written document to the same effect is to be thereafter prepared and signed does not alter the binding validity of the original contract.

However, when the original contract is incomplete because essential provisions intended to govern the contractual relationship have not been settled or agreed upon; or the contract is too general or uncertain to be valid in itself and is dependent on the making of a formal contract; or the understanding or intention of the parties, even if there is no uncertainty as to the terms of their agreement, is that their legal obligations are to be deferred until a formal contract has been approved and executed, the original or preliminary agreement cannot constitute an enforceable contract. In other words, in such circumstances the "contract to make a contract" is not a contract at all. The execution of the contemplated formal document is not intended only as a solemn record or memorial of an already complete and binding contract but is essential to the formation of the contract itself ...

[19] Richardson also relies on a passage from a decision of this Court in support of its argument that the contract in the case at bar was not finalized until it was confirmed in writing. In *Megill-Stephenson Co. Ltd. v. Woo et al.* (1989), 58 Man.R. (2d) 302, Huband J.A. wrote at para. 19 in dealing with the Statute of Frauds:

The Statute of Frauds came into being to prevent disputes where an alleged contract had not been reduced into writing. The requirement to put the agreement into written form in turn requires that the parties be reasonably certain as to the terms of the contract. For policy reasons the British Parliament concluded that it should not be left to the courts to weigh conflicting claims based on oral evidence, and then attempting to restructure a contract on a foundation of conflicting testimony. While the Statute of Frauds has been repealed in this jurisdiction, the idea lying behind it remains valid. The courts should be reluctant to impose binding contracts on parties based upon conversations, particularly where the usual practice has been to reduce such contracts into writing.

[20] And finally, and with more emphasis, Richardson referred the Court to the decision of the Supreme Court of Canada in *Harvey v. Perry*, [1953] 1 S.C.R. 233. In another decision dealing with the Statute of Frauds, Estey J. writes at pp. 241–42:

> In cases of this type the respondent (pl.) must establish a contract concluded between the parties and a note or memorandum sufficient to satisfy the requirements of the Statute of Frauds. *Hussey v. Horne-Payne* [(1879), 4 App. Cas. 311 at 316]. The parties here negotiated, in part, at Saginaw, but mainly through correspondence. It is, therefore, essential to examine the evidence and the entire correspondence, both to ascertain whether the parties had agreed and, if so, whether there is a sufficient memorandum to meet the Statute of Frauds.
>
> The letter of September 2, the proposed agreement enclosed therewith and respondent's solicitors' letter of September 9, might support a conclusion that the parties had agreed, but, when read, as they must be, with respondent's solicitors' letter of September 13 and the proposed agreement enclosed therewith, it is clear that the respondent had not agreed. The minds of the parties had not met. There was no consensus ad idem because the respondent was still negotiating for better terms.
>
> The position of the respondent is analogous to that of the plaintiff in *Bristol, Cardiff and Swansea Aerated Bread Co. v. Maggs* [(1890), 44 Ch. Div. 616]. There, after an agreement, as evidenced by two letters, had been arrived at, the vendor's (defendant's) solicitors submitted an agreement for approval and the purchaser's (plaintiff's) solicitors inserted a new clause which the vendor refused to agree to. Thereafter the purchaser sought to accept the original offer and to enforce the contract. Kay J. stated at p. 624:
>
> > Their position, therefore, is, that they were not satisfied with the terms of

the two letters, but themselves reopened the matter by negotiating for another most important advantage; and having thus treated the two letters as part of an incomplete bargain, it would be most inequitable to allow them to say, "Although we thus treated the matter as incomplete and a negotiation only, yet the Defendant had no right to do so, but was bound by a completed contract."

> In my opinion, the decision of *Hussey v. Horne-Payne* (*supra*) completely covers this case. I understand it to mean, that if two letters standing alone would be evidence of a sufficient contract, yet a negotiation for an important term of the purchase and sale carried on afterwards is enough to shew that the contract was not complete; and, so far as my own judgment is concerned, I entirely agree in the justice and equity of such a rule.

And at p. 243:

> This case is distinguishable upon its facts from that of *Perry v. Suffields, Limited* [[1916] 2 Ch. 187]. There the vendor was granted specific performance of a contract contained in two letters of February 23 and March 3, 1915. The defendant's solicitors sent a draft agreement in a letter in which they stated, in part: "We do not know whether it incorporates quite all the terms agreed, as Mr. Perry has not seen it and we have not had very full instructions from him." The draft contract contained clauses at variance with that agreed upon and when it was contended that this amounted to a reopening of the arrangement between the parties Lord Cozens-Hardy dismissed that contention and stated at p. 193:
>
> > The solicitor frankly said he was not sure that he was fully instructed, and his attempt to alter the contract contained in those letters by making a new contract containing different terms as to price, as to fixing a date for completion, and as to the postponement of completion until after the completion of another contract for the purchase of a portion of the property by the Rugby Urban District Council seems to me to be entirely outside the question.
>
> The letter of September 2 and the agreement enclosed therewith, signed by the respondent, were admittedly prepared upon his instructions. The position is, therefore, quite different from that in *Perry v. Suffields, Limited*, in that here the respondent is not submitting a proposed contract, with a request that errors and omissions be corrected, but rather does so for

the purpose of obtaining terms more satisfactory from his point of view than those already agreed upon.

[21] I do not take issue with the principles established in these decisions which Richardson relies upon. What, however, must not be forgotten is that all of these principles find their roots in factual situations. The case before us is no different. There are contract cases that make their way before the courts in which great and sometimes innovative principles of law are established. This is not such a case. The determination of this case is to be found on the facts, and absent an overriding and palpable error by a trial judge, an appellate court should not interfere with fact findings of a trial judge. See *Geffen v. Goodman Estate*, [1991] 2 S.C.R. 353; *Caners v. Eli Lilly Canada Inc.* (1996), 110 Man.R. (2d) 95 (C.A.).

[22] In *G. Scammell & Nephew Ltd. v. Ouston et al.*, [1941] A.C. 251 (H.L.) at 268–69, Lord Wright puts into succinct language the circumstances in which a court should interfere and find that a contract between two parties did not exist:

> There are in my opinion two grounds on which the court ought to hold that there was never a contract. The first is that the language used was so obscure and so incapable of any definite or precise meaning that the court is unable to attribute to the parties any particular contractual intention. The object of the court is to do justice between the parties, and the court will do its best, if satisfied that there was an ascertainable and determinate intention to contract, to give effect to that intention, looking at substance and not mere form. It will not be deterred by mere difficulties of interpretation. Difficulty is not synonymous with ambiguity so long as any definite meaning can be extracted. But the test of intention is to be found in the words used. If these words, considered however broadly and untechnically and with due regard to all the just implications, fail to evince any definite meaning on which the court can safely act, the court has no choice but to say that there is no contract. Such a position is not often found. ...
>
> But I think the other reason, which is that the parties never in intention nor even in appearance reached an agreement, is a still sounder reason against enforcing the claim. In truth, in my opinion, their agreement was inchoate and never got beyond negotiations.

[23] Richardson's argument on the issue of the safe income was that Gendis was attempting to change the agreement to now gain an advantage that previously was theirs. Richardson, however, fails to con-

vince me that such is the case as the price had been agreed upon and safe income payable to Gendis could in no way increase the amount that Richardson had already agreed to pay. The advantage that Richardson had with regards to the issue of safe income existed during the course of negotiations, and Richardson attempted to use that advantage to secure a deal at a lower cost. By increasing its offer Richardson cannot now claim that they are paying too much or that it has lost an advantage in negotiation. Richardson, on its own free will, gave away the advantage that it now claims it has been deprived of.

[24] Richardson's argument on the safe income issue is even more difficult to accept when it is contrasted with the evidence given by George Richardson himself as to why the issue of safe income was even broached with Gendis. On October 22, 1999 Mr. Richardson testified (vol. 5, p. 75 of transcript):

> Q In fact, prior to February 26th Richardson Oil & Gas Limited had, independent of Gendis, researched the idea of structuring the sale so as to deliver safe income to Gendis, hadn't you?
> A Correct.
> Q And the purpose of putting such a structure together was simply to be of assistance to Gendis, wasn't it?
> A Correct.
> Q You were really just looking at that structure because you wanted to make sure that Gendis got the highest return possible; isn't that, sir (sic)?
> A I'd have to agree with that, yes. We were trying to be helpful.

[25] There is further evidence of the contradiction between the Richardson position on trial and at appeal on this issue and the facts as found in the read-ins from the discovery of George Richardson. Starting at Q 230 we find:

> Q You were looking at means of structuring the sale that might be tax friendly?
> A For Gendis.
> Q Yes.
> A (Witness nodding.)
> Q Had Gendis asked you to do that, or is this something that you were doing at your own
> —
> A Something we were doing to be of assistance to them.
> Q Do you disagree with what I am saying, that is to say that one of the reasons you were doing this was to try and identify a method of completing the sale that would perhaps give you some basis for convincing Gendis to lower their price on the Tundra shares?

A No, I won't agree with that. We were going to offer them an opportunity that we thought they would be familiar with, but an opportunity to enhance their bottom line, given our offer.

[26] The argument advanced by Richardson on the issue of safe income simply does not correspond with the facts or the evidence in this case. This argument is no more convincing to me than it was to the trial judge. In the words of Lord Wright in Scammell, there existed an ascertainable and determinative intention to contract between Richardson and Gendis and that intention was clear, precise and fixed. The trial judge made no error in finding that a valid and binding contract existed. I would, therefore, dismiss this ground of appeal.

[27] Richardson also raised the issue of the basis on which the incentive payment was to be paid. The trial judge made a clear finding of fact on this issue and there is no reason to interfere with it. In any event, that issue is conceded by Richardson in para. 42 of its appeal factum:

> In his judgment, Barkman J., after his review of the evidence, concluded that Mr. George Richardson and Mr. MacKenzie had agreed that the prices to be used in determining whether the deferred compensation would be payable was WTI expressed in Canadian dollars rather than Tundra's Realized Price. Recognizing the heavy onus in overturning a finding of fact and the relative unimportance of the finding to the ultimate disposition of this case, this factum does not intend to challenge that finding.

[28] The next issue raised by Richardson, and which can be considered as an extension of the ongoing negotiations argument, deals with the import of clause 9. The best reason to reject the bona fides of this argument is the evidence of George Richardson himself. In vol. 5 at p. 73 of the transcript commencing at line 19 we read:

> Q My point, Mr. Richardson, I supposed, is simply this. Once again, the wording in paragraph 9 was of no concern to you. If you had an agreement and the written agreement that was sent over to you reflected the deal that you had made, clause 9 wouldn't have stood in the way of you signing it, would it?
> A That's correct.

> Q I mean, clearly your justification for failing to close rests on two things and two things only, that is to say, the inclusion of that safe income clause that you object to, right?
> A Correct.
> Q And the use of WTI as a benchmark, right?
> A Correct.

[29] There is no more merit to this argument than there was to the safe income argument.

[30] The last issue raised by Richardson was that the trial judge erred in his award of damages, and specifically that he failed to find that Gendis should have mitigated its damages. The trial judge made the following finding on this issue at para. 30:

> The defendant argued that the legal principle of mitigation of damages should be applied in this case. The law is clear that, if the plaintiff, in the circumstances of the case, could have reduced the damages suffered, then its claim for damages must be reduced accordingly. I am satisfied that the circumstances of this case did not facilitate the reduction of the plaintiff's damages because of the fact that, even if the plaintiff had been able to sell its shares to a third party, the price obtainable would likely not have been more than $29 million (Exhibit 8), the valuation established by the defendant. Therefore, under the shareholders' agreement (Exhibit 1), the defendant would have paid the plaintiff $29 million, which, under the circumstances here, would have increased the damages suffered by the plaintiff.

[31] I agree with this finding. Considering the fact that what was attempted to be sold was an interest in a two-partner company with specific provisions to sell to an outside interest, the position being advanced by Richardson is not realistic. Apart from arguing that Gendis should have mitigated, Richardson led no evidence to demonstrate that the sale of the Gendis shares to a third party was a viable alternative. Logic and common business sense support the inference that a third party purchaser would not even bother with the simple effort of conducting a due diligence. As pointed out by Gendis, shares which are the subject of litigation and which net only a stalemate interest are not in high demand, particularly when the other litigating partner has a right of first refusal.

[32] I would, therefore, dismiss the appeal on all grounds, with costs to Gendis.

(e) *Electricity Corporation of New Zealand Limited v. Fletcher Challenge Energy Limited*†

Court of Appeal of New Zealand

[BLANCHARD J. for the Majority):]

[1] Electricity Corporation of New Zealand Ltd (ECNZ) appeals against a declaratory order of the High Court at Wellington that a document called a Heads of Agreement (HoA) signed on behalf of Fletcher Challenge Energy Ltd (FCE) and ECNZ on 28 February 1997 is a valid and binding contract for the sale and purchase of gas. It also appeals a finding that it is in breach of an obligation in the HoA to use all reasonable endeavours to agree on a full sale and purchase agreement within three months of the date on which the HoA was executed.

· · · ·

[3] In 1997 the offshore Maui field, majority owned by FCE, was by a considerable distance the largest oil and gas field in New Zealand. Production from that field was expected to continue until 2009. A smaller but significant offshore field known as Kupe had not yet been developed. However, if development were to proceed in the near future, Kupe was expected to be a producing field until 2011. After 2011 the position was uncertain both in relation to these two fields and generally.

[4] As part of the Government's reform of the electricity industry, ECNZ, which was a state owned enterprise, had been required to divest itself of certain generating assets. It found itself short of gas to fuel a power station which it owned at Huntly. The Huntly station is capable of being fuelled either with gas or coal. It is connected by a pipeline to the Maui Field. ECNZ also had plans to build a new combined cycle gas turbine power plant at Huntly, which would be gas fuelled and was anticipated to be a much more efficient producer than the existing Huntly station.

[5] Negotiations between FCE and ECNZ over the long-term supply of gas to Huntly had broken down in 1997. Part of the difficulty, as the judgment below records (at para [15]), was FCE's inability to provide that supply in addition to its existing commitments.

[6] Western Mining Corporation Ltd (WMC) held a 40% interest in the Kupe field and had called for tenders for the purchase of that interest. Both FCE and ECNZ submitted bids. The judgment records that they were "closely competing". WMC called for a second round of bidding, to close on 28 February 1997.

[7] In the meantime FCE managed to acquire the 20% interest in Kupe held by the Norcen group. It remained interested in WMC's interest through which it could obtain the operatorship of the field. But at the same time FCE wanted to limit its financial exposure to Kupe. It appears to have been concerned by the level of anticipated capital costs of developing the field.

[8] Against this background, including particularly the lack of any source for the acquisition of a gas supply other than Kupe and the FCE controlled Maui, the parties entered into discussions. Representatives met at the ECNZ offices in Wellington on 27 and 28 February in an attempt to negotiate an agreement for a long-term gas supply for Huntly. Those representatives were Messrs McLaughlin, Taylor and Boshier of ECNZ and Kirk and Russell of FCE.

[9] On 28 February while these talks were still underway, Mr Hugh Fletcher, Chief Executive Officer of the Fletcher Challenge Group and Mr Dave Frow, his counterpart at ECNZ, respectively signed and endorsed agreement on a letter from FCE to ECNZ (the Fletcher/Frow letter). The letter is expressed to be an "attempt at capturing the agreed proposal". It is in four parts. In the first part the letter states that ECNZ and FCE would that day resubmit their first round bids to WMC. If either bid was accepted, they would each buy the shares in the Kupe field in the proportions of 25.75% for ECNZ and 14.25% for FCE.

[10] The second part of the letter read:

(ii) By the end of today, ECNZ and Fletcher Challenge Energy will enter into the Heads of Agreement for long term gas supply. This

† [2002] 2 NZLR 433.

Heads of Agreement will specify all essential terms for it to be a binding agreement, including annual quantities, max/min flow rates, start date, duration, prices throughout, force majeure terms. This Heads of Agreement will be conditional on ECNZ Board approval within eight days.

[11] In the third part of the letter ECNZ and FCE set out certain terms relating to the Kupe field, including a commitment from ECNZ to support FCE's bid to replace WMC as the field's operator.

[12] In the last part of the letter the parties agreed that in the event of ambiguity or uncertainty Messrs Frow and Fletcher would "interpret the current intent and that will prevail".

[13] Later on the same day, 28 February, the HoA was signed on behalf of ECNZ by Mr Taylor, its General Manager, Business Development, and on behalf of FCE by Mr Kirk, its General [Manager], Marketing and Commercial.

[14] The HoA is set out in full in a schedule to the judgments. It has four unusual features. The words "to be agreed" appear against the efficiency factor (K) in the formula for calculating the liability of FCE for non-delivery of gas (other than due to force majeure). The words "Not agreed" appear under the marginal heading "Force Majeure" and in the text of that item there is the statement ("Not agreed: Extension to National Grid"). Below the marginal heading "Prepaid Gas Relief" there is the notation "not agreed". Finally, above the signatures, there is the following:

Agreed (except where indicated)

[15] There are two matters stated to be "Conditions Precedent". The first is the securing of the 40% Kupe stake. The second is "ECNZ's Board Approval".

[16] There is also an item called "Time Frame for Proceeding" which reads:

FCE/ECNZ to use all reasonable endeavours to agree a full sale and purchase agreement within three months of the date of this agreement.

[17] The bids were re-submitted to WMC in accordance with the Fletcher/Frow letter and on 4 March WMC advised that FCE's bid had been accepted.

[18] On 12 March Messrs Fletcher and Frow re-signed an amended version of their letter. The first part of the letter was altered to remove some portions which had placed restrictions on voting in the joint venture. It seems this was thought likely to attract the disapproval of the Commerce Commission. The second part of the letter was amended to read as follows (with the changes as italicised):

(ii) By the end of today, ECNZ and Fletcher Challenge Energy will enter into the Heads of Agreement for long term gas supply. *The gas to be supplied under this Agreement will be sourced by Fletcher Challenge Energy from a variety of sources available to it.* This Heads of Agreement will specify all essential terms for it to be a binding agreement, including annual quantities, max/min flow rates, start date, duration, prices throughout, force majeure terms. This Heads of Agreement will be condition [*sic*] on ECNZ Board approval *within thirteen days.*

[19] There was no change to parts three and four of the letter.

[20] The extension of the date for obtaining ECNZ Board approval was made at the request of ECNZ. Its Board met on the same day, 12 March. A resolution was passed in the following terms:

RESOLVED
that
(i) the Heads of Agreement for the contract for the sale of gas between FCE and ECNZ be approved, subject to challenging the provision that FCE should only deliver gas in the period 2011–2017 if such delivery were to be economic;
(ii) the Committee of the Board comprising of Messrs Cushing, Gentry and Wu and that that Committee be authorised to approve the final contract for the Sale and Purchase of the Gas with Fletcher Challenge Energy and to authorise the execution of that document.

[21] It was the uncontested evidence of Mr Kirk of FCE that he was told by Mr Taylor of ECNZ in a telephone call on 13 March that ECNZ's Board had given approval to the HoA. He was not told about the qualification concerning gas deliveries from 2011 to 2017. FCE did not learn of this qualification until after this proceeding had been commenced.

[22] The parties became pre-occupied for a while with completing the Kupe interest purchase. That was achieved on 27 March. It was not until 3 April that they met to begin their endeavours to agree the "full sale and purchase agreement". As a first step, each side prepared a list of issues requiring agreement. These were not, as listed, restricted to the matters stated in the HoA as to be agreed or not agreed.

[23] Further discussions were delayed until May by a Commerce Commission investigation into the parties' acquisition of WMC's Kupe interest. About three weeks into the negotiations which then ensued, ECNZ, concerned to have a secure supply of gas until 2017, raised with FCE the question of the "economic test", which formed the basis upon which FCE could decline to deliver gas after 30 September 2011 under the "Preferred Customer" obligation in the HoA ("FCE will deliver gas only if delivery is economic"). FCE objected to the test proposed by ECNZ which was a net present value test extending to FCE's entire gas and liquids business in New Zealand. As Mr Russell of FCE put it in his evidence:

> Under the test posed by ECNZ, if the net present value of the whole of FCE's gas and liquids revenues in New Zealand, taking into account revenues from, and the costs of, the supply of gas to ECNZ, was positive, then FCE would have to supply gas to ECNZ. In other words, FCE would be forced under that test to cross-subsidise the delivery of gas to ECNZ with its revenues from all its other gas and liquids activities in New Zealand if the price ECNZ paid to FCE was not sufficient in and of itself to cover the cost of delivering the gas to ECNZ. And, in other words, FCE would be required to supply ECNZ with gas except to the extent that to do so would place FCE in a net loss situation over the whole of its gas and liquids business in New Zealand.

[24] The negotiations in the end appear to have broken down principally over this question. In the meantime, developments in the electricity market had altered ECNZ's view about the prices set under the HoA. Lower price forecasts predicting future over-supply of electricity coupled with the development of the Government's plans for further re-structuring of ECNZ and the electricity market made the gas supply from FCE a less attractive proposition.

[25] Eventually, although the parties continued their discussions and proposals flowed to and fro between them, an impasse was reached in January 1998. The negotiations collapsed. ECNZ took the position that the HoA did not constitute a legally binding contract and declined to proceed with the purchase of gas. FCE instituted this proceeding seeking declarations that the HoA was binding on ECNZ and that, whether or not that was so, ECNZ was in breach of a binding obligation to use "all reasonable endeavours" to agree on the full sale and purchase agreement.

. . . .

ARGUMENT FOR APPELLANT

[35] Mr Craddock QC, for ECNZ, stated what he said were the fundamental issues in the case in this way:

> Assessed objectively on 28 February 1997:
> [a] had the parties agreed all the terms they regarded as essential;
> [b] did the parties intend to be finally and exclusively bound to a contract on the terms agreed in the HoA excluding those terms not agreed;
> and, if so, was the HoA legally complete?

[36] It was submitted that the parties had failed to reach agreement on a number of terms they considered essential to their bargain:

> [a] the efficiency factor (K) was still "to be agreed";
> [b] an additional clause was needed "to cover non supply liabilities";
> [c] force majeure terms were "not agreed" either generally or at least in respect of the extension to the National Grid;
> [d] repayment terms for pre-paid gas (in the case of force majeure and non-delivery) were stated to be "not agreed";
> [e] the HoA did not contain minimum flow rates (compare the Fletcher/Frow letter which included in essential terms "max/min flow rates"), nor did it prescribe a maximum hourly flow rate.

The terms had been stated generally to be "Agreed (except where indicated)." Counsel submitted that the parties were clearly not *ad idem* on terms which they regarded as essential to any contract. It was for them to determine what was essential to their bargain. If both parties or either party regarded a term as essential then it was.

[37] The appellant submitted also that, upon an objective assessment of the documents, it is clear that the parties did not intend to be immediately bound by the HoA. They had recorded that lack of agreement and their intention to continue negotiating. They remained in a state of negotiation. Counsel submitted that the HoA simply recorded the point in the negotiation which they had reached. They had not provided for agreement on outstanding issues to be reached by resort to an expert or an arbitrator or by another mechanism.

. . . .

[39] Mr Craddock said that it could not possibly be the case that ECNZ intended to bind itself finally and conclusively to a 17-year multi-billion dollar gas contract without reaching agreement on a force majeure term, minimum flow rates (even if these were zero), a formula for calculating non-delivery liabilities, a clause dealing with other liabilities, a prepaid gas relief term, a clause defining price-escalation, a term defining the economic test and the rest of the other terms which the appellant submitted were uncertain.

[40] And even if the parties had intended to be bound, it was the appellant's submission that their negotiations did not reach a point of sufficient certainty to be binding in law. Counsel took the Court to several provisions, including that for the delivery of gas after 2011 only if "economic" for FCE, which he said were incapable of interpretation.

. . . .

ARGUMENT FOR RESPONDENT

[43] Mr Wilson QC, for FCE, submitted that the appellant's argument had subordinated the question of intention to be bound to the question of completeness and had thus inverted the proper approach. It was the respondent's contention that the approach of the Judge was correct in law; that he had first determined that the parties intended to be bound and only then had sought to give effect to their intention, following the modern approach to contract formation. The terms in the Fletcher/Frow letter were said to be merely illustrative of the types of terms which might be agreed in order to create a binding HoA; the signatories to the letter were not attempting to define the essential terms. Their object was merely to ensure that the HoA would be binding when signed. It was open to the appointed negotiators to come to a different view on what was essential, accepting as they did so that the HoA was necessarily an imperfect document because of the limited time available to work out its terms. The position taken by the negotiators had been confirmed by the re-signing of the letter when the CEOs knew that not all of the terms mentioned in their letter had been covered.

[44] It was said that each party had elected to take a risk on the outcome of the unresolved matters. That risk was outweighed by the perceived value of getting an agreement which in fact included all terms essential in law or thought by the parties to be essential. Omission or non-agreement on other mat-

ters therefore did not prevent effect being given to the intention of the parties to be bound. The existence of the "not agreeds" ought, it was said, to be relevant only to the likelihood that the parties intended to be bound or to whether any matter not agreed was objectively essential.

[45] Mr Wilson referred to ECNZ's need for gas, with the only two sources being Maui (controlled by FCE) and Kupe. ECNZ had been exposed to the risk that FCE would put in a higher bid. It could not afford to miss out on Kupe because, if it did, FCE could then have named its own price for gas supplies.

[46] Mr Wilson asked why ECNZ would have made the agreement subject to its Board's approval if there had been no intention that it be binding. He explained FCE's attitude to the subsequent negotiations towards a full agreement as deriving from their view that while the HoA was a binding contract, a full agreement would cure its imperfections and be a much more satisfactory basis for the long-term relationship.

[47] Because the parties intended to be bound at the time of signature (described by Mr Wilson as the "key point"), it was proper for Wild J to take the view that, by a process of implication and interpretation, the contract could be found to be complete or made to be complete. While the Judge had proceeded actually to resolve the alleged incompleteness and uncertainty, it was not necessary to go that far. The Court had only to form the view that these matters were capable of resolution should the need arise during the performance of the contract. All the allegedly incomplete or uncertain terms were either capable of being rendered certain or were not essential to the bargain. The HoA, it was said, contained all the terms needed to make it enforceable. It was not unworkable in the sense of being objectively impossible to perform.

. . . .

THE CORRECT LEGAL APPROACH

[50] The question whether negotiating parties intended the product of their negotiation to be immediately binding upon them, either conditionally or unconditionally, cannot sensibly be divorced from a consideration of the terms expressed or implicit in that product. They may have embarked upon their negotiation with every intention on both sides that a contract will result, yet have failed to attain that objective because of an inability to agree on particu-

lar terms and on the bargain as a whole. In other cases, which are much less common, the intention may remain but somehow the parties fail to reach agreement on a term or terms without which there is insufficient structure to create a binding contract. This latter situation is uncommon because normally negotiating parties will have an appreciation of what basic terms they need to reach agreement upon in order to form a contract of the particular type which they are negotiating. It is comparatively rare that, having an intention to contract immediately, not only do they fail to deal expressly with an essential or fundamental term but it also proves impossible for the Court to determine the contractual intent in that regard by implication of a term or by reference to what was reasonable in the particular circumstances or to some other objective standard.

[51] A contract is not legally incomplete merely because consequential matters have been omitted, particularly when they relate to questions of contingency and risk allocation. The parties may have thought it unnecessary to the essence of their bargain to reach agreement upon such matters or it may have been difficult or even impossible to predict what might arise in the future, particularly under a long term contract. It may therefore have been thought satisfactory — and it would often be more economically efficient — to leave such matters to be worked out if necessary in the course of the performance of the contract.

[52] But even where the parties are *ad idem* concerning all terms essential to the formation of a contract — the basic structure of a contract of the type under negotiation is found to have been present in the terms which have been agreed — they still may not have achieved formation of a contract if there are other unagreed matters which the parties themselves regard as a prerequisite to any agreement and in respect of which they have reserved to themselves alone the power of agreement. In such cases, what is missing at the end of the negotiation is the intention to contract, not a legally essential element of a bargain.

[53] The prerequisites to formation of a contract are therefore:

(a) An intention to be immediately bound (at the point when the bargain is said to have been agreed); and

(b) An agreement, express or found by implication, or the means of achieving an agreement (e.g. an arbitration clause), on every term which

(i) was legally essential to the formation of such a bargain; or

(ii) was regarded by the parties themselves as essential to their particular bargain.

A term is to be regarded by the parties as essential if one party maintains the position that there must be agreement upon it and manifests accordingly to the other party.

[54] Whether the parties intended to enter into a contract and whether they have succeeded in doing so are questions to be determined objectively. In considering whether the negotiating parties have actually formed a contract, it is permissible to look beyond the words of their "agreement" to the background circumstances from which it arose — the matrix of facts. This can include statements the parties made orally or in writing in the course of their negotiations and drafts of the intended contractual document.

· · · ·

[57] It is also very important, in considering the intention of the parties to be bound, to bear in mind the dynamics of the negotiation process and the internal inter-relationship of the terms of a commercial bargain. Tamberlin J of the Federal Court of Australia made the following valuable observation in *Seven Cable Television Pty Ltd v Telstra Corporation Ltd* (2000) 171 ALR 89, 114 (para [97]):

> When parties are negotiating in order to arrive at a contract to govern their legal relations the process is often complex, especially in cases of detailed and wide ranging agreements intended to endure over many years. In the course of negotiations there will generally be a constant and ongoing process of adjustment and readjustment of the positions adopted by the parties on particular clauses. This process sometimes involves a series of mutual "trade-offs" whereby a concession is made by one party in respect of one provision in exchange for the giving of a concession by the other party in respect of a different provision. It will also involve compromise and adjustment so that it is often difficult to determine whether at any particular point of time prior to execution of a final agreement the parties have entered into contractual relations. Before a final contract is made it is also difficult to detach any particular provision from its context and say that a final agreement has been reached on that particular clause as a discrete agreement.

[58] The Court has an entirely neutral approach when determining whether the parties intended to

enter into a contract. Having decided that they had that intention, however, the Court's attitude will change. It will then do its best to give effect to their intention and, if at all possible, to uphold the contract despite any omissions or ambiguities (*Hillas & Co Ltd v Arcos Ltd* (1932) 147 LT 503; [1932] All ER Rep 494; *R & J Dempster Ltd v Motherwell Bridge and Engineering Co Ltd* 1964 SC 308 and *Attorney-General v Barker Bros Ltd* [1976] 2 NZLR 495). We agree with the way in which Anderson J expressed the position in *Anaconda Nickel Ltd v Tarmoola Australia Pty Ltd* (2000) 22 WAR 101, 132–3:

> I think it is fair to say, speaking very generally, that where the parties intended to make a final and binding contract the approach of the courts to questions of uncertainty and incompleteness is rather different from the approach that is taken when the uncertainty or incompleteness goes to contractual intention. Where the parties intended to make an immediately binding agreement, and believe they have done so, the courts will strive to uphold it despite the omission of terms or lack of clarity: see *Trustees Executors & Agency Co Ltd v Peters* (1960) 102 CLR 537; *Upper Hunter County District Council v Australian Chilling & Freezing Co Ltd* (1968) 118 CLR 429; *Meehan v Jones* (1982) 149 CLR 571. However, the principle that courts should be the upholders and not the destroyers of bargains, which is the principle that underlies this approach, is not applicable where the issue to be decided is whether the parties intended to form a concluded bargain. In determining that issue, the court is not being asked to enforce a contract, but to decide whether or not the parties intended to make one. That inquiry need not be approached with any predisposition in favour of upholding anything. The question is whether there is anything to uphold.

. . . .

[62] We agree with Professor McLauchlan (*Rethinking Agreements to Agree* (1998) 18 NZULR 77, 85) that "an agreement to agree will not be held void for uncertainty if the parties have provided a workable formula or objective standard or a machinery (such as arbitration) for determining the matter which has been left open". We also agree with him that the court can step in and apply the formula or standard if the parties fail to agree or can substitute other machinery if the designated machinery breaks down.

[63] However, if essential matters (i.e. legally essential or regarded as essential by the parties) have not

been agreed upon and are not determinable by recourse to a mechanism or to a formula or agreed standard, it may be beyond the ability of the Court to fill the gap in the express terms, even with the assistance of expert evidence. ...

It will be a matter of fact and degree in each case whether the gap left by the parties is simply too wide to be filled. The Court can supplement, enlarge or clarify the express terms but it cannot properly engage in an exercise of effectively making the contract for the parties by imposing terms which they have not themselves agreed to and for which there are no reliable objective criteria.

[64] Where the intention to contract is found to have existed, the Court may supply an omission by implying a term.

. . . .

[66] It follows that merely because an important term is deferred to be settled on a future occasion, that does not mean that there is no intention to be bound. In such circumstances, provided the Court is satisfied that the parties did intend to enter immediately into a contractual relationship, it will do its best to find a means of giving effect to that intention by determining, if possible, the outstanding matter.

DID THE PARTIES INTEND THE HoA TO BE A CONTRACT?

[68] There can be no doubt that ECNZ and FCE both went into the negotiations on 27 and 28 February intent on concluding an agreement in the form of a heads of agreement. They must have appreciated that a relatively sketchy, perhaps incomplete, document was likely to result from the hurried negotiations. But it is clear from the Fletcher/Frow letter that the companies embarked on the negotiations with every intention of completing a binding deal.

[69] We accept also that the negotiators had authority to determine what matters were to be regarded as essential to any binding contract. We do not read the Fletcher/Frow letter as doing more than illustrating the kinds of things which might emerge as being essential. Whatever Mr Fletcher and Mr Frow may have contemplated, they appear to have left it to Mr Kirk and Mr Taylor to make the final determination by signing the HoA, subject of course to the opportunity to be reserved to ECNZ's Board to withhold its approval.

[70] The critical matter is whether the negotiators achieved their objective of agreeing on all terms they (or either of them) considered essential; whether, by signifying that certain matters had not been agreed they were indicating that essential matters remained outstanding or, alternatively, were withdrawing those matters from the list of what was, at the end of the negotiation, still regarded as essential. Did they, at the end of the negotiations on the HoA, intend to have an immediately binding contract?

[71] We consider that it is very significant in a document which on its face appeared incomplete — where items were actually marked "not agreed" — that the negotiators did not record that their agreement was to be regarded as complete, or legally binding. ... Nor did they provide for any machinery, such as an independent expert or an arbitrator, to resolve the matters on which they had not agreed.

. . . .

[73] The HoA has the appearance of a memorandum listing the points which have been agreed, those which have not been agreed and those which the parties are content to put to one side for the moment, together with a statement of their intention to negotiate a full (i.e complete) agreement within three months. ...

[74] The HoA accordingly seems to us to be in the nature of a progress report from the negotiators, containing also a statement on the course intended to be followed in order to complete the agreement. Both sides were evidently very confident of ultimately reaching that full agreement. However, it seems to us very probable that, if the negotiators had been asked before placing their signatures on the HoA whether, in the unexpected event of failure to do so, the HoA was to stand on its own as the contractual document to govern the parties' relationship until 2017, both Mr Kirk and Mr Taylor would have answered in the negative. They had simply reached an important staging post on the way to final agreement.

. . . .

[83] For these reasons, although we do not agree with the criticism made of the Judge that he approached the question of contractual intent with a predisposition to find that there was a contract, we have concluded that he erred in finding that the HoA was intended to be a binding contract.

. . . .

[THOMAS J (dissenting):]

INTRODUCTION

[120] I do not doubt that when the senior executives signed the Heads of Agreement (HoA) on behalf of Fletcher Challenge Energy Ltd (FCE) and Electricity Corporation of New Zealand Ltd (ECNZ) on 28 February 1997 they intended to be bound by that agreement. The HoA was to be binding until superseded by a full agreement which the parties contemplated would, with "all reasonable endeavours", be completed within a relatively short time. Arguments and evidence that the HoA was intended to be binding are overwhelming. Nor was the HoA so incomplete or uncertain that the courts would decline to enforce it.

[121] It follows that I would dismiss the appeal and endorse the declaratory orders made by Wild J in the Court below to the effect that the HoA is a valid and binding contract for the sale and purchase of gas in accordance with its terms. I would also support his finding that ECNZ is in breach of its obligation under the HoA to use all reasonable endeavours to agree to a full agreement. While, as will subsequently appear, there are certain aspects of his judgment with which I am not wholly in accord, I consider Wild J's judgment to be a first-rate judgment. ...

[122] What happened in this case can be discerned with tolerable certainty. The Chief Executives of FCE and ECNZ deliberately set out to reach accord on a number of matters. They negotiated a broad agreement which was recorded in their letter of 28 February 1997. It provided, inter alia, the framework by which a binding agreement would be concluded relating to a long-term agreement for the supply of gas from FCE to ECNZ. The senior executives did their Chief Executive's bidding and negotiated and signed the HoA. They reported their success back to the Chief Executives. The Chief Executives shook hands on the deal. They had a drink together to celebrate their success. Both parties acted on the HoA and acknowledged that the HoA was intended to be binding. Negotiations were set in train to complete a full agreement. But market conditions changed significantly. The price of electricity dropped and it appeared that it would remain depressed for a number of years. ECNZ no longer regarded the agreement as commercially favourable. It set about making demands in negotiation which FCE considered unrealistic and which it could not possibly agree to. Negotiations stalled. When challenged by FCE,

ECNZ sought to withdraw from the agreement. It raised numerous arguments designed to avoid liability, many of which lacked sufficient substance to be pressed on appeal in this Court.

. . . .

[124] I therefore differ from the majority's view that the HoA is not a binding agreement. ...

. . . .

THE CORRECT APPROACH

. . . .

[127] No case law need be cited, beyond that relied upon by Wild J, to arrive at the correct approach. It is long-established. The first question is whether the parties intended to be bound at the time of their agreement. The intention of the parties is paramount and the courts must give effect to that intention. The second question, which follows if they did intend to be bound, is whether, notwithstanding that contractual intention, the contract is so incomplete or uncertain as to be unenforceable at law. (See D.W. McLauchlan, supra, at 78). Of course, the fact matters have been deferred for future agreement or a number of significant matters have not been agreed may be an indication that the parties did not have the requisite contractual intention. But where there are otherwise compelling arguments and evidence pointing to that contractual intention it should be accepted that the parties have struck a bargain. The absence of matters which have been deferred are then relevant to the second question, that is, whether the contract as it stands is so incomplete or uncertain as to be incapable of being given legal effect.

[128] Adhering to this approach serves the law's purpose. It enables the law to give effect to the reasonable expectations of commercial men and women by giving legal effect to their bargains. The law, as Lord Tomlin observed in *Hillas & Co Ltd v Arcos Ltd* [1932] All ER Rep. 494, at 499, does not then incur the reproach of being the destroyer of bargains. Bargains are the essence of commerce and they should not be frustrated by the courts unless the incompleteness or uncertainty of the bargain renders the contract incapable of enforcement. At issue, is the autonomy of the will of the parties. The courts cannot work wonders, but they can positively seek to serve the interests of commerce and the reasonable

expectations of commercial men and women by facilitating their deliberate and intended transactions.

[129] With respect, I believe that the majority's decision fails the law in this regard. Closely analysed, their decision rests upon the fact that two matters stipulated in the agreement[:] *force majeure* relating to the National Grid and pre-paid gas relief, were marked "not agreed" in the HoA. (See paras [72] to [78]). Yet, when addressing the question whether the terms agreed upon by the parties were sufficient in law, the majority hold that the absence of either provision would not render the HoA unenforceable. (I deal later with the supposition that because the negotiators marked these clauses "not agreed" the parties must have considered them essential). The failure to reach agreement on the force majeure provision did not mean that the contract was legally "incomplete". (See paras [86] to [88]). Similarly, the agreement could operate without a provision relating to pre-paid gas relief. (See para [89]). The result is incongruent. The HoA is denied binding force essentially because the parties did not agree on two provisions, the absence of which did not render the parties' agreement incomplete or uncertain!

HEADS OF AGREEMENT

[130] There is another respect in which I consider that commerce is ill-served by a decision denying the HoA binding force. Heads of agreement are an integral part of commercial activity. They, and the regularity with which business men and women resort to them, are a commercial reality. Sometimes they are complete. More often than not, however, they leave important matters to be decided later. As Lord Lloyd (then Lloyd LJ), who was for a time a distinguished Judge of the Commercial Court in the United Kingdom has stated, parties may agree to be bound now while deferring important matters to be agreed later. "It happens," he said, "every day when parties enter into so-called 'heads of agreement'". See *Pagnan S.p.A v Feed Products Ltd* [1987] 2 Lloyd's Rep 601, at 619.

[131] Experience indicates why heads of agreement are an essential feature of commercial activity. Commercial agreements are frequently complex documents, but what is crucial is the essence of the bargain. Doing the initial deal or bargain is the task of senior managers. They are the deal-makers. Often the circumstances require the bargain to be "struck under great pressure of events and time" (Johan Steyn, "Contract Law: Fulfilling the Reasonable Expectations of Honest Men" (1997) 113 LQR

433, at 439). Heads of agreement suffice to complete a binding transaction. The managers, the deal-makers, then move to other productive areas of the company's business, leaving the core agreement to be expanded into a comprehensive document by subordinate executives and the parties' legal advisers.

[132] Naturally, the chief executives or deal makers will focus on the essential elements of a proposed agreement. Contingencies will frequently be incompletely dealt with in that the contract will fail to specify a party's obligation on the occurrence of a future contingency or fail to address a future contingency at all. (See David Goddard, "Long-Term Contracts: A Law and Economics Perspective" (1997) NZ Law Rev 423, at 426). Provisions to cover both forms of contingency deal with the allocation of risk and, if no explicit provision is agreed, the parties accept the risk involved. By and large essential terms do not relate to contingencies. There are various reasons why this is so: by definition, the contingency may be a remote possibility and may never occur; the sensible outcome, should the contingency occur, may be able to be determined by agreement or, failing agreement, by resorting to the common law; the appropriate provision may be a "boiler plate" clause or one that can readily be determined by reference to industry practice; or the parties may simply not be prepared to risk jeopardising a favourable bargain, the essential elements of which have been agreed, by arguing about a contingency which is remote and may never occur. Thus, it is not uncommon for commercial parties to enter into heads of agreement which have gaps, but which are intended to be binding pending the completion of a more comprehensive agreement. Where the heads of agreement are not intended to be binding, but only the forerunner to a formal contract, commercial prudence (if not the sense of self-preservation of the executives carrying out the negotiation) will ordinarily dictate that this conditional status be clearly spelt out.

[133] There is nothing novel in this perception. Take, for example, Lord Wright's speech in *Hillas & Co Ltd v Arcos Ltd*, supra. The learned law Lord affirmed, at 503, that "[b]usiness men often record the most important agreements in "crude and summary fashion", and (at 504) that "in contracts for future performance over a period, the parties may not be able nor may they desire to specify many matters of detail, but leave them to be adjusted in the working out of the contract." Thus, the notion that the adversarial ethic prevails in commercial negotiations relating to a prospective deal is misconceived. Indeed, in the context of a prospective

deal it is a myth. More often than not business men and women approach such negotiations with a "win/win" objective and outlook. A bargain can be struck which, certainly overall and notwithstanding the inevitable and unresolved risks involved, will be perceived to be advantageous to both parties.

[134] Mr Craddock sought to make much of the argument that the parties could not feasibly have intended to create legal relations by a mere heads of agreement in respect of a contract allegedly worth 1.2 to 1.8 billion dollars spanning a period of 17 years. They would need certainty on numerous risk and mitigation provisions so that financiers could rely on the contract as guaranteeing a secure supply of gas. This argument prompts a number of points.

- First, the submission runs counter to the description of heads of agreement and their important function in commerce which I have just set out. I do not doubt that it may appear surprising to persons who are not engaged in commerce that such a vast matter can be concluded in such a short form. But it is not surprising to anyone with commercial experience, direct or indirect, who has seen such deals completed with a shake of the hands and a heads of agreement, or even an exchange of letters.

- Secondly, it is to be borne in mind that the negotiators envisaged that, with all reasonable endeavours, a "full" agreement would be able to be completed within three months. There is no reason, therefore, why they should not have intended the HoA to have binding force pending the completion of the full agreement. Failure to reach that agreement does not change their intention to be bound by the HoA.

- Thirdly, the parties themselves contemplated that an HoA containing all essential terms would be sufficient to record a binding agreement. The majority agree that it is clear from the Fletcher/Frow letter that ECNZ and FCE embarked on the negotiations with every intention of completing a binding deal. (Para [68]). If, then, this was their intention at that time, they must have accepted that a binding agreement worth in excess of a billion dollars and spanning 17 years could be completed by way of a heads of agreement.

[135] Hence, heads of agreement, unless qualified to the contrary, are what they purport to be, the "heads" of the "agreement" reached. If heads of agreement entered into in the circumstances of this case are not to be honoured by the parties and

enforced by the courts a valuable and essential commercial tool will be seriously prejudiced.

[136] Consequently, I am reluctant to endorse any approach which would tend to restrict the utility of heads of agreement. Of course, the courts can say that, if parties wish to give effect to their intention to be bound, they can expressly say so, and if they do not say so they cannot blame the courts for not giving effect to their intention. But such a response is outmoded. It suggests that the law will lay down the rules and commerce can abide by those rules or come asunder; not that the law should seek to serve the needs and realities of commerce. No doubt those of a formalistic persuasion will applaud such a negative approach on the ground that it provides "certainty and predictability" in the law. But it will never be explained how it is that denying parties who have manifested an intention to be bound the binding force which they seek for their contract facilitates certainty and predictability. On the contrary, one would think that if parties manifest an intention to be bound they deserve the certainty of knowing that the courts will recognise their intention and endeavour to give effect to that intention.

[137] One further point can be made under this heading. No one would suggest that the courts should "make" the contract for the parties. Of course, the courts cannot and must not do that. Judges must be scrupulous not to fill gaps in the contract in a way which may not reflect the intention of the parties. But this caution should not be pressed to the extent that it becomes an argument *in terrorem*. The caution is more critically relevant to the second question referred to above, that is, whether, notwithstanding the parties' contractual intention, the contract is so incomplete or uncertain as to be unenforceable at law. A court is not making the contract or filling in a gap in the contract should it determine that the parties intended to be bound. Of course, the courts must not hold that a contract is binding where the parties have no intention to be bound, but it determines that question on the basis of an objective assessment of the intention of the parties and not on the basis that one party is able to specify a list of matters which have not been decided. As already stated, the fact that there are matters which have been deferred for future agreement or that a number of significant matters may not have been agreed may be an indication that the parties did not have the requisite contractual intention. But sight should not be lost of the fact that the focus of the initial question is the intention of the parties and not the content of the contract.

. . . .

INTENTION TO BE BOUND — A DISCRETE JURAL ACT

[139] As I consider it is clear that the parties intended to be bound when they completed the HoA, I do not propose to enter at length into the debate whether that question is to be determined objectively or subjectively. The majority state that the question is to be determined objectively. (Para [54]). I consider, however, that much of the objective/subjective dichotomy is misplaced in the present context. The question whether the parties intended to create legal relations cannot be determined by simply examining the HoA, in its matrix, as if the question was one of contractual interpretation. The nature of the question[:] did the parties intend to enter into a binding agreement, makes it necessary to go beyond the agreement itself. As Lloyd LJ said in the *Pagnan* case, supra, at 619, "It is for the parties to decide whether they wish to be bound and, if so, by what terms, whether important or unimportant". They are the "masters of their contractual fate."

[140] Certainly, the exercise cannot be subjective in the sense that the court listens to the opposing claims of each party and, as a matter of credibility, prefers the evidence of one party to the other. Some objective reference is required to determine the parties' true intention outside the credibility of their competing claims. That objective reference can only come from the commercial context or purpose of the agreement, the agreement itself, and reliable evidence extrinsic to the agreement.

. . . .

[145] To sum up, then, my approach to the question whether the parties intended to be bound is the same, or substantially the same, as the approach succinctly articulated by McHugh JA in *Air Great Lakes Pty Ltd & Others v K S Easter (Holdings) Pty Ltd* [1985] 2 NSWLR 309, at 337:

> The intention to create a legally binding contract <u>although a matter to be proved objectively, may, nevertheless, in my opinion, be proved by what the parties said and did as well as what they wrote.</u> The intention may be proved in that way even in a case where the document is intended to comprise all the terms of the bargain. <u>This is because the intention to be bound is a jural act separate and distinct from the terms of their bargain.</u> (Emphasis added).

. . . .

THE PARTIES INTENDED TO BE BOUND

[147] I turn now to examine the arguments and evidence of the parties' intention which I believe to be overwhelming. The headings are listed in the table of contents preceding this judgment.

1) The commercial context and purpose of the HoA

[148] In my view, the commercial context and commercial purpose of an agreement are critical considerations in determining whether it was intended to be binding. In this regard the commercial context and purpose of the HoA indicate that the parties must have intended to be bound by that document. An HoA which was no more than a step in the process of negotiations or in the nature of a progress report from the negotiators is not consistent with the commercial context and would not have served the commercial purpose which the parties sought to achieve.

[149] Both FCE and ECNZ were in a difficult position. The supply of commercial oil and gas in New Zealand is limited. FCE held a 68.5 per cent interest in the largest oil and gas field, Maui, but that field was expected to be depleted by 2009. The company was therefore bent on acquiring a larger interest in the Kupe field which was expected to last until 2011. It wished to purchase the 40 per cent interest held by the Western Mining Company Ltd. But Western Mining sought to sell that interest by open tender. A further 20 per cent interest which FCE acquired at the time from two other parties did not eliminate its need to acquire this share. But the acquisition would place FCE in a dilemma. If successful in requiring Western Mining's 40 per cent share, the company would then hold a 62.5 per cent share in Kupe. This share represented a larger capital exposure than was prudent or FCE desired. Hence, the attraction of an agreement with ECNZ to divide the Western Mining share should either company be the successful bidder. Either that or, in order to protect its existing interest and its future supply of gas, it had to be the successful bidder itself.

[150] For its part, ECNZ had been subject to restrictions on its generating capacity imposed by the Government in 1994 in an effort to promote competition in the electricity market. As a result of further restructuring, a competitive market had been established by the end of 1996. But ECNZ was left short of gas to fuel its remaining power stations, in particular, the Huntly station which was connected to the Maui field. Its supply to that station, which was the station's only supply, was due to end in 2002. ECNZ therefore initiated discussions with FCE to obtain a gas supply for Huntly beyond that date. Negotiations continued throughout 1996, but these negotiations had not resulted in agreement because of FCE's inability to supply the gas ECNZ needed in the long term.

[151] The acquisition of the interest in Kupe was therefore critical to both companies. Hence, the arrangement evolved whereby FCE and ECNZ would resubmit their previous bids and then, irrespective of which company succeeded, participate in the additional supply on an agreed percentage basis. The arrangement was important to both companies[:] to FCE if it was to secure the larger interest in Kupe, and to ECNZ if it was not to be put in the position of having to purchase gas from FCE in the future on FCE's terms. (See majority's judgment, para [45].)

[152] Without doubt, the deferred open tender inspired a concentrated effort by both companies to reach agreement. Their respective Chief Executives met and reached the agreement recorded in the Fletcher/Frow letter dated 28 February 1997. The parties were given a day to complete a heads of agreement, including all essential terms for it to be a "binding agreement", for long-term gas supply. The letter embraced not only the agreed tendering and completion of the HoA, but also the development of Kupe in a manner "consistent with each party meeting its obligations" under the HoA.

[153] Thus, the commercial context was such that FCE and ECNZ had to seek an immediate binding agreement. It was to the commercial advantage of both to do so. The shared basis of the Western Mining interest was critical to both companies, and the commercial purpose evident in the Fletcher/Frow letter would not be achieved unless the parties were able to complete a binding HoA. Neither the commercial context nor the purpose of the agreement left any scope for a heads of agreement that was nothing more than a step in the process of negotiations or a progress report from the negotiators on the course intended to be followed in order to complete the agreement. An interim document of this kind would not have completed the arrangement contemplated by the Fletcher/Frow letter, and it

would not have achieved the commercial advantage both parties regarded as essential.

2) The Fletcher/Frow letter

[154] The HoA was part of the wider arrangement recorded in the Fletcher/Frow letter. The terms of that letter are therefore of assistance in determining the intention of the parties. It records the outcome of conversations between the two Chief Executives and sets out the "agreed proposal". The conversations followed a meeting between Mr Kirk, the General Manager Marketing and Commercial of FCE and Mr Taylor, the General Manager, Business Development of ECNZ (the ultimate signatories to the HoA) in late January or early February. Mr Taylor is said to have advised Mr Kirk that ECNZ was very interested in developing a joint approach with FCE to obtain the Kupe interest, provided that FCE also entered into a gas supply contract with ECNZ after that company's existing contract with another supplier came to an end in 2002.

[155] The letter first confirms the bidding agreement and the respective share each company would take of Western Mining's interest should either of their bids be accepted. It was agreed that each party would own and pay for the shares or underlying assets in the proportions of 25.75 per cent to ECNZ and 14.25 per cent to FCE. Detailed points follow to govern the relationship of the parties in this event. (Para (i)). But this agreement does not stand alone. Part of the "agreed proposal" is the requirement that by the end of the day the parties will have entered into the HoA for long-term gas supply. (Para (ii)). The HoA is to include all the essential terms for it to be a "binding agreement". The HoA does not make the agreement conditional on anything other than Western Mining's stake in Kupe being secured by either FCE or ECNZ and the ECNZ Board's approval. Then, in para (iii), it is recited that both ECNZ and FCE "desire the development of Kupe in a manner which is consistent with each party meeting its obligations under the agreement in (ii) above," that is, the obligations of each party under the HoA. Finally, the parties agree that in the event of any ambiguity or uncertainty Messrs Frow and Fletcher will interpret the current intent, and their determination is to prevail.

[156] It is difficult to read this letter and not conclude that the parties intended the HoA to be binding. Lengthy negotiations had taken place the previous year which, although unsuccessful, had resulted in a significant measure of agreement in the

"term sheet" which had been prepared by the negotiators. Wild J specifically rejected the evidence of Mr McLaughlin and held that most of the terms in the HoA were drawn from the term sheet. (Para [48]). The groundwork done in those negotiations made it possible for the parties to conclude the HoA over two days. (Para [49]). But there was, of course, nothing binding about the term sheet. In contrast, the HoA was to be binding. Had a binding HoA not been completed there would have been no deal. Both FCE and ECNZ would have been free to submit higher bids. The letter did not contemplate that the HoA would be a step in the negotiations or provide what was in effect a progress report from the negotiators. This document was not a term sheet.

. . . .

3) The terms of the HoA

[158] The terms of the HoA also indicate that the parties intended to be bound. They headed their document "FCE/ECNZ Gas Contract: Heads of Agreement". Then, two conditions precedent are stipulated. The first presupposes that the FCE/ECNZ Kupe joint venture will secure the 40 per cent stake being sold by Western Mining. This condition is essential to provide access to the gas which is then made subject to the HoA. The second condition precedent is ECNZ's Board approval. During the course of negotiating the terms of the HoA, the ECNZ negotiators consulted with members of the ECNZ Board as to the content of the HoA. They reported back that they were comfortable with the terms agreed but insisted that they still required the condition precedent. As Wild J observes, there was no point in including conditions precedent if the parties did not intend the HoA to bind them upon execution. A condition precedent was simply not necessary if either party was free to regard the HoA as a step in the negotiating process or something in the nature of a progress report from the negotiators. There is considerable point in the rhetorical question originally asked by FCE and recorded by Wild J (para [46]) to this effect: what was intended to become unconditionally binding once the ECNZ Board had approved the HoA?

[159] The HoA is a relatively detailed heads of agreement. Throughout, language appropriate to an agreement intended to be binding is consistently utilised. There are no qualifications, such as agreement to use best endeavours, in relation to any of the obligations set out in the document (other than to agree to a "full" agreement). The obligations are

stipulated in absolute terms. All but two terms are "agreed". (See below). Under the heading "Time frame for proceeding", FCE and ECNZ are to use all reasonable endeavours to agree to a "full sale and purchase agreement". The HoA is not made subject to that agreement and it is described as a "full ... agreement", suggesting an elaboration of what has been agreed. The time frame refers to the three months by which the negotiators expected the full agreement to be completed. The fact it was thought a period of three months was all that would be necessary to complete the "full" agreement itself indicates that the negotiators did not anticipate any real problems in converting the HoA into that agreement. Because the HoA would stand, the essential bargain would stand and the area for further dispute would be substantially reduced.

[160] Finally, the agreement concludes with the words "Agreed (except where indicated)." The negotiators saw fit to insert these words at the end of the HoA and above their signatures. They were strictly unnecessary as the signatures would have indicated agreement on all terms other than those marked "not agreed" and "to be agreed". The natural meaning to ascribe to the phrase is that, other than in the excepted respects, the rest of the HoA has been agreed, that is, agreed in the sense of being binding on the parties. To restrict the phrase to meaning agreed to be essential or agreed for further negotiation would not make sense. What point would there be in noting general agreement and excepting the two provisions that had not been agreed if it were intended that the whole HoA was not agreed?

4) The re-signing of the Fletcher/Frow letter

[161] The amendments made to the Fletcher/Frow letter which was re-signed by the Chief Executives on 12 March are recounted in the majority's judgment. (Para [18]). I can agree with the majority that the need to avoid any criticism from the Commerce Commission would have been the reason for making the amendments and backdating the letter. But I cannot agree that it does not provide legitimate evidence of the parties' intention. The letter stipulating that the parties would enter into an HoA specifying "all essential terms for it to be a binding agreement" was re-signed after the HoA had been signed. At that time the Chief Executives were fully aware of the contents of the HoA. They knew that two provisions had been marked "not agreed" and one provision had been noted "to be agreed". But they also

knew exactly what had been agreed and must have been satisfied that all terms essential for it to be a "binding agreement" had been included in the document. Why would the Chief Executives have re-signed the letter in the same form on 12 March if the HoA had failed to meet the critical requirement which they had stipulated in their original letter of 28 February?

[162] Conversely, if the HoA had been no more than a step in the negotiating process or in the nature of a progress report from the negotiators it would simply not have fulfilled the Chief Executive's explicit requirement that it be a binding agreement. The re-signing would simply not have made sense. Indeed, one may also question why the parties would have re-signed and backdated an amended letter to meet a perceived concern about the reaction of the Commerce Commission if it had been no more than a record of the parties' negotiations toward a full agreement.

[Note: Justice Thomas then reviewed key items of evidence and facts that he considered supported the conclusion that the parties intended to be bound. These included:

- FCE and ECNZ acted on the agreement by:
  - Resubmitting their previous tender
  - Giving effect to the agreed shares in the Kupe field

- The ECNZ board gave its approval to the agreement and appointed a committee to oversee the finalization of the contract and to authorize execution of it without referral back to the full board. In his words, "this resolution is consistent with the Board recognizing that the bargain had been struck." At para. 170.

- Supporting extrinsic evidence, including
  - The executive summary for the ECNZ board, which referred to the Heads of Agreement as 'entered into force' specifying all 'necessary terms for it to be a binding agreement.'
  - A background paper for the ECNZ Board recognizing that binding arrangements were already in place.
  - Mr Frow's report to the ECNZ Board indicating that the CEOs had 'agreed to do the deal' and that heads of agreement were concluded.
  - ECNZ Board minutes relating to the "FCE Gas Contract" as part of the Kupe acquisition proposal.

- Subsequent conduct including
  - The course of negotiations — with all ECNZ documentation referring to the heads of agreement as a contract and the further drafting as an exercise being undertaken as one of drafting the full agreement with care, given its long-term nature and to ensure that there was no shift in the material value agreed, not of negotiating or renegotiating the essential bargain
  - Media releases and communications with the Minister of Energy referring to "the legally binding Heads of Agreement"

- The 'speaking silence', by which Thomas J. meant the absence of any files or documents suggesting that there was no intention to be legally bound by the Heads of Agreement.

Thomas J. then referred to the question of the provisions marked "not agreed" and the view of the majority that the Heads of Agreement were in the nature of a "progress report" from "negotiators", continuing:]

[218] There are a number of reasons why I must respectfully decline to support this reasoning.

[219] First, it seems to me that the majority's construction does not squarely confront the strength of the arguments and evidence confirming that the parties intended to be bound by the HoA until it was superseded by the "full" agreement which they contemplated would be completed within three months by the use of all reasonable endeavours: the commercial context and purpose of the HoA, the terms of the Fletcher/Frow letter, the terms of the HoA itself, the fact that the Fletcher/Frow letter was re-signed after the HoA had been completed, the fact that both parties acted on the agreement as if it were binding, and the fact that the ECNZ Board approved the HoA reserving only the right to "challenge" a particular feature of the HoA in drawing up the "full" agreement. In effect, the majority's construction is equivalent to saying that the HoA was subject to a formal contract. It clearly was not that, a conclusion which would seem to be put beyond doubt by the extrinsic evidence which cannot be satisfactorily explained away.

[220] In the context of a detailed HoA containing what the General Manager of ECNZ described as "the essential terms of the gas contract", the inability of the negotiators to reach agreement on two terms does not negate the agreement arrived at on the essential terms. As Mr Wilson submitted, working to

a whiteboard within a dramatically short time to complete agreement, it is as if these not agreed matters had simply been erased by the negotiators as negotiations proceeded to the more critical issues. The matters remained to be agreed, if possible, as part of the "full" agreement, but the fact that they were deferred at this stage does not necessarily mean that the rest of the agreement was not intended to stand pending that full agreement.

[221] Secondly, it seems to me that the majority's construction is at least partially undermined by their subsequent conclusion that the absence of a force majeure provision relating to the National Grid and the absence of a pre-paid gas relief provision would not render the agreement incomplete. Why should it be odd for the negotiators to defer items which are not essential in order to complete an urgent deal? It happens with heads of agreement which are undoubtedly intended to be binding every day.

[222] Thirdly, nor is it telling that no machinery was included in the HoA to enable these two terms to be resolved if the parties were unable to agree. Contemplating that all reasonable endeavours on the part of both parties would enable a full agreement to be reached, the negotiators may well not have wanted to resort to arbitration or the like. The sanction lay in the fact that the HoA was intended to be binding: it remained in force until replaced by full agreement containing terms the parties had been able to agree upon.

[223] Fourthly, how can the majority's claim that the fact the two clauses were marked "not agreed" is an indication of their importance and that they were regarded as essential terms be substantiated? The fact they were marked "not agreed" can just as well indicate that they were not considered important or essential, and in context that must surely be the preferred interpretation. (See above.) Why should terms, the absence of which would not render the HoA incomplete, be regarded as essential by the parties? This suggestion seems to [...] me, with respect, to represent an improbable leap of reason. The conclusion that non-essential terms were regarded by the negotiators as essential terms because they were marked "not agreed", with the result that the rest of the HoA becomes a step in the negotiating process or report of the negotiators as to progress made, is untenable and flies in the face of all the arguments and evidence to the contrary.

[224] Fifthly, some meaning must be given to the words "Agreed (except as otherwise indicated)" immediately above Mr Taylor and Mr Kirk's signa-

tures. Those words may have been included out of caution, but they are unnecessary to simply denote that all but two provisions have been agreed to. The signatures would have achieved that purpose. The more probable interpretation having regard to the commercial context and purpose of the HoA is that the parties were making it clear that, other than as expressly noted, the terms of the HoA had been agreed as essential and binding terms. (See above, para [41]).

[225] Nor, in the sixth place, do I consider that anything significant can be read into the difference in wording between "not agreed" and "to be agreed". (See majority judgment, para [72]). A provision can be left open in an agreement to be determined at a future date. In fact the K factor can only properly be determined at a future time. (See majority judgment, para [91] and [92]).

[226] Seventhly, while I agree that both parties were confident of reaching agreement, I utterly disagree with the proposition that, if the negotiators had been asked before signing whether, in the unexpected event of a failure to reach agreement on the full agreement, the HoA would stand on its own as the contractual document to govern the parties' relationship until 2017, both Mr Kirk and Mr Taylor would have answered in the negative. (Para [74]). This assessment is also contrary to the arguments and evidence I have touched upon in this judgment.

[227] In posing the question whether the negotiators would have intended the HoA to govern the parties' relationship until 2017, and receiving a negative answer, the majority stipulate the "unexpected event of failing to reach full agreement". But what if the question is changed slightly? If the negotiators had been asked before placing their signatures on the HoA whether, in the event that the other party changed its mind about the commercial desirability of the deal and therefore decided not to proceed with it, the HoA was intended to be a binding agreement, would Mr Kirk and Mr Taylor then have answered in the negative? Of course not. It is certain that they would have said the HoA was binding and would remain binding until the full agreement was completed. Neither party would be free to ignore the binding agreement after it had become unconditional.

[228] The answer which I suggest Mr Kirk and Mr Taylor would have given is indicated by the majority's acceptance of the fact that the negotiators were very confident of completing the full agreement. The parties did not anticipate for one moment that full

agreement would not be reached, and for good reason; the essential terms had been agreed in the HoA and were to the advantage of both parties. Thus, they would have said that the HoA would stand on its own until it had been replaced by the full agreement within the anticipated three months. If, contrary to their expectations, the full agreement did not eventuate, the HoA would, being binding and in force, continue to operate. It would necessarily continue to govern the purchase and supply of the gas in the long-term.

[229] Moreover, the proposition to the effect that Mr Kirk and Mr Taylor, faced with a prescient bystander able to tell them that the "full" agreement would never be completed, would agree that the HoA was not binding injects a speculative element into the question of determining whether the parties intended to be bound. If this proposition is accepted, the parties' actual or objective intention is replaced by the Court second-guessing the parties, that is, speculating what the parties' intention would have been if they had shared a different expectation. It is like saying to the parties; "Yes, we accept that you intended to create legal relations alright, but if you had known about such and such or been able to foretell the future you would not have had that intention." In fact, their intention to create legal relations remains intact. It is infinitely preferable to accept that the parties intended to be bound when they concluded the HoA and to then consider the second question; whether that agreement is sufficiently complete and certain to be enforceable at law. (I note that ECNZ have not pleaded or argued mistake).

[230] Eighthly, the fact that when FCE and ECNZ negotiated the full agreement they did not "pick up where they left off" but treated themselves as free to renegotiate agreed terms does not mean that they did not intend the HoA to be binding. With the essential terms agreed, the inherent value of the agreement to each party had been determined. Both parties desired the commercial advantage the long-term gas contract gave them. Why would they place that agreement in jeopardy by renegotiating a new set of terms, including those that had obviously been agreed? The answer has to be that the renegotiation of terms, including the agreed terms, did not place the agreement in jeopardy. In other words, in the process of completing a comprehensive agreement, the parties could, if they chose, seek to renegotiate the terms agreed to in the HoA simply because they were agreed and binding. Failure to renegotiate agreement on any term did not leave a vacuum. (See

also para [74] above noting that the parties at the outset spoke of the pending negotiations and emphasised the care required in "drafting" the full agreement. Negotiation, and renegotiation within the bounds of the inherent value of the agreement to the parties, was not inimical to the preparation of the full agreement).

[231] Nor do I accept for one moment the view that the HoA was binding is contrary to the normal negotiating process, or the dynamic of that process, as elaborated by the majority. (Paras [57] and [77]). Of course, there is an interrelationship between one term and another in a contract. A party will adjust and readjust its position, and may compromise its position, before reaching a final agreement. But this is not to say that parties cannot reach agreement in a heads of agreement, even though there may be important matters still to be agreed. (See above). The heads of agreement itself can, and is likely to, reflect that process of adjustment, readjustment and compromise. As Mr Wilson submitted, this process is precisely what happened here. It is why the Chief Executives insisted upon the HoA containing all essential terms to make it binding. These terms fixed the value of the agreement to the parties. Once agreed and binding, neither party in the course of negotiating or renegotiating the "full" agreement would permit the value of the bargain it had made to be diminished.

[232] In concluding this section, may I respectfully urge that it is possible to make altogether too much of the fact that two items were marked "not agreed" in an agreement in which all the essential matters had been agreed and which the parties contemplated would, with all reasonable endeavours, be converted into a full agreement.

THE AGREEMENT IS COMPLETE AND CERTAIN

[233] As I have already indicated, I agree with the majority that the HoA was not incomplete because of the absence of agreement as to the *force majeure* and pre-paid gas relief provisions. I also agree that the notation "not agreed" in respect of *force majeure* applied only to the extension to the National Grid. (Para [86] to [87]). Failure to reach agreement on the extension of the *force majeure* clause to the National Grid did not mean that the contract was legally incomplete. (Para [88]). So, too, the agreement could operate without a pre-paid gas relief provision. (Para [89]).

. . . .

CONCLUSION

[245] I repeat what I said at the outset that the arguments and evidence that the HoA was intended to be binding are overwhelming. It seems to me that the highest the contrary case can be stated is to say that, although the parties clearly intended to be bound, they would not have had that intention if they had appreciated that the "full" agreement might or would not be completed, whether due to the default of one party or otherwise. Their overt intention, in other words, was based on an assumption which permits the Court to redefine their intention. As I have sought to show, that view is untenable for a number of reasons, not the least being that the parties' intention is paramount and, having been objectively determined, the Court is obliged to move to the second question and determine whether the contract is so incomplete and uncertain as to be unenforceable.

[246] In his excellent article, which bears repeated reference, "Does Legal Formalism Hold Sway in England?" (1996) 49 II Current Legal Problems, 45, Lord Steyn expressed the view (at 47) that formalism in the sense of an exclusive reliance on formalist methods has not been exorcised in England, but it is on the wane. Is it possible that in this case the exorcist may be knocking at the door? Undue adherence to formalism, it seems to me, is required in the context of contract formation to sanction any of the following notions:

- The notion that the object of the courts' inquiry is or can be something other than the actual intention of the parties, objectively assessed; or
- The notion that the courts can impute an "objective" intention to the parties which is not their actual intention; or
- The notion that the "subjective" evidence which the courts will disregard is not limited to what the parties say about their intention to be bound, but extends to evidence of what they said and did which points to their intention; and
- The notion that the scope of the inquiry is to be restricted to an examination of the terms of the agreement, or that otherwise relevant and reliable evidence is to be excluded, by reference to rules pertaining to the objective interpretation of contractual terms.

. . . .

[250] ... I consider that it is important that the law should endeavour to meet the needs of commerce rather than require commerce to meet rules laid down by the law. It should meet the reasonable expectations of business men and women rather than require the law to meet the possibly overly legalistic expectations of men and women in the law. The realities of commerce should be recognised, and where the law does not accord with those realities it should be made to give way to a more responsive legal approach.

[251] I would like to think that this is the path which New Zealand would wish to follow as an independent judicial system. If and when it is able to do so, I am confident that, in a case such as the present, the Court will reject the influence of lingering formalism and decline to artificially restrict the scope of the inquiry so as to admit of an outcome which is at variance with the true intention of the parties.

(f)　E-link(s) and Further Reading

- E.W. Thomas, "Case Study: *Fletcher Challenge Energy v. ECNZ [2002]" in The Judicial Process* (Cambridge: Cambridge University Press, 2005) at 287–99 (e-book).

B. Terms and Exemptions

(g)　*L'Estrange v. F Graucob Ltd.*†

U.K. King's Bench

On 7 February 1933, the plaintiff signed an agreement, called a "sales agreement," whereby she agreed to buy from the defendants an automatic cigarette machine and to pay for the same by an initial payment of 8 pounds 15s and eighteen later instalments of 3 pounds 19s 11d. It was a term of the agreement that, if the plaintiff fell into arrears with the instalments, all the remaining payments should immediately become due. The agreement contained the following clause:

> This agreement contains all the terms and conditions under which I agree to purchase the machine specified above, and any express or implied condition statement or warranty, statutory or otherwise, not stated herein is hereby excluded.

This clause was in small print, and was not read by the plaintiff. On February 9 the defendants sent to the plaintiff an "order confirmation" signed by them, and on March 28 they delivered the machine to her.

The machine did not work satisfactorily, and after the defendants had several times attempted, without success, to repair it, the plaintiff declined to go on with the contract, and on May 8 she wrote to the defendants that she had decided to forfeit the

---

† [1934] All ER Rep 16. (Appeal from Llandudno County Court.)

amounts already paid by her, and asked them to remove the machine. This they refused to do.

On May 25 the plaintiff brought this action, claiming [return] of instalments paid to date, as money paid for a consideration which had failed, by reason of the machine being unfit for the purpose for which it was intended. This was denied by the defendants in their defence. Later, the plaintiff delivered an amended claim alleging breach of an implied warranty that the machine was reasonably fit for the purpose for which it was intended. The defendants counterclaimed 71 pounds 18s 6d, the balance of the agreed price of the machine.

At the trial the county court judge gave judgment for the plaintiff on her claim for 70 pounds as damages for breach of warranty, and for the defendants on the counterclaim for 71 pounds 18s 6d, the balance of the price. He found that when the plaintiff signed the sales agreement she had not read and did not know the contents of that document, except the amount of the price and the terms of payment. She did not know that the document contained conditions relating to the terms of the contract, and that the defendants had not done all that was reasonably sufficient to give the plaintiff notice of the conditions; and that the machine was defective: and he held that there was an implied warranty of fitness which had been broken. For these reasons he held that the defendants were not entitled to rely upon the clause which excluded implied warranties. The defendants appealed.

[SCRUTTON L.J.:]

... As to the defence that no action would lie for breach of implied warranty, the defendants relied upon the following clause in the contract:

> This agreement contains all the terms and conditions under which I agree to purchase the machine specified above and any express or implied condition, statement, or warranty, statutory or otherwise not stated herein is hereby excluded.

A clause of that sort has been before the courts for some time. The first reported case in which it made its appearance seems to be *Wallis, Son and Wells v Pratt and Haynes*[1] where the exclusion clause mentioned only "warranty," and it was held that it did not exclude conditions. In the more recent case of *Andrews Bros (Bournemouth) Ltd v Singer & Co*[2] where the draftsman had put into the contract of sale a clause which excluded only implied conditions, warranties, and liabilities, it was held that the clause did not apply to an express term describing the arti-

cle, and did not exempt the seller from liability where he delivered an article of a different description. The clause here in question would seem to have been intended to go further than any of the previous clauses, and in order to avoid the result of these decisions, to include all terms denoting collateral stipulations.

The main question raised is whether that clause formed part of the contract. If it did, it clearly excluded any condition or warranty. In the course of the argument in the county court reference was made to the railway passenger and cloak-room ticket cases, such as *Richardson Spence & Co v Rowntree*[3]. In that case LORD HERSCHELL, LC, laid down the law applicable to these cases and stated the three questions which should be left to the jury. In the present case the learned judge asked himself the three questions appropriate to these cases, and in answering them has found as facts: (i) that the plaintiff knew that there was printed material on the document which she signed; (ii) that she did not know that the document contained conditions relating to the contract; and (iii) that the defendants did not do what was reasonably sufficient to bring these conditions to the notice of the plaintiff.

The present case is not a ticket case, and it is distinguishable from the ticket cases. In *Parker v South Eastern Rail Co*[4] MELLISH, LJ, laid down in a few sentences the law which is applicable to this case. He there said (2 CPD at p 421):

> In an ordinary case, where an action is brought on a written agreement which is signed by the defendant, the agreement is proved by proving his signature, and, in the absence of fraud, it is wholly immaterial that he has not read the agreement and does not know its contents.

Having said that, he goes on to deal with the ticket cases, where there is no signature to the contractual document, the document being simply handed by the one party to the other, and continues:

> The parties may, however, reduce their agreement into writing, so that the writing constitutes the sole evidence of the agreement, without signing it; but in that case there must be evidence independently of the agreement itself to prove that the defendant has assented to it. In that case, also, if it is proved that the defendant has assented to the writing constituting the agreement between the parties, it is, in the absence of fraud, immaterial that the defendant had not read the agreement and did not know its contents.

In cases in which the contract is contained in a railway ticket or other unsigned document, it is necessary to prove that an alleged party was aware, or ought to have been aware, of its terms and conditions. These cases have no application when the document has been signed. When a document containing contractual terms is signed, then, in the absence of fraud, or, I will add, misrepresentation, the party signing it is bound, and it is wholly immaterial whether he has read the document or not.

The plaintiff contended at the trial that she was induced by misrepresentation to sign the contract without knowing its terms, and that on that ground they are not binding upon her. The learned judge in his judgment makes no mention of that contention of the plaintiff, and he pronounces no finding as to the alleged misrepresentation. There is a further difficulty. Fraud is not mentioned in the pleadings, and I strongly object to deal with allegations of fraud where fraud is not expressly pleaded. I have read the evidence with care, and it contains no material upon which fraud could be found. The plaintiff, no doubt, alleged that the defendants' agent represented to her that the document which was given her to be signed was an order form, but, according to the defendants' evidence, no such statement was made to her by the agent. Moreover, whether the plaintiff was or was not told that the document was an order form, it was, in fact, an order form, and an order form is a contractual document. It may be either an acceptance or a proposal which may be accepted, but it always contains some contractual terms. There is no evidence that the plaintiff was induced to sign the contract by misrepresentation.

In this case the plaintiff has signed a document headed "sales agreement," which she admits had to do with an intended purchase and contained a clause excluding all conditions and warranties. That being so, the plaintiff, having put her signature to the document and not having been induced to do so by any fraud or misrepresentation, cannot be heard to say that she is not bound by the terms of the document because she has not read them.

The county court judge has given judgment for the defendants on the counterclaim for the balance of the price, 71 pounds 18s 6d. I do not see how he could have done that unless he found that the contract included the clause in small print providing that, if any instalment of the price should not be duly paid, all the remaining instalments should fall due for immediate payment. That judgment on the counterclaim must stand....

[MAUGHAM L.J.:]

I regret the decision to which I have come, but I am bound by legal rules and cannot decide the case on other considerations.

The material question is whether or not there was a contract in writing between the plaintiff and the defendants in the terms contained in the document which she signed. In the case of a formal contract between seller and buyer, such as a deed, there is a presumption which puts it beyond doubt that the parties intended that the document should contain the terms of their contract. This document is not a formal instrument of that character, yet, in my opinion, having been signed, it may well constitute a contract in writing....

I deal with this case on the footing that when the order confirmation was signed by the defendants confirming the order form which had been signed by the plaintiff, there was then a signed contract in writing between the parties. If that is so, then, subject to certain contingencies, there is no doubt that it was wholly immaterial whether the plaintiff read the small print or not. There can be no dispute as to the soundness in law of the statement of MELLISH, LJ, in *Parker v South Eastern Rail Co*[4] which has been read by my learned brother, to the effect that where a party has signed a written agreement it is immaterial to the question of his liability under it that he has not read it and does not know its contents. That is true in any case in which the agreement is held to be an agreement in writing.

There are, however, two possibilities to be kept in view. The first is that it might be proved that the document, though signed by the plaintiff, was signed in circumstances which made it not her act. That is known as the case of "non est factum." I do not think it is necessary to add anything to what SCRUTTON, LJ, has already said about that. The written document admittedly related to the purchase of the machine by the plaintiff. Even if she was told that it was an order form, she could not be heard to say that it did not affect her because she did not know its contents.

Another possibility is that the plaintiff might have been induced to sign the document by misrepresentation. She contended that she was so induced to sign the document inasmuch as (i) she was assured that it was an order form, (ii) that at the time when she signed it she knew nothing of the conditions which it contained. The second of these contentions is unavailing by reason of the fact that the document was in writing signed by the plaintiff. As to the first contention it is true that the document was an order form. But, further, if the statement that it was an order form could be treated as a representation that it contained no clause expressly excluding all conditions and warranties, the answer would be that there is no evidence to prove that that statement was made by or on behalf of the defendants.

In this case it is, in my view, an irrelevant circumstance that the plaintiff did not read, or hear of, the parts of the sales document which are in small print, and that document should have effect accord-ing to its terms. I may add, however, that I could wish that the contract had been in a simpler and more usual form. It is unfortunate that the important clause excluding conditions and warranties is in such small print. I also think that the order confirmation form should have contained an express statement to the effect that it was exclusive of all conditions and warranties. I agree that the appeal should be allowed.

Appeal allowed.

(h) *Thornton v. Shoe Lane Parking Limited*†

U.K. Court of Appeal

[LORD DENNING, The Master of the Rolls:]

In 1964 Mr. Thornton, who was a free-lance trumpeter of the highest quality, had an engagement with the B.B.C. at Farringdon Hall. He drove to the City in his motorcar and went to park it at a multi-storey automatic car park. It had only been open a few months. He had never gone there before. There was a notice on the outside headed "Shoe Lane Parking". It gave the parking charges: "5/ for two hours; 7/6d. for three hours", and so forth; and at the bottoms "All cars parked at owner's risk". Mr. Thornton drove up to the entrance. There was not a man in attendance. There was a traffic light which showed red. As he drove in and got to the appropriate place, the traffic light turned green and a ticket was pushed out from the machine. Mr. Thornton took it. He drove on into the garage. The motorcar was taken up by mechanical means to a floor above. Mr. Thornton left it there and went off to keep his appointment with the B.B.C. Three hours later Mr. Thornton came back. He went to the office and paid the charge for the time the car was there. His car was brought down from the upper floor. He went to put his belongings into the boot of the car. But unfortunately there was an accident. Mr. Thornton was severely injured. The Judge has found it was half his own fault, but half the fault of the Shoe Lane Parking Ltd. The Judge awarded him £3,637 6s. 11d.

On this appeal the garage company do not contest the Judge's findings about the accident. They acknowledge that they were at fault, but they claim that they are protected by some exempting conditions. They rely on the ticket which was issued to Mr. Thornton by the machine. They say that it was a contractual document and that it incorporated a condition which exempts them from liability to him. The ticket was headed "Shoe Lane Parking". Just below there was a "box" in which was automatically recorded the time when the car went into the garage. There was a notice alongside: "Please present this ticket to cashier to claim your car". Just below the time, there was some small print in the left hand corner which said: "This ticket is issued subject to the conditions of issue as displayed on the premises". That is all.

Mr. Thornton says he looked at the ticket to see the time on it, and put it in his pocket. He could see there was printing on the ticket, but he did not read it. He only read the time. He did not read the words which said that the ticket was issued subject to the conditions as displayed on the premises.

If Mr. Thornton had read those words on the ticket and had looked round the premises to see where the conditions were displayed, he would have had to have driven his car on into the garage and walked round. Then he would have found, on a pillar opposite the ticket machine, a set of printed con-

---

† [1971] 2 QB 163.

ditions in a panel. He would also have found, in the paying office (to be visited when coming back for the car) two more panels containing the printed conditions. If he had the time to read the conditions — it would take him a very considerable time — he would read this.

> CONDITIONS: The following are the conditions upon which alone motor vehicles are accepted for parking:
>
> 1. The customer agrees to pay the charges of Shoe Lane Parking Developments Limited, and so on.
>
> 2. The Customer is deemed to be fully insured at all times against all risks (including, without prejudice to the generality of the foregoing, fire, damage and theft, whether due to the negligence of others or not) and the Company shall not be responsible or liable for any loss or misdelivery of or damage of whatever kind to the Customer's motor vehicle, or any articles carried therein or thereon or of or to any accessories carried thereon or therein or injury to the Customer or any other person occurring; when the Customer's motor vehicle is in the Parking Building howsoever that loss, misdelivery, damage or injury shall be caused; and it is agreed and understood that the Customer's motor vehicle is parked and permitted by the Company to be parked in the Parking Building in accordance with this Licence entirely at the Customer's risk.

There is a lot more. I have only read about one-tenth of the conditions. The important thing to notice is that the Company seeks by this condition to exempt themselves from liability, not only to damage to the car, but also for injury to the customer howsoever caused. The condition talks about insurance. It is well known that the customer is usually insured against damage to the car. But he is not insured against damage to himself. If the condition is incorporated into the contract of parking, it means that Mr. Thornton will be unable to recover any damages for his personal injuries which were caused by the negligence of the company.

We have been referred to the ticket cases of former times from *Parker v. The South Eastern Railway Co.* (1877 2 C.P.D. 416) to *McCutcheon v. MacBrayne Ltd.* (1964 1 W.L.R. 125). They were concerned with railways, steamships and cloakrooms where booking clerks issued tickets to customers who took them away without reading them. In those cases the issue of the ticket was regarded as an <u>offer</u> by the company. If the customer took it and retained it without objection, his act was regarded as an <u>acceptance</u> of the offer: see *Watkins v. Rymill* (1883) 10 Q.B.D. at page 188; *Thompson v. L.M.S.*, (1930) 1 K.B. at page 47. These cases were based on the theory that the customer, on being handed the ticket, could refuse it and decline to enter into a contract on those terms. He could ask for his money back. That theory was, of course, a fiction. No customer in a thousand ever read the conditions. If he had stopped to do so, he would have missed the train or the boat.

None of those cases has any application to a ticket which is issued by an automatic machine. The customer pays his money and gets a ticket. He cannot refuse it. He cannot get his money back. He may protest to the machine, even swear at it. But it will remain unmoved. He is committed beyond recall. He was committed at the very moment when he put his money into the machine. The contract was concluded at that time. It can be translated into offer and acceptance in this way: the offer is made when the proprietor of the machine holds it out as being ready to receive the money. The acceptance takes place when the customer puts his money into the slot. The terms of the offer are contained in the notice placed on or near the machine stating what is offered for the money. The customer is bound by those terms as long as they are sufficiently brought to his notice before-hand, but not otherwise. He is not bound by the terms printed on the ticket if they differ from the notice, because the ticket comes too late. The contract has already been made: see *Olley v. Marlborough Court* (1949 1 K.B. 532). The ticket is no more than a voucher or receipt for the money that has been paid (as in the deckchair case, *Chapelton v. Barry U.D.C.* ... 1940 1 K.B. 532), on terms which have been offered and accepted before the ticket is issued.

In the present case the offer was contained in the notice at the entrance giving the charges for garaging and saying "at owner's risk", i.e. at the risk of the owner so far as damage to the car was concerned. The offer was accepted when Mr. Thornton drove up to the entrance and, by the movement of his car, turned the light from red to green, and the ticket was thrust at him. The contract was then concluded, and it could not be altered by any words printed on the ticket itself. In particular, it could not be altered so as to exempt the company from liability for personal injury due to their negligence.

Assuming, however, that an automatic machine is a booking clerk in disguise — so that the old fashioned ticket cases still apply to it. We then have to go back to the three questions put by Lord Justice Mellish in *Parker v. The South Eastern Railway Co.* (1877) 2 C.P.D. at page 423, subject to this qualification: Lord Justice Mellish used the word "conditions" in the plural, whereas it would be more apt to use the word "condition" in the singular, as indeed the Lord Justice himself did on the next page. After all, the only condition that matters for this purpose is the exempting condition. It is no use telling the customer that the ticket is issued subject to some "conditions" or other, without more: for he may reasonably regard "conditions" in general as merely regulatory, and not as taking away his rights, unless the exempting condition is drawn specifically to his attention. (Alternatively, if the plural "conditions" is used, it would be better prefaced with the word "exempting", because the exempting conditions are the only conditions that matter for this purpose.) Telescoping the three questions, they come to this: the customer is bound by the exempting condition if he knows that the ticket is issued subject to it; or, if the company did what was reasonably sufficient to give him notice of it.

Mr. Machin admitted here that the company did not do what was reasonably sufficient to give Mr. Thornton notice of the exempting condition. That admission was properly made. I do not pause to inquire whether the exempting condition is void for unreasonableness. All I say is that it is so wide and so destructive of rights that the Court should not hold any man bound by it unless it is drawn to his attention in the most explicit way. It is an instance of what I had in mind in *Spurling v. Bradshaw.* 1956, 1 W.L.R. at page 466. In order to give sufficient notice, it would need to be printed in red ink with a red hand pointing to it — or something equally startling.

But, although reasonable notice of it was not given, Mr. Machin said that this case came within the second question propounded by Lord Justice Mellish, namely that Mr. Thornton "knew or believed that the writing contained conditions". There was no finding to that effect. The burden was on the company to prove it, and they did not do so. Certainly there was no evidence that Mr. Thornton knew of this exempting condition. He is not, therefore, bound by it.

Mr. Machin relied on a case in this Court last year — *Mendelssohn v. Normand Ltd.* (1970 1 K.B. 177). Mr. Mendelssohn parked his car in the Cumberland Garage at Marble Arch, and was given a ticket which contained an exempting condition. There was no discussion as to whether the condition formed part of the contract. It was conceded that it did. That is shown by the report in the Law Reports at page 180. Yet the garage company were not entitled to rely on the exempting condition for the reasons there given.

That case does not touch the present, where the whole question is whether the exempting condition formed part of the contract. I do not think it did. Mr. Thornton did not know of the condition, and the company did not do what was reasonably sufficient to give him notice of it.

I do not think the garage company can escape liability by reason of the exemption condition. I would, therefore, dismiss the appeal.

[Sir GORDON WILLMER]

I have reached the same conclusion, and there is very little for me to add. It seems to me that the really distinguishing feature of this case is the fact that the ticket on which reliance is placed was issued out of an automatic machine. I think it is right to say — at any rate, it is the fact so far as the cases that have been called to our attention are concerned — that in all the previous so-called "ticket cases" the ticket has been proffered by a human hand, and there has always been at least the notional opportunity for the customer to say — if he did not like the conditions — "I do not like your conditions: I will not have this ticket." But in the case of a ticket which is proffered by an automatic machine, there is something quite irrevocable about the process. There can be no *locus poenitentiae.* I do not propose to say any more upon the difficult question which has been raised as to the precise moment when a contract was concluded in this case; but at least it seems to me that any attempt to introduce conditions after the irrevocable step has been taken of causing the machine to operate must be doomed to failure. It may be that those who operate garages of this nature, as well as those who install other types of automatic machines, should give their attention to this problem. But it seems to me that the learned Judge below was on the right track when he said, towards the end of his judgment, that in this sort of case, if you do desire to impose upon your customers stringent conditions such as these, the least you can do is to post a prominent notice at the entrance to the premises, warning your customers that there are conditions which will apply. So far as the rest of the case is concerned, I agree with what has been said by my Lords and do not wish to add anything further.

Appeal dismissed with costs.

(i) *Tilden Rent-A-Car Co. v. Clendenning*†

Ontario Court of Appeal

[DUBIN J.A.:]

Upon his arrival at Vancouver airport, Mr. Clendenning, a resident of Woodstock, Ontario, attended upon the office of Tilden Rent-A-Car Company for the purpose of renting a car while he was in Vancouver. He was an experienced traveller and had used Tilden Rent-A-Car Company on many prior occasions. He provided the clerk employed at the airport office of Tilden Rent-A-Car Company with the minimum information which was asked of him, and produced his American Express credit card. He was asked by the clerk whether he desired additional coverage, and, as was his practice, he said "yes". A contract was submitted to him for his signature, which he signed in the presence of the clerk, and he returned the contract to her. She placed his copy of it in an envelope and gave him the keys to the car. He then placed the contract in the glove compartment of the vehicle. He did not read the terms of the contract before signing it, as was readily apparent to the clerk, and in fact he did not read the contract until this litigation was commenced, nor had he read a copy of a similar contract on any prior occasion.

The issue on the appeal is whether the defendant is liable for the damage caused to the automobile while being driven by him by reason of the exclusionary provisions which appear in the contract.

On the front of the contract are two relevant clauses set forth in box form. They are as follows:

15 COLLISION DAMAGE WAIVER BY CUSTOMERS INITIALS "J.C."

In consideration of the payment of $2.00 per day customers liability for damage to rented vehicle including windshield is limited to NIL. But notwithstanding payment of said fee, customer shall be fully liable for all collision damage if vehicle is used, operated or driven in violation of any of the provisions of this rental agreement or off highways serviced by federal, provincial, or municipal governments, and for all damages to vehicle by striking overhead objects.

16 I, the undersigned have read and received a copy of above and reverse side of this contract

Signature of customer or employee of customer
"John T. Clendenning"
(Emphasis added.)

On the back of the contract in particularly small type and so faint in the customer's copy as to be hardly legible, there are a series of conditions, the relevant ones being as follows:

6. The customer agrees not to use the vehicle in violation of any law, ordinance, rule or regulation of any public authority.

7. The customer agrees that the vehicle will not be operated:
(a) By any person who has drunk or consumed any intoxicating liquor, whatever be the quantity, or who is under the influence of drugs or narcotics;

The rented vehicle was damaged while being driven by Mr. Clendenning in Vancouver. His evidence at trial, which was accepted by the trial Judge, was to the effect that in endeavouring to avoid a collision with another vehicle and acting out of a sudden emergency, he drove the car into a pole. He stated that although he had pleaded guilty to a charge of driving while impaired in Vancouver, he did so on the advice of counsel, and at the time of the impact he was capable of the proper control of the motor vehicle. This evidence was also accepted by the trial Judge.

Mr. Clendenning testified that on earlier occasions when he had inquired as to what added coverage he would receive for the payment of $2 per day, he had been advised that "such payment provided full non-deductible coverage". It is to be observed that the portion of the contract reproduced above does provide that "In consideration of the payment of $2.00 per day customers liability for damage to rented vehicle including windshield is limited to NIL".

A witness called on behalf of the plaintiff gave evidence as to the instructions given to its employees as to what was to be said by them to their customers about the conditions in the contract. He stated that unless inquiries were made, nothing was to be

---

† (1978), 18 O.R. (2d) 601.

said by its clerks to the customer with respect to the exclusionary conditions. He went on to state that if inquiries were made, the clerks were instructed to advise the customer that by the payment of the $2 additional fee the customer had complete coverage "unless he were intoxicated, or unless he committed an offence under the Criminal Code such as intoxication".

Mr. Clendenning acknowledged that he had assumed, either by what had been told to him in the past or otherwise, that he would not be responsible for any damage to the vehicle on payment of the extra premium unless such damage was caused by reason of his being so intoxicated as to be incapable of the proper control of the vehicle, a provision with which he was familiar as being a statutory provision in his own insurance contract.

The provisions fastening liability for damage to the vehicle on the hirer, as contained in the clauses hereinbefore referred to, are completely inconsistent with the express terms which purport to provide complete coverage for damage to the vehicle in exchange for the additional premium. It is to be noted, for example, that if the driver of the vehicle exceeded the speed-limit even by one mile per hour, or parked the vehicle in a no-parking area, or even had one glass of wine or one bottle of beer, the contract purports to make the hirer completely responsible for all damage to the vehicle. Indeed, if the vehicle at the time of any damage to it was being driven off a federal, provincial or municipal highway, such as a shopping plaza for instance, the hirer purportedly would be responsible for all damage to the vehicle.

Mr. Clendenning stated that if he had known of the full terms of the written instrument, he would not have entered into such a contract. Having regard to the findings made by the trial Judge, it is apparent that Mr. Clendenning had not in fact acquiesced to such terms.

It was urged that the rights of the parties were governed by what has come to be known as "the rule in *L'Estrange v. F. Graucob, Ltd.*", [1934] 2 K.B. 394, and in particular the following portion from the judgment of Scrutton, L.J., at p. 403:

> In cases in which the contract is contained in a railway ticket or other unsigned document, it is necessary to prove that an alleged party was aware, or ought to have been aware, of its terms and conditions. These cases have no application when the document has been signed. When a document containing contractual terms is signed, then, in the absence of fraud, or, I will add, misrepresentation, the party signing it is bound, and

it is wholly immaterial whether he has read the document or not. (Emphasis added.)

In the same case Maugham, L.J., added at p. 406:

> There can be no dispute as to the soundness in law of the statement of Mellish L.J. in *Parker v. South Eastern Ry. Co.*, 2 C.P.D. 416, 421, which has been read by my learned brother, to the effect that where a party has signed a written agreement it is immaterial to the question of his liability under it that he has not read it and does not know its contents. That is true in any case in which the agreement is held to be an agreement in writing.
>
> There are, however, two possibilities to be kept in view. The first is that it might be proved that the document, though signed by the plaintiff, was signed in circumstances which made it not her act. That is known as the case of Non est factum.

And at p. 407:

> Another possibility is that the plaintiff might have been induced to sign the document by misrepresentation.

Consensus ad idem is as much a part of the law of written contracts as it is of oral contracts. The signature to a contract is only one way of manifesting assent to contractual terms. However, in the case of *L'Estrange v. F. Graucob, Ltd.*, there was in fact no *consensus ad idem*. Miss L'Estrange was a proprietor of a cafe. Two salesmen of the defendant company persuaded her to order a cigarette machine to be sold to her by their employer. They produced an order form which Miss L'Estrange signed without reading all of its terms. Amongst the many clauses in the document signed by her, there was included a paragraph, with respect to which she was completely unaware, which stated "any express or implied condition, statement, or warranty, statutory or otherwise not stated herein is hereby excluded". In her action against the company she alleged that the article sold to her was unfit for the purposes for which it was sold and contrary to the Sale of Goods Act. The company successfully defended on the basis of that exemption clause.

Although the subject of critical analysis by learned authors (see, for example, J. R. Spencer, "Signature, Consent, and the Rule in *L'Estrange v. Graucob*", [1973] C.L.J. 104), the case has survived, and it is now said that it applies to all contracts irrespective of the circumstances under which they are entered into, if they are signed by the party who seeks to escape their provisions.

Thus, it was submitted that the ticket cases, which in the circumstances of this case would afford a ready defence for the hirer of the automobile, are not applicable.

As is pointed out in Waddams, The Law of Contracts, at p. 191:

> From the 19th century until recent times an extraordinary status has been accorded to the signed document that will be seen in retrospect, it is suggested, to have been excessive.

The justification for the rule in *L'Estrange v. F. Graucob, Ltd.*, appears to have been founded upon the objective theory of contracts, by which means parties are bound to a contract in writing by measuring their conduct by outward appearance rather than what the parties inwardly meant to decide. This, in turn, stems from the classic statement of Blackburn, J., in *Smith v. Hughes* (1871), L.R. 6 Q.B. 597 at p. 607:

> I apprehend that if one of the parties intends to make a contract on one set of terms, and the other intends to make a contract on another set of terms, or, as it is sometimes expressed, if the parties are not ad idem, there is no contract, unless the circumstances are such as to preclude one of the parties from denying that he has agreed to the terms of the other. The rule of law is that stated in *Freeman v. Cooke* (1848), 2 Ex. 654, 154 E.R. 652. If, whatever a man's real intention may be, he so conducts himself that a reasonable man would believe that he was assenting to the terms proposed by the other party, and that other party upon that belief enters into the contract with him, the man thus conducting himself would be equally bound as if he had intended to agree to the other party's terms. (Emphasis added.)

Even accepting the objective theory to determine whether Mr. Clendenning had entered into a contract which included all the terms of the written instrument, it is to be observed that an essential part of that test is whether the other party entered into the contract in the belief that Mr. Clendenning was assenting to all such terms. In the instant case, it was apparent to the employee of Tilden-Rent-A-Car that Mr. Clendenning had not in fact read the document in its entirety before he signed it. It follows under such circumstances that Tilden-Rent-A-Car cannot rely on provisions of the contract which it had no reason to believe were being assented to by the other contracting party.

As stated in Waddams, The Law of Contracts, p. 191:

One who signs a written document cannot complain if the other party reasonably relies on the signature as a manifestation of assent to the contents, or ascribes to words he uses their reasonable meaning. But the other side of the same coin is that only a reasonable expectation will be protected. If the party seeking to enforce the document knew or had reason to know of the other's mistake the document should not be enforced.

In ordinary commercial practice where there is frequently a sense of formality in the transaction, and where there is a full opportunity for the parties to consider the terms of the proposed contract submitted for signature, it might well be safe to assume that the party who attaches his signature to the contract intends by so doing to acknowledge his acquiescence to its terms, and that the other party entered into the contract upon that belief. This can hardly be said, however, where the contract is entered into in circumstances such as were present in this case.

A transaction, such as this one, is invariably carried out in a hurried, informal manner. The speed with which the transaction is completed is said to be one of the attractive features of the services provided.

The clauses relied on in this case, as I have already stated, are inconsistent with the over-all purpose for which the contract is entered into by the hirer. Under such circumstances, something more should be done by the party submitting the contract for signature than merely handing it over to be signed.

In an analogous situation Lord Devlin in the case of *McCutcheon v. David MacBrayne Ltd.*, [1964] 1 W.L.R. 125, commented as follows, at pp. 132–4:

> It would be a strangely generous set of conditions in which the persistent reader, after wading through the verbiage, could not find something to protect the carrier against "any loss ... wheresoever or whensoever occurring"; and condition 19 by itself is enough to absolve the respondents several times over for all their negligence. It is conceded that if the form had been signed as usual, the appellant would have had no case. But, by a stroke of ill luck for the respondents, it was upon this day of all days that they omitted to get Mr. McSporran to sign the conditions. What difference does that make?
>
> If it were possible for your Lordships to escape from the world of make-believe which the law has created into the real world in which transactions of this sort are actually done, the answer would be short and simple. It should make no difference whatever. This sort of document is not meant to be read, still less to be

understood. Its signature is in truth about as significant as a handshake that marks the formal conclusion of a bargain.

   ... Unless your Lordships are to disapprove the decision of the Court of Appeal in *L'Estrange v. F. Graucob Ltd.*, [1934] 2 K.B. 394, C.A. — and there has been no suggestion in this case that you should — the law is clear ... that a signature to a contract is conclusive. (Emphasis added.)

An analysis of the Canadian cases, however, indicates that the approach in this country has not been so rigid. In the case of *Colonial Investment Co. of Winnipeg, Man. v. Borland*, [1911] 1 W.W.R. 171 at p. 189, 19 W.L.R. 588, 5 Alta. L.R. at p. 72 [affirmed 6 D.L.R. 21, 2 W.W.R. 960, 22 W.L.R. 145, 5 Alta. L.R. 71], Beck, J., set forth the following propositions:

Consensus ad idem is essential to the creation of a contract, whether oral, in writing or under seal, subject to this, that as between the immediate parties (and merely voluntary assigns) apparent — as distinguished from real — consent will on the ground of estoppel effect a binding obligation unless the party denying the obligation proves:

(1) That the other party knew at the time of the making of the alleged contract that the mind of the denying party did not accompany the expression of his consent; or

(2) Such facts and circumstances as show that it was not reasonable and natural for the other party to suppose that the denying party was giving his real consent and he did not in fact give it;

In commenting on the *Colonial Investment Co. of Winnipeg v. Borland* case, Spencer, in the article above cited, observes at p. 121:

It is instructive to compare a Canadian approach to the problem of confusing documents which are signed but not fully understood.

And at p. 122 the author concludes his article with the following analysis:

Policy considerations, but of different kinds, no doubt lay behind both the Canadian and the English approaches to this problem. The Canadian court was impressed by the abuses which would result — and, in England, have resulted — from enabling companies to hold ignorant signatories to the letter of sweeping exemption clauses contained in contracts in standard form. The English courts, however, were much more impressed with the danger of furnishing an easy line of defence by which liars could evade contractual liabilities freely assumed. It would be very dangerous to allow a man over the age of legal infancy to escape from the legal effect of a document he has, after reading it, signed, in the absence of any express misrepresentation by the other party of that legal effect. Forty years later, most lawyers would admit that the English courts made a bad choice between two evils.

The significance of the circumstances under which a contract is entered into is noted by Taschereau, J., in *Provident Savings Life Ass'ce Society of New York v. Mowat et al.* (1902), 32 S.C.R. 147, as follows at p. 162:

As remarked by Mr. Justice Maclennan [27 O.A.R. 675]:

The case of a formal instrument like the present, prepared and executed, after a long negotiation, and correspondence delivered and accepted, and acted upon for years, is wholly different from the cases relating to railways and steamship and cloak-room tickets, in which it has been held that conditions qualifying the principal contract of carriage or bailment, not sufficiently brought to the attention of the passenger or bailor are not binding upon him. Such contracts are usually made in moments of more or less haste and confusion and stand by themselves.

I see no real distinction in contracts such as these, where the signature by itself does not truly represent an acquiescence of unusual and onerous terms which are inconsistent with the true object of the contract, and the ticket cases....

In commenting on [various related cases].... Professor Waddams makes the following observations, at pp. 590–1:

These cases suggest that there is a special onus on the supplier to point out any terms in a printed form which differ from what the consumer might reasonably expect. If he fails to do so, he will be guilty of a "misrepresentation by omission", and the court will strike down clauses which "differ from the ordinary understanding of mankind" or (and sometimes this is the same thing) clauses which are "unreasonable or oppressive". If this principle is accepted, the rule about written documents might be restated as follows: the signer is bound by the terms of the document if, and only if, the other party believes on reasonable grounds that those terms truly express the signer's intention. This principle retains the role of signed documents as a means of protecting reasonable expectations; what it does not allow is that a party should rely on a printed document to contradict what he knows, or ought to know, is the understanding of the other party. Again this principle seems to be particularly applicable in situations involving the distribution of goods and services to consumers, though it is by no means confined to such situations. In modern commercial practice, many standard form printed documents are signed without being read or understood. In many cases the parties seeking to rely on the terms of the contract know or ought to know that the signature of a party to the contract does not represent the true intention of the signer, and that the party signing is unaware of the stringent and onerous provisions which the standard form contains. Under such circumstances, I am of the opinion that the party seeking to rely on such terms should not be able to do so in the absence of first having taken reasonable measures to draw such terms to the attention of the other party, and, in the absence of such reasonable measures, it is not necessary for the party denying knowledge of such terms to prove either fraud, misrepresentation or non est factum.

In the case at bar, Tilden Rent-A-Car took no steps to alert Mr. Clendenning to the onerous provisions in the standard form of contract presented by it. The clerk could not help but have known that Mr. Clendenning had not in fact read the contract before signing it. Indeed the form of the contract itself with the important provisions on the reverse side and in very small type would discourage even the most cautious customer from endeavouring to read and understand it. Mr. Clendenning was in fact unaware of the exempting provisions. Under such circumstances, it was not open to Tilden Rent-A-Car to rely on those clauses, and it was not incumbent

on Mr. Clendenning to establish fraud, misrepresentation or non est factum. Having paid the premium, he was not liable for any damage to the vehicle while being driven by him.

As Lord Denning stated in *Neuchatel Asphalte Co. Ltd. v. Barnett*, [1957] 1 W.L.R. 356 at p. 360: "We do not allow printed forms to be made a trap for the unwary."

In this case the trial Judge held that "the rule in *L'Estrange v. Graucob*" governed. He dismissed the action, however, on the ground that Tilden Rent-A-Car had by their prior oral representations misrepresented the terms of the contract. He imputed into the contract the assumption of Mr. Clendenning that by the payment of the premium he was "provided full non-deductible coverage unless at the time of the damage he was operating the automobile while under the influence of intoxicating liquor to such an extent as to be for the time incapable of the proper control of the automobile". Having found that Mr. Clendenning had not breached such a provision, the action was dismissed.

For the reasons already expressed, I do not think that in the circumstances of this case "the rule in *L'Estrange v. Graucob*" governed, and it was not incumbent upon Mr. Clendenning to prove misrepresentation.

In any event, if "the rule *in L'Estrange v. Graucob*" were applicable, it was in error, in my respectful opinion, to impute into the contract a provision which Tilden Rent-A-Car had not in fact represented as being a term of the contract.

... In the result, therefore, I would dismiss the appeal with costs.

(j) *Tercon Contractors Ltd. v. British Columbia (Transportation and Highways)*†

Supreme Court of Canada

[CROMWELL J. (for the majority of the court on the application of the exclusion clause):]

[Note: In the result, the majority of the judges concurred with Cromwell J. that BC was liable for damages for breach of contract. Cromwell J. accepted the legal framework for construction of exclusionary clauses as set out by Binnie J. but disagreed as to the application of the exclusionary clause in this contract. In the view of Binnie J. writ-

---

† 2010 SCC 4.

ing for the minority on this point, the exclusion clause did cover the situation, was not unreasonable, and protected BC from liability.]

. . . .

II. BRIEF OVERVIEW OF THE FACTS

[9] I will have to set out more factual detail as part of my analysis. For now, a very brief summary will suffice. In 2000, the Ministry of Transportation and Highways (the "Province") issued a request for expressions of interest ("RFEI") for designing and building a highway in northwestern British Columbia. Six teams made submissions, including Tercon and Brentwood Enterprises Ltd. Later that year, the Province informed the six proponents that it now intended to design the highway itself and would issue a request for proposals ("RFP") for its construction.

[10] The RFP was formally issued on January 15, 2001. Under its terms, only the six original proponents were eligible to submit a proposal. The RFP also included a clause excluding all claims for damages "as a result of participating in this RFP" (s. 2:10).

[11] Unable to submit a competitive bid on its own, Brentwood teamed up with Emil Anderson Construction Co. ("EAC"), which was not a qualified bidder, and together they submitted a bid in Brentwood's name. Brentwood and Tercon were the two shortlisted proponents and the Ministry ultimately selected Brentwood as the preferred proponent.

[12] Tercon brought an action seeking damages, alleging that the Ministry had considered and accepted an ineligible bid and that but for that breach, it would have been awarded the contract. The trial judge agreed and awarded roughly $3.5 million in damages and prejudgment interest. As noted, the Court of Appeal reversed and Tercon appeals by leave of the Court.

III. ISSUES

[13] The issues for decision are whether the trial judge erred in finding that:

1. the Province breached the tendering contract by entertaining a bid from an ineligible bidder.
2. the exclusion clause does not bar the appellant's claim for damages for the breaches of the tendering contract found by the trial judge.

IV. ANALYSIS

. . . .

B. The Exclusion Clause

1. Introduction

[60] As noted, the RFP includes an exclusion clause which reads as follows:

> **2.10** ... Except as expressly and specifically permitted in these Instructions to Proponents, <u>no Proponent shall have any claim for compensation of any kind whatsoever, as a result of participating in this RFP</u>, and by submitting a Proposal each Proponent shall be deemed to have agreed that it has no claim. [Emphasis added.]

[61] The trial judge held that as a matter of construction, the clause did not bar recovery for the breaches she had found. The clause, in her view, was ambiguous and, applying the *contra proferentem* principle, she resolved the ambiguity in Tercon's favour. She also found that the Province's breach was fundamental and that it was not fair or reasonable to enforce the exclusion clause in light of the nature of the Province's breach. The Province contends that the judge erred both with respect to the construction of the clause and her application of the doctrine of fundamental breach.

[62] On the issue of fundamental breach in relation to exclusion clauses, my view is that the time has come to lay this doctrine to rest, as Dickson C.J. was inclined to do more than 20 years ago: *Hunter Engineering Co. v. Syncrude Canada Ltd.*, [1989] 1 S.C.R. 426, at p. 462. I agree with the analytical approach that should be followed when tackling an issue relating to the applicability of an exclusion clause set out by my colleague Binnie J. However, I respectfully do not agree with him on the question of the proper interpretation of the clause in issue here. In my view, the clause does not exclude Tercon's claim for damages, and even if I am wrong about that, the clause is at best ambiguous and should be construed *contra proferentem* as the trial judge held. As a result of my conclusion on the interpretation issue, I do not have to go on to apply the rest of the analytical framework set out by Binnie J.

[63] In my view, the exclusion clause does not cover the Province's breaches in this case. The RFP process put in place by the Province was premised on a closed list of bidders; a contest with an ineligible bidder was not part of the RFP process and was in fact expressly precluded by its terms. A "Contract A"

could not arise as a result of submission of a bid from any other party. However, as a result of how the Province proceeded, the very premise of its own RFP process was missing, and the work was awarded to a party who could not be a participant in the RFP process. That is what Tercon is complaining about. Tercon's claim is not barred by the exclusion clause because the clause only applies to claims arising "as a result of participating in [the] RFP", not to claims resulting from the participation of other, ineligible parties. Moreover, the words of this exclusion clause, in my view, are not effective to limit liability for breach of the Province's implied duty of fairness to bidders. I will explain my conclusion by turning first to a brief account of the key legal principles and then to the facts of the case.

2. *Legal Principles*

[64] The key principle of contractual interpretation here is that the words of one provision must not be read in isolation but should be considered in harmony with the rest of the contract and in light of its purposes and commercial context....

[65] In a similar way, it is necessary in the present case to consider the exclusion clause in the RFP in light of its purposes and commercial context as well as of its overall terms. The question is whether the exclusion of compensation for claims resulting from "participating in this RFP", properly interpreted, excludes liability for the Province having unfairly considered a bid from a bidder who was not supposed to have been participating in the RFP process at all.

3. *Application to this Case*

[66] Having regard to both the text of the clause in its broader context and to the purposes and commercial context of the RFP, my view is that this claim does not fall within the terms of the exclusion clause.

[67] To begin, it is helpful to recall that in interpreting tendering contracts, the Court has been careful to consider the special commercial context of tendering. Effective tendering ultimately depends on the integrity and business efficacy of the tendering process: see, e. g., *Martel*, at para. 88; *M.J.B.*, at para. 41; *Double N Earthmovers Ltd.*, at para. 106. As Iacobucci and Major JJ. put it in *Martel*, at para. 116, "it is imperative that all bidders be treated on an equal footing.... Parties should at the very least be confident that their initial bids will not be skewed by some underlying advantage in the drafting of the

call for tenders conferred upon only one potential bidder".

. . . .

[69] One aspect that is generally seen as contributing to the integrity and business efficacy of the tendering process is the requirement that only compliant bids be considered. As noted earlier, such a requirement has often been implied because, as the Court said in *M.J.B.*, it makes little sense to think that a bidder would comply with the bidding process if the owner could circumscribe it by accepting a non-compliant bid. Respectfully, it seems to me to make even less sense to think that eligible bidders would participate in the RFP if the Province could avoid liability for ignoring an express term concerning eligibility to bid on which the entire RFP was premised and which was mandated by the statutorily approved process.

[70] The closed list of bidders was the foundation of this RFP and there were important competitive advantages to a bidder who could side-step that limitation. Thus, it seems to me that both the integrity and the business efficacy of the tendering process support an interpretation that would allow the exclusion clause to operate compatibly with the eligibility limitations that were at the very root of the RFP.

. . . .

[75] The Province would have us interpret the phrase excluding compensation "as a result of participating in this RFP" to mean that compensation is excluded that results from "submitting a Proposal". However, that interpretation is not consistent with the wording of the clause as a whole. The clause concludes with the phrase that "by submitting a Proposal each Proponent shall be deemed to have agreed that it has no claim". If the phrases "participating in this RFP" and "submitting a Proposal" were intended to mean the same thing, it is hard to understand why different words were used in the same short clause to express the same idea. The fact that the Minister had approved a closed list of participants strengthens the usual inference that the use of different words was deliberate so as not to exclude compensation for a departure from that basic eligibility requirement.

. . . .

[79] If I am wrong about my interpretation of the clause, I would hold, as did the trial judge, that its language is at least ambiguous. If, as the Province

contends, the phrase "participating in this RFP" could reasonably mean "submitting a Proposal", that phrase could also reasonably mean "competing against the other eligible participants". Any ambiguity in the context of this contract requires that the clause be interpreted against the Province and in favour of Tercon under the principle *contra proferentem*: see, e.g. *Hillis Oil and Sales Ltd. v. Wynn's Canada, Ltd.*, [1986] 1 S.C.R. 57, at pp. 68–69. Following this approach, the clause would not apply to bar Tercon's damages claim.

V.   DISPOSITION

[80] I conclude that the judge did not err in finding that the Province breached the tendering contract or in finding that Tercon's remedy in damages for that breach was not precluded by the exclusion clause in the contract. I would therefore allow the appeal, set aside the order of the Court of Appeal and restore the judgment of the trial judge. The parties advise that the question of costs has been resolved between them and that therefore no order in relation to costs is required.

[Binnie J. (for McLachlin C.J., Abella and Rothstein JJ.):]

[81] The important legal issue raised by this appeal is whether, and in what circumstances, a court will deny a defendant contract breaker the benefit of an exclusion of liability clause to which the innocent party, not being under any sort of disability, has agreed. Traditionally, this has involved consideration of what is known as the doctrine of fundamental breach, a doctrine which Dickson C.J. in *Hunter Engineering Co. v. Syncrude Canada Ltd.*, [1989 1 S.C.R. 426, suggested should be laid to rest 21 years ago (p. 462).

[82] On this occasion we should again attempt to shut the coffin on the jargon associated with "fundamental breach". Categorizing a contract breach as "fundamental" or "immense" or "colossal" is not particularly helpful. Rather, the principle is that a court has no discretion to refuse to enforce a valid and applicable contractual exclusion clause unless the plaintiff (here the appellant Tercon) can point to some paramount consideration of public policy sufficient to override the public interest in freedom of [contract] and defeat what would otherwise be the contractual rights of the parties. Tercon points to the public interest in the transparency and integrity of the government tendering process (in this case, for a highway construction contract) but in my view such a concern, while important, did not render unenforceable the terms of the contract Tercon agreed to. There is nothing inherently unreasonable about exclusion clauses. Tercon is a large and sophisticated corporation. Unlike my colleague Justice Cromwell, I would hold that the respondent Ministry's conduct, while in breach of its contractual obligations, fell within the terms of the exclusion clause. In turn, there is no reason why the clause should not be enforced. I would dismiss the appeal.

I.   OVERVIEW

.   .   .   .

[86] I accept, as did the courts below, that the respondent Ministry breached the terms of its own RFP when it contracted with Brentwood, knowing the work would be carried out by a co-venture with Brentwood and EAC. The addition of EAC, a bigger contractor with greater financial resources than Brentwood, created a stronger competitor for Tercon than Brentwood alone. However, I also agree with the B.C. Court of Appeal that the exclusion of compensation clause is clear and unambiguous and that no legal ground or rule of law permits us to override the freedom of the parties to contract (or to decline to contract) with respect to this particular term, or to relieve Tercon against its operation in this case.

.   .   .   .

III.   TERCON'S CLAIM FOR RELIEF FROM THE EXCLUSIONARY CLAUSE IT AGREED TO

.   .   .   .

A.   The Statutory Argument

.   .   .   .

[102] In the ordinary world of commerce, as Dickson C.J. commented in *Hunter*, "clauses limiting or excluding liability are negotiated as part of the general contract. As they do with all other contractual terms, the parties bargain for the consequences of deficient performance" (p. 461). Moreover, as Mr. Hall points out, "[t]here are many valid reasons for contracting parties to use exemption clauses, most notably to allocate risks" (G.R. Hall, *Canadian Contractual Interpretation Law* (2007), at p. 243). Tercon for example is a sophisticated and experienced con-

tractor and if it decided that it was in its commercial interest to proceed with the bid despite the exclusion of compensation clause, that was its prerogative and nothing in the "policy of the Act" barred the parties' agreement on that point.

. . . .

B. The Doctrine of the Fundamental Breach

[104] The trial judge considered the applicability of the doctrine of fundamental breach. Tercon argued that the Ministry, by reason of its fundamental breach, had forfeited the protection of the exclusion of compensation clause.

[105] The leading case is *Hunter* which also dealt with an exclusion of liability clause. The appellants Hunter Engineering and Allis-Chalmers Canada Ltd. supplied gearboxes used to drive conveyor belts at Syncrude's tar sands operations in Northern Alberta. The gearboxes proved to be defective. At issue was a broad exclusion of warranty clause that limited time for suit and the level of recovery available against Allis-Chalmers (i.e. no recovery beyond the unit price of the defective products). Dickson C.J. observed: "In the face of the contractual provisions, Allis-Chalmers can only be found liable under the doctrine of fundamental breach" (p. 451).

[106] This doctrine was largely the creation of Lord Denning in the 1950s (see, e.g., *Karsales (Harrow) Ltd. v. Wallis*, [1956] 1 W.L.R. 936 (C.A.)). It was said to be a rule of law that operated independently of the intention of the parties in circumstances where the defendant had so egregiously breached the contract as to deny the plaintiff substantially the whole of its benefit. In such a case, according to the doctrine, the innocent party was excused from further performance but the defendant could still be held liable for the consequences of its "fundamental" breach even if the parties had excluded liability by clear and express language. See generally S.M. Waddams, *The Law of Contracts* (5th ed. 2005), at para. 478; J.D. McCamus, *The Law of Contracts* (2005), at pp. 765 *et seq.*

[107] The five-judge *Hunter* Court was unanimous in the result and gave effect to the exclusion clause at issue. Dickson C.J. and Wilson J. both emphasized that there is nothing inherently unreasonable about exclusion clauses and that they should be applied unless there is a compelling reason not to give effect to the words selected by the parties. At that point, there was some divergence of opinion.

[108] Dickson C.J. (La Forest J. concurring) observed that the doctrine of fundamental breach had "spawned a host of difficulties" (p. 460), the most obvious being the difficulty in determining whether a particular breach is fundamental. The doctrine obliged the parties to engage in "games of characterization" (p. 460) which distracted from the real question of what agreement the parties themselves intended. Accordingly, in his view, the doctrine should be "laid to rest". The situations in which the doctrine is invoked could be addressed more directly and effectively through the doctrine of "unconscionability", as assessed at the time the contract was made:

> It is preferable to interpret the terms of the contract, in an attempt to determine exactly what the parties agreed. If on its true construction the contract excludes liability for the kind of breach that occurred, the party in breach will generally be saved from liability. Only where the contract is unconscionable, as might arise from situations of unequal bargaining power between the parties, should the courts interfere with agreements the parties have freely concluded. [p. 462]

Dickson C.J. explained that "[t]he courts do not blindly enforce harsh or unconscionable bargains" (p. 462), but "there is much to be gained by addressing directly the protection of the weak from over-reaching by the strong, rather than relying on the artificial legal doctrine of 'fundamental breach'" (p. 462). To enforce an exclusion clause in such circumstances could tarnish the institutional integrity of the court. In that respect, it would be contrary to public policy. However, a *valid* exclusion clause would be enforced according to its terms.

[109] Wilson J. (L'Heureux-Dubé J. concurring) disagreed. In her view, the courts retain some residual discretion to refuse to enforce exclusion clauses in cases of fundamental breach where the doctrine of *pre*-breach unconscionability (favoured by Dickson C.J.) did not apply. Importantly, she rejected the imposition of a general standard of reasonableness in the judicial scrutiny of exclusion clauses, affirming that "the courts ... are quite unsuited to assess the fairness or reasonableness of contractual provisions as the parties negotiated them" (p. 508). Wilson J. considered it more desirable to develop through the common law a *post*-breach analysis seeking a "balance between the obvious desirability of allowing the parties to make their own bargains ... and the obvious undesirability of having the courts used to enforce bargains in favour of parties who are totally repudiating such bargains themselves" (p. 510).

[110] Wilson J. contemplated a two-stage test, in which the threshold step is the identification of a fundamental breach where "the foundation of the contract has been undermined, where the very thing bargained for has not been provided" (p. 500). Having found a fundamental breach to exist, the exclusion clause would *not* automatically be set aside, but the court should go on to assess whether, having regard to the circumstances of the breach, the party in fundamental breach should escape liability:

> Exclusion clauses do not automatically lose their validity in the event of a fundamental breach by virtue of some hard and fast rule of law. They should be given their natural and true construction so that the meaning and effect of the exclusion clause the parties agreed to at the time the contract was entered into is fully understood and appreciated. But, in my view, the court must still decide, having ascertained the parties' intention at the time the contract was made, whether or not to give effect to it in the context of subsequent events such as a fundamental breach committed by the party seeking its enforcement through the courts.... [T]he question essentially is: in the circumstances that have happened should the court lend its aid to A to hold B to this clause? [Emphasis added; pp. 510–11.]

[111] Wilson J. reiterated that "as a general rule" courts should give effect to exclusion clauses *even in the case of fundamental breach* (p. 515). Nevertheless, a residual discretion to withhold enforcement exists:

> Lord Wilberforce [in *Photo Production Ltd. v. Securicor Transport Ltd.*, [1980] A.C. 827 (H.L.)] may be right that parties of equal bargaining power should be left to live with their bargains regardless of subsequent events. I believe, however, that there is some virtue in a residual power residing in the court to withhold its assistance on policy grounds in appropriate circumstances. [Emphasis added; p. 517]

Wilson J. made it clear that such circumstances of disentitlement would be rare. She acknowledged that an exclusion clause might well be accepted with open eyes by a party "very anxious to get" the contract (p. 509). However, Wilson J. did not elaborate further on what such circumstances might be because she found in *Hunter* itself that no reason existed to refuse the defendant Allis-Chalmers the benefit of the exclusion clause.

[112] The fifth judge, McIntyre J., in a crisp two-paragraph judgment, agreed with the conclusion of Wilson J. in respect of the exclusion clause issue but found it "unnecessary to deal further with the concept of fundamental breach in this case" (p. 481).

[113] The law was left in this seemingly bifurcated state until *Guarantee Co. of North America v. Gordon Capital Corp.*, [1999] 3 S.C.R. 423. In that case, the Court breathed some life into the dying doctrine of fundamental breach while nevertheless affirming (once again) that whether or not a "fundamental breach prevents the breaching party from continuing to rely on an exclusion clause is a matter of construction rather than a rule of law" (at para. 52). In other words, the question was whether the parties *intended* at the time of contract formation that the exclusion or limitation clause would apply "in circumstances of contractual breach, whether fundamental or otherwise" (para. 63). The Court thus emphasized that what was important was not the label ("fundamental or otherwise") but the intent of the contracting parties when they made their bargain. "The only limitation placed upon enforcing the contract as written in the event of a fundamental breach", the Court in *Guarantee Trust* continued,

> would be to refuse to enforce an exclusion, of liability in circumstances where to do so would be unconscionable, according to Dickson C.J., or [note the disjunctive "or"] unfair, unreasonable or otherwise contrary to public policy, according to Wilson J. [Emphasis added; para. 52.] ...

What has given rise to some concern is not the reference to "public policy", whose role in the enforcement of contracts has never been doubted, but to the more general ideas of "unfair" and "unreasonable", which seemingly confer on courts a very broad after-the-fact discretion.

. . . .

[116] While memorably described as an unruly horse, public policy is nevertheless fundamental to contract law, both to contractual formation and enforcement and (occasionally) to the court's relief *against* enforcement. As Duff C.J. observed:

It is the duty of the courts to give effect to contracts and testamentary dispositions according to the settled rules and principles of law, since we are under a reign of law; but there are cases in which rules of law cannot have their normal operation because the law itself recognizes some paramount consideration of public policy which over-rides the interest and what otherwise would be the rights and powers of the individual. (*Re Millar Estate*, [1938] S.C.R. 1, at p. 4)

[117] As Duff C.J. recognized, freedom of contract will often, but not always, trump other societal values. The residual power of a court to decline enforcement exists but, in the interest of certainty and stability of contractual relations, it will rarely be exercised. Duff C.J. adopted the view that public policy "should be invoked only in clear cases in which the harm to the public is substantially incontestable, and does not depend upon the idiosyncratic inferences of a few judicial minds" (p. 7). While he was referring to public policy considerations pertaining to the nature of the *entire contract*, I accept that there may be well-accepted public policy considerations that relate directly to the nature of the *breach*, and thus trigger the court's narrow jurisdiction to give relief against an exclusion clause.

[118] There are cases where the exercise of what Professor Waddams calls the "ultimate power" to refuse to enforce a contract may be justified, even in the commercial context. Freedom of contract, like any freedom, may be abused. Take the case of the milk supplier who adulterates its baby formula with a toxic compound to increase its profitability at the cost of sick or dead babies. In China, such people were shot. In Canada, should the courts give effect to a contractual clause excluding civil liability in such a situation? I do not think so. Then there are the people, also fortunately resident elsewhere, who recklessly sold toxic cooking oil to unsuspecting consumers, creating a public health crisis of enormous magnitude. Should the courts enforce an exclusion clause to eliminate contractual liability for the resulting losses in such circumstances? The answer is no, but the contract breaker's conduct need not rise to the level of criminality or fraud to justify a finding of abuse.

[119] A less extreme example in the commercial context is *Plas-Tex Canada Ltd. v. Dow Chemical of Canada Ltd.*, 2004 ABCA 309, 245 D.L.R. (4th) 650. The Alberta Court of Appeal refused to enforce an exclusion clause where the defendant Dow knowingly supplied defective plastic resin to a customer who used it to fabricate natural gas pipelines. Instead of disclosing its prior knowledge of the defect to the buyer, Dow chose to try to protect itself by relying upon limitation of liability clauses in its sales contracts. After some years, the pipelines began to degrade, with considerable damage to property and risk to human health from leaks and explosions. The court concluded that "a party to a contract will not be permitted to engage in unconscionable conduct secure in the knowledge that no liability can be imposed upon it because of an exclusionary clause" (para. 53). (See also McCamus, at p. 774, and Hall, at p. 243). What was demonstrated in *Plas-Tex* was that the defendant Dow was so contemptuous of its contractual obligation and reckless as to the consequences of the breach as to forfeit the assistance of the court. The public policy that favours freedom of contract was outweighed by the public policy that seeks to curb its abuse.

[120] Conduct approaching serious criminality or egregious fraud are but examples of well-accepted and "substantially incontestable" considerations of public policy that may override the countervailing public policy that favours freedom of contract. Where this type of misconduct is reflected in the breach of contract, all of the circumstances should be examined very carefully by the court. Such misconduct may disable the defendant from hiding behind the exclusion clause. But a plaintiff who seeks to avoid the effect of an exclusion clause must identify the overriding public policy that it says outweighs the public interest in the enforcement of the contract. In the present case, for the reasons discussed below, I do not believe Tercon has identified a relevant public policy that fulfills this requirement.

[121] The present state of the law, in summary, requires a series of enquiries to be addressed when a plaintiff seeks to escape the effect of an exclusion clause or other contractual terms to which it had previously agreed.

[122] The first issue, of course, is whether as a matter of interpretation the exclusion clause even *applies* to the circumstances established in evidence. This will depend on the Court's assessment of the intention of the parties as expressed in the contract. If the exclusion clause does not apply, there is obviously no need to proceed further with this analysis. If the exclusion clause applies, the second issue is whether the exclusion clause was unconscionable at the time the contract was made, "as might arise from situations of unequal bargaining power between the parties" (*Hunter*, at p. 462). This second issue has to do with contract formation, not breach.

[123] If the exclusion clause is held to be valid and applicable, the Court may undertake a third enquiry, namely whether the Court should nevertheless refuse to enforce the valid exclusion clause because of the existence of an overriding public policy, proof of which lies on the party seeking to avoid enforcement of the clause, that outweighs the very strong public interest in the enforcement of contracts.

IV. APPLICATION TO THE FACTS OF THIS CASE

. . . .

B. What is the Proper Interpretation of the Exclusion of Compensation Clause and Did the Ministry's Conduct Fall Within its Terms?

[127] It is at this stage that I part company with my colleague Cromwell J. The exclusion clause is contained in the RFP and provides as follows:

2:10 ...

> Except as expressly and specifically permitted in these Instructions to Proponents, no Proponent shall have any claim for compensation of any kind whatsoever, as a result of participating in this RFP, and by submitting a Proposal each Proponent shall be deemed to have agreed that it has no claim.

In my view, "participating in this RFP" began with "submitting a Proposal" for consideration. The RFP process consisted of more than the final selection of the winning bid and Tercon participated in it. Tercon's bid *was* considered. To deny that such participation occurred on the ground that in the end the Ministry chose a Brentwood joint venture (ineligible) instead of Brentwood itself (eligible) would, I believe, take the Court up the dead end identified by Wilson J. in *Hunter*:

> ... exclusion clauses, like all contractual provisions, should be given their natural and true construction. Great uncertainty and needless complications in the drafting of contracts will obviously result if courts give exclusion clauses strained and artificial interpretations in order, indirectly and obliquely, to avoid the impact of what seems to them *ex post facto* to have been an unfair and unreasonable clause. [p. 509]

Professor McCamus expresses a similar thought:

> ... the law concerning exculpatory clauses is likely to be more rather than less predictable if the underlying concern is openly recognized, as it is in *Hunter*, rather than suppressed and achieved indirectly through the subterfuge of strained interpretation of such terms. [p. 778]

[128] I accept the trial judge's view that the Ministry was at fault in its performance of the RFP, but the conclusion that the process thereby ceased to be the RFP process appears to me, with due respect to colleagues of a different view, to be a "strained and artificial interpretatio[n] in order, indirectly and obliquely, to avoid the impact of what seems to them *ex post facto* to have been an unfair and unreasonable clause".

[129] As a matter of interpretation, I agree with Donald J.A. speaking for the unanimous court below:

> The [trial] judge said the word "participating" was ambiguous. With deference, I do not find it so. The sense it conveys is the contractor's involvement in the RFP/contract A <u>stage</u> of the process. I fail to see how "participating" could bear any other meaning. [Emphasis added; para. 16.]

Accordingly, I conclude that on the face of it, the exclusion clause applies to the facts described in the evidence before us.

C. Was the Claim Excluding Compensation Unconscionable at the Time Contract A was Made?

[130] At this point, the focus turns to contract formation. Tercon advances two arguments: firstly, that it suffered from an inequality of bargaining power and secondly, (as mentioned) that the exclusion clause violates public policy as reflected in the *Transportation Act*.

(1) Unequal Bargaining Power

[131] In *Hunter*, Dickson C.J. stated, at p. 462: "Only where the contract is unconscionable, as might arise from situations of unequal bargaining power between the parties, should the courts interfere with agreements the parties have freely concluded." Applying that test to the case before him, he concluded:

> I have no doubt that unconscionability is not an issue in this case. Both Allis-Chalmers and Syncrude are large and commercially sophisticated companies. Both parties knew or should have known what they were doing and what they had bargained for when they entered into the contract. [p. 464]

While Tercon is not on the same level of power and authority as the Ministry, Tercon is a major contractor and is well able to look after itself in a commercial context. It need not bid if it doesn't like what is proposed. There was no relevant imbalance in bargaining power.

. . . .

D. Assuming the Validity of the Exclusion Clause at the Time the Contract was Made, is There Any Overriding Public Policy That Would Justify the Court's Refusal to Enforce it?

[135] If the exclusion clause is not invalid from the outset, I do not believe the Ministry's performance can be characterized as so aberrant as to forfeit the protection of the contractual exclusion clause on the basis of some overriding public policy. While there is a public interest in a fair and transparent tendering process, it cannot be ratcheted up to defeat the enforcement of Contract A in this case. There *was* an RFP process and Tercon participated in it.

[136] Assertions of ineligible bidders and ineligible bids are the bread and butter of construction litigation. If a claim to defeat the exclusion clause succeeds here on the basis that the owner selected a joint venture consisting of an eligible bidder with an ineligible bidder, so also by a parity of reasoning should an exclusion clause be set aside if the owner accepted a bid ineligible on other grounds. There would be little room left for the exclusion clause to operate. A more sensible and realistic view is that the parties here expected, even if they didn't like it, that the exclusion of compensation clause would operate even where the eligibility criteria in respect of the bid (including the bidder) were not complied with.

[137] While the Ministry's conduct was in breach of Contract A, that conduct was not so extreme as to engage some overriding and paramount public interest in curbing contractual abuse as in the *Plas-Tex* case. Brentwood was not an outsider to the RFP process. It was a legitimate competitor. All bidders knew that the road contract (i.e. Contract B) would not be performed by the proponent alone. The work required a large "team" of different trades and personnel to perform. The issue was whether EAC would be on the job as a major sub-contractor (to which Tercon could not have objected) or identified with Brentwood as a joint venture "proponent" with

EAC. All bidders were made aware of a certain flexibility with respect to the composition of any proponent's "team". Section 2.8(b) of the RFP provided that if "a material change has occurred to the Proponent since its qualification under the RFEI, including if the composition of the Proponent's team members has changed, ... the Ministry may request [further information and] ... reserves the right to disqualify that Proponent, and reject its Proposal". Equally, "[i]f a qualified Proponent is concerned that it has undergone a material change, the Proponent can, at its election, make a preliminary submission to the Ministry, in advance of the Closing Date, and before submitting a Proposal.... The Ministry will, within three working days of receipt of the preliminary submission give a written decision as to whether the Proponent is still qualified to submit a Proposal."

. . . .

[141] The construction industry in British Columbia is run by knowledgeable and sophisticated people who bid upon and enter government contracts with eyes wide open. No statute in British Columbia and no principle of the common law override their ability in this case to agree on a tendering process including a limitation or exclusion of remedies for breach of its rules. A contractor who does not think it is in its business interest to bid on the terms offered is free to decline to participate. As Donald J.A. pointed out, if enough contractors refuse to participate, the Ministry would be forced to change its approach. So long as contractors are willing to bid on such terms, I do not think it is the court's job to rescue them from the consequences of their decision to do so. Tercon's loss of anticipated profit is a paper loss. In my view, its claim is barred by the terms of the contract it agreed to.

V.   DISPOSITION

[142] I would dismiss the appeal without costs.

7 Consideration and Evolution in Agreement

(a) *Stilk v. Myrick*†

U.K. King's Bench

This was an action for seaman's wages, on a voyage from London to the Baltic and back.

By the ship's articles, executed before the commencement of the voyage, the plaintiff was to be paid at the rate of £5 a month; and the principal question in the cause was, whether he was entitled to a higher rate of wages? In the course of the voyage two of the men deserted and the captain having in vain attempted to supply their places at Cronstadt, there entered into an agreement with the rest of the crew, that they should have the wages of the two who had deserted equally divided among them, if he could not procure two other hands at Gottenburgh. This was found impossible; and the ship was worked back to London by the plaintiff and eight more of the original crew, with whom the agreement had been made at Cronstadt.

Garrow for the defendant insisted, that this agreement was contrary to public policy, and utterly void. In West India voyages, crews are often thinned greatly by death and desertion; and if a promise of advanced wages were valid, exorbitant claims would be set up on all such occasions. This ground was strongly taken by Lord Kenyon in *Harris v. Watson*, Peak. Cas. 72, where that learned Judge held, that no action would lie at the suit of a sailor on a promise of a captain to pay him extra wages, in consideration of his doing more than the ordinary share of duty in navigating the ship; and his Lordship said, that if such a promise could be enforced, sailors would in many cases suffer a ship to sink unless the captain would accede to any extravagant demand they might think proper to make.

The Attorney-General, *contra*, distinguished this case from *Harris v. Watson*, as the agreement here was made on shore, when there was no danger or pressing emergency, and when the captain could not be supposed to be under any constraint or apprehension. The mariners were not to be permitted on any sudden danger to force concessions from the captain; but why should they be deprived of the compensation he voluntarily offers them in perfect security for their extra labour during the remainder of the voyage?

[LORD ELLENBOROUGH:]

I think *Harris v. Watson* was rightly decided; but I doubt whether the ground of public policy, upon which Lord Kenyon is stated to have proceeded, be the true principle on which the decision is to be supported. Here, I say, the agreement is void for want of consideration. There was no consideration for the ulterior pay promised to the mariners who remained with the ship. Before they sailed from London they had undertaken to do all that they could under all the emergencies of the voyage. They had sold all their services till the voyage should be completed. If they had been at liberty to quit the vessel at Cronstadt, the case would have been quite different; or if the captain had capriciously discharged the two men who were wanting, the others might not have been compellable to take the whole duty upon them-

---

† [1809] EWHC KB J58, (1809) 170 ER 1168.

selves, and their agreeing to do so might have been a sufficient consideration for the promise of an advance of wages. But the desertion of a part of the crew is to be considered an emergency of the voyage as much as their death; and those who remain are bound by the terms of their original contract to exert themselves to the utmost to bring the ship in safety to her destined port. Therefore, without looking to the policy of this agreement, I think it is void for want of consideration, and that the plaintiff can only recover at the rate of £5 a month.

Verdict accordingly.[1]

Note 1

> But where a seaman performs some service beyond the scope of his original contract, the case is otherwise. Thus before the ransoming of ships was prohibited, a promise by the captain of a captured ship to pay monthly wages to one of the sailors, in order to induce him to become a hostage, was held binding on the owners, although they abandoned the ship and cargo. *Yates v. Hall*, 1 T. R. 73. A seaman at monthly wages, who is impressed or inters from a merchant ship into the royal navy during a voyage is not entitled to wages to the time of his quitting the ship, unless the voyage be completed. *Anon. coram* Lord Ellenborough, at Guildhall, December 11th 1806. Action for seaman's wages: The plaintiff entered on board the defendant's ship at Shields, and was to have the monthly wages of £6, 3s. The ship was bound to Gibraltar with a cargo of coals, and she arrived there in safety. She then sailed for Zante, where she was to take a cargo, with which she was to return to England. In the course of this voyage, the plaintiff was impressed; and before it was completed the ship was captured. The defendant had paid into Court the amount of the plaintiff's wages to Gibraltar; and the question was, whether anything more was due? On the part of the plaintiff, it was contended that by virtue of stat. 2 Geo. II. C. 36, s. 13, he was entitled to recover his wages from his leaving Gibraltar to the period of his being impressed. It is thereby enacted "that nothing in that Act contained shall extend, or be construed to extend, to debar any seaman or mariner belonging to any merchant ship or vessel, from entering or being entered into the service of his Majesty, his heirs &c. on board of any of his or their ships or vessels; nor shall such seaman or mariner for such entry forfeit the wages due to him during the term of his service in such merchant ship or vessel." And even before the passing of that statute, it was held by Holt, C.J. (*Wiggins v. Ingleton*, 2 Ld. Raym. 1211) that an impressed seaman is entitled to his wages *pro tanto*. It followed, that the plaintiff was entitled to payment at the time when he left the ship, and therefore that he could not be affected by the subsequent casualties of the voyage. But Lord Ellenborough held, that the plaintiff was not placed in a better situation than the other seamen; and was not entitled to any apportionment of wages for his service during a voyage which had not been completed.

(b) *Central London Property Trust Limited v. High Trees House Limited*[†]

U.K. King's Bench

[DENNING, J. stated the facts:]

By a lease under seal made on September 24, 1937, the plaintiffs, Central London Property Trust Ltd., granted to the defendants, High Trees House Ltd., a subsidiary of the plaintiff company, a tenancy of a block of flats for the term of ninety-nine years from September 29, 1937, at a ground rent of 2,500*l.* a year. The block of flats was a new one and had not been fully occupied at the beginning of the war owing to the absence of people from London. With war conditions prevailing, it was apparent to those responsible that the rent reserved under the lease could not be paid out of the profits of the flats and, accordingly, discussions took place between the directors of the two companies concerned, which were closely associated, and an arrangement was made between them which was put into writing.

On January 3, 1940, the plaintiffs wrote to the defendants in these terms, "we confirm the arrangement made between us by which the ground rent should be reduced as from the commencement of the lease to 1,250*l.* per annum," and on April 2, 1940, a confirmatory resolution to the same effect was passed by the plaintiff company. On March 20, 1941, a receiver was appointed by the debenture holders of the plaintiffs and on his death on February 28, 1944, his place was taken by his partner. The defendants paid the reduced rent from 1941 down to the beginning of 1945 by which time all the flats in the block were fully let, and continued to pay it thereafter. In September, 1945, the then receiver of

---

† [1947] KB 130.

the plaintiff company looked into the matter of the lease and ascertained that the rent actually reserved by it was 2,500*l*. On September 21, 1945, he wrote to the defendants saying that rent must be paid at the full rate and claiming that arrears amounting to 7,916*l*. were due. Subsequently, he instituted the present friendly proceedings to test the legal position in regard to the rate at which rent was payable. In the action the plaintiffs sought to recover 625*l*., being the amount represented by the difference between rent at the rate of 2,500*l*. and 1,250*l*. per annum for the quarters ending September 29, and December 25, 1945.

By their defence the defendants pleaded (1.) that the letter of January 3, 1940, constituted an agreement that the rent reserved should be 1,250*l*. only, and that such agreement related to the whole term of the lease, (2.) they pleaded in the alternative that the plaintiff company were estopped from alleging that the rent exceeded 1,250*l*. per annum and (3.) as a further alternative, that by failing to demand rent in excess of 1,250*l*. before their letter of September 21, 1945 (received by the defendants on September 24), they had waived their rights in respect of any rent, in excess of that at the rate of 1,250*l*., which had accrued up to September 24, 1945.

[and continued]

If I were to consider this matter without regard to recent developments in the law, there is no doubt that had the plaintiffs claimed it, they would have been entitled to recover ground rent at the rate of 2,500*l*. a year from the beginning of the term, since the lease under which it was payable was a lease under seal which, according to the old common law, could not be varied by an agreement by parol (whether in writing or not), but only by deed. Equity, however stepped in, and said that if there has been a variation of a deed by a simple contract (which in the case of a lease required to be in writing would have to be evidenced by writing), the courts may give effect to it as is shown in *Berry v. Berry* [1929] 2 K.B. 316. That equitable doctrine, however, could hardly apply in the present case because the variation here might be said to have been made without consideration. With regard to estoppel, the representation made in relation to reducing the rent, was not a representation of an existing fact. It was a representation, in effect, as to the future, namely, that payment of the rent would not be enforced at the full rate but only at the reduced rate. Such a representation would not give rise to an estoppel, because, as was said in *Jorden v.*

Money (1854) 5 H.L.C. 185, a representation as to the future must be embodied as a contract or be nothing.

But what is the position in view of developments in the law in recent years? The law has not been standing still since *Jorden v. Money* (1854) 5 H.L.C. 185. There has been a series of decisions over the last fifty years which, although they are said to be cases of estoppel are not really such. They are cases in which a promise was made which was intended to create legal relations and which, to the knowledge of the person making the promise, was going to be acted on by the person to whom it was made and which was in fact so acted on. In such cases the courts have said that the promise must be honoured. The cases to which I particularly desire to refer are: *Fenner v. Blake* [1900] 1 Q.B. 426, *In re Wickham* (1917) 34 T.L.R. 158, *Re William Porter & Co., Ltd.* [1937] 2 All E.R. 361 and *Buttery v. Pickard* [1946] W.N. 25. As I have said they are not cases of estoppel in the strict sense. They are really promises — promises intended to be binding, intended to be acted on, and in fact acted on. *Jorden v. Money* (1854) 5 H.L.C. 185 can be distinguished, because there the promisor made it clear that she did not intend to be legally bound, whereas in the cases to which I refer the proper inference was that the promisor did intend to be bound. In each case the court held the promise to be binding on the party making it, even though under the old common law it might be difficult to find any consideration for it.

The courts have not gone so far as to give a cause of action in damages for the breach of such a promise, but they have refused to allow the party making it to act inconsistently with it. It is in that sense, and that sense only, that such a promise gives rise to an estoppel. The decisions are a natural result of the fusion of law and equity: for the cases of *Hughes v. Metropolitan Ry. Co.* (1877) 2 App. Cas. 439, 448, Birmingham and *District Land Co. v. London & North Western Ry. Co.* (1888) 40 Ch.D. 268, 286 and *Salisbury (Marquess) v. Gilmore* [1942] 2 K.B. 38, 51, afford a sufficient basis for saying that a party would not be allowed in equity to go back on such a promise. In my opinion, the time has now come for the validity of such a promise to be recognized. The logical consequence, no doubt is that a promise to accept a smaller sum in discharge of a larger sum, if acted upon, is binding notwithstanding the absence of consideration: and if the fusion of law and equity leads to this result, so much the better. That aspect was not considered in *Foakes v. Beer* (1884) 9 App. Cas. 605. At this time of day however, when law and equity have been joined together for over seventy years, principles must be reconsidered in the light of their combined effect. It is to be noticed that in the Sixth Interim Report of the Law Revision Committee, pars. 35, 40, it is recommended that such a promise as that to which I have referred, should be enforceable in law even though no consideration for it has been given by the promisee. It seems to me that, to the extent I have mentioned that result has now been achieved by the decisions of the courts.

I am satisfied that a promise such as that to which I have referred is binding and the only question remaining for my consideration is the scope of the promise in the present case. I am satisfied on all the evidence that the promise here was that the ground rent should be reduced to 1,250*l.* a year as a temporary expedient while the block of flats was not fully, or substantially fully let, owing to the conditions prevailing. That means that the reduction in the rent applied throughout the years down to the end of 1944, but early in 1945 it is plain that the flats were fully let, and, indeed the rents received from them (many of them not being affected by the Rent Restrictions Acts), were increased beyond the figure at which it was originally contemplated that they would be let. At all events the rent from them must have been very considerable. I find that the conditions prevailing at the time when the reduction in rent was made, had completely passed away by the early months of 1945. I am satisfied that the promise was understood by all parties only to apply under the conditions prevailing at the time when it was made, namely, when the flats were only partially let, and that it did not extend any further than that. When the flats became fully let, early in 1945, the reduction ceased to apply.

In those circumstances, under the law as I hold it, it seems to me that rent is payable at the full rate for the quarters ending September 29 and December 25, 1945.

If the case had been one of estoppel, it might be said that in any event the estoppel would cease when the conditions to which the representation applied came to an end, or it also might be said that it would only come to an end on notice. In either case it is only a way of ascertaining what is the scope of the representation. I prefer to apply the principle that a promise intended to be binding, intended to be acted on and in fact acted on, is binding so far as its terms properly apply. Here it was binding as covering the period down to the early part of 1945, and as from that time full rent is payable.

I therefore give judgment for the plaintiff company for the amount claimed.

(c) *Gilbert Steel Ltd. v. University Construction Ltd.*†

Ontario Court of Appeal

[WILSON, J.A., for the Court;]

[1] This is an appeal from the order of Mr. Justice Pennell dismissing the plaintiff's action for damages for breach of an oral agreement for the supply of fabricated steel bars to be incorporated into apartment buildings being constructed by the defendant. The case raises some fundamental principles of contract law.

[2] The circumstances giving rise to the action are as follows. On September 4, 1968, the plaintiff entered into a written contract to deliver to the defendant fabricated steel for apartment buildings to be erected at three separate sites referred to in the contract as the "Flavin, Tectate and University projects". The price fixed by that contract was $153 per ton for "Hard grade" and $159 per ton for "Grade 60,000". Deliveries for the Flavin and Tectate projects were completed in August, 1969, and October, 1969, respectively, and paid for at the agreed-upon prices.

[3] Two apartment buildings calling for the supply of 3,000 tons of fabricated steel were to be erected at the University site. However, prior to the defendant's notifying the plaintiff of its intention to commence construction on the first of these two buildings, the

---

† [1976] O.J. No. 2087, 12 O.R. (2d) 19, 67 D.L.R. (3d) 606.

owners of the steel mill announced an increase in the price of unfabricated steel. They also gave warning of a further increase to come. The plaintiff approached the defendant about a new contract for the University project and a written contract dated October 22, 1969, was entered into for the supply of fabricated steel for the first building. The new price was $156 per ton for "Hard grade" and $165 per ton for "Grade 60,000". In fact this increase in price did not reflect the full amount of the initial increase announced by the mill owners.

[4] On March 1, 1970, while the building under construction was still far from completion, the mill owners announced the second increase in price and a further discussion took place between John Gilbert and his brother Harry representing the plaintiff and Mendel Tenenbaum and Hersz Tenenbaum representing the defendant with respect to the price to be paid for the steel required to complete the first building. It is this discussion which the plaintiff alleges resulted in a binding oral agreement that the defendant would pay $166 per ton for "Hard grade" and $178 per ton for "Grade 60,000". Although the plaintiff submitted to the defendant a written contract embodying these revised prices following their meeting, the contract was not executed. It contained, in addition to the increased prices, two new clauses which the trial Judge found had not been the subject of any discussion with the defendant but were unilaterally imported into the document by the plaintiff. The trial Judge also found, however, that the defendant agreed at the meeting to pay the increased price.

[5] From March 12, 1970, until the completion of the first building the defendant accepted deliveries of the steel against invoices which reflected the revised prices but, in making payments on account, it remitted cheques in rounded amounts which at the date of the issuance of the writ resulted in a balance owing to the plaintiff in accordance with the invoices.

[6] Having found on the evidence that the defendant had orally agreed to pay the increased prices, the legal issue confronting Mr. Justice Pennell was whether that agreement was legally binding upon the defendant or whether it failed for want of consideration. Counsel for the defendant submitted at the trial that past consideration is no consideration and that the plaintiff was already obliged before the alleged oral agreement was entered into to deliver the steel at the original prices agreed to in the written contract of October 22, 1969. Where then was

the quid pro quo for the defendant's promise to pay more?

[7] Counsel for the plaintiff sought to supply this omission from the evidence of Hersz Tenenbaum who, during the course of discussions which took place in September, 1970, with a view to a contract for the supply of steel for the second building at the University site, asked whether the plaintiff would give him "a good price" on steel for this building. Plaintiff's counsel argued that the promise of a good price on the second building was the consideration the defendant received for agreeing to pay the increased price on the first. The trial Judge rejected this submission and found the oral agreement unenforceable for want of consideration. In the course of his reasons for judgment the trial Judge adverted briefly to an alternate submission made by the plaintiff's counsel. He said:

> I should, in conclusion, mention a further point which was argued with ingenuity by Mr. Morphy. His contention was that the consideration for the oral agreement was the mutual abandonment of right under the prior agreement in writing. I must say, with respect, that this argument is not without its attraction for me.

[8] On the appeal Mr. Morphy picked up and elaborated upon this submission which had intrigued the trial Judge. In launching his main attack on the trial Judge's finding that the oral agreement was unenforceable for want of consideration, he submitted that the facts of this case evidenced not a purported oral variation of a written contract which failed for want of consideration but an implied rescission of the written contract and the creation of a whole new contract, albeit oral, which was subsequently reneged on by the defendant. The consideration for this new oral agreement, submitted Mr. Morphy, was the mutual agreement to abandon the previous written contract and to assume the obligations under the new oral one. Mr. Morphy submitted to the Court for its consideration two lines of authority, the first line illustrated by the leading case of *Stilk v. Myrick* (1809), 2 Camp. 317, 170 E.R. 1168, in which the subsequent agreement was held to be merely a variation of the earlier agreement and accordingly failed for want of consideration, and the other line illustrated by *Morris v. Baron, & Co.*, [1918] A.C. 1, in which the subsequent agreement was held to have rescinded the former one and was therefore supported by the mutual agreement to abandon the old obligations and substitute the new. Mr. Morphy invited us to find that the oral agreement to pay the increased price for steel fell into the second cate-

gory. There was, he acknowledged, no express rescission of the written contract but price is such a fundamental term of a contract for the supply of goods that the substitution of a new price must connote a new contract and impliedly rescind the old.

[9] It is impossible to accept Mr. Morphy's submission in face of the evidence adduced at the trial. It is clear that the sole reason for the discussions between the parties in March, 1970, concerning the supply of steel to complete the first building at the University site was the increase in the price of steel by the mill owners. No changes other than the change in price were discussed. The trial Judge found that the other two changes sought to be introduced into the written document submitted by the plaintiff to the defendant for signature following the discussions had not even been mentioned at the meeting. Moreover, although repeated references were made at trial by the Gilbert brothers to the fact that the parties had made a "new contract" in March, 1970, it seems fairly clear from the evidence when read as a whole that the "new contract" referred to was the agreement to pay the increased price for the steel, i.e., the agreement which effected the variation of the written contract and not a new contract in the sense of a contract replacing in toto the original contract of October 22, 1969.

[10] I am not persuaded that either of the parties intended by their discussions in March, 1970, to rescind their original contract and replace it with a new one. Indeed, it is significant that no such plea was made in the statement of claim which confined itself to an allegation that "it was orally agreed in March 1970 that the prices as set forth in the said contract [i.e., of October 22, 1969] would be varied ....." Accordingly, consideration for the oral agreement is not to be found in a mutual agreement to abandon the earlier written contract and assume the obligations under the new oral one.

[11] Nor can I find consideration in the vague references in the evidence to the possibility that the plaintiff would give the defendant "a good price" on the steel for the second building if it went along with the increased prices on the first. The plaintiff, in my opinion, fell far short of making any commitment in this regard.

[12] Counsel for the appellant put before us as an alternate source of consideration for the agreement to pay the increased price, the increased credit afforded by the plaintiff to the defendant as a result of the increased price. The argument went something

like this. Whereas previously the defendant had credit outstanding for 60 days in the amount owed on the original prices, after the oral agreement was made he had credit outstanding for 60 days in the amount owed on the higher prices. Therefore, there was consideration flowing from the promisee and the law does not inquire into its sufficiency. Reliance was placed by counsel on the decision of Chief Justice Meredith in *Kilbuck Coal Co. v. Turner & Robinson* (1915), 7 O.W.N. 673. This case, however, is clearly distinguishable from the case at bar, as Mr. Justice Pennell pointed out in his reasons, on the basis of the force majeure clause which had relieved the plaintiff of its obligations under the original contract. In undertaking to supply coal despite the strike the plaintiff was unquestionably providing consideration of real substance in that case. I cannot accept counsel's contention, ingenious as it is, that the increased credit inherent in the increased price constituted consideration flowing from the promisee for the promisor's agreement to pay the increased price.

[13] The final submission put forward by counsel for the appellant was that the defendant, by his conduct in not repudiating the invoices reflecting the increase in price when and as they were received, had in effect acquiesced in such increase and should not subsequently be permitted to repudiate it. There would appear to be two answers to this submission. The first is summed up in the maxim that estoppel can never be used as a sword but only as a shield. A plaintiff cannot found his claim in estoppel. Secondarily, however, it should perhaps be pointed out that in order to found an estoppel the plaintiff must show, not only that the conduct of the defendant was clearly referable to the defendant's having given up its right to insist on the original prices, but also that the plaintiff relied on the defendant's conduct to its detriment. I do not think the plaintiff can discharge either of these burdens on the facts of this case.

[14] In summary, I concur in the findings of the trial Judge that the oral agreement made by the parties in March, 1970, was an agreement to vary the written contract of October 22, 1969, and that it must fail for want of consideration.

[15] Argument was directed on the appeal to the question of interest, a matter not dealt with by the trial Judge. The written contract of October 22, 1969, is silent on the subject of interest although it specifies in the terms of payment "net 60 days from date of invoice". I have considered whether it is to be implied from these words that interest will be

exigible if the amount owing is not paid within the 60-day period. Such meagre authority as exists on the meaning of "net" in different contexts does not appear to be helpful. Generally it has reference to the amount established after all proper expenses or deductions have been allowed for. However, it is also commonly used to mean the "rock-bottom price" from which no discount will be given. "Net" may not be an apt word to use in connection with an extension of credit but I have concluded that this is what the parties had in mind in this case. Payment could be deferred by the defendant for the 60-day period free of any sanction but after the expiry of that period, interest would be exigible. Since no rate is specified I find that interest is payable on overdue amounts at the statutory rate of 5% per annum. I attach no significance to the notation "1% per month interest on overdue accounts" on the invoices received by the defendant at the increased prices on the basis that interest cannot be imposed unilaterally in this manner.

[16] The judgment of Pennell, J., should be varied to provide that the plaintiff shall have judgment for interest at the rate of 5% on the payments which were overdue for more than 60 days under the contract dated October 22, 1969. Subject to this variation the appeal should be dismissed with costs.

[17] The respondent cross-appealed on the subject of costs. The trial Judge made no order as to costs although the defendant was successful in the action. Mr. Starkman submits that, in failing to award costs to his successful client, Mr. Justice Pennell did not exercise his discretion with respect to costs judicially. A review of Mr. Justice Pennell's reasons for judgment indicates that he was motivated to withhold costs by his assessment of the conduct of the defendant which led up to this litigation and, since he was in a better position than this Court to make such an assessment, I see no reason to interfere with his disposition as to the costs at trial.

[18] The cross-appeal should accordingly be dismissed. There will be no order as to costs of the cross-appeal.

Appeal and cross-appeal dismissed.

EDITOR'S NOTE

[19] The passage quoted on p. 21 will not be found in the report of the trial judgment ([1973] 3 O.R. 268 et seq.). Some two months after those reasons were published the concluding paragraphs were revised by the trial Judge at the common request of counsel, but the revision was not brought to our attention. The concluding paragraphs on p. 279, from the paragraph beginning "I have postponed to this stage ..." to the end, were deleted and the following substituted:

I should, in conclusion, mention a further point which was argued with ingenuity by Mr. Morphy. His contention was that the consideration for the oral agreement was the mutual abandonment of right under the prior agreement in writing. I must say, with respect, that this argument is not without its attraction for me. I am conscious that my views have changed with frequency during the helpful argument of Mr. Morphy. The defendant itself was evidently impressed with the belief that some advantage would come to it from a promise to pay an increased price of steel. But I am unable to discern an advantage, however technical or trivial, to which the defendant was not already entitled. Here the plaintiff was contributing nothing but the fulfilment of its duty; the plaintiff could not have done less without being guilty of a wrong. On the part of the defendant, it was a promise to the ear to be broken on the demand for payment, a teasing illusion perhaps intended as wine to warm the plaintiff to its obligations. Grappling with my own ignorance and limitations, I have come to the conclusion that the defendant's promise is unenforceable against it for lack of consideration. I cannot abandon ancient principles. I cannot breathe the breath of life into a contract that never was.

For the reasons above given I feel constrained to dismiss the action. I make no order as to costs.

(d) *Williams v. Roffey Brothers & Nicholls (Contractors) Ltd.*†

Court of Appeal (Civil Division)

[GLIDEWELL, L.J.:]

This is an appeal against the decision of Mr. Rupert Jackson Q.C., an assistant recorder, given on 31st January 1989 at Kingston-upon-Thames County Court, entering judgment for the plaintiff for £3,500 damages with £1,400 interest and costs and dismissing the defendants' counterclaim.

THE FACTS

The plaintiff is a carpenter. The defendants are building contractors who in September 1985 had entered into a contract with Shepherds Bush Housing Association Ltd. to refurbish a block of flats called Twynholm Mansions, Lillie Road, London S.W.6. The defendants were the main contractors for the works. There are 28 flats in Twynholm Mansions, but the work of refurbishment was to be carried out in 27 of the flats.

The defendants engaged the plaintiff to carry out the carpentry work in the refurbishment of the 27 flats, including work to the structure of the roof. Originally the plaintiff was engaged on three separate sub-contracts, but these were all superseded by a sub-contract in writing made on 21st January 1986 by which the plaintiff undertook to provide the labour for the carpentry work to the roof of the block and for the first and second fix carpentry work required in each of the 27 flats for a total price of £20,000.

The judge found that, though there was no express term providing for payment to be made in stages, the contract of 21st January 1986 was subject to an implied term that the defendants would make interim payments to the plaintiff, related to the amount of work done, at reasonable intervals.

The plaintiff and his men began work on 10th October 1985. The judge found that by 9th April 1986 the plaintiff had completed the work to the roof, had carried out the first fix to all 27 flats, and had substantially completed the second fix to 9 flats. By this date the defendants had made interim payments totalling £16,200.

It is common ground that by the end of March 1986 the plaintiff was in financial difficulty. The judge found that there were two reasons for this, namely:

(i) That the agreed price of £20,000 was too low to enable the plaintiff to operate satisfactorily and at a profit. Mr. Cottrell, a Surveyor employed by the defendants said in evidence that a reasonable price for the works would have been £23,783.

(ii) That the plaintiff failed to supervise his workmen adequately.

The defendants, as they made clear, were concerned lest the plaintiff did not complete the carpentry work on time. The main contract contained a penalty clause. The judge found that on 9th April 1986 the defendants promised to pay the plaintiff the further sum of £10,300, in addition to the £20,000, to be paid at the rate of £575 for each flat in which the carpentry work was completed.

The plaintiff and his men continued work on the flats until the end of May 1986. By that date the defendants, after their promise on 9th April 1986, had made only one further payment of £1,500. At the end of May the plaintiff ceased work on the flats. I will describe later the work which, according to the judge's findings, then remained to be done. Suffice it to say that the defendants engaged other carpenters to complete the work, but in the result incurred one week's time penalty in their contract with the building owners.

THE ACTION

The plaintiff commenced this action by specially endorsed writ on 10th May 1987. He originally claimed the sum of £32,708.70. In a re-amended statement of claim served on 3rd March 1986 his claim was reduced to £10,847.07. It was, I think, at about this time that the matter was transferred to the county court.

It is not necessary to refer to the statement of claim. On every important issue on which the plain-

---

† [1989] EWCA Civ 5 (23 November 1989), [1991] 1 QB 1.

tiff's case differed from that of the defendants, the judge found that the plaintiff was mistaken, and preferred the evidence for the defendants. In particular, the plaintiff denied the defendants' promise of 9th April 1986 to pay him an additional £10,300, instead alleging an earlier and different agreement which the judge found had not been made.

In the amended defence the defendants' promise to pay an additional £10,300 was pleaded as part of paragraph 5 in the following terms:

> ... In or about the month of May 1986 at a meeting at the offices of the defendants between Mr. Hooper and the plaintiff on the one hand and Mr. Cottrell and Mr. Roffey on the other it was agreed that the defendants would pay the plaintiff an extra £10,300 over and above the contract sum of £20,000. 9 flats had been first and second fixed completely at the date of this meeting and there were 18 flats left that had been first fixed but on which the second fixing had not been completed. The sum of £10,300 was to be paid at a rate of £575 per flat to be paid on the completion of each flat.

The defence then alleged that neither the balance of the original contract sum nor the £10,300 addition was payable until the work was completed, that the plaintiff did not complete the work before he left the site, and thus that no further sum was due to him. By their amended counterclaim the defendants claimed that the plaintiff was in breach of contract in ceasing work at the end of May 1986, as a result of which they had suffered damage to the extent of £18,121.46.

THE JUDGE'S CONCLUSIONS

The judge found that the defendants' promise to pay an additional £10,300, at the rate of £575 per completed flat, was part of an oral agreement made between the plaintiff and the defendants on 9th April 1986, by way of variation to the original contract.

The judge also found that before the plaintiff ceased work at the end of May 1986 the carpentry in 17 flats had been substantially (but not totally) completed. This means that between the making of the agreement on 9th April 1986 and the date when the plaintiff ceased work, eight further flats were substantially completed.

The judge calculated that this entitled the plaintiff to receive £4,600 (8 × £575) "less some small deduction for defective and incomplete items". He held that the plaintiff was also entitled to a reasonable proportion of the £2,200 which was outstanding

from the original contract sum. (I believe this figure should be £2,300, but this makes no practical difference). Adding these two amounts, he decided that the plaintiff was entitled to further payments totalling £5,000 against which he had only received £1,500, and that the defendants were therefore in breach of contract, entitling the plaintiff to cease work.

THE ISSUES

Before us Mr. Evans for the defendants advances two arguments. His principal submission is that the defendants' admitted promise to pay an additional £10,300, at the rate of £575 per completed flat, is unenforceable since there was no consideration for it. This issue was not raised in the defence, but we are told that the argument was advanced at the trial without objection, and that there was equally no objection to it being argued before us.

Mr. Evans' secondary argument is that the additional payment was only payable as each flat was completed. On the judge's findings, 8 further flats had been "substantially" completed. Substantial completion was something less than completion. Thus none of the 8 flats had been completed, and no further payment was yet due from the defendants. I will deal with this subsidiary argument first.

. . . .

Was there consideration for the defendants' promise made on 9th April 1986 to pay an additional price at the rate of £575 per completed flat?

The judge made the following findings of fact which are relevant on this issue.

(i) The sub-contract price agreed was too low to enable the plaintiff to operate satisfactorily and at a profit. Mr. Cottrell, the defendants' surveyor, agreed that this was so.

(ii) Mr. Roffey (managing director of the defendants) was persuaded by Mr. Cottrell that the defendants should pay a bonus to the plaintiff. The figure agreed at the meeting on 9th April 1986 was 610,300.

The judge quoted and accepted the evidence of Mr. Cottrell to the effect that a main contractor who agrees too low a price with a sub-contractor is acting contrary to his own interests. He will never get the job finished without paying more money.

The judge therefore concluded:

> In my view where the original sub-contract price is too low, and the parties subsequently agree that the additional monies shall be paid to the subcontractor, this agreement is in the interests of both parties. This is what happened in the present case, and in my opinion the agreement of 9th April 1986 does not fail for lack of consideration.

In his address to us, Mr. Evans outlined the benefits to his clients the defendants which arose from their agreement to pay the additional £10,300 as:

(i) seeking to ensure that the plaintiff continued work and did not stop in breach of the subcontract;

(ii) avoiding the penalty for delay;

(iii) avoiding the trouble and expense of engaging other people to complete the carpentry work. However, Mr. Evans submits that, though his clients may have derived, or hoped to derive, practical benefits from their agreement to pay the "bonus", they derived no benefit in law, since the plaintiff was promising to do no more than he was already bound to do by his subcontract i.e. continue with the carpentry work and complete it on time. Thus there was no consideration for the agreement.

Mr. Evans relies on the principle of law which, traditionally, is based on the decision in *Stilk v. Myrick* (1809) 2 Camp. 317. That was a decision at first instance of Lord Ellenborough C.J. On a voyage to the Baltic, two seamen deserted. The captain agreed with the rest of the crew that if they worked the ship back to London without the two seamen being replaced, he would divide between them the pay which would have been due to the two deserters. On arrival at London this extra pay was refused, and the plaintiff's action to recover his extra pay was dismissed. Counsel for the defendant argued that such an agreement was contrary to public policy, but the Chief Justice's judgment (as reported in Campbell's Reports) was based on lack of consideration. It reads:

> I think *Harris v. Watson* was rightly decided; but I doubt whether the ground of public policy, upon which Lord Kenyon is stated to have proceeded, be the true principle on which the decision is to be supported. Here, I say the agreement is void for want of consideration. There was no consideration for the ulterior pay promised to the mariners who remained with the

ship. Before they sailed from London they had undertaken to do all they could under the emergencies of the voyage. They had sold all their services till the voyage should be completed. If they had been at liberty to quit the vessel at *Cronstadt*, the case would have been quite different; or if the captain had capriciously discharged the two men who were wanting, the others might not have been compellable to take the whole duty upon themselves, and their agreeing to do so might have been a sufficient consideration for the promise of an advance of wages. But the desertion of a part of the crew is to be considered an emergency of the voyage as much as their death, and those who remain are bound by the terms of their original contract to exert themselves to the utmost to bring the ship in safety to her destination port. Therefore, without looking to the policy of this agreement, I think it is void for want of consideration, and that the plaintiff can only recover at the rate of £5 a month.

In *North Ocean Shipping Co. Ltd. v. Hyundai Construction Co. Ltd.* [1979] Q.B. 705 Mocatta J. regarded the general principle of the decision in *Stilk v. Myrick* as still being good law. He referred to two earlier decisions of this court, dealing with wholly different subjects, in which Denning L.J., as he then was, sought to escape from the confines of the rule, but was not accompanied in his attempt by the other members of the court.

In *Ward v. Byham* [1956] 1 WLR 496 the plaintiff and the defendant lived together unmarried for five years, during which time the plaintiff bore their child. After the parties ended their relationship, the defendant promised to pay the plaintiff £1 per week to maintain the child, provided that she was well looked after and happy. The defendant paid this sum for some months, but ceased to pay when the plaintiff married another man. On her suing for the amount due at £1 per week, he pleaded that there was no consideration for his agreement to pay for the plaintiff to maintain her child, since she was obliged by law to do so — see section 42 of the National Assistance Act 1948. The county court judge upheld the plaintiff mother's claim, and this court dismissed the defendant's appeal.

Denning L.J. said at page 498:

> I approach the case, therefore, on the footing that the mother, in looking after the child, is only doing what she is legally bound to do. Even so, I think that there was sufficient consideration to support the promise. I have always thought that a promise to perform an existing duty, or the performance of it, should be regarded as

good consideration, because it is a benefit to the person to whom it is given. Take this very case. It is as much a benefit for the father to have the child looked after by the mother as by a neighbour. If he gets the benefit for which he stipulated, he ought to honour his promise; and he ought not to avoid it by saying that the mother was herself under a duty to maintain the child.

I regard the father's promise in this case as what is sometimes called a unilateral contract, a promise in return for an act, a promise by the father to pay £1 a week in return for the mother's looking after the child. Once the mother embarked on the task of looking after the child, there was a binding contract. So long as she looked after the child, she would be entitled to £1 a week. The case seems to me to be within the decision of *Hicks v. Gregory*, on which the judge relied. I would dismiss the appeal.

However, Morris L.J. put it rather differently. He said:

... Mr. Lane submits that there was a duty on the mother to support the child; that no affiliation proceedings were in prospect or were contemplated; and that the effect of the arrangement that followed the letter was that the father was merely agreeing to pay a bounty to the mother.

It seems to me that the terms of the letter negative those submissions, for the husband says 'providing you can prove that she' — that is Carol — 'will be well looked after and happy and also that she is allowed to decide for herself whether or not she wishes to come and live with you'. The father goes on to say that Carol is then well and happy and looking much stronger than ever before. 'If you decide what to do let me know as soon as possible'. It seems to me, therefore, that the father was saying, in effect: Irrespective of what may be the strict legal position, what I am asking is that you shall prove that Carol will be well looked after and happy, and also that you must agree that Carol is to be allowed to decide for herself whether or not she wishes to come and live with you. If those conditions were fulfilled the father was agreeable to pay. Upon those terms, which in effect became operative, the father agreed to pay £1 a week. In my judgment, there was ample consideration there to be found for his promise, which I think was binding.

Parker L.J. agreed. As I read the judgment of Morris L.J., he and Parker L.J. held that, though in maintaining the child the plaintiff was doing no more than she was obliged to do by law, nevertheless her promise that the child would be well looked after and happy was a practical benefit to the father which amounted to consideration for his promise.

In *Williams v. Williams* [1957] 1 W.L.R. 148, a wife left her husband, and he promised to make her a weekly payment for her maintenance. On his failing to honour his promise, the wife claimed the arrears of payment, but her husband pleaded that, since the wife was guilty of desertion she was bound to maintain herself, and thus there was no consideration for his promise. Denning L.J. (at page 151) reiterated his view that

a promise to perform an existing duty is, I think, sufficient consideration to support a promise, so long as there is nothing in the transaction which is contrary to the public interest.

However, the other members of the court (Hodson and Morris L.JJ.) declined to agree with this expression of view, though agreeing with Denning L.J. in finding that there was consideration because the wife's desertion might not have been permanent, and thus there was a benefit to the husband.

It was suggested to us in argument that, since the development of the doctrine of promissory estoppel, it may well be possible for a person to whom a promise has been made, on which he has relied, to make an additional payment for services which he is in any event bound to render under an existing contract or by operation of law, to show that the promisor is estopped from claiming that there was no consideration for his promise. However, the application of the doctrine of promissory estoppel to facts such as those of the present case has not yet been fully developed; see e.g. the judgment of Lloyd J. (as he then was) in *The Proodos C.* [1980] 2 Ll.L.R. 390 at 392. Moreover, this point was not argued in the court below, nor was it more than adumbrated before us. Interesting though it is, no reliance can in my view be placed on this concept in the present case.

There is, however, another legal concept of relatively recent development which is relevant, namely, that of economic duress. Clearly if a sub-contractor has agreed to undertake work at a fixed price, and before he has completed the work declines to continue with it unless the contractor agrees to pay an increased price, the subcontractor may be held guilty of securing the contractor's promise by taking unfair advantage of the difficulties he will cause if he does not complete the work. In such a case an agreement to pay an increased price may well be voidable because it was entered into under duress. Thus this concept may provide another answer in law to the question of policy which has troubled the courts since before *Stilk v. Myrick*, and no doubt led at the date of that decision to a rigid adherence to the doctrine of consideration.

This possible application of the concept of economic duress was referred to by Lord Scarman, delivering the judgment of the Judicial Committee of the Privy Council in *Pao On v. Lau Yiu Long* [1989] A.C. 614. He said at page 632B-F:

> Their Lordships do not doubt that a promise to perform, or the performance of, a pre-existing contractual obligation to a third party can be valid consideration. In *New Zealand Shipping Co. Ltd. V. A.M. Satterthwaite & Co. Ltd (The Eurymedon)* [1975] AC 154, 168 the rule and the reason for the rule were stated:
>
>> An agreement to do an act which the promisor is under an existing obligation to a third party to do, may quite well amount to valid consideration ... the promisee obtains the benefit of a direct obligation.... This proposition is illustrated and supported by *Scotson v. Pegg* (1861) 6 H. & N. 295 which their Lordships consider to be good law.
>
> Unless, therefore, the guarantee was void as having been made for an illegal consideration or voidable on the ground of economic duress, the extrinsic evidence establishes that it was supported by valid consideration.
>
> Mr. Leggatt for the defendants submits that the consideration is illegal as being against public policy. He submits that to secure a party's promise by a threat of repudiation of a pre-existing contractual obligation owed to another can be and in the circumstances of this case was, an abuse of a dominant bargaining position and so contrary to public policy. [...] This submission found favour with the majority in the Court of Appeal. Their Lordships, however, considered it misconceived.

Lord Scarman then referred to *Stilk v. Myrick* and its predecessor *Harris v. Watson* (1791) Peake 102, and to *Williams v. Williams* before turning to the development of this branch of the law in the United States of America. He then said at page 634B–635B:

> Their Lordships' knowledge of this developing branch of American law is necessarily limited. In their judgment it would be carrying audacity to the point of foolhardiness for them to attempt to extract from the American case law a principle to provide an answer to the question now under consideration. That question, their Lordships repeat, is whether, in a case where duress is not established, public policy may nevertheless invalidate the consideration if there has been a threat to repudiate a pre-existing contractual obligation or an unfair use of a dominating bargaining position. Their Lordships' conclusion is that where businessmen are negotiating at arms' length it is unnecessary for the achievement of justice, and unhelpful in the development of the law, to invoke such a rule of public policy. It would also create unacceptable anomaly. It is unnecessary because justice requires that men, who have negotiated at arm's length, be held to their bargains unless it can be shown that their consent was vitiated by fraud, mistake or duress. If a promise is induced by coercion of a man's will, the doctrine of duress suffices to do justice. The party coerced, if he chooses and acts in time, can avoid the contract. If there is no coercion, there can be no reason for avoiding the contract where there is shown to be a real consideration which is otherwise legal.
>
> Such a rule of public policy as is now being considered would be unhelpful because it would render the law uncertain. It would become a question of fact and degree to determine in each case whether there had been, short of duress, an unfair use of a strong bargaining position. It would create anomaly because, if public policy invalidates the consideration, the effect is to make the contract void. But unless the facts are such as to support a plea of 'non est factum', which is not suggested in this case, duress does no more than confer upon the victim the opportunity if taken in time, to avoid the contract. It would be strange if conduct less than duress could render a contract void, whereas duress does no more than render a contract voidable. Indeed, it is the defendants' case in this appeal that such an anomaly is the correct result. Their case is that the plaintiffs, having lost by cancellation the safeguard of the subsidiary agreement, are without the safeguard of the guarantee because its consideration is contrary to public policy, and that they are debarred from restoration to their position under the subsidiary agreement because the guarantee is void, not voidable. The logical consequence of Mr. Leggatt's submission is that the safeguard which all were at all times agreed the plaintiffs should have — the safeguard against fall in value of the share — has been lost by the application of a rule of public policy. The law is not, in their Lordships' judgment, reduced to countenancing such stark injustice; nor is it necessary, when one bears in mind the protection offered otherwise by the law to one who contracts in ignorance of what he is doing or under duress. Accordingly, the submission that the additional consideration established by the extrinsic evidence is invalid on the ground of public policy is rejected.

It is true that *Pao On* is a case of a tripartite relationship i.e. a promise by A to perform a pre-existing contractual obligation owed to B, in return for a promise of payment by C. But Lord Scarman's words at page 634/5 seem to me to be of general application, equally applicable to a promise made by one of the original two parties to a contract.

Accordingly, following the view of the majority in *Ward v. Byham* and of the whole court in *Williams v. Williams* and that of the Privy Council in *Pao On* the present state of the law on this subject can be expressed in the following proposition:

(i)   if A has entered into a contract with B to do work for, or to supply goods or services to, B in return for payment by B; and

(ii) at some stage before A has completely performed his obligations under the contract B has reason to doubt whether A will, or will be able to, complete his side of the bargain; and

(iii) B thereupon promises A an additional payment in return for A's promise to perform his contractual obligations on time; and

(iv) as a result of giving his promise, B obtains in practice a benefit, or obviates a disbenefit; and

(v)   B's promise is not given as a result of economic duress or fraud on the part of A; then

(vi) the benefit to B is capable of being consideration for B's promise, so that the promise will be legally binding.

As I have said, Mr. Evans accepts that in the present case by promising to pay the extra £10,300 his client secured benefits. There is no finding, and no suggestion, that in this case the promise was given as a result of fraud or duress.

If it be objected that the propositions above contravene the principle in *Stilk v. Myrick*, I answer that in my view they do not; they refine, and limit the application of that principle, but they leave the principle unscathed e.g. where B secures no benefit by his promise. It is not in my view surprising that a principle enunciated in relation to the rigours of sea-faring life during the Napoleonic wars should be subjected during the succeeding 180 years to a process of refinement and limitation in its application in the present day.

It is therefore my opinion that on his findings of fact in the present case, the judge was entitled to hold, as he did, that the defendants' promise to pay the extra £10,300 was supported by valuable consideration, and thus constituted an enforceable agreement.

As a subsidiary argument, Mr. Evans submits that on the facts of the present case the consideration, even if otherwise good, did not "move from the promisee". This submission is based on the principle illustrated in the decision in *Tweddle v. Atkinson* (1861) 1 B. & S. 393. My understanding of the meaning of the requirement that "consideration must move from the promisee" is that such consideration must be provided by the promisee, or arise out of his contractual relationship with the promisor. It is consideration provided by somebody else, not a party to the contract, which does not 'move from the promisee'. This was the situation in *Tweddle v. Atkinson*, but it is, of course, not the situation in the present case. Here the benefits to the defendants arose out of their agreement of 9th April 1986 with the plaintiff, the promisee. In this respect I would adopt the following passage from Chitty on Contracts, 25th edition, paragraph 173, and refer to the authorities there cited:

> The requirement that consideration must move from the promisee is most generally satisfied where some detriment is suffered by him e.g. where he parts with money or goods, or renders services, in exchange for the promise. But the requirement may be equally well satisfied where the promisee confers a benefit on the promisor without in fact suffering any detriment.

That is the situation in this case.

I repeat, therefore, my opinion that the judge was, as a matter of law, entitled to hold that there was valid consideration to support the agreement under which the defendants promised to pay an additional £10,300 at the rate of £575 per flat.

For these reasons I would dismiss this appeal.

. . . .

[PURCHAS, L.J.:]

The history and circumstances under which this appeal comes before the court have been set out in the judgment of Glidewell L.J. whose exposition I gratefully adopt. I repeat here only for ease of reference the significant features of the factual matrix against which the parties came together on 9th April 1986.

Evidence given by Mr. Cottrell, the defendants' surveyor, established that, to their knowledge, the original contract price was too low to enable the plaintiff to operate satisfactorily and at a profit by something a little over £3,780. It was also known that the plaintiff was falling short in the supervision of his own labour force with the result that productivity fell and his financial difficulties had been aggravated. A further difficulty, which the judge found had arisen by the time of the meeting in April, was that the plaintiff had been paid for more than 80% of the work but had not completed anything like this percentage. These facts were all obviously known to the plaintiff as well as the defendants. Also known to the defendants through Mr. Cottrell, and probably also appreciated by the plaintiff, was that the carpentry work to be executed by the plaintiff was on what was known as "the critical path of the [defendants'] global operations". Failure to complete this work by the plaintiff, in accordance with the contract, would seriously prejudice the defendants as main contractors vis-a-vis the owners for whom they were working.

In these circumstances there were clearly incentives to both parties to make a further arrangement in order to relieve the plaintiff of his financial difficulties and also to ensure that the plaintiff was in a position, or alternatively was willing, to continue with the sub-contract works to a reasonable and timely completion. Against this context the judge found that on 9th April 1986 a meeting took place between the plaintiff and a man called Hooper, on the one hand, and Mr. Cottrell and Mr. Roffey on the other hand. The arrangement was that the respondents would pay the plaintiff an extra £10,300 by way of increasing the lump sum for the total work. It was further agreed that the sum of £10,300 was to be paid at the rate of £575 per flat on the completion of each flat. This arrangement was beneficial to both sides. By completing one flat at a time rather than half completing all the flats the plaintiff was able to receive moneys on account and the respondents were able to direct their other trades to do work in the completed flats which otherwise would have been held up until the plaintiff had completed his work.

The point of some difficulty which arises on this appeal is whether the judge was correct in his conclusion that the agreement reached on 9th April failed for lack of consideration within the principle established by the old cases of *Stilk v. Myrick* [1809] 2 Camp. 317 approving *Harris v. Watson* [1791] Peake 102. Mr. Makey, who appeared for the plaintiff, was bold enough to submit that *Harris v. Watson*, albeit a decision of Lord Kenyon, was a case tried at the Guildhall at Nisi Prius in the Court of King's Bench and that *Stilk v. Myrick* was a decision also at Nisi Prius albeit a judgment of no less a judge than Lord Ellenborough and that, therefore, this court was bound by neither authority. I feel I must say at once that, for my part, I would not be prepared to overrule two cases of such veneration

involving judgments of judges of such distinction except on the strongest possible grounds since they form a pillar stone of the law of contract which has been observed over the years and is still recognised in principle in recent authority: see the decision of *Stilk v. Myrick* to be found in *North Ocean Shipping Co. Ltd. v. Hyundai Construction Co. Ltd.* [1979] 1 Q.B. 705 at page 712 per Mocatta J. With respect, I agree with his view of the two judgments by Denning L.J. (as he then was) in *Ward v. Byham* [1956] 1 W.L.R. 498 and *Williams v. Williams* [1957] 1 W.L.R. 148 in concluding that these judgments do not provide a sound basis for avoiding the rule in *Stilk v. Myrick*. Although this rule has been the subject of some criticism it is still clearly recognised in current textbooks of authority: see Chitty on Contract and Cheshire and Fifoot Law of Contract. By the same token I find myself unable to accept the attractive invitation offered by Mr. Makey to follow the decision of the Supreme Court of New Hampshire in *Watkins and Sons Inc. v. Carrig* (1941) 21 A.2d 591.

In my judgment, therefore, the rule in *Stilk v. Myrick* remains valid as a matter of principle, namely that a contract not under seal must be supported by consideration. Thus, where the agreement upon which reliance is placed provides that an extra payment is to be made for work to be done by the payee which he is already obliged to perform then unless some other consideration is detected to support the agreement to pay the extra sum that agreement will not be enforceable. The two cases, *Harris v. Watson* and *Stilk v. Myrick* involved circumstances of a very special nature, namely the extraordinary conditions existing at the turn of the eighteenth century under which seamen had to serve their contracts of employment on the high seas. There were strong public policy grounds at that time to protect the master and owners of a ship from being held to ransom by disaffected crews. Thus, the decision that the promise to pay extra wages even in the circumstances established in those cases, was not supported by consideration is readily understandable. Of course, conditions today on the high seas have changed dramatically and it is at least questionable, as Mr. Makey submitted, whether these cases might not well have been decided differently if they were tried today. The modern cases tend to depend more upon the defence of duress in a commercial context rather than lack of consideration for the second agreement. In the present case the question of duress does not arise. The initiative in coming to the agreement of 9th April came from Mr. Cottrell and not from the plaintiff. It would not, therefore, lie in the defendants' mouth to assert a defence of duress. Nevertheless, the court is more ready in the presence of this defence being available in the commercial context to look for mutual advantages which would amount to sufficient consideration to support the second agreement under which the extra money is paid. Although the passage cited below from the speech of Lord Hailsham of St. Marylebone L.C. in *Woodhouse A.C. Israel Cocoa Ltd. S.A. v. Nigerian Produce Marketing Co Ltd.* [1972] A.C. 741 was strictly obiter dicta I respectfully adopt it as an indication of the approach to be made in modern times. The case involved an agreement to vary the currency in which the buyer's obligation should be met which was subsequently affected by a depreciation in the currency involved. The case was decided on an issue of estoppel but Lord Hailsham commented on the other issue, namely the variation of the original contract in the following terms at page 757:

> If the exchange of letters was not variation, I believe it was nothing. The buyers asked for a variation in the mode of discharge of a contract of sale. If the proposal meant what they claimed, and was accepted and acted upon, I venture to think that the vendors would have been bound by their acceptance at least until they gave reasonable notice to terminate, and I imagine that a modern court would have found no difficulty in discovering consideration for such a promise. Business men know their own business best even when they appear to grant an indulgence, and in the present case I do not think that there would have been insuperable difficulty in spelling out consideration from the earlier correspondence.

In the light of those authorities the question now must be addressed: Was there evidence upon which the judge was entitled to find that there was sufficient consideration to support the agreement of 9th April, as set out in the passage from his judgment already set out in the judgment of Glidewell L.J.? The references to this problem in Chitty on Contracts, 25th edition, General Principles, are not wholly without some conflict amongst themselves. In paragraph 1491 the learned editors turn to the question of consideration to support an agreement to vary an existing contract:

> In many cases, consideration can be found in the mutual abandonment of existing rights or the conferment of new benefits by each party on the other.

Reference is made to the *Woodhouse* case to which I have already referred:

For example, an alteration of the money of account in a contract proposed or made by one party and accepted by the other is binding on both parties, since either may benefit from the variation.... However, an agreement whereby one party undertakes an additional obligation, but the other party is merely bound to perform his existing obligations, or an agreement whereby one party undertakes an additional obligation, but for the benefit of that party alone, will not be effective to vary the contract as no consideration is present.

These statements are based upon *Stilk v. Myrick* and *The Syrus Shipping Co. S.A. v. Elaghill Trading Co.* [1982] Lloyds Rep. 390. Reference is also made to paragraph 185 earlier in the textbook where the case of *Stilk v. Myrick* is considered at some length. On the other hand, at paragraph 173 the learned editors make this proposition:

> The requirement that consideration must move from the promisee is most generally satisfied where some detriment is suffered by him: e.g. where he parts with money or goods, or renders services, in exchange for the promise. But the requirement may equally well be satisfied where the promisee confers a benefit on the promisor without in <u>fact</u> suffering any detriment. For example, in *De la Bere v. Pearson Ltd.* [1908] 1 K.B. 287 the defendants owned a newspaper and invited readers to apply for financial advice on the terms that the defendants should be entitled to publish the readers' letters and their own replies.

This is an accurate recital of the facts in *De la Bere v. Pearson Ltd.* but when the argument and judgments are read the case turned on issues other than consideration, namely remoteness of damage, etc. So the case is doubtful support for the proposition made in this paragraph.

The question must be posed: What consideration has moved from the plaintiff to support the promise to pay the extra £10,300 added to the lump sum provision? In the particular circumstances which I have outlined above, there was clearly a commercial advantage to both sides from a pragmatic point of view in reaching the agreement of 9th April. The defendants were on risk that as a result of the bargain they had struck the plaintiff would not or indeed possibly could not comply with his existing obligations without further finance. As a result of the agreement the defendants secured their position commercially. There was, however, no obligation added to the contractual duties imposed upon the plaintiff under the original contact. Prima facie this would appear to be a classic *Stilk v. Myrick* case. It was, however, open to the plaintiff to be in deliberate breach of the contract in order to "cut his losses" commercially. In normal circumstances the suggestion that a contracting party can rely upon his own breach to establish consideration is distinctly unattractive. In many cases it obviously would be and if there was any element of duress brought upon the other contracting party under the modern development of this branch of the law the proposed breaker of the contract would not benefit. With some hesitation and comforted by the passage from the speech of Lord Hailsham, to which I have referred, I consider that the modern approach to the question of consideration would be that where there were benefits derived by each party to a contract of variation even though one party did not suffer a detriment this would not be fatal to the establishing of sufficient consideration to support the agreement. If both parties benefit from an agreement it is not necessary that each also suffers a detriment. In my judgment, on the facts as found by the judge, he was entitled to reach the conclusion that consideration existed and in those circumstances I would not disturb that finding. This is sufficient to determine the appeal. The judge found as a fact that the flats were "substantially completed" and that payment was due to the plaintiff in respect of the number of flats substantially completed which left an outstanding amount due from the defendants to the plaintiff in the absence of the payment of which the plaintiff was entitled to remove from the site. For these reasons and for the reasons which have already been given by Glidewell L.J. I would dismiss this appeal.

Order: Appeal dismissed, with costs; leave to appeal to House of Lords granted.

(e)   Contract Law in Perspective[†]

Linda Mulcahy

CONSIDERATION AND ESTOPPEL

Introduction

In this chapter, we look at another key component which the judiciary look for in contracts — consideration. The doctrine is fundamental to the classical model, which expects every contract to involve an *exchange* which comes about as a result of striking a bargain. It is the mechanism through which the judiciary have sought to distinguish between gifts and legally enforceable exchanges. A lot of what has been written about the doctrine of consideration makes it seem as though it is a very complex notion. In fact the key concept behind it is very simple. If you want to enforce a contract, you must give something to the other party and receive something in return.

It is important to understand from the start that evidence of consideration may be needed more than once in the life of a commercial relationship. Whenever the parties need to vary the terms of the original agreement, they will need to provide fresh consideration as, in the eyes of traditionalists, this is a fresh deal. It will be seen that it is this condition which has caused the most tension between the requirements of doctrine and the needs and practices of the business community. We learnt when looking at the work of Macaulay and others in Chapter 4 that business people are not as concerned with formalities as lawyers. The commercial pressures or tight deadlines which they work with on a daily basis mean that they are often prepared to accept changes to contractual arrangements without even considering what they need to do to make the variation legally binding.

Attempts have been made to circumvent the rigour of the consideration doctrine by the development of the equitable doctrine of promissory estoppel. One of the most significant characteristics of the doctrine is the fact that it shifts the conceptual focus away from the notion of exchange to that of reliance. Where the latter is concerned, the emphasis is on whether a party has acted reasonably when relying on an undertaking relating to variation of the

† Linda Mulcahy, *Contract Law in Perspective*, 5th ed. (London and New York: Routledge-Cavendish, 2008) at pp. 85–90. [Notes/references omitted.] Reproduced by permission of Taylor & Francis Books UK.

contractual terms rather than looking for a fresh exchange. The notion of reliance has been much discussed in academic circles as an alternative to understanding contractual obligations as exchanges. Estoppel is one of the areas in which this thinking has found its way into doctrine. As a result the comparison of these two models is a major focus of this chapter and a theme which we carry over to the next, when we look at the problems of misrepresentation in pre-contractual negotiations.

Contract As Bargain and Exchange

We shall start with an exploration of the fact that traditionally the common law concept of contract has been founded on the concept of exchange and bargain. What this means is that, for a contract to be enforceable, each of the parties to it must give something and receive something. Every time you buy a newspaper you give money in exchange for it but the thing you exchange does not have to be a material object. I get paid a monthly salary in exchange for the services I provide as a lecturer. Those of you who have taken out student loans have been given money in exchange for a promise to pay it back. It might also be the case that a person promises *not* to do something (forbearance) by way of providing consideration. This would be the case, for instance, if I agreed not to bring a lawsuit to recover a sum of money owed to me if the debtor agreed to pay by instalments over a 12-month period together with interest. The principle underlying all the examples given so far is that both the parties to a contract have to achieve something as a result of the exchange. Lack of exchange renders informal, gratuitous promises or gifts unenforceable at law because they lack the required *reciprocity*.

A promise to do something in the future can also amount to consideration. The ability to enforce a contract which relies on an exchange of promises about things yet to be performed marked an important stepping stone in the law of contract. Critically, it allows for forward planning in the commercial sector. Consider the example of the building of Wembley stadium. The contracts between Wembley National Stadium Limited and the construction company Multiplex were legally enforceable *before* construction actually started. The contract was formed on the basis that Multiplex *promised* to construct the stadium and Wembley National Stadium Limited *promised* to pay them for the work. At this stage the contract is said to be *executory*. Actual performance of the act (or the forbearance) embodied in such a promise amounts to *executed* consideration. In other words the contract is executed when the promise is performed. In the case of a unilateral contract, it is executed when a promise is exchanged for a completed act.

Contract law textbooks reveal centuries of 'leading' cases on consideration, which deal with a variety of legal propositions and exceptions regarding the nature of this contractual requirement. However, for an introductory study of the law as it operates *today*, it is doubtful if full attention needs be given to the extensive and complicated accumulation of 'old' case law on consideration. Points from such cases do still arise but more often than not, modern cases tend to demonstrate moves in judicial thinking *away from* strict theories. Lord Denning (1979) expressed the view that the effect of the doctrine of promissory estoppel since 1947:

> has been to do away with the doctrine of consideration in all but a handful of cases. During the 16 years while I have been Master of the Rolls I do not recall any case in which it has arisen or been discussed.

Taking these statements as our cue, we will confine ourselves to an examination of consideration's main features and then proceed to a closer look at promissory estoppel and other moves away from traditional models.

Economic Value

The consideration supplied by the parties must be something of value in the eyes of the law to make it binding. Generally speaking, value has been taken by the courts to mean *economic* value. The economic value of consideration is usually obvious and this is probably the main reason why few consideration disputes reach the courts. Services and goods are generally exchanged for the going market rate. However, it is important to recognise that the courts are willing to acknowledge nominal economic consideration such as peppercorn rent. This is because the notion of freedom of contract which dominates the classical model of contract is based on the principle that it is not the job of the courts to police whether a contract is a *good* bargain. They are only there to ensure that there is some bargain. In other words, party autonomy trumps judicial meddling. It has been long argued that the parties should be free to set their own price or promise in accordance with the value they personally attach to the exchange. This position demonstrates a clear logic. If contract reflects a bargain which has been struck, then it is for the parties to do the bargaining and determine what suits them best. It is for this reason that the agreement between Angie, Georgie and Polly to pay the latter double the market rate in wages would be enforceable in the courts. According to judicial authority, the adequacy of the consideration is for the parties to consider at the time of making the agreement, not for the court when it is sought to be enforced.

Whilst this general approach to bargains continues to frame the case law, nowadays, the courts are more sensitive to the ways in which imbalances of bargaining strength and the use of excessive commercial pressure or undue influence can undermine the notion of free exchange. The result is that, in some cases, a grossly inadequate consideration may militate against a court's sense of fair bargain. In *Lloyd's Bank Ltd v Bundy* (1975), although Lord Denning stated that 'no bargain will be upset which is the result of the ordinary interplay of forces', the court struck down a contract of guarantee by which the defendant, an elderly farmer not well versed in business affairs, mortgaged his house as security for the debts of his son's business. This was done at a time when the company was already in dire financial straits, and not long before its eventual collapse. It was felt that, in the circumstances, the consideration moving from the bank was grossly inadequate and, at the late stage at which the guarantee was given, all that the company gained was a short respite from impending doom. The legislature has also played an increasingly active role in the regulation of exchange in certain contexts, such as carriage of goods by sea, rents and interest rates.

Bargain and the Timing of Consideration

The classical view of contract expects consideration to be exchanged as part of a bargaining process. Thus it is said that something wholly performed *before* an agreement is reached cannot amount to consideration. Instead, it is known as *past* consideration. The idea rests on the idea that, if something has been voluntarily given before the bargaining begins, then this should be treated as a voluntary gift or service. For example, if I give you some legal advice in connection with problems you are having with your landlord and two weeks later you agree to pay me for it, this does not amount to an exchange which would be recognised as a contract. My voluntary contribution occurred before the subject of money was discussed. Put simply its bargaining value was used up or spent in advance. The

service was offered at a time when we had no expectation of exchange or bargain.

However, in a business context, it may be argued that, if the service was requested, it might have been understood by the parties that payment would be forthcoming. In these circumstances the courts have been prepared to allow that a later express promise to pay merely confirms and quantifies an earlier implied promise on your part: see *Re Casey's Patents* (1892). However, this alternative reading of such situations I has proved controversial and is seen by some as undermining the whole notion of *contemporaneous* bargain on which traditional reasoning is based.

The sort of problems which might arise in connection with this rule in the commercial sector are illustrated in *Pao On v Lau Yiu Long* (1980). In this case, the defendants made a contract with the claimants. They sold shares to the claimant who in exchange promised not to put them on the market for at least 12 months. The defendants, who retained a large block of shares in the same company, had required this, as they did not wish to see the value of their holding depressed by a sudden sale of the claimant's shares. The defendants later promised to indemnify the claimant against any loss he might incur if the shares fell in value during the year. The Privy Council was willing to marry together the claimant's promise not to sell, albeit given as part of the original contract of sale, and the defendants' subsequent promise to indemnify. It has been said that the claimant was 'only getting what he was really, morally and commercially, entitled to'. The case also supports the growing idea that, in appropriate circumstances, the court should have regard to a *continuing commercial relationship* between parties rather than concentrating on 'discrete' transactions or arrangements within that relationship, a proposition which sits comfortably with the arguments of relational contract theorists.

Consideration and Existing Contractual Duties

It follows from what has been said about past consideration that a party can not offer up as consideration something that they have a pre-existing duty to do. If a duty already exists, then this 'consideration', like past consideration, has already been used and spent. The position can be outlined by using an example from the case study in Chapter 2. Chelsea agreed to carry out certain obligations as a shop assistant for Angie and Georgie at a fixed weekly wage for a five-year period. As a result of severe financial pressures on their business, Angie and Georgie find they are unable to pay Chelsea at the agreed rate. Rather than terminating her employment, they agree to pay Chelsea a lower wage for the same work. Because she enjoys her work and would find it difficult to find another job locally, Chelsea agrees to the change. Is the variation of the contract binding in law? The traditional viewpoint would be that it is not. Each new or varied contract requires fresh consideration, and Chelsea has already agreed to offer up her services in exchange for an agreed wage and for a fixed term. It might be useful to think of the issue in two stages. There is an original contractual agreement followed by a variation of it. According to traditional reasoning, the variation can only stand if Chelsea agrees to do *more* for Angie and Georgie in exchange for their new promise. This would be a new agreement with additional consideration for the second contract.

The problem the courts are faced with is that the parties to a contract often change the terms of performance without any reference to the formal requirements of this doctrine. In the majority of cases this happens because of a change in circumstances or market conditions. These cases serve to remind us that it is extremely difficult for the parties to an ongoing commercial relationship to predict what will happen in the future at the time of making their contract. Many have claimed that the English law of contract with its emphasis on exchange and the 'moment of responsibility' has paid insufficient attention to the need for flexibility in ongoing commercial relationships Despite these concerns a strict line on this issue has been taken in much of the case law. So for instance, in *Stilk v Myrick* (1809), a crew had been engaged to sail a vessel from London to the Baltic and back at the rate of £5 a month. Following the desertion ... of two of the 11 crew members, the captain promised to share the deserters' wages among the remaining crew if they would work the ship back to London. But when the ship returned its owners refused to honour the captain's promise. It was held that the seamen's claim for the extra pay failed for lack of consideration. The crew were already bound by their contract to meet the normal emergencies of the voyage and were doing no more than their duty in sailing the ship back. Similar facts arose in *Hartley v Ponsonby* (1857), except that in this case 17 out of 36 crew deserted and the voyage became very hazardous. The extra danger in this case was used to justify a different decision from that in *Stilk v Myrick* (1809). It was held that, because of the new danger, the remaining crew had been discharged from their original contract and were free therefore to enter a new one at higher wages which reflected the extra risk.

A number of subsequent cases have re-opened the debate about past consideration and questioned the basis on which this aspect of the doctrine is based. In the 1950s Lord Denning made a radical departure from the traditional stance. He felt able to find that such a promise was good consideration in two cases where a party merely promised to perform an existing legal duty in return for a promise. In *Ward v Byham* (1956), a case involving a pre-existing statutory duty, he argued: 'I have always thought that a promise to perform an existing duty, or the performance of it, should be regarded as good consideration, because it is a benefit to the person to whom it is given' (p. 320). And in *Williams v Williams* (1957) which involved a matrimonial dispute he opined:

> Now I agree that, in promising to maintain herself while she was in desertion, the wife was only promising to do that which she was already bound to do. Nevertheless, a promise to perform an existing duty is, I think, sufficient consideration to support a promise, so long as there is nothing in the transaction which is contrary to the public interest. (p. 307)

The cases shift the focus from strict formulae of fresh bargain and new exchange to a more pragmatic discussion of whether there is any *practical benefit* to the person to whom the promise is given, regardless of whether the consideration has already been 'used'. The only limitation imposed by Denning was that there should be no public policy reasons for not enforcing the promise.

These points re-emerge in the more recent case of *Williams v Roffey Bros and Nicholls (Contractors) Ltd* (1991) which has excited considerable interest in the issue. In that case, Roffey, as main contractors entered into a contract with a housing association for the refurbishment of a block of flats. Roffey subcontracted the carpentry work to Williams for £20,000. Part way through the work, Williams was in financial difficulties because he had tendered too low and had failed to supervise his workmen properly. There was a distinct possibility that Williams would not complete on time or would stop work altogether. Facing a penalty clause in the main contract for late completion, Roffey agreed to pay Williams a further £10,300 at a rate of £575 per flat completed in order to get the job completed. The carpentry work on eight more flats was finished but, with only a further £1,500 having been paid by Roffey, Williams stopped work and sued for damages in respect of the eight completions. In line with the judgement In *Stilk v Myrick* (809), Roffey argued that Williams had provided no consideration to support their promise of additional payment and Williams was merely doing what he was already obliged to do.

The Court of Appeal held that Roffey *was* bound by their promise. Approving the decision in *Stilk v Myrick*, they nonetheless argued that the present case could be distinguished because something new was being offered up. In the view of Glidewell LJ, as long as the promisee obtains a practical benefit under the revised agreement and there is no economic duress or fraud, then the promise to do what Williams was already bound to do can constitute good consideration. In his view, there were a number of reasons why the benefits obtained and detriment avoided by the main contractors offered a new element. Firstly, they ensured that the claimant continued work and did not stop in breach of the sub-contract. Secondly, it allowed the main contractor to avoid the penalty for delay in the main contract. Finally, it allowed them to avoid the trouble and expense of engaging other people to complete the carpentry work.

The decisions demonstrate a willingness on the part of the judiciary to enforce arrangements which reflect good business sense in changing market conditions. The main contractor, when giving his promise of additional payment, is making the best of a bad job, and the variation in the arrangements is of benefit to him. In his estimation it is less disadvantageous to pay the sub-contractor more than to run the very real risk of having to pay his client even more under the terms of the penalty clause in the main contract. On this basis, the court leaves the parties to their rearrangement. The case also takes account of the long-term commercial inevitability of the renegotiation of terms during the performance of the contract. Treating each variation of terms as a new contract requiring fresh consideration may be a logical approach to contracts where an ongoing relationship of dependence does not exist. But, as *Williams v Roffey* shows, an overly formalistic approach to the issue in all contracts can create an absurd situation in which the law undermines perfectly fair and logical alterations which benefit both parties. This view of the case can be seen, in more technical language, in the words of Russell LJ: 'Consideration there must be but in my judgment the courts nowadays should be more ready to find its existence so as to reflect the intention of the parties to the contract where the bargaining powers are not unequal' (p. 18). This view is far from being new. Over 60 years ago, the American realists insisted that a true understanding of business law's purpose assumes an understanding of the facts of business life.

The reasoning in *Williams v Roffey* has not gone uncriticised (see for instance *South Caribbean Trading Co v Trafigura Beheer*, 2005) but it has been instrumental in spurning some interesting debates about the legitimacy of doctrines which fail to reflect the realities of the commercial sector in which such variations, negotiated in the absence of duress or undue pressure are common.

(f)   Estoppel and Relational Contracts†

T. Brettel Dawson

A relational contract schema developed by Ian MacNeil draws out points of tension and change in contract law, which are relevant to identifying trends in the current estoppel developments. He defined contracts as 'the relations among parties to the process of projecting exchange into the future'. In this way he focuses on the contractual or exchange behaviour of the parties rather than the boundaries of legal definitions. Equally, exchange is viewed as being 'embedded in relations' rather than arising from the discrete transactions of classical law. Reciprocity and solidarity are fundamental contractual behaviours maintaining these relations. Contractual obligation is set in a normative context requiring *inter alia* role integrity, planning, effectuation of consent, flexibility and the creation and restraint of power.

†   From "Estoppel and Obligation: The Modern Role of Estoppel by Convention" (1989) 9:1 Legal Studies 16 at 29–30. [Notes/references omitted.] Reproduced with permission.

253

In a relational contract, MacNeil argues, four particularly relational norms are significant. First is role integrity:

> ... in such circumstances, role integrity is more than simply keeping the role (as contractor) honest; if the role is to serve its social function as a foundation of reliance and expectations, maintaining it in the sense of keeping it together in a coherent piece, is a major job of social engineering.'[70]

A second norm is preservation of the relation over the life of the exchange. Third, is harmonisation of relational conflict. This requires that flexibility be built into the terms of the relation itself and is premised upon high levels of good faith and trust between the participants. This, in turn, relates back to reciprocity, which requires that the parties derive mutual benefit from the exchange and may adjust their relation to ensure fair distribution of the exchange surplus.

The fourth relational norm is characterised as conformity with '*supra* contract norms' which reflect the range of social and political choices constituting social structure.[71] In itself this is not novel, as contract laws necessarily recognise obligations consistent with underlying economic structures of exchange, entitlement and distribution.[72] However, MacNeil emphasises the integration of contractual analysis with the world of production and social relations:

in on-going contractual relations, we find such broad norms as distributive justice, liberty, social equality and inequality, and procedural justice, to mention some of the more vital ... at this point, just as contractual relations exceed the capacities of the neo-classical contract law system, so too the issues exceed the capacities of neo-classical contract law scholars. They must become something else — anthropologists, economists, political theorists, and philosophers — to do reasonable justice to the issues raised in contractual relations.[73]

Such relational norms cannot be accommodated within classical contract law. Even at its broadest, neo-classical contract law remains designed to facilitate discrete transactions, rather than to support the legal effect of actions taken in the context of relations. In the US faced with parallel development in s 90 promissory estoppel developments, Farber and Matheson proposed a new rule of obligation to deal directly with the relational issues arising in these cases. This 'revised rule of obligation' would:

> accept the fundamental fact that commitments are often made to promote economic activity and obtain economic benefits without any specific bargained-for exchange ... the proposed rule is simply that commitments made in furtherance of economic activity should be enforced ... (this) is a major departure from traditional contract law ... (but) the rule sounds within contract law, and operates within its traditional area of concern — promissory economic exchange.[74]

III

Unjust Enrichment

OVERVIEW

The third main division in the private law of Obligations is unjust enrichment. Although the newcomer to the taxonomy, it has an ancient pedigree, as evidenced by the continuing reference to the foundational case of *Moses v. Macpherlan*, 1760. In this case, Jacob had issued promissory notes (much like cheques) to Moses, who later endorsed these over to Macpherlan on the express understanding that Macpherlan would only seek payment from Jacob. In strictly legal terms, Moses was alternatively liable to pay on the notes based on his endorsement of them. For some reason lost to history, Macpherlan decided to sue Moses for the money owing on the notes and won summary judgment. Moses then brought an action of his own against Macpherlan in the Court of Queen's Bench, alleging that Macpherlan owed him the money won in the lower court. In effect he was asking Macpherlan to give him back the money because he was not entitled to have it or to keep it. Moses won his case, effectively overhauling the decision in the other proceedings. In the course of his reasons in favour of Moses, Lord Mansfield, one of England's finest commercial law judges of the time (a time associated with the Industrial Revolution and the emergence of new commercial activities), stated that Macpherlan "ought in justice [to] refund the money *mala fide* (in bad faith) obtained." In other Law Reports, Lord Mansfield is recorded saying, "This kind of equitable action, to recover back money, which ought not in justice to be kept, is very beneficial, and therefore much encouraged. It lies only for money which, *ex aequo et bono*, the defendant ought to refund." In his view, "[The action] lies for money paid by mistake; or upon a consideration which happens to fail; or for money got through imposition, (express, or implied); or extortion; or oppression; or an undue advantage taken of the plaintiff's situation, contrary to laws made for the protection of persons under those circumstances.... In one word, the gist of this kind of action is, that the defendant, upon the circumstances of the case, is <u>obliged by the ties of natural justice and equity</u> to <u>refund</u> the money."

Lines of cases raising similar concerns developed in a diffuse way and were regarded as exceptions or additions to contract law rules (indeed, there was for a time talk of 'quasi-contract law'). The spirit of Lord Mansfield re-appeared in the oft-quoted words of Lord Wright in his 1943 decision in *Fibrosa Spolka*. The case itself was of little import, but what matters about it is that Lord Wright stated the rationale for obligation in these terms: "[A]ny civilised system of law is found to provide remedies for unjust enrichment, that is to prevent a man from retaining the money of or some benefit derived from another which it is against conscience that he should keep. Such remedies are generically different from remedies in contract and tort and are now recognized to fall within a third category of the common law."

In the United States work was also being done at this time to analyze and link together the various instances of these concerns. John McCamus, co-author of a leading Canadian text in this area, notes the prescient work of Scott and Seavey for the American Law Institute's *Restatement of the Law of Restitution* (1937):

> The *Restatement* brought together much of the old law of quasi-contract and a variety of equitable doctrines, most notably much of the law relating to constructive trust, under the "Restitution" banner on the theory that these bodies of doctrine had much more in common than their disparate origins in common law and equity would suggest. Indeed, the Institute was said to have adopted "the conviction that [these bodies of doctrine] are all subject to one unitary principle which heretofore has not had general recognition, principle being, of course, the principle against unjust enrichment."

The initial name for this branch of the law of obligations was "Restitution", given the strong association in the cases with 'making good' or restoring the inappropriately obtained benefit. Over time, it has come to be called "Unjust Enrichment" as a more accurate reflection of the common principle.

At this point of its development, there are two streams in the jurisprudence of unjust enrichment. The first relates to defective transactions. Mitchell McInnes, a Canadian scholar, has explained this thread in the following terms:

> Restitution has typically been triggered by a defective intention: the claimant's (person who wants their money back or payment for goods or services) intention in effecting the 'impugned' or ineffective transaction was impaired by error, qualified by some subsequently disappointing condition; it allows a person to resile from a transaction that was not the product of informed choice.[1]

Patrick Atiyah has grouped these sorts of situations as being ones where "some misfire has occurred, some untoward and unplanned benefit has been rendered. Is it right that the beneficiary should pay for it, or are there grounds on which it is more just that he should be permitted to retain an unpaid-for benefit?"[2] Some of the legal doctrines grouped in this area of unjust enrichment include mistake, duress, waiver of tort; transactions ineffective in common law; compulsory discharge of another's liability and necessitous intervention. McInnes has pointed out that "[u]nless a legal system is to adopt the simple, though unattractive solution of merely allowing the gains and losses to lie where they fall, it must find an alternative means of governing such transactions."[3] At stake is the equilibrium of the market (and contract law) as the mechanism of exchange.

The second stream in the jurisprudence of unjust enrichment draws more directly on concepts originating in the Court of Equity. In the extract contained in Chapter 9, Ziff explains Equity as "a cognate set of rules, separate from the common law", giving rise to rights enforceable in a court of equity (e.g., Chancery). Equity was the guardian of the 'weak and unprotected', a court of 'conscience' and remedial in scope, addressing defects, undue harshness or omissions in the common law. In this thread of unjust enrichment the situations group around problems rooted in mistakes outside of contractual settings, breach of fiduciary duty, breach of confidence, obtaining profits from wrongs and sharing the value of property to which one has contributed by labour or money in a common venture in the absence of being on the title.

Within the United States and Canada, at least, the law of restitution is now firmly established as a third branch of the private law of obligations. The unifying principle across both threads of originating jurisprudence and which in effect 'fuses' together the law in this area that where there has been an enrichment, a corresponding deprivation, and the absence of any juristic reason — such as a contract or disposition of law — for the enrichment.

In this Part there are two chapters. The first loosely focuses on the emergence of unjust enrichment as a branch of private law, with a focus on mistaken payments and defective transactions. The second chapter addresses the equitable stream more closely, with a focus on division of property held in the name of one partner to a marriage or common law relationship when the relationship breaks down. The recent decision of the Supreme Court of Canada in *Kerr v. Baranow*, 2011 brings many of the threads together in a clear restatement of its own in regard to this area of the law. Readers should also look for a decision to be issued by the Supreme Court of Canada in a Quebec case known informally as "Eric v. Lola", in which similar questions have been raised but in the context of Quebec Civil Law. The United Kingdom has also recently updated its approach in this area (which had been mired in very technical trust law analysis) in the decision of *Kernott v. Jones*, [2011] UKSC 53.

Notes

1. Mitchell McInnes, "Unjust Factors, Juristic Reasons and Contracts in Anglo-Canadian Law" in *Re-examining Contract and Unjust Enrichment*, ed., Paula Giliker (Boston: Martinus Nijhoff, 2007) 23 at 27.
2. Patrick Atiyah, "Contracts, Promises and the Law of Obligations" (1978) 94 LQR 193 at 198.
3. McInnes, *supra* n1 at 29.

LEARNING OBJECTIVES

At the conclusion of this Part, readers should be able to

- explain and illustrate why and how the law has decided to look beyond 'strict legal rights' in contract or property law to allow remedies;
- outline the policy tensions that courts in Canada have navigated in establishing the scope of the principle of unjust enrichment, including certainty and choice;
- state and define the meaning of the three components of the unjust enrichment principle;
- connect the development of property rights on the breakdown of conjugal relationships with evolving forms of family law and principles of equality;
- outline the remedies available in unjust enrichment, distinguishing between constructive trust, damages and 'restitution'.

(a)   Unjust Enrichment: Its Role and Its Limits†

John D. McCamus

> A person who has been unjustly enriched at the expense of another is required to make restitution to the other. (American Law Institute, *Restatement of the Law of Restitution, 1937*)

2.   THE TAXONOMER

In 1889, the indefatigable nineteenth century, American treatise writer, Joel Prentiss Bishop,[4] published what may well be his least remembered contribution to the genre, *Commentaries on the Non-Contract Law*.[5] Though one suspects that this work may not have enjoyed a wide readership, it is nonetheless a fascinating work for the student of taxonomy. Bishop begins his treatise with a brief discussion of the need for and nature of legal taxonomy:[6]

> The division of our law into various subjects, and of each subject into its particular titles and subtitles, is matter simply of convenience to writer and reader; it constitutes no part of the law itself. The law is a seamless and partitionless whole. But it is a thing so vast that the mind can have no valuable comprehension of it, except in parts artificially separated from the mass for examination and study. And every writer is entitled to make for himself the divisions best adapted to his particular methods and objects. Practically, in most instances, there will be discovered a common professional usage, which it will be most convenient for both writer and reader to follow.

The law of non-contract, in Bishop's conception of it, was to include what remained of the private law of

obligations once the law of contract itself had been removed. Thus, it covered virtually all of what was then, as now, considered to be the law of torts. It touched upon, as well, some subjects that might now be considered restitutionary in nature. As Bishop explained,[7]

> Its sphere extends beyond torts, which it includes, to whatever else is within a group of fundamental principles regulating things not bargained about. Therein it follows a natural division in the legal field, instead of driving a mere artificial furrow.

.   .   .   .

Thirty-six years in the making, breath-taking in its scope and ambition, *Commentaries on the Non-Contract Law* is, in its own way, a work of brilliance. It is sad to record, therefore, that as an experiment in taxonomy, it was nonetheless an abysmal failure. Like many another brilliant failure, however, it offers useful instruction to others engaged in the same line of work.

In 1937, the American Law Institute published its much more successful experiment in the reorganization of legal rules, the *Restatement of Restitution*. Unique among the restatements published by the Institute, the *Restatement of Restitution* created a new legal subject. As is well known, the reporters or draftsmen of the *Restatement* were two distinguished American legal academics, Warren A. Seavey and Austin W. Scott. In the early pages of the *Restatement* and in an article published in the Law Quar-

---

† From D. Waters (ed.), *Fiduciaries and Trusts 1993* (Toronto: Carswell & Co., 1993) 129 at 131, 132–37, 143–44. [Footnotes omitted.] Reprinted by permission of author and Carswell, a division of Thomson Reuters Canada Limited.

terly Review,[9] Seavey and Scott explain the nature and scope of their project. The *Restatement* brought together much of the old law of quasi-contract and a variety of equitable doctrines, most notably much of the law relating to constructive trust, under the "Restitution" banner on the theory that these bodies of doctrine had much more in common than their disparate origins in common law and equity would suggest. Indeed, the Institute was said to have adopted "the conviction that [these bodies of doctrine] are all subject to one unitary principle which heretofore has not had general recognition,"[10] that principle being, of course, the principle against unjust enrichment. In Part I of the *Restatement*, the authors offered an account of the existing doctrine, whether of common law or equitable origins, treating such subjects as the recovery of benefits conferred upon another as a result of a mistake, coercion, or fraud, the recovery of benefits conferred in situations where the conferrer anticipated receiving something in return which did not materialize and the recovery of the value of services rendered in necessitous circumstances. Part II of the *Restatement* focuses particularly on the rules relating to the constructive trust and might have been more helpfully titled, as Seavey and Scott pointed out, "Rights in Property Created as the Result of a Right to Restitution."

Recognition of restitution as a distinct branch, division of or subject of the law was part of a larger recognition of "the tripartite division of the law into contract, torts and restitution, the division being made with reference to the purposes which each subject serves in protecting one of three fundamental interests."[12] The fundamental interest protected by contract law was said to be "that a person is entitled to receive what another has promised him or promised another for him."[13] The fundamental postulate of tort law is "that a person has a right not to be harmed by another" with the result that the law requires "a wrong-doer to give such compensation to the person harmed as will be substantially equivalent to the harm done".[14] The third postulate, underlying restitutionary doctrine, is, of course, the principle against unjust enrichment.

The objective to be served by bringing the material together and restating it in this fashion was that "of making clear the principles underlying this group and of attempting to give to it the individual life and development which its importance demands."[15] The subject had not previously received adequate treatment. The accidents of English legal history had scattered it "through many sections of the digests and in treatises on apparently diverse subjects".[16] In short, the objective was essentially one of reorganiza-

tion and restatement of hitherto neglected material whose unity was to be found in describing them all as instances of recovery of an unjust enrichment.

. . . .

In the present context, it is appropriate to ask whether any more precise view can be gained of the role envisioned by Seavey and Scott for the unjust enrichment principle. Seavey and Scott, like many who have followed in their footsteps, treat this matter somewhat Delphically. It is plain that Seavey and Scott think that the unjust enrichment principle and the underlying postulates of contract and tort provide a useful device for organizing the exposition and study of the basic doctrines of private law. It is also plain that they conceive of the principle as something other than the rules set out in the decided cases. The basic postulates offer "merely a brief thumb-nail sketch indicating extent rather than giving precise boundaries."[20] Yet, at the same time, it is clear that Seavey and Scott do not view the unjust enrichment principle as merely one of a possible range of taxonomic devices, including, for example, alphabetical order, from which a selection has been arbitrarily made.[21]

> The subject of restitution is not properly or adequately described merely by a description of the purpose or interest which gives life to the rules. It is an organism growing in accordance with the principle which causes it to exist; a statement of the principle is not a description of what it produces.

If contract law is, in some sense, animated by a general disposition to enforce bargained-for promises, restitution cases are animated by a general disposition to reverse unjust enrichment. To find out which types of promises are, in fact, enforced and which enrichments are, in fact, reversed it is necessary to consult the decided cases.

. . . .

... In England and Australia judicial acceptance of the utility of the unjust enrichment analysis has come only slowly. In recent years, however, leading decisions of the highest courts in England and Australia have adopted the unjust enrichment analysis.[24] In Canada, I shall not resist from observing, the unjust enrichment principle has enjoyed a much longer and a much richer career than elsewhere in the Commonwealth. In a remarkable series of cases beginning with *Deglman v. Guaranty Trust Co. of Canada*[25] and continuing, most recently, with the decision in *Peel (Regional Municipality) v. A.G.*

(Ontario),[26] the Supreme Court of Canada has openly and, especially in recent years, enthusiastically embraced the basic features of the *Restatement* model and woven them into the fabric of Canadian restitutionary doctrine.

If the unjust enrichment principle has thus enjoyed some Commonwealth success, especially in Canada, in reordering the taxonomy of private law, it is nonetheless a striking fact of contemporary academic literature on the subject, especially in England, that it continues to be preoccupied, to a significant degree, with questions of taxonomy....

Another contributing factor, however, must be the articulate and sophisticated opposition to the restitution project offered by one of England's most influential private law scholars, Professor Patrick Atiyah. In *The Rise and Fall of Freedom of Contract*,[28] Professor Atiyah offered a critique of the development of this new branch of law as part of a larger critique of the tripartite division of the common law into contract, tort and restitution. It will not be possible to portray adequately the richness of Professor Atiyah's larger critique in the present context. Nonetheless, a brief sketch will be helpful. Professor Atiyah's principal thesis constitutes an attack on the classical model of contract law. More particularly, he criticizes the centrality of promise as a foundation for contractual liability and rejects as unsatisfactory the expectancy measure of relief in contract cases for a variety of reasons.[29] He further argues that the distinctions among these three branches of the law are or should be collapsing as a result of the decline of the classical model of contract law (which included protection of bare expectancy as one of its features) and its replacement by a resurgence of benefit-based and reliance-based liabilities. In the course of a brief account of the evolution of judicial thought concerning quasi-contract, Atiyah noted the arrival of the restitution treatise by Goff and Jones and its acceptance of the basic idea that the unjust enrichment principle underlies this branch of the law. Professor Atiyah then went on to observe:[30]

> Nevertheless, it may be suggested that this development is as misconceived as all the earlier attempts to state the basis of the law relating to such liabilities. It is misconceived, in my view, because it fails to recognize the very substantial and close relationship between contractual and restitutionary liabilities. As I have rejected the notion that contractual liabilities are all promise-based and have insisted that where part executed contracts are enforced, the liability is primarily benefit-based or reliance-based, it is evident that I cannot support a move towards a total theoretical separation of contract from restitution.

In any case, it must be said that there is little sign yet of any wholehearted acceptance by English lawyers of a new branch of law entitled the Law of Restitution, and based on unjust enrichment ideas. The reality is that unjust enrichment has become a more important underlying idea of the law, for it is only another phrase for the concept of benefit-based liability, but the developments have been occurring interstitially in all branches of the law. In contract, in tort, in family law, in the law of property, in company law, the same development has been occurring. The various cases show little sign of coming together to cohere into one new body of law, and this may be just as well.

Professor Atiyah ends this study by concluding "that the time is plainly ripe for a new theoretical structure for contract, which will place it more firmly in association with the rest of the law of obligations."[31] Indeed, the new structure he has in mind for contract involves nothing less than a restructuring of the entire law of obligations. As he suggests elsewhere, the "great divide between duties which are voluntarily assumed and duties which are imposed by law" which underlies the current structure of the divisions of the law of obligations is an over-simplification.[32]

> A more adequate and more unifying conceptual structure for the law of obligations can be built around the inter-relationships between the concepts of reciprocal benefits, acts of reasonable reliance, and voluntary human conduct.

It will be evident that Professor Atiyah's attack was not so much an attack on the unjust enrichment principle *per se* — indeed it was part of his thesis that unjust enrichment or benefit-based liabilities have invaded many fields of law — rather it was his view that the isolation of a particular division or subject of the law based on this principle was misconceived.

．　．　．　．

3.　THEORY OF LIABILITY

．　．　．　．

When we examine the common sense lying behind the contract cases, a number of interesting features of the general principle emerge. First, it appears unlikely that there is any one single reason of policy that would justify the enforcement of the many different kinds of undertakings that are enforced at common law. The justifications for enforcing commercial contracts for the sale of goods, agreements of compromise, separation agreements and agreements which restrain trade but not unduly so are likely to have slightly or perhaps significantly different contours. Although consent is likely to form a significant part of the justification in each case, it is evident that there are many "contractual" obligations imposed on parties to which their actual consent is more assumed than real. Nonetheless, without examining the case in support of this proposition more carefully, there would appear to be, at the very least, "family resemblances"[51] among the various justifications given for the enforcement of undertakings. The policy reasons for the imposition of implied undertakings are likely to be closely related to the policy reasons for enforcing express obligations. There are also, obviously, reasons of convenience for including the enforcement of implied undertakings in our account of consensual obligation even if the basic theory of obligation cannot offer a complete explanation or justification for the imposition of liability. In sum, while the general principle is indeed vague, there exists nonetheless the possibility of giving it a content which is something other than the particular rules arising from the decided cases.

If the general principle can thus be said to have some content, it also appears to have some utility as a theory of liability insofar as it serves as a reminder or elliptical reference to the policy considerations favouring the enforcement of undertakings. To be sure, explicit references to the general principle are likely to be rare, at least in the contracts jurisprudence. Some things are so widely accepted that they need not be explicitly stated. In a difficult case, however, resort to the basic principle may be thought to be helpful. The important decision of Devlin J. in *St. John Shipping Corp. v. Joseph Rank Ltd.*[52] illustrates the point. It may be recalled that in the course of determining whether to enforce a contract for the carriage of goods by sea which had been performed unlawfully, Devlin J. invoked the general principle and suggested that departures from it should be countenanced only on "serious and sufficient grounds".[53]

Against this background, we can turn to the unjust enrichment principle and consider whether significant responses can be made to the charges of "void for vagueness" and "circularity". Without exploring the evidence in detail, it is my impression that the common sense and policy considerations lying behind the rules articulated in the various topics brought together by Seavey and Scott can, indeed, be usefully referred to, in a generalized way, as constituting a principle against unjust enrichment. Thus, a thoughtful explanation of the reasons for granting recovery of a payment made under mistake of fact is likely to make reference to the unintentional nature of the transfer and the windfall nature of the defendant's benefit. A similar discussion of money extracted by duress would likely refer to the same considerations and might add that it is inappropriate, for various reasons, to allow the defendant to profit from wrongful conduct of this kind. And so on. Although, as in the case of contract, the list of policy considerations will no doubt vary to some extent from one context to the next, I suspect that references to the windfall benefits issue and to the desirability of disgorging the profits of wrongdoing would repeat themselves throughout the exercise. If this is so, the unjust enrichment principle would, indeed, appear to be a useful shorthand reference to the policy considerations supporting the imposition of liability in the domain identified by Seavey and Scott as restitutionary in nature. Like *pacta sunt servanda*, the principle against unjust enrichment can indeed be given some content. The allegation of "circularity" is undermined by the empirical nature of this approach. The relevance of the unjust enrichment principle for these purposes can be tested by examining the reasons underlying the imposition of liability in restitution cases and asking whether the unjust enrichment principle is, in fact, a useful reference to recurrent justificatory reasons.

(b) *Moses v. Macpherlan*[†]

Court of King's Bench

Moses had four notes of one Chapman Jacob, dated 11th July, 1757, value 30s. each. Macpherlan, 7th November, 1758, prevailed upon Moses to indorse these notes to him, upon an express written agreement to indemnify Moses against all consequences of such indorsement, and that no suit should be

---

† (1760) S.C. 2 Burr. 1005. [Notes omitted.]

brought against Moses the indorser, but only against Jacob the drawer. Notwithstanding which, Macpherlan brought four actions in the Court of Conscience upon these very notes against Moses; and, upon trial of the first, the commissioners refused to go into any evidence of this agreement; whereupon the plaintiff recovered, and the defendant paid in the whole 6 *l.* And now Moses, the defendant below, brought indebitatus assumpsit against Macpherlan, the plaintiff below, for money had and received to his use, and obtained a verdict for 6 *l.*, subject to the opinion of this Court.

Morton (for defendant Macpherlan) argued, that indebitatus assumpsit would not lie upon a judgment recovered in an Inferior Court of a final jurisdiction; and cited Cro. Jac. 218; and I Bulstr. 152: the remedy in this case being a special action on the case for breach of the agreement.

Norton, contra, that this action would well lie, the remedy by action on assumpsit being of the most liberal and beneficial kind.

On the argument, Mansfield, C.J., doubted if the action would lie, after a judgment in the Court of Conscience; but wished to extend this remedial action as far as might be: to which Dennison, J., agreed, and inclined strongly that the action would lie. Foster, J., was afraid of the consequences of overhauling the judgment of a Court of a competent jurisdiction. Wilmot, J., was clear that the action would not lie; because this action always arises from a contract of re-payment, implied by law; and it would be absurd, if the law were to raise an implication in one Court, contrary to its own express judgment in another Court. He compared this action to the title De Solutione Indebiti, Inst. 3, 28, s. 6; and De Condictione Indebiti in Cod. and Dig.[p] in which there was always an exception causæ judicati; and this reason given for it, ne actiones resuscitentur.

[Lord Mansfield, C.J. for the court:]

It has been objected to this action: 1st, that debt will not lie upon this ground of complaint; therefore indebitatus assumpsit will not lie. But there is no foundation for this argument. It is held, indeed, in *Slade's case*, 4 Rep. 93, that where debt will lie, assumpsit will also lie; but the negative doctrine, e converso, is not any where held; it is rather a general rule, that where debt will not lie, indebitatus assumpsit will.[q] 2dly, that in this case no implied contract can arise, where upon to ground all assumpsit. But surely, if a man is bona fide obliged to refund whatever money be has unlawfully received, an implied debt is thereby raised, quasi ex

contractu. 3dly, that where money is recovered in a Court having a competent jurisdiction, it cannot be overhauled in another Court, but by writ of error or false judgment. But the verdict given in this cause is consistent with the determination of the Court of Conscience. The commissioners determined merely upon the indorsement, and refused to go into the collateral matter of the agreement; in which they did right; else, upon such & matter as a note of 30s., they might go into a large and extensive account; and might settle the balance of a series of mercantile transactions, much superior to their conusance.[r] And yet, though the judgment was right, the iniquity of keeping the money so adjudged to be paid may appear in another Court. Suppose an insurer is condemned to pay money on the death of a person who afterwards appears to be alive; would not a new action lie for him, against the person who recovered upon the former judgment[s]? The admission that an action will lie upon the express agreement, is conclusive upon this case. For the great benefit of this action (upon an implied contract) is, that the plaintiff need not set out the particular circumstances, on which, ex æquo et bono, he demands a satisfaction; but may declare generally for money had and received to his use, and may give the special matter in evidence. And it is equally beneficial to defendant, who may give in evidence any equitable matter, in order to discharge himself. Therefore, if it stood merely upon principles, there is no reason why the plaintiff should be confined to his action on the special agreement, and be debarred his remedy on the assumpsit implied by law. But the point has been expressly determined in *Dutch and Warren*, M. 7 Geo. I, Common Pleas[t]: wherein it was held, that it was at the election of the party, either to affirm an express contract, by bringing an action on the special agreement, or to disaffirm it, and rest on an implied one, by bringing indebitatus assumpsit. In this case, the plaintiff had paid to the defendant 262 *l.* 10*s.* for five shares in copper mines, to be transferred on the 22d of February, which defendant failed to do. Plaintiff brought indebitatus assumpsit, for money had and received to his use: and the jury, who in these actions can go into all the equity of the transaction, gave him 175 *l.* only, which he recovered; being the value which the shares had fallen to on the said 22d of February. Therefore we are all of opinion, that the defendant ought in justice to refund this money thus mala fide recovered; and though an action on the agreement would also have indemnified him for his costs in the Court below, yet he may waive this advantage and pursue the present remedy.

The postea must be delivered to the plaintiff.[v]

(c) *Deglman v. Guaranty Trust Co. of Canada and Constantineau*†

Supreme Court of Canada

[RAND J. (for Rinfret C.J. and of Taschereau and Rand JJ.):]

In this appeal the narrow question is raised as to the nature of part performance which will enable the court to order specific performance of a contract relating to lands unenforceable at law by reason of s. 4 of the Statute of Frauds. The respondent Constantineau claims the benefit of such a contract and the appellant represents the next of kin other than the respondent of the deceased, Laura Brunet, who [resists] it.

The respondent was the nephew of the deceased. Both lived in Ottawa. When he was about 20 years of age, and while attending a technical school, for six months of the school year 1934–35 he lived with his aunt at No. 550 Besserer Street. Both that and the house on the adjoining lot, No. 548, were owned by the aunt and it was during this time that she is claimed to have agreed that if the nephew would be good to her and do such services for her as she might from time to time request during her lifetime she would make adequate provision for him in her will, and in particular that she would leave to him the premises at No. 548. While staying with her the nephew did the chores around both houses which, except for an apartment used by his aunt, were occupied by tenants. When the term ended he returned to the home of his mother on another street. In the autumn of that year he worked on the national highway in the northern part of Ontario. In the spring of 1936 he took a job on a railway at a point outside of Ottawa and at the end of that year, returning to Ottawa, he obtained a position with the city police force. In 1941 he married. At no time did he live at the house No. 548 or, apart from the six months, at the house No. 550.

The performance consisted of taking his aunt about in her own or his automobile on trips to Montreal and elsewhere, and on pleasure drives, of doing odd jobs about the two houses, and of various accommodations such as errands and minor services for her personal needs. These circumstances,

Spence J. at trial and the Court of Appeal, finding a contract, have held to be sufficient grounds for disregarding the prohibition of the statute.

The leading case on this question is *Maddison v. Alderson*. The facts there were much stronger than those before us. The plaintiff, giving up all prospects of any other course of life, had spent over twenty years as housekeeper of the intestate until his death without wages on the strength of his promise to leave her the manor on which they lived. A defectively executed will made her a beneficiary to the extent of a life interest in all his property, real and personal. The House of Lords held that, assuming a contract, there had been no such part performance as would answer s. 4.

The Lord Chancellor, Earl Selborne, states the principle in these words:

> All the acts done must be referred to the actual contract, which is the measure and test of their legal and equitable character and consequence.

At p. 479, referring to the rule that payment of the purchase price is not sufficient, he says:

> The best explanation of it seems to be, that the payment of money is an equivocal act, not (in itself) until the connection is established by parol testimony, indicative of a contract concerning land.... All the authorities show that the acts relied upon as part performance must be unequivocally, and in their own nature referable to some such agreement as that alleged.

Lord O'Hagan, at p. 485, uses this language:

> It must be unequivocal. It must have relation to the one agreement relied upon, and to no other when it must be such, in Lord Hardwicke's words, "as could be done with no other view or design than to perform that agreement".

At p. 489 Lord Blackburn, speaking of the delivery of possession as removing the bar of the statute, says:

> This is, I think, in effect to construe the fourth section of the Statute of Frauds as if it con-

---

† [1954] S.C.R. 725.

tained these words, "or unless possession of the land shall be given and accepted". Notwithstanding the very high authority of those who have decided those cases, I should not hesitate if it was res integra in refusing to interpolate such words or put such a construction on the statute.

I am quite unable to distinguish that authority from the matter before us. Here, as there, the acts of performance by themselves are wholly neutral and have no more relation to a contract connected with premises No. 548 than with those of No. 550 or than to mere expectation that his aunt would requite his solicitude in her will, or that they were given gratuitously or on terms that the time and outlays would be compensated in money. In relation to specific performance, strict pleading would seem to require a demonstrated connection between the acts of performance and a dealing with the land before evidence of the terms of any agreement is admissible. This exception of part performance is an anomaly; it is based on equities resulting from the acts done; but unless we are to say that, after performance by one party, any refusal to perform by the other gives rise to them, which would in large measure write off the section, we must draw the line where those acts are referable and referable only to the contract alleged. The facts here are almost the classical case against which the statute was aimed: they have been found to be truly stated and I accept that; but it is the nature of the proof that is condemned, not the facts, and their truth at law is irrelevant. Against this, equity intervenes only in circumstances that are not present here.

There remains the question of recovery for the services rendered on the basis of a *quantum meruit*. On the findings of both courts below the services were not given gratuitously but on the footing of a contractual relation: they were to be paid for. The statute in such a case does not touch the principle of restitution against what would otherwise be an unjust enrichment of the defendant at the expense of the plaintiff. This is exemplified in the simple case of part or full payment in money as the price under an oral contract; it would be inequitable to allow the promissor to keep both the land and the money and the other party to the bargain is entitled to recover what he has paid. Similarly is it in the case of services given.

This matter is elaborated exhaustively in the Restatement of the Law of Contract issued by the American Law Institute and Professor Williston's monumental work on Contracts in vol. 2, s. 536 deals with the same topic. On the principles there laid down the respondent is entitled to recover for

his services and outlays what the deceased would have had to pay for them on a purely business basis to any other person in the position of the respondent. The evidence covers generally and perhaps in the only way possible the particulars, but enough is shown to enable the court to make a fair determination of the amount called for; and since it would be to the benefit of the other beneficiaries to bring an end to this litigation, I think we should not hesitate to do that by fixing the amount to be allowed. This I place at the sum of $3,000.

The appeal will therefore be allowed and the judgment modified by declaring the respondent entitled to recover against the respondent administrator the sum of $3,000, all costs will be paid out of the estate, those of the administrator as between solicitor and client.

[CARTWRIGHT J. (for Estey, Locke, Cartwright and Fauteux JJ.), after reviewing the law on part performance and the Statute of Frauds with respect to land:]

An interpretation similar to that in *McNeil v. Corbett* was placed upon the decision in *Maddison v. Alderson* by Turgeon J.A., with whom Haultain C.J.S. and Lamont and McKay JJ.A. agreed, in *Re Meston, Meston v. Gray et al.* At page 888, Turgeon J.A. said:

> ... In order to exclude the operation of the Statute of Frauds, the part performance relied upon must be unequivocally referable to the contract asserted. The acts performed must speak for themselves, and must point unmistakably to a contract affecting the ownership or the tenure of the land and to nothing else.

I have already expressed the view that the acts relied upon by the respondent in the case at bar are not unequivocally and in their own nature referable to any dealing with the land in question and on this point the appellant is entitled to succeed.

It remains to consider the respondent's alternative claim to recover for the value of the services which he performed for the deceased and the possible application to such a claim of the Statute of Limitations.

I agree with the conclusion of my brother Rand that the respondent is entitled to recover the value of these services from the respondent administrator. This right appears to me to be based, not on the contract, but on an obligation imposed by law.

In *Fibrosa Spolka Akcyjna v. Fairbairn Lawson Combe Barbour Ltd.*, Lord Wright said, at page 61:

It is clear that any civilized system of law is bound to provide remedies for cases of what has been called unjust enrichment or unjust benefit, that is to prevent a man from retaining the money of or some benefit derived from another which it is against conscience that he should keep. Such remedies in English law are generically different from remedies in contract or in tort, and are now recognized to fall within a third category of the common law which has been called quasi-contract or restitution.

and at page 62:

Lord Mansfield does not say that the law implies a promise. The law implies a debt or obligation which is a different thing. In fact, he denies that there is a contract; the obligation is as efficacious as if it were upon a contract. The obligation is a creation of the law, just as much as an obligation in tort. The obligation belongs to a third class, distinct from either contract or tort though it resembles contract rather than tort.

Lord Wright's judgment appears to me to be in agreement with the view stated in Williston on Contracts referred to by my brother Rand.

In *Scott v. Pattison* the plaintiff served the defendant under a contract for service not to be performed within one year which was held not to be enforceable by reason of the Statute of Frauds. It was held that he could nonetheless sue in *assumpsit* on an implied contract to pay him according to his deserts. While I respectfully agree with the result arrived at in *Scott v. Pattison* I do not think it is accurate to say that there was an implied promise. In my view it was correctly decided in *Britain v. Rossiter* that where there is an express contract between the parties which turns out to be unenforceable by reason of the Statute of Frauds no other contract between the parties can be implied from the doing of acts in performance of the express but unenforceable contract. At page 127 Brett L.J., after stating that the express contract although unenforceable was not void but continued to exist, said:

It seems to me impossible that a new contract can be implied from the doing of acts which were clearly done in performance of the first contract only, and to infer from them a fresh contract would be to draw an inference contrary to the fact. It is a proposition which cannot be disputed that no new contract can be implied from acts done under an express contract, which is still subsisting; all that can be said is that no one can be charged upon the original contract because it is not in writing.

Cotton L.J., at pages 129 and 130 and Thesiger L.J. at page 133 expressed the same view. In the case at bar all the acts for which the respondent asks to be paid under his alternative claim were clearly done in performance of the existing but unenforceable contract with the deceased that she would devise 548 Besserer Street to him, and to infer from them a fresh contract to pay the value of the services in money would be, in the words of Brett L.J. quoted above, to draw an inference contrary to the fact. In my opinion when the Statute of Frauds was pleaded the express contract was thereby rendered unenforceable, but, the deceased having received the benefits of the full performance of the contract by the respondent, the law imposed upon her, and so on her estate, the obligation to pay the fair value of the services rendered to her.

If this is, as I think, the right view of the nature of the obligation upon which the respondent's claim rests it follows that the Statute of Limitations can have no application.

For the above reasons I would dispose of the appeal as proposed by my brother Rand.

Appeal allowed with costs.

(d) *Peel (Regional Municipality) v. Canada; Peel (Regional Municipality) v. Ontario*†

Supreme Court of Canada

[McLACHLIN J. (for La Forest, Sopinka, Gonthier, Cory, McLachlin and Iacobucci JJ.:]

This appeal arises from a financial dispute involving three different levels of government — federal, pro-

---

† [1992] 3 S.C.R. 762.

vincial and municipal. The federal government passed a law requiring the municipality to meet certain expenses should a court so order. The courts so ordered. The municipality, protesting *inter alia* that the federal law was unconstitutional, paid. The courts eventually ruled that the federal law was unconstitutional. The municipality now sues both the federal and provincial governments to get its money back. It is established that the municipality cannot sue in tort: it has long been recognized that the enactment of legislation *ultra vires* a legislature's competence does not give rise to damages for breach of a "duty of care" — *Welbridge Holdings Ltd. v. Metropolitan Corporation of Greater Winnipeg*, [1971] S.C.R. 957, at p. 969. The municipality, however, claims that it has an action under the doctrine of unjust enrichment. That is the question which we must now consider.

THE FACTS

As with most restitutionary claims, the particular facts of the case are of great importance to the ultimate decision of whether or not the Court will extend to the plaintiff the relief it seeks. A detailed summary of the relevant facts is thus warranted.

First enacted in 1908, the *Juvenile Delinquents Act*, R.S.C. 1970, c. J-3 (replaced in 1984 by the *Young Offenders Act*, R.S.C., 1985, c. Y-1) conferred upon "juvenile court judges" the jurisdiction to issue a variety of orders upon finding that a particular child had committed a "delinquent act"; these alternative orders were set out in s. 20(1) of the Act. Section 20(2) of the Act empowered these judges to order that the parent(s) of the child or the municipality in which the child is situate "contribute to the child's support such sum as the court may determine"; where the municipality is so ordered, it was authorized by s. 20(2) to recover from the parent(s) any sum paid by it pursuant thereto.

The appellant municipality came into being on January 1, 1974, under the authority of the *Regional Municipality of Peel Act*, S.O. 1973, c. 60. Section 66 of that Act, (R.S.O. 1980, c. 440, s. 70) clarified the orders made under s. 20(2) of the *Juvenile Delinquents Act*:

> 66. Where an order is made under subsection 2 of section 20 of the *Juvenile Delinquents Act* (Canada) upon an area municipality, such order shall be considered to be an order upon the Regional Corporation, and the sums of money required to be paid under such order shall be paid by the Regional Corporation and not by the area municipality.

Between 1974 and 1982, the Family Court judges in the Peel District purported to direct, pursuant to s. 20(1)(*d*)–(*f*) of the *Juvenile Delinquents Act*, that a number of juveniles be placed in various "group homes"; these homes were for the most part "Viking House" institutions. The Family Court judges appear to have believed that the 'group home' setting was the most appropriate disposition and wished to ensure the direct placement of the juveniles in such facility rather than placement of these children with the Children's Aid Society ("CAS"), which could determine whether placement in a group home was warranted. The evidence indicates because the CAS insisted on the authority to determine whether the child should in fact be placed in a group home, and once such decision was made to decide the particular home and the date which the child should be removed, the Family Court judges in the District decided to 'by-pass' the CAS and directly place the juvenile. The judges relied upon s. 20(2) of the Act to order the appellant municipality to pay the *per diem* rate that each group home charged for the care of the child. Between 1974 and 1982, the municipality paid out a total of $2,036,131.37 under such orders. The municipality's payments under these orders, after deduction of the *ex gratia* amounts paid the municipality by the province (1976–1982), totalled $1,166,814.22; this is the amount claimed here.

The municipality protested these orders; it instituted an action in the Ontario courts which challenged the jurisdiction of the Family Court judges to direct that the juveniles be placed in a group home on two grounds. First, the municipality claimed that the court lacked the statutory authority to make such orders on the basis that a "group home" is not an individual or institution to which a child may be committed under s. 20(1). Second, the municipality challenged Parliament's jurisdiction under s. 20(2) to order a municipality to contribute to the support of a juvenile. J. Holland J. found that the Family Court judges lacked the statutory jurisdiction to order the juveniles to group homes; in *obiter*, he found s. 20(2) *intra vires* Parliament.

In the wake of this ruling, a meeting took place at the Ministry of Community and Social Services at which provincial and municipal officials, Chief Judge Andrews of the Family Court and certain representatives of "Viking Houses" were in attendance. At the request of the province, the municipality agreed to continue paying the children's maintenance costs and to refrain from seeking immediate recovery from Viking Houses pending negotiations between all parties at the meeting as to an equitable cost sharing arrangement. The province agreed to contribute to 50% of the municipality's costs which would result from such orders in the future; it met this obligation. The respondent federal government was not included in any of the appellant's protests or in these negotiations.

On April 21, 1977, the Court of Appeal affirmed the judgment of J. Holland J. in its entirety, and declared the orders invalid. The Supreme Court confirmed the appeal judgment but refrained, however, from pronouncing upon the constitutional validity of s. 20(2): *Attorney General for Ontario v. Regional Municipality of Peel*, [1979] 2 S.C.R. 1134.

In a parallel proceeding commenced shortly after the judgment of J. Holland J., referred to above, the appellant challenged an order which — to comply with J. Holland J.'s decision — placed the juvenile in the custody of a named staff member of a Viking House facility (a "suitable person" under s. 20(1)(d)) in which the judge wished the child to be cared for. The validity of this order was upheld at trial and on appeal. On further appeal, this Court struck down s. 20(2) of the Act, so far as it purported to authorize the imposition of the financial cost of the disposition on a municipality, as *ultra vires* Parliament: *Regional Municipality of Peel v. MacKenzie*, [1982] 2 S.C.R. 9.

Having been vindicated in its contention that the direction to support juveniles under authority of the *Juvenile Delinquents Act* was *ultra vires*, the municipality commenced proceedings for restitution from the provincial and federal governments. In the Federal Court, the trial judge found in the appellant municipality's favour, ordering that the federal government reimburse the municipality in the amount of $1,166,814.22. The Federal Court of Appeal, however, found that the appellant had failed to establish that Parliament was legally obligated to pay for the juveniles subject to these orders and thus had not made out its claim in restitution. As a result, the municipality had no right of recoupment from the federal government. The proceedings against the province played out in a similar fashion. At trial, the Ontario Supreme Court ordered that the province reimburse the municipality in the above amount but the Court of Appeal reversed the trial judgment because the municipality had failed to meet the elements of a claim in restitution.

The municipality appeals to this Court from both judgments. It seeks reimbursement of what it paid out pursuant to the invalid orders plus interest thereupon.

LEGISLATION

The orders for which payment was demanded of the municipality were made under s. 20 of the (then) *Juvenile Delinquents Act* which read as follows:

> **20.**(1) In the case of a child adjudged to be a juvenile delinquent the court may, in its discretion, take either one or more of the several courses of action hereinafter in this section set out, as it may in its judgment deem proper in the circumstances of the case:
>
> . . . .
>
> (d) commit the child to the care or custody of a probation officer or of any other suitable person;
>
> (f) cause the child to be placed in a suitable family home as a foster home, subject to the friendly supervision of a probation officer and the further order of the court;
>
> (g) impose upon the delinquent such further or other conditions as may be deemed advisable;
>
> (h) commit the child to the charge of any children's aid society, duly organized under an Act of the legislature of the province and approved by the lieutenant governor in council, or, in any municipality in which there is no children's aid society, to the charge of the superintendent, if there is one; or
>
> (i) commit the child to an industrial school duly approved by the lieutenant governor in council.
>
> (2) In every such case it is within the power of the court to make an order upon the parent or parents of the child, or upon the municipality to which the child belongs, to contribute to the child's support such sum as the court may determine, and where such order is made upon the municipality, the municipality may from time to time recover from the parent or parents any sum or sums paid by it pursuant to such order.

Section 16(1) of the *Family Law Reform Act, 1978*, R.S.O. 1980, c. 152, (now s. 31(1) of the *Family Law Act*, S.O. 1986, c. 4) imposed the following obligation on the parent(s) to support his/her child:

> **16.**(1) Every parent has an obligation, to the extent the parent is capable of doing so, to provide support, in accordance with need, for his or her child who is unmarried and is under the age of eighteen years.
>
> (2) The obligation under subsection (1) does not extend to a child who, being of the age of sixteen years or over, has withdrawn from parental control.
>
> . . . .

ANALYSIS

Overview

The concept of restitution for unjust enrichment in the common law world has evolved over the past century from a collection of fact-specific categories in which recovery was permitted, toward a body of law unified by a single set of coherent rules applicable to all cases. The evolving state of the law of restitution manifests itself in a series of tensions, all reflected in the present appeal.

The first set of tensions is theoretical. There are two distinct doctrinal approaches to restitution at common law. The first is the traditional "category" approach. It involves looking to see if the case fits into any of the categories of cases in which previous recovery has been allowed, and then applying the criteria applicable to a given category to see whether the claim is established. The second approach, which might be called the "principled" approach, developed only in recent years. It relies on criteria which are said to be present in all cases of unjust enrichment: (1) benefit to the defendant; (2) corresponding detriment to the plaintiff; and (3) the absence of any juridical reason for the defendant's retention of the benefit: *Pettkus v. Becker*, [1980] 2 S.C.R. 834.

The arguments before us reflect these distinct doctrinal approaches. The municipality, finding it difficult to bring its case within the traditional categories, emphasizes the general "principled" approach to unjust enrichment, asking that the court apply those general principles in an expansive fashion. The federal and provincial governments, on the other hand, argue that the municipality must fail because it is unable to bring itself within a recognized category of recovery.

The second set of tensions is jurisprudential in nature. I refer to the tension between the need for certainty in the law and the need to do justice in the individual case; the tension between the need for predictable rules upon which people can predicate their conduct and the desire to allow recovery where, and only where, retention of the benefit would in all the circumstances be unjust. This jurisprudential tension corresponds to the doctrinal tension discussed above. An approach based on traditional categories has the advantage of being predictable. Its supporters conjure up "frightful images ... of judges roaming willy-nilly over the restitutionary landscape with only their inner voices to guide them." (McInnes, "Incontrovertible Benefits and the Canadian Law of Restitution" (1990) 12 *Advocates' Q.* 323, at p. 352). Those advocating the approach of general principle, on the other hand, are more ready to concede that

in some cases, the court may have to make decisions based on the equities of the particular case before them. The term "unjust", as well as the term "absence of juristic reason" in the third requirement of the general test, lend themselves to this approach.

Once again, the arguments before us reflect these tensions. The municipality emphasizes the "injustice" of being unable to recover payments which the federal legislation required it to make, where the legislation was later held to be *ultra vires*. The federal and provincial governments, on the other hand, emphasize the absence of any legal precedent for requiring them to reimburse expenses incurred as a result of *ultra vires* legislation.

The third set of tensions lies on the philosophical — policy level. The traditional reluctance of the law to permit recovery to a plaintiff who had provided non-contractual benefits to another was founded on a philosophy of robust individualism which expected every person to look out after his or her own interests and which placed premium on the right to choose how to spend one's money. As one nineteenth century judge (Pollock, C.B. in *Taylor v. Laird* (1856), 25 L.J. Ex. 329, at p. 332) put it: "One cleans another's shoes; what can the other do but put them on?" The new approach of general principle, on the other hand, questions the merits of this view and the quality of justice which it entails. It shrinks from the harsh consequences of individualism and seeks to effect justice where fairness requires restoration of the benefit conferred.

The arguments before us reflect this tension too. The municipality emphasizes the injustice of its situation; the federal and provincial governments argue that they never voted to spend their money on supporting these children in group homes and assert that the municipality's situation is the unfortunate but occasionally inevitable by-product of a federal system where legislatures from time to time are found to have exceeded their powers.

This case presents the Court with the difficult task of mediating between, if not resolving, the conflicting views of the proper scope of the doctrine of unjust enrichment. It is my conclusion that we must choose a middle path; one which acknowledges the importance of proceeding on general principles but seeks to reconcile the principles with the established categories of recovery; one which charts a predictable course without falling into the trap of excessive formalism; one which recognizes the importance of the right to choose where to spend one's money while taking account of legitimate expectations and what, in the light of those expectations, is fair.

THE ARGUMENTS ON CLASSES OF TRADITIONAL RECOVERY AND THE GENERAL PRINCIPLE OF RESTITUTION

The modern law of restitution finds its roots in the 16th century writ of *indebitatus assumpsit* which, as a form of trespass on the case, was returnable in the Court of King's Bench, as opposed to the Court of Common Pleas where all regular debt actions had to be instituted. Maddaugh and McCamus, *The Law of Restitution* (1990), note at p. 5 that from the Writ's birth in *Slade's Case* (1602), 4 Co. Rep. 92b, 76 E.R. 1074, a number of "standard forms of general *assumpsit* were developed depending upon the type of circumstance giving rise to the original 'indebtedness'"; the standard forms were called the 'common counts':

> Of these common counts, four have come to form the basis of the vast majority of common law actions in quasi-contract: (i) *money had and received to the plaintiff's use*, where money is paid directly to the defendant; (ii) *money paid to the defendant's use*, where money is paid, not to the defendant but to a third party for the defendant's benefit; (iii) *quantum meruit*; and (iv) *quantum valebat*, where services or goods, respectively, are bestowed by the plaintiff upon the defendant.

The Court of Chancery, or Equity, also played an important role in the development of the modern law of restitution. Maddaugh and McCamus consider equity's most fundamental contribution to be the development of the remedial constructive trust as a means by which the unjust enrichment of a defendant may be avoided. Late 19th and 20th century courts faced the arduous task of making sense of the diverse branches of restitution and of creating some general principle upon which to ground restitutionary relief.

The courts found the required unifying principle in the concept of unjust enrichment. The American *Restatement of the Law of Restitution: Quasi Contracts and Constructive Trusts*, 1937, states the principle simply at p. 12: "A person who has been unjustly enriched at the expense of another is required to make restitution to the other." A leading commonwealth text offers the following elaboration:

> [Unjust enrichment] presupposes three things: first, that the defendant has been enriched by the receipt of *a benefit*; secondly, that he has been so enriched *at the plaintiff's expense*; and thirdly, that it would seem *unjust* to allow him to retain the benefit. (Goff and Jones, *The Law of Restitution* (3rd ed. 1986), at p. 16.)

These three requirements, somewhat differently articulated, have been recognized as the basis of the action for unjust enrichment by this Court: e.g., *Pettkus v. Becker, supra.*

At the heart of the doctrine of unjust enrichment, whether expressed in terms of the traditional categories of recovery or general principle, lies the notion of restoration of a benefit which justice does not permit one to retain. As Goff and Jones, *supra*, put it at p. 12: "Most mature systems of law have found it necessary to provide, outside the fields of contract and civil wrongs, for the restoration of benefits on grounds of unjust enrichment". Thus for recovery to lie, something must have been given, whether goods, services or money. The thing which is given must have been received and retained by the defendant. And the retention must be without juristic justification, to quote Dickson J. in *Pettkus v. Becker.*

The tri-partite principle of general application which this Court has recognized as the basis of the cause of action for unjust enrichment is thus seen to have grown out of the traditional categories of recovery. It is informed by them. It is capable, however, of going beyond them, allowing the law to develop in a flexible way as required to meet changing perceptions of justice.

It follows from this that the traditional categories of recovery, while instructive, are not the final determinants of whether a claim lies. In most cases, the traditional categories of recovery can be reconciled with the general principles enunciated in *Pettkus v. Becker, supra*. But new situations can arise which do not fit into an established category of recovery but nevertheless merit recognition on the basis of the general rule.

It is suggested that the case at bar falls into, or is analogous to, the following classes of cases where recovery has been allowed: (1) a benefit conferred under compulsion; (2) a benefit conferred out of necessity; (3) a benefit conferred as a result of an ineffective transaction; and (4) a benefit conferred at the request of the defendant. The distinctions between these categories turn mainly on the circumstances giving rise to the conferral of the benefit, which in turn affect the absence of a juristic reason for permitting the defendant to retain the benefit. It seems clear that the municipality in this case made the payments under statutory compulsion. It may also be argued that it did so out of necessity, since someone had to care for the children in question. In some ways payment under an invalid statute may be likened to payment under an ineffective transaction. And if one rejects the compulsion argument, one might argue that the federal and provincial governments requested the payments.

The difficulty lies not in establishing that the plaintiff made payments which might potentially attract the doctrine of unjust enrichment. The difficulty lies rather in establishing that the payments conferred a "benefit" on the federal and provincial governments which represents an unjust retention or enrichment. As Professors Goff and Jones note: "In restitution it is not material that the plaintiff has suffered a loss if the defendant has gained no benefit." (See Goff and Jones, *The Law of Restitution, supra*, at p. 16.) As already noted, the concept of restoration of a benefit retained without juristic reason lies at the heart of the doctrine of unjust enrichment. The word "restitution" implies that something has been given to someone which must be returned or the value of which must be restored by the recipient. The word "enrichment" similarly connotes a tangible benefit. It follows that without a benefit which has "enriched" the defendant and which can be restored to the donor in specie or by money, no recovery lies for unjust enrichment.

Since the establishment of such a benefit is essential for recovery under any of the traditional categories, as well as under the general test for recovery which this Court has adopted, the remainder of these reasons focus on that concept. To date, the cases have recognized two types of benefit. The most common case involves the positive conferral of a benefit upon the defendant, for example the payment of money. But a benefit may also be 'negative' in the sense that the benefit conferred upon the defendant is that he or she was spared an expense which he or she would have been required to undertake, i.e., the discharge of a legal liability.

It is useful to begin by looking at the sort of benefit required for recovery under the category which fits most closely with the facts in this case, that of payment made under compulsion of law. The courts have consistently held that for a benefit to be established in this class of case, it must be shown that the plaintiff's payments discharged the defendant's liability. (See, for example, Fridman and McLeod, *Restitution* (1982), at p. 347, and *Brook's Wharf and Bull Wharf, Ltd. v. Goodman Brothers*, [1937] 1 K.B. 534.)

As regards the traditional requirement that the plaintiff have discharged the defendant's liability, Goff and Jones, *supra*, state at pp. 320 and 324:

> Compulsion is not enough in itself to enable a plaintiff to recover. He must also, by reason of the compulsion, have paid money which the defendant is primarily liable to pay, *so that the latter obtained the benefit of the payment by the discharge of his liability.*

> At first sight it is puzzling that the plaintiff's payment should be capable of discharging the defendant's liability in these cases, for a stranger cannot discharge the debt of another without that other's authority. The present cases can only be explained on the ground that the law compels the plaintiff to make the payment and therefore enables him, although a stranger, to discharge the liability of the defendant. It is for this reason, we suggest, that the doctrine is limited to those cases where the plaintiff has been compelled *by law* to make the payment; if he were not, for example, if his goods had been *wrongfully* taken in distress for rent, it appears that his payment would not of itself discharge the liability of the person primarily liable to pay.

> ...

> If no liability has been discharged, it is irrelevant that the plaintiff, in the performance of a duty or otherwise, has incidentally conferred some benefit on the defendant by his payment. For it is a limiting principle of restitution that the mere conferring of some incidental benefit, while discharging an obligation to another, does not in itself give rise to any right to be recouped. [Emphasis in original.]

The municipality acknowledges that it cannot meet the test for benefit in the category of payment under compulsion of law, nor indeed, in any of the traditional categories of recovery. The requirement that the plaintiff have discharged the defendant's legal liability is simply not met in the sense required by the traditional tests. There was no constitutional obligation on either the federal or provincial government to provide for the care of these children; as the courts below noted, the power to legislate does not give rise to an obligation to legislate. Nor were the federal or provincial governments under a statutory or legal liability to provide for the care of the children. The provincial statutes relied on by the municipality as evidence of the province's obligation generally create a discretion in the province to finance the acquisition or construction of institutions for the care of children and in some cases to finance the operation of these institutions in cooperation with others. The benefit which the federal government is said to have received is the care of 'prisoners' which it might otherwise have had to provide itself (even though they are not obliged to, provincial prisons house many persons convicted of federal offences), and a more general "political" benefit of having the goals of its legislation furthered. The benefit which the province is said to have received is the discharge of responsibilities which it might have undertaken because conscience required that someone do so. So there was no legal liability on either government as required by the traditional tests.

Unable to meet the traditional tests, the municipality turns to the general principles governing recovery for unjust enrichment enunciated by this Court in cases such as *Pettkus v. Becker, supra*. It argues that the third condition of the traditional rule has been revised by the Canadian jurisprudence so as to require only that the plaintiff's payments have discharged a political, social or moral responsibility of the defendant, for which the defendant was primarily liable; the plaintiff need not have discharged a liability enforceable at law. Stated otherwise, a defendant may be found to have benefitted from the payment of a certain sum even though the defendant had the option of whether or not it wished to incur this expenditure. It is in the failure to accept this proposition that the appellate courts below are said to have erred.

The question thus reduces to this: how should "benefit" in the general test for recovery for unjust enrichment be defined? More particularly, can it encompass payments which fall short of discharging the defendant's legal liability?

. . . .

Notwithstanding the absence of authority, some scholars (Goff and Jones, Maddaugh and McCamus) perceive a 'whittling away' of the hard and fast rule barring recovery absent proof of a defendant's legal obligation to undertake the expense or perform the act which the plaintiff claims to have accomplished on the defendant's behalf. They suggest that where the plaintiff has conferred on the defendant an "incontrovertible benefit" recovery should be available even in the absence of a defendant's legal liability. An "incontrovertible benefit" is found in the gain of "a demonstrable financial benefit" or the saving of an "inevitable expense". At pages 21–22 of *The Law of Restitution, supra*, Goff and Jones state:

> To allow recovery because a defendant has been incontrovertibly benefited is to accept that he must make restitution even though he did not request or freely accept the benefit. In the past, the principle embodied in Bowen L.J.'s well known dictum in *Falcke's* case, that "liabilities are not to be forced on people behind their backs any more than you can confer a benefit upon a man against his will," has been regarded as paramount. Free choice must be preserved inviolate. To accept the principle of incontrovertible benefit is to admit a limited and, in our view, desirable exception. <u>The burden will always</u>

<u>be on the plaintiff to show that he did not act officiously, that the particular defendant has gained a demonstrable financial benefit or has been saved an inevitable expense and that it will not be a hardship to the defendant, in the circumstances of the case, to make restitution.</u> [Emphasis added.]

An "incontrovertible benefit" is an unquestionable benefit, a benefit which is demonstrably apparent and not subject to debate and conjecture. Where the benefit is not clear and manifest, it would be wrong to make the defendant pay, since he or she might well have preferred to decline the benefit if given the choice. According to Justice Gautreau of the District Court of Ontario, where an unjust benefit is found "one discharges another's debt that is owed to a third party or discharges another's contractual or statutory duty": Gautreau, "When Are Enrichments Unjust?" (1989), 10 *Advocates' Q*. 258, at p. 269. The late Justice Gautreau cites this Court's decision in *Carleton (County of) v. Ottawa (City of), supra*, as an example of such a case but adds the following pertinent remarks at pp. 270–71:

> While the principle of freedom of choice is ordinarily important, it loses its force if the benefit is an incontrovertible benefit, <u>because it only makes sense that the defendant would not have realistically declined the enrichment</u>. For example, choice is not a real issue if the benefit consists of money paid to the defendant or paid to a third party to satisfy the debt of the defendant that was owing to the third party. In either case there has been an <u>unquestionable</u> benefit to the defendant. In the first case, he can return it or repay it if he chooses; in the second, he had no choice but to pay it, the only difference is that the payee has changed. Likewise, the principle of freedom of choice is a spent force if the benefit covers an expense that the defendant would have been put to in any event, and, as an issue, it is weak if the defendant subsequently adopts and capitalizes on the enrichment by turning it to account through sale or profitable commercial use.
>
> The principle of incontrovertible benefit is not the antithesis of freedom of choice. It is not in competition with the latter; rather, it exists when freedom of choice as a problem is absent. [Emphasis added.]

Gautreau's comment takes us back to the terms of the traditional test; the discharge of a legal liability creates an "unquestionable" benefit because the law allowed the defendant no choice. Payment of an amount which the defendant was under no legal obligation to discharge is quite another matter.

The same requirement of inevitable expense is reflected in McInnes' discussion of the notion of incontrovertible benefit: McInnes, *supra*. He asserts, at p. 346, that "restitutionary relief should be available to one who has saved another an inevitable or necessary expense (whether factually or legally based)." *Arguendo*, he suggests that recovery may lie where one "has discharged an obligation which the obligee would likely have paid another to discharge." He goes on, at p. 347, to caution that "although otherwise warranted, restitutionary relief should be denied if the benefit was conferred officiously, or if liability would amount to a hardship for the recipient of the benefit." McInnes concludes at p. 362 that the caselaw provides only theoretical and not express support for the incontrovertible benefit doctrine and suggests that, as such relief is "somewhat extraordinary", it "should not be imposed unless the equities of the circumstances demand it."

It is thus apparent that any relaxation on the traditional requirement of discharge of legal obligation which may be effected through the concept of "incontrovertible benefit" is limited to situations where it is clear on the facts (on a balance of probabilities) that had the plaintiff not paid, the defendant would have done so. Otherwise, the benefit is not incontrovertible.

While not much discussed by common law authorities to date, it appears that a further feature which the benefit must possess if it is to support a claim for unjust enrichment, is that it be more than an incidental blow-by. A secondary collateral benefit will not suffice. To permit recovery for incidental collateral benefits would be to admit of the possibility that a plaintiff could recover twice — once from the person who is the immediate beneficiary of the payment or benefit (the parents of the juveniles placed in group homes in this case), and again from the person who reaped an incidental benefit. See, for example, Fridman and McLeod, *supra*, at p. 361; Maddaugh and McCamus, *supra*, at p. 717; and, Gautreau, *supra*, at pp. 265 *et seq.* It would also open the doors to claims against an undefined class of persons who, while not the recipients of the payment or work conferred by the plaintiff, indirectly benefit from it. This the courts have declined to do. The cases in which claims for unjust enrichment have been made out generally deal with benefits conferred directly and specifically on the defendant, such as the services rendered for the defendant or money paid to the defendant. This limit is also recognized in other jurisdictions. For example, German restitutionary law confines recovery to cases of direct

benefits: Zwiegert and Kötz, *Introduction to Comparative Law*, vol. II (2nd ed. 1987), at pp. 234–35.

Where does this discussion of "benefit" in the doctrine of unjust enrichment bring us? Accepting for the purposes of argument that the law of restitution should be extended to incontrovertible benefits, the municipality still falls short of the law's mark. The benefit conferred is not incontrovertible in the sense in which Goff and Jones define that concept; the municipality has not shown that either level of government being sued "gained a demonstrable financial benefit or has been saved an inevitable expense." Nor is it "unquestionable", to use Gautreau's test; the federal and provincial governments were under no legal obligation and their contention that they were not benefited at all, or in any event to the value of the payments made, has sufficient merit to require, at the least, serious consideration. It was neither inevitable nor likely, in McInnes' phrase, that in the absence of a scheme which required payment by the municipality the federal or provincial government would have made such payments; an entirely different scheme could have been adopted, for example.

To admit recovery in this case would be to extend the concept of benefit in the law of unjust enrichment much further than contemplated by any of the authorities to date. It would open the door to recovery wherever a payment has been made under compulsion of law which arguably has an incidental beneficial effect of a non-pecuniary nature. In short, it would take the law of unjust enrichment far beyond the concept of restoration of property, money, or services unfairly retained, which lies at its core.

To elaborate, Parliament was clearly aware of and relied upon the obligation of parents to support their children, expressly acknowledged in s. 16(1) of the (then) *Family Law Reform Act*, because s. 20(2) of the *Juvenile Delinquents Act* provided that the municipality could recover any expenditures ordered under s. 20(2) from the parent or parents responsible. The fact that the municipality's payments can be said to have furthered Canada's general interest in the welfare of its citizens or its more particular interest in the effective administration of its scheme for the regulation of criminal conduct by minors is an insufficient "correlative link" upon which to found recovery even on the application of the broader 'incontrovertible benefit' doctrine; it falls short of proof of a "demonstrable financial benefit" or proof that the federal government was saved an "inevitable expense". The principle of freedom of choice, referred to by Gautreau, *supra*, and Maddaugh and

McCamus, *supra*, is not a "spent force" in this instance — the municipality has failed to establish that its payments covered an expense that the federal government "would have been put to in any event" nor did it proffer any evidence that the Canadian government "capitalized" in any direct fashion upon these payments. On close examination, even McInnes' proposition, at p. 346, that "restitutionary relief should be available to one who has saved another an inevitable or necessary expense (whether factually or legally based) or, arguably, has discharged an obligation which the obligee would likely have paid another to discharge", does not assist the municipality in this instance. Federal government (financial) support of the juveniles' stay in the group homes in Peel was not "inevitable". Neither was this expense "necessary", first and foremost, given the host of dispositions available to judges under s. 20, and second, given the municipality's statutory authority to seek reimbursement from the children's parents. The legislative scheme set up by Parliament is proof positive that Parliament did not believe it had any obligation to provide financial support for the juveniles assigned to group homes; any obligation it had to the provinces in this regard was created by a voluntary federal-provincial agreement to which the appellant was not privy. These facts confirm that any benefit received by the Government of Canada from the municipality's payments was incidental or indirect; the federal government had no greater responsibility for the welfare of these children than did the municipality from whence they came and cannot be found liable in restitution.

The same inability to establish an incontrovertible benefit bedevils the municipality's claim against the province. The fact that the appellant's payments necessarily furthered the province's general interest in the welfare of its citizens or its more specific interest in the protection and supervision of children residing within its boundaries is, for the reasons already outlined, not a sufficient basis upon which to found recovery even if the Court were to apply the 'incontrovertible benefit' doctrine.

The appellant is unable to establish on a balance of probabilities that the provincial government has received "a demonstrable <u>financial</u> benefit" nor has it established that the province was spared an <u>inevitable expense.</u> The paucity of evidence as to both the types of institutions sought to be created under the provincial legislation said to evidence the province's obligation and as to the <u>functional equivalence</u> of these institutions to "Viking House" facilities, combined with the absence of proof that such institutions were actually in existence at the material times, makes it difficult for this Court to give credence to the appellant's claim that in lieu of the invalid orders, the juveniles would have been placed in the care of such provincial institutions, and thus the province was enriched by foregoing this expense. I am in agreement with the Ontario Court of Appeal that a more probable alternative order would have placed the juvenile delinquents at issue directly in the custody of a foster home, an order which would <u>not</u> necessarily involve any cost to the Government of Ontario, or into the custody of the CAS. Such an eventuality is, however, still too speculative for proof on the balance of probabilities — the standard which the appellant must meet.

Even if the Court could say with sufficient certainty, for example, that the children would have <u>necessarily</u> been handed over to the charge of the CAS, the financial responsibility for these children would have been shared between the municipality, the province and the federal government on application of the Canada Assistance Plan. The practical effect of the Canada Assistance Plan, as all parties seem to be agreed, was that the appellant would have been responsible for 20% of the cost of the support of juveniles committed to the charge of the CAS; the province would have been responsible, ultimately, for 30% of that cost, while the other 50% would have been borne by the federal government by way of transfer payments. Assuming this scenario sufficiently proven, it may be useful to ask whether the province therefore benefitted <u>in a practical sense</u> by the municipality's expenditures.

It is important to recall the facts at this juncture. Once it was determined by J. Holland J., in 1977, that the Family Court judges had been invalidly placing the juveniles in group homes, the respondent province met with the appellant and certain other parties to discuss cost-sharing arrangements. The municipality agreed to meet the expenses directed by current and subsequent s. 20(2) orders. The province agreed to reimburse the municipality for 50% of the costs imposed upon it by all s. 20(2) orders made subsequent to J. Holland J.'s decision. The evidence is that the province met this undertaking (1977–82), paying to the municipality a total of $843,986.65. Of the total amount paid by the appellant pursuant to s. 20(2) orders between 1974 and 1982, the province's reimbursement of the appellant, totalling $869,317.15, constituted 42.6% of that amount. Such reimbursement was available to all municipalities in Ontario subject to s. 20(2) orders under the *Juvenile Delinquents Act*. In light of these facts, it would be difficult for the Court — even if the appellant could establish on a balance of probabilities what alternative course Family Court judges in Peel would have elected — to find that the province benefited, in the end, in a practical sense.

As with its claim against the respondent federal government, the appellant has failed to establish that its payments to the specified group homes covered an expense that the province "would have been put to in any event", nor did it lead sufficient evidence by which to establish on a balance of probabilities that the province was saved an "inevitable or necessary expense", whether factually or legally based. As found by the Court of Appeal, the appellant has, at most, shown that its payments may have relieved the province of some obligation or debt that might have arisen.

THE ARGUMENT ON INJUSTICE

The municipality is reduced in the final analysis to the contention that it should recover the payments which it made from the federal and provincial governments because this is what the dictates of justice and fairness require; stated otherwise, it would be unjust for the federal and provincial governments to escape these payments. This argument raises two questions. First, where the legal tests for recovery are clearly not met, can recovery be awarded on the basis of justice or fairness alone? Second, if courts can grant judgment on the basis of justice alone, does justice so require in this case?

On my review of the authorities, the first question must be answered in the negative. The courts' concern to strike an appropriate balance between predictability in the law and justice in the individual case has led them in this area, as in others, to choose a middle course between the extremes of inflexible rules and case by case "palm tree" justice. The middle course consists in adhering to legal principles, but recognizing that those principles must be sufficiently flexible to permit recovery where justice so requires having regard to the reasonable expectations of the parties in all the circumstances of the case as well as to public policy. Such flexibility is found in the three-part test for recovery enunciated by this Court in cases such as *Pettkus v. Becker, supra*. Thus recovery cannot be predicated on the bare assertion that fairness so requires. A general congruence with accepted principle must be demonstrated as well.

This is not to say that the concepts of justice and equity play no role in determining whether recovery lies. It is rather to say that the law defines what is so unjust as to require disgorgement in terms of benefit, corresponding detriment and absence of juristic reason for retention. Such definition is required to preserve a measure of certainty in the law, as well as to ensure due consideration of factors such as the legitimate expectation of the parties, the right of parties to order their affairs by contract, and the right of legislators in a federal system to act in accordance with their best judgment without fear of unforeseen future liabilities.

Additionally, conscience and fairness may play a role in the development of the relevant legal principles. When questions arise as to the scope of the principles, the balance of equities between the parties may determine the outcome. Thus Maddaugh and McCamus (*The Law of Restitution* (1990), "Compulsory Discharge of Another's Liability"), considering a series of cases where the defendant shared a legal liability for the payment made with the plaintiff, opine at p. 740 that "[s]o long as that benefit is bestowed by a plaintiff in circumstances such that the defendant cannot, in all good conscience, retain it, restitutionary relief ought to be awarded." But this is quite different from the assertion that "good conscience" is the only requirement for recovery.

But even if justice without more were admitted as the basis of recovery, the municipality in this case would fail on the second question. The facts fall short of establishing that justice requires that the federal and provincial governments reimburse the municipality for payments under the ineffective law.

The concept of "injustice" in the context of the law of restitution harkens back to the Aristotelian notion of correcting a balance or equilibrium that had been disrupted. The restitutive form of justice is distinct from the analysis particular to tort and contract law, in the sense that questions of duty, standards, and culpability are not a central focus in restitution. Speaking in highly general terms, Stevens suggests that contract and tort claims deal with punitive or distributive measures, whereas restitution claims deal with an "unusual receipt *and* a retention of value" ("Restitution, Property, and the Cause of Action in Unjust Enrichment: Getting By With Fewer Things (Part I)" (1989), 39 *U.T.L.J.* 258, at p. 271; see also Wingfield, "The Prevention of Unjust Enrichment: or How Shylock Gets His Comeuppance" (1988), 13 *Queen's L.J.* 126, at p. 134). Thus, restitution, more narrowly than tort or contract, focuses on re-establishing equality as between two parties, as a response to a disruption of equilibrium through a subtraction or taking. This observation has dual ramifications for the concept of "injustice" in the context of restitution. First, the injustice lies in one person's retaining something which he or she ought not to retain, requiring that the scales be righted. Second, the required injustice must take into account not only what is fair to the plaintiff; it must also consider what is fair to the defendant. It is not enough that the plaintiff has made a payment or rendered services which it was not obliged to make or render; it must also be shown that the defendant as a consequence is in possession of a benefit, and it is fair and just for the defendant to disgorge that benefit.

The municipality has shown that it expended monies under a statute which was *ultra vires*. This may seem unfair, considered in the abstract. But in the context of the law of restitution, no injustice is established. The payments did not confer on the federal and provincial governments benefits which must be returned to right the balance between the parties; the benefits were conferred on the children of the Regional Municipality of Peel and their parents.

Of equal importance, fairness must embrace not only the situation of the claimant, but the position of those from whom payment is claimed. It is far from clear that ordering payment to the municipality would be fair to the federal and provincial governments and the taxpayers who would ultimately foot the account.

The ordering of one level of government to pay large sums of money to another level of government because one level has suffered by obeying the invalid legislation of the other is a complex question, involving political as well as legal issues. It is further complicated by the fact that all the governments act as the representatives of the electorate in the name of the Crown. This complex matrix of considerations renders problematic any assertion that justice and fairness demand that the federal and provincial governments reimburse the Regional Municipality of Peel for expenditures made under the invalid legislation.

. . . .

CONCLUSION

I would dismiss the appellant's appeal both as against the respondent Her Majesty The Queen in Right of Canada and as against the respondent Her Majesty The Queen in Right of Ontario. Due to the peculiar circumstances in which these appeals have arisen, I would however exercise this Court's discretion and refrain from ordering costs in the cause.

Appeals dismissed.

(a)   The Essence of Modern Equity and The Trust[†]

Bruce Ziff

(A)   INTRODUCTION

It is now possible to describe the nucleus around which today's equitable principles revolve. Equity continues to serve its initial function as a gloss on an imperfect common law. As such, it remains a tool for reform.[73] Equity and law remain fused, procedurally, though their substantive doctrines are distinct. This is not to say that principles of law and equity do not influence each other as they develop; they do,[74] perhaps more so in recent times than before. Accordingly, there is today a confluence of these separate streams of justice in some areas.[75] That is a natural result of the fact that the same judges apply and refine both law and equity. Yet, it has been cautioned that "[t]here might be room for concern if one were indiscriminately attempting to meld the whole of the two systems"[76] and to treat them as fully integrated for all purposes. Differences remain, irreconcilable conflicts between law and equity can therefore still emerge, and these are resolved in favour of equity. Alberta law explicitly declares that "[i]n all matters in which there is any conflict or variance between the rules of equity and common law with reference to the same matter, the rules of equity prevail".[77] That provision merely codifies a long-standing principle.

Equity continues to focus on the conscience, creating, on one view, mere personal (or *in personam*) rights enforceable against an individual. In theory, therefore, these rights are not proprietary (or *in rem*). However, the effect of recognizing the rights of enforcement of the *cestui que trust* is normally described as creating an equitable interest in property that has been impressed with a trust.[78] The result of that characterization is that equitable rights are regarded as proprietary. Even so, in important respects an equitable interest is more fragile than a legal entitlement. A right in equity is dependent on the availability of equitable remedies,[79] the granting or withholding of which is still a matter of judicial discretion. Additionally, equity will not impose an obligation against a *bona fide* purchaser for value of a legal interest who had no notice of an antecedent equitable claim. Such a person acquires the legal title free from the obligations of equity.[80]

(B)   MODERN DEPLOYMENT OF THE TRUST[81]

The ancient functions of the use have been eclipsed over time, but the modern trust possesses its own vitality as a mechanism of private law estate planning and commercial practice. For example, a trust can be set up to allow property to be held for the benefit of minor children or other dependants. In general, protective trusts can be established to allow a person to enjoy the benefit of trust income while preventing that beneficiary from having full control over the property. It was seen (in Chapter 5) that when rights over real property are divided between present and future owners, the interposition of a trust can provide one means of regulating the management of the

---

† From Bruce Ziff, *Principles of Property Law*, Fifth Edition (Toronto: Carswell, 2010) at 225–40. [Footnotes omitted.] Reprinted by permission of author and Carswell, a division of Thomson Reuters Canada Limited.

settled property.[82] Similarly, trusts can be deployed in a testamentary context to allow for the management of a decedent's estate. Property can be donated to charity via a trust. A trust is useful in this context because there are principles of equity (and statute law) that create special (generally advantageous) rules for charitable trusts.[83]

Within the commercial realm, pension plans, mutual fund investments, debt security, indeed many types of financial ventures, can be undertaken by using a trust instrument in some way. The trust can also serve as a form of business organization.[84] The administration of trusts is itself a field of commercial endeavour. Trusts are sometimes created under statute as a means of effecting public policy.[85] The trust can be of value in tax planning, that is, it can be invoked to assist in the ordering of one's (personal or business) affairs in a way that minimizes tax liability. Indeed, it has been offered that "[t]he trust is the estate planning vehicle *par excellence*".[86] This, plainly, is the strongest analogue to the early deployment of uses as a means of circumventing the exaction of feudal dues.

This overview intimates that trusts are principally of value to wealthy organizations or individuals, and that for others they are of marginal utility.[87] In the main that reading is accurate. By the same token, it should be recognized that trusts can arise in wholly mundane circumstances, involving modest items. Even something as ostensibly worthless as season tickets to see the Calgary Flames play hockey can be the subject of a trust.[88] Moreover, charitable trusts facilitate the redistribution of wealth, and as such these are concerned with more than just elite practices. As we will soon see,[89] principles of equity in Canada have become increasingly directed toward the prevention of unjust enrichment. In this way the trust has affected the lives of many Canadians.

It is possible that the trust can help to provide a response to environmental concerns. In the United States, what is termed the public trust doctrine has traditionally been invoked as a means of ensuring public access to navigable waters and shores by treating the title to these places as being held in trust by the state for the public at large. In some states it has emerged as a more extensive basis for environmental control, its scope extending "from beaches and rivers to lakes, tributaries, riparian banks, and now encompass[ing] aquifers, marshes, wetlands, springs, and groundwater".[90] There may be lessons here for Canada.[91]

Equitable principles have played a prominent role in the ever-developing field of Aboriginal law. The Crown is cast in the role of fiduciary (an equi-

table construct) each and every time it assumes discretionary control over specific Aboriginal interests.[92] And equity's protective side has been invoked as a way to respond to wrongful acts of cultural appropriation that fall outside of mainstream laws such as copyright.[93] Still, these principles can be two-edged swords. As noticed before, the privileging of *bona fide* purchasers of legal title has been used to insulate current non-Aboriginal owners of parcels that happen to be situated on traditional Aboriginal territories.[94]

Expressly created trusts (such as those that we have discussed above[95]) are regulated by a vast battery of principles concerning such matters as the required formalities, other issues as to the correct constitution of the trust, and the rights, responsibilities, and powers of trustees.[96] These matters are beyond the purview of this text. However, there are two kinds of trust that are germane to topics that are covered elsewhere in the book — resulting and constructive trusts. These are introduced below.

(C)   RESULTING TRUSTS[97]

A resulting trust can arise in several ways. It may occur when the beneficial entitlement under a trust has not been fully or properly disposed of by the settlor. In addition, when property is gratuitously conferred by A to B, a resulting trust may be found in favour of A. It may also arise as a result of what is sometimes called 'common intention'. These are general propositions that merit further elaboration.

Turning to the first situation, if, in a grant of property on trust, some element of the beneficial interest is not transferred, it will result back to the settlor. Consider a gift by A 'to the Baker Trust Co. in fee simple, in trust for C for life'. Reviewing what was said above, Baker Trust Co. is installed as the trustee; because it is a corporation, its interest would not be executed by the *Statute of Uses*. Baker would hold the legal title on trust for C, the beneficiary, for life. Notice that the remainder of the beneficial fee simple estate after the grant of the equitable life estate to C is unaccounted for in the settlement. That portion of the equitable title, not having been given away, results back to the settlor (A). It likely does not belong to Baker, which holds only the legal estate, although it might have been given a beneficial interest had the settlor been inclined to do so. Similarly, assume that property is conveyed on trust, 'for my first child to turn 21 years of age'. Until the age condition is met, the equitable title cannot pass to the intended beneficiary. In the meantime, the beneficial interest results back to the settlor. It will spring forward if the appointed time arrives.

A resulting trust can also arise if a deed of trust is somehow ineffective, such that it fails totally or partially. That might occur when, for example, the trust is found to contravene public policy, or if it was created through the perpetration of fraud or duress. Here, as in the case of an incomplete transfer of the beneficial interest, normally[98] the equitable title results back to the settlor.[99]

Another type of resulting trust involves gratuitous transfers. As a general rule, when A buys property and places title to it in the name of B, a resulting trust is presumed to arise in favour of A. The same is true when A voluntarily transfers property that she or he presently owns to B. In both of these situations the legal title is in B, who may even be registered as the owner. However, equity will treat that interest as subordinate to the resulting trust held by A; B is regarded as a bare trustee. One could even take the analysis further. If a resulting trust occurs here, then B is, by definition, holding in trust for (to the use of) A; the *Statute of Uses* should be invoked by such a gift. If so, A winds up with not just the equitable title (via the resulting trust), but the legal title as well (by virtue of the Statute).[100]

The presumption of resulting trust is an instantiation of the maxim that equity presumes bargains and not gifts; it leans against treating a transfer as a donation. But the presumption that arises in these circumstances serves merely a protective function and is not designed to impose a prohibition on gift-giving. The presumption of resulting trust can be rebutted by showing that a gift was truly intended.[101] If that is proven, then the legal and equitable titles are held by the donee (B in the example), and no trust arises.

The presumption of resulting trust is the general rule. However, in some circumstances the position is reversed, and a presumption of advancement (or gift) obtains.[102] Whether this presumption applies depends on the nature of the relationship of the parties to the transaction. For example, a gift is presumed in a transfer of property from parent to a minor child.[103] An advancement is likewise presumed when an individual stands in the place of a parent (*in loco parentis*).[104] When the presumption of advancement is engaged, the child will be presumed to have been given both the legal and equitable interests. That reading of the transaction can be rebutted, and a resulting trust found in favour of the parent, if it can be shown that a gift was not intended. However, for an adult child, even one

still dependent on parental support, the presumption of advancement is not invoked. In other words, a resulting trust arises unless an intention to give a gift can be proven on the balance of probabilities.[105]

Traditionally an advancement was presumed when a husband purchased property in the name of his wife, but not *vice versa*. In other words, a gift by H to W triggered a rebuttable presumption of advancement in favour of W. In a gift from W to H, a resulting trust was presumed, also in favour of W. An advancement has also been applied to engaged couples.[106] In the case of cohabiting spouses the conventional view has been that the presumption of advancement does not apply,[107] though there is authority to the contrary.[108]

In some jurisdictions the rules governing transfers between spouses have been reformed by statute. The general approach has been to render the rules gender-neutral and to limit or abolish the application of the presumption of advancement. For example, in proceedings under Alberta's *Matrimonial Property Act* for a division of property, the presumption of resulting trust generally applies to transfers made by one spouse to the other.[109] An exception exists for assets that are purchased by the spouses as joint owners: in that case the presumption is that both hold a share of the equitable title.[110] In other words, here a gift is presumed.

On the judicial front, the presumption of advancement, as it applies between spouses, is surely at death's door. In the Supreme Court of Canada decision in *Rathwell v. Rathwell*, discussed below, it was said that the "old presumption of advancement has ceased to embody any credible inference of intention".[111] That is weighty language, coming as it does from the Supreme Court, and it may well point to the end of the doctrine. Some courts, mindful of this *dictum*, have treated the presumption as still extant, while at the same time noting that its significance has declined; hence, less has been demanded to support a rebuttal.[112] It certainly has no place when the spouses have separated.[113] As the years pass it is increasingly difficult to imagine that the old rule operates at all.[114] However, I would have thought that the most likely intention in transfers between spouses is to bestow a gift. I would therefore prefer a gender-neutral rule that presumes an advancement.[115]

The 'common intention' resulting trust is a variant on the idea that a trust arises in favour of the party advancing the purchase price.[116] That form of resulting trust has been found in cases in which it is shown that the party on title intended some other person (usually the spouse of the legal owner) to share beneficial ownership. What normally triggers the trust is an agreement, often only implicit, sometimes quite fictional, that the non-titled spouse should acquire some proprietary right owing to that person's contributions to the acquisition, preservation, or enhancement of the property. In the past, the recognition of the common intention resulting trust served as a way of rewarding the non-monetary contributions of one spouse, when title was held by the other. It remains important in England mainly in relation to unmarried cohabitants.[117] As we will see below, that function has been overtaken since the late-1970s by the emergence of two very robust equitable concepts: the doctrine of unjust enrichment and the remedial constructive trust. In Chapter 9, the role played by marital property laws in responding to these situations will also be explained.

(D) CONSTRUCTIVE TRUSTS

(i) Conventional Forms

A constructive trust is one imposed by equity. Influenced by the orthodox English position, the constructive trust in Canada was at one time regarded as having a narrow compass. In this traditional or institutional form, the constructive trust is situation-based; that is, it arises in a number of established specific instances. For example, an express trustee who wrongfully obtains profits from his or her position will, for that act of infidelity, hold those monies under a constructive trust. A person who unlawfully meddles with trust property, when that person knew or ought to have known of the trust, will be treated as a (constructive) trustee *de son tort*. Likewise, a constructive trust may be imposed to prevent a wrongdoer from profiting from a crime.[118]

These illustrations[119] suggest that a constructive trust arises in those instances in which equity wishes to respond to various modes of unconscionable conduct. While that is a common ingredient, it is not always a necessary one. A vendor in a standard house transaction normally assumes the position of a constructive trustee prior to the closing of the transaction. Accordingly, the vendor must maintain the property and not deal with it in a manner that would be detrimental to the interests of the purchaser. However, the position of the vendor is not in all respects identical to that of other constructive trustees. Until the price is paid in full, an array of beneficial rights may still be enjoyed by the vendor, including rights to possession and to any rents or profits derived from the property.

The purchaser acquires this equitable interest (through a constructive trust) *if* equity would be prepared to order specific performance of the contract of sale.[120] The word *if* is stressed because of developments in the Canadian law of specific performance. In *Semelhago v. Paramadevan*, Sopinka J. stated that it was no longer appropriate to assume that specific performance would issue as a matter of course as the remedy in land sales. Rather, the plaintiff must demonstrate that damages would not provide adequate recompense because, centrally, the property at issue is unique.[121] One can imagine situations in which [commercial] property may lack that special quality, but the law applies to residential sales as well. One house or condominium in a development may, sadly, be just like many others in that neighbourhood.[122]

Justice Sopinka's statement, though *obiter dictum*, has been taken very seriously by Canadian courts, especially in relation to commercial land sales.[123] It stresses equity's place within the juridical world as a supplement to the common law. Equity is needed in this setting when damages at law will not make the innocent party whole. That party will be required to stop the bleeding, that is, to mitigate the damages resulting from a breach.

However, I am not convinced that the law is now better. The ruling has given rise to plenty of reported case law in which nuanced arguments about uniqueness and the adequacy of damages have surfaced. Ordering performance places the court in the potential position of having to supervise compliance. However, in generic real estate closing [scenarios] typically all that the order is mandating is that the land in question be transferred to the purchaser. Indeed, an award of damages can raise thorny issues as to quantum,[124] and may demand more monitoring from the judicial system if the defendant is a recalcitrant judgment-debtor.

I suspect that vendors are, as a rule, happier to pay or receive damages (as the case may be) than purchasers, but there is no obvious reason why one group should be preferred over the other. We injure purchasers by dashing their expectations, and injure them further by requiring that they mitigate their financial losses. I see the wisdom of promoting mitigation, but prefer that deals close as planned unless there is a very good reason to do otherwise. The Alberta Law Reform Institute has taken the same stance.[125]

The English jurisprudence demonstrates rote familiarity with the situations in which constructive trusts have previously been imposed. And even though the situations in which English law is prepared to impose a trust do not form a closed set, there has been resistance to the expansion of the concept beyond its established domain. One English response, cautiously developed and invoked, has been the recognition of a residual category of constructive trusts based on good conscience.[126]

In Canada, the institutional constructive trust continues to apply, and it is now clear beyond dispute that the good conscience trust is part of that package.[127] Moreover, the idea of good conscience may be the best overarching description or common denominator of the institutional constructive trusts that now exist or may later be recognized. In the leading Canadian case of *Soulos v. Korkontzilas*, McLachlin J. (as she then was) outlined four criteria that would determine whether the good conscience constructive trust was appropriate:

(1) The defendant must have been under an equitable obligation, that is, an obligation of the type that courts of equity have enforced, in relation to the activities giving rise to the assets in his hands;

(2) The assets in the hands of the defendant must be shown to have resulted from deemed or actual agency activities of the defendant in breach of his equitable obligation to the plaintiff;

(3) The plaintiff must show a legitimate reason for seeking a proprietary remedy, either personal or related to the need to ensure that others like the defendant remain faithful to their duties[; and]

(4) There must be no factors which would render imposition of a constructive trust unjust in all the circumstances of the case; *e.g.*, the interests of intervening creditors must be protected.[128]

(ii) Remedial

Prior to the *Soulos* decision, another form of flexible constructive trust had already been devised in Canada as a means of responding to unjust enrichment.[129] Like the good conscience constructive trust, it is available in a variety of circumstances beyond purview of the traditional institutional constructive trust. The use of the remedial constructive trust as a means of responding to unjust enrichment has provided a basis for compensating those engaged in (otherwise unrewarded) household labour. Specifically, the imposition of this form of trust has been used to furnish a proprietary remedy as payment for such work. However, its application has been much broader: it has also been applied in a commercial context. This type of remedial trust, influenced by American law, is a relatively recent innovation in

Canada. A helpful way of understanding its present complexion is through a brief historical review, beginning with the infamous decision of the Supreme Court of Canada in *Murdoch v. Murdoch*.[130]

Murdoch involved a claim by a wife to an interest in her husband's ranch properties. In that case the wife had worked with her husband as a hired hand on various ranches from 1943 to 1947. During that period, both of their pay packets were given to the husband. In 1947 the husband and his father purchased a guest ranch. That holding was sold in 1951, and a second property was later purchased by the husband, with the title to that land being taken in his name alone. This property was paid for with the proceeds of sale from the first property, together with money drawn from the wife's bank account. The wife had obtained that money from her mother. Several other parcels were later acquired, and these properties were operated collectively as a ranch.

Mrs. Murdoch worked tirelessly: for five months of the year, while her husband was away on business, she attended to the daily ranching chores (which included various forms of arduous physical labour). When the marriage broke down she claimed an interest in the ranch, based partly on the financial contributions made prior to the purchase of the lands, and partly on the indirect contributions that she had provided through her work. Her action failed.

A majority of the Supreme Court assessed the claims on the basis of whether or not a *resulting* trust arose. In the view of the majority, the necessary intention required to create a resulting trust could not be found on the facts. Remarkable as the wife's contributions appeared to be, Mr. Murdoch testified that these were no more than would be expected of an ordinary ranch wife in the circumstances. That characterization seems to have been accepted by the trial judge and the majority of the Supreme Court. Her work could not therefore support a finding that there was a common intention that title was to be shared.

Additionally, the Supreme Court apparently discounted the financial contributions made by the wife during the early years of the marriage when the spouses had both worked as hired hands. It was held that the first property was bought by the husband with his own assets. The money received from the wife's bank account was found to be a loan from the wife's mother. In dissent, Laskin J. (as he then was) was prepared to hold that a constructive trust should be imposed. His Lordship concluded that it was necessary to respond to the unjust enrichment enjoyed by the husband. Unlike the majority, Laskin J. was prepared to take into account the wife's contributions before the lands were purchased, as well as her participation in the ranching operations over the years. The *Murdoch* case was more than a harsh judgment;[131] it became a *cause celebre*, and was a catalyst in the process of family property reform that was already underway in Canada.[132] Through Laskin J.'s dissent, the seeds had also been sown for the growth of a new conceptualization of the constructive trust. Equitable doctrines underwent a rapid transition after *Murdoch*, starting with the Supreme Court judgment in *Rathwell v. Rathwell*,[133] which was decided only a few years later. There, a claim similar in nature to that advanced in *Murdoch* succeeded. While all members of the Court were able to find a resulting trust based on an implied common intention, a three-member minority went further. They endorsed the existence in Canada of a general doctrine of unjust enrichment, applicable when the facts display: (i) an enrichment; (ii) a corresponding deprivation; and (iii) the absence of a juristic reason for the enrichment. One of the ways in which this unjust enrichment can be remedied, it was said, would be to treat the legal owner as holding part of the legal title on a constructive trust for the party suffering the deprivation.

In *Pettkus v. Becker*,[134] a case involving a *de facto* relationship that lasted almost 20 years, the minority position in *Rathwell* was adopted by a majority of the Supreme Court. From that point on the doctrine of unjust enrichment, with the remedy of constructive trust in aid, has been firmly entrenched in Canadian law. Only a few years after *Murdoch*, equitable principles had changed so dramatically that it is almost certain that Mrs. Murdoch would have received a share in the ranch (probably half of it) had her case been litigated in the wake of *Pettkus v. Becker*.[135]

An issue often present in these cases relates to whether or not the provision of domestic services, of the sort normally undertaken by spouses during cohabitation, could serve as the basis for an unjust enrichment suit. In these earlier cases there had always been some additional, often monumental, contribution to the material well-being of the parties. In *Peter v. Beblow*[136] the Supreme Court of Canada sustained a claim of unjust enrichment based on conventional domestic labour.

In this case the parties had cohabited for 12 years, during which Catherine Peter had undertaken most of the domestic work. William Beblow, in whose name the family home was registered, had maintained and improved the property in the ways

that owners customarily do. Over the course of the relationship the mortgage on the home was paid off; Beblow also bought a houseboat and van during that period. Ms. Peter purchased a parcel of land with money earned during the currency of the relationship. When the parties separated the beneficial title to the Beblow house came into question. In the result, the Court found that Mr. Beblow had been unjustly enriched by Ms. Peter's contributions and that a proprietary remedy was appropriate. Due to the extent of the contributions to the overall financial welfare of the family, the entire equity in the home was awarded to Ms. Peter. Ultimately, the Supreme Court of Canada upheld that order.

The elements of unjust enrichment were present: the housekeeping constituted a benefit to Beblow; there was no compensation to Peter (the deprivation); plus, there was no obligation to provide the services, and no other plausible reason to deny compensation. Her work in the home was not regarded as having been provided as a gift. The suggestion that ordinary household services cannot support a claim of unjust enrichment was repudiated, given the basic principles of that doctrine, and the obvious value of such contributions. (Prior to this relationship, Beblow had hired a housekeeper to perform some of the work that was later undertaken by Peter.) The idea that domestic services cannot found a claim was flatly rejected as "a pernicious one that systematically devalues the contributions which women tend to make to the family economy".[137] It was added that such a notion had in the past "contributed to the phenomenon of the feminization of poverty".[138]

A finding of unjust enrichment does not invariably lead to the imposition of a constructive trust. Another option open to a court is to award monetary compensation.[139] And the granting of an interest in land need not amount to the fee simple estate; in some circumstances a more limited interest (*e.g.*, a life estate) may be the most appropriate response. In *Beblow*, the Supreme Court held as well that for a constructive trust to be ordered, whether in family law cases or otherwise,[140] a court should find that (i) a monetary compensation is inadequate; and (ii) that a link exists between the services rendered and the property in dispute.[141] (These are general rules: because equity is inherently flexible, they are not rigid requirements.) The nature of the requisite causal connection remains vague. A minor or indirect contribution should not be sufficient to prompt the constructive trust remedy.

In *Beblow* the contributions had been substantial, and they were found to be sufficiently connected to the family home, presumably because Ms. Peter's contributions allowed Beblow to pay off the mortgage and improve the property. A money payment was held to be inadequate given the nature of her work in the home and the chance that a damages award might not be paid. The measure of her assistance, based on the manner in which it enhanced the holdings of the parties,[142] was treated as roughly equivalent to the value of the family home. For this reason the home was awarded to Ms. Peter.

That outcome does seem extreme: Beblow, the sole legal owner of the house, wound up with no rights to that property.[143] In granting the award the Supreme Court suggested that the proper course was to consider the manner in which the contributions of Ms. Peter enhanced the value of all of the family assets. Having done so, one of these assets, the home, was segregated out and made the subject of the trust. She was also living in the home after the separation. Still, this left Beblow with very little (mainly a van, a houseboat, and his veteran's allowance).

Another consideration in disputes of this nature is the extent to which the benefits received by the claimant during cohabitation should be taken into account. The non-owning party in many of these cases has lived rent-free, while the owner of the property may have paid all of the current expenses associated with the upkeep of the home. It is obviously important that this side of the balance sheet not be overlooked. After all, if it is unrealistic to suppose that the cohabitee in a case like *Beblow* is intending to make a gift of services, then the same must be true of the tangible benefits provided by the other party.[144] In the *Beblow* case the trial judge divided the financial contributions of Peter by 50%, presumably to take account of the benefits that she had received from Beblow.[145]

The third requirement — the presence or absence of a juristic reason to allow the enrichment to stand — is both vague and vital. There are myriad instances when events cause someone to gain and another to lose. The juristic element tells us when some results are to be regarded as unjust. There are two obvious problems here: first, it is hard to know what counts as a good reason. Second, if the plaintiff must demonstrate that no such reason exists, this entails proving a negative, which is in theory a tricky matter: try proving that you have never been to the north pole (assuming you haven't been there).

To respond to these concerns the current approach is to bifurcate the onus of proof. As a general rule, the plaintiff must initially show that no previously recognized juristic reason to deny recovery applies to the present case. The established reasons include a contract, a disposition by operation of law, an intended gift by the plaintiff, and any other valid obligation founded in the common law, equity, or statute. If it is shown that there is no juristic reason from among this set, the plaintiff has made out a *prima facie* case under the juristic reason component. The defendant then bears a *de facto* burden to establish that a novel juristic reason exists. In considering such claims, regard should be paid to the reasonable expectations of the parties, as well as basic public policy issues. At the end of the day, a court might decide that: (i) a new category of juristic reason should be acknowledged; or (ii) a special reason (but no new category) exists in the present case that would prompt the court to deny relief to the plaintiff; or (iii) the defendant has simply failed to rebut the presumption of entitlement raised by the plaintiff.[146]

The story of the emergence of the remedial constructive trust as a response to unjust enrichment conveys a profoundly significant theme. It was argued in *Peter v. Beblow* that because matrimonial property legislation excluded certain couples from the right to seek a division of family assets under these statutory schemes, the courts should not use the equitable doctrine of unjust enrichment to infuse such a right through equitable channels. In response it was said that "[i]t is precisely where an injustice arises without a legal remedy that equity finds a role".[147]

That reply leads the discussion back to the starting point of this chapter. The growth of the remedial constructive trust in Canada cuts to the core of equity as a curative gloss on the common law. At the same time, the reluctance of English law to follow a similar course of development is premised on another part of the saga of equity. The open-ended nature of unjust enrichment principles reminds some of a much earlier epoch when equity was decried as varying with the length of the Chancellor's foot.[148] These opposing attitudes reflect the tension that often emerges between the need for certainty and flexibility in property law, and in the law generally.

(b) *Murdoch v. Murdoch*†

Supreme Court of Canada

[LASKIN J. (*dissenting*):]

The substantive issue in this appeal is whether the appellant wife is entitled to an interest in certain assets, including land, standing in the name of her husband from whom she is separated. She asserts an equitable claim, by way of a resulting or a constructive trust, to a one-half interest, by reason of her contribution of money and labour over many years to the acquisition of those assets.

In her pleadings, by an amendment allowed at trial, the appellant also alleged a partnership, and the reasons of the trial judge dismissing her claim focus mainly on that allegation. The only sentence in his brief reasons that could conceivably relate to the issue as argued in this Court was one coupling his rejection of the allegation of partnership with a refusal to find that (in his words) "a relationship existed which would give the plaintiff the right to claim as a joint owner in equity in any of the farm assets". Although I do not regard this as meeting the case advanced on behalf of the appellant, it appears to be founded on the trial judge's view that there was "a normal husband and wife relationship until the parties separated". On the evidence, to which I will refer, I cannot share the trial judge's appreciation of normalcy. The wife's contribution, in physical labour at least, to the assets amassed in the name of the husband can only be characterized as extraordinary. In so far as the trial judge's holding against the appellant rests on his view that she discharged a role that was not beyond what is normally expected of a wife, I disagree with it and approach her claim on a different footing.

I am the less reluctant to do so because the Alberta Appellate Division did not deal with the merits and hence this Court is, in fact, the first appellate Court in respect to them. The Alberta Appellate Division held that the wife was precluded from pursuing her appeal on her claim for a division of property because she had accepted payments of alimony under a judgment of the trial judge in a separate action for judicial separation and alimony which was consolidated for trial with the claim now in appeal. It relied upon *Pigott v. Pigott*, which, in my view, is inapplicable. In the *Pigott* case, interim alimony was fixed by taking into account what the husband had been directed to pay under a previous partition order. The husband did not appeal the interim alimony order but sought to appeal the partition order which he had invoked in having the amount of interim alimony reduced. The Ontario Court of Appeal quashed the appeal because he had acted upon the partition order to his advantage. No such situation is present here. There has been no appeal by the husband from the order for alimony, and the wife was certainly entitled to take the fruits of the judgment as it stood and to ask for more. She was not in the position of approbating and reprobating at the same time, as was the husband in the *Pigott* case.

I have had the advantage in preparing these reasons of reading those written by my brother Martland. Since the conclusions which I draw from the facts lead me to a different result in law from that which he has reached, it is best that I make my own summary to indicate how and why my view differs from his.

Central to my assessment is the uncontradicted evidence of the physical labour which the wife contributed to the spouses' well-being and evidence of what she otherwise put into the matrimonial stock. First, as to the physical labour. For some four years after the marriage in November 1943, the spouses worked on various ranches, hiring themselves out as a couple. The husband broke horses and looked after cattle and the wife did the cooking for the work crews and assisted her husband in some of his work. They were paid $100 per month, which was received by the husband, and got their board and lodging. In 1947, the husband and the wife's father bought a piece of ranch property jointly, each putting up $3,000. Some of this — the parties do not agree in their evidence as to how much — came from their earnings as a hired couple. This property, the Bragg Creek property, was operated as a dude ranch until it was sold in 1951 and the husband realized $3,500 as his share of the proceeds.

During most of the period of ownership of the Bragg Creek property the husband was an employee

---

† [1975] 1 S.C.R. 423. (Appeal dismissed with costs, Laskin J. dissenting.)

of a stock association, working for it during the day away from home for some five months of the year. He remained so employed up to the time the spouses separated in October 1968 and was still so employed at the time of the trial. In the result, it was the wife who, during her husband's absence for the five months of the year, performed the work which was involved in operating the dude ranch as a joint venture with the wife's father. Thus, she accompanied guests on pack trips, on fishing and hunting hikes and did other necessary chores around the ranch.

Her contribution of physical labour beyond ordinary housekeeping duties continued during the some four years that the spouses rented a property known as the Sturrock farm in which they had grazing rights and the right to mow and dispose of the hay on the property. One of the factual issues in this case concerned the source of the money, about $5,000 used to prepay the rent on the Sturrock farm, and I will return to this later in these reasons.

In 1956, the spouses bought the 160-acre Ward property, on which they had been living as tenants, for $4,500, making a down payment of $3,000. Again, there was a difference of view by the parties as to the source of this money. Undeniably, however, the wife again did a husband's work, during his periods of absence, in operating this ranch property. The Ward property was sold in late 1958 for $8,000 and the Brockway property consisting of 480 acres, three quarter-sections, was bought for $25,000. A down payment was made of $10,000 but of this sum $3,800 represented the purchase price of farm machinery which was part of the deal. The balance of the purchase price was payable in annual instalments of $2,000 for the first year and $1,000 per year thereafter. Again, the wife did her husband's work on this property during the periods he was away on his stock association work.

The wife filed a caveat in 1964 against one of the Brockway quarter-sections as an assertion of an interest under *The Dower Act*, R.S.A. 1955, c. 90. Relations between the spouses had deteriorated by that time, and they were severed completely in 1968 after the wife refused her husband's request to release the caveat to enable him to sell the Brockway property. Subsequently there was a physical clash which resulted in the hospitalization of the wife. The parties separated, with the husband remaining in possession of the Brockway property and everything in and on it. The wife was left with nothing, and her two actions followed.

The wife's contribution of physical labour to the various ranching operations on the properties successively occupied by the spouses is detailed in her evidence in chief as follows:

> Q. Now, you said earlier that you did certain kinds of work on ranches. We haven't dealt with the Ward property, the Sturrock property and the Brockway property. Did you do any work on those properties?
> A. Yes, I worked on all of them.
> Q. Could you tell the court, as briefly as you can, the nature of the work you did?
> A. Haying, raking, swathing, moving, driving trucks and tractors and teams, quietening horses, taking cattle back and forth to the reserve, dehorning, vaccinating, branding, anything that was to be done. I worked outside with him, just as a man would, anything that was to be done.
> Q. Was your husband away from these properties?
> A. Yes, for five months every year.
> Q. Five months of every year?
> A. Yes. He worked for the Stock Association in the Forestry Service.
> Q. So that you would do the chores and other work around the farm?
> A. I did until our son was old enough, then he helped, but until we had him I did it on my own, except for the few, you know, two or three weeks in the summer time when we would hire extra help then for stacking, but I was always still out there helping to rake and take lunches and gas out into the field.

The respondent husband admitted on discovery that his wife did the necessary chores while he was away on his other work, and his evidence in chief on this matter was as follows:

> Q. Over the years what were your wife's activities around the ranch?
> A. Oh, just about what the ordinary rancher's wife does. Most of them can do most anything.

This answer appears to be the basis of the trial judge's conclusion that the wife made only a normal contribution as wife to the matrimonial regime, a conclusion carrying the legal signification that it gave her no foundation, upon the breakdown of the marriage, to claim an outright interest in the assets, standing in her husband's name, which were accumulated during the cohabitation of the spouses.

The evidence as to the wife's financial contribution falls into several categories. It is clear that the remuneration paid to the husband for the period that the spouses were engaged as a couple was in part earnings of the wife, and the husband used some of the money in making the down payment on the Bragg Creek property. The proceeds of the sale of that property were in part at least used for the purchase of the Ward property, and the proceeds of the sale of that property were used in part for the down payment on the Brockway property. It is undeniable, therefore, that the appellant wife made a financial contribution, that was more than nominal, to the various purchases of property taken in the husband's name. The trial judge, unfortunately, failed to deal with this although it was plain enough on the record.

A second type of financial contribution made by the wife was in the purchase of all household furniture and appliances, save a stove which the husband bought. The wife was not allowed to take any of those articles with her when she and her husband separated. There is no contradiction of her evidence that it was her money that purchased the household effects. The trial judge made no reference to this matter in his reasons but it is a factor in the case which operates in the wife's favour.

A third situation involving an alleged financial contribution by the wife relates to the prepayment of rent on the Sturrock farm and to the down payment on the Ward property. The mother of the appellant wife had come into some insurance money on the death of her husband and she gave the money to her daughter who banked it in her name. The daughter drew on this account to provide $4,000 for the rent on the Sturrock farm and $2,000 as a down payment on the Ward property. The husband's position was that these outlays were by way of a loan to him from his mother-in-law and that, as indicated by his records, he so treated them and had made repayments accordingly. The trial judge dealt with the conflicting evidence on this matter as follows:

> The money that Mrs. Nash received by way of insurance policies on her husband's life I find was turned over by her to the plaintiff and was banked by the plaintiff in her name. I find no quarrel with the suggestion of Mrs. Nash that this money was considered to be her daughter's money to use as her daughter saw fit. However, this relationship between the mother and daughter was a relationship between them, and was not a relationship which involved the defendant. I accept the defendant's evidence that, in so far as he was concerned, the moneys that he received from time to time to assist in purchasing land or paying rent or purchasing cattle or use for other farm or ranch expenses, he understood to belong to Mrs. Nash, and he understood and treated that money at all times as a loan made to him.

Although clarity could have been better served if this is intended as a finding that the money was a loan from the wife's mother, I need not quarrel with it in the view that I take of this case.

The position as between the parties at the time of their separation was, therefore, that the wife had contributed considerable physical labour to the building up of the assets claimed by the husband as his own and had also made a modest financial contribution to their acquisition. The legal question is whether she can now claim a one-half or any interest in them when the husband has legal title and possession, [and] denies any arrangement for the sharing of the assets and the wife is unable to produce any effective writing to support a division in her favour.

The legal proposition upon which the respondent husband rests is that his wife's work earned her nothing in a share of the assets in his name when it had not been recognized by him in a way that would demand an apportionment, that is by proof of an agreement or at least of a common intention that she should share in the acquisitions. In my view, this is to state too narrowly the law that should apply to the present case.

The case is one where the spouses over a period of some fifteen years improved their lot in life through progressively larger acquisitions of ranch property to which the wife contributed necessary labour in seeing that the ranches were productive. There is no reason to treat this contribution as any less significant than a direct financial contribution, which to a much lesser degree she also made. The relations of husband and wife in such circumstances should not be allowed to rest on the mere obligation of support and shelter which arises from the fact of marriage, where the husband is able so to provide for an impecunious wife, nor on her statutory dower rights under the law of Alberta. They represent a minimum, and reflect the law's protection for a dependent wife. I do not regard them as exhausting a wife's claim upon her husband where she has, as here, been anything but dependent.

The most relevant decision in this country to date on the point in issue here has been the judgment of the Alberta Appellate Division in *Trueman v. Trueman*. Counsel for the respondent husband invited this Court to say that the case was wrongly decided or, if not, that it was distinguishable on its facts so as to exclude in the present case the application of the legal principles upon which it proceeded. The findings of fact in the *Trueman* case were that the husband had provided the down payment for the purchase of the farm on which the spouses built the matrimonial home but that the wife assisted materially in the building of the house, and worked in the field operating the farm machinery thus helping in the realization of the revenue which was used to pay the purchase price of the farm. No hired man was employed and in working as she did (her husband was frequently ill and unable to work) she assumed duties beyond what a farm wife was expected to do. I point to this view of the Alberta Appellate Division in contrast to the assessment of the wife's work in the present case by the trial judge, an assessment which, I have already indicated, is unacceptable.

In holding that the wife (who sued for a declaration after dissolution of her marriage) was entitled to a one-half interest in the farm property, Johnson J.A. speaking for the Court founded himself on principles stated by Lord Reid in *Pettitt v. Pettitt*, as expanded in *Gissing v. Gissing*, at p. 896. He also concluded that a declaration in favour of the appellant wife on the facts in the case was quite consistent with what was said by Judson J. for the majority of this Court in *Thompson v. Thompson*. I wish to examine the foregoing three cases and other authorities, including recent English cases on the subject under review.

I begin with *Thompson v. Thompson* where there was a division of opinion in the provincial Court of Appeal and in this Court on whether on the evidence the wife had made a financial contribution to the purchase of the property on which the matrimonial home was built. The trial judge had found that the husband had purchased the land with his own money, and this view was sustained by a majority of this Court speaking through Judson J. The majority reasons did not advert to a point taken by Kerwin C.J.C. in dissent that the spouses had each expended physical labour in building the house and in working the land in conjunction with others. Three points emerge from the reasons of Judson J. First, he rejects the view that any financial contribution by the wife entitles her to a one-half interest. I agree that there can be no such arbitrary division, and recent English cases indicate that the extent of a wife's interest must depend on the extent of her contribution: see, for example, *Gissing v. Gissing*, at p. 897; *Falconer v. Falconer*, at p. 452 where Lord Denning, after adverting to *Gissing v. Gissing*, said: "It is not in every case that the parties hold in equal shares. Regard must be had to their respective contributions. This confirms the practice of this Court. In quite a few cases we have not given half-and-half but something different."

I agree as well with the second point that emerges from the reasons of Judson J. in the *Thompson* case, and that is that a joint assets doctrine cannot be founded on the discretionary power given by s. 12 of the Ontario *Married Women's Property Act*, now R.S.O. 1970, c. 262, for the adjudication on summary application of disputes between husband and wife as to title to or possession of property. This same view was taken some years later by the House of Lords in *Pettitt v. Pettitt*, in respect of the prototype provision in the similarly named English Act. We are not concerned with such a provision here not only because it is not invoked in this case but because no such provision exists in any relevant Alberta legislation.

The third point in the *Thompson* case is that to which Johnson J.A. in the Alberta Appellate Division referred and which, he found, did not inhibit his freedom to make an order in favour of the wife on a trust basis. After dealing with and rejecting the proposition that any contribution, however modest, entitled the wife to a one-half interest Judson J. went on as follows (at p. 13 of [1961] S.C.R.):

> But no case has yet held that, in the absence of some financial contribution, the wife is entitled to a proprietary interest from the mere fact of marriage and cohabitation and the fact the property in question is the matrimonial home. Yet, if the principle is sound when it is based on a financial contribution, no matter how modest, there seems to be no logical objection to its application and the exercise of the same discretion when there is no financial contribution when the other attributes of the matrimonial partnership are present. However, if one accepts the finding of the learned trial judge, the basis for the application of the rule at its present stage of development in England is not to be found in the present case.

I read this passage as emphasizing the illogic of an arbitrary half-interest division in favour of a wife who has made little or no financial contribution. It does not relate to the equity considerations that may warrant a Court in declaring some entitlement in a wife who has contributed substantially in money or in labour to the acquisition of property taken in the husband's name.

Certainly, to say that a wife has no invariable right to a half-interest by reason of a financial contribution however modest is not to say that she must be denied any interest, where her contribution in money or in money's worth has been substantial, merely because legal title is in the husband. We are nearing a century (and it is more than that as to some States of the United States: see Schouler, *Marriage, Divorce, Separation and Domestic Relations*, vol.

1, 6th ed., 1921, at pp. 311 ff.) since married women's property legislation was enacted in England and in Canada. It offered merely mute testimony to the independent legal personality and capacity of the wife. As was said in a recent piece of periodical literature on the subject (see Foster and Freed, *Marital Property Reform: Partnership of Co Equals?*, in (1973) 169 New York L.J. for March 5, 23 and April 27) "it is relatively meaningless for a wife to acquire legal capacity to own property if she does not have any, or to become entitled to keep her own wages if she is forced to stay at home and raise children, or employment opportunities are limited...."

No doubt, legislative action may be the better way to lay down policies and prescribe conditions under which and the extent to which spouses should share in property acquired by either or both during marriage. But the better way is not the only way; and if the exercise of a traditional jurisdiction by the Courts can conduce to equitable sharing, it should not be withheld merely because difficulties in particular cases and the making of distinctions may result in a slower and perhaps more painful evolution of principle.

A Court with equitable jurisdiction is on solid ground in translating into money's worth a contribution of labour by one spouse to the acquisition of property taken in the name of the other, especially when such labour is not simply housekeeping, which might be said to be merely a reflection of the marriage bond. It is unnecessary in such a situation to invoke present-day thinking as to the co-equality of the spouses to support an apportionment in favour of the wife. It can be grounded on known principles whose adaptability has, in other situations, been certified by this Court: *cf. Deglman v. Guaranty Trust Co. of Canada and Constantineau.* The Court is not being asked in this case to declare an interest in the appellant merely because she is a wife and a mother; nor is there here an implicit plea for a community property regime to be introduced by judicial fiat. Common law jurisdictions in the United States, which also has community property States, have recognized that it is within a court's equity powers to adjudicate property rights between husband and wife: see Clark, *Law of Domestic Relations in the United States*, 1968, at pp. 449 ff. In *Garver v. Garver*, the Supreme Court of Kansas in drawing a distinction between alimony (as based on the husband's common law obligation to support his wife) and division of property said (at p. 410), "division of property ... has for its basis the wife's right to a just and equitable share of that property which has been accumulated by the parties as a result of their joint efforts during the years of the marriage to serve their mutual needs"; and see also *Engebretsen v. Engebretsen*, which is factually similar to the present case. Since, in my view, the wife has clearly established here a factual basis for a share in the Brockway property, the only remaining question is whether there are any obstacles in legal principle against a declaration in her favour.

The House of Lords canvassed this and other matters in the *Pettitt* and *Gissing* cases. As Lord Reid pointed out in the latter case, much wider questions were raised in the two cases than were necessary for the decisions in them, but this was because of the unsatisfactory state of the law as it had been developing in the English courts. The *Pettitt* case, on its facts, involved a claim by a husband to a beneficial interest in land purchased by his wife by reason of improvements made to a house thereon. His claim was disallowed, however, because there was no evidence of an agreement or of any common intention that the husband should have an interest by reason of the work he did on the house which the wife alone had purchased; such an agreement or common intention was held to be necessary where improvements, at least if not substantial, were concerned. Subsequent legislation, s. 37 of the *Matrimonial Proceedings and Property Act*, 1970 (U.K.), c. 45, has outflanked the *Pettitt* case by providing that subject to any agreement to the contrary a spouse who has contributed substantially in money or money's worth to the improvement of real or personal property in which either or both has or have a beneficial interest is entitled to a share or enlarged share, as the case may be, in the beneficial interest. In the *Gissing* case, the House of Lords agreed with the finding of the trial judge that the claiming divorced wife had not made, either directly or indirectly, any substantial contribution to the purchase of the house standing in her former husband's name and hence it rejected her contention that she was entitled to a beneficial interest. The facts in the present case distinguish it markedly from the *Pettitt* and *Gissing* cases.

The wider questions raised in those cases included, first, the effect of s. 17 of the *Married Women's Property Act* (similar to s. 12 of the Ontario Act referred to in the *Thompson* case), a matter irrelevant to the present appeal, and, second, the circumstances under which trust doctrines could be invoked to support claims by one spouse or former spouse to an interest in property formally held as to legal title by the other. It is this second matter that controls the disposition of the present appeal.

On one point, a starting point, there can be no dispute. The fact that legal title is vested in a person does not necessarily exclude beneficial interests in others. Evidence of a common intention before or at the time of acquisition, qualifying the formal legal title, is generally admissible. A long-established presumption of a resulting trust operates in equity in favour of a purchaser who takes title in another's name, and this presumption, a rebuttable one, is equally operable in favour of one who contributes some but not all of the purchase money. This is as true in the relations of husband and wife as it is in the relations of strangers. (For present purposes, it is unnecessary to consider the effect of the presumption of advancement on an alleged resulting trust in favour of a husband, it is the wife who is claiming here.)

What complicates the application of a presumption of a resulting trust, in its ordinary signification arising from a contribution of purchase money to the acquisition of property, is that in the case of husband and wife the contribution may relate only to a deposit on property which has to be carried on mortgage or instalment payments for many years; that where the spouses have lived together for some years after the acquisition, without any thought having been given to formalizing a division of interests claimed upon the breakdown or dissolution of the marriage, the presumption (as a mere inference from the fact of payment of money) is considerably weakened if not entirely dissipated; and that there is no historical anchorage for it where the contribution of money is indirect or the contribution consists of physical labour. Attribution of a common intention to the spouses in such circumstances (where evidence of the existence of such an intention at the material time is lacking) and resort to the resulting trust to give it sanction seem to me to be quite artificial.

The appropriate mechanism to give relief to a wife who cannot prove a common intention or to a wife whose contribution to the acquisition of property is physical labour rather than purchase money is the constructive trust which does not depend on evidence of intention. Perhaps the resulting trust should be as readily available in the case of a contribution of physical labour as in the case of a financial contribution, but the historical roots of the inference that is raised in the latter case do not exist in the former. It is unnecessary to bend or adapt them to the desired end because the constructive trust more easily serves the purpose. As is pointed out by Scott, *Law of Trusts*, 3rd ed., 1967, vol. 5, at p. 3215, "a constructive trust is imposed where a person holding title to property is subject to an equitable duty to convey it to another on the ground that he would be injustly enriched if he were permitted to retain it .... The basis of the constructive trust is the unjust enrichment which would result if the person having the property were permitted to retain it. Ordinarily, a constructive trust arises without regard to the intention of the person who transferred the property"; and, again, at p. 3413, quoting Judge Cardozo "a constructive trust is the formula through which the conscience of equity finds expression. When property has been acquired in such circumstances that the holder of the legal title may not in good conscience retain the beneficial interest, equity converts him into a trustee."

Why the device of the constructive trust is more appropriate in a case like the present one is pointed up by what Lord Reid said in the *Gissing* case, at p. 896 of [1971] A.C., as follows:

> As I understand it, the competing view is that, when the wife makes direct contributions to the purchase by paying something either to the vendor or to the building society which is financing the purchase, she gets a beneficial interest in the house although nothing was ever said or agreed about this at the time: but that, when her contributions are only indirect by way of paying sums which the husband would otherwise have had to pay, she gets nothing unless at the time of the acquisition there was some agreement that she should get a share. I can see no good reason for this distinction and I think that in many cases it would be unworkable.

It appears to me that Lord Diplock in the *Pettitt* case viewed the matter in the same way in speaking as he did (although this view did not attract majority support) at p. 823 of [1970] A.C.:

> Unless it is possible to infer from the conduct of the spouses at the time of their concerted action in relation to acquisition or improvement of the family asset that they did form an actual common intention as to the legal consequences of their acts upon the proprietary rights in the asset the court must impute to them a constructive common intention which is that which in the court's opinion would have been formed by reasonable spouses.

Although later English cases have continued to speak in terms of the resulting trust both where the financial contribution has been direct (see *Heseltine v. Heseltine*, and where it has been indirect (see *Falconer v. Falconer*, some of them are more easily explicable on the basis of a constructive trust: see *Hargrave v. Newton*: cf. *Hussey v. Palmer*. What has emerged in the recent cases as the law is that if contributions are established, they supply the basis for a beneficial interest without the necessity of proving in addition an agreement (see *Hazell v. Hazell*, and that the contributions may be indirect or take the form of physical labour (see *In re Cummins*.

It is the fact that the great majority of the decided cases concern the matrimonial home, but the applicable law is not limited to that kind of property: see *In re Cummins, supra*. In making the substantial contribution of physical labour, as well as a financial contribution, to the acquisition of successive properties culminating in the acquisition of the Brockway land, the wife has, in my view, established a right to an interest which it would be inequitable to deny and which, if denied, would result in the unjust enrichment of her husband. Denial would equate her strenuous labours with mere housekeeping chores which, an English Court has held, will not *per se* support a constructive trust: see *Kowalczuk v.*

Kowalczuk. Moreover, the evidence in the present case is consistent with a pooling of effort by the spouses to establish themselves in a ranch operation.

Having regard to what each put into the various ventures in labour and money, beginning with their hiring out as a couple working for wages, I would declare that the wife is beneficially entitled to an interest in the Brockway property and that the husband is under an obligation as a constructive trustee to convey that interest to her. Rather than fix the size of her interest arbitrarily, I would refer the case back for inquiry and report for that purpose. I am not called upon in this appeal to determine the effect of this declaration upon the award of alimony in her favour or its relation to her statutory dower rights.

I would allow this appeal with costs to the wife throughout.

(c) *Rathwell v. Rathwell*†

Supreme Court of Canada

[DICKSON J. (for Laskin C.J. and Spence and Dickson JJ.):]

I

This appeal affords the Court an opportunity of again considering the juridical basis for the resolution of matrimonial property disputes. The settlement of such disputes has been bedevilled by conflicting doctrine and a continuing struggle between the "justice and equity" school, with *Rimmer v. Rimmer*, the leading case and Lord Denning the dominant exponent, and the "intent" school, reflected in several of the speeches delivered in the House of Lords in *Pettitt v. Pettitt* and *Gissing v. Gissing*, and in the judgment of this Court in *Murdoch v. Murdoch*. The charge raised against the former school is that of dispensing "palmtree" justice; against the latter school, that of [meaningless] ritual in searching for a phantom intent. In England, in spite of apparent reversal in *Pettitt* and in *Gissing*, the justice and equity tide flowed unabated until, in 1970, Parliament effectively removed matrimonial property dis-

putes in England from the common law by enacting the *Matrimonial Proceedings and Property Act*, 1970, c. 45, the relevant provisions of which are now contained in the *Matrimonial Causes Act*, 1973, c. 18.

In earlier days the view was taken that on marriage "man and woman are one and that one is the man." The introduction generally of *Married Women's Property Acts* made it possible for wives to hold separate property but did little otherwise to improve the lot of married women. The custom by which real estate acquired by a married couple was taken in the name of the husband, coupled with the reverence paid to registered title, militated against wives. The view expressed in *Rimmer* that matrimonial property ought not to be governed by the strict considerations commonly applied between strangers survived *Gissing* and *Pettitt*, but was coldly received by this Court in *Thompson v. Thompson*.

Many factors, legal and non-legal, have emerged to modify the position of earlier days. Among these factors are a more enlightened attitude toward the status of women, altered life-styles, dynamic socioeconomic changes. Increasingly, the work of a woman in the management of the home and rearing of the children, as wife and mother, is recognized as an economic contribution to the family unit.

Canadian legislatures generally have given little or no guidance for the resolution of matrimonial property disputes, with the result that laws applied are perforce judge-made laws. An exception will be found in an amendment (1974–75 (Sask.), c. 29) to *The Married Women's Property Act of Saskatchewan*, R.S.S. 1965, c. 340, which came into force on May 19, 1975, after the trial in the present case.

On the legal front, acceptance of the notion of restitution and unjust enrichment in Canadian jurisprudence (*Deglman v. Guaranty Trust Company*) has opened the way to recognition of the constructive trust as an available and useful remedial tool in resolving matrimonial property disputes. Lacking that, a court is reduced to searching for actual, inferred or, possibly, imputed agreement (common intent) when the plain fact is that there rarely is agreement because the parties do not turn their minds to the eventuality of separation and divorce. With these prefatory observations I turn to the facts of the instant appeal.

II

Mr. and Mrs. Rathwell were married on July 4, 1944. He was a soldier, 24 years of age. She was an administrative clerk in the Royal Canadian Air Force, 21 years of age. Six months later she left the Air Force and went to live with his parents on their farm in the Tompkins District in the Province of Saskatchewan. He was posted overseas. Following return to Canada and discharge from the Army, he and his wife decided to make farming their way of life.

They opened a joint bank account in which their wartime savings (about $700 each) were deposited. It was the only account they ever had. During their married life all the moneys they received, or to which either became entitled, went into the joint account and all payments, for whatever purpose, were made therefrom.

In 1946, moneys from the joint account were used to provide the $780 initial payment on two quarter-sections of land (SE ¼ Section 20; SW Section 21: Township 13, Range 20, West 3rd) purchased under the *Veterans' Land Act*, R.S.C. 1970, c. V-4. The balance of the purchase price, amounting to $4,020, was paid by delivery each year of one-sixth of the grain harvested.

A second land purchase, also under the *Veterans' Land Act*, was made in 1947 and consisted of two adjoining quarter-sections (NW Section 17, SW ½ Section 20: in the same Township and Range). The down payment of $1,000 again came from the joint account and the balance of $6,000 was met by crop share payments.

A third purchase was made in 1958 (S½ Section 12; N½ Section 1; Part SE¼ Section 1: Township 13, Range 21, West 3rd). The price was $7,000 of which $4,000 was paid from the joint account. The balance was satisfied through farm work, such as combining, seeding and summer fallowing, done by Mr. Rathwell for the vendor of the land.

Title to all of the lands to which I have referred issued in Mr. Rathwell's name, in 1957 and 1959. There was no discussion between him and his wife concerning beneficial ownership of the land, apart from the statement by him from time to time that the lands were "ours".

It is clear from the evidence that Mr. and Mrs. Rathwell worked hard; they saved their money and they bought land. According to Mr. Rathwell, they were "working together as a husband and wife in the farming business." The venture was a "joint effort" in which, Mr. Rathwell said, he and his wife "worked as a team, to start with." Mr. Rathwell acknowledged that his wife contributed "to an extent." It was to a considerable extent. Mrs. Rathwell did the chores when her husband was busy on the land; she looked after the garden and canned the produce; she milked cows and sold the cream; she drove machinery, bailed hay, provided meals and transportation for hired help and kept the books and records of the farming operation. Often, while Mr. Rathwell worked the fields, she fulfilled his obligations under a contract to drive the school bus. She raised and educated four children. Mr. Justice Woods, of the Saskatchewan Court of Appeal, made the observation, which I think correct[, that] to grain-belt farmers, the kitchen was just as much an integral part of the farming operation as the feed lot, or the machine shed.

Marital difficulties led to the separation of Mr. and Mrs. Rathwell in 1967. Thereafter, Mr. Rathwell, with the agreement of his wife, leased the lands to their son, Duane, and mortgaged part of the lands to raise money for the purchase of other property for Duane. Mrs. Rathwell, to further her son's interests, released her homestead rights to the mortgagee.

Although Mr. Rathwell ceased farming in 1970, he acquired from his mother, in 1971, two further quarter-sections of land (NW ¼ Section 6, Township 15, Range 22, W. 3rd; NE Section 35, Township 14, Range 23, W. 3rd) for $2,000. The acquisition was largely by way of gift, as the value of the land far exceeded the price paid.

III

Mrs. Rathwell commenced an action in the Saskatchewan Courts for a declaration that she had an interest in one-half of all real and personal property owned by her husband, and for an accounting of all income and benefits returned by the property. Disbery J. dismissed the action and, in doing so, made the following significant findings of fact: (i) that the joint bank account was "a common purse intended for the use of both of them"; (ii) that Mrs. Rathwell made no contribution to the acquisition of the real or personal farm assets by way of labour; (iii) that there was no agreement between the parties that Mrs. Rathwell was to have a proprietary interest in the farm assets; (iv) that taken as a whole the evidence rebutted any presumption of interest of the wife created by the fact of her contribution to the joint account.

The Court of Appeal for Saskatchewan reversed the trial judge. Woods J.A. noted that it was "very clear to me that there was an agreement to share at the start and that it carried through until the marital differences developed"; on that basis he was prepared to award Mrs. Rathwell a one-half interest in all the lands — excepting those acquired from Mr. Rathwell's mother — and an accounting. Hall J.A. agreed with that result, but his reasoning differed from that of Mr. Justice Woods. He was of the opinion that there was no evidence as to intention at the time the joint bank account was opened, nor at the time the first land purchase was made; that through her monetary contribution Mrs. Rathwell acquired an interest in subsequent deposits to the joint account and in all purchases of land made from the joint account. Brownridge J.A. found evidence of an agreement to share in the assets Mrs. Rathwell helped create; alternatively, if common intention were lacking, Mrs. Rathwell could assert an equitable claim in constructive trust against the two purchases made in 1946 and 1947. Mr. Justice Brownridge did not explain why he differed from the other members of the Court in failing to find a trust in favour of Mrs. Rathwell in respect of the land, the subject of the third purchase.

IV

In broad terms matrimonial property disputes are much alike, differing only in detail. Matrimonial property, *i.e.* property acquired during matrimony (I avoid the term "family assets" with its doctrinal connotations) is ordinarily the subject-matter of the conflict. One or other, or both, of the spouses may have contributed financially to the purchase. One or other may have contributed freely given labour. The contribution may have been direct, or indirect in the sense of permitting the acquisition of an asset which would otherwise [not] have been acquired. Such an indirect contribution may have been in money, or it may have been in other forms as, for example, through caring for the home and family. The property is acquired during a period when there is marital accord. When this gives way to discord, problems arise in respect of property division. There is seldom prior express agreement. There is rarely implied agreement or common intention, apart from the general intention of building a life together. It is not in the nature of things for young married people to contemplate the break-up of their marriage and the division, in that event, of assets acquired by common effort during wedlock.

It would be wrong to think that the long line of cases on these matters is thoroughly consistent. It is not, as many distinguished academic commentators have been at pains to point out. One cannot help but notice as well the number of successful appeals. All of this suggests an uncertain and unstable state of law, but there is a certain inevitability about this in family law matters. The economic and human variables in a society are bound to be diffuse.

The need for certainty in matrimonial property disputes is unquestionable, but it is a certainty of legal principle hedging in a judicial discretion capable of redressing injustice and relieving oppression.

One limit to the exercise of that discretion is clear. If the husband and wife have agreed from the time of acquisition to hold the property in distinct shares on the basis of their contribution to the purchase price, or on some other basis, the plain duty of the court is to give effect to this agreement.

Another limit is equally clear. There is not, in the absence of legislative enactment, any such doctrine as "family assets" as was contended for in *Appleton v. Appleton.* The mere fact of marriage does not bring any pre-nuptial property into community ownership, or give the courts a discretion to apportion it on marital breakdown.

A third limit: Although equity is said to favour equality, it is not every contribution which will entitle a spouse to a one-half interest in the matrimonial property. The extent of the interest will be proportionate to the contribution, direct or indirect, of the spouse. Where the contributions are unequal, the shares will be unequal. A spouse who fails to make a contribution has no claim in justice to assets acquired wholly by the efforts of the other spouse.

Canadian common law does not recognize the concept of community of property, resulting from the sole fact of marriage. In the absence of legislative provision to that effect, it is not proper for a court to upset current matrimonial property practice by acting as if such an institution existed. This is a point of great importance and needs re-emphasis here. See *Pettitt v. Pettitt, supra,* at p. 803. But it must also be noted that there is a considerable distinction between judicial legislation of community of property and judicial enforcement of the equitable doctrines of resulting and constructive trust. It is understandable that confusion between the two should arise in matrimonial property disputes for the apparent net effect of each is normally a divestiture of property, or an interest in it, and transfer from the titled to the non-titled spouse. The essential difference, however, is that the divestiture from community of property has as its source the fact of marriage; the divestiture in trust arises out of a common intention (resulting trust), or out of inequitable withholding resulting in an unjust enrichment (constructive trust).

V

In the well-known work, *Underhill's Law Relating to Trusts and Trustees* (12th ed.), it is said (at p. 9) that trusts may be created:

> (i) intentionally by the act of the settlor, in which case they are called express trusts, or
> (ii) by implication of a court of equity, where the legal title to property is in one person and the equitable right to the beneficial enjoyment thereof is in another, in which case they are called constructive trusts.

Resulting trusts are treated under the head of constructive trusts, for the reason, it is said, that it would be extremely confusing to divide them into such as depend on intention, and such as do not.

Notwithstanding the reluctance, the distinction is of practical importance. Constructive trusts are analyzed by the author as either resulting trusts, in which the equitable interest springs back or results to a settlor or his representatives, or non-resulting trusts; a resulting trust will be presumed in favour of a person who is proved to have paid the purchase money for real property in the character of purchaser if the real property is conveyed to another.

Maitland, on the other hand, suggested a division into trusts and quasi-trusts, thereby reflecting what is certainly true, that particular trusts arise by will of the settlor, and others arise independently of that will, by operation of law: Maitland, *Equity* (1936), at p. 74. This latter division is particularly important where trusts of land are concerned, for by s. 7 of the English *Statute of Frauds* (received in Saskatchewan in 1870: *Balaberda v. Mucha*) trusts created by operation of law are exempt from the requirement of being evidenced by writing. Quasi-trusts are further divisible into resulting trusts and constructive trusts.

In England whenever the resolution of property disputes falls to be decided according to trust law, the phrase "implied, resulting or constructive trust" is used, with little apparent effort to distinguish the several types. Yet, they are different. Except in situations where there is a failure to exhaust the beneficial interest on the transfer of property, which is not the case in matrimonial property disputes, a resulting trust is concerned with the intent of the transferor: see *In re Vandervell's Trusts (No. 2)*, at pp. 294–5. In constructive trust the court imposes, irrespective of the intention of the parties but in accordance with good conscience, a duty upon A to hold title for B.

In the United States, where the concept of unjust enrichment enjoys a much greater acceptance than in England, the constructive trust, regarded as remedial, appears to have afforded a more flexible and satisfactory doctrinal base than the classical English institutional approach. Dean Roscoe Pound has referred to constructive trust as "purely a remedial institution" (33 Harv. L. Rev. 421).

VI

Resulting trusts are as firmly grounded in the settlor's intent as are express trusts, but with this difference — that the intent is inferred, or is presumed as a matter of law from the circumstances of the case. That is very old doctrine, stated by Lord Hardwicke in *Hill v. Bishop of London*. The law presumes that the holder of the legal title was not intended to take beneficially. There are certain situations — such as purchase in the name of another — where the law unfailingly raises the presumption of resulting trust: *Dyer v. Dyer; Barton v. Muir; The Venture.* The presumption has always been regarded as rebuttable: *Rider v. Kidder.*

If at the dissolution of a marriage one spouse alone holds title to property, it is relevant for the court to ask whether or not there was a common intention, or agreement, that the other spouse was to take a beneficial interest in the property and, if so, what interest? Such agreements, as I have indicated, can rarely be evidenced concretely. It is relevant and necessary for the courts to look to the facts and circumstances surrounding the acquisition, or improvement, of the property. If the wife without title has contributed, directly or indirectly, in money or money's worth, to acquisition or improvement, the doctrine of resulting trusts is engaged. An interest in the property is presumed to result to the one advancing the purchase moneys, or part of the purchase moneys. The principle is expressed thus in 19 Halsbury (3rd. ed.) para. 1372:

> 1372. Property purchased wholly or partly with wife's money. Where property is bought with money belonging to a wife and conveyed to her husband, there is a resulting trust in favour of the wife in the absence of proof by the husband of a contrary intention on her part.
>
> ...
>
> Where property is purchased in the name of the husband or the wife, as a continuing provision for them during their joint lives, and both the husband and wife contribute towards the purchase price, the property belongs beneficially to the husband and wife in equal shares, in the absence of evidence justifying a determination that the beneficial interests belong to them in some other shares.

To the same effect, see *Thompson v. Thompson, supra,* in which Cartwright J., although in dissent, did not differ from other members of the Court in saying, at p. 9:

> When the husband used moneys of which the wife was joint owner with him to purchase a property and took the deed thereof in his own name there arose a rebuttable presumption that he held as trustee for himself and his wife jointly.

The position is the same in respect of both spouses. In present social conditions the old presumption of advancement has ceased to embody any credible inference of intention: see *Pettitt v. Pettitt, supra,* at pp. 793, 811, 815 and 824.

The presumption of a resulting trust is sometimes explained as the fact of contribution evidencing an agreement; it has also been explained as a constructive agreement. All of this is settled law: *Murdoch v. Murdoch, supra; Gissing v. Gissing, supra; Pettitt v. Pettitt, supra.* The courts are looking for a common intention manifested by acts or words that property is acquired as a trustee.

If there is a contribution in money or money's worth, but absence of evidence of an agreement or common intention as to the quantum of the interest, doubts may arise as to the extent of the share of each spouse in the property. Lord Reid, in *Pettitt's* case, *supra,* at p. 794, said that the respective shares might be determined in this manner: "... you ask what reasonable people in the shoes of the spouses would have agreed if they had directed their minds to the question of what claim the contributing spouse ought to have." This is a sensible solution and I would adopt it.

The difficulty experienced in the cases is the situation where no agreement or common intention is evidenced, and the contribution of the spouse without title can be characterized as performance of the usual duties growing out of matrimony. There are many examples of this. There is the class of case where one spouse spends week-ends or evenings making small repairs to the family home: *Appleton v. Appleton, supra; Pettitt v. Pettitt, supra,* or contributes money to such repairs: *Re Taylor.* There is the case where one spouse may go out to work, making contributions to family expenses enabling the other spouse to acquire and pay for the matrimonial home: *Rimmer v. Rimmer, supra; Fribance v. Fribance;* or the case where one spouse may work in a family business and receive no wage or title to property: *Re Cummins.* There is also the case where a business may be a joint effort, such as a farm and, though title may issue to one spouse only, the business only succeeds through the efforts of both husband and wife: *Trueman v. Trueman; Murdoch v. Murdoch, supra; Fiedler v. Fiedler.* Some of these situations may be analyzed as agreement or common intention situations. Such intention is generally presumed from a financial contribution. The doctrine of resulting trusts applies. In others a common intention is clearly lacking and cannot be presumed. The doctrine of the resulting trust then cannot apply. It is here that we must turn to the doctrine of constructive trust.

VII

The constructive trust encompasses a more uncertain amplitude than the resulting trust. English law has long treated it as an analogous institution to the express trust arising in certain definite situations such as the assumption of trustee duties by a stranger to a trust, the participation in the fraud of a trustee by a stranger, and reception and dealing with trust property by a stranger in ways inconsistent with the trust: *Barnes v. Addy; Soar v. Ashwell.* The hallmark of the constructive trust is that it is imposed irrespective of intention; indeed, it is imposed quite against the wishes of the constructive trustee.

The examples mentioned above are situations where a man against his will is brought within the express trusteeship institution, but in the United States the constructive trust has never been so limited. Its amplitude oversteps the substantive trust machinery. It is a remedial mechanism.

The constructive trust amounts to a third head of obligation, quite distinct from contract and tort, in which the court subjects "a person holding title to property..., to an equitable duty to convey it to another on the ground that he would be unjustly enriched if he were permitted to retain it"; *Murdoch v. Murdoch* at p. 455, *per* Laskin J., citing Scott, *Law of Trusts* (3d), Vol. 5, at p. 3215. The constructive trust is an obligation of great elasticity and generality.

Where a common intention is clearly lacking and cannot be presumed, but a spouse does contribute to family life, the court has the difficult task of deciding whether there is any casual connection between the contribution and the disputed asset. It has to assess whether the contribution was such as enabled the spouse with title to acquire the asset in dispute. That will be a question of fact to be found in the circumstances of the particular case. If the answer is affirmative, then the spouse with title becomes accountable as a constructive trustee. The court will assess the contributions made by each spouse and make a fair, equitable distribution having regard to the respective contributions. The relief is part of the equitable jurisdiction of the court and does not depend on evidence of intention. As expressed by Professor Scott in an article entitled "Constructive Trusts" (1955), 71 L.Q.Rev. 39 at p. 41:

> The court does not give relief because a constructive trust has been created; but the court gives relief because otherwise the defendant would be unjustly enriched; and because the court gives this relief it declares that the defendant is chargeable as a constructive trustee.

Or, as expressed by Lord Denning, M.R. in *Hussey v. Palmer*, at pp. 1289–90:

> ... it is a trust imposed by law whenever justice and good conscience require it. It is a liberal process, founded upon large principles of equity to be applied in cases where the legal owner cannot conscientiously keep the property for himself alone, but ought to allow another to have the property or the benefit of it or a share in it. The trust may arise at the outset when the property is acquired, or later on, as the circumstances may require. It is an equitable remedy by which the court can enable an aggrieved party to obtain restitution.

Lord Diplock, in a passage quoted with approval in this Court in *Murdoch v. Murdoch*, at p. 438, said that a trust is created "whenever the trustee has so conducted himself that it would be inequitable to allow him to deny to the *cestui que trust* a beneficial interest in the land acquired".

The constructive trust, as so envisaged, comprehends the imposition of trust machinery by the court in order to achieve a result consonant with good conscience. As a matter of principle, the court will not allow any man unjustly to appropriate to himself the value earned by the labours of another. That principle is not defeated by the existence of a matrimonial relationship between the parties; but, for the principle to succeed, the facts must display an enrichment, a corresponding deprivation, and the absence of any juristic reason — such as a contract or disposition of law — for the enrichment. Thus, if the parties have agreed that the one holding legal title is to take beneficially an action in restitution cannot succeed: *Peter Kiewit Sons' Co. of Canada v. Eakins Construction Ltd.* at pp. 368–9; see also *Restatement of the Law of Restitution*, (1936), s. 160.

The emergence of the constructive trust in matrimonial property disputes reflects a diminishing preoccupation with the formalities of real property law and individual property rights and the substitution of an attitude more in keeping with the realities of contemporary family life. The manner in which title is registered may, or may not, be of significance in determining beneficial ownership. The state of legal title may merely reflect conformity with regulatory requirements, such as those under the *Veterans' Land Act*, which stipulate that the veteran must make the application; it may, on the other hand, be a matter of utmost indifference to the spouses as to which name appears on the title, so long as happy marriage subsists; the manner in which title is recorded may simply reflect the conveyancing in vogue at the time as, for example, the practice in Western Canada of placing title to farmland in the name of the husband. The state of title may be entirely fortuitous; it should not be taken as decisive against the non-titled party.

VIII

It seems to me that Mrs. Rathwell must succeed whether one applies classical doctrine or constructive trust. Each is available to sustain her claim. The presumption of common intention from her contribution in money and money's worth entitles her to succeed in resulting trust. Her husband's unjust enrichment entitles her to succeed in constructive trust.

Mr. Rathwell advanced, in support of the position that the presumption that a resulting trust had been rebutted, the following points: (i) Mrs. Rathwell had never questioned the registration of title in his name; (ii) she had delayed inordinately in advancing a claim; (iii) the filing of homestead caveats against the SW¼ Section 21 and NW¼ Section 17 and a further caveat against the SE¼ Section 20; in the last-mentioned caveat she claimed a one-tenth interest in the SE¼ Section 20 on the ground that she had advanced one-tenth of the purchase price. The caveats were filed following a threat by Mr. Rathwell to sell all the lands; they were filed for the purpose of giving notice of her claim to an interest in the three quarter-sections. Her assertion at that time to a claim [of] something less than her present alleged entitlement does not defeat the latter. None of the three grounds has merit.

Counsel for Mr. Rathwell submits that the courts will limit the application of the doctrine of resulting trust to the "matrimonial property", and not extend it to "business property", because to do otherwise is, in effect, to declare a partnership between the husband and wife. I do not think that what we are dealing with here is the husband's business property. It is matrimonial property in the true sense. It is fair to say that most of the cases in which the wife has succeeded in establishing her interest in land have been concerned with matrimonial homes, but this is not exclusively so: see *Nixon v. Nixon* (market stall); *Re Cummins, supra,* (vegetable shop); *Dillon v. Dillon* (combined dwelling and service station). I do not know what term one might properly apply to the Rathwell properties — "family farm", or "farming business", and with all respect to those of a contrary view, I do not think it matters. In one sense, it was a family farm, in another a business, in another it was a way of life. The property was all operated as one family unit by Mr. and Mrs. Rathwell working together.

An attempt was made to analogize a law firm to a farming operation and the *in terrorem* argument was advanced that if the interest of a wife is given recognition in what was said to be a farming business operation, why not also in respect of a law practice. I am not much persuaded by that line of argument. If and when a case is presented in which a wife has worked continuously and effectively with her husband in the development of a law practice, the respective rights and obligations of husband and wife can be considered. I must say, though, that I cannot think of any reason in principle why a wife should not, in the proper case, share in the proceeds of the sale of a law practice, if she worked together with her husband in the development of the practice.

In the present case all three justices of appeal reversed the findings of Disbery J. as to the absence of common intention. Two of the justices found positive evidence of an agreement that Mrs. Rathwell was to acquire an interest. Halt LA. found no evidence capable of rebutting the presumption of resulting trust occasioned by purchase from the joint account. The findings in both lower Courts are concurrent that the joint account was a common pool.

It was contended by Mr. Rathwell that the Saskatchewan Court of Appeal erred in law in overruling a finding of fact by the trial judge that the presumption of resulting trust in favour of Mrs. Rathwell had been rebutted on the evidence. I can find no evidence capable of rebutting the presumption that Mrs. Rathwell, as a contributor to the purchase price, would take an interest in the lands. Although an appellate court should be slow to reverse findings of fact below, there is no doubt as to the right to do so when, after full consideration, the court concludes that the judgment below is plainly wrong. *Coghlan v. Cumberland*; *Annable v. Coventry*.

IX

It is conceded by Mr. Rathwell that the down payment for the first acquired property came from the joint bank account to which Mrs. Rathwell contributed one-half of the initial funds.

Where a husband and wife have a joint bank account, the beneficial ownership of money in it, and of assets acquired from it, will depend upon the intention of the parties. *Jones v. Maynard* is authority for the proposition that when the intention is that the account is to be a pool of their resources, or in the words of the trial judge in the present proceedings, "a common purse", the money in it will be treated as belonging to them jointly and if investments are purchased out of the account in the name of the husband, he holds a one-half interest in them as trustee for the wife. It is true that in *Re Bishop, National Provincial Bank Ltd. v. Bishop*, Stamp J. said that so far as the decision in *Jones v. Maynard* related to investments, it was based on its own particular facts and, in general, where spouses open a joint account on terms that cheques may be drawn by either, then (unless the account is kept for some specific or limited purpose) each spouse can draw on it for his or her own benefit, and any investment purchased out of the account belongs to the spouse in whose name the purchase was made. I have difficulty in understanding the basis upon which it can be said that the joint owner who reaches the bank first can divert jointly-owned funds to the purchase of investments upon which the other joint owner will have no claim. In a decision of this Court *Re Daly; Daly v. Brown*, at p. 148, a joint bank account case, McLellan J. said: "In a case of joint tenancy neither party is exclusive owner of the whole. Neither can appropriate the whole to himself."

Mr. Rathwell gave the following evidence with respect to the opening of, and the operation of, the joint account:

> Q. And you purchased these through the Veterans' Land Act, did you?
> A. Right.
> Q. It was in the neighbourhood of $700.00 you had to pay as down payment then?
> A. Mhm.
> Q. Where did you get that money from? A. We had a joint account.
> Q. With your wife? A. With my wife.
> Q. And who had deposited money in that account? A. Both of us, as far as I'm concerned.
> Q. So this was a joint effort between you and your wife?
> A. This was a joint effort.

In the absence of agreement to the contrary, a one-half interest in any investment purchased by a husband from a common pool of funds, in the circumstances of the case at bar, will be considered to be held by him for the benefit of his wife. Legal title will be held in trust for both parties jointly. As to the first land purchase, Mrs. Rathwell's direct financial contribution is clear. As to the second and third purchases, Mrs. Rathwell's claim to a beneficial interest can rest on her continuing one-half interest in the joint bank account and the use of funds therefrom to effect the purchase. Moneys deposited to the account represented the proceeds from the sale of the produce from land of which she was a one-half owner. The proceeds were impressed with a trust in her favour. I agree with the views expressed by Hall J.A. on this point in the following passage from his judgment:

> All of the remaining payments on the first parcel of land purchased were made from the produce of the land itself. All of the deposits subsequently made to the joint account came from the proceeds of the farming operation. The appellant, therefore, had a proprietary interest in all of the subsequent deposits that were made, and all of the subsequent purchases made out of the joint account. To state it briefly, the fact that all of the subsequent cash flow which passed through the joint account was generated by the

initial investment supports the claim of the appellant that she had an interest in the assets held by the respondent.

It is well established that an accretion to property held in trust forms part of the capital of the trust property for the benefit of those beneficially interested in it.

The proper quantum inference to make in respect of the second and third purchases, as with the first, is a half-share held on resulting trust. No presumption of resulting trust arises with respect to the purchase from Mr. Rathwell's mother. This purchase was made subsequent to severance of the joint account and separation of the parties. Mrs. Rathwell cannot, therefore, be taken to have contributed to its acquisition either by capital or labour.

X

Analyzing the facts from the remedial perspective of constructive trust, it is clear that only through the efforts of Mrs. Rathwell was Mr. Rathwell able to acquire the lands in question. Assuming, *arguendo*, that Mrs. Rathwell had made no capital contribution to the acquisitions, it would be unjust, in all of the circumstances, to allow Mr. Rathwell to retain the benefits of his wife's labours. His acquisition of legal title was made possible only through "joint effort" and "team work" as he himself testified; he cannot now deny his wife's beneficial entitlement.

In a similar argument to that advanced in respect of resulting trust it was urged that if Mrs. Rathwell was accorded any interest in the land by the application of constructive trust, such interest should be limited to the homestead, or failing that, to the two quarter-sections comprised in the first purchase. It is difficult to find a rational basis for any such limitation. The Rathwells worked on and operated all of the land as one farm, a family farm in which husband and wife shared control and operating responsibilities. Although the causal connection may be clearer when the couple save money to buy the house in which they reside, there is no reason on the authorities, or in principle, why the application of a constructive trust should be confined to a homestead, or to a matrimonial home. The outcome in a matrimonial property case should not depend upon the nature of the property in dispute. The principles should apply to any real estate, or interest therein, and as well to personal property. The property which is subject to the trust in Mrs. Rathwell's favour is all of the property acquired in whole, or in part, from the contributions, direct and indirect, of Mrs. Rathwell.

XI

It was argued that Mrs. Rathwell should be denied a proprietary interest because she was awarded $250 per month maintenance. I agree with the Saskatchewan Court of Appeal in the present case that an order for alimony and maintenance in her favour does not bar a wife from seeking a further order declaring that she has an equitable proprietary interest. The two forms of relief are obtained in separate actions based on different legal rights. They are related only to the extent that the wife's success in the latter proceeding may permit the husband to seek a change in the award of alimony and maintenance in the earlier proceeding.

XII

The crucial question remains whether Mrs. Rathwell can succeed in this appeal in the face of the *Thompson* and *Murdoch* decisions of this Court. The judgment in *Thompson v. Thompson* was generally regarded as rejecting the line of lower court decisions that followed *Rimmer v. Rimmer*. In *Thompson*, Judson J., for a majority of the Court, (Kerwin C.J. and Cartwright J. dissenting) stated that the *Rimmer* case, and those which followed it, stood for the proposition that, at p. 13: "... if it is found that the wife makes any contribution to the purchase of the matrimonial home, she is the owner of a one-half interest and not merely of an interest proportionate to her contribution as in *Re Rogers*." Mr. Justice Judson continued with these words, at p. 13:

> But no case has yet held that, in the absence of some financial contribution, the wife is entitled to a proprietary interest from the mere fact of marriage and cohabitation and the fact the property in question is the matrimonial home. Yet, if the principle is sound when it is based on a financial contribution, no matter how modest, there seems to be no logical objection to its application and the exercise of the same discretion when there is no financial contribution when the other attributes of the matrimonial partnership are present. However, if one accepts the finding of the learned trial judge, [no financial contribution by the wife] the basis for the application of the rule at its present stage of development in England is not to be found in the present case.

The present Chief Justice of this Court, then Laskin J., dissenting in *Murdoch v. Murdoch*, considered that three points emerged from the reasons of Judson J. in *Thompson*: (i) rejection of the view that *any* financial contribution by the wife entitled her to

a one-half interest; (ii) a joint assets doctrine cannot be founded on the discretionary power given by s. 12 of the Ontario *Married Women's Property Act* (s. 22 of the Saskatchewan *Married Women's Property Act*, R.S.S. 1965, c. 340); (iii) the passage quoted above emphasized the illogic of an arbitrary half-interest division in favour of a wife who has made little, or no financial contribution. I would not take issue with any of these points.

The Thompson case was considered by this Court in *Murdoch v. Murdoch, supra*. The majority judgment in *Murdoch* was delivered by Martland J., who had this to say, at p. 433:

> Reverting to the *Thompson* case, it was decided that, on the finding of the trial judge that it was the husband who had provided the purchase money, and who took title in his own name, there was no basis for the imposition of a trust. *The finding of the trial judge in the present case rebuts the appellant's contention that the respondent accepted contributions from her toward the purchase price of the property.* The finding is that the funds received from her bank account were regarded by the respondent as loans from Mrs. Nash, which he recognizes as payable, and there is ample evidence on which that finding could properly be made. *If a financial contribution is necessary in order to found the appellant's claim, it has not been established on the facts of this case.* (Emphasis added.)

The absence of a financial contribution was considered to be important by the majority of the Court in *Murdoch* in the present case financial contribution is undisputed.

Mrs. Murdoch also founded her argument on the Alberta appellate decision in *Trueman v. Trueman*, in which a wife was awarded a one-half interest in matrimonial property notwithstanding the absence of any direct financial contribution by her. Mrs. Murdoch contended that her claim could rest, apart from financial contribution, on the work performed by her in connection with her husband's ranching activities. Mr. Justice Martland reviewed the *Trueman* case in detail and concluded, at p. 436:

> Assuming that the conclusion reached in the *Truman* case was, on its facts, correct, it does not follow that the appellant should succeed in the present appeal. The English decisions in *Pettitt* and *Gissing*, as well as those to which reference *was* made *in* the *Thompson* case, were all concerned with the determination of interests in what has been called the matrimonial home. The *Trueman* case dealt with a claim for an interest in the family "homestead". The present case involves a claim to an interest in three quarter-

sections of land and in all the other assets of the respondent. It is, in substance, a claim to a one-half interest in the respondent's ranching business and it is probably for that reason that the action, as formulated, sought a declaration of a partnership interest.

The above discussion by Martland J. is directed to the claim advanced by Mrs. Murdoch for a declaration of a partnership interest. Such a claim is not put forward in the present case. It is also worthy of note that *Murdoch* did not overrule *Trueman*.

In *Murdoch*, a distinction was drawn between a family "homestead" (at issue in the *Trueman* case) and the claim advanced by Mrs. Murdoch to a one-half interest in three quarter-sections of land and all the other assets, referred to by Martland J. as the "respondent's ranching business".

As I have stated earlier, if resulting or constructive trust applies, there is no reason in principle why it should be limited to the homestead. Mrs. Rathwell's contribution was to the entire farm, not merely to one hundred and sixty acres of homestead. Homestead legislation was introduced to protect a wife, not to be used arbitrarily for denying her rights to which she would otherwise be entitled.

Another point of difficulty in *Murdoch* arises through the adoption of common intention as the central test, and what might be regarded as implicit

rejection by the majority of the Court of the concept of constructive trust of which Laskin J. spoke. The issue of constructive trust was not advanced by counsel in any Court during the *Murdoch* litigation. At trial the claim was based on equal partnership, or in the alternative, on the contractual doctrine of *quantum meruit*. In the Court of Appeal, and in this Court, the case for Mrs. Murdoch was based on resulting trust and partnership. The issue of constructive trust never had a thorough airing before either of the lower Courts or in this Court. To this extent *Murdoch* did not deny the possibility of an action in constructive trust. In the present case the issue of constructive trust was thoroughly argued before the Court of Appeal and this Court, and it constituted one of the express grounds of decision in the Court of Appeal.

However, having recognized that the *Murdoch* decision is distinguishable in various ways, I wish also to say this: to the extent that *Murdoch* stands for the proposition that a wife's labour cannot constitute a contribution in money's worth and to the extent that *Murdoch* stands in the way of recognition of constructive trust as a powerful remedial instrument for redress of injustice, I would not, with utmost respect, follow *Murdoch*.

I would dismiss the appeal with costs.

(d) *Pettkus v. Becker*[†]

Supreme Court of Canada

[DICKSON J. (for Laskin C.J. and Dickson, Estey, McIntyre, Chouinard and Lamer JJ.):

The appellant, Lothar Pettkus, through toil and thrift, developed over the years a successful beekeeping business. He now owns two rural Ontario properties, where the business is conducted, and he has the proceeds from the sale, in 1974, of a third property, located in the Province of Quebec. It is not to his efforts alone, however, that success can be attributed. The respondent, Rosa Becker, through her labour and earnings, contributed substantially to the good fortune of the common enterprise. She

lived with Mr. Pettkus from 1955 to 1974, save for a separation in 1972. They were never married. When the relationship sundered in late 1974, Miss Becker commenced this action, in which she sought a declaration of entitlement to a one-half interest in the lands and a share in the beekeeping business.

I.   THE FACTS

Mr. Pettkus and Miss Becker came to Canada from central Europe, separately, as immigrants, in 1954. He had $17 upon arrival. They met in Montreal in 1955. Shortly thereafter, Mr. Pettkus moved in with

† [1980] 2 S.C.R. 834.

Miss Becker, on her invitation. She was thirty years old and he was twenty-five. He was earning $75 per week; she was earning $25 to $28 per week, later increased to $67 per week.

A short time after they began living together, Miss Becker expressed the desire that they be married. Mr. Pettkus replied that he might consider marriage after they knew each other better. Thereafter, the question of marriage was not raised, though within a few years Mr. Pettkus began to introduce Miss Becker as his wife and to claim her as such for income tax purposes.

From 1955 to 1960 both parties worked for others. Mr. Pettkus supplemented his income by repairing and restoring motor vehicles. Throughout the period Miss Becker paid the rent. She bought the food and clothing and looked after other living expenses. This enabled Mr. Pettkus to save his entire income, which he regularly deposited in a bank account in his name. There was no agreement at any time to share either monies or property placed in his name. The parties lived frugally. Due to their husbandry and parsimonious lifestyle, $12,000 had been saved by 1960 and deposited in Mr. Pettkus' bank account.

The two travelled to Western Canada in June 1960. Expenses were shared. One of the reasons for the trip was to locate a suitable farm at which to start a beekeeping business. They spent some time working at a beekeeper's farm.

They returned to Montreal, however, in the early autumn of 1960. Miss Becker continued to pay the apartment rent out of her income until October 1960. From then until May 1961, Mr. Pettkus paid rent and household expenses, Miss Becker being jobless. In April 1961, she fell sick and required hospitalization.

In April 1961, they decided to buy a farm at Franklin Centre, Quebec, for $5,000. The purchase money came out of the bank account of Mr. Pettkus. Title was taken in his name. The floor and roof of the farmhouse were in need of repair. Miss Becker used her money to purchase flooring materials and she assisted in laying the floor and installing a bathroom.

For about six months during 1961 Miss Becker received unemployment insurance cheques, the proceeds of which were used to defray household expenses. Through two successive winters she lived in Montreal and earned approximately $100 per month as a babysitter. These earnings also went toward household expenses.

After purchasing the farm at Franklin Centre the parties established a beekeeping business. Both worked in the business, making frames for the hives, moving the bees to the orchards of neighbouring farmers in the spring, checking the hives during the summer, bringing in the frames for honey extraction during July and August, and the bees for winter storage in autumn. Receipts from sales of honey were handled by Mr. Pettkus; payments for purchases of bee hives and equipment were made from his bank account.

The physical participation by Miss Becker in the bee operation continued over a period of about fourteen years. She ran the extracting process. She also, for a time, raised a few chickens, pheasants and geese. In 1968, and later, the parties hired others to assist in moving the bees and bringing in the honey. Most of the honey was sold to wholesalers, though Miss Becker sold some from door to door.

In August 1971, with a view to expanding the business a vacant property was purchased in East Hawkesbury, Ontario, at a price of $1,300. The purchase monies were derived from the Franklin Centre honey operation. Funds to complete the purchase were withdrawn from the bank account of Mr. Pettkus. Title to the newly acquired property was taken in his name.

In 1973 a further property was purchased, in West Hawkesbury, Ontario, in the name of Mr. Pettkus. The price was $5,500. The purchase monies came from the Franklin Centre operation, together with a $1,900 contribution made by Miss Becker, to which I will again later refer. Nineteen seventy-three was a prosperous year, yielding some 65,000 pounds of honey, producing net revenue in excess of $30,000.

In the early 1970's the relationship between the parties began to deteriorate. In 1972 Miss Becker left Mr. Pettkus, allegedly because of mistreatment. She was away for three months. At her departure, Mr. Pettkus threw $3,000 on the floor.

He told her to take the money, a 1966 [Volkswagen], forty beehives containing bees, and "get lost". The beehives represented less than ten percent of the total number of hives then in the business.

Soon thereafter, Mr. Pettkus asked Miss Becker to return. In January, 1973, she agreed, on condition he see a marriage counselor, make a will in her favor and provide her with $500 per year so long as she stayed with him. It was also agreed that Mr. Pettkus would establish a joint bank account for household expenses, in which receipts from retail sales of honey would be deposited. Miss Becker returned; she brought back the car and $1,900 remaining out of the $3,000 she had earlier received. The $1,900 was deposited in Mr. Pettkus' account.

She also brought the forty bee hives but the bees had died in the interim.

In February 1974 the parties moved into a house on the West Hawkesbury property, built in part by them and in part by contractors. The money needed for construction came from the honey business, with minimal purchases of materials by Miss Becker.

The relationship continued to deteriorate and on October 4, 1974 Miss Becker [again] left, this time permanently, after an incident in which she alleged that she had been beaten and otherwise abused. She took the car and approximately $2,600 in cash, from honey sales. Shortly thereafter the present action was launched.

At trial, Miss Becker was awarded forty beehives, without bees, together with $1,500, representing earnings from those hives for 1973 and 1974.

The Ontario Court of Appeal varied the judgment at trial by awarding Miss Becker a one-half interest in the lands owned by Mr. Pettkus and in the beekeeping business.

II   RESULTING TRUST

This appeal affords the Court an opportunity to clarify the equivocal state in which the law of matrimonial property was left, following *Rathwell v. Rathwell* [[1978] 2 S.C.R. 436].

Broadly speaking, it may be said that the principles which have guided development of recent Canadian case law are to be found in two decisions of the House of Lords: *Pettitt v. Pettitt* [[1970] A.C. 777] and *Gissing v. Gissing* [[1971] A.C. 886]. In neither judgment does a majority opinion emerge. Though it is not necessary to embark upon a detailed analysis of the two cases, the legacy of *Pettitt* and *Gissing* should be noted. First, the decisions upheld the judicial quest for that fugitive common intention which must be proved in order to establish beneficial entitlement to matrimonial property. Second, the Law Lords did not feel free to ascribe or impute an intention to the parties, not supported by evidence, in order to achieve "equity" in the division of assets of partners to a marriage. Third, in *Gissing* four of the Law Lords spoke of "implied, constructive or resulting trust" without distinction.

A majority of the Court in *Murdoch v. Murdoch* [[1975] 1 S.C.R. 423] adopted the "common intention" concept of Lord Diplock in *Gissing*:

Difficult as they are to solve, however, these problems as to the amount of the share of a spouse in the beneficial interest in a matrimonial home where the legal estate is vested solely in the other spouse, only arise in [cases] where the court is satisfied by the words or conduct of the parties that it was their common intention that the beneficial interest was not to belong solely to the spouse in whom the legal estate was vested but was to be shared between them in some proportion or other. [p. 438]

In *Murdoch*, it was held that there was no evidence of common intention. In *Rathwell, supra* common intention was held to exist. Although the notion of common intention was endorsed in *Murdoch* and in *Rathwell*, many difficulties, chronicled in the cases and in the legal literature on the subject, inhered in the application of the doctrine in matrimonial property disputes. The sought-for "common intention" is rarely, if ever, express; the courts must glean 'phantom intent' from the conduct of the parties. The most relevant conduct is that pertaining to the financial arrangements in the acquisition of property. Failing evidence of direct contribution by a spouse, there may be evidence of indirect benefits conferred: where, for example, one partner pays for the necessaries while the other retires the mortgage loan over a period of years, *Fribance v. Fribance* [[1957] 1 All E.R. 357].

The artificiality of the common intention approach has been stressed. Professor Donovan Waters in a comment in (1975), 53 Can. Bar Rev. 366 stated:

In other words, this "discovery" of an implied common intention prior to the acquisition is in many cases a mere vehicle or formula for giving the wife a just and equitable share in the disputed asset. It is in fact a constructive trust approach masquerading as a resulting trust approach, [at p. 368]

Professor Waters also observed, in a discussion of the resulting trust and constructive trust doctrines:

After all, in few cases will the inferring of an agreement be impossible or unreasonable, and, where it is so, justice and equity may well come to the same conclusion as that produced by the law of resulting trusts. But too often the resulting trust theory produces a result at odds with what would seem the more desirable outcome, or there is a fight through the appeal courts, and then what may well be difference of judicial opinion on the factual merits becomes a difference on the subtleties of the law of trusts, [at p. 377]

In *Murdoch v. Murdoch*, Laskin J., as he was then, introduced in a matrimonial property dispute the concept of constructive trust to prevent unjust enrichment. It is imposed without reference to intention to create a trust, and its purpose is to remedy a result otherwise unjust. It is a broad and flexible equitable tool which permits courts to gauge all the circumstances of the case, including the respective contributions of the parties, and to determine beneficial entitlement. It was described this way in *Rathwell*, at p. 455:

> The constructive trust, as so envisaged, comprehends the imposition of trust machinery by the court in order to achieve a result consonant with good conscience. As a matter of principle, the court will not allow any man unjustly to appropriate to himself the value earned by the labours of another. That principle is not defeated by the existence of a matrimonial relationship between the parties; but, for the principle to succeed, the facts must display an enrichment, a corresponding deprivation, and the absence of any juristic reason — such as a contract or disposition of law — for the enrichment.

Although the resulting trust approach will often afford a wife the relief she seeks, the resulting trust is not available, as Professor Waters points out, (at p. 374): "where the imputation of intention is impossible or unreasonable". One cannot imply an intention that the wife should have an interest if her conduct before or after the acquisition of the property is "wholly ambiguous", or its association with the alleged agreement "altogether tenuous". Where evidence is inconsistent with resulting trust, the court has the choice of denying a remedy or accepting the constructive trust.

Turning then to the present case and common intention, the evidence is clear that Mr. Pettkus and Miss Becker had no express arrangement for sharing economic gain. She conceded there was no specific arrangement with respect to the use of her money. She said[,] "No, we just saved together. It was meant to be together, it was ours". The arrangement "was without saying anything ... there was nothing talked over...." She testified she was not interested in the amount Mr. Pettkus had in the bank. In response to the question[,] "but he never told that what he was saving was yours?" she replied: "I never asked".

It is apparent Mr. Pettkus took a negative view of Miss Becker's entitlement. His testimony makes it clear that he never regarded her as his wife. The finances of each were completely separate, except for the joint account opened for the retail sales of honey. Mr. Pettkus was asked in cross-examination:

"you both saved together?", and replied: "I saved, she didn't". Uncommitted to marriage or to a permanent relationship it would be difficult to ascribe to Mr. Pettkus an intention, express or implied, to share his savings. Miss Becker said they were to "save together" but the truth is that Mr. Pettkus saved at the expense of Miss Becker.

With respect to the period from 1955 until the spring of 1961, the trial judge found:

> Now the Plaintiff claims a share in the said farm on the ground that at the beginning of their relationship they had implicitly agreed to carry on a common enterprise, the Plaintiff paying the living expenses and the Defendant doing the saving. I am sure that the Plaintiff wouldn't have voiced such a proposition explicitly at the time, bent as she was on marriage, for fear of scaring away a prospective husband. <u>I find that her contribution to the household expenses during the first few years of their relationship was in the nature of risk capital invested in the hope of seducing a younger Defendant into marriage.</u>
>
> Moreover, the evidence does not clearly show that from 1955 to May, 1961, the Plaintiff contributed more than the Defendant to the overall expenses of the household, so that <u>I find that the $12,000 accumulated by the Defendant was due to his superior salary, his frugal living and his off job gains from repairs.</u> It is to be noted that the Plaintiff made also some savings. [Emphasis added.]

Whatever the passage may lack in point of gallantry, the words underlined represent findings of fact by the trial judge, negating common intention.

As to the contribution by Miss Becker to the beekeeping business, the trial judge found:

> As the honey business is a seasonal one, the Defendant continued his side line, repairs of German cars but both businesses were not enough sometimes to keep the household solvent so that the Plaintiff had to work outside a few times. I also find that during that period the Plaintiff helped the Defendant to a certain degree in the operation of the honey business, especially during the extracting period but such help was seasonal and marginal as the Defendant employed outside help in the peak periods.

The trial judge dealt with Miss Becker's claim to a part interest in the Ontario properties, for the 1971 to 1974 period, in the following manner:

> The Plaintiff alleges that those sums came from the Franklin Centre honey operation and claims a part interest in those Ontario properties on account of her active participation in the honey

business. Once again, it would never have occurred to the Plaintiff to make such a claim explicitly at the time because such <u>a trust wasn't in the contemplation of either party, even implicitly.</u> [Emphasis added.]

Again there is a rejection of the notion of implied intention and resulting trust. At trial, Mr. Pettkus testified:

> Q. All right. Now did you ever have any discussions with her as to whether or not she had an interest in either your garage business or your bee business?
>
> A. It was all mine. She had no interest in the business, no.
>
> Q. Did she ever suggest that she did?
>
> A. No.

With regard to the arrangement under which Miss Becker was to receive $500 per year, Mr. Pettkus testified:

> A. Well, I knew the whole business is in my name and she has nothing so I figured it's only fair to give her a little bit of money and I figured the five hundred dollars, pay for all the expenses and she would have five hundred dollars every year as long as she stayed with me and if there's a good crop if there's no crop well of course I can't pay.

In the view of the Ontario Court of Appeal, speaking through Madam Justice Wilson, the trial judge vastly underrated the contribution made by Miss Becker over the years. She had made possible the acquisition of the Franklin Centre property and she had worked side by side with him for fourteen years building up the beekeeping operation.

The trial judge held there was no common intention, either express or implied. It is important to note that the Ontario Court of Appeal did not overrule that finding.

I am not prepared to infer, or presume, common intention when the trial judge has made an explicit finding to the contrary and the appellate court has not disturbed the finding. Accordingly, I am of the view that Miss Becker's claim grounded upon resulting trust must fail. If she is to succeed at all, constructive trust emerges as the sole juridical foundation for her claim.

III CONSTRUCTIVE TRUST

The principle of unjust enrichment lies at the heart of the constructive trust. "Unjust enrichment" has played a role in Anglo-American legal writing for centuries. Lord Mansfield, in the case of *Moses v.*

Macferlan [(1760), 2 Burr. 1005] put the matter in these words: "... the gist of this kind of action is, that the defendant, upon the circumstances of the case, is *obliged by the ties of natural justice and equity to refund* the money". It would be undesirable, and indeed impossible, to attempt to define all the circumstances in which an unjust enrichment might arise.... The great advantage of ancient principles of equity is their flexibility: the judiciary is thus able to shape these malleable principles so as to accommodate the changing needs and mores of society, in order to achieve justice. The constructive trust has proven to be a useful tool in the judicial armoury....

How then does one approach the question of unjust enrichment in matrimonial causes? In *Rathwell*, I ventured to suggest there are three requirements to be satisfied before an unjust enrichment can be said to exist: an enrichment, a corresponding deprivation and absence of any juristic reason for the enrichment. This approach, it seems to me, is supported by general principles of equity that have been fashioned by the courts for centuries, though, admittedly, not in the context of matrimonial property controversies.

The common law has never been willing to compensate a plaintiff on the sole basis that his actions have benefited another. Lord Halsbury scotched this heresy in the case of *The Ruabon Steamship Company, Limited v. London Assurance* [[1900] A.C. 6] with these words: ".... I cannot understand how it can be asserted that it is part of the common law that where one person gets some advantage from the act of another a right of contribution towards the expense from that act arises on behalf of the person who has done it." (p. 10) Lord Macnaghten, in the same case, put it this way: "there is no principle of law which requires that a person should contribute to an outlay merely because he has derived a material benefit from it[.]" (p. 15) It is not enough for the court simply to determine that one spouse has benefited at the hands of another and then to require restitution. It must, in addition, be evident that the retention of the benefit would be "unjust" in the circumstances of the case.

Miss Becker supported Mr. Pettkus for 5 years. She then worked on the farm for about 14 years. The compelling inference from the facts is that she believed she had some interest in the farm and that that expectation was reasonable in the circumstances. Mr. Pettkus would seem to have recognized in Miss Becker some property interest, through the payment to her of compensation, however modest. There is no evidence to indicate that he ever informed her that all her work performed over the nineteen years was being performed on a gratuitous basis. He freely accepted the benefits conferred upon him through her financial support and her labour.

On these facts, the first two requirements laid down in *Rathwell* have clearly been satisfied: Mr. Pettkus has had the benefit of nineteen years of unpaid labour, while Miss Becker has received little or nothing in return. As for the third requirement, I hold that where one person in a relationship tantamount to spousal prejudices herself in the reasonable expectation of receiving an interest in property and the other person in the relationship freely accepts benefits conferred by the first person in circumstances where he knows or ought to have known of that reasonable expectation, it would be unjust to allow the recipient of the benefit to retain it.

I conclude, consonant with the judgment of the Court of Appeal, that this is a case for the application of constructive trust. As Madam Justice Wilson noted, "the parties lived together as husband and wife, although unmarried for almost twenty years during which period she not only made possible the acquisition of their first property in Franklin Centre during the lean years, but worked side by side with him for fourteen years building up the beekeeping operation which was their main source of livelihood".

Madam Justice Wilson had no difficulty in finding that a constructive trust arose in favour of the respondent by virtue of "joint effort" and "teamwork", as a result of which Mr. Pettkus was able to acquire the Franklin Centre property, and subsequently the East Hawkesbury and West Hawkesbury properties. The Ontario Court of Appeal imposed

the constructive trust in the interests of justice and, with respect, I would do the same.

. . . .

VII RESPECTIVE PROPORTIONS

Although equity is said to favour equality, as stated in *Rathwell* it is not every contribution which will entitle a spouse to a one-half interest in the property. The extent of the interest must be proportionate to the contribution, direct or indirect, of the claimant. Where the contributions are unequal, the shares will be unequal.

It could be argued that Mr. Pettkus contributed somewhat more to the material fortunes of the joint enterprise than Miss Becker but it must be recognized that each started with nothing; each worked continuously, unremittingly and sedulously in the joint effort. Physically, Miss Becker pulled her fair share of the load; weighing only 87 pounds, she assisted in moving hives weighing 80 pounds. Any difference in quality or quantum of contribution was small. The Ontario Court of Appeal in its discretion favoured an even division and I would not alter that disposition, other than to note that in any accounting regard should be had to the $2,600, and the car, which Miss Becker received on separation in 1974.

. . . .

I would dismiss the appeal with costs to the respondent.

[Also note: some judges dissented in this case and wrote separate opinions.]

(e) *Kerr v. Baranow*†

Supreme Court of Canada

[CROMWELL J. (for the Court):]

I. INTRODUCTION

[1] In a series of cases spanning 30 years, the Court has wrestled with the financial and property rights of parties on the breakdown of a marriage or domestic relationship. Now, for married spouses, comprehen-

sive matrimonial property statutes enacted in the late 1970s and 1980s provide the applicable legal framework. But for unmarried persons in domestic relationships in most common law provinces, judge-made law was and remains the only option. The main legal mechanisms available to parties and courts have been the resulting trust and the action in unjust enrichment.

† [2011] 1 S.C.R. 269, 2011 SCC 10.

[2] In the early cases of the 1970s, the parties and the courts turned to the resulting trust. The underlying legal principle was that contributions to the acquisition of a property, which were not reflected in the legal title, could nonetheless give rise to a property interest. Added to this underlying notion was the idea that a resulting trust could arise based on the "common intention" of the parties that the non-owner partner was intended to have an interest. The resulting trust soon proved to be an unsatisfactory legal solution for many domestic property disputes, but claims continue to be advanced and decided on that basis.

[3] As the doctrinal problems and practical limitations of the resulting trust became clearer, parties and courts turned increasingly to the emerging law of unjust enrichment. As the law developed, unjust enrichment carried with it the possibility of a remedial constructive trust. In order to successfully prove a claim for unjust enrichment, the claimant must show that the defendant has been enriched, the claimant suffered a corresponding detriment, and there is no "juristic reason" for the enrichment. This claim has become the pre-eminent vehicle for addressing the financial consequences of the breakdown of domestic relationships. However, various issues continue to create controversy, and these two appeals, argued consecutively, provide the Court with the opportunity to address them.

[4] In the *Kerr* appeal, a couple in their late 60s separated after a common law relationship of more than 25 years. Both had worked through much of that time and each had contributed in various ways to their mutual welfare. Ms. Kerr claimed support and a share of property held in her partner's name based on resulting trust and unjust enrichment principles. The trial judge awarded her one-third of the value of the couple's residence, grounded in both resulting trust and unjust enrichment claims (2007 BCSC 1863, 47 R.F.L. (6th) 103). He did not address, other than in passing, Mr. Baranow's counterclaim that Ms. Kerr had been unjustly enriched at his expense. The judge also ordered substantial monthly support for Ms. Kerr pursuant to statute, effective as of the date she applied to the court for relief. However, the resulting trust and unjust enrichment conclusions of the trial judge were set aside by the British Columbia Court of Appeal (2009 BCCA 111, 93 B.C.L.R. (4th) 201). Both lower courts addressed the role of the parties' common intention and reasonable expectations. The appeal to this Court raises the questions of the role of resulting trust law in these types of disputes, as well as

how an unjust enrichment analysis should take account of the mutual conferral of benefits and what role the parties' intentions and expectations play in that analysis. This Court is also called upon to decide whether the award of spousal support should be effective as of the date of application, as found by the trial judge, the date the trial began, as ordered by the Court of Appeal, or some other date.

[5] In the *Vanasse* appeal, the central problem is how to quantify a monetary award for unjust enrichment. It is agreed that Mr. Seguin was unjustly enriched by the contributions of his partner, Ms. Vanasse; the two lived in a common law relationship for about 12 years and had two children together during this time. The trial judge valued the extent of the enrichment by determining what proportion of Mr. Seguin's increased wealth was due to Ms. Vanasse's efforts as an equal contributor to the family venture (2008 CanLII 35922). The Court of Appeal set aside this finding and, while ordering a new trial, directed that the proper approach to valuation was to place a monetary value on the services provided by Ms. Vanasse to the family, taking due account of Mr. Seguin's own contributions by way of set-off (2009 ONCA 595, 252 O.A.C. 218). In short, the Court of Appeal held that Ms. Vanasse should be treated as an unpaid employee, not a co-venturer. The appeal to this Court challenges this conclusion.

[6] These appeals require us to resolve five main issues. The first concerns the role of the "common intention" resulting trust in claims by domestic partners. In my view, it is time to recognize that the "common intention" approach to resulting trust has no further role to play in the resolution of property claims by domestic partners on the breakdown of their relationship.

[7] The second issue concerns the nature of the money remedy for a successful unjust enrichment claim. Some courts take the view that if the claimant's contribution cannot be linked to specific property, a money remedy must always be assessed on a fee-for-services basis. Other courts have taken a more flexible approach. In my view, where both parties have worked together for the common good, with each making extensive, but different, contributions to the welfare of the other and, as a result, have accumulated assets, the money remedy for unjust enrichment should reflect that reality. The money remedy in those circumstances should not be based on a minute totting up of the give and take of daily domestic life, but rather should treat the claimant as a co-venturer, not as the hired help.

[8] The third area requiring clarification relates to mutual benefit conferral. Many domestic relationships involve the mutual conferral of benefits, in the sense that each contributes in various ways to the welfare of the other. The question is how and at what point in the unjust enrichment analysis should this mutual conferral of benefits be taken into account? For reasons I will develop below, this issue should, with a small exception, be addressed at the defence and remedy stage.

[9] Fourth, there is the question of what role the parties' reasonable or legitimate expectations play in the unjust enrichment analysis. My view is that they have a limited role, and must be considered in relation to whether there is a juristic reason for the enrichment.

[10] Finally, there is the issue of the appropriate date for the commencement of spousal support. In my respectful view, the Court of Appeal erred in setting aside the trial judge's selection of the date of application in the circumstances of the *Kerr* appeal.

[11] I will first address the law of resulting trusts as it applies to the breakdown of a marriage-like relationship. Next, I will turn to the law of unjust enrichment in this context. Finally, I will address the specific issues raised in the two appeals.

II. RESULTING TRUSTS

[12] The resulting trust played an important role in the early years of the Court's jurisprudence relating to property rights following the breakdown of intimate personal relationships. This is not surprising; it had been settled law since at least 1788 in England (and likely long before) that the trust of a legal estate, whether in the names of the purchaser or others, "results" to the person who advances the purchase money: *Dyer v. Dyer* (1788), 2 Cox Eq. Cas. 92, at p. 93, 30 E.R. 42. The resulting trust, therefore, seemed a promising vehicle to address claims that one party's contribution to the acquisition of property was not reflected in the legal title.

[13] The resulting trust jurisprudence in domestic property cases developed into what has been called "a purely Canadian invention", the "common intention" resulting trust: A H. Oosterhoff, et al., *Oosterhoff on Trusts: Text, Commentary and Materials* (7th ed. 2009) at p. 642. While this vehicle has largely been eclipsed by the law of unjust enrichment since the decision of the Court in *Pettkus v. Becker*, [1980] 2 S.C.R. 834, claims based on the "common intention" resulting trust continue to be advanced. In

the *Kerr* appeal, for example, the trial judge justified the imposition of a resulting trust, in part, on the basis that the parties had a common intention that Mr. Baranow would hold title to the property by way of a resulting trust for Ms. Kerr. The Court of Appeal, while reversing the trial judge's finding of fact on this point, implicitly accepted the ongoing vitality of the common intention resulting trust.

[14] However promising this common intention resulting trust approach looked at the beginning, doctrinal and practical problems soon became apparent and have been the subject of comment by the Court and scholars: see, e.g., *Pettkus*, at pp. 842–43....

[15] In this Court, since *Pettkus*, the common intention resulting trust remains intact but unused. While traditional resulting trust principles may well have a role to play in the resolution of property disputes between unmarried domestic partners, the time has come to acknowledge that there is no continuing role for the common intention resulting trust. To explain why, I must first put the question in the context of some basic principles about resulting trusts.

[16] That task is not as easy as it should be; there is not much one can say about resulting trusts without a well-grounded fear of contradiction. There is debate about how they should be classified and how they arise, let alone about many of the finer points: see, for example, *Rathwell v. Rathwell*, [1978] 2 S.C.R. 436, at pp. 449–50.... However, it is widely accepted that the underlying notion of the resulting trust is that it is imposed "to return property to the person who gave it and is entitled to it beneficially, from someone else who has title to it. Thus, the beneficial interest 'results' (jumps back) to the true owner": Oosterhoff, at p. 25. There is also widespread agreement that, traditionally, resulting trusts arose where there had been a gratuitous transfer or where the purposes set out by an express or implied trust failed to exhaust the trust property: *Waters'*, at p. 21.

[17] Resulting trusts arising from gratuitous transfers are the ones relevant to domestic situations. The traditional view was they arose in two types of situations: the gratuitous transfer of property from one partner to the other, and the joint contribution by two partners to the acquisition of property, title to which is in the name of only one of them. In either case, the transfer is gratuitous, in the first case because there was no consideration for the transfer of the property, and in the second case because there was no consideration for the contribution to the acquisition of the property.

. . . .

[21] That brings me to the "common intention" resulting trust. It figured prominently in the majority judgment in *Murdoch v. Murdoch*, [1975] 1 S.C.R. 423. Quoting from Lord Diplock's speech in *Gissing v. Gissing*, [1970] 2 All E.R. 780 (H.L.), at pp. 789 and 793, Martland J. held for the majority that, absent a financial contribution to the acquisition of the contested property, a resulting trust could only arise "where the court is satisfied by the words or conduct of the parties that it was their common intention that the beneficial interest was not to belong solely to the spouse in whom the legal estate was vested but was to be shared between them in some proportion or other": *Murdoch*, at p. 438.

[22] This approach was repeated and followed by a majority of the Court three years later in *Rathwell*, at pp. 451–53, although the Court also unanimously found there had been a direct financial contribution by the claimant. In *Rathwell*, there is, as well, some blurring of the notions of contribution and common intention; there are references to the fact that a presumption of resulting trust is sometimes explained by saying that the fact of contribution evidences the common intention to share ownership: see p. 452, *per* Dickson J. (as he then was); p. 474, *per* Ritchie J. This blurring is also evident in the reasons of the Court of Appeal in *Kerr*, where the court said, at para. 42, that "a resulting trust is an equitable doctrine that, by operation of law, imposes a trust on a party who holds legal title to property that was gratuitously transferred to that party by another <u>and where there is evidence of a common intention that the property was to be shared by both parties</u>" (emphasis added).

[23] The Court's development of the common intention resulting trust ended with *Pettkus*, in which Dickson J. (as he then was) noted the "many difficulties, chronicled in the cases and in the legal literature" as well as the "artificiality of the common intention approach" to resulting trusts: at pp. 842–3. He also clearly rejected the notion that the requisite common intention could be attributed to the parties where such an intention was negated by the evidence: p. 847. The import of *Pettkus* was that the law of unjust enrichment, coupled with the remedial constructive trust, became the more flexible and appropriate lens through which to view property and financial disputes in domestic situations. As Ms. Kerr stated in her factum, the "approach enunciated in *Pettkus v. Becker* has become the dominant legal

paradigm for the resolution of property disputes between common law spouses" (para. 100).

[24] This, in my view, is as it should be, and the time has come to say that the common intention resulting trust has no further role to play in the resolution of domestic cases. I say this for four reasons.

[25] First, as the abundant scholarly criticism demonstrates, the common intention resulting trust is doctrinally unsound. It is inconsistent with the underlying principles of resulting trust law. Where the issue of intention is relevant to the finding of resulting trust, it is the intention of the grantor or contributor alone that counts.... The underlying principles of resulting trust law also make it hard to accommodate situations in which the contribution made by the claimant was not in the form of property or closely linked to its acquisition. The point of the resulting trust is that the claimant is asking for his or her own property back, or for the recognition of his or her proportionate interest in the asset which the other has acquired with that property.... The final doctrinal problem is that the relevant time for ascertaining intention is the time of acquisition of the property. As a result, it is hard to see how a resulting trust can arise from contributions made over time to the improvement of an existing asset, or contributions in kind over time for its maintenance. As Oosterhoff succinctly puts it at p. 652, a resulting trust is inappropriate in these circumstances because its imposition, in effect, forces one party to give up beneficial ownership which he or she enjoyed before the improvement or maintenance occurred.

. . . .

[28] Finally, as the development of the law since *Pettkus* has shown, the principles of unjust enrichment, coupled with the possible remedy of a constructive trust, provide a much less artificial, more comprehensive and more principled basis to address the wide variety of circumstances that lead to claims arising out of domestic partnerships. There is no need for any artificial inquiry into common intent. Claims for compensation as well as for property interests may be addressed. Contributions of all kinds and made at all times may be justly considered. The equities of the particular case are considered transparently and according to principle, rather than masquerading behind often artificial attempts to find common intent to support what the court thinks for unstated reasons is a just result.

. . . .

III. UNJUST ENRICHMENT

A. Introduction

[30] The law of unjust enrichment has been the primary vehicle to address claims of inequitable distribution of assets on the breakdown of a domestic relationship. In a series of decisions, the Court has developed a sturdy framework within which to address these claims. However, a number of doctrinal and practical issues require further attention. I will first briefly set out the existing framework, then articulate the issues that in my view require further attention, and finally propose the ways in which they should be addressed.

B. The Legal Framework for Unjust Enrichment Claims

[31] At the heart of the doctrine of unjust enrichment lies the notion of restoring a benefit which justice does not permit one to retain: *Peel (Regional Municipality) v. Canada*, [1992] 3 S.C.R. 762, at p. 788. For recovery, something must have been given by the plaintiff and received and retained by the defendant without juristic reason. A series of categories developed in which retention of a conferred benefit was considered unjust. These included, for example: benefits conferred under mistakes of fact or law; under compulsion; out of necessity; as a result of ineffective transactions; or at the defendant's request: see *Peel*, at p. 789; see generally, G. H. L. Fridman, *Restitution* (2nd ed. 1992), c. 3–5, 7, 8 and 10; and Lord Goff of Chieveley and G. Jones, *The Law of Restitution* (7th ed., 2007), c. 4–11, 17 and 19–26).

[32] Canadian law, however, does not limit unjust enrichment claims to these categories. It permits recovery whenever the plaintiff can establish three elements: an enrichment of or benefit to the defendant, a corresponding deprivation of the plaintiff, and the absence of a juristic reason for the enrichment: *Pettkus*; *Peel*, at p. 784. By retaining the existing categories, while recognizing other claims that fall within the principles underlying unjust enrichment, the law is able "to develop in a flexible way as required to meet changing perceptions of justice": *Peel*, at p. 788.

[33] The application of unjust enrichment principles to claims by domestic partners was resisted until the Court's 1980 decision in *Pettkus*. In applying unjust enrichment principles to domestic claims, however, the Court has been clear that there is and should be no separate line of authority for "family" cases developed within the law of unjust enrichment. Rather, concern for clarity and doctrinal integrity mandate that "the basic principles governing the rights and remedies for unjust enrichment remain the same for all cases" (*Peter v. Beblow*, [1993] 1 S.C.R. 980, at p. 997).

[34] Although the legal principles remain constant across subject areas, they must be applied in the particular factual and social context out of which the claim arises. The Court in *Peter* was unanimously of the view that the courts "should exercise flexibility and common sense when applying equitable principles to family law issues with due sensitivity to the special circumstances that can arise in such cases" (p. 997, *per* McLachlin J. (as she then was); see also p. 1023, *per* Cory J.). Thus, while the underlying legal principles of the law of unjust enrichment are the same for all cases, the courts must apply those common principles in ways that respond to the particular context in which they are to operate.

[35] It will be helpful to review, briefly, the current state of the law with respect to each of the elements of an unjust enrichment claim and note the particular issues in relation to each that arise in claims by domestic partners.

C. The Elements of an Unjust Enrichment Claim

(1) Enrichment and Corresponding Deprivation

[36] The first and second steps in the unjust enrichment analysis concern first, whether the defendant has been enriched by the plaintiff and second, whether the plaintiff has suffered a corresponding deprivation.

[37] The Court has taken a straightforward economic approach to the first two elements — enrichment and corresponding deprivation. Accordingly, other considerations, such as moral and policy questions, are appropriately dealt with at the juristic reason stage of the analysis: see *Peter*, at p. 990, referring to *Pettkus*, *Sorochan v. Sorochan*, [1986] 2 S.C.R. 38, and *Peel*, affirmed in *Garland v. Consumers' Gas Co.*, 2004 SCC 25, [2004] 1 S.C.R. 629, at para. 31.

[38] For the first requirement — enrichment — the plaintiff must show that he or she gave something to the defendant which the defendant received and retained. The benefit need not be retained permanently, but there must be a benefit which has enriched the defendant and which can be restored to

the plaintiff *in specie* or by money. Moreover, the benefit must be tangible. It may be positive or negative, the latter in the sense that the benefit conferred on the defendant spares him or her an expense he or she would have had to undertake (*Peel*, at pp. 788 and 790; *Garland*, at paras. 31 and 37).

[39] Turning to the second element — a *corresponding* deprivation — the plaintiff's loss is material only if the defendant has gained a benefit or been enriched (*Peel*, at pp. 789–90). That is why the second requirement obligates the plaintiff to establish not simply that the defendant has been enriched, but also that the enrichment corresponds to a deprivation which the plaintiff has suffered (*Pettkus*, at p. 852; *Rathwell*, at p. 455).

(2) Absence of Juristic Reason

[40] The third element of an unjust enrichment claim is that the benefit and corresponding detriment must have occurred without a juristic reason. To put it simply, this means that there is no reason in law or justice for the defendant's retention of the benefit conferred by the plaintiff, making its retention "unjust" in the circumstances of the case: see *Pettkus*, at p. 848; *Rathwell*, at p. 456; *Sorochan*, at p. 44; *Peter*, at p. 987; *Peel*, at pp. 784 and 788; *Garland*, at para. 30.

[41] Juristic reasons to deny recovery may be the intention to make a gift (referred to as a "donative intent"), a contract, or a disposition of law (*Peter*, at pp. 990–91; *Garland*, at para. 44; *Rathwell*, at p. 455). The latter category generally includes circumstances where the enrichment of the defendant at the plaintiff's expense is required by law, such as where a valid statute denies recovery (P.D. Maddaugh, and J. D. McCamus, *The Law of Restitution* (1990), at p. 46; *Reference re Goods and Services Tax*, [1992] 2 S.C.R. 445; *Mack v. Canada (Attorney General)* (2002), 60 O.R. (3d) 737 (C.A.)). However, just as the Court has resisted a purely categorical approach to unjust enrichment claims, it has also refused to limit juristic reasons to a closed list. This third stage of the unjust enrichment analysis provides for due consideration of the autonomy of the parties, including factors such as "the legitimate expectation of the parties, the right of parties to order their affairs by contract (*Peel*, at p. 803).

[42] A critical early question in domestic claims was whether the provision of domestic services could support a claim for unjust enrichment. After some doubts, the matter was conclusively resolved in *Peter*, where the Court held that they could. A spouse or domestic partner generally has no duty, at common law, equity, or by statute, to perform work or services for the other. It follows, on a straightforward economic approach, that there is no reason to distinguish domestic services from other contributions (*Peter*, at pp. 991 and 993; *Sorochan*, at p. 46). They constitute an enrichment because such services are of great value to the family and to the other spouse; any other conclusion devalues contributions, mostly by women, to the family economy (*Peter*, at p. 993). The unpaid provision of services (including domestic services) or labour may also constitute a deprivation because the full-time devotion of one's labour and earnings without compensation may readily be viewed as such. The Court rejected the view that such services could not found an unjust enrichment claim because they are performed out of "natural love and affection". (*Peter*, at pp. 989–95, *per* McLachlin J., and pp. 1012–16, *per* Cory J.).

[43] In *Garland*, the Court set out a two-step analysis for the absence of juristic reason. It is important to remember that what prompted this development was to ensure that the juristic reason analysis was not "purely subjective", thereby building into the unjust enrichment analysis an unacceptable "[immeasurable] judicial discretion" that would permit "case by case 'palm tree' justice": *Garland*, at para. 40. The first step of the juristic reason analysis applies the established categories of juristic reasons; in their absence, the second step permits consideration of the reasonable expectations of the parties and public policy considerations to assess whether recovery should be denied:

> First, the plaintiff must show that no juristic reason from an established category exists to deny recovery [...] The established categories that can constitute juristic reasons include a contract (*Pettkus*, *supra*), a disposition of law (*Pettkus*, *supra*), a donative intent (*Peter*, *supra*), and other valid common law, equitable or statutory obligations (*Peter*, *supra*). If there is no juristic reason from an established category, then the plaintiff has made out a *prima facie* case under the juristic reason component of the analysis.
>
> The *prima facie* case is rebuttable, however, where the defendant can show that there is another reason to deny recovery. As a result, there is a *de facto* burden of proof placed on the defendant to show the reason why the enrichment should be retained. This stage of the analysis thus provides for a category of residual defence in which courts can look to all of the circumstances of the transaction in order to determine whether there is another reason to deny recovery.

As part of the defendant's attempt to rebut, courts should have regard to two factors: the reasonable expectations of the parties, and public policy considerations. [paras. 44–46]

[44] Thus, at the juristic reason stage of the analysis, if the case falls outside the existing categories, the court may take into account the legitimate expectations of the parties (*Pettkus*, at p. 849) and moral and policy-based arguments about whether particular enrichments are unjust (*Peter*, at p. 990). For example, in *Peter*, it was at this stage that the Court considered and rejected the argument that the provision of domestic and childcare services should not give rise to equitable claims against the other spouse in a marital or quasi-marital relationship (pp. 993–95). Overall, the test for juristic reason is flexible, and the relevant factors to consider will depend on the situation before the court (*Peter*, at p. 990).

[45] Policy arguments concerning individual autonomy may arise under the second branch of the juristic reason analysis. In the context of claims for unjust enrichment, this has led to questions regarding how (and when) factors relating to the manner in which the parties organized their relationship should be taken into account. It has been argued, for example, that the legislative decision to exclude unmarried couples from property division legislation indicates the court should not use the equitable doctrine of unjust enrichment to address their property and asset disputes. However, the court in *Peter* rejected this argument, noting that it misapprehended the role of equity. As McLachlin J. put it at p. 994, "It is precisely where an injustice arises without a legal remedy that equity finds a role." (See also *Nova Scotia (Attorney General) v. Walsh*, 2002 SCC 83, [2002] 4 S.C.R. 325, at para. 61.)

(3) Remedy

[46] Remedies for unjust enrichment are restitutionary in nature; that is, the object of the remedy is to require the defendant to repay or reverse the unjustified enrichment. A successful claim for unjust enrichment may attract either a "personal restitutionary award" or a "restitutionary proprietary award". In other words, the plaintiff may be entitled to a monetary or a proprietary remedy (*Lac Minerals Ltd. v. International Corona Resources Ltd.*, [1989] 2 S.C.R. 574, at p. 669, *per* La Forest J.).

(A) MONETARY AWARD

[47] The first remedy to consider is always a monetary award (*Peter*, at pp. 987 and 999). In most cases, it will be sufficient to remedy the unjust enrichment. However, calculation of such an award is far from straightforward. Two issues have given rise to disagreement and difficulty in domestic unjust enrichment claims.

[48] First, the fact that many domestic claims of unjust enrichment arise out of relationships in which there has been a mutual conferral of benefits gives rise to difficulties in determining what will constitute adequate compensation. While the value of domestic services is not questioned (*Peter*; *Sorochan*), it is unjust to pay attention only to the contributions of one party in assessing an appropriate remedy. This is not only an important issue of principle; in practice, it is enormously difficult for the parties and the court to "create, retroactively, a notional ledger to record and value every service rendered by each party to the other" (R. E. Scane, "Relationships 'Tantamount to Spousal', Unjust Enrichment, and Constructive Trusts" (1991), 70 *Can. Bar Rev.* 260, at p. 281)....

[49] A second difficulty arises from the fact that some courts and commentators have read *Peter* as holding that when a monetary award is appropriate, it must invariably be calculated on the basis of the monetary value of the unpaid services. This is often referred to as the *quantum meruit*, or "value received" or "fee-for-services" approach. This was followed in *Bell v. Bailey* (2001), 203 D.L.R. (4th) 589, (Ont. C.A.). Other appellate courts have held that monetary relief may be assessed more flexibly — in effect, on a value survived basis — by reference, for example, to the overall increase in the couple's wealth during the relationship: *Wilson v. Fotsch*, 2010 BCCA 226, 319 D.L.R. (4th) 26, at para. 50; *Pickelein v. Gillmore* (1997), 30 B.C.L.R. (3d) 44 (C.A.); *Harrison v. Kalinocha* (1994), 90 B.C.L.R. (2d) 273 (C.A.); *MacFarlane v. Smith*, 2003 NBCA 6, 256 N.B.R. (2d) 108, at paras. 31–34 and 41–43; *Shannon v. Gidden*, 1999 BCCA 539, 71 B.C.L.R. (3d) 40, at para. 37. With respect to inconsistencies in how *in personam* relief for unjust enrichment may be quantified, see also: *Matrimonial Property Law in Canada*, vol 1, by J.G. McLeod and A.A. Mamo, eds. (loose-leaf), at pp. 40.78–40.79.

(B) PROPRIETARY AWARD

[50] The Court has recognized that, in some cases, when a monetary award is inappropriate or insufficient, a proprietary remedy may be required. *Pettkus* is responsible for an important remedial feature of the Canadian law of unjust enrichment: the development of the remedial constructive trust. Imposed without reference to intention to create a trust, the

constructive trust is a broad and flexible equitable tool used to determine beneficial entitlement to property (*Pettkus*, at pp. 843–44 and 847–48). Where the plaintiff can demonstrate a link or causal connection between his or her contributions and the acquisition, preservation, maintenance or improvement of the disputed property, a share of the property proportionate to the unjust enrichment can be impressed with a constructive trust in his or her favour (*Pettkus*, at pp. 852–53; *Sorochan*, at p. 50). *Pettkus* made clear that these principles apply equally to unmarried cohabitants, since "[t]he equitable principle on which the remedy of constructive trusts rests is broad and general; its purpose is to prevent unjust enrichment in whatever circumstances it occurs" (pp. 850–51).

[51] As to the nature of the link required between the contribution and the property, the Court has consistently held that the plaintiff must demonstrate a "sufficiently substantial and direct" link, a "causal connection" or a "nexus" between the plaintiff's contributions and the property which is the subject matter of the trust (*Peter*, at pp. 988, 997 and 999; *Pettkus* at p. 852; *Sorochan*, at pp. 47–50; *Rathwell*, at p. 454). A minor or indirect contribution will not suffice (*Peter*, at p. 997). As Dickson C.J. put it in *Sorochan*, the primary focus is on whether the contributions have a "clear proprietary relationship" (p. 50, citing Professor McLeod's annotation of *Herman v. Smith* (1984), 42 R.F.L. (2d) 154, at p. 156). Indirect contributions of money and direct contributions of labour may suffice, provided that a connection is established between the plaintiff's deprivation and the acquisition, preservation, maintenance, or improvement of the property (*Sorochan*, at p. 50; *Pettkus*, at p. 852).

[52] The plaintiff must also establish that a monetary award would be insufficient in the circumstances (*Peter*, at p. 999). In this regard, the court may take into account the probability of recovery, as well as whether there is a reason to grant the plaintiff the additional rights that flow from recognition of property rights (*Lac Minerals*, at p. 678, *per* La Forest J.).

[53] The extent of the constructive trust interest should be proportionate to the claimant's contributions. Where the contributions are unequal, the shares will be unequal (*Pettkus*, at pp. 852–53; *Rathwell*, at p. 448; *Peter*, at pp. 998–99). As Dickson J. put it in *Rathwell*, "The court will assess the contributions made by each spouse and make a fair,

equitable distribution having regard to the respective contributions" (p. 454).

D.   Areas Needing Clarification

[54] While the law of unjust enrichment sets out a sturdy legal framework within which to address claims by domestic partners, three areas continue to generate controversy and require clarification. As mentioned earlier, these are as follows: the approach to the assessment of a monetary award for a successful unjust enrichment claim, how and where to address the mutual benefit problem, and the role of the parties' reasonable or legitimate expectations. I will address these in turn.

E.   Is a Monetary Award Restricted to Quantum Meruit?

(1) Introduction

[55] As noted earlier, remedies for unjust enrichment may either be proprietary (normally a remedial constructive trust) or personal (normally a money remedy). Once the choice has been made to award a monetary rather than a proprietary remedy, the question of how to quantify that monetary remedy arises. Some courts have held that monetary relief must always be calculated based on a value received or *quantum meruit* basis (*Bell*), while others have held that monetary relief may also be based on a value survived (i.e. by reference to the value of property) approach (*Wilson*; *Pickelein*; *Harrison*; *MacFarlane*; *Shannon*). If, as some courts have held, a monetary remedy must invariably be quantified on a *quantum meruit* basis, the remedial choice in unjust enrichment cases becomes whether to impose a constructive trust or order a monetary remedy calculated on a *quantum meruit* basis. One scholar has referred to this approach as the false dichotomy between constructive trust and *quantum meruit* (McCamus, at pp. 375–76). Scholars have also noted this area of uncertainty in the case law, and have suggested that an *in personam* remedy using the value survived measure is a plausible alternative to the constructive trust (McCamus, at p. 377; P. Birks, *An Introduction to the Law of Restitution* (1985), at pp. 394–95). As I will explain below, *Peter* is said to have established this dichotomy of remedial choice. However, in my view, the focus in *Peter* was on the availability of the constructive trust remedy, and that case should not be taken as limiting the calculation of monetary relief for unjust enrichment to a *quantum meruit* basis. In appropriate circumstances, monetary relief may be assessed on a value survived basis.

[56] I will first briefly describe the genesis of the purported limitation on the monetary remedy. Then I will explain why, in my view, it should be rejected. Finally, I will set out my views on how money remedies for unjust enrichment claims in domestic situations should be approached.

(2) *The Remedial Dichotomy*

[57] As noted, there is a widespread, although not unanimous, view that there are only two choices of remedy for an unjust enrichment: a monetary award, assessed on a fee-for-services basis; or a proprietary one (generally taking the form of a remedial constructive trust), where the claimant can show that the benefit conferred contributed to the acquisition, preservation, maintenance, or improvement of specific property. Some brief comments in *Peter* seem to have spawned this idea, which is reflected in a number of appellate authorities. For instance, in the *Vanasse* appeal, the Ontario Court of Appeal reasoned that since Ms. Vanasse could not show that her contributions were linked to specific property, her claim had to be quantified on a fee-for-services basis. I respectfully do not agree that monetary awards for unjust enrichment must always be calculated in this way.

(3) *Why the Remedial Dichotomy Should Be Rejected*

[58] In my view, restricting the money remedy to a fee-for-services calculation is inappropriate for four reasons. First, it fails to reflect the reality of the lives of many domestic partners. Second, it is inconsistent with the inherent flexibility of unjust enrichment. Third, it ignores the historical basis of *quantum meruit* claims. Finally, it is not mandated by the Court's judgment in *Peter*. For those reasons, this remedial dichotomy should be rejected. The discussion which follows is concerned only with the quantification of a monetary remedy for unjust enrichment; the law relating to when a proprietary remedy should be granted is well established and remains unchanged.

(A) LIFE EXPERIENCE

[59] The remedial dichotomy would be appropriate if, in fact, the bases of all domestic unjust enrichment claims fit into only two categories — those where the enrichment consists of the provision of unpaid services, and those where it consists of an unrecognized contribution to the acquisition, improvement, maintenance or preservation of specific property. To be sure, those two bases for unjust enrichment claims exist. However, all unjust enrichment cases cannot be neatly divided into these two categories.

[60] At least one other basis for an unjust enrichment claim is easy to identify. It consists of cases in which the contributions of both parties over time have resulted in an accumulation of wealth. The unjust enrichment occurs following the breakdown of their relationship when one party retains a disproportionate share of the assets which are the product of their joint efforts. The required link between the contributions and a specific property may not exist, making it inappropriate to confer a proprietary remedy. However, there may clearly be a link between the joint efforts of the parties and the accumulation of wealth; in other words, a link between the "value received" and the "value surviving", as McLachlin J. put it in *Peter*, at pp. 1000–1001. Thus, where there is a relationship that can be described as a "joint family venture", and the joint efforts of the parties are linked to the accumulation of wealth, the unjust enrichment should be thought of as leaving one party with a disproportionate share of the jointly earned assets.

[61] There is nothing new about the notion of a joint family venture in which both parties contribute to their overall accumulation of wealth. It was recognition of this reality that contributed to comprehensive matrimonial property legislative reform in the late 1970s and early 1980s. As the Court put it in *Clarke v. Clarke*, [1990] 2 S.C.R. 795, at p. 807 (in relation to Nova Scotia's *Matrimonial Property Act*), ". . . the Act supports the equality of both parties to a marriage and <u>recognized the joint contribution of the spouses, be it financial or otherwise, to that enterprise.</u> . . . The Act is accordingly remedial in nature. It was designed to alleviate the inequities of the past when the contribution made by women to the economic survival and growth of the family was not recognized" (emphasis added).

[62] Unlike much matrimonial property legislation, the law of unjust enrichment does not mandate a presumption of equal sharing. However, the law of unjust enrichment can and should respond to the social reality identified by the legislature that many domestic relationships are more realistically viewed as a joint venture to which the parties jointly contribute.

[63] This reality has also been recognized many times and in many contexts by the Court. For instance, in *Murdoch*, Laskin J. (as he then was), in

dissent, would have imposed constructive trust relief, on the basis that the facts were "consistent with a pooling of effort by the spouses" to establish themselves in a ranch operation (p. 457), and that the spouses had worked together for fifteen years to improve "their lot in life through progressively larger acquisitions of ranch property" (p. 446). Similarly, in *Rathwell*, a majority of the judges agreed that Mr. and Mrs. Rathwell had pooled their efforts to accumulate wealth as a team. Dickson J. emphasized that the parties had together "decided to make farming their way of life" (p. 444), and that the acquisition of property in Mr. Rathwell's name was only made possible through their "joint effort" and "team work" (p. 461).

[64] A similar recognition is evident in *Pettkus* and *Peter*.

[65] In *Pettkus*, the parties developed a successful beekeeping business, the profits from which they used to acquire real property. Dickson J., writing for the majority of the Court, emphasized facts suggestive of a domestic and financial partnership. He observed that "each started with nothing; each worked continuously, unremittingly and sedulously in the joint effort" (p. 853); that each contributed to the "good fortune of the common enterprise" (p. 838); that Wilson J.A. (as she then was) at the Court of Appeal had found the wealth they accumulated was through "joint effort" and "teamwork" (p. 849); and finally, that "[t]heir lives and their economic well-being were fully integrated" (p. 850).

[66] I agree with Professor McCamus that the Court in *Pettkus* was "satisfied that the parties were engaged in a common venture in which they expected to share the benefits flowing from the wealth that they jointly created" (p. 367). Put another way, Mr. Pettkus was not unjustly enriched because Ms. Becker had a precise expectation of obtaining a legal interest in certain properties, but rather because they were in reality partners in a common venture.

[67] The significance of the fact that wealth had been acquired through joint effort was again at the forefront of the analysis in *Peter* where the parties lived together for 12 years in a common law relationship. While Mr. Beblow generated most of the family income and also contributed to the maintenance of the property, Ms. Peter did all of the domestic work (including raising the six children of their blended family), helped with property maintenance, and was solely responsible for the property when Mr. Beblow was away. The reality of their joint venture was acknowledged when McLachlin J.

wrote that the "joint family venture, in effect, was no different from the farm which was the subject of the trust in *Pettkus v. Becker*" (p. 1001).

[68] The Court's recognition of the joint family venture is evident in three other places in *Peter*. First, in reference to the appropriateness of the "value survived" measure of relief, McLachlin J. observed, "[I]t is more likely that a couple expects to share in the wealth generated from their partnership, rather than to receive compensation for the services performed during the relationship" (p. 999). Second, and also related to valuing the extent of the unjust enrichment, McLachlin J. noted that, in a case where both parties had contributed to the "family venture", it was appropriate to look to all of the family assets, rather than simply one of them, to approximate the value of the claimant's contributions to that family venture (p. 1001). Third, the Court's justification for affirming the value of domestic services was, in part, based on reasoning that such services are often proffered in the context of a common venture (p. 993).

[69] Relationships of this nature are common in our life experience. For many domestic relationships, the couple's venture may only sensibly be viewed as a joint one, making it highly artificial in theory and extremely difficult in practice to do a detailed accounting of the contributions made and benefits received on a fee-for-services basis. Of course, this is a relationship-specific issue; there can be no presumption one way or the other. However, the legal consequences of the breakdown of a domestic relationship should reflect realistically the way people live their lives. It should not impose on them the need to engage in an artificial balance sheet approach which does not reflect the true nature of their relationship.

(B) FLEXIBILITY

[70] Maintaining a strict remedial dichotomy is inconsistent with the Court's approach to equitable remedies in general, and to its development of remedies for unjust enrichment in particular.

[71] The Court has often emphasized the flexibility of equitable remedies and the need to fashion remedies that respond to various situations in principled and realistic ways. So, for example, when speaking of equitable compensation for breach of confidence, Binnie J. affirmed that "the Court has ample jurisdiction to fashion appropriate relief out of the full gamut of available remedies, including appropriate financial compensation": *Cadbury Schweppes Inc. v. FBI Foods Ltd.*, [1999] 1 S.C.R. 142, at para. 61. At

para. 24, he noted the broad approach to equitable remedies for breach of confidence taken by the Court in *Lac Minerals*. In doing so, he cited this statement with approval: ". . . the remedy that follows [once liability is established] should be the one that is most appropriate on the facts of the case rather than one derived from history or over-categorization" (from J. D. Davies, "Duties of Confidence and Loyalty", [1990] *Lloyds' Mar. & Com. L.Q.* 4, at p. 5). Similarly, in the context of the constructive trust, McLachlin J. (as she then was) noted that "[e]quitable remedies are flexible; their award is based on what is just in all the circumstances of the case": *Soulos v. Korkontzilas*, [1997] 2 S.C.R. 217, at para. 34.

[72] Turning specifically to remedies for unjust enrichment, I refer to Binnie J.'s comments in *Pacific National Investments Ltd. v. Victoria (City)*, 2004 SCC 75, [2004] 3 S.C.R. 575 at para. 13. He noted that the doctrine of unjust enrichment, while predicated on clearly defined principles, "retains a large measure of remedial flexibility to deal with different circumstances according to principles rooted in fairness and good conscience". Moreover, the Court has recognized that, given the wide variety of circumstances addressed by the traditional categories of unjust enrichment, as well as the flexibility of the broader, principled approach, its development has been characterized by, and indeed requires, recourse to a number of different sorts of remedies depending on the circumstances: see *Peter*, at p. 987; *Sorochan*, at p. 47.

[73] Thus, the remedy should mirror the flexibility inherent in the unjust enrichment principle itself, so as to allow the court to respond appropriately to the substance of the problem put before it. This means that a monetary remedy must match, as best it can, the extent of the enrichment unjustly retained by the defendant. There is no reason to think that the wide range of circumstances that may give rise to unjust enrichment claims will necessarily fall into one or other of the two remedial options into which some have tried to force them.

(C) HISTORY

[74] Imposing a strict remedial dichotomy is also inconsistent with the historical development of the unjust enrichment principle. Unjust enrichment developed through several particular categories of cases. *Quantum meruit*, the origin of the fee-for-services award, was only one of them. *Quantum meruit* originated as a common law claim for compensation for benefits conferred under an agreement which,

while apparently binding, was rendered ineffective for a reason recognized at common law. The scope of the claim was expanded over time, and the measure of a *quantum meruit* award was flexible. It might be assessed, for example, by the cost to the plaintiff of providing the service, the market value of the benefit, or even the value placed on the benefit by the recipient: P.D. Maddaugh and J.D. McCamus, *The Law of Restitution* (loose-leaf), vol. 1 at § 4:200.30. The important point, however, is that *quantum meruit* is simply one of the established categories of unjust enrichment claims. There is no reason in principle why one of the traditional categories of unjust enrichment should be used to force the monetary remedy for all present domestic unjust enrichment cases into a remedial straitjacket.

.   .   .   .

(4) The Approach to the Monetary Remedy

[80] The next step in the legal development of this area should be to move away from the false remedial dichotomy between *quantum meruit* and constructive trust, and to return to the underlying principles governing the law of unjust enrichment. These underlying principles focus on properly characterizing the nature of the unjust enrichment giving rise to the claim. As I have mentioned above, not all unjust enrichments arising between domestic partners fit comfortably into either a "fee-for-services" or "a share of specific property" mold. Where the unjust enrichment is best characterized as an unjust retention of a disproportionate share of assets accumulated during the course of what McLachlin J. referred to in *Peter* (at p. 1001) as a "joint family venture" to which both partners have contributed, the monetary remedy should reflect that fact.

[81] In such cases, the basis of the unjust enrichment is the retention of an inappropriately disproportionate amount of wealth by one party when the parties have been engaged in a joint family venture and there is a clear link between the claimant's contributions to the joint venture and the accumulation of wealth. Irrespective of the status of legal title to particular assets, the parties in those circumstances are realistically viewed as "creating wealth in a common enterprise that will assist in sustaining their relationship, their well-being and their family life" (McCamus, at p. 366). The wealth created during the period of cohabitation will be treated as the fruit of their domestic and financial relationship, though not necessarily by the parties in equal measure. Since the spouses are domestic and financial partners, there is

no need for "duelling *quantum meruits*". In such cases, the unjust enrichment is understood to arise because the party who leaves the relationship with a disproportionate share of the wealth is denying to the claimant a reasonable share of the wealth accumulated in the course of the relationship through their joint efforts. The monetary award for unjust enrichment should be assessed by determining the proportionate contribution of the claimant to the accumulation of the wealth.

[82] This flexible approach to the money remedy in unjust enrichment cases is fully consistent with *Walsh*. While that case was focused on constitutional issues that are not before us in this case, the majority judgment was clearly not intended to freeze the law of unjust enrichment in domestic cases; the judgment indicates that the law of unjust enrichment, including the remedial constructive trust, is the preferable method of responding to the inequities brought about by the breakdown of a common law relationship, since the remedies for unjust enrichment "are tailored to the parties' specific situation and grievances" (para. 61). In short, while emphasizing respect for autonomy as an important value, the Court at the same time approved of the continued development of the law of unjust enrichment in order to respond to the plethora of forms and functions of common law relationships.

. . . .

[84] It is not the purpose of the law of unjust enrichment to replicate for unmarried partners the legislative presumption that married partners are engaged in a joint family venture. However, there is no reason in principle why remedies for unjust enrichment should fail to reflect that reality in the lives and relationships of unmarried partners.

[85] I conclude, therefore, that the common law of unjust enrichment should recognize and respond to the reality that there are unmarried domestic arrangements that are partnerships; the remedy in such cases should address the disproportionate retention of assets acquired through joint efforts with another person. This sort of sharing, of course, should not be presumed, nor will it be presumed that wealth acquired by mutual effort will be shared equally. Cohabitation does not, in itself, under the common law of unjust enrichment, entitle one party to a share of the other's property or any other relief. However, where wealth is accumulated as a result of joint effort, as evidenced by the nature of the parties' relationship and their dealings with each other,

the law of unjust enrichment should reflect that reality.

[86] Thus the rejection of the remedial dichotomy leads us to consider in what circumstances an unjust enrichment may be appropriately characterized as a failure to share equitably assets acquired through the parties' joint efforts. While this approach will need further refinement in future cases, I offer the following as a broad outline of when this characterization of an unjust enrichment will be appropriate.

(5) Identifying Unjust Enrichment Arising From a Joint Family Venture

[87] My view is that when the parties have been engaged in a joint family venture, and the claimant's contributions to it are linked to the generation of wealth, a monetary award for unjust enrichment should be calculated according to the share of the accumulated wealth proportionate to the claimant's contributions. In order to apply this approach, it is first necessary to identify whether the parties have, in fact, been engaged in a joint family venture. In the preceding section, I reviewed the many occasions on which the existence of a joint family venture has been recognized. From this rich set of factual circumstances, what emerge as the hallmarks of such a relationship?

[88] It is critical to note that cohabiting couples are not a homogeneous group. It follows that the analysis must take into account the particular circumstances of each particular relationship. Furthermore, as previously stated, there can be no presumption of a joint family venture. The goal is for the law of unjust enrichment to attach just consequences to the way the parties have lived their lives, not to treat them as if they ought to have lived some other way or conducted their relationship on some different basis. A joint family venture can only be identified by the court when its existence, in fact, is well-grounded in the evidence. The emphasis should be on how the parties actually lived their lives, not on their *ex post facto* assertions or the court's view of how they ought to have done so.

[89] In undertaking this analysis, it may be helpful to consider the evidence under four main headings: mutual effort, economic integration, actual intent and priority of the family. There is, of course, overlap among factors that may be relevant under these headings and there is no closed list of relevant factors. What follows is not a checklist of conditions for finding (or not finding) that the parties were engaged in a joint family venture. These headings,

and the factors grouped under them, simply provide a useful way to approach a global analysis of the evidence and some examples of the relevant factors that may be taken into account in deciding whether or not the parties were engaged in a joint family venture. The absence of the factors I have set out, and many other relevant considerations, may well negate that conclusion.

(A) MUTUAL EFFORT

[90] One set of factors concerns whether the parties worked collaboratively towards common goals. Indicators such as the pooling of effort and team work, the decision to have and raise children together, and the length of the relationship may all point towards the extent, if any, to which the parties have formed a true partnership and jointly worked towards important mutual goals.

[91] Joint contributions, or contributions to a common pool, may provide evidence of joint effort. For instance, in *Murdoch*, central to Laskin J.'s constructive trust analysis was that the parties had pooled their efforts to establish themselves in a ranch operation. Joint contributions were also an important aspect of the Court's analyses in *Peter*, *Sorochan*, and *Pettkus*. Pooling of efforts and resources, whether capital or income, has also been noted in the appellate case law (see, for example, *Birmingham v. Ferguson*, 2004 CanLII 4764 (Ont. C.A.); *McDougall v. Gesell Estate*, 2001 MBCA 3, 153 Man. R. (2d) 54, at para. 14). The use of parties' funds entirely for family purposes may be indicative of the pooling of resources: *McDougall*. The parties may also be said to be pooling their resources where one spouse takes on all, or a greater proportion, of the domestic labour, freeing the other spouse from those responsibilities, and enabling him or her to pursue activities in the paid workforce (see *Nasser v. Mayer-Nasser* (2000), 5 R.F.L. (5th) 100 (Ont. C.A.) and *Panara v. Di Ascenzo*, 2005 ABCA 47, 361 A.R. 382, at para. 27).

(B) ECONOMIC INTEGRATION<

[92] Another group of factors, related to those in the first group, concerns the degree of economic interdependence and integration that characterized the parties' relationship (*Birmingham*; *Pettkus*; *Nasser*). The more extensive the integration of the couple's finances, economic interests and economic well-being, the more likely it is that they should be considered as having been engaged in a joint family venture. For example, the existence of a joint bank account that was used as a "common purse", as well

as the fact that the family farm was operated by the family unit, were key factors in Dickson J.'s analysis in *Rathwell*. The sharing of expenses and the amassing of a common pool of savings may also be relevant considerations (see *Wilson; Panara*).

[93] The parties' conduct may further indicate a sense of collectivity, mutuality, and prioritization of the overall welfare of the family unit over the individual interests of the individual members (McCamus, at p. 366). These and other factors may indicate that the economic well-being and lives of the parties are largely integrated (see, for example, *Pettkus*, at p. 850).

(C) ACTUAL INTENT

[94] Underpinning the law of unjust enrichment is an appropriate concern for the autonomy of the parties, and this is a particularly important consideration in relation to domestic partnerships. While domestic partners might not marry for a host of reasons, one of them may be the deliberate choice not to have their lives economically intertwined. Thus, in considering whether there is a joint family venture, the actual intentions of the parties must be given considerable weight. Those intentions may have been expressed by the parties or may be inferred from their conduct. The important point, however, is that the quest is for their actual intent as expressed or inferred, not for what in the court's view "reasonable" parties *ought* to have intended in the same circumstances. Courts must be vigilant not to impose their own views, under the guise of inferred intent, in order to reach a certain result.

[95] Courts may infer from the parties' conduct that they intended to share in the wealth they jointly created (P. Parkinson, "Beyond *Pettkus* v. *Becker*: Quantifying Relief for Unjust Enrichment" (1993), 43 U.T.L.J. 217, at p. 245). The conduct of the parties may show that they intended the domestic and professional spheres of their lives to be part of a larger, common venture (*Pettkus; Peter; Sorochan*). In some cases, courts have explicitly labelled the relationship as a "partnership" in the social and economic sense (*Panara*, at para. 71; *McDougall*, at para. 14). Similarly, the intention to engage in a joint family venture may be inferred where the parties accepted that their relationship was "equivalent to marriage" (*Birmingham*, at para. 1), or where the parties held themselves out to the public as married (*Sorochan*). The stability of the relationship may be a relevant factor as may the length of cohabitation (*Nasser; Sorochan; Birmingham*). When parties have lived together in a stable relationship for a lengthy period,

it may be nearly impossible to engage in a precise weighing of the benefits conferred within the relationship (*McDougall*; *Nasser*).

[96] The title to property may also reflect an intent to share wealth, or some portion of it, equitably. This may be the case where the parties are joint tenants of property. Even where title is registered to one of the parties, acceptance of the view that wealth will be shared may be evident from other aspects of the parties' conduct. For example, there may have been little concern with the details of title and accounting of monies spent for household expenses, renovations, taxes, insurance, and so on. Plans for property distribution on death, whether in a will or a verbal discussion, may also indicate that the parties saw one another as domestic and economic partners.

[97] The parties' actual intent may also negate the existence of a joint family venture, or support the conclusion that particular assets were to be held independently. Once again, it is the parties' actual intent, express or inferred from the evidence, that is the relevant consideration.

(D) PRIORITY OF THE FAMILY

[98] A final category of factors to consider in determining whether the parties were in fact engaged in a joint family venture is whether and to what extent they have given priority to the family in their decision making. A relevant question is whether there has been in some sense detrimental reliance on the relationship, by one or both of the parties, for the sake of the family. As Professor McCamus puts it, the question is whether the parties have been "[p]roceeding on the basis of understandings or assumptions about a shared future which may or may not be articulated" (p. 365). The focus is on contributions to the domestic and financial partnership, and particularly financial sacrifices made by the parties for the welfare of the collective or family unit. Whether the roles of the parties fall into the traditional wage earner/homemaker division, or whether both parties are employed and share domestic responsibilities, it is frequently the case that one party relies on the success and stability of the relationship for future economic security, to his or her own economic detriment (Parkinson, at p. 243). This may occur in a number of ways including: leaving the workforce for a period of time to raise children; relocating for the benefit of the other party's career (and giving up employment and employment-related networks as a result); foregoing career or educational advancement for the benefit of the family or rela-

tionship; and accepting underemployment in order to balance the financial and domestic needs of the family unit.

[99] As I see it, giving priority to the family is not associated exclusively with the actions of the more financially dependent spouse. The spouse with the higher income may also make financial sacrifices (for example, foregoing a promotion for the benefit of family life), which may be indicative that the parties saw the relationship as a domestic and financial partnership. As Professor Parkinson puts it, the joint family venture may be identified where

> [o]ne party has encouraged the other to rely to her detriment by leaving the workforce or forgoing other career opportunities for the sake of the relationship, and the breakdown of the relationship leaves her in a worse position than she would otherwise have been had she not acted in this way to her economic detriment. [p. 256].

(6) Summary of Quantum Meruit Versus Constructive Trust

[100] I conclude:

1. The monetary remedy for unjust enrichment is not restricted to an award based on a fee-for-services approach.

2. Where the unjust enrichment is most realistically characterized as one party retaining a disproportionate share of assets resulting from a joint family venture, and a monetary award is appropriate, it should be calculated on the basis of the share of those assets proportionate to the claimant's contributions.

3. To be entitled to a monetary remedy of this nature, the claimant must show both (a) that there was, in fact, a joint family venture, and (b) that there is a link between his or her contributions to it and the accumulation of assets and/or wealth.

4. Whether there was a joint family venture is a question of fact and may be assessed by having regard to all of the relevant circumstances, including factors relating to (a) mutual effort, (b) economic integration, (c) actual intent and (d) priority of the family.

F. Mutual Benefit Conferral

(1) Introduction

[101] As discussed earlier, the unjust enrichment analysis in domestic situations is often complicated by the fact that there has been a mutual conferral of

benefits; each party in almost all cases confers benefits on the other: Parkinson, at p. 222. Of course, a claimant cannot expect both to get back something given to the defendant and retain something received from him or her: Birks, at p. 415. The unjust enrichment analysis must take account of this common sense proposition. How and where in the analysis should this be done?

[102] The answer is fairly straightforward when the essence of the unjust enrichment claim is that one party has emerged from the relationship with a disproportionate share of assets accumulated through their joint efforts. These are the cases of a joint family venture in which the mutual efforts of the parties have resulted in an accumulation of wealth. The remedy is a share of that wealth proportionate to the claimant's contributions. Once the claimant has established his or her contribution to a joint family venture, and a link between that contribution and the accumulation of wealth, the respective contributions of the parties are taken into account in determining the claimant's proportionate share. While determining the proportionate contributions of the parties is not an exact science, it generally does not call for a minute examination of the give and take of daily life. It calls, rather, for the reasoned exercise of judgment in light of all of the evidence.

[103] Mutual benefit conferral, however, gives rise to more practical problems in an unjust enrichment claim where the appropriate remedy is a money award based on a fee-for-services-provided approach. The fact that the defendant has also provided services to the claimant may be seen as a factor relevant at all stages of the unjust enrichment analysis. Some courts have considered benefits received by the claimant as part of the benefit/detriment analysis (for example, at the Court of Appeal in *Peter v. Beblow* (1990), 50 B.C.L.R. (2d) 266). Others have looked at mutual benefits as an aspect of the juristic reason inquiry (for example, *Ford v. Werden* (1996), 27 B.C.L.R. (3d) 169 (C.A.), and the Court of Appeal judgment in *Kerr*). Still others have looked at mutual benefits in relation to both juristic reason and at the remedy stage (for example, as proposed in *Wilson*). It is apparent that some clarity and consistency is necessary with respect to this issue.

[104] In my view, there is much to be said about the approach to the mutual benefit analysis mapped out by Huddart J.A. in *Wilson*. Specifically, I would adopt her conclusions that mutual enrichments should mainly be considered at the defence and remedy stages, but that they may be considered at the

juristic reason stage to the extent that the provision of reciprocal benefits constitutes relevant evidence of the existence (or non-existence) of juristic reason for the enrichment (para. 9). This approach is consistent with the authorities from this Court, and provides a straightforward and just method of ensuring that mutual benefit conferral is fully taken into account without short-circuiting the proper unjust enrichment analysis. I will briefly set out why, in my view, this approach is sound.

. . . .

G. Reasonable or Legitimate Expectations

[117] The final point that requires some clarification relates to the role of the parties' reasonable expectations in the domestic context. My conclusion is that, while in the early domestic unjust enrichment cases the parties' reasonable expectations played an important role in the juristic reason analysis, the development of the law, and particularly the Court's judgment in *Garland*, has led to a more limited and clearly circumscribed role for those expectations.

[118] In the early cases of domestic unjust enrichment claims, the reasonable expectations of the claimant and the defendant's knowledge of those expectations were central to the juristic reason analysis. For example, in *Pettkus*, when Dickson J. came to the juristic reason step in the analysis, he said that "where one person in a relationship tantamount to spousal prejudices herself in the reasonable expectation of receiving an interest in property and the other person in the relationship freely accepts benefits conferred by the first person in circumstances where he knows or ought to have known of that reasonable expectation, it would be unjust to allow the recipient of the benefit to retain it" (p. 849). Similarly, in *Sorochan*, at p. 46, precisely the same reasoning was invoked to show that there was no juristic reason for the enrichment.

[119] In these cases, central to the Court's concern was whether it was just to require the defendant to pay — in fact to surrender an interest in property — for services not expressly requested. The Court's answer was that it would indeed be unjust for the defendant to retain the benefits, given that he had continued to accept the services when he knew or ought to have known that the claimant was providing them with the reasonable expectation of reward.

[120] The Court's resort to reasonable expectations and the defendant's knowledge of them in these

cases is analogous to the "free acceptance" principle. The notion of free acceptance has been invoked to extend restitutionary recovery beyond the traditional sorts of *quantum meruit* claims in which services had either been requested or provided under an unenforceable agreement. The law's traditional reluctance to provide a remedy for claims where no request was made was based on the tenet that a person should generally not be required, in effect, to pay for services that he or she did not request, and perhaps did not want. However, this concern carries much less weight when the person receiving the services knew that they were being provided, had no reasonable belief that they were a gift, and yet continued to freely accept them: see P. Birks, *Unjust Enrichment* (2nd ed. 2005), at pp. 56–57.

[121] The need to engage in this analysis of the claimant's reasonable expectations and the defendant's knowledge thereof with respect to domestic services has, in my view, now been overtaken by developments in the law. *Garland*, as noted, mandated a two-step approach to the juristic reason analysis. The first step requires the claimant to show that the benefit was not conferred for any existing category of juristic reasons. Significantly, the fact that the defendant also provided services to the claimant is not one of the existing categories. Nor is the fact that the services were provided pursuant to the parties' reasonable expectations. However, the fact that the parties reasonably expected the services to be provided might afford relevant evidence in relation to whether the case falls within one of the traditional categories, for example a contract or gift. Other than in that way, mutual benefit conferral and the parties' reasonable expectations have a very limited role to play at the first step in the juristic reason analysis set out in *Garland*.

[122] However, different considerations arise at the second step. Following *Peter* and *Garland*, the parties' reasonable or legitimate expectations have a critical role to play when the defendant seeks to establish a new juristic reason, whether case-specific or categorical. As Iacobucci J. put it in *Garland*, this introduces a category of residual situations in which "courts can look to all of the circumstances of the transaction in order to determine whether there is another reason to deny recovery" (para. 45). Specifically, it is here that the court should consider the parties' reasonable expectations and questions of policy.

. . . . .

[124] To summarize:

1. The parties' reasonable or legitimate expectations have little role to play in deciding whether the services were provided for a juristic reason within the existing categories.

2. In some cases, the facts that mutual benefits were conferred or that the benefits were provided pursuant to the parties' reasonable expectations may be relevant evidence of whether one of the existing categories of juristic reasons is present. An example might be whether there was a contract for the provision of the benefits. However, generally the existence of mutual benefits flowing from the defendant to the claimant will not be considered at the juristic reason stage of the analysis.

3. The parties' reasonable or legitimate expectations have a role to play at the second step of the juristic reason analysis, that is, where the defendant bears the burden of establishing that there is a juristic reason for retaining the benefit which does not fall within the existing categories. It is the mutual or legitimate expectations of both parties that must be considered, and not simply the expectations of either the claimant or the defendant. The question is whether the parties' expectations show that retention of the benefits is just.

[125] I will now turn to the two cases at bar. [Note: only *Vanasse v. Seguin* is included in this edited version of the case.]

IV. THE *VANASSE* APPEAL

A. Introduction

[126] In the Vanasse appeal, the main issue is how to quantify a monetary award for unjust enrichment. The trial judge awarded a share of the net increase in the family's wealth during the period of unjust enrichment. The Court of Appeal held that this was the wrong approach, finding that the trial judge ought to have performed a *quantum meruit* calculation in which the value that each party received from the other was assessed and set off. This required an evaluation of the defendant Mr. Seguin's non-financial contributions to the relationship which, in the view of the Court of Appeal, the trial judge failed to perform. As the record did not permit the court to apply the correct legal principles to the facts, it ordered a new hearing with respect to compensation and consequential changes to spousal support.

[127] In this Court, the appellant Ms. Vanasse raises two issues:

1. Did the Court of Appeal err by insisting on a strict *quantum meruit* (i.e. "value received") approach to quantify the monetary award for unjust enrichment?
2. Did the Court of Appeal err in finding that the trial judge had failed to consider relevant evidence of Mr. Seguin's contributions?

[128] In my view, the appeal should be allowed and the trial judge's order restored. For the reasons I have developed above, my view is that money compensation for unjust enrichment need not always, as a matter of principle, be calculated on a *quantum meruit* basis. The trial judge here, although not labelling it as such, found that there was a joint family venture and that there was a link between Ms. Vanasse's contribution to it and the substantial accumulation of wealth which the family achieved. In my view, the trial judge made a reasonable assessment of the monetary award appropriate to reverse this unjust enrichment, taking due account of Mr. Seguin's undoubted and substantial contributions.

B. Brief Overview of the Facts and Proceedings

[129] The background facts of this case are largely undisputed. The parties lived together in a common law relationship for approximately 12 years, from 1993 until March 2005. Together, they had two children who were aged 8 and 10 at the time of trial.

[130] During approximately the first four years of their relationship (1993 to 1997), the parties diligently pursued their respective careers, Ms. Vanasse with the Canadian Security Intelligence Service ("CSIS") and Mr. Seguin with Fastlane Technologies Inc., marketing a network operating system he had developed.

[131] In March of 1997, Ms. Vanasse took a leave of absence to move with Mr. Seguin to Halifax, where Fastlane had relocated for important business reasons. During the next three and one-half years, the parties had two children; Ms. Vanasse took care of the domestic labour, while Mr. Seguin devoted himself to developing Fastlane. The family moved back to Ottawa in 1998, where Mr. Seguin purchased a home and registered it in the names of both parties as joint tenants. In September 2000, Fastlane was sold and Mr. Seguin netted approximately $11 million. He placed the funds in a holding company,

with which he continued to develop business and investment opportunities.

[132] After the sale of Fastlane, Ms. Vanasse continued to assume most of the domestic responsibilities, although Mr. Seguin was more available to assist. He continued to manage the finances.

[133] The parties separated on March 27, 2005. At that time, they were in starkly contrasting financial positions: Ms. Vanasse's net worth had gone from about $40,000 at the time she and Mr. Seguin started living together, to about $332,000 at the time of separation; Mr. Seguin had come into the relationship with about $94,000, and his net worth at the time of separation was about $8,450,000.

[134] Ms. Vanasse brought proceedings in the Superior Court of Justice. In addition to seeking orders with respect to spousal support and child custody, Ms. Vanasse claimed unjust enrichment. She argued that Mr. Seguin had been unjustly enriched because he retained virtually all of the funds from the sale of Fastlane, even though she had contributed to their acquisition through benefits she conferred in the form of domestic and childcare services. She alleged her contributions allowed Mr. Seguin to dedicate most of his time and energy to Fastlane. She sought relief by way of constructive trust in Mr. Seguin's remaining one half interest in the family home, and a one-half interest in the investment assets held by Mr. Seguin's holding company.

[135] Mr. Seguin contested the unjust enrichment claim. While conceding he had been enriched during the roughly three-year period where he was working outside the home full time and Ms. Vanasse was working at home full time (May 1997 to September 2000), he argued there was no corresponding deprivation because he had given her a one-half interest in the family home and approximately $44,000 in Registered Retirement Saving Plans ("RRSPs"). In the alternative, Mr. Seguin submitted that a constructive trust remedy was inappropriate because there was no link between Ms. Vanasse's contributions and the property of Fastlane.

[136] The trial judge, Blishen J., concluded that the relationship of the parties could be divided into three distinct periods: (1) From the commencement of cohabitation in 1993 until March 1997 when Ms. Vanasse left her job at CSIS; (2) From March 1997 to September 2000, during which both children were born and Fastlane was sold; and (3) From September 2000 to the separation of the parties in March 2005. She concluded that neither party had been

unjustly enriched in the first or third periods; she held that their contributions to the relationship during these periods had been proportionate. In the first period, there were no children of the relationship and both parties were focused on their careers; in the third period, both parents were home and their contributions had been proportional.

[137] In the second period, however, the trial judge concluded that Mr. Seguin had been unjustly enriched by Ms. Vanasse. Ms. Vanasse had been in charge of the domestic side of the household, including caring for their two children. She had not been a "nanny/housekeeper" and, as the trial judge held, throughout the relationship she had been at least "an equal contributor to the family enterprise". The trial judge concluded that Ms. Vanasse's contributions during this second period "significantly benefited Mr. Seguin and were not proportional" (para. 139).

[138] The trial judge found as fact that Ms. Vanasse's efforts during this second period were directly linked to Mr. Seguin's business success. She stated, at para. 91, that

> Mr. Seguin was enriched by Ms. Vanasse's running of the household, providing child care for two young children and looking after all the necessary appointments and needs of the children. Mr. Seguin could not have made the efforts he did to build up the company but for Ms. Vanasse's assumption of these responsibilities. Mr. Seguin reaped the benefits of Ms. Vanasse's efforts by being able to focus his time, energy and efforts on Fastlane. [Emphasis added.]

Again at para. 137, the trial judge found that

> Mr. Seguin was unjustly enriched and Ms. Vanasse deprived for three and one-half years of their relationship, during which time Mr. Seguin often worked day and night and traveled frequently while in Halifax. Mr. Seguin could not have succeeded, as he did, and built up the company, as he did, without Ms. Vanasse assuming the vast majority of childcare and household responsibilities. Mr. Seguin could not have devoted his time to Fastlane but for Ms. Vanasse's assumption of those responsibilities. . . . Mr. Seguin reaped the benefit of Ms. Vanasse's efforts by being able to focus all of his considerable energies and talents on making Fastlane a success. [Emphasis added.]

[139] The trial judge concluded that a monetary award in this case was appropriate, given Mr. Seguin's ability to pay, and lack of a sufficiently direct and substantial link between Ms. Vanasse's contributions and Fastlane or Mr. Seguin's holding company, as required to impose a remedial constructive trust.

[140] With respect to quantification, Blishen J. noted that Ms. Vanasse had received a one-half interest in the family home, but concluded that this was not adequate compensation for her contributions. The trial judge compared the net worths of the parties and determined that Ms. Vanasse was entitled to a one-half interest in the prorated increase in Mr. Seguin's net worth during the period of the unjust enrichment. She reasoned that his net worth had increased by about $8.4 million dollars over the 12 years of the relationship. Although she noted that the most significant increase took place when Fastlane was sold towards the end of the period of unjust enrichment, she nonetheless prorated the increase over the full 12 years of the relationship, yielding a figure of about $700,000 per year. Starting with the $2.45 million increase attributable to the three and one-half years of unjust enrichment, the trial judge awarded Ms. Vanasse 50 percent of that amount, less the value of her interest in the family home and her RRSPs. This produced an award of just under $1 million.

[141] Mr. Seguin did not appeal Blishen J.'s unjust enrichment finding, and conceded unjust enrichment between 1997 and 2000 on appeal. Therefore, the trial judge's findings that there had been an unjust enrichment during that period and that there was no unjust enrichment during the other periods are not in issue. The sole issue for determination in this Court is the propriety of the trial judge's monetary award for the unjust enrichment which she found to have occurred.

C. Analysis

(1) Was the Trial Judge Required to Use a Quantum Meruit Approach to Calculate the Monetary Award?

[142] I agree with the appellant that a monetary award for unjust enrichment need not, as a matter of principle, always be calculated on a fee-for-services basis. As I have set out earlier, an unjust enrichment is best characterized as one party leaving the relationship with a disproportionate share of wealth that accumulated as a result of the parties' joint efforts. This will be so when the parties were engaged in a joint family venture and where there is a link between the contributions of the claimant and

the accumulation of wealth. When this is the case, the amount of the enrichment should be assessed by determining the claimant's proportionate contribution to that accumulated wealth. As the trial judge saw it, this was exactly the situation of Ms. Vanasse and Mr. Seguin.

(2) Existence of a Joint Family Venture

[143] The trial judge, after a six-day trial, concluded that "Ms. Vanasse was not a nanny/housekeeper". She found that Ms. Vanasse had been at least "an equal contributor to the family enterprise" throughout the relationship and that, during the period of unjust enrichment, her contributions "significantly benefited Mr. Seguin" (para. 139).

[144] The trial judge, of course, did not review the evidence under the headings that I have suggested will be helpful in identifying a joint family venture, namely "mutual effort", "economic integration", "actual intent" and "priority of the family". However, her findings of fact and analysis indicate that the unjust enrichment of Mr. Seguin at the expense of Ms. Vanasse ought to be characterized as the retention by Mr. Seguin of a disproportionate share of the wealth generated from a joint family venture. The judge's findings fit conveniently under the headings I have suggested.

(A) MUTUAL EFFORT

[145] There are several factors in this case which suggest that, throughout their relationship, the parties were working collaboratively towards common goals. First, as previously mentioned, the trial judge found that Ms. Vanasse's role was not as a "nanny/ housekeeper" but rather as at least an equal contributor throughout the relationship. The parties made important decisions keeping the overall welfare of the family at the forefront: the decision to move to Halifax, the decision to move back to Ottawa, and the decision that Ms. Vanasse would not return to work after the sale of Fastlane are all clear examples. The parties pooled their efforts for the benefit of their family unit. As the trial judge found, during the second stage of their relationship from March 1997 to September 2000, the division of labour was such that Ms. Vanasse was almost entirely responsible for running the home and caring for the children, while Mr. Seguin worked long hours and managed the family finances. The trial judge found that it was through their joint efforts that they were able to raise a young family and acquire wealth. As she put it, "Mr. Seguin could not have made the efforts he did to build up the company but for Ms.

Vanasse's assumption of these responsibilities" (para. 91). While Mr. Seguin's long hours and extensive travel reduced somewhat in September 1998 when the parties returned to Ottawa, the basic division of labour remained the same.

[146] Notably, the period of unjust enrichment corresponds to the time during which the parties had two children together (in 1997 and 1999), a further indicator that they were working together to achieve common goals. The length of the relationship is also relevant, and their 12-year cohabitation is a significant period of time. Finally, the trial judge described the arrangement between the parties as a "family enterprise", to which Ms. Vanasse was "at least, an equal contributor" (paras. 138–39).

(B) ECONOMIC INTEGRATION

[147] The trial judge found that "[t]his was not a situation of economic interdependence" (para. 105). That said, there was a pooling of resources. Ms. Vanasse was not employed and did not contribute financially to the family after the children were born, and thus was financially dependent on Mr. Seguin. The family home was registered jointly, and the parties had a joint chequing account. As the trial judge put it, "She was 'the C.E.O. of the kids' and he was 'the C.E.O. of the finances'" (para. 105).

(C) ACTUAL INTENT

[148] The actual intent of the parties in a domestic relationship, as expressed by the parties or inferred from their conduct, must be given considerable weight in determining whether there was a joint family venture. There are a number of findings of fact that indicate these parties considered their relationship to be a joint family venture.

[149] While a promise to marry or the discussion of legal marriage is by no means a prerequisite for the identification of a joint family venture, in this case the parties' intentions with respect to marriage strongly suggest that they viewed themselves as the equivalent of a married couple. Mr. Seguin proposed to Ms. Vanasse in July 1996 and they exchanged rings. While they were "devoted to one another and still in love", a wedding date was never set (para. 14). Mr. Seguin raised the topic of marriage again when Ms. Vanasse found out she was pregnant with their first child. Although they never married, the trial judge found that there had been "mutual expectations [of marriage] during the first few years of their 12 year relationship" (para. 64). Mr. Seguin continued to address Ms. Vanasse as "my future

wife", and she was viewed by the outside world as such (para. 33).

[150] The trial judge also referred to statements made by Mr. Seguin that were strongly indicative of his view that there was a joint family venture. As the trial judge put it, at para. 28, upon the sale of Fastlane

> Mr. Seguin became a wealthy man. He told Ms. Vanasse that they would never have to worry about finances as their parents did; their children could go to the best schools and they could live a good life without financial concerns.

Again, at para. 98:

> After the sale of the company, Mr. Seguin indicated they could retire, the children could go to the best schools and the family would be well cared for. The family took travel vacations, enjoyed luxury cars, bought a large cabin cruiser which they used for summer vacations and purchased condominiums at Mont-Tremblant.

[151] While the trial judge viewed Mr. Seguin's promises and reassurances as contributing to a reasonable expectation on the part of Ms. Vanasse that she was to share in the increase of his net worth during the period of unjust enrichment, in my view these comments are more appropriately characterized as a reflection of the reality that there was a joint family venture, to which the couple jointly contributed for their mutual benefit and the benefit of their children.

(D) PRIORITY OF THE FAMILY

[152] There is a strong inference from the factual findings that, to Mr. Seguin's knowledge, Ms. Vanasse relied on the relationship to her detriment. As the trial judge found, in 1997 Ms. Vanasse gave up a lucrative and exciting career with CSIS, where she was training to be an intelligence officer, to move to Halifax with Mr. Seguin. In many ways this was a sacrifice on her part; she left her career, gave up her own income, and moved away from her family and friends. Mr. Seguin had moved to Halifax in order to relocate Fastlane for business reasons. Ms. Vanasse then stayed home and cared for their two small children. As I have already explained, during the period of the unjust enrichment, Ms. Vanasse was responsible for a disproportionate share of the domestic labour. It was these domestic contributions that, in part, permitted Mr. Seguin to focus on his work with Fastlane. Later, in 2003, the "family's decision" was for Ms. Vanasse to remain home after her leave from CSIS had expired (para. 198). Ms.

Vanasse's financial position at the breakdown of the relationship indicates she relied on the relationship to her economic detriment. This is all evidence supporting the conclusion that the parties were, in fact, operating as a joint family venture.

[153] As a final point, I would refer to the arguments made by Mr. Seguin, which were accepted by the Court of Appeal, that the trial judge failed to give adequate weight to sacrifices Mr. Seguin made for the benefit of the relationship. Later in my reasons, I will address the question of whether the trial judge actually failed in this regard. However, the points raised by Mr. Seguin to support this argument actually serve to reinforce the conclusion that there was a joint family venture. Mr. Seguin specifically notes a number of factors, including: agreeing to step down as CEO of Fastlane in September 1997 to make himself more available to Ms. Vanasse, causing friction with his co-workers and partners, and reducing his remuneration; agreeing to relocate to Ottawa at Ms. Vanasse's request in 1998; and making increased efforts to work at home more and travel less after moving back to Ottawa. These facts are indicative of the sense of mutuality in the parties' social and financial relationship. In short, they support the identification of a joint family venture.

(E) CONCLUSION ON IDENTIFICATION OF THE JOINT FAMILY VENTURE

[154] In my view, the trial judge's findings of fact clearly show that Ms. Vanasse and Mr. Seguin engaged in a joint family venture. The remaining question is whether there was a link between Ms. Vanasse's contributions to it and the accumulation of wealth.

(3) *Link to Accumulation of Wealth*

[155] The trial judge made a clear finding that there was a link between Ms. Vanasse's contributions and the family's accumulation of wealth.

[156] I have referred earlier, in some detail, to the trial judge's findings in this regard. However, to repeat, her conclusion is expressed particularly clearly at para. 91 of her reasons:

> Mr. Seguin could not have made the efforts he did to build up the company but for Ms. Vanasse's assumption of these [household and child-rearing] responsibilities. Mr. Seguin reaped the benefits of Ms. Vanasse's efforts by being able to focus his time, energy and efforts on Fastlane.

[157] Given that and similar findings, I conclude that not only were these parties engaged in a joint family venture, but that there was a clear link between Ms. Vanasse's contribution to it and the accumulation of wealth. The unjust enrichment is thus best viewed as Mr. Seguin leaving the relationship with a disproportionate share of the wealth accumulated as a result of their joint efforts.

(4) Calculation of the Award

[158] The main focus of the appeal was on whether the award ought to have been calculated on a *quantum meruit* basis. Very little was argued before this Court regarding the way the trial judge approached her calculation of a proportionate share of the parties' accumulated wealth. I conclude that the trial judge's approach was reasonable in the circumstances, but I stress that I do not hold out her approach as necessarily being a template for future cases. Within the legal principles I have outlined, there may be many ways in which an award may be quantified reasonably. I prefer not to make any more general statements about the quantification process in the context of this appeal, except this. Provided that the correct legal principles are applied, and the findings of fact are not tainted by clear and determinative error, a trial judge's assessment of damages is treated with considerable deference on appeal: see, e.g., *Nance v. British Columbia Electric Railway Co.*, [1951] A.C. 601 (P.C.). A reasoned and careful exercise of judgment by the trial judge as to the appropriate monetary award to remedy an unjust enrichment should be treated with the same defer-

ence. There are two final specific points that I must address.

[159] Mr. Seguin submits, very briefly, that a proper application of the "value survived" approach in this case would require a careful determination of the contributions by third parties to the growth of Fastlane during the period his own contributions were diminished, as a result of what counsel characterizes as Ms. Vanasse's "demands" that he reduce his hours and move back to Ottawa. This argument is premised on the notion that the money he received from the sale was not justly his to share with Ms. Vanasse. I cannot accept this premise. Unexplained is why he received more than his share when the company was sold or why, having received more than he was due, Ms. Vanasse is still not entitled to an equitable share of what he actually received.

[160] Second, there is the finding of the Court of Appeal that the trial judge failed to take into account evidence of Mr. Seguin's numerous and significant non-financial contributions to the family. I respectfully cannot accept this view. The trial judge specifically alluded to these contributions in her reasons. Moreover, by confining the period of unjust enrichment to the three and one-half year period, the trial judge took into account the periods during which Ms. Vanasse's contributions were not disproportionate to Mr. Seguin's. In my view, the trial judge took a realistic and practical view of the evidence before her and gave sufficient consideration to Mr. Seguin's contributions.

IV

Conscience in Private Law

OVERVIEW

This final Part of the materials turns attention to residual principles and preoccupations in the private law of obligations. These principles are 'cross-cutting' in that they are apparent or in operation in situations engaging the law torts, contracts and unjust enrichment. However, they do stand alone as distinct branches of obligation. These principles include reliance, trust, confidence and unconscionability. They have coalesced into doctrines such as estoppel and inequality of bargaining power. They are reflected in a body of law establishing the duties of fiduciaries (those entrusted to care of the interests of others). These ideas are examined in three chapters.

The first chapter addresses reliance. It includes material on the doctrine of proprietary estoppel (which operates in relation to property rights, and in particular where common law rights are inconsistent with a course of conduct arising from reliance on shared understandings). This doctrine applies in commercial relationships, and also in personal, family-type relationships where its application has been more expansive because of the often added layer of vulnerability and detriment. The interesting divergence of Canada, which has tended to address these situations within the law of unjust enrichment, from other parts of the Commonwealth is examined in this chapter.

The argument in this section of the book is that private law is concerned not only with individual transactions but also with the integrity of social and economic relationships. This is explicitly covered in the second chapter (Chapter 11) in this Part, which addresses Fiduciary Obligations. Rotman claims, in the extract in Chapter 11, that "the broad social and economic goals of fiduciary obligations are far more ambitious than those of contract or unjust enrichment; they are a tool which maintains the visibility of interdependent societies by preserving the integrity of important social and economic interactions of high trust and confidence."[1] In his view, fiduciary law looks beyond self-interest and allows individuals to trust that their interests will be cared for by others, mandates 'other regarding behaviour', and balances "implicit dependency and peculiar vulnerability."[2] Much earlier, renowned U.S. judge Benjamin Cardozo stated, "The fiduciary concept is part of a pervasive policy of the law to protect the integrity of commercial organizations."[3] The Supreme Court of Canada has weighed in on these matters as well, stating in *Hodgkinson v. Simms*, which is also included in this chapter, "not all relationships are characterized by a dynamic of mutual autonomy, and that the marketplace cannot always [be left to] set the rules.... By [responding to regulate social institutions and enterprises], the law thereby helps to strengthen them."[4] We examine leading cases in this area of the law — not to provide a comprehensive survey of the law but to identify the principles animating legal development in this area.

The final chapter in this Part addresses a controversial area of private law — the scope of the law's intervention when there is an inequality of bargaining power. Generally these situations involve one party labouring under a personal vulnerability that correlates to systemic social inequality, such as being old and infirm, or a married woman, or an Aboriginal person. When and why does the law intervene? How important is it that a person may have signed a contract? On what grounds might the contract be set aside? This case study allows us to engage with the vision of one of England's greatest (and certainly most colourful) judges of the twentieth century, Lord Denning. His attempt to synthesize disparate themes in private law into an overarching principle in the famous case of *Lloyd's Bank v. Bundy* continues to attract supporters and detractors. We also use this final chapter to explore the role of theory in better understanding the contours and development of private law. How do rules interact with policies? How do policies inter-relate with normative social visions? On what basis do judges make, interpret and apply legal rules? In this way, the book returns to the dialogue about how the principles of tort and contract law were conceived and continue to change. However, we use a case study based on jurisprudence on the question of when financial guarantees given by wives secured against the family home, to support loans to their husbands' businesses, are enforceable. The way in which the issues and resolution of the issues arising is examined using a number of theories, including law and economics, critical legal studies and feminist legal theory. At the end of the case study, we hope that readers will better appreciate the interplay of social context (and our understandings and debates about it) with legal rules in private law.

Notes

1. Leonard Rotman, "The Fiduciary Concept, Contract Law and Unjust Enrichment", *Re-examining Contract and Unjust Enrichment*, ed., Paula Giliker (Boston: Martinus Nijhoff, 2007) at 87 at 92.
2. Ibid., at 92.

3. *Beatty v. Guggenheim Exploration Co*, 122 NE 378 at 380 (NYCA, 1919).
4. *Hodgkinson v. Simms*, [1994] 3 S.C.R. 377 at para 9.

LEARNING OBJECTIVES

At the conclusion of this Part, readers should be able to

- identify when the principle of reliance has been upheld in private law;
- define the doctrine of proprietary estoppel as an example of the reliance principle;
- explain the relationship between unjust enrichment and estoppel comparing and contrasting judicial approaches to the problem of unconscionability;
- define the concept of fiduciary relationship and state the duties of a fiduciary;
- state the indicia (or indicators) of the presence of fiduciary obligation derived from the decision of Justice Wilson in *Frame v. Smith*;
- differentiate the purposes of the law of unjust enrichment and fiduciary obligation;
- state Lord Denning's concept of 'inequality of bargaining power' as a unifying principle;
- compare and contrast the legal reasons (or bases) for decision as between Lord Denning and Lord Justice Sachs in *Lloyds Bank v. Bundy*;
- identify and explain several theories about the operation of private law;
- compare and contrast legal reasoning based on different theories as it applies to a legal problem about whether to uphold a contract.

10 Reliance

(a) Reliance†

Stephen Waddams

Reliance on the promises and assertions of others, express or implied, is very common in human affairs, and its protection has been a prominent feature of Anglo-American law. Effective protection has often been afforded by contract law, but in a number of circumstances reliance occurs in the absence of an enforceable contract, and here other legal concepts have been deployed. But it has not proved possible to explain the protection of reliance in terms of any other single legal concept.

Very frequently one person makes an assertion on which another relies. In a wide variety of circumstances the courts have held that the person making the assertion is precluded from later contradicting it. The clearest examples relate to statements of fact. If a deadline for enrolment in a university programme is imminent, and a prospective student is informed by the university, before the deadline and while spaces remain in the programme, that she is duly enrolled, the university is estopped (i.e., precluded), after the deadline has passed, from denying the truth of the information, even if the student in fact was not duly enrolled, and even in the face of a mandatory rule in the most stringent language imaginable to the effect that no student shall in any circumstances be enrolled after the deadline. It will be seen from this example that the principle of estoppel is capable of having far-reaching effects on other legal rules, and it has often been the source of obligations that are not assignable to any of the usual divisions shown on diagrams or maps.[1] Lord Goff has said (2001) that 'in the end I am inclined to think that the many circumstances capable of giving rise to an estoppel cannot be accommodated within a single formula, and that it is unconscionability which provides the link between them'.[2] By this he meant that the underlying reason for estoppel is that it would be unfair for a person, having made an assertion that induces another to act to her detriment, to go back on the assertion.

The effect of estoppel is to protect the plaintiff from harm, and to that extent there is an affinity with tort, but there is no need for proof of wrongdoing: the assertion may be due to an honest and perfectly reasonable mistakē (due to computer malfunction, for example). The Privy Council put it in this way (1892):

> The law of this country gives no countenance to the doctrine that in order to create estoppel the person whose acts or declarations induced another to act in a particular way must have been under no mistake himself, or must have intended to mislead or deceive ... [T]he principle on which the law ... rest[s] is, that it would be most inequitable and unjust to him that if another, by a representation made, or by conduct amounting to a representation, has induced him to act as he would not otherwise have done, the person who made the representation should be allowed to deny or repudiate the effect of his former statement, to the loss and injury of the person who acted on it.[3]

Estoppel clearly has a close relation to contract: the words or conduct of one person that induce

---

† From Stephen Waddams, *Dimensions of Private Law* (Cambridge: Cambridge University Press, 2003) at 57–69. [Notes/references omitted.] Reprinted with the permission of Cambridge University Press.

expectations in another give rise to a legal obligation. Yet the obligation is not purely contractual. Neither promise nor bargain have been required, nor has the remedy been always equivalent to the plaintiff's expectation. Moreover, if the concept of estoppel were applicable to a promise standing alone, it would largely have subsumed contract law. In a number of instances estoppel has indeed been a means of enforcing promises. An important example is the Australian case of *Waltons Stores (Interstate) Ltd* v. *Maher*[4] (1987), where an owner of land demolished a building and commenced construction of a new one to the specifications of a prospective tenant. No binding lease was ever effected, but the prospective tenant was held to be estopped (in the view of the majority of the court) from retreating from an implied promise to complete the contract.

One of the simplest imaginable examples of reliance arises when a landowner promises to give the land to another person (for example, a relative) and the other person, relying on the promise, builds on the land. The promisor (or, as it has more usually been, his or her estate) then seeks to revoke the promise. These facts have presented a problem for Anglo-American law because the transaction, being gratuitous, is not enforceable as a contract. Property has not been legally transferred; neither is the promisor guilty of any tort. Nevertheless the courts of equity gave a remedy to the promisee.[5] These cases could not be reconciled with orthodox contract doctrine and have therefore been ignored or marginalized by many writers on contract law. They have usually been described as cases of proprietary estoppel, but this phrase is scarcely explanatory. In some of the cases avoidance of unjust enrichment was evidently a crucial factor: in the leading case of *Dillwyn* v. *Llewelyn*[6] for example (1862), the plaintiff had expended the very large sum of £20,000 in improving land that was originally worth only £1,500. One of the considerations in the mind of a court faced with such facts has been the enrichment that would enure to the defendant if no measure of enforcement were available, and one of the reasons for favouring proprietary estoppel as a rule is that unjust enrichment is *very apt* to occur in such circumstances, and so the rule tends to prevent unjust enrichment. But unjust enrichment has not been present in every particular case,[7] and the remedy has not normally been measured by enrichment. As Peter Birks wrote (1985), 'the doctrine has a *dimension* to it which has nothing to do with restitution/unjust enrichment'.[8] This is true, but it does not follow that considerations of unjust enrichment have been irrelevant. Many of the cases have had the effect of pro-

tecting reliance, but the measure of recovery is not, where the plaintiff becomes effectively the owner of the land, restricted to out-of-pocket loss. Non-contractual reliance has sometimes been protected by concepts of wrongdoing, but in these cases there is no wrongdoing in the ordinary sense. Though the phrase 'equitable fraud' has sometimes been employed, no actual proof of wrongdoing has been required: the defendant acts fraudulently, in the eyes of equity, by failing to do what is just. As expressed in *Wilmott* v. *Barber* (1880), 'the plaintiff must prove that he [the defendant] has acted fraudulently, *or* that there has been such an acquiescence on his part as would make it fraudulent for him *now* to assert his legal rights'.[9]

The word 'fraudulent' in the last clause of this passage means 'unjust', and cannot be explained except in terms of concepts other than wrongdoing. The defendant must, by action or inaction, induce the plaintiff's reliance, but no proof of intention to mislead or deceive is required.[10] The only 'fraud' required to be proved is an unwillingness to do what equity considers just. A similar comment may be made in relation to the concept of unconscionability, earlier mentioned.[11] If equity protects the plaintiff's reliance, it will be, by that very fact, against conscience for the defendant to defeat it. 'Inequitable', 'fraudulent', 'unconscionable', and 'unconscientious' have been, in this context, four ways of saying the same thing.[12]

Reasons have been mentioned why the cases considered here cannot readily be assimilated into contract law, namely, that there is no bargain, no consideration, and, in the ordinary common and legal use of the word, no contract. But there is another reason, and that is that no promise has been required: it has been sufficient that the defendant acquiesced in the plaintiffs reliance in circumstances where, having done so, it was unreasonable to leave the reliance unprotected.[13] Definitions of contract law based on the concept of promise have not therefore been able to accommodate these cases.

In one of the leading cases on this question, *Ramsden* v. *Dyson*[14] (1866), the House of Lords spoke not in terms of promise but of 'expectation created or encouraged' and reliance occurring 'with the knowledge of the [defendant] and without objection by him'.[15] In the passage earlier quoted from *Wilmott* v. *Barber* it was said to be sufficient for the plaintiff to prove 'such an *acquiescence* on his [the defendant's] part as would make it fraudulent for him now to assert his legal rights'.[16] In the twentieth-century case of *Crabb* v. *Arun District Council*[17] (1976) the plaintiff divided his land on the strength of an expectation that an essential right of way would be granted by the defendant. There had been inconclusive discussions on this question, and the trial judge found that, though there had been 'agreement in principle', the defendant had given 'no definite assurance' and made 'no firm commitment'. But the defendant put up gates at the point where the right of way was contemplated, leading the plaintiff to believe that a right of way would be given. The Court of Appeal held that this was sufficient:

> The defendants knew that the plaintiff *intended* to sell the two portions separately and that he would need an access at [the point where the gates were erected]. Seeing that they knew of his intention — and they did nothing to disabuse him but rather confirmed it by erecting gates ... — it was their conduct which led him to act as he did: and this raises an equity in his favour against him.[18]

A further reason why cases of this sort cannot be readily assimilated to contract law is the extent of the remedy, which is not necessarily equivalent to enforcement of the plaintiffs full expectation. In the *Crabb* case the court said on this point, 'Here equity is displayed at its most flexible',[19] contemplating that the court might require payment by the plaintiff of a reasonable price for the right of way, though on the facts of the case this was not done because the plaintiff had lost the use of the land pending resolution of the dispute.

In these cases, as in the others considered in earlier chapters, it can be seen that several legal concepts have operated simultaneously and cumulatively. The plaintiff could state no case for recovery in contract, for there was no contract. Nor (without the help of estoppel, or until the court would 'raise an equity') could the plaintiff claim the land as his or her property, because title was vested in the defendant. Nor was the defendant guilty of wrongdoing (in the ordinary sense of the word), for he or she had no legal obligation to perform the promise. Nor has there been in every case an unjust enrichment. Yet the cumulative impact of these concepts has been sufficiently persuasive. In a recent case (2001) the English Court of Appeal emphasized the interrelationship of concepts on this question. The trial judge had dismissed the claim primarily because he found that there was no irrevocable promise or 'mutual understanding' between the parties. The Court of Appeal reversed the decision on the ground that the various relevant considerations, though each in itself insufficient, might have a cumulative effect:

the quality of the relevant assurances may influence the issue of reliance, ... reliance and detriment are often intertwined, and... whether there is a distinct need for a 'mutual understanding' may depend on how the other elements are formulated and understood. Moreover the fundamental principle that equity is concerned to prevent unconscionable conduct permeates all the elements of the doctrine. In the end the court must look at the matter in the round.... [T]he cumulative effect of the judge's findings and of the undisputed evidence is that ... Mr Gillett had an exceptionally strong claim on Mr Holt's conscience.[20]

Similar questions have arisen, and similar solutions have been adopted, in respect of unenforceable contracts. The Statute of Frauds,[21] enacted in 1677 in order to prevent the fraudulent assertion of contractual obligations, provided that certain contracts, notably contracts for the sale of interests in land, were unenforceable unless evidenced by a signed writing. Where a purchaser under an oral contract took possession of the land and built on it, and the landowner subsequently repudiated the contract, considerations arose similar to those discussed in the preceding paragraphs. The purchaser's reliance and the vendor's enrichment were considerations tending strongly in favour of the purchaser; against these had to be set the express statutory provision that the contract was unenforceable. But this point was in turn weakened because the very acts constituting the reliance and causing the enrichment — taking possession and building — tended themselves to show that the contract had probably been made and therefore might be said to satisfy the underlying purpose for which the Statute of Frauds had been enacted, though not, of course, the actual requirements of the statute itself. In such circumstances, by what was misleadingly called the doctrine of part performance, the courts of equity enforced the contract. Neither reliance alone, nor enrichment alone, nor proof of the contract alone (except by a signed writing) could support this result. Frederick Pollock (1876) said that the plaintiff's right rested 'not on a contract but on a principle akin to estoppel', though adding that 'the practical result is that the agreement is enforced'.[22] A century later the difficulty of classification was again noted and described as 'an uneasy oscillation between regarding the doctrine [of part performance] as a principle vindicating conscientious dealing and as a rule of evidence'.[23] These comments show that the cases cannot be allocated to a single category, or explained by a single concept, but that, cumulatively, various reasons have been effective.[24]

Closely related to these cases are those of informal instructions for disposition of property after death, called, by 'a not altogether felicitous expression',[25] secret trusts. The typical case has been of a testator leaving property to a person by will, having privately instructed the person to give the property, in whole or in part, to some other person. Enforcement of such a gift appears on the face of it to contravene the Wills Act, which requires a will to be executed according to certain formalities, and, in cases involving oral instructions relating to land, to contravene also the Statute of Frauds. Nevertheless the courts of equity have enforced the intended gifts in these cases by requiring the person named in the will to hold the property on trust for the intended donee.

The justice of this result has rarely been doubted, but the precise reason is difficult to explain in terms of legal concepts. The question, as Lord Buckmaster said in 1929, 'is one which in various forms has for over 200 years been the subject of vexed controversy'.[26] It cannot be explained in terms of property because the intended gift has not been completed according to the necessary legal formalities: 'it is because there is no one to whom the law can give relief ... that relief, if any, must be sought in equity'.[27] Reference has been made in many of the cases to prevention of fraud, but, as elsewhere in equity, this does not mean actual wrongdoing: the fraud is the refusal to recognize the trust that equity imposes:

> It was contended ... that the fraud for the avoidance of which the trust is enforced, must be the personal fraud of the legatee, but I think the answer is that, if it would be a fraud on the part of the legatees to refuse to carry out the trust, the residuary legatees cannot take advantage of and thus make themselves parties to such fraud.[28]

Considerations of unjust enrichment have been prominent in these cases,[29] as the words 'take advantage of', just quoted, indicate, but it is not obvious, without assuming the result, that the enrichment is at the expense of the intended beneficiary rather than of the estate.[30] Restitution *to the estate* would, of course, be a most unattractive prospect, for it would completely defeat the testator's intention. Thus, considerations of intention and agreement are also relevant, and, as Peter Jaffey has pointed out,[31] there is a very close affinity between these cases and those of promises in favour of third party beneficiaries discussed in the last chapter.[32]

From the example earlier given of the university official who assures a student that she is enrolled it will be seen that the line between statement of fact and promise is indistinct. The official who makes the assertion might say 'your name is already on the list', or she might say 'I will enter your name on the list today (before the deadline)', or she might say 'I will accept your application tomorrow (after the deadline)'; the first of these utterances is a statement of fact; the last two are promises, but they all have the same practical effect of inducing the student to let the deadline pass. Lord St Leonards made this point in 1854 in a case where a bondholder promised not to enforce the bond, and the obligor changed his position in reliance. The majority held that there was no estoppel because this was a promise and not a statement of fact, but Lord St Leonards pointed out in dissent that there is scarcely a practical distinction between saying 'I have cancelled the bond, or have destroyed it or burnt it' and 'I have got the bond, but you may safely rely on it that I never intend to use it'.[33]

Protection was given to reliance on such promises in a number of nineteenth-century English and American cases.[34] In a New York case (1920) Justice Cardozo gave the hypothetical example of a land sale contract under which the seller agrees to change the wallpaper of a room, but, the buyer subsequently indicating that new wallpaper is not required, the seller accordingly leaves the old wallpaper in place. The buyer would not be permitted on the day of closing (completion) to reinstate his original contractual rights without notice so as to put the seller in default. Justice Cardozo added that (on reasonable notice) (the buyer may change his mind again and revert to his agreement. He may not summarily rescind because of the breach which he has encouraged.'[35] This comment shows that Cardozo derived his principle not from any map or scheme, but from very general considerations of justice. He plainly did not consider that the buyer's indication amounted to a binding contract: on the contrary, he said that the 'buyer may change his mind'.

The relation of estoppel with other grounds of obligations presents difficult conceptual problems. Estoppel standing alone does not state a complete reason for imposing an obligation.[36] Conceptually speaking, it is more akin to a rule of evidence than to a substantive ground of obligation. The effect of estoppel has been, as we have seen, to protect reliance in various circumstances, but if every instance of reliance raised an estoppel, it would subsume much of contract law. In order to avert this consequence, various limits have been suggested, but none of them has been found entirely satisfactory. It has been suggested that estoppel applies only to statements of fact and not to promises,[37] but the distinction is hard to put into practice,[38] hard to justify in principle, and does not correspond with many of the actual decisions.[39] It has been suggested that estoppel can only operate as a defence or part of a cause of action, not as a cause of action in itself, and it has been linked, through the common law concept of waiver, with the idea of relinquishment of rights.[40] It is true that estoppel is an 'auxiliary' concept in the sense that it does not in itself seem to state a complete cause of action, but it is often a matter of chance which party is plaintiff and which defendant in litigation, and in practice, as we have seen in the examples discussed, estoppel often has had the practical effect of creating an obligation in favour of plaintiffs.[41]

In American jurisdictions the concept of promissory estoppel was widely used in a variety of contexts, particularly in order to enforce charitable subscriptions. In the first *Restatement of Contracts* (1932) a section (s. 90) was included as follows:

> A promise which the promisor should reasonably expect to induce action or forbearance of a definite and substantial character on the part of the promisee and which does induce such action or forbearance is binding if injustice can be avoided only by enforcement of the promise.

An important practical and theoretical question relates to the proper remedy. If reliance is the reason for enforcing the promise, there is a strong argument for restricting the remedy to the extent of the reliance. The point may be illustrated by considering a gratuitous promise to give valuable land on which the promisee then erects a small building; the effect of enforcing the promise in full would be to go much further than protection of reliance, substantially to enforce an incomplete gift, and to give the promisee the benefit of a bargain that had not been made.[42] Section 90 of the first *Restatement* said that the promise 'is binding'. In its context this meant fully binding, like other contractual obligations, and this reflected Williston's view.[43] Corbin, on the other hand, took the more flexible view that the remedy might be adjusted according to the extent of the promisee's reliance.[44] The question of classification was crucial here. Williston would no doubt have said that a limited remedy for reliance might be appropriate somewhere in the law, but not in a restatement of *contracts*. Corbin's view prevailed, however, in the *Second Restatement*, where the significant words were added at the end of the section:

'The remedy granted for breach may be limited as justice requires.'

The question whether the principle thus stated is truly 'part' of the law of contracts has not been answered, just because the question assumes a definitional precision that has been absent from the history of Anglo-American law. A complicating factor is that in jurisdictions where reliance has not been recognized as a ground of liability, other concepts have been enlarged: many cases that fall in American jurisdictions under section 90 of the *Restatement* have been categorized in English law, with some stretching of the concept of bargain, as unilateral contracts. If contract is defined strictly as bargain, the reliance principle is not properly part of contract law, for there is often no bargain; if contract is defined as consisting of promises fully enforceable as a matter of right, the principle (as qualified in the *Second Restatement*) must similarly be excluded, for the promisee's right is only to protection of reliance; if contracts are restricted to obligations voluntarily assumed by persons of full capacity, estoppel must be excluded, for, as Pollock pointed out, persons lacking contractual capacity (such as minors, or, in the days of Pollock's first edition, married women) may be estopped;[45] if contracts are taken to include all promises enforceable in whole or in part, then the principle is included, but it could plausibly be argued that the principle should then be stated in wider terms than 'promises', since it applies also to protect reliance on representations of fact, and on conduct amounting to silent acquiescence. But there is no other obvious location on any map of the law of obligations so far devised to which the principle could be readily allocated, for it requires neither wrongdoing nor unjust enrichment; as the principle is certainly of vital interest to every student of contract law, it has retained its closest associations there, but for pragmatic rather than theoretical reasons.

In 1970 Professor Grant Gilmore gave a series of lectures in Ohio, subsequently published as *The Death of Contract*, in which he suggested that section 90 of the *Restatement* could absorb the whole of contract law, which could disappear as an independent concept:

> What is happening is that 'contract' is being reabsorbed into the mainstream of 'tort'.... By passing through the magic gate of s. 90, it seems, we can rid ourselves of all the technical limitations of contract theory.[46]

The consequence of this approach would be to enforce only promises on which there had been actual reliance, and to give a right of enforcement only to the extent of that reliance. Shortly afterwards, in England, Patrick Atiyah was advancing the similar thesis that there was no justification for enforcement of promises except to the extent of actual proved reliance.[47]

These suggestions aroused considerable academic interest, but had little impact on judicial decisions. Their effect would have been to reduce the remedy for breach of contract to the measure of the promisee's reliance, and to remove altogether the enforcement of purely executory contracts. It is true to say that protection of reliance has been an important effect of contract law, but it is a considerable step from that proposition to the conclusion that protection of reliance must be the *sole* purpose and effect of contract law. The proposals are of interest from the point of view of the present study, in that they suggest a simplification of legal concepts by abolishing the concept of 'contract'. But simplification of concepts, standing alone, is a very weak reason for making substantial legal changes, and for discarding legal rules found, over several centuries, to have answered the needs of justice. Convenience and elegance of concepts are not the primary ends to be attained by the legal system.

If, indeed, it could be convincingly claimed that the proposed changes were insubstantial in practice and merely restated in more convenient or elegant form the actual past practice of the courts, there would be a stronger case for the proposed simplification, but historical evidence does not support that claim. The principle suggested by Gilmore and Atiyah would cast doubt on many features of Anglo-American contract law as it has been administered in the past, notably the availability of specific enforcement, the enforceability of formal contracts, the ability of parties to treat their transactions as final, and the contractual allocation of risks;[48] it would be likely to reduce very substantially the degree to which contractual parties could, in practice, plan their actions with firm confidence that the counter-performance promised, or its equivalent, would be forthcoming.[49]

Where one party withdraws from contractual negotiations before formation of a binding contract, a remedy has sometimes been given to the other party for expenses incurred in anticipation of the contract. These cases are difficult to classify, as Ewan McKendrick has pointed out, mentioning, as possible bases of liability, 'breach of contract, unjust enrichment, tort, equitable or promissory estoppel, unjust sacrifice, *culpa in contrahendo* [fault in contracting], and breach of a duty of good faith and fair dealing'.[50] Where there is no corresponding benefit to the defendant it is difficult to explain liability as depending on unjust enrichment.[51] The fact that a contract was contemplated is important, but contractual principles alone do not explain the result, for, by hypothesis, the primary contract contemplated is not binding, and the implication of a secondary contract to pay a reasonable compensation is open to the observation that it is fictitious.[52] The idea of fault is present in the suggestion in some of the cases of the relevance of the defendant's unreasonable conduct in breaking off negotiations, with the implication that if the plaintiff had broken off negotiations there would be no liability;[53] yet it is not in itself a wrong to withdraw from incomplete negotiations, even for selfish reasons.[54] Goff and Jones concluded that 'it is not easy to glean any clear principles from this body of case law'.[55] As Jack Beatson has said, 'even within the law of restitution it is not possible to explain everything by reference to the principle of unjust enrichment, and ... a further principle based on the need to protect injurious reliance is the basis for some restitutionary claims'.[56]

Estoppel, though it can, as we have seen, have far-reaching effects, does not itself describe any ground of obligation; it prevents a party from making certain assertions. For this reason estoppel can only operate in the framework of an otherwise recognized cause of action. The claimant must assert a cause of action that *if not contradicted* would be sufficient to support the result sought; the defendant may then be precluded from adducing the contradictory evidence. Estoppel has been effective where the parties are in some sort of near-contractual relationship, or where they have had dealings in respect of identifiable property, but it falls short of a rule that reliance will always be protected.

(b) *Taylor Fashions Ltd v. Liverpool Victoria Friendly Society*†

England and Wales High Court

[1] Giving judgment, OLIVER J said that he had before him two summonses, both claiming new leases under the Landlord and Tenant Act 1954, but these summonses had not yet been adjourned into court because it was necessary first to determine claims made by the plaintiffs for specific performance and other relief. The background was as follows. The summonses under the 1954 Act related to claims for new leases of business premises in Bournemouth known as 20, 21 and 22 Westover Road. The plaintiffs in the first summons were Taylor Fashions Ltd ('Taylors'), the tenants of no 22. The plaintiffs in the second summons were Old & Campbell Ltd ('Olds'), the tenants of nos 20 and 21. The defendants to both summonses were the Liverpool Victoria Friendly Society, the freeholders and the landlords of the plaintiffs.

[2] The present judgment was concerned with the plaintiffs' primary claims, not with the 1954 Act summonses. It would be seen that a question at the root of the matters with which he (his Lordship) had to deal was the exercisability of an option contained in the demise of no 22 to renew the term for a further 14 years after the expiry of the original term in 1976. This question was common to the cases of both plaintiffs. The defendants claimed that the option was void against them for want of registration under the Land Charges Act 1925, although apart from this all the relevant conditions for the exercise of the option had been fulfilled. The defendants had accordingly declined to renew the leases of nos 20 and 22 and had purported to exercise a right to break the lease of no 21, a right which only arose upon the non-exercise by Taylors of the option of renewal in respect of no 22. The defendants had served notices on the plaintiffs in respect of all three leases, to which the plaintiffs had replied by the claims for new leases under the 1954 Act already mentioned. The defendants' case did not impress one as overburdened with merit, but if they were right in law, and if there was no equity which assisted the plaintiffs, it was no part of a judge's function to impose his own idiosyncratic code of commercial morality. He was not criticising those who had the

conduct of the defendants' affairs. They had a fiduciary responsibility for the management of the affairs of others.

[3] It was necessary to give more detailed consideration to the factual background. Nos 21 and 22 Westover Road, Bournemouth, consisted of a building of four storeys and a basement in a favoured part of Bournemouth's shopping area, both premises being used as retail clothing stores, no 21 for gentlemen's tailoring and outfitting, no 22 as a ladies' fashion store. Prior to 1949 the building was owned by Olds, but in 1948 they decided to raise finance by making certain dispositions. The upshot was that the freehold of nos 21 and 22 became vested in the defendants, the Liverpool Victoria Friendly Society, subject to a lease of no 21 back to Olds for 42 years from December 25 1948 and subject to a lease of no 22 to Taylors (who had acquired the ladies' fashion business) for 28 years from December 25 1948. The lease of no 22 contained the critical provision that if the tenants should install a lift in accordance with permission given in the lease they should, subject to certain conditions as to the timing of the request and compliance with covenants, have an option for the renewal of their lease for a further term of 14 years from December 25 1976, the original date of expiry. The lease of no 21 to Olds for a term of 42 years from December 25 1948 contained a provision that if the tenants of no 22 should not exercise their option of renewal for a further 14 years, then the landlords should have the option of terminating the lease of no 21 at the end of 28 years. In that event both leases would terminate on December 25 1976.

[4] Almost at once Taylors set about carrying out extensive improvements to no 22 for which they applied and received the landlords' consent. They also prepared plans and obtained estimates for the installation of the lift, involving substantial expenditure. This was done in the belief that there was in existence a valid and enforceable option which would provide Taylors with a total term of 32 years. There was no doubt that the defendants knew that the lift was going to be installed before the work was done

---

† [1979] EWHC Ch 1, [1982] QB 133.

and must have been aware that the existence of the option would be at least a relevant consideration in Taylors' undertaking the work and expenditure. The carrying out of the work was known to and acquiesced in by the defendants. At the time of the discussions on the siting and construction of the lift and while the work was being done the defendants did not suspect, and had no reason to suspect, that there might be a question as to the validity of the option for renewal. If Taylors had known that there were grounds for contesting such validity they *might* (but it was not possible to find as a fact that they *would*) have decided not to carry out the work on the lift.

[5] It was relevant to mention at this point an event which had nothing to do with any of the parties but which had an important bearing on this litigation. This was the decision of Buckley J (as he then was) in the case of *Beesly* v *Hallwood Estates* [1960] 1 WLR 549 to the effect that an option to renew contained in a lease was registrable as a land charge under the Land Charges Act 1925 and was void against a purchaser of the reversion if not registered. It had to be recalled that before this decision the view of the legal profession, based no doubt on the notes in the then current edition of *Wolstenholme & Cherry*, was that an option to renew, being a covenant which touched and concerned the land and therefore ran with the reversion, did not require to be registered in order to bind a purchaser of the reversion. It is common ground that, so far as the parties to the present transactions were concerned, the significance of the decision was not appreciated by anybody. In fact this unconsciousness endured for a number of years.

[6] The next transaction which needed to be mentioned was the taking of a lease by Olds of the adjoining property at no 20 in furtherance of a plan of expansion by Olds. The lease of no 20 to Olds was tied in with the other leases. It was executed on March 22 1963 and provided for a term of 14 years with an option to renew for a further 14 years, with the usual conditions as to prior notice and compliance with covenants, provided that the option to renew in respect of no 22 had been exercised. If the tenants of no 22 did not exercise their option then the option to renew the lease of no 20 was not exercisable by Olds. In committing themselves to the lease of no 20, and incurring the expenditure which this involved, Olds were relying on the continued exercisability of the option to Taylors under the lease of no 22 and they would not have proceeded if they had been aware that this underlying assumption

was invalid. It was also clear that, at this time, that assumption was shared by the defendants themselves. It was not until 1975 that they became aware that the option might be void against them for want of registration.

[7] On June 7 1976 Taylors served notice on the defendants exercising or purporting to exercise their option to renew in the lease of no 22 and they now claimed specific performance of that option. Olds now also claimed specific performance of the option contained in the 1963 lease relating to no 20 and an appropriate declaration as regards the clause in the lease of 1949 (which provided that if the option in respect of no 22 was not exercised the landlords could terminate the lease of no 21 at the end of the original 28 years' term).

[8] The points which arose for decision in the light of the record of events were the following:

(1) Was Taylors' option, as the defendants now claimed and the plaintiffs contest, void against the defendants for want of registration?
(2) If so, were the defendants estopped as against Taylors from relying on this ground of invalidity having regard to the expenditure incurred by Taylors with the defendants' concurrence?
(3) If the option was unenforceable against the defendants, had it nevertheless been 'exercised' for the purpose of the break and renewal clauses in the lease of 1949 to Olds?
(4) If it had not, were the defendants estopped as against Olds from relying on the invalidity of an option which in their own grants they had asserted to be subsisting?

[9] It had been submitted by Mr Scott, for Taylors, that the Land Charges Act 1925 did not affect contractual obligations which, ever since the Grantees of Reversions Act 1540, had run with the land and remained binding at law quite regardless of any question of notice. This view, however, was not tenable so far as options for renewal were concerned since the decision in *Beesly* v *Hallwood Estates Ltd* above mentioned, a decision which had been accepted as correct in two Court of Appeal decisions, *Greene* v *Church Commissioners for England* [1974] Ch 467 and *Kitney* v *MEPC Ltd* [1977] 1 WLR 981.

[10] It was, therefore, necessary to approach the case on the footing that, whatever the parties may have thought, the option to renew was in fact void against the defendants. That raised the issue of estoppel mentioned in the second and fourth questions set out

above. The relevant principle of estoppel had been formulated by Mr Essayan as follows: 'If A, under an expectation created or encouraged by B that A shall have a certain interest in land, thereafter on the faith of such expectation and with the knowledge of B and without objection by him, acts to his detriment in connection with such land, a court of equity will compel B to give effect to such expectation.' From here, however, there was a critical division of opinion. The plaintiffs contended that the court had to look at the conduct of the party sought to be estopped and ask whether what he was now seeking to do was unconscionable. The defendants contended that it was an essential feature of this particular equitable doctrine that the party alleged to be estopped must, before the assertion that his strict rights could be considered unconscionable, be aware both of what his strict rights were and of the fact that the other party is acting in the belief that they will not be enforced against him. The defendants cited in support of their contention a number of authorities including the often-cited judgment of Fry J (as he then was) in *Willmott* v *Barber* (1880) 15 Ch D 96 in which he set out what are described as the five 'probanda' for establishing the equitable doctrine which would make it 'fraudulent' for a person to insist on his strict legal rights. The authorities, particularly more recent ones, however, appeared to support a much wider equitable jurisdiction to interfere in cases where the assertion of strict legal rights would be regarded by the court as unconscionable.

[11] After an exhaustive review of the authorities, his Lordship concluded that it was not an essential element of this category of estoppel that the party estopped, although he must have known of the other party's belief, must have known that that belief was mistaken. In the recent case of *Shaw* v *Applegate* [1977] 1 WLR 970 Buckley LJ at p 978, referring to Fry J's 'probanda' in *Willmott* v *Barber*, said: 'So I do not, as at present advised, think it is clear that it is essential to find all the five tests set out by Fry J literally applicable and satisfied in any particular case. The real test, I think, must be whether, upon the facts of the particular case, the situation has become such that it would be dishonest or unconscionable for the plaintiff, or the person having the right sought to be enforced, to continue to seek to enforce it.'

[12] The question therefore was whether, in all the circumstances, it was unconscionable for the defendants to seek to take advantage of the mistake which, at the material time, everybody shared. The cases of the two plaintiffs had to be considered separately.

In [13] the case of Taylors there were two difficulties. The first was the difficulty of imputing to the defendants either encouragement or acquiescence in regard to Taylors' belief in the validity of the option. The defendants came into the picture as purchasers of the reversion on an existing lease and subject to all its expressed obligations so far as enforceable against them. In installing the lift Taylors were simply doing what was contemplated by the lease and the defendants could not lawfully object to the work and could not be under any duty to communicate to Taylors what the defendants did not know themselves, namely, that the option was unenforceable because of non-registration. The second difficulty was that, although Taylors believed that the option was valid, it was not possible to say that they would have decided not to do the work if they had thought otherwise. It was even less possible to say that the defendants were, or must have been, aware that Taylors would not have done it. It was therefore necessary, although with some regret, to dismiss Taylors' claim for specific performance.

[14] The case of Olds was very different. First of all, the defendants obtained the freehold from them at a price which was calculated, so far as Olds were concerned, on the footing that the break clause in the 1949 lease was to operate, and the term of the leaseback was to be reduced from 42 to 28 years, only in the event of the non-exercise of an option assumed to be subsisting when the lease was granted. Secondly, in the 1963 transaction Olds were encouraged by the defendants to expend a very large sum on no 21, and to take a lease of the adjoining premises (no 20), upon the faith of the expectation, encouraged by the defendants, that they would be entitled to renew in a particular event which Olds were invited to believe was at least possible. It would be most inequitable if the defendants, having put forward Taylors' option as a valid option in two documents, under each of which they were the grantors, and having encouraged Olds to incur expenditure and alter their position irrevocably by taking additional premises on the faith of that supposition, were now to be permitted to resile and to assert, as they wished to do, that they were, and had been all along, entitled to frustrate the expectation which they themselves created and that the right which they themselves stated to exist did not, at any material time, have any existence in fact. It followed that Olds' claim to specific performance succeeded.

[15] Two further points should perhaps be mentioned. It might be that, apart from the kind of estoppel which had been discussed, the defendants

were also estopped, as regards Olds, by their own deeds. Although estoppel by deed normally arose from recitals, it could be created by a clear and distinct averment in the operative part. It was a necessary inference from the wording of the 1963 deed that the tenants of no 22 had an option. The second point was Mr Essayan's contention that in construing the two leases to Olds the references to the tenants of no 22 'exercising' their option could be taken as references to their taking the necessary steps to give them a contractual right to a new lease, even though it could not result in a new lease effective against the defendants; the option could still produce contractual obligations between the original parties. However, the correct construction appeared to be that 'exercise' meant an effective exercise entitling the tenants of no 22 to a new term.

[16] The result was, therefore, that (1) the claim of Taylors for specific performance of the option in the

lease of no 22 must be dismissed; (2) there would be a declaration in favour of Olds that the break clause in the 1949 lease of no 21 was non-operative; and (3) a decree for specific performance of the option for renewal in the 1963 lease of no 20 to Olds would be granted.

[17] The judge accordingly ordered that the claim by Taylors for specific performance of the option to renew in respect of no 22 be dismissed with costs, leaving the issue under the Landlord and Tenant Act 1954 outstanding. He made a declaration in favour of Olds that the two notices purporting to be notices under section 25 of the 1954 Act affecting their premises were null and void on the grounds (a) in respect of no 20, that the plaintiffs had validly exercised their option to renew the lease, and (b) in respect of no 21, that the defendants' right to terminate the tenancy had not arisen; the defendants to pay the costs.

(c)   *Gillett v. Holt*†

England and Wales Court of Appeal (Civil Division)

[WALKER L.J.:]

THE FACTS

The undisputed background facts have some unusual features. In 1952, when Mr Gillett first met the first defendant Mr Kenneth Holt, the former was a schoolboy aged 12 and the latter was a gentleman farmer (and a bachelor) aged 38. Mr Holt's father had been a farmer in Lincolnshire, but the family money came from shipping interests in Liverpool. Mr Holt himself began farming on his own in 1936, as tenant of a mixed farm of 536 acres known as The Limes, Baumber. The farmhouse at The Limes is a substantial house and Mr Holt has lived there since 1936. The landlord, from 1947, was Merton College Oxford. Since these disputes arose Mr Holt has, through a company, acquired the freehold of The Limes.

    Mr Holt had two brothers (one of whom was killed in the 1914–18 war) and one sister but he did

not have any nephews or nieces who might have been expected to benefit from his estate. The surviving brother, Mr Noel Holt, who was born in 1911, plays a peripheral part in the story. Both he and Mr Holt's housekeeper, Miss Hilda Bell (who died before the trial) gave witness statements to Mr Gillett's solicitors and these were admitted in evidence at the trial.

    In 1952 Mr Gillett moved with his parents from Skegness to Woodhall Spa on his father's promotion from police constable to police sergeant. Mr Gillett senior (who also plays a peripheral part in the story) went on to be a police inspector and, after his retirement, the chairman of the East Lindsey District Council. Mr Gillett junior went to Queen Elizabeth's Grammar School at Horncastle. He first met Mr Holt at Woodhall Spa golf club when he was earning some pocket money as a caddie. He became Mr Holt's regular caddie and a friendship developed between them. Mr Gillett said in his witness statement that despite the difference in their ages they

---

†   [2000] EWCA Civ 66, [2001] 1 Ch 210 (CAEW).

got on well. During his teenage years Mr Gillett was a regular visitor to The Limes, helping on the farm and sometimes staying at the house. Mr Holt was introduced to Mr Gillett's parents and got on well with them. They sometimes played bowls together. Mr Gillett senior acknowledged that he was initially concerned about Mr Holt's relationship with his son but that after meeting Mr Holt's housekeeper he was reassured.

When Mr Gillett junior was 15 Mr Holt proposed that he should leave school and work full-time for Mr Holt. The proposal was that he should work at The Limes for a year and then go to agricultural college near Lincoln. Mr Gillett's headmaster was against the plan, as he was expected to take 'O' and 'A' levels, and his parents had misgivings about it. But they overcame their misgivings and in December 1956, when he was just 16, Mr Gillett went to work for Mr Holt, living at The Limes from January 1957. He took his meals with Mr Holt and the house-keeper (a predecessor of Miss Bell, who arrived in 1961). He did not in the end go to agricultural college because Mr Holt thought that he could learn more at The Limes. Mr Holt (from 1957 through his company K A Holt Ltd — "KAHL") employed a foreman and four or five other men but Mr Gillett was treated as a trainee rather than a farm labourer. He was made responsible for the payroll and Mr Holt took him to Nottingham and introduced him to Mr Holt's accountant who explained PAYE to him.

During the years when he might have been expected to be studying for his 'A' levels, or in further education, Mr Gillett learned a great deal about farming, partly from his practical training at The Limes and partly from evening courses and study which he undertook on his own initiative (he said that Mr Holt was not a believer in college learning). By 1960, when he was twenty, he had introduced a new bookkeeping system and had been given a degree of responsibility for purchasing spares. This was extended over the next two or three years to responsibility for negotiating supplies of fuel, seeds, fertilisers and sprays, and for buying and selling machinery and livestock. He introduced Mr Holt to bee-keeping, which had been a schoolboy hobby of his, and at Mr Holt's suggestion he began his own business of keeping laying poultry and selling eggs. He also enjoyed an active social life with Mr Holt, with many outdoor activities ranging from golf to shooting and speedboat racing. The only activity from which Mr Gillett was largely excluded was fishing for salmon and trout, which became an abiding interest of Mr Holt's from about 1960, taking him on regular trips to Scotland.

In 1958 or 1959 Mr Holt approached Merton College to ask whether it would sell the freehold reversion to the farm. When the college declined this approach Mr Holt asked whether the tenancy could be put in the joint names of himself and Mr Gillett. The college declined that also (unsurprisingly, if only because Mr Gillett was still under full age as the law then stood). Mr Holt then made the suggestion, both to Mr Gillett and to his parents, that he (Mr Holt) should adopt him in order to give Mr Gillett a right of succession to the agricultural tenancy. Nothing came of this but it is an indication of Mr Holt's feelings and it is part of the background to the assurances and understandings on which Mr Gillett relied in the main action.

In May 1963 Mr Holt acquired another freehold farm of 236 acres, White House Farm, Waddingworth. This was conveyed into Mr Holt's own name, not to KAHL. When Mr Gillett was between 18 and 20 Mr Holt was clearly of central importance both to Mr Gillett's working life and to his social life. Mr Gillett had some girl friends, but Mr Holt did not encourage them. Then in 1961 at Horncastle Young Farmers Mr Gillett met and became friendly with Sally Wingate, the daughter of a tenant farmer on a nearby estate. After some initial coolness on both sides she put herself out to become friends with Mr Holt, and Mr Holt became friendly both with her and with her father and mother (until their deaths in 1971 and 1984 respectively). Mr Gillett and Miss Wingate became very close friends and at Easter 1964 they became engaged.

They broke the news to Mr Holt who was at first shocked but returned the next day to his usual friendly manner. During 1964 Mr Gillett senior was transferred from Woodhall Spa to Boston and he and his wife moved away from the district for about three years. In the summer Mr Holt told Mr Gillett that he (Mr Holt) was going fishing in Iceland and that Mr Gillett (then aged 24) would be in charge of the harvest. Mr Holt went fishing and Mr Gillett got the harvest in successfully. On his return Mr Holt congratulated Mr Gillett and, according to Mr Gillett, from then on he retired from day to day involvement in the work of the farm.

Then occurred the first of seven incidents which the judge recorded ([1998] 3 AER at pp. 930–2) as assurances given by Mr Holt and relied on by Mr Gillett. The judge accepted the Gilletts' account as factually accurate. The first incident (and some supporting material from the same period) were described as follows by the judge,

<u>1964 Harvest</u>

Mr Gillett says that he and Sally (then his fiancée) were taken to dinner by Mr Holt at the Golf Hotel Woodhall Spa. The discussion was in line with earlier indications but was 'more specific'. Mr Holt explained that 'as time progressed I would be involved more and more with the farming business and in due course I would take over the complete running of the farm and when he died the farming business would be left to me in its entirety.' Mrs Gillett remembers Mr Holt saying that Mr Gillett was going to be in full charge of the farm in due course and "that he also wanted to leave the farm to Geoff".

.　.　.　.

In December 1964 Mr and Mrs Gillett were married. Before their marriage, but after the dinner with Mr Holt, they had agreed to buy a bungalow called Rose Bank at Thimbleby, a little over two miles from The Limes. It cost £2,250, provided by a 95 per cent mortgage from the Abbey National and the balance from Mr Gillett's savings. Mr Gillett was before his marriage being paid £15 a week by KAHL, but this was raised to £17 on his marriage. This was one of the few points on which the judge found Mr Gillett's recollection to be at fault. He also had a modest pension plan arranged by Mr Holt. Mr Gillett's evidence was that he and his wife found it difficult to keep up with their mortgage payments, even with help from her earnings. Their first child, Robert, was born on 18 April 1971.

Robert's christening was the occasion of the second assurance relied on by Mr Gillett in the main action. The judge made the following finding about this,

<u>1971 Robert's Christening</u>

Mr Holt attended the christening as Robert's godfather and gave a speech. The Statement of Claim (para 27) alleges that he stated words to the effect that 'Robert's birth would enable the farm to continue to the next generation'. This wording accords with Mr Gillett's evidence. He says it did not surprise him because it was already well settled between them that 'I would eventually succeed to his farming business'. The evidence of Sally and Mr Gillett senior is to similar effect.

Shortly before Robert's birth there had been an important change in that Mr Holt's company KAHL, acquired further freehold property and Mr and Mrs Gillett went to live there. They sold Rose Bank for about £4,000, leaving a net equity in their hands of

about £1,500. The purchase of the new land (103 acres and a farmhouse, then called Hatton Farm, Baumber, now The Beeches) was negotiated and carried through by Mr Gillett, with Mr Holt's approval. The price was £28,000 financed by an increased overdraft (which Mr Gillett negotiated as being preferable to an inflexible mortgage loan). The farmhouse (renamed The Beeches) was in a poor state and the Gilletts carried out repairs and improvements, some at the expense of KAHL and some at their own expense.

On 16 March 1973 their second son Andrew was born. A few months later a new company, G&H Farms Ltd ("G&H") was formed. Mr Holt and Mr Gillett each had 45 per cent of the shares and Mr Holt's brother Noel the remaining 10 per cent (which was transferred to Mrs Gillett in 1991). The directors were Mr Holt and Mr Gillett (who in 1973 were aged 59 and 33 respectively). The idea for the company came from Mr Holt's accountant in Nottingham, Mr Ray, who suggested that the new company could hire machinery out to KAHL and build up liquid assets derived from it, and so achieve a legitimate saving of estate duty on Mr Holt's death (this was before the replacement of estate duty by capital transfer tax, and a raft of new reliefs for agricultural and business assets, transformed tax planning for farmers). Mr Holt's concerns about tax planning may have been prompted partly by the partition, during 1973, of the Holt family trust, which made a substantial addition to Mr Holt's disposable assets. Mr Holt freely discussed these matters with Mr and Mrs Gillett, who assisted Mr Holt with the secretarial side of managing his investments and in the preparation of his tax returns. The Gilletts had in 1967 formed a company of their own, Horncastle Secretarial Services Ltd, which was run by Mrs Gillett and provided secretarial and bookkeeping services, mainly to farmers (including KAHL). It ceased trading in 1980 but Mrs Gillett continued to work for KAHL and became its employee in 1986.

During the first part of 1974 Mr Holt must have written again to Merton because there was a letter dated 30 April 1974 from the Estates Bursar to him. It began,

> The College policy for re-letting farms to sons of tenants before the death or retirement of the father has, for the last twelve years been that until the father dies or retires completely, no change can be made. This may seem harsh but there are reasons for it.

Then after some explanation of the college policy it went on,

With regard to Limes Farm, I hope that you will remain our tenant for a great number of years. If your tenancy did end, then the College would have to decide whether to sell or re-let, as I am sure we would not wish to farm it ourselves. As you know we have no other land near Baumber with which to amalgamate and 543 acres is rapidly becoming a small unit for the type of land. The College might be tempted to sell but if it did not then we would want a tenant and Mr Gillett, who I have got to know quite well over the last few years and who I know would make an excellent tenant so long as he had the necessary finance, would stand a very good chance of getting the tenancy.

The next three instances of assurances given by Mr Holt to Mr Gillett occurred in 1973, 1974 and 1975, and again the judge's findings about these should be set out in full:

Christmas 1973

According to the Statement of Claim (para 32) Mr Holt held a dinner for Mr and Mrs Gillett at which he 'repeated once again that he would bequeath all his assets' to Mr Gillett, and 'specifically stated' that he believed that his non-farming assets would be sufficient to pay the tax liability on the estate 'leaving (at the least) the entirety of his farming business to be passed to the plaintiff free of liability to tax'.

The evidence does not go so far. According to Mr Gillett's statement, Mr Holt 're-iterated all he had said about leaving K A Holt Ltd to Sally and me on his death and the formation of G&H Farms Ltd'. As I understood his answers in cross-examination, he did not suggest that the representation extended to 'all his assets'. The other assets came into the conversation, because Mr Holt 'thought it would be possible' to use them to enable the Farm to be passed on free of tax; he was in consultation with his solicitors and accountants about this. According to Mrs Gillett, Mr Holt said that he was 'looking into the best way of passing assets over but he was worried about the tax side of it'.

1974 Golf Hotel Dinner

According to the Statement of Claim (para 34) Mr Holt told Mr Gillett that he had appointed him executor of his Will, and showed him some papers which 'appeared to indicate' that he had 'bequeathed his entire estate' to Mr Gillett. Again Mr Gillett's evidence is less specific. His statement says that at a dinner at the Golf Hotel, Mr Holt said that 'he had now made his Will in our favour', with him as one of the executors. Shortly afterwards, at the Limes, Mr Holt showed him a document which he understood to be this will, but he was not given it to read.

1975 Discussion of The Beeches

Mr Gillett says that he asked Ken for something in writing to confirm that the Beeches Farm would be theirs. He was told 'that was not necessary as it was all going to be ours anyway'. Mr Gillett was disappointed but after discussing it with his wife and parents decided 'that Ken was a man of his word so I accepted his assurances'. His statement supports the Statement of Claim in this respect (para 35). In cross-examination he said that he understood this as a representation that the farming business would come to him on Mr Holt's death.

The last of these episodes is referred to in the notice of appeal as 'The Beeches incident'.

It does not appear from the documents disclosed on discovery that Mr Holt had by this stage made a will in favour of Mr and Mrs Gillett. The official announcement (in November 1974) of the proposed replacement of estate duty by capital transfer tax, with partially retrospective effect, had a chilling effect on tax planning at that time. But there is a draft will of Mr Holt prepared in February 1976 appointing Mr Gillett and two others (Mr George Grant, a local farmer, and Mr Wormald, a Liverpool solicitor) as executors and (after numerous pecuniary legacies and specific legacies of chattels, many to the members of the Gillett family) settling the residuary estate on trusts under which Mr and Mrs Gillett took successive life interests, with ulterior trusts of capital in favour of their children (and an ultimate trust, if no child attained a vested interest, for Mr and Mrs Gillett in equal shares). Another similar draft will, but with Mr Noel Holt as one of the executors in place of Mr Grant, and Mr William Pinfold, another partner in Alsop Stevens, in place of Mr Wormald, was prepared in March 1977. It is probable but not certain (and may not ultimately be significant) that wills in these forms were executed by Mr Holt, and destroyed when revoked by a new will. At that time Mr Holt was taking a lot of advice on tax planning from different quarters, primarily Alsop Stevens (his Liverpool solicitors), Prior & Palmer (his Nottingham accountants) and a firm of insurance brokers. The judge summarized the slow progress in arriving at a tax-planning strategy and implementing it ([1998] 3 AER at p. 920):

By September 1978 this had crystallised into a decision in principle to give 20% of the shares in KAHL to Mr Gillett, to sell White House Farm to KAHL, and (subject to tax considerations) to channel future machinery purchases through G&H. The transfer of the shares in KAHL was not implemented until the end of

1983 when Mr and Mrs Gillett were given 10% each of the shares in KAHL.

These decisions were documented at the time in the minutes of a meeting held at The Limes on 27 September 1978. The meeting was attended by Mr Holt, his brother Noel (who took the chair), Mr Palmer and Mr Kennedy of Prior & Palmer, Mr Pinfold of Alsop Stevens and (for part of the meeting) Mr Gillett.

Shortly afterwards Mr Gillett, at Mr Holt's request, visited Mr Palmer and expressed some doubts about the effect of the proposals on the liquidity of the farming business, especially as KAHL was losing its tenancy of a farm called Greenfield Farm. He is also recorded by Mr Palmer (in a letter to Mr Pinfold) as having expressed personal anxieties:

> He has also pointed out that the whole family has a record of longevity, and he envisages the possibility that he, Gillett, may reach retirement age before anything really happens. I pointed out to him that this is highly unlikely, and in any case if it go anywhere near that I am sure Ken Holt, having voluntarily taken these steps to try and help Gillett, would do something about it. I also pointed out that Gillett himself, is not immortal, and if we went too far handing things over at this stage we could well be landed with the classical situation that Ken Holt could be stripped of a large part of his fortune. I begged him to drive carefully on the way back to Baumber.

Mr Pinfold's response was that Mr Gillett should be grateful for anything. Mr Kennedy replied on 15 December saying at the beginning of a long letter,

> I do not think that Mr Gillett's comments are necessarily in contradiction of our main conclusion. I think that Peter Palmer and I both tend to agree with the comments in your letter of 28 November that Mr Gillett is in a way tending to look his gift horse in the mouth. Nevertheless, he is the business manager used to thinking chiefly in terms of the business and his comments do have some bearing on our proposals.
>
> I was myself unaware of the pending loss of Greenfield Farm and this will obviously have a material effect on the results of the business unless an alternative can be found.

The letter then continued with detailed financial projections. This exchange of correspondence is interesting as showing the perceptions of detached professionals whose instructions came from Mr Holt.

In 1979 Merton College was again asked about transferring Mr Holt's tenancy of The Limes into the joint names of himself and Mr Gillett, but again this approach came to nothing. The Estates Bursar wrote to Mr Holt,

> I fully understand your desire to secure Mr Gillett's future and I feel it is good of you to be so concerned on his behalf. I am afraid, however, that it would be quite contrary to the College's policy to create a joint tenancy with him.

Mr Gillett's own view of the matter appears from some manuscript notes which he prepared, probably in 1981, for a presentation to Mr Holt (which did not in the event happen, so that the notes were not used). The judge set out part of the notes as an expression of what he called Mr Gillett's frustrations ([1998] 3 AER at p. 923):

> After a long series of intermittent discussions no conclusion has been reached. During this protracted period I have accepted a lower salary in anticipation of a substantial capital involvement over the years. I believe the time has come that a satisfactory solution must be reached as my total involvement in the farm must not be allowed to wane. As you are aware I have been for some time frustrated because of your policy of non-expansion. I ask myself at 40 years old just what on earth I will do with my untapped energy for the times on the farm when it is slack.

But the judge commented that there was no evidence before 1992 that his frustrations were reflected in any failings in the management of the farm. In particular, Mr Gillett's decision in 1987 to develop on some of the land at The Beeches what he called the Countryside Companions project — a project for farm diversification first into wild flower seed, and then into the growing of native trees and shrubs, and fish farming — was taken with Mr Holt's blessing and support, although Mr Holt did not wish to be a shareholder or director in Countryside Companions (an unlimited company).

There was a good deal of evidence before the judge (uncontradicted by any evidence from the defendants, since they elected to call no evidence) that Mr Gillett, so far from neglecting the farm business, was energetic, skilful and innovative. One example of many to be found in Mr Gillett's long witness statement is his collaboration with ICI in developing a new means of transporting and handling fertiliser:

In 1973 I hit on an idea to make easier the handling of bulk fertiliser. I was fed up with all the work involved in lifting bags of fertiliser, generally packed in 1 cwt bags. Farm mechanisation was increasingly happening and my simple idea was to use bigger bags which could be lifted by a tractor fitted with fork lifting gear. I discussed this with a contact at ICI which led to trials on the farm in which we co-operated with ICI. The result was the 'big bag' system now universally in use on farms.

In 1984 Mr Holt celebrated his seventieth birthday. His birthday party on 24 March 1984 was the occasion of the sixth assurance on which Mr Gillett relied in his pleadings. The judge made this finding about it:

Mr Holt's 70th birthday party (March 1984)

According to the Statement of Claim (para 42) there was a party organised by Mr and Mrs Gillett. Mr Holt said that he was pleased that they and their children 'had a very secure future'. This wording accords with Mr Gillett's statement.

On 9 June 1986 Mr Holt made a new will. This is the first executed will disclosed on discovery but it probably revoked a will in the form of the draft prepared in March 1977. It appointed as executors Mr Noel Holt, Mr Gillett and Mr Pinfold. It contained no pecuniary or specific gifts and left the entire residuary estate to Mr Gillett absolutely (with alternative gifts to Mrs Gillett or to their children at 21 in equal shares, if the gift to Mr Gillett failed).

The seventh and last assurance pleaded by Mr Gillett was made in 1989 when Mr Holt had to go into hospital. The judge made this finding:

1989 Mr Holt's operation

According to the Statement of Claim (para 43), on 21st June 1989, Mr Holt had to go to hospital in Lincoln for a prostate operation. He was taken there by Mr and Mrs Gillett. He told them that, if anything went wrong with the operation, 'it is all yours, but I would like you to look after all the people who have worked for me'. Again this is supported by Mr Gillett's statement.

A few months after Mr Holt's operation in 1989 Mr and Mrs Gillett celebrated their silver wedding by going on a round the world cruise. Mr Holt was sufficiently recovered to have their younger son Andrew (then 16) to stay with him, and Mr Holt wrote affectionate letters to the elder son, Robert, signing himself 'Love from Uncle Ken'. So in 1990 there were still very warm relations between Mr Holt

and the Gilletts, and in 1991 Mr Holt made a codicil appointing Mr Grant as an executor in place of his brother Mr Noel Holt, but otherwise confirming his will.

In 1992, however, things began to change, and relations between Mr Holt and the Gilletts deteriorated rapidly until the final rupture on 27 November 1995, when Mr and Mrs Gillett were summarily dismissed by KAHL after a police investigation (which resulted in no criminal charges) and a disciplinary hearing.

The primary cause of this dramatic change, after friendships which went back 43 years as between Mr Holt and Mr Gillett, and at least 31 years as between Mr Holt and Mrs Gillett, was the appearance on the scene in 1992 of Mr David Wood, the second defendant. He was then a trainee solicitor with Roythorne & Co of Spalding. That firm, principally in the person of Mr Alan Plummer, appears to have played a major part in initiating the police investigation and conducting the disciplinary hearing against Mr and Mrs Gillett. It has also acted for Mr Holt and Mr Wood in this litigation. But all Mr Holt's testamentary instruments appear to have been prepared by Alsop Stevens (or its successor Alsop Wilkinson).

The judge's findings in relation to Mr Wood were as follows:

As for the period after 1992, there is no doubt that the primary cause of the rift was the change in Mr Holt's affections, brought about by Mr Wood's appearance on the scene. This is not just the view of the Gillett family, but it is supported by Mrs Bell (Mr Holt's housekeeper since 1961) and his brother, Noel. From Mrs Bell's evidence it is clear that Mr Holt's relationship with Mr Wood developed into something of an obsession, which was of concern to his family and other friends. Not having heard Mr Holt or Mr Wood (although they were sitting together at the back of the court for most of the trial), I have no reason to doubt her account. By February 1994 this relationship had developed sufficiently for Mr Wood to have replaced Mr Gillett as the principal beneficiary under Mr Holt's will.

In that will Mr Wood became an executor in place of Mr Gillett. Mr Gillett and members of his family took pecuniary legacies totalling £120,000, but White House Farm, Mr Holt's shares in KAHL and G&H and his residuary estate were left to Mr Wood. There was a provision for Mr and Mrs Gillett to occupy the farmhouse and garden at The Beeches for as long as they wished. It is not clear whether this provision was mandatory or precatory in nature.

In Mr Holt's next will dated 5 April 1995 the legacies to the Gilletts had been reduced to £60,000 but the rest of the will was in substantially similar form. By 20 November 1995, a week before the disciplinary hearing, the legacies to the Gilletts and the provision for them to stay in The Beeches farmhouse had disappeared.

[As to the substance of the complaints made against Mr and Mrs Gillett at the disciplinary hearing, the judge noted that they were found to be without merit.]

After his dismissal Mr Gillett commenced the main action against Mr Holt, and (after Mr Gillett learned of lifetime dispositions made by Mr Holt in favour of Mr Wood) the proceedings were amended to join Mr Wood as second defendant. The other proceedings (a s 459 petition in respect of KAHL issued by Mr Gillett, a s 459 petition in respect of G&H issued by Mr Holt, and the possession proceedings in respect of The Beeches commenced by KAHL with a counterclaim for a declaration) also followed. These matters were heard together during twelve days of hearings in April and May 1998 (and would no doubt have taken longer but for the defendants' decision, described by the judge [1998] 3 AER at pp. 921–2, not to call any evidence). The amended statement of claim pleaded the claim in terms of contract as well as estoppel, but the former claim was abandoned at trial.

THE JUDGMENT AND THE NOTICE OF APPEAL

In his reserved judgment the judge made numerous findings of fact (the most important of which are set out above). He made those findings on the basis that the Gilletts and their witnesses had told the truth, apart from a few errors of recollection. Nevertheless he reached the conclusion that the main action must be dismissed. He set out his reasons as follows ([1998] 3 AER at p. 932, in a paragraph headed 'Conclusions'):

> It is not in dispute that for a long period Mr Holt intended to leave the bulk of his estate to the Gilletts; and that he both made that intention known to Mr Gillett, and gave effect to it in wills executed by him. (The precise extent of the property covered by those statements from time to time is less clear.) What I am unable to find in the representations reviewed above is anything which could reasonably be construed as an irrevocable promise that the Gilletts would inherit, regardless of any

change in circumstances. Nor do I believe that Mr Gillett himself did so construe them. In cross-examination, he accepted that if circumstances had changed materially, for example if Mr Holt had married and had children, he could not have complained if Mr Holt had made some provision for them. No doubt it was because of this insecurity that he pressed for something more formal in relation to the Beeches. On that he was unsuccessful. He must have been well aware that his expectations, however reasonable, were dependent on Mr Holt's continuing good will, and had no legally enforceable foundation.

> In those circumstances the claim based on proprietary estoppel must fail.

The judge went on to say that the claim would in any event have failed because Mr Gillett had not proved himself to have suffered sufficient detriment, in reliance on Mr Holt's assurances, to give rise to a proprietary estoppel.

PROPRIETARY ESTOPPEL

This judgment considers the relevant principles of law, and the judge's application of them to the facts which he found.... But although the judgment is, for convenience, divided into several sections with headings which give a rough indication of the subject-matter, it is important to note at the outset that the doctrine of proprietary estoppel cannot be treated as subdivided into three or four watertight compartments. .. Moreover the fundamental principle that equity is concerned to prevent unconscionable conduct permeates all the elements of the doctrine. In the end the court must look at the matter in the round.

In his discussion of the law the judge took as his starting point the decision of Mr Edward Nugee QC in *Re Basham* [1986] 1 WLR 1498. In that case the claimant and her husband had helped her mother and her stepfather in all sorts of ways throughout the claimant's adult life. She received no remuneration but understood that she would inherit her stepfather's property when he died. After her mother's death in 1976, and until her stepfather's death in 1982, she and her husband lived near the cottage to which her stepfather had moved (but never lived in the cottage). The claimant was told by her stepfather that 'she would lose nothing' by her help and (a few days before his death) that she was to have the cottage. The deputy judge held that she was entitled, by proprietary estoppel, to the whole of the estate of her stepfather (who died intestate). He rejected the submission that the principle could not extend beyond cases where the claimant already had enjoyment of an identified item of property (see at pp. 1509–10). In that context he referred to the well-known judgment of Oliver J in *Taylors Fashions v Liverpool Victoria Trustees* (1979) [1982] QB 133. That judgment has been described as 'a watershed in the development of proprietary estoppel,' In it Oliver J stated (at p. 151) that in the light of the more recent cases the principle

> requires a very much broader approach which is directed rather at ascertaining whether, in particular individual circumstances, it would be unconscionable for a party to be permitted to deny that which, knowingly or unknowingly, he has allowed or encouraged another to assume to his detriment than to enquiring whether the circumstances can be fitted within the confines of some preconceived formula serving as a universal yardstick of unconscionable behaviour.

[Another] case in which *Re Basham* has been referred to in this court is *Wayling v Jones* (1993) 69 P&CR 170. It concerned an assurance ('It'll all be yours one day') given by the elder partner in a male homosexual relationship to his younger partner. Balcombe LJ (at p. 172) cited Mr Nugee's statement of principle in *Re Basham* (at p. 1503) as having been accepted by the parties:

> The plaintiff relies on proprietary estoppel; the principle of which in its broadest form may be stated as follows: where one person (A) has acted to his detriment on the faith of a belief which was known to and encouraged by another person (B) that he either has or is going to be given a right in or over B's property B cannot insist on his strict legal rights if to do so would be inconsistent with A's belief.

Balcombe LJ went on (at p. 173) to state the relevant principles as to reliance and detriment:

> (1) There must be a sufficient link between the promises relied upon and the conduct which constitutes the detriment — see *Eves v Eves* [1975] 1 WLR 1338, 1345 in particular per Brightman J in *Grant v Edwards* [1986] Ch 638 at 648–649; 655–657; 656, per Nourse LJ and per Browne-Wilkinson V-C and in particular the passage where he equates the principles applicable in cases of constructive trust to those of proprietary estoppel.
>
> (2) The promises relied upon do not have to be the sole inducement for the conduct: it is sufficient if they are an inducement — *Amalgamated Property Co v Texas Bank* [1982] QB 84, 104–5.
>
> (3) Once it has been established that promises were made, and that there has been conduct by

the plaintiff of such a nature that inducement may be inferred then the burden of proof shifts to the defendants to establish that he did not rely on the promises — *Greasley v Cooke* [1986] 1 WLR 1306; *Grant v Edwards* [1986] Ch 638, 657.

IRREVOCABILITY OF ASSURANCES

. . . .

[Note: Citing discussion with respect to a disputed case, *Taylor v Dickens*, Lord Justice Walker cited Carnwath J in ([1998] 3 AER at p. 929)] that the advice to the claimant in 'not to count his chickens before they were hatched' is

> an apt statement of how, in normal circumstances, and in the absence of a specific promise, any reasonable person would regard — and should be expected by the law to regard — a representation by a living person as to his intentions for his will.

In the generality of cases that is no doubt correct, and it is notorious that some elderly persons of means derive enjoyment from the possession of testamentary power, and from dropping hints as to their intentions, without any question of an estoppel arising. But in this case Mr Holt's assurances were repeated over a long period, usually before the assembled company on special family occasions, and some of them (such as 'it was all going to be ours anyway' on the occasion of the Beeches incident) were completely unambiguous. With all respect to the judge, I cannot accept the conclusion which he reached on this point ([1998] 3 AER at p. 932, a passage which I have already quoted). The judge attached weight to the Beeches incident in reaching his conclusion. To my mind it is highly significant, but its significance goes the other way. I find it wholly understandable that Mr and Mrs Gillett, then ten years married and with two young sons, may have been worried about their home and their future depending on no more than oral assurances, however emphatic, from Mr Holt. The bitterly fought and ruinously expensive litigation which has ensued shows how right they would have been to be worried. But Mr Gillett, after discussing the matter with his wife and his parents, decided to rely on Mr Holt's assurances because 'Ken was a man of his word'. Plainly the assurances given on this occasion were intended to be relied on, and were in fact relied on. In any event reliance would be presumed....

. . . .

... As already noted, it is the other party's detrimental reliance on the promise which makes it irrevocable. To that extent the judge seems to have misdirected himself as to what he was looking for in the facts.

Mr Gillett was cross-examined at length about some increasingly improbable eventualities: that Mr Holt would marry his housekeeper, that he would have children, that his elderly sister would suddenly lose all her investments and turn to him for help. Mr Gillett naturally enough conceded that in those circumstances Mr Holt could or would have made some provision for these moral obligations. But he stuck resolutely to the promises made to him (transcript of 27 April 1998, p. 24),

> I am aware that promises were made by Mr Holt to me and I continued through 40 years of my life on the basis of those promises

and on the next page,

> This was a partnership arrangement effectively between Ken and [me] over many, many years and hypothetical situations like that are inappropriate I would have thought.

The last two sentences of the 'Conclusion' paragraph begin "No doubt it was because of this insecurity...." and "He must have been well aware...." Neither of these sentences can readily be described as a simple finding of primary fact. Moreover the second sentence does, with great respect to the judge, beg the whole question, because Mr Gillett was not in the witness box to take part in a seminar on the elements of proprietary estoppel (although parts of his cross-examination suggest otherwise). He was there to give evidence, which was largely unchallenged and which the judge accepted, about the assurances made to him and his detrimental reliance on them. Whether those assurances put his expectations on a legally enforceable foundation was not a question for him. But unfortunately he was right in his instinct that his lack of success in getting Mr Holt to give him anything more formal might lead to tears.

. . . .

MUTUAL UNDERSTANDING AND RELIANCE

The judge below's approach seems also to have been influenced by the need to find what he called (at p. 929e)

> a mutual understanding — which may be expressed or inferred from conduct — between

promisor and promisee, both as to the content of the promise and as to what the promisee is doing, or may be expected to do, in reliance on it.

Similarly he set out his view (at p. 932j) that

> the *Basham* principle requires some mutual understanding as to the quid pro quo [i.e. the consideration] for the promise.

... I think that the judge may have been too influenced by the cases on mutual wills in which a definite agreement is an essential part of the doctrine. There is of course a kernel of truth, indeed a considerable nugget of truth in this approach, because there must be a sufficient link between the promises relied on and the conduct which constitutes the detriment. In cases where the detriment involves the claimant moving house ... or otherwise taking some particular course of action at the other party's request, the link is, in the nature of things, going to have some resemblance to the process of offer and acceptance leading to a mutual understanding. But in other cases well within the mainstream of proprietary estoppel, such as *Inwards v Baker* [1965] 2 QB 29 and the 19th century decisions which this court applied in that case, there is nothing like a bargain as to what particular interest is to be granted, or when it is to be granted, or by what type of disposition it is to be granted. The link is provided by the bare fact of A encouraging B to incur expenditure on A's land.

The judge seems to have recognised this point when he said,

> It may be easier to infer a fixed intent when the subject matter is a particular property, which the plaintiff has been allowed to enjoy in return for services, than a whole estate.

But when he got to his conclusion he was taking too restricted a view of the first essential element of this very flexible doctrine. If it had been necessary to find a mutual understanding in this case, the judge might readily have found it in Mr Holt promising to reward Mr Gillett for his past, present and future loyalty and hard work which (backed up by that of Mrs Gillett) made Mr Holt's life more pleasant and prosperous. That seems to have been the general theme of the speech which Mr Holt made on the occasion of his 70th birthday party in 1984. It also seems to be reflected in an exchange in Mr Martin's cross-examination of Mr Gillett (transcript of 27 April 1988, p. 24),

Q Let us take an example, you say, as I understand it, that Ken's promises were not a one-
way street. You had obligations too. You
were obliged to provide companionship and
keep on working for him?
A Yes, that's fair.

But particular findings of that sort were not necessary because Mr Gillett had abandoned his claim
in contract.

DETRIMENT

It is therefore necessary to go on to consider detriment. The judge would have decided the case
against Mr Gillett on this point also, as he indicated
at the end of his judgment in the main action
([1998] 3 AER at pp. 932g–936c). The judge devoted
almost all of this part of his judgment to an analysis
of whether Mr Gillett was substantially underpaid
between 1965 and 1995. He dealt with the other
matters relied on as detriment in a manner which
Mr McDonnell has described as perfunctory.

. . . .

Professor Giles [an expert called at the trial]
concluded that over the whole period from 1964 to
1995 Mr Gillett had received earnings and benefits
amounting to about 80 per cent of the average disclosed by the survey, whereas his above-average level
of responsibility would have justified earnings and
benefits 5 to 10 per cent above the average. The
judge noted and accepted two main criticisms of this
conclusion, in addition to the small size of the sample on which the average was based: first, that some
of Mrs Gillett's earnings from KAHL were in effect
a redistribution of those of her husband; and second,
that no account was taken of the time which Mr
Gillett was, after 1988, devoting to the business of
Countryside Companions. The judge said that he was
not persuaded, on the evidence, that Mr Gillett did
in fact receive less than a reasonable wage for his
services as a manager, or that he did so as part of
an understanding related to his expectations, and
that conclusion has not been seriously challenged in
this court. The judge then said,

> Various other matters were relied on by Mr
> Gillett in support of his case of 'detriment': for
> example, his refusal of enquiries from other
> employers, the limited provision made for his
> pension, the domestic tasks undertaken by him
> and Sally for Mr Holt, and the money spent by
> him on improving the Beeches. Against that, he
> acknowledges that Mr Holt was generous with

gifts to the family, in paying Robert's school
fees, and in other ways. It is impossible and
inappropriate to attempt to weigh the balance of
advantage and disadvantage. The Gilletts decided
at an early stage that their future lay with Mr
Holt, and as with most human relationships that
involved obligations and compensations. I cannot
find in them such a balance of 'detriment' as
to support the case for a legally enforceable
obligation.

Both sides agree that the element of detriment
is an essential ingredient of proprietary estoppel. ...
The overwhelming weight of authority shows
that detriment is required. But the authorities also
show that it is not a narrow or technical concept.
The detriment need not consist of the expenditure of
money or other quantifiable financial detriment, so
long as it is something substantial. The requirement
must be approached as part of a broad inquiry as to
whether repudiation of an assurance is or is not
unconscionable in all the circumstances.

. . . .

... If in a situation like that in *Inwards v Baker*,
a man is encouraged to build a bungalow on his
father's land and does so, the question of detriment
is, so long as no dispute arises, equivocal. Viewed
from one angle (which ignores the assurance implicit
in the encouragement) the son suffers the detriment
of spending his own money in improving land which
he does not own. But viewed from another angle
(which takes account of the assurance) he is getting
the benefit of a free building plot. If and when the
father (or his personal representative) decides to go
back on the assurance and assert an adverse claim
then (as Dixon J put it)

> if [the assertion] is allowed, his own original
> change of position will operate as a detriment.

The matters which Mr Gillett pleaded as
detriment, and on which he adduced evidence of
detriment, included, apart from the level of his
remuneration, (i) his continuing in Mr Holt's
employment (through KAHL) and not seeking or
accepting offers of employment elsewhere, or going
into business on his own account; (ii) carrying out
tasks and spending time beyond the normal scope
of an employee's duty; (iii) taking no substantial
steps to secure his future wealth, either by larger
pension contributions or otherwise; and (iv) expenditure on improving the Beeches farmhouse which was,
Mr Gillett said, barely habitable when it was first
acquired by KAHL in 1971. That company paid for

some structural work, with a local authority improvement grant, but Mr Gillett paid for new fittings and materials and carried out a good deal of the work himself. ... After listening to lengthy submissions about the judgment, and after reading much of Mr Gillett's evidence both in his witness statement and under cross-examination, I am left with the feeling that the judge, despite his very clear and careful judgment, did not stand back and look at the matter in the round. Had he done so I think he would have recognised that Mr Gillett's case on detriment (on the facts found by the judge, and on Mr Gillett's uncontradicted evidence) was an unusually compelling one.

In my judgment the cumulative effect of the judge's findings and of the undisputed evidence is that by 1975 (the year of the Beeches incident) Mr Gillett had an exceptionally strong claim on Mr Holt's conscience. Mr Gillett was then 35. He had left school before he was 16, without taking any of the examinations which might otherwise have given him academic qualifications, against the advice of his headmaster and in the face of his parents' doubts, in order to work for and live with a 42 year-old bachelor who was socially superior to, and very much wealthier than, his own parents. Mr Holt seriously raised the possibility of adopting him. Mr Holt's influence extended to Mr Gillett's social and private life and it seems to have been only through the diplomacy of Miss Sally Wingate (as she then was) that Mr Holt came to tolerate, and then accept, the notion of Mr Gillett having a girlfriend. Mr Holt had said that he would arrange for Mr Gillett to go to agricultural college but then did not arrange it, and it was only through Mr Gillett's own hard work and determination that he learned additional skills at evening classes. He proved himself by getting in the harvest in 1964 when Mr Holt was away fishing. All these matters preceded the first of the seven assurances on which Mr Gillett relied, so they are in a sense no more than background. But they are very important background because they refute Mr Martin's suggestion (placed in the forefront of his skeleton argument) that Mr Gillett's claim should be regarded as a 'startling' claim by someone who was no more than an employee. On the contrary, Mr McDonnell was not putting it too high when he said that for thirty years Mr and Mrs Gillett and their sons provided Mr Holt with a sort of surrogate family.

However a surrogate family of that sort is not the same as a birth family, and it is clear that Mr Gillett and his wife must often have been aware of the ambivalence of their position. Mr Holt was generous but it was the generosity of the patron; his will prevailed; Mr and Mrs Gillett were expected to, and did, subordinate their wishes to his (compare *Re Basham* [1986] 1 WLR 1498, 1505H). One telling example of this was over the education of their sons. Mr Holt decided that he would like to pay for the Gilletts' elder son, Robert, to go to Mr Holt's old school (Greshams in Norfolk). The offer did not extend to their younger son, Andrew, and the Gilletts not unnaturally felt that if one boy was to go to boarding school then both should go. In the end Robert went to Greshams and Andrew to a less well-known boarding school at Grimsby, and Mr and Mrs Gillett used some maturing short-term endowment policies and increased their overdraft in order to bear half the combined cost of the school fees and extras.

Mr Gillett also incurred substantial expenditure on the farmhouse at The Beeches, most of it after the clear assurance which Mr Holt gave him when, in 1975, he ventured to ask for something in writing: "that was not necessary as it was all going to be ours anyway". This was after the Gilletts had sold their own small house at Thimbleby and so had stepped off the property-owning ladder which they had got on to in 1964.

... Mr Gillett and his wife devoted the best years of their lives to working for Mr Holt and his company, showing loyalty and devotion to his business interests, his social life and his personal wishes, on the strength of clear and repeated assurances of testamentary benefits. They received (in 1983) 20 percent of the shares in KAHL, which must be regarded as received in anticipation of, and on account of, such benefits. Then in 1995 they had the bitter humiliation of summary dismissal and a police investigation of alleged dishonesty which the defendants called no evidence to justify at trial. I do not find Mr Gillett's claim startling.... I would find it startling if the law did not give a remedy in such circumstances.

SATISFYING THE EQUITY

Since Mr Gillett has established his claim to equitable relief, this court must decide what is the most appropriate form for the relief to take. The aim is (as Sir Arthur Hobhouse said in *Plimmer v Mayor of Wellington* (1884) 9 App Cas 699, 714) to "look at the circumstances in each case to decide in what way the equity can be satisfied". The court approaches this task in a cautious way, in order to achieve what Scarman LJ (in *Crabb v Arun DC* [1976] Ch 179, 198) called "the minimum equity to do justice to the plaintiff". The wide range of possible relief appears from Snell's Equity 30th ed. pp. 641–3.

In this case the satisfaction of the equity presents unusually difficult problems. Often (as in *Inwards v Baker* or *Re Basham*) the property in dispute is a small house or a small house and some modest savings and the litigants are not wealthy enough to be much troubled by inheritance tax, capital gains tax or Schedule E tax on 'golden handshakes'. In this case, by contrast, it is necessary to take account of taxes and the constraints of company law. Since the litigation began Mr Holt has made some very substantial gifts in favour of Mr Wood. These have involved some complex manoeuvres (although these seem to have been inspired by legitimate tax-planning considerations, and not by a desire to put assets beyond Mr Gillett's reach). It is therefore necessary to summarize the present position (as it was explained to this court on instructions).

· · · ·

[After doing so, Lord Justice Walker concluded:]

The Substance of the Result to Be Achieved

Mr and Mrs Gillett are to be entitled to the freehold of the whole of The Beeches (that is the farmhouse, the land occupied by Countryside Companions and the land farmed under contract by Aubourn) together with the sum of £100,000 to compensate for the exclusion of Mr Gillett from all the rest of the farming business. That figure represents an overall assessment of what the justice of the case requires, taking account of numerous matters large and small, including Mr Gillett's exceptionally long and devoted service on the one hand and the element of acceleration on the other hand. Liability for rent in respect of The Beeches will cease at once but Aubourn will be entitled to get in this year's harvest unless the parties agree otherwise. The bank mortgage must be discharged or shifted to other assets of KAHL. The £100,000 will carry interest at 5 per cent per annum from today. I do not exclude the possibility of some or all of that sum being satisfied (by agreement between the parties) by the transfer of other assets in specie, but I recognise that the layout of the properties, and the need for a clean break, may make such an agreement unlikely. It seems clear that the freehold of The Beeches plus £100,000 must exceed the net assets value of the Gilletts' 20 per cent shareholdings in KAHL; but to the extent that it does not exceed that value, the distribution must be made either in satisfaction of (or otherwise in consideration of) their shareholdings.

(d) *Yeoman's Row Management Limited v. Cobbe*†

U.K. House of Lords

[LORD SCOTT OF FOSCOTE:]

[2] The essence of the problem to be resolved in this case can be quite shortly stated. A is the owner of land with potential for residential development and enters into negotiations with B for the sale of the land to B. They reach an oral "agreement in principle" on the core terms of the sale but no written contract, or even a draft contract for discussion, is produced. There remain some terms still to be agreed. The structure of the agreement in principle that A and B have reached is that B, at his own expense, will make and prosecute an application for the desired residential development and that, if the desired planning permission is obtained, A will sell the land to B, or more probably to a company nominated by B, for an agreed up-front price, £x. B will then, again at his own expense, develop the land in accordance with the planning permission, sell off the residential units, and, when the gross proceeds of sale received by B equals £2x, any further gross proceeds of sale will be divided equally between A and B. Pursuant to this agreement in principle B makes and prosecutes an application for planning permission for the residential development that A and he

---

† [2008] UKHL 55.

have agreed upon. B is encouraged by A to do so. In doing so B spends a considerable sum of money as well, of course, as a considerable amount of time. The application is successful and the desired planning permission is obtained. A then seeks to re-negotiate the core financial terms of the sale, asking, in particular, for a substantial increase in the sum of money that would represent £x. B is unwilling to commit himself to the proposed new financial terms and A is unwilling to proceed on the basis of the originally agreed financial terms. So B commences legal proceedings. The question for your Lordships is what relief, in the circumstances described, B should be granted, for, I believe, none of your Lordships considers that he would not be entitled to any.

. . . .

THE FACTS

[5] A, in the present case, is the appellant company, Yeoman's Row Management Ltd. B is the respondent, Mr Cobbe. He is an experienced property developer. The property in question consists of a block of, originally, thirteen flats, one of which has, since 1983, been the home of Mrs Lisle-Mainwaring and, until his fairly recent death, her husband. In about 1986 Mr and Mrs Lisle-Mainwaring, no doubt recognising the development potential of the property, decided to purchase it. They used the appellant company, of which they were the directors and shareholders, as the vehicle by means of which to do so. First, however, Mrs Lisle-Mainwaring acquired a long leasehold interest in her flat (and, later, two other flats with which her flat was then physically combined into one unit). Then, in April 1998, the property was transferred to the appellant company subject to Mrs Lisle-Mainwaring's long lease and to the tenancies of the other flats, five of which were held on Rent Act protected tenancies. Negotiations with Mr Cobbe about the development of the property began in February 2001. It was Mrs Lisle-Mainwaring who, on behalf of the appellant, played the leading role in the negotiations that led, towards the end of 2002, to an oral agreement in principle being reached between her and Mr Cobbe. This agreement replaced an earlier agreement in principle that she and Mr Cobbe had reached and is, for that reason, referred to in the judgments of the trial judge, Etherton J, and Mummery LJ in the Court of Appeal as "the second agreement". I shall, for convenience, also do so.

[6] The substance of the second agreement was (i) that Mr Cobbe, at his own expense, would apply for planning permission to demolish the existing block of flats and to erect, in its place, a terrace of six houses, (ii) that, upon the grant of planning permission and the obtaining of vacant possession, the property would be sold to Mr Cobbe, or to a company nominated by him, for an up-front payment to the appellant of £12 million, (iii) and that Mr Cobbe, or the nominee company, would develop the property in accordance with the planning permission and (iv) would sell the six houses and pay to the appellant 50 per cent of the amount, if any, by which the gross proceeds of sale exceeded £24 million. So, in effect, Mr Cobbe was to take the risk, first, that planning permission might be refused, in which case his expenditure and time spent in seeking to obtain the planning permission would be wasted, and, secondly, that the gross proceeds of sale, after deduction of the cost of obtaining planning permission, the £12 million and the building and other costs of development, might leave him with an inadequate profit or even none at all. The amount that he, or his nominee company, would have to pay as the up-front price would clearly have constituted an important element in his calculations.

[7] The oral agreement in principle that had been reached, i.e. the core terms, did not cover everything that would have been expected in due course to be dealt with in a formal written contract. It must have been expected, for example, that Mrs Lisle-Mainwaring would have wanted some provision to be included in the formal contract regarding the reasonably expeditious commencement and progress of the development and, also, some security and timetable for the payment of the appellant's share of the excess over £24 million of the gross proceeds of sale. The nature of the transaction would plainly have excluded reliance on a vendor's lien. Mr Cobbe, for his part, would probably have wanted some contractual assurance as to the timing of the availability of vacant possession of the block of flats. These would not have been expected to have been difficult matters on which to reach agreement but were all matters for future discussion, and the outcome of future negotiations has always an inherent uncertainty.

[8] Planning permission for the demolition of the existing block of flats and the erection of a terrace of six houses on the site was formally granted on 5 April 2004 but the Council resolution approving the grant had been passed on 17 March 2004 and Mrs Lisle-Mainwaring on 18 March announced her dissatisfaction with the financial terms of the second agreement and demanded an up-front price of £20 million in place of the originally agreed £12 million.

She suggested that the appellant's share of the proceeds of sale of the development should become 40 per cent of the amount by which the gross proceeds exceeded £40 million. Mr Cobbe at first agreed to these changes but subsequently, after further reflection on the commercial implications, withdrew his agreement, and insisted on adherence to the financial terms of the second agreement. Mrs Lisle-Mainwaring refused to proceed on those terms and the *impasse* led to Mr Cobbe commencing the proceedings which are now before the House.

[Note: Lord Scott decided that Mr Cobbe should not receive a proprietary remedy but instead a personal remedy to compensate him for his costs and time (a *quantum meruit*). His judgment became the leading decision insofar as the majority of judges concurred with his reasoning and result. That said, it has attracted scholarly criticism for perhaps muddling the principles and remedies available. Lord Walker's decision, while concurring in the result reached, is arguably a more lucid exposition of this area of the law and is more applicable to our study in this chapter. It follows:]

[LORD WALKER OF GESTINGTHORPE:]

[46] Equitable estoppel is a flexible doctrine which the Court can use, in appropriate circumstances, to prevent injustice caused by the vagaries and inconstancy of human nature. But it is not a sort of joker or wild card to be used whenever the Court disapproves of the conduct of a litigant who seems to have the law on his side. Flexible though it is, the doctrine must be formulated and applied in a disciplined and principled way. Certainty is important in property transactions. As Deane J said in the High Court of Australia in *Muschinski v Dodds* (1985) 160 CLR 583, 615–616,

> Under the law of [Australia] — as, I venture to think, under the present law of England — proprietary rights fall to be governed by principles of law and not by some mix of judicial discretion, subjective views about which party 'ought to win' and 'the formless void of individual moral opinion'.

[47] The principle has been applied in quite a wide variety of factual situations, sometimes of a domestic nature, sometimes commercial. Any formulation of the principle must, if it is to be comprehensive, be expressed in such general terms as to give little idea of what it is really about — what Lord Hoffmann (comparing estoppel with legitimate expectation in *R (Reprotech (Pebsham) Ltd) v East Sussex County*

Council [2003] 1 WLR 348, para 35) referred to as "the moral values which underlie the private law concept of estoppel."

[48] The authors of Gray and Gray (para 10.189) propose a classification which Mr Ivory QC (for the respondent, Mr Cobbe) adopted in his printed case:

> The concatenation of ideas underlying proprietary estoppel emerges from three broad, and not entirely distinct, categories of circumstance. These categories comprise (1) the 'imperfect gift' cases, (2) the 'common expectation' cases, and (3) the 'unilateral mistake' cases. These cases alike present the essential characteristics of proprietary estoppel, but each class of case in its turn gives a heightened emphasis to one or other of the constituent elements of representation, reliance and unconscionable disadvantage. The tendency in the modern case law is to synthesise the jurisprudence of proprietary estoppel in a more unified doctrine of 'detrimental reliance'.

I may have made a small personal contribution to that tendency. But the difficulty and importance of this appeal, and the very full examination of the authorities which counsel have undertaken, remind me that synthesis and unification, however desirable as objectives, have their dangers. Without embarking on anything like an exhaustive review of the case law, I propose to look at some of the key authorities with Gray and Gray's suggested taxonomy in mind.

. . . .

[51] Cases of unilateral mistake occurred quite frequently in the 19th century, when the construction of canals and railways, coupled with the complexity of unregistered conveyancing in those days, made it not uncommon for building works to be carried out on land whose owner (or part-owner) had not agreed to the works. An example is *Rochdale Canal Company v King* (1853) 16 Beav 630, 633–637, in which Sir John Romilly MR said

> The principle on which the Defendants rely is one often recognised by this Court, namely, that if one man stand by and encourage another, though but passively, to lay out money, under an erroneous opinion of title, or under the obvious expectation that no obstacle will afterwards be interposed in the way of his enjoyment, the Court will not permit any subsequent interference with it, by him who formally promoted and encouraged those acts of which he now either complains or seeks to take advantage. This is the rule laid down in *Dann v Spurrier* (7 Ves

231), *Powell v Thomas* (6 Hare 300), and many other cases, to which it is unnecessary to refer, because the principle is clear.

[52] The great case of *Ramsden v Dyson* (1866) LR 1 HL 129 has, rightly, been closely examined in the course of the appeal. The Vice-Chancellor had held that two tenants of Sir John Ramsden, the owner of a large estate near Huddersfield, were entitled to long leases of plots on the estate. They ostensibly held the plots as tenants at will only, but they had spent their own money in building on the strength of assurances, said to have been given to them by the landowner's agent, that they would never be disturbed. This House reversed that decision by a majority ... Lord Kingsdown's statement of the law (at p. 170, emphasising the element of encouragement) has often been preferred ... [Note: the passage to which Lord Walker was referring is as follows: "If a man, under a verbal agreement with a landlord for a certain interest in land, or, what amounts to the same thing, under an expectation, created or encouraged by the landlord, that he shall have a certain interest, takes possession of such land, with the consent of the landlord, and upon the faith of such promise or expectation, with the knowledge of the landlord, and without objection by him, lays out money upon the land, a Court of equity will compel the landlord to give effect to such promise or expectation."]

[54] *Plimmer v Mayor, Councillors and Citizens of the City of Wellington* (1884) 9 App Cas 699 was a common expectation case. Mr Plimmer seems to have been a businessman of some substance, and he was dealing with the provincial government, but their arrangements seem to have been attended by a high degree of informality. In that respect it is in striking contrast to *Attorney General of Hong Kong v Humphreys Estate (Queen's Gardens)* [1987] AC 114, discussed below. In *Plimmer* the nub of the Privy Council's decision appears at p. 712:

> In the present case, the equity is not claimed because the landowner has stood by in silence while his tenant has spent money on his land. This is a case in which the landowner has, for his own purposes, requested the tenant to make the improvements. The Government were engaged in the important work of introducing immigrants into the colony. For some reason, not now apparent, they were not prepared to make landing-places of their own, and in fact they did not do so until the year 1863. So they applied to John Plimmer to make his landing place more commodious by substantial extension of his jetty and the erection of a warehouse for baggage. Is it to be said that, when he had incurred the expense of doing the work asked for, the Government could turn round and revoke his licence at their will? Could they in July, 1856, have deprived him summarily of the use of the jetty? It would be in a high degree unjust that they should do so, and that the parties should have intended such a result is, in the absence of evidence, incredible.

[55] In *Plimmer* the opinion of the Privy Council, delivered by Sir Arthur Hobhouse, is of interest because it discusses (at pp. 710–712) the case of *Ramsden v Dyson* at some length, and rejects the argument (based on Lord Cranworth's speech) that some sort of unilateral mistake is necessary in every case. *Plimmer* is also important for the discussion (at pp. 713–714) of the Court's discretion as to the remedy to be granted in any case where an equitable estoppel is established.

.   .   .   .

[Lord Walker noted the confusion introduced by the so-called five probanda in *Willmot v. Barber* (1880) and continued:]

[58] In *Taylor's Fashions* Oliver J analysed the authorities in a masterly way and put this part of the law back on the right track. ... Oliver J discussed *Ramsden v Dyson* at some length and followed the preference shown by the Privy Council in *Plimmer* for Lord Kingsdown's analysis ...

[59] Towards the end of his judgment Oliver J made some important general observations (at pp. 151–152):

> Furthermore the more recent cases indicate, in my judgment, that the application of the *Ramsden v Dyson* LR 1 HL 129 principle — whether you call it proprietary estoppel, estoppel by acquiescence or estoppel by encouragement is really immaterial — requires a very much broader approach which is directed rather at ascertaining whether, in particular individual circumstances, it would be unconscionable for a party to be permitted to deny that which, knowingly, or unknowingly, he has allowed or encouraged another to assume to his detriment than to enquiring whether the circumstances can be fitted within the confines of some preconceived formula serving as a universal yardstick for every form of unconscionable behaviour.

This passage certainly favours a broad or unified approach to equitable estoppel. But it is emphatically not a licence for abandoning careful analysis for unprincipled and subjective judicial opinion. It is worth noting that on this part of the case Oliver J analysed over twenty authorities spanning more than two centuries.

[60] The last authority that calls for close examination is *Attorney General of Hong Kong v Humphreys Estate (Queen's Gardens) Ltd* [1987] AC 114. It was concerned with protracted (and ultimately abortive) negotiations for an exchange of valuable property between the Government of Hong Kong (which was to acquire a block of flats to house senior civil servants) and a large property developer (which was to take a Crown lease of Queen's Gardens in order to develop it, together with other land already owned by the developer). An agreement in principle had been reached in discussions recorded in lengthy written correspondence, which unsurprisingly referred to the agreement in principle as being "subject to contract". Experienced lawyers were acting on both sides, and they and their clients were well aware that an enforceable contract would come into existence only on exchange of contracts as finally agreed between the lawyers.

[61] Despite that both sides incurred expenditure in the expectation that a contract would eventually be entered into. The Government took possession of the flats and spent money on them; the developer entered Queen's Gardens and carried out work at its expense. But each side was acting at its own risk, because each knew perfectly well that it had no enforceable rights against the other. The Government's main witness, Mr Ward, was a surveyor who accepted that he was not a party to the negotiations under which the Government moved into the flats and that he had no authority to take decisions. The parties' knowledge that neither had any enforceable rights was fatal to the Government's claim to rely on equitable estoppel. Lord Templeman, delivering the opinion of the Board, summarised the position at p. 124:

> Their Lordships accept that the Government acted to their detriment and to the knowledge of HKL in the hope that HKL would not withdraw from the agreement in principle. But in order to found an estoppel the Government must go further. First the Government must show that HKL created or encouraged a belief or expectation on the part of the Government that HKL would not withdraw from the agreement in principle. Secondly the Government must show that the Government relied on that belief or expectation. Their Lordships agree with the courts of Hong Kong that the Government fail on both counts.

[62] In reaching that conclusion the Privy Council naturally referred to, and placed some reliance on, the use of the phrase "subject to contract" in the correspondence between the parties. But in my opinion that was simply a routine acknowledgement of what both parties knew very well in any event: that they were involved in a complex process of negotiation which might come to nothing (as occurred when the Hong Kong property market fell sharply in 1984). The Government of Hong Kong was at pains, as appears from the documents quoted by the Privy Council (and still more from the fuller quotations from the documents in the judgments in the Hong Kong Court of Appeal, [1986] HKLR 669), to emphasise on every occasion that it was not committing itself in any way. By the same token, it could not expect the developer to be committing itself, either in law or in equity. It could not be unconscionable for the developer to follow a course which the Government repeatedly insisted was open to itself.

[63] ... This case is, in the terminology used by Gray and Gray, a case of "common expectation" if it is anything. The critical issue, to my mind, is whether there was, on the judge's findings, a common expectation of the type capable of raising an equitable estoppel. ...

. . . .

[65] In *Plimmer* the Privy Council (at p. 712, the passage I have already quoted) regarded it as an irresistible inference that Mr Plimmer thought that his compliance with the Government's request gave him a right to security of tenure, even if the duration of that security was uncertain. It is not enough to hope, or even to have a confident expectation, that the person who has given assurances will eventually do the proper thing.

[66] The point that hopes by themselves are not enough is made most clearly in cases with a commercial context, of which *Attorney General of Hong Kong* is the most striking example. It does not appear so often in cases with more of a domestic or family flavour, from *Inwards v Baker* [1965] 2 QB 29 and *Pascoe v Turner* [1979] 1 WLR 431 to *Windeler v Whitehall* [1990] 2 FLR 505, *Gillett v Holt* [2001] Ch 210, *Grundy v Ottey* [2003] WTLR 1253, *Jennings v Rice* [2003] 1 P & CR 8 and *Lissimore v Downing* [2003] 2 FLR 308. The son who built the bungalow in *Inwards v Baker*, the young farm manager in *Gillett v Holt*, the elderly country neighbour in *Jennings v Rice* and the female companions in the other three cases almost certainly did not take any

legal advice until after the events relied on as creating the estoppel. They may not have had a clear idea of the quantum of what they expected to get (in *Grundy v Ottey*, unusually, the expected quantum was precisely defined). But in those cases in which an estoppel was established, the claimant believed that the assurance on which he or she relied was binding and irrevocable.

[67] It may possibly be that some of the domestic cases might have been decided differently if the nature of the claimant's belief had been an issue vigorously investigated in cross-examination. In *Gillett v Holt* there was such cross-examination ([2001] Ch 210, 229),

> Mr Gillett was cross-examined at length about some increasingly improbable eventualities: that Mr Holt would marry his housekeeper, that he would have children, that his elderly sister would suddenly lose all her investments and turn to him for help. Mr Gillett naturally enough conceded that in those circumstances Mr Holt could or would have made some provision for these moral obligations. But, in giving evidence, he stuck resolutely to the promises made to him ... Mr Gillett was not in the witness box to take part in a seminar on the elements of proprietary estoppel (although parts of his cross-examination suggest otherwise). He was there to give evidence, which was largely unchallenged and which the judge accepted, about the assurances made to him and his detrimental reliance on them.

In most of these cases the controversial issues tend to be whether any sufficient assurance was made, and whether it was causally relevant (often cross-examination is directed towards establishing that the claimant would have done the same in any case, out of friendship or family feeling).

[68] It is unprofitable to trawl through the authorities on domestic arrangements in order to compare the forms of words used by judges to describe the claimants' expectations in cases where this issue (hope or something more?) was not squarely raised. But the fact that the issue is seldom raised is not, I think, coincidental. In the commercial context, the claimant is typically a business person with access to legal advice and what he or she is expecting to get is a *contract*. In the domestic or family context, the typical claimant is not a business person and is not receiving legal advice. What he or she wants and expects to get is an *interest* in immovable property, often for long-term occupation as a home. The focus is not on intangible legal rights but on the tangible property which he or she expects to get. The typical

domestic claimant does not stop to reflect (until disappointed expectations lead to litigation) whether some further legal transaction (such as a grant by deed, or the making of a will or codicil) is necessary to complete the promised title.

[69] The judge's findings of fact, which are not challenged in any significant respect, need to be examined with these points in mind. His findings are clearly identified and set out in paras 62 to 84 of his judgment. To say that they are dispassionate is not to suggest that they are in any way unfocused; quite the reverse.

[70] The crucial findings, to my mind, are in paras 68 to 70:

> 68. On the other hand, I find that, from the end of 2002 until the grant of the Planning Permission on 17 March 2004, Mr Cobbe believed the following: that the ... Agreement comprised all the critical commercial terms, that any outstanding terms were of secondary importance and in the nature of legal mechanics, which would inevitably be agreed one way or another, and that Mrs Lisle-Mainwaring was, and regarded herself as, bound in honour to enter into a formal written contract embodying the terms of the ... Agreement if Mr Cobbe obtained planning permission for the development of the Property by its demolition and its replacement by six houses.
>
> 69. I also accept Mr Cobbe's evidence that he himself felt the ... Agreement was binding on him in honour. I reject the submission of Mr Seitler to the contrary based on the oral evidence of Mr McMahon, as to what Mr McMahon had been told by, and the general impression that was given to him by, Mr Cobbe, and on a note made by Mr Cobbe in 2004 concerning the First Agreement and its termination.
>
> 70. Mr Cobbe envisaged that, if Mrs Lisle-Mainwaring decided not to proceed with the development of the Property, prior to planning permission being granted, he would be reimbursed his reasonable expenditure. If she did not withdraw, and such planning permission was refused, he would not be reimbursed.

[71] So the judge found that Mr Cobbe believed that Mrs Lisle-Mainwaring was, and regarded herself as, bound in honour to enter into a formal written contract if planning permission was granted; and that Mr Cobbe regarded himself as similarly bound. It is implicit — in my view necessarily and deliberately implicit — in the judge's carefully chosen language that neither Mrs Lisle-Mainwaring nor Mr Cobbe regarded herself or himself as legally bound. They were both very experienced in property matters

and they knew perfectly well that that was not the position.

[72] Another unusual feature of this case is the judge's finding that Mr Cobbe believed that he would be reimbursed his reasonable expenditure if Mrs Lisle-Mainwaring decided to withdraw from the arrangement before planning permission was granted. This emphasis on the actual grant of planning permission as the crucial condition produces a strange result: would it be conscionable for Mrs Lisle-Mainwaring to withdraw (subject only to reimbursement) at a stage when 99% of the work necessary to obtain planning permission had been done, and success was virtually certain, but unconscionable to do so once success had actually been achieved? This feature of the arrangement emphasises the risk which Mr Cobbe was undertaking, in deciding to rely on Mrs Lisle Mainwaring's sense of honour.

[73] The judge then proceeded to analyse the position (paras 85–129 of his judgment), stating at the outset his conclusion that the facts did give rise to a proprietary estoppel in favour of Mr Cobbe. The judge's analysis is lengthy and closely-reasoned but there are, as I see it, three main themes.

[74] The first is the importance (para 86) of Mr Cobbe's

> belief that, even though the Second Agreement was not a legally binding and enforceable contract, Mrs Lisle Mainwaring regarded it as binding.

The judge did not add "in honour only" but that was necessarily implicit. Mr Cobbe knew enough about the law of property, and about Mrs Lisle-Mainwaring's astuteness, to know that there was no legally binding contract between them, and that Mrs Lisle-Mainwaring would not regard an obligation arising in honour only as legally binding. This point then re-emerged in para 123, near the end of the judge's analysis, with a reference to Mr Cobbe's belief that the arrangement "would be honoured, even though it was not legally binding." "Honour" is used, as a verb, to describe compliance with both contractual and non-contractual promises, and so its use rather elides the difference between them.

.   .   .   .

[81] In my opinion none of these cases casts any doubt on the general principle laid down by this House in *Ramsden v Dyson*, that conscious reliance on honour alone will not give rise to an estoppel.

Nor do they cast doubt on the general principle that the court should be very slow to introduce uncertainty into commercial transactions by over-ready use of equitable concepts such as fiduciary obligations and equitable estoppel. That applies to commercial negotiations whether or not they are expressly stated to be subject to contract.

[82] The judge went on to consider how he should exercise his discretion so as to give effect to the estoppel which he had found to be established. The difficulties that he encountered are a further indication, I think, of the incongruity of trying to apply the doctrine of equitable estoppel to a complicated commercial negotiation in which one crucial element — how Mr Cobbe was going to fund the project, and provide security both for the funding and for Mrs Lisle-Mainwaring's overage interest — had hardly been addressed.

.   .   .   .

[86] My reasons for differing from the courts below *[Ed note: both the trial judge and an unanimous Court of Appeal had found an estoppel]* are three-fold (although, as always seems to happen in this area of law, the points are not completely distinct; they rub shoulders together). They broadly correspond to the first four grounds of appeal in the Court of Appeal, but taking the first and second grounds together.

[87] The informal bargain made in this case was unusually complex, as both courts below acknowledged. When a claim based on equitable estoppel is made in a domestic setting the informal bargain or understanding is typically on the following lines: if you live here as my carer/companion/lover you will have a home for life. The expectation is of acquiring and keeping an interest in an identified property. In this case, by contrast, Mr Cobbe was expecting to get a contract. Under that contract he (or much more probably a company controlled by him) would have been entitled to acquire the property for a down-payment of £12m, but only as part of a deal under which the block of flats on the site was to be demolished, the site cleared, and six very expensive townhouses were to be erected instead, and sold for the best prices that they would fetch. The interests of Mrs Lisle-Mainwaring and YRML were not restricted to the £12m down-payment. She was to receive a further sum amounting (together with the £12m) to one-half of the gross proceeds of sale of the six townhouses. She would expect this future sum to be secured on the property. The bank or other institution providing the development finance would

also expect its lending to be fully secured. At some point a very large sum of money was going to be secured on an empty site. None of these matters seems to have been under negotiation before the deal collapsed in March 2004. Mr Ivory made a virtue of that point, arguing that the absence of any active negotiations between September 2002 and March 2004 shows that the parties did not expect to encounter any difficulty in agreeing these matters. It is more likely, to my mind, that they both accepted that there was no point in tackling them until planning permission had been obtained.

[88] I have already mentioned the judge's finding that Mr Cobbe believed (para 68),

> that the Second Agreement comprised all the critical commercial terms, that any outstanding terms were of secondary importance and in the nature of legal mechanics, which would inevitably be agreed one way or another.

Mr Dowding did not directly attack this conclusion, but he did submit (to my mind convincingly) that the matters which were not agreed (or even under negotiation) were far from trivial. The fact that one or both parties may have expected that all outstanding points would be resolved does not mean that that outcome was certain or near-certain (as is confirmed by recent events in the mortgage lending and property sectors).

. . . .

[91] When examined in that way, Mr Cobbe's case seems to me to fail on the simple but fundamental point that, as persons experienced in the property world, both parties knew that there was no legally binding contract, and that either was therefore free to discontinue the negotiations without legal liability — that is liability in equity as well as at law, to echo the words of Lord Cranworth quoted in para 53 above. Mr Cobbe was therefore running a risk, but he stood to make a handsome profit if the deal went ahead, and the market stayed favourable. He may have thought that any attempt to get Mrs Lisle-Mainwaring to enter into a written contract before the grant of planning permission would be counter-productive. Whatever his reasons for doing so, the fact is that he ran a commercial risk, with his eyes

open, and the outcome has proved unfortunate for him. It is true that he did not expressly state, at the time, that he was relying solely on Mrs Lisle-Mainwaring's sense of honour, but to draw that sort of distinction in a commercial context would be as unrealistic, in my opinion, as to draw a firm distinction depending on whether the formula "subject to contract" had or had not actually been used.

[92] Mr Dowding devoted a separate section of his printed case to arguing that even if the elements for an estoppel were in other respects present, it would not in any event be unconscionable for Mrs Lisle-Mainwaring to insist on her legal rights. That argument raises the question whether "unconscionability" is a separate element in making out a case of estoppel, or whether to regard it as a separate element would be what Professor Peter Birks once called "a fifth wheel on the coach" (Birks & Pretto (eds) Breach of Trust (2002) p. 226). But Birks was there criticising the use of "unconscionable" to describe a *state of mind* (*Bank of Credit & Commerce International (Overseas) Ltd v Akindele* [2001] Ch 437, 455). Here it is being used (as in my opinion it should always be used) as an objective value judgment on *behaviour* (regardless of the state of mind of the individual in question). As such it does in my opinion play a very important part in the doctrine of equitable estoppel, in unifying and confirming, as it were, the other elements. If the other elements appear to be present but the result does not shock the conscience of the court, the analysis needs to be looked at again. In this case Mrs Lisle-Mainwaring's conduct was unattractive. She chose to stand on her rights rather than respecting her non-binding assurances, while Mr Cobbe continued to spend time and effort, between Christmas 2003 and March 2004, in obtaining planning permission. But Mr Cobbe knew that she was bound in honour only, and so in the eyes of equity her conduct, although unattractive, was not unconscionable.

[93] ... I would (in common, as I understand it, with all of your Lordships) allow this appeal and direct an inquiry with a view to reimbursing Mr Cobbe on a generous scale not only for his out of pocket expenditure in seeking and obtaining planning permission, but also for his time and trouble in doing so.

(e) Promissory Estoppel, Proprietary Estoppel and Constructive Trust in Canada: "What's in a name?"†

Jane Matthews Glenn

That which we call a rose
By any other name would smell as sweet.[1]

INTRODUCTION

The common law is like an English country garden, where a wide variety of plants of all shapes, sizes, colours, provenance and purpose thrive together in apparent disorder but with striking overall effect. Most of the plants are native species of ancient lineage, although judicious pruning and cross-fertilization have often changed their original aspect and adapted them to new uses; some of the plants have been transplanted from elsewhere, and their survival has depended on the suitability of soil and climate as well as the care and attention of gardeners.

England and other common law Commonwealth jurisdictions, except Canada, have concentrated much care and attention on cultivation of the doctrine of estoppel, so that there is now a profusion of estoppels, with promissory and proprietary estoppel having pride of place; none of these jurisdictions has shown particular interest in cultivating the remedial constructive trust. Common law Canada, on the other hand, has tended to ignore estoppel, being content to import English examples without more, and has concentrated its attention on cultivation of the constructive trust, particularly a vigorous American-style remedial constructive trust.

The range of plants in an English country garden makes them often difficult to classify — to determine whether they are plants of different genera, different species of the same genus, or simply different varieties of the same species. So it is with the common law. This paper looks at promissory estoppel, proprietary estoppel and the remedial constructive trust — more precisely, the unjust enrichment constructive trust — with a view to determining whether, like plants, they are fundamentally different, somewhat similar or basically the same.

. . . . .

I. HISTORICAL DEVELOPMENT

All three concepts — promissory and proprietary estoppel, and the constructive trust — were developed by the courts of equity to attenuate injustices resulting from application of strict legal rules, with these rules being basically contractual in the case of promissory estoppel and proprietary in the cases of proprietary estoppel and constructive trusts. All three trace their origins back to at least the eighteenth century, if not earlier, although these early roots are strongest in the case of constructive trusts. Both proprietary and promissory estoppel were rationalized by late nineteenth century court decisions. And all three concepts were further shaped by the influence of Lord Denning in the latter half of the twentieth century.

Promissory estoppel: The precursor of promissory estoppel, estoppel by representation, is ancient, although promissory estoppel itself did not emerge until the late nineteenth century, notably in the 1877 House of Lords' decision in *Hughes v. Metropolitan Railway Co.*[4] It then lay more or less dormant until it was taken up by Lord Denning in *Central London Property Trust Ltd. v. High Trees House Ltd.,* decided in 1946,[5] and was refined subsequently. *High Trees* is generally regarded as the English high-water mark of promissory estoppel, and the most interesting doctrinal developments in regard to it since then have come from Australia, with courts and scholars there advocating unification of the various types of estoppel — including promissory and proprietary estoppel — into one overarching concept.[6]

Proprietary estoppel: Proprietary estoppel owes its main impetus to an 1866 House of Lords' case, *Ramsden v. Dyson.* Lord Cranworth, speaking for the majority, there articulated the equitable principle in narrowly circumscribed terms based on mistake:

> If a stranger begins to build on my land supposing it to be his own, and I, perceiving his mistake, abstain from setting him right, and leave him to persevere in his error, a Court of equity will not allow me afterwards to assert my title to

† (2007) 30 Dalhousie L.J. 141 at 142–48, 151, 154, 157–63. [Notes/references omitted.] Reproduced with permission of the author.

the land on which he had expended money on the supposition that the land was his own....

But it will be observed that to raise such an equity two things are required, first, that the person expending the money supposes himself to be building on his own land; and, secondly, that the real owner at the time of the expenditure knows that the land belongs to him and not to the person expending the money in the belief that he is the owner.[7] The idea of mistake was emphasized in 1880 by Fry J. in *Wilmott v. Barber*, in his oft-cited statement of the five "probanda" to be demonstrated by the person seeking to raise an estoppel: (1) that the plaintiff must have made a mistake as to his legal rights; (2) that he have expended some money or done some other act to his detriment on the faith of his mistaken belief; (3) that the defendant (the person sought to be estopped) know of the existence of his own right which is inconsistent with the right claimed by the plaintiff; (4) that the defendant know of the plaintiff's mistaken belief of his rights; and (5) that the defendant have encouraged the plaintiff in his expenditure of money or other acts, either directly or by abstaining from asserting his legal right.[8] This mistake-based approach is sometimes called "estoppel by acquiescence" and is clearly accepted in Canada today.[9]

... Constructive trust: Equity's long association with the trust, which dates back to at least the fifteenth century, means that the constructive trust as an institutional complement to the express trust developed continuously and incrementally, to encompass different categories of defendants; this took place largely between the seventeenth and nineteenth centuries,[12] without the periods of quiescence experienced with promissory and proprietary estoppel. Indeed, the 1726 touchstone case of *Keech v. Sandford*[13] continues to be taught and cited today. England flirted briefly with the idea of a remedial constructive trust in the 1960s and 1970s, again under the influence of Lord Denning,[14] but it was the Supreme Court of Canada that put the doctrine on a principled footing in its 1980 landmark decision in *Pettkus v. Becker*.[15]

II.   PRINCIPLES

Promissory estoppel, proprietary estoppel and constructive trust are creatures of equity, and equity is a court of conscience. Unconscionability, and the remedying of unconscionable conduct, is thus said to be the unifying principle for the two estoppels,[16] as each originates with a holding out by one party and has at its heart the detrimental reliance on this holding out by the other party. Similarly, good conscience is identified by the Supreme Court as the "common concept unifying the various instances in which a constructive trust may be found",[17] whether it be a remedial constructive trust imposed in situations of unjust enrichment of one party by another or an institutional constructive trust imposed in more disparate, category-based, situations.[18]

Promissory estoppel: Promissory estoppel is an equitable extension of the older "estoppel by representation." Both have three basic elements: a representation by one party to another; action by the other party in reliance on the representation; and resulting detriment to the party acting in reliance. The requirements concerning reliance and detriment are substantially similar in the two cases,[19] and the Supreme Court of Canada recently described them as follows:

> Detrimental reliance encompasses two distinct, but interrelated, concepts: reliance and detriment. The former requires a finding that the party seeking to establish the estoppel changed his or her course of conduct by acting or abstaining from acting in reliance upon the assumption, thereby altering his or her legal position. If the first step is met, the second requires a finding that, should the other party be allowed to abandon the assumption, detriment will be suffered by the estoppel raiser because of the change from his or her assumed position.[20]

. . . .

The emphasis on representation, or holding out, thus gives promissory estoppel, as all other estoppels, a certain flavour of unilateralism: the representation, or holding out, is by one party and the action in reliance is by another and subsequent to the holding out. However, a certain element of mutuality is also required, as the statement or conduct must be known to the other party and acted upon. This is described as "crossing the line."

> All estoppels must involve some statement or conduct by the party alleged to be estopped on which the alleged representee was entitled to rely and did rely. In this sense *all estoppels may be regarded as requiring some manifest representation which crosses the line between representor and representee, either by statement or conduct....*
>
> There cannot be any estoppel unless the alleged representor has said or done something, or failed to do something, with the result that — across the line between the parties — his action or inaction has produced some belief or expectation in the mind of the alleged representee, so that, depending on the circumstances, it would thereafter no longer be right to allow the alleged

representor to resile by challenging the belief or expectation which he has engendered.[24]

The mutuality is strongest in "estoppel by convention," identified by the Supreme Court of Canada in *Ryan v. Moore* as a form of estoppel by representation of fact or promissory estoppel (the Court also included proprietary estoppel in the list) requiring not just a representation by one party to the other, but a common assumption shared by both parties: "[t]he crucial requirement for estoppel by convention, which distinguishes it from the other types of estoppel, is that at the material time both parties must be of 'like mind.'... Mutual assent is what distinguishes the estoppel by convention from other types of estoppel."[25]

Proprietary estoppel: The constituent elements of proprietary estoppel are substantially the same as promissory estoppel: a holding out or representation (either by words, action or inaction) by one person to another, whether it be about an existing state of facts or a promise about future action; action in reliance on that holding out by the other; and resulting detriment to the party acting in reliance.[49] The essential differences between the two are, firstly, that proprietary estoppel requires that the representation be made by a property owner in relation to land and, secondly, that proprietary estoppel can be used as a sword as well as a shield (and is sometimes described as a "quasi-estoppel" for this reason). Indeed, the similarities between the two types of estoppel are so strong that proprietary estoppel is sometimes referred to as a simple subset of promissory estoppel: "Proprietary estoppel is a form of promissory estoppel. It is commonly supposed that estoppel cannot give rise to a cause of action, but proprietary estoppel appears to be an exception to that rule."[50] That proprietary estoppel can be used as a sword as well as a shield was clearly affirmed by the British Columbia Court of Appeal in *Zelmer v. Victor Projects Ltd*[51] in 1997, an affirmation relied on in other cases subsequently.

．　．　．　．

The reason for the paucity of such cases in Canada, when compared with England, Australia and other Commonwealth jurisdictions, is that they would usually be decided here on the basis of a remedial constructive trust. As Fridman put it:

> Canadian developments, in effect, have married the original constructive trust idea to the proprietary or equitable estoppel idea to produce something that is now quite distinct from both ...

Canadian decisions regard those who have provided money, work or services, leading to or assisting in the acquisition, creation or expansion of wealth or property, as the beneficiaries of a constructive trust imposed on the one who was legal owner of the resulting wealth or property. Where an English court might have resolved the issue by invoking the doctrine of estoppel, Canadian courts have dealt with the question of 'compensation' by utilising the constructive trust.[67] *Constructive trust:* Canada, like England, has long recognized the existence of a constructive trust as an institutional complement to the express trust in a variety of situations. These situations include unauthorized gains by a fiduciary, intermeddling in trust property by third parties, breaches of confidence, profiting from corporate and other opportunities, obtaining secret commissions and bribes, contracts for the sale of land, and so on.[68] Many but not all of these situations involve a pre-existing fiduciary relationship. The Supreme Court of Canada, by a slim majority, recently reaffirmed the continued recognition of the "institutional" constructive trust in Canada, and rationalized its application.[69]

But it is not the institutional constructive trust that is of interest as a comparator to promissory and proprietary estoppel, but rather the "remedial" constructive trust. The constructive trust as a remedy for unjust enrichment was developed slowly by the Supreme Court of Canada through a number of decisions, and was accepted for the first time by a majority of the Court in 1980 in *Pettkus v. Becker*. There Dickson J., speaking for six of the nine judges, identified unjust enrichment as lying "at the heart of the constructive trust," and set out the requirements for finding one:

> [T]here are three requirements to be satisfied before an unjust enrichment can be said to exist: an enrichment, a corresponding deprivation and absence of any juristic reason for the enrichment. This approach, it seems to me, is supported by general principles of equity that have been fashioned by the courts for centuries ... [70]

Enrichment and deprivation are relatively easy to identify and apply, and the Supreme Court takes a "straightforward economic approach" to them.[71] The former was described by McLachlin J. in *Regional Municipality of Peel v. Canada* as consisting of a tangible benefit conferred by the plaintiff on the defendant; it can be either a positive benefit, such as the payment of money, in which case the enrichment is presumed, or a negative benefit, such as relieving the defendant from an expense which must otherwise be paid (e.g., paying all household expenses, renovating or maintaining the property, assuming the burden of caring for young children or elderly parents, etc.), in which case the benefit must be proved.[72] Detriment comprises lost opportunity, and is assumed in the case of financial contribution but must be proved in the case of the contribution of care and services.[73]

The third requirement — absence of juristic reason for the enrichment — is the most difficult to assess. Dickson J. described it in *Pettkus v. Becker* in terms akin to proprietary estoppel (estoppel by acquiescence):

> As for the third requirement, I hold that where one person in a relationship ... prejudices herself in the reasonable expectation of receiving an interest in property and the other person in the relationship freely accepts benefits conferred by the first person in circumstances where he knows or ought to have known of that reasonable expectation, it would be unjust to allow the recipient of the benefit to retain it.[74]

McLachlin J. expanded upon this in *Peter v. Beblow:* "It is in connection with the third element — absence of juristic reason for the enrichment — that ... the court must consider whether the enrichment and detriment, morally neutral in themselves, are 'unjust.'"[75] And most recently, Iacobucci J. suggested a two-step approach in *Garland v. Consumers' Gas Co.:* firstly, that the plaintiff make out a *prima facie* case by proving the absence of an "established category" of juristic reasons (which include "a contract ... a disposition of law ... a donative intent ... and other valid common law, equitable or statutory obligations"); and secondly, that the *de facto* burden of proof would then shift to the defendant to rebut the presumption of unjustness thus raised by pointing to other circumstances which might constitute a valid juristic reason for the enrichment. The court would assess the circumstances raised in rebuttal by looking to two factors, "the reasonable expectations of the parties" and "public policy considerations."[76]

Unjust enrichment, for its part, can be used only as a sword, not a shield. This flows from its role as a cause of action and is not discussed in the cases.

The remedial constructive trust is now firmly established in Canada. It has been applied and further developed by the Supreme Court in a number of cases since *Pettkus v. Becker*, not just in decisions concerned with family property[77] but also in commercial and other disputes.[78] English courts, on the other hand, have eschewed the remedial constructive trust since the retirement of Lord Denning,[79] in favour of either a "common intention" constructive

trust when the plaintiff can prove direct financial contribution[80] or proprietary estoppel otherwise.

III. REMEDIES

Promissory estoppel: Because Canadian courts limit promissory estoppel to the role of defence to a main action, it does not give rise to any particular remedial issues. The defence is either successful, or not; the person making the representation is either estopped from going back on it, or not; and the main action proceeds apace and gives rise to the remedies appropriate to it. Canadian courts thus do not have to deal with the issue of principle of whether the appropriate estoppel remedy should reflect expectation of gain or simply compensate for loss flowing from the reliance. ...

Proprietary estoppel: The English cases show that the remedies available to the injured party under the doctrine of proprietary estoppel are varied and effective. They can be either personal or proprietary in nature, and the proprietary remedies can range from awarding an equitable charge or lien on the land, to recognizing an easement over property or a leasehold or life estate in it, through to awarding a share in the freehold title to the property, or the title itself — with or even without compensation to the landowner.[82] ...

Because Canadian courts tend to turn to the constructive trust to remedy cases of unjust enrichment arising from improvements made to the property of another, most of the recent Canadian appellate-level proprietary estoppel cases have awarded only limited interests in land, most often easements[84] requiring payment of compensation in one instance.[85]

Constructive trust: The constructive trust raises remedial questions similar to those raised by proprietary estoppel.[87] In fact, imposing a trust is just one of a panoply of measures to remedy an unjust enrichment, some of which are personal (e.g., compensation for labour performed or goods provided, accounting for profits) and some of which are proprietary (e.g., a lien or a trust). As La Forest J. expressed it in *Lac Minerals:* "While ... '[t]he principle of unjust enrichment lies at the heart of the constructive trust' ... the converse is not true. The constructive trust does not lie at the heart of the law of restitution. It is but one remedy, and will only be imposed in appropriate circumstances."[88] The court is thus free to choose the most appropriate remedy, with a proprietary remedy (the trust) being imposed where a monetary remedy would be inadequate and the nexus between the detriment and the property in question is sufficient.[89] Generally speaking, a proprietary remedy is quantified using the "value survived" approach, while a monetary remedy calls for the "value received" approach unless this would be unfair in the circumstances (particularly in a rising market in a family context).[90] These two approaches, which correspond loosely to the difference between equity and debt, echo the estoppel distinction between remedies based on expectation of gain or compensation for loss.[91]

· · · ·

CONCLUSIONS

What can we conclude about these three concepts, and the interrelationship between them? Are they, like plants, fundamentally different, somewhat similar or basically the same? At the most general level, the three are admittedly fundamentally different, as was mentioned in the introduction, as one (promissory estoppel) is a defence to an action, another (proprietary estoppel) a cause of action as well as a defence,[96] and the third (constructive trust) simply a remedy to a cause of action. But closer examination reveals certain underlying similarities among them.

A first-blush look at language and definitional elements suggests that the closest pairing is between the two estoppels, with the remedial — or unjust enrichment — trust being only somewhat similar to them. The estoppels are defined from the point of view of estoppel claimants, and focus on the detriment suffered by them: in this sense, they are framed in terms of unjust impoverishment.[97] In contrast, the remedial constructive trust is a response to unjust enrichment, and thus focuses on the benefit received by defendants. But this difference between estoppel and constructive trust is more apparent than real because unjust impoverishment and unjust enrichment are here two sides of the same coin. The definition of unjust enrichment is explicit about this, and includes the need for a counterbalancing detriment (or deprivation) as part of the formula; and a counterbalancing benefit to the reneging party would

seem implicitly part of estoppel, as the main reason for going back on one's word would be to obtain a benefit. The definitions of all three — promissory estoppel, proprietary estoppel and the unjust enrichment which is behind a constructive trust — are [more] similar than initially appears. Their similarity is further supported by the fact that their underlying principles, and especially the grounding of all three in matters of conscience, are basically the same.

However, a more detailed look at remedies and especially procedure — the sword/shield distinction — suggests that the closest pairing is between proprietary estoppel and the constructive trust, with promissory estoppel being the odd concept out.

As for remedies, both proprietary estoppel and unjust enrichment can give rise to proprietary remedies in appropriate circumstances, and timing is an issue for both. Most attention has focused on the time prior to judgment, and on the effect an eventual proprietary remedy can have on third party dealings taking place in this period. But a closer analysis suggests that there are three phases to consider — pre-judgment, post-judgment but pre-execution, and post-execution — with the claimant having different property interests at each stage.

· · · ·

A final, and more general, suggestion is that it seems odd, even unprincipled, to make a fundamental difference in the doctrine of estoppel between promises relating to land and other promises, and to give more weight to the former than the latter, in the context of a legal system that places more formal requirements on dealings with property, especially land, than on other dealings. Why should the law of contract insist on a peppercorn when the law of property can overlook the need for seals, writings, registration, properly attested wills, and so on? Is it because equity has made greater substantive incursions into property law than into contract law, and the shield/sword distinction between promissory and proprietary estoppel is simply a reflection of the difference between law's formalism and equity's flexibility? Should fusion of the two courts now attenuate this distinction?

(a)   *Canadian Aero Service Ltd v. O'Malley*[†]

Supreme Court of Canada

[LASKIN J.:]

This appeal arises out of a claim by the plaintiff-appellant (hereinafter referred to as Canaero) that the defendants had improperly taken the fruits of a corporate opportunity in which Canaero had a prior and continuing interest. The allegation against the defendants O'Malley and Zarzycki is that while directors or officers of Canaero they had devoted effort and planning in respect of the particular corporate opportunity as representatives of Canaero, but had subsequently wrongfully taken the benefit thereof in breach of a fiduciary duty to Canaero. The defendant Wells, who had been a director of Canaero but never an officer, was brought into the action as an associate of the other individual defendants in an alleged scheme to deprive Canaero of the corporate opportunity which it had been developing through O'Malley and Zarzycki; and the defendant Terra Surveys Limited was joined as the vehicle through which the individual defendants in fact obtained the benefit for which Canaero had been negotiating.

. . . .

Canaero was incorporated in 1948 under the *Companies* Act of Canada as a wholly-owned subsidiary of Aero Service Corporation, a United States company whose main business, like that of Canaero and other subsidiaries, was topographical mapping and geophysical exploration. In 1961, the parent Aero and its subsidiaries came under the control of another United States corporation, Litton Industries Inc. O'Malley joined Aero Service Corporation in 1936 and, apart from army service, remained with it until 1950 when he became general manager and president of Canaero whose head office was in Ottawa. He returned to the parent Aero company in 1957, but rejoined Canaero in 1964 as president and chief executive officer, and remained as such until he resigned on August 19, 1966. Acknowledgement and acceptance of the resignation followed on August 26, 1966.

Zarzycki, who attained a widely respected reputation in geodesy, joined Canaero in 1953, soon becoming chief engineer. He was named executive vice-president in 1964 and made a director in March 1965. He resigned these posts on August 22, 1966, and received the acknowledgment and acceptance of his resignation in a letter of August 29, 1966.

. . . .

The defendant Terra Surveys Limited was incorporated on August 16, 1966, following a luncheon meeting of O'Malley, Zarzycki and Wells on August 6, 1966, at which the suggestion to form a company of their own was made by Wells to O'Malley and Zarzycki. To Wells' knowledge, the latter were discontented at Canaero by reason of the limitations upon their authority and the scope of independent action imposed by the Litton company, and they also feared loss of position if Canaero should fail to get contracts. Nominal directors and officers of the new company were appointed, but O'Malley and Zarzycki

[†] [1974] S.C.R. 592.

became major shareholders when common stock was issued on September 12, 1966. One share was issued to Wells at this time but he made a further investment in the new company on November 6, 1966. There is no doubt that Terra Surveys Limited was conceived as a company through which O'Malley and Zarzycki could pursue the same objects that animated Canaero. O'Malley became president of Terra Surveys Limited and Zarzycki became executive vice-president shortly after its incorporation.

The legal issues in this appeal concern what I shall call the Guyana project, the topographical mapping and aerial photographing of parts of Guyana (known as British Guiana until its independence on May 25, 1965) to be financed through an external aid grant or loan from the Government of Canada under its programme of aid to developing countries. Terra Surveys Limited, in association with Survair Limited and another company, succeeded in obtaining the contract for the Guyana project which Canaero had been pursuing through O'Malley and Zarzycki, among others, for a number of years. There is a coincidence of dates and events surrounding the maturing and realization of that project, and the departure of O'Malley and Zarzycki from Canaero, their involvement with Wells in the incorporation of Terra Surveys Limited and its success, almost immediately thereafter, in obtaining the contract for the project. The significance of this coincidence is related, first, to the nature of the duty owed to Canaero by O'Malley and Zarzycki by reason of their positions with that company and, second, to the continuation of the duty, if any, upon a severance of relationship.

The coincidence aforementioned emerges from a review of the activities of Canaero in respect of the Guyana project. The business in which Canaero and other like companies were engaged involved technical, administrative and even diplomatic capabilities because, in the main, their dealings were with governments, both of countries seeking foreign aid for development and of countries, like United States and Canada, which had programmes for such aid. Companies like Canaero risked initiative and expenditure in preparatory work for projects without any assurance of return in the form of contracts; they saw their business as not only bidding on projects ripe for realization, but as also embracing suggestion and development of projects for which they would later seek approval and contracts to carry them out. In this latter aspect, the development of a project involved negotiation with officials of the country for whose benefit it was intended and the establishment of a receptive accord with a country offering aid for such matters. Of course, a suggested project was more likely to be viewed favourably if its technical and administrative aspects were well worked out in the course of its presentation for governmental approval.

Canaero's interest in promoting a project in Guyana for the development of its natural resources, and in particular electrical energy, began in 1961. It had done work in nearby Surinam (or Dutch Guiana) where conditions were similar. It envisaged extensive aerial photography and mapping of the country which, apart from the populated coastal area, was covered by dense jungle. Promotional work to persuade the local authorities that Canaero was best equipped to carry out the topographical mapping was done by O'Malley and by another associate of the parent Aero. A local agent, one Gavin B. Kennard, was engaged by Canaero. In May 1962, Zarzycki spent three days in Guyana in the interests of Canaero, obtaining information, examining existing geographical surveys and meeting government officials. He submitted a report on his visit to Canaero and to the parent Aero company.

Between 1962 and 1964 Canaero did magnetometer and electromagnetometer surveys in Guyana on behalf of the United Nations, and it envisaged either the United Nations or the United States as the funding agency to support the topographical mapping project that it was evolving as a result of its contacts in Guyana and Zarzycki's visit and report. Political conditions in Guyana after Zarzycki's visit in May 1962 did not conduce to furtherance of the project and activity thereon was suspended.

It was resumed in 1965 when it appeared that funds for it might be made available under Canada's external aid programme. The United States had adopted a policy in this area of awarding contracts to United States firms. The record in this case includes a letter of October 22, 1968, after the events which gave rise to this litigation, in which the Canadian Secretary of State for External Affairs wrote that Canada's external aid policy was to require contractors to be incorporated in Canada, managed and operated from Canada and to employ Canadian personnel; and although preference in awarding external aid contracts was given to Canadian controlled firms, this was not an absolute requirement of eligibility to obtain such contracts. Canaero would hence have been eligible at that time for an award of a contract and, inferentially, in 1966 as well.

Zarzycki returned to Guyana on July 14, 1965, and remained there until July 18, 1965. By July 26, 1965, he completed a proposal for topographical mapping of the country, a proposal that the Government thereof might use in seeking Canadian financial aid. Copies went to a Guyana cabinet minister, to the Canadian High Commissioner there and to the External Aid Office in Ottawa. Zarzycki in his evidence described the proposal as more sales-slanted than technical. The technical aspects were none the less covered; for example, the report recommended the use of an aerodist, a recently invented airborne electronic distance-measuring device. Zarzycki had previously urged that Canaero purchase one as a needed piece of equipment which other subsidiaries of Litton Industries Inc. could also use. Canaero placed an order for an aerodist, at a cost of $75,000, on or about July 15, 1966.

A few days earlier, on July 10, 1966, to be exact, an internal communication to the acting director-general of the Canadian External Aid Office, one Peter Towe, informed him that the Governments of Guyana and Canada had agreed in principle on a loan to Guyana for a topographical survey and mapping. The Prime Minister of Guyana had come to Ottawa early in July, 1966, for discussion on that among other matters. O'Malley had felt that if the assistance from Canada was by way of a loan Guyana would have the major say in naming the contractor, and this would make Canaero's chances better than if the assistance was by way of grant because then the selection would be determined by Canada. Although a loan was authorized, its terms were very liberal, and it was decided that Canada would select the contractor with the concurrence of Guyana, after examining proposals from a number of designated companies which would be invited to bid. An official of the Department of Mines and Technical Surveys visited Guyana and prepared specifications for the project which was approved by the Cabinet on August 10, 1966. Towe was informed by departmental letter of August 18, 1966, of a recommendation that Canaero, Lockwood Survey Corporation, Spartan Air Services Limited and Survair Limited be invited to submit proposals for the project. There was a pencilled note on the side of the letter, apparently added later, [with] the following words: "general photogramy Terra Ltd.".

The Canadian External Aid Office by letter of August 23, 1966, invited five companies to bid on the Guyana project. Survair Limited was dropped from the originally recommended group of four companies, and Terra Surveys Limited and General Photogrammetric Services Limited were added. A briefing on the specifications for the project was held by the Department of Mines and Technical Surveys on August 29, 1966. Zarzycki and another represented Terra Surveys Limited at this briefing.

O'Malley and Zarzycki pursued the Guyana project on behalf of Canaero up to July 25, 1966, but did nothing thereon for Canaero thereafter. On July 9, 1966, they had met with the Prime Minister of Guyana during his visit to Ottawa, and on July 13, 1966, they had met with Towe (who had previously been informed of the inter-governmental agreement in principle on the Guyana project) and learned from him that the project was on foot. O'Malley had written to Kennard, Canaero's Guyana agent, on July 15, 1966, that he felt the job was a certainty for Canaero. By letter of the same date to Towe, O'Malley wrote that Zarzycki had spent about 20 days in Georgetown, Guyana, on two successive visits to inventory the data available and determine the use to which the control survey and mapping would be put, and that he had subsequently prepared a proposal for a geodetic network and topographical mapping which was submitted to the Honourable Robert Jordan (the appropriate Guyanese cabinet minister) on July 27, 1965. On July 22, 1966, O'Malley wrote to an officer of the parent company that the Prime Minister of Guyana had advised him that "the Canadian Government would honour the project". Finally, on July 25, 1966, O'Malley wrote to Kennard to ask if he could learn what position Guyana was taking on the selection of a contractor, that is whether it proposed to make the selection with Canada's concurrence or whether it would leave the selection to Canada subject to its concurrence.

Thereafter the record of events, subject to one exception, concerns the involvement of O'Malley and Zarzycki with Wells in the incorporation of Terra Surveys Limited, their resignations from their positions with Canaero and their successful intervention through Terra Surveys Limited into the Guyana project. As of the date of O'Malley's letter of resignation, August 19, 1966, Terra Surveys Limited had a post office box and a favourable bank reference. Zarzycki had then not yet formally resigned as had O'Malley but had made the decision to do so. O'Malley informed the Canadian External Aid Office on August 22, 1966, of the new company which he, Zarzycki and Wells had formed.

The exception in the record of events just recited concerns a visit of Zarzycki, his "regular trip to the External Aid Office" (to use his own words), to the man in charge of the Caribbean area. This was on or about August 13, 1966, after his return from holidays and after the luncheon meeting with O'Malley and Wells that led to the incorporation of Terra. The purpose of the visit related to two project possibilities in the Caribbean area for Canaero, that in Guyana and one in Ecuador. Zarzycki then received confirmation of what he had earlier learned from Towe, namely, that the Guyana project had been approved in principle.

Despite having lost O'Malley and Zarzycki and also a senior employee[,] Turner (who joined the Terra venture and attended the briefing session on August 29, 1966, on its behalf with Zarzycki), Canaero associated itself with Spartan Air Services Limited in the latter's proposal on the Guyana project which was submitted under date of September 12, 1966. Prior to this submission, representatives of these two companies visited Guyana to assure officials there that Canaero was involved in the preparation of the Spartan proposal and was supporting it.

Terra Surveys Limited submitted its proposal on September 12, 1966, through Zarzycki, having sent a letter on that date to the External Aid Office setting out its qualifications. A report on the various proposals submitted was issued on September 16, 1966, by the Canadian government officer who had visited Guyana and had prepared the specifications for the project. He recommended that Terra Surveys Limited be the contractor, and included in his report the following observations upon its capabilities:

> This project is one of the most demanding that has been undertaken in the Canadian technical assistance program. The parts of the operation most seriously affected by the difficult conditions are the establishment of survey control and the procurement of the aerial photography, and the success of the project will depend greatly on the ability of the company selected to complete these two phases satisfactorily. The subsequent operations are somewhat less complex and are dependent on the successful completion of the initial phases. Furthermore, should the project lag in these phases, further resources are readily available in other companies in Canada.
>
> In my discussions with senior survey officials in Guyana, I was informed that an accurate framework of survey control was required to form the base for the topographical mapping now urgently required and in addition to permit the orderly completion of the national coverage in the future. Our experience is that the Aerodist system can provide the precision and density of control required more economically than any other method developed to date. Operational experience with this equipment by Canadian commercial companies has been extremely limited and has only been gained on projects where they acted in a support role to Surveys and Mapping Branch engineers. This has been kept in mind in the examination of the proposals in evaluating the plans of approach presented for this phase....

The proposals for the control surveys and topographical mapping project in Guyana submitted to the Director General on September 12, 1966 by Lock-wood Survey Corporation, Spartan Air Services Limited and Terra Surveys Limited have been carefully reviewed.

Representatives of General Photogrammetric Services Limited and Canadian Aero Services Limited submitted no proposals. However, Spartan Air Services Limited has indicated that they intend to make use of equipment and services of Canadian Aero Service Limited while Terra Surveys Limited has stated that they intend to subcontract compilation and draughting work to General Photogrammetric Services Limited....

Terra Surveys Limited has submitted a detailed proposal outlining their assessment of the major points to be considered in undertaking the proposed project in Guyana and their solution. It concludes with their proposed plan of operations and associated time schedule and is accompanied by a summary of what the Government of Guyana may expect to receive as well as the support it will be expected to provide....

Although Terra, like other Canadian companies, has had no practical experience in planning and executing a similar type of Aerodist project, the proposal indicates that its authors have studied the subject very thoroughly and in preparing their plan of operation have also taken conditions peculiar to Guyana into account....

Dr. J. M. Zarzycki is named as the project manager. He is known internationally as an outstanding photogrammetric engineer and has developed and successfully used an aerial triangulation procedure utilizing superwide angle photography, the Wild B. 8 and auxiliary data. Like most photogrammetric operations it requires good work by technicians but its success or failure hinges on the professional judgment and supervision of the engineer. Dr. Zarzycki has demonstrated this ability most clearly in past years.

Mr. M. H. Turner is to assist Dr. Zarzycki. He gained extensive experience in different field operations in Africa and has shown his ability to establish excellent working relationships with the senior survey officials as well as carrying out very difficult survey tasks. The Aerodist project will call for a high degree of theoretical knowledge in geodesy as well as practical management ability. This can be provided by Messrs. Turner and Zarzycki....

The proposal submitted by Terra Surveys Limited covered the operation in much greater detail than might normally be expected. However, the suggestions put forward indicate that all aspects of the operation have been most carefully reviewed and the plan of operation well thought out. The sections of the Terra proposal dealing with Aerodist indicate a more complete understanding of the problems in the field and subsequent operations than the other two proposals.

The treatment of many aspects of the project varies very little in the three proposals. However, appreciable differences do appear in the key phases of aerial photography and Aerodist control as explained in the preceding paragraphs. My assessment is that Terra Surveys Limited, in combination with Survair Limited and General Photogrammetric Services Limited, is best fitted to undertake this very difficult operation.

In the result, Terra Surveys Limited negotiated a contract with the External Aid Office, and on November 26, 1966, entered into an agreement with the Government of Guyana to carry out the project for the sum of $2,300,000. This was the amount indicated in the proposal of July 26, 1965, prepared by Zarzycki on behalf of Canaero.

．　．　．　．

There are four issues that arise for consideration on the facts so far recited. There is, first, the determination of the relationship of O'Malley and Zarzycki to Canaero. Second, there is the duty or duties, if any, owed by them to Canaero by reason of the ascertained [relationship]. Third, there is the question whether there has been any breach of duty, if any is owing, by reason of the conduct of O'Malley and Zarzycki in acting through Terra to secure the contract for the Guyana project; and, fourth, there is the question of liability for breach of duty if established.

... I do not think it matters whether O'Malley and Zarzycki were properly appointed as directors of Canaero or whether they did or did not act as directors. What is not in doubt is that they acted respectively as president and executive vice-president of Canaero for about two years prior to their resignations. To paraphrase the findings of the trial judge in this respect, they acted in those positions and their remuneration and responsibilities verified their status as senior officers of Canaero. They were "top management" and not mere employees whose duty to their employer, unless enlarged by contract, consisted only of respect for trade secrets and for confidentiality of customer lists. Theirs was a larger, more exacting duty which, unless modified by statute or by contract (and there is nothing of this sort here), was similar to that owed to a corporate employer by its directors. I adopt what is said on this point by Gower, *Principles of Modern Company Law*, 3rd ed., 1969, at p. 518 as follows:

... these duties, except in so far as they depend on statutory provisions expressly limited to directors, are not so restricted but apply equally to any officials of the company who are authorized to act on its behalf, and in particular to those acting in a managerial capacity.

The distinction taken between agents and servants of an employer is apt here, and I am unable to appreciate the basis upon which the Ontario Court of Appeal concluded that O'Malley and Zarzycki were mere employees, that is servants of Canaero rather than agents. Although they were subject to supervision of the officers of the controlling company, their positions as senior officers of a subsidiary, which was a working organization, charged them with initiatives and with responsibilities far removed from the obedient role of servants.

It follows that O'Malley and Zarzycki stood in a fiduciary relationship to Canaero, which in its generality betokens loyalty, good faith and avoidance of a conflict of duty and self-interest. Descending from the generality, the fiduciary relationship goes at least this far: a director or a senior officer like O'Malley or Zarzycki is precluded from obtaining for himself, either secretly or without the approval of the company (which would have to be properly manifested upon full disclosure of the facts), any property or business advantage either belonging to the company or for which it has been negotiating; and especially is this so where the director or officer is a participant in the negotiations on behalf of the company.

An examination of the case law in this Court and in the Courts of other like jurisdictions on the fiduciary duties of directors and senior officers shows the pervasiveness of a strict ethic in this area of the law. In my opinion, this ethic disqualifies a director or senior officer from usurping for himself or diverting to another person or company with whom or with which he is associated a maturing business opportunity which his company is actively pursuing; he is also precluded from so acting even after his resignation where the resignation may fairly be said to have been prompted or influenced by a wish to acquire for himself the opportunity sought by the company, or where it was his position with the company rather than a fresh initiative that led him to the opportunity which he later acquired.

It is this fiduciary duty which is invoked by the appellant in this case and which is resisted by the respondents on the grounds that the duty as formulated is not nor should be part of our law and that, in any event, the facts of the present case do not fall within its scope.

This Court considered the issue of fiduciary duty of directors in *Zwicker v. Stanbury* [[1953] 2 S.C.R. 438], where it found apt for the purposes of that case certain general statements of law by Viscount Sankey and by Lord Russell of Killowen in *Regal (Hastings) Ltd. v. Gulliver* [[1942] 1 All E.R. 378], at pp. 381 and 389. These statements, reflecting basic principle which is not challenged in the present case, are represented in the following passages:

Per Viscount Sankey:

In my view, the respondents were in a fiduciary position and their liability to account does not depend upon proof of *mala fides*. The general rule of equity is that no one who has duties of a fiduciary nature to perform is allowed to enter into engagements in which he has or can have a personal interest conflicting with the interests of those whom he is bound to protect. If he holds any property so acquired as trustee, he is bound to account for it to his *cestui que trust*. The earlier cases are concerned with trusts of specific property: *Keech v. Sandford* ((1726), Sel.Cas. Ch. 61) per Lord King, L.C. The rule, however, applies to agents, as, for example, solicitors and directors, when acting in a fiduciary capacity.

Per Lord Russell of Killowen:

In the result, I am of opinion that the directors standing in a fiduciary relationship to Regal in regard to the exercise of their powers as directors, and having obtained these shares by reason and only by reason of the fact that they were directors of Regal and in the course of the execution of that office, are accountable for the profits which they have made out of them. The equitable rule laid down in *Keech v. Sandford* [supra] and *Ex p. James* ((1803), 8 Ves. 337), and similar authorities applies ... in full force. It was contended that these cases were distinguishable by reason of the fact that it was impossible for Regal to get the shares owing to lack of funds, and that the directors in taking the shares were really acting as members of the public. I cannot accept this argument. It was impossible for the *cestui que trust* in *Keech v. Sandford* to obtain the lease, nevertheless the trustee was accountable. The suggestion that the directors were applying simply as members of the public is a travesty of the facts. They could, had they wished, have protected themselves by a resolution (either antecedent or subsequent) of the Regal share-holders in general meeting. In default of such approval, the liability to account must remain.

I need not pause to consider whether on the facts in *Regal (Hastings) Ltd. v. Gulliver* the equitable

principle was overzealously applied; see, for example, Gower, *op. cit.*, at pp.535–537. What I would observe is that the principle, or, indeed, principles, as stated, grew out of older cases concerned with fiduciaries other than directors or managing officers of a modern corporation, and I do not therefore regard them as providing a rigid measure whose literal terms must be met in assessing succeeding cases. In my opinion, neither the conflict test, referred to by Viscount Sankey, nor the test of accountability for profits acquired by reason only of being directors and in the course of execution of the office, reflected in the passage quoted from Lord Russell of Killowen, should be considered as the exclusive touchstones of liability. In this, as in other branches of the law, new fact situations may require a reformulation of existing principle to maintain its vigour in the new setting.

The reaping of a profit by a person at a company's expense while a director thereof is, of course, an adequate ground upon which to hold the director accountable. Yet there may be situations where a profit must be disgorged, although not gained at the expense of the company, on the ground that a director must not be allowed to use his position as such to make a profit even if it was not open to the company, as for example, by reason of legal disability, to participate in the transaction. An analogous situation, albeit not involving a director, existed for all practical purposes in the case of *Phipps v. Boardman* [[1967] 2 A.C. 46], which also supports the view that liability to account does not depend on proof of an actual conflict of duty and self-interest. Another, quite recent, illustration of a liability to account where the company itself had failed to obtain a business contract and hence could not be regarded as having been deprived of a business opportunity is *Industrial Development Consultants Ltd. v. Cooley* [[1972] 2 All E.R. 162], a judgment of a Court of first instance. There, the managing director, who was allowed to resign his position on a false assertion of ill health, subsequently got the contract for himself. That case is thus also illustrative of the situation where a director's resignation is prompted by a decision to obtain for himself the business contract denied to his company and where he does obtain it without disclosing his intention.

What these decisions indicate is an updating of the equitable principle whose roots lie in the general standards that I have already mentioned, namely, loyalty, good faith and avoidance of a conflict of duty and self-interest. Strict application against directors and senior management officials is simply recognition of the degree of control which their positions give them in corporate operations, a control which rises above day-to-day accountability to owning shareholders and which comes under some scrutiny only at annual general or at special meetings. It is a necessary supplement, in the public interest, of statutory regulation and accountability which themselves are, at one and the same time, an acknowledgment of the importance of the corporation in the life of the community and of the need to compel obedience by it and by its promoters, directors and managers to norms of exemplary behaviour.

· · · ·

The view taken by the trial judge, and affirmed by the Court of Appeal (which quoted the same passage from the reasons of Lord Russell of Killowen in *Regal (Hastings) Ltd. v. Gulliver*), tended to obscure the difference between the survival of fiduciary duty after resignation and the right to use non-confidential information acquired in the course of employment and as a result of experience. I do not see that either the question of the confidentiality of the information acquired by O'Malley and Zarzycki in the course of their work for Canaero on the Guyana project or the question of copyright is relevant to the enforcement against them of a fiduciary duty. The fact that breach of confidence or violation of copyright may itself afford a ground of relief does not make either one a necessary ingredient of a successful claim for breach of fiduciary duty.

· · · ·

In my opinion, the fiduciary duty upon O'Malley and Zarzycki, if it survived their departure from Canaero, would be reduced to an absurdity if it could be evaded merely because the Guyana project had been varied in some details when it became the subject of invited proposals, or merely because Zarzycki met the variations by appropriate changes in what he prepared for Canaero in 1965 and what he proposed for Terra in 1966. I do not regard it as necessary to look for substantial resemblances. Their presence would be a factor to be considered on the issue of breach of fiduciary duty but they are not *a sine qua* non. The cardinal fact is that the one project, the same project which Zarzycki had pursued for Canaero, was the subject of his Terra proposal. It was that business opportunity, in line with its general pursuits, which Canaero sought through O'Malley and Zarzycki. There is no suggestion that there had been such a change of objective as to make the project for which proposals were invited from Canaero, Terra and others a different one from

that which Canaero had been developing with a view to obtaining the contract for itself.

Again, whether or not Terra was incorporated for the purpose of intercepting the contract for the Guyana project is not central to the issue of breach of fiduciary duty. Honesty of purpose is no more a defence in that respect than it would be in respect of personal interception of the contract by O'Malley and Zarzycki. This is fundamental in the enforcement of fiduciary duty where the fiduciaries are acting against the interests of their principal. Then it is urged that Canaero could not in any event have obtained the contract, and that O'Malley and Zarzycki left Canaero as an ultimate response to their dissatisfaction with that company and with the restrictions that they were under in managing it. There was, however, no certain knowledge at the time O'Malley and Zarzycki resigned that the Guyana project was beyond Canaero's grasp. Canaero had not abandoned its hope of capturing it, even if Wells was of opinion, expressed during his luncheon with O'Malley and Zarzycki on August 6, 1966, that it would not get a foreign aid contract from the Canadian Government. Although it was contended that O'Malley and Zarzycki did not know of the imminence of the approval of the Guyana project, their ready run for it, when it was approved at about the time of their resignations and at a time when they knew of Canaero's continuing interest, are factors to be considered in deciding whether they were still under a fiduciary duty not to seek to procure for themselves or for their newly-formed company the business opportunity which they had nurtured for Canaero.

· · · ·

... As in other cases in this developing branch of the law, the particular facts may determine the shape of the principle of decision without setting fixed limits to it. So it is in the present case. Accepting the facts found by the trial judge, I find no obstructing considerations to the conclusion that O'Malley and Zarzycki continued, after their resignations, to be under a fiduciary duty to respect Canaero's priority, as against them and their instrument Terra, in seeking to capture the contract for the Guyana project. They entered the lists in the heat of the maturation of the project, known to them to be under active Government consideration when they resigned from Canaero and when they proposed to bid on behalf of Terra.

In holding that on the facts found by the trial judge, there was a breach of fiduciary duty by

O'Malley and Zarzycki which survived their resignations I am not to be taken as laying down any rule of liability to be read as if it were a statute. The general standards of loyalty, good faith and avoidance of a conflict of duty and self-interest to which the conduct of a director or senior officer must conform, must be tested in each case by many factors which it would be reckless to attempt to enumerate exhaustively. Among them are the factor of position or office held, the nature of the corporate opportunity, its ripeness, its specificness and the director's or managerial officer's relation to it, the amount of knowledge possessed, the circumstances in which it was obtained and whether it was special or, indeed, even private, the factor of time in the continuation of fiduciary duty where the alleged breach occurs after termination of the relationship with the company, and the circumstances under which the relationship was terminated, that is whether by retirement or resignation or discharge.

. . . .

There remains the question of the appropriate relief against O'Malley and Zarzycki, and against Terra through which they acted in breach of fiduciary duty. In fixing the damages at $125,000, the trial judge based himself on a claim for damages related only to the loss of the contract for the Guyana project, this being the extent of Canaero's claim as he understood it. No claim for a different amount or for relief on a different basis, as, for example, to hold Terra as constructive trustee for Canaero in respect of the execution of the Guyana contract, was made in this Court. Counsel for the respondents, although conceding that there was evidence of Terra's likely profit from the Guyana contract, emphasized the trial judge's finding that Canaero could not have obtained the contract itself in view of its association with Spartan Air Services Limited in the submission of a proposal. It was his submission that there was no evidence that that proposal would have been accepted if Terra's had been rejected and, in any event, there was no evidence of Canaero's likely share of the profit.

Liability of O'Malley and Zarzycki for breach of fiduciary duty does not depend upon proof by Canaero that, but for their intervention, it would have obtained the Guyana contract; nor is it a condition of recovery of damages that Canaero establish what its profit would have been or what it has lost by failing to realize the corporate opportunity in question. It is entitled to compel the faithless fiduciaries to answer for their default according to their gain. Whether the damages awarded here be viewed as an accounting of profits or, what amounts to the same thing, as based on unjust enrichment, I would not interfere with the quantum. The appeal is, accordingly, allowed against all defendants and judgment should be entered against them for $125,000. ...

(b) *Frame v. Smith*†

Supreme Court of Canada

[La FOREST JJ. (for Dickson C.J. and Beetz, McIntyre, Lamer and La Forest JJ.:]

[1] The issue in this case is whether the appellant has a right of action against his former spouse and her present husband for interfering with his access to his children.

BACKGROUND

[2] This appeal arises out of a motion to strike out a statement of claim on the ground that it discloses no cause of action. That being the case, it must be assumed, for the purposes of the motion, that the facts pleaded are true. The most salient of these are as follows.

[3] Richard Frame and Eleanor Smith were formerly husband and wife and had three children, now aged 24, 19 and 18. The couple separated in 1970, and in 1971 a Manitoba court granted the wife custody of the children, with generous visiting privileges to her husband. Later orders of access were issued in Ontario in 1974 and 1975. According to the husband,

---

† [1987] 2 S.C.R. 99. (Appeal from a judgment of the Ontario Court of Appeal dismissing an appeal from a judgment of Boland J. granting an order to strike for want of a reasonable cause of action.)

however, his former wife has done everything in her power to frustrate his access to the children. She has moved between Winnipeg, Toronto, Denver and Ottawa, making access and visitation, in his words, impossible. She changed the children's surname and religion, told them that the appellant was not their father, forbade telephone conversation with him, and intercepted his letters to them. The husband alleges that as a result of his former wife's conduct he has undergone considerable expense and has suffered severe emotional and psychic distress. He claims that she and her present husband are liable for any damages flowing from their wrongful interference with the legal relationship he had with his children. Accordingly, he seeks recovery not only of his out-of-pocket expenses (estimated at $25,000), but of general and punitive damages in the sum of $1,000,000 and $500,000 respectively. The endorsement on the writ of summons reads as follows:

> The Plaintiff's claim is for damages as a result of the defendants' failure to permit the plaintiff to exercise the right to access to his children or alternatively, damages relating to the defendants' wilful denial or refusal to permit the plaintiff from exercising his lawful right to access to his children or alternatively, damages arising from the defendants' conspiracy to commit acts in order to prevent the plaintiff from exercising his legal rights and for damages related to the plaintiff's loss of opportunity to develop a meaningful human relationship and have social companionship and contact with his children and to provide and give to the said children proper parental love, care and guidance.

. . . .

POSSIBLE TORT LIABILITY

[6] Despite their deep human and social importance, the interest of parents in the love and companionship of their children and the reciprocal interest of children in the love and companionship of their parents were not, at common law, accorded specific protection. The *Restatement of the Law of Torts* (1938), s. 699, puts the parent's common law position in these words: "One who, without more, alienates from its parents the affection of a child, whether a minor or of full age, is not liable to the child's parent." There were the old actions of enticement, harbouring, or seduction or loss of services that gave some protection to a father's interest in his children, but these actions had a distinctly pecuniary flavour. In any event, they have now been abolished in Ontario

by the *Family Law Reform Act*, R.S.O. 1980, c. 152, s. 69(4).

[7] In the United States, a separate tort of "alienation of affections" was developed to protect the reciprocal interest of spouses in one another's companionship, but from the mid-1930's onward, it began to fall into disfavour and, along with the traditional actions already mentioned, was abolished in many of the states. It simply did not sit well in an age of "rapidly shifting husbands and wives and ever-increasing family catastrophes"; for an account, see Alan Milner, "Injuries to Consortium in Modern Anglo-American Law" (1958), 7 *Int. & Comp. Law Q.* 417, especially at pp. 435–36. The extension of the tort in a few state courts to allow parents to sue for the loss of affection of their children received anything but universal approval; see Milner, ibid.; Clay A. Mosberg, Note, "A Parent's Cause of Action for the Alienation of a Child's Affection" (1973–74), 22 *Kan. L. Rev.* 684. Opening the gates to a multiplicity of actions within the family circle and against close family friends was not viewed as an undiluted good. Indeed, in Michigan, one of the few states where this extension was made, the State legislature went out of its way to abolish it; see Mosberg, ibid., at pp. 689 — 90. In Canada, this Court, in *Kungl v. Schiefer*, [1962] S.C.R. 443, rejected an action by a husband to recover damages for the alienation of the affection of his wife, holding that no such tort existed in Canada. In this, it followed the lead of the English courts where, in *Gottlieb v. Gleiser*, [1957] 3 All E.R. 715, Denning L.J. made it clear that such domestic matters lie outside the realm of the law altogether.

[8] The husband in the present case also sought to rely on the tort of conspiracy but as my colleague Justice Wilson explains in her judgment, there are grave disadvantages associated with applying this tort to circumstances like the present. Further, as she notes, this Court has made it clear that it does not look kindly upon the extension of this tort, which it regards as an anomaly, see, *Canada Cement LaFarge Ltd. v. British Columbia Lightweight Aggregate Ltd.* [1983] 1 S.C.R. 452, at p. 473, *per* Estey J. Wilson J., in her judgment, has also adequately disposed of the possibility of other existing torts applying to the circumstances of this case. It is also doubtful, as she observes, that a parent had at common law a right of access, as opposed to custody, upon which an action could be grounded. There is no pecuniary interest here, and, in any event, any possible interest seems to be very much akin to that which

would have been protected by the rejected tort of alienation of affections.

[9] It would, of course, be possible for the courts to devise a new tort to meet the situation. And the temptation to do so is clearly present, for one cannot help but feel sympathy for the appellant and others in like situations. But there are formidable arguments against the creation of such a remedy. I have already mentioned the undesirability of provoking suits within the family circle. The spectacle of parents not only suing their former spouses but also the grandparents, and aunts and uncles of their children, to say nothing of close family friends, for interfering with rights of access is one that invites one to pause. The disruption of the familial and social environment so important to a child's welfare may well have been considered reason enough for the law's inaction, though there are others.

[10] There are also serious difficulties in defining such a tort. At what stage and for what actions should one be able to claim interference with access? Is advice or encouragement to a child sufficient? It is notorious that free, and not always disinterested and wise advice abounds in a family setting. There are degrees of interference, of course, and some interference is malicious and some is not, but where the line is to be drawn defies specification. It seems to me that there is no clear boundary between ordinary interruptions to access and sustained, putatively actionable interference, and where the point is reached where permissible advice intended for the child's benefit stops and malicious obstruction begins is virtually impossible to divine. This is especially so because, as Alan Milner, ibid., at p. 429, has pointed out, "when there is dislike, a desire to injure is never far behind." Besides, the awarding of damages will do little to bring back love and companionship, but it may, in some cases, well deprive a child of the support he or she might otherwise obtain from a custodial parent and relatives. If, on the other hand, the action is generally limited to the recovery of expenses, it will be of little use to most parents given the costs, in time and money, of court actions. These and other practical considerations are sufficient to raise serious doubts about whether an action at law is the appropriate way to deal with this type of situation. This probably explains the reticence of the courts in finding a remedy at common law.

[11] But what really determines the matter, in my view, is that any possible judicial initiative has been overtaken by legislative action. In all the provinces (and at the federal level for that matter), legislation has been enacted to deal with the modern phenomenon of frequent family breakdowns and, in particular, to provide for custody of, and access to children. In Ontario, the *Children's Law Reform Act*, R.S.O. 1980, c. 68, as amended by the *Children's Law Reform Amendment Act, 1982*, S.O. 1982, c. 20, now deals with the matter in a comprehensive manner. In particular, the courts are given the role of ensuring that issues involving custody of, and access to children are determined on the basis of the best interests of the children (see ss. 19(*a*), 24(1)). Numerous remedies are provided for the enforcement of orders granting custody or access. The court can give such directions as it considers appropriate for the supervision of those having custody of, or access to the children (s. 35). It may, on application, make an order restraining any person from molesting, annoying or harassing the applicant or a child in the applicant's custody (s. 36). It may also empower the applicant or someone on his or her behalf to apprehend a child to give effect to the applicant's entitlement to custody or access (s. 37(1)). In certain circumstances, it may direct the sheriff or the police to do so (s. 37(2)), and empower them to enter and search any place where they have reasonable and probable grounds for believing the child may be, and to use such assistance or force as may be reasonable in the circumstances (s. 37(5)). The court may also take steps to prevent a child from being removed from the province (s. 38). In addition to its powers in respect of contempt, the court is empowered to impose a fine or imprisonment for wilful contempt of, or resistance to its process or orders in respect of custody or access (s. 39).

[12] It seems obvious to me that the Legislature intended to devise a comprehensive scheme for dealing with these issues. If it had contemplated additional support by civil action, it would have made provision for this, especially given the rudimentary state of the common law. Indeed, as we saw, the Legislature in a separate statute (the *Family Law Reform Act*) went out of its way to abolish all the relevant, if inadequate, remedies then existing at common law. Gray J. in *Schrenk, supra*, assumed that an action like the present fell within the ambit of these abolished common law remedies, and I agree that the statute shows a clear disposition not to permit recourse to the courts for civil actions of this nature. There is more here than the usual presumption that the Legislature must be taken to have known the pre-existing law. It had acted on the basis of a *Report on Family Law* (1969) prepared by the Ontario Law Reform Commission.

[14] More generally, what the present action appears to contemplate is the enforcement of a statutory duty, or what amounts to the same thing, an order made by virtue of a statutory discretion, by means of a civil action rather than by means of the remedies provided by the Act. ...

[15] There is no need today to supplement legislative action in this way. Indeed, to do so may well do violence to the comprehensive statutory scheme provided by the Legislature ...

[16] In my view, therefore, the appellant husband has not established a proper basis for an action in tort.

POSSIBLE FIDUCIARY OBLIGATION

[17] Much of what I have already stated seems to me, with respect, to apply with equal force to the possibility, about which this Court invited counsel to make additional submissions, that the appellant may have an action for a breach of a fiduciary obligation arising out of the court order granting him access to the child. All the reasons for not permitting a tort action apply equally to an action for the breach of such an obligation. The Legislature created the rights of custody and access and, as we saw, provided a whole array of remedies for enforcing them, from directions for supervising access, to restraining orders against interference, to apprehending the child, if necessary by permitting entries into premises and searches by the police or the sheriff, to fines and imprisonment. Why the legislature should be thought to have intended enforcement by an action for breach of a fiduciary obligation when there is a failure to comply with an access order, when an intention to permit a tortious action will not be implied, I fail to understand. All the more so when the Legislature has taken pains to abolish all non-statutory actions that had any obvious relevance to the matter. Indeed there are in my view stronger reasons to doubt that the Legislature would have contemplated recourse to this action. It is extremely ill-defined and it would scarcely be one that would immediately leap to mind.

[18] There is no greater clarity as to when an action for a breach of fiduciary obligation would arise than is the case respecting possible tortious action for interference with access. Even if one assumes that not every breach of the right of access can give rise to an action, at what point precisely does an action arise? As I noted in discussing a possible tort action, precision is virtually impossible in this area. The fact that the court may have some discretion in awarding damages does not alter the fact that there may be a wide area of conduct that might be thought by litigants to warrant suit. These are but a few of the uncertainties that surround this amorphous remedy. These uncertainties have the potential to generate pyrrhic, excessive and often needless litigation.

[19] Permitting such an action may well be violative of the express direction of the Act that custody of, and access to children should, in situations like these, be accorded solely on the basis of the children's best interests. The Legislature may well have thought that allowing a civil action would have this effect. I might mention here that the courts will not permit violence to be done indirectly to a legislative scheme. In other contexts, not only have they refused to allow a tort action, but they have gone further and not permitted what had traditionally been permissible contractual actions; see, for example, *St. Anne Nackawic, supra.*

[20] In sum, it is by no means certain that permitting civil actions against the custodial parents can be said to be in the best interests of the child, whether this be by creating a tort or recognizing a fiduciary relationship arising out of a court order. Resort even to fines and imprisonment, which is permitted by the Act, has been described as not "entirely appropriate"; see James G. McLeod, "Annotation" to *O'Byrne v. Koresec* (1986), 2 R.F.L. (3d) 104, at p. 105. That is because these may encroach on the resources of the custodial parent and because the child may suffer from the knowledge that one parent has taken such drastic action against the other. This applies, and in some respects with greater force to a legal action. Damages can impose a far greater financial burden than the fine of up to $1,000 which may be imposed under the Act (s. 39(1)). Furthermore, though the imprisonment of one parent at the behest of the other may be damaging to the child, litigation by one against the other over a protracted period may well be even more damaging.

[21] For these reasons, I cannot accept that a breach of the statutorily authorized order in the present case gives rise to a fiduciary relationship on which a cause of action can be grounded.

CONCLUSION

[22] No possible basis for a cause of action having been presented, I would dismiss the appeal with costs.

[WILSON J. (dissenting):]

[23] The central issue in this case is whether the courts should recognize a common law parental right of access to children or, alternatively, a right to recover damages for interference with an order for access made by a court pursuant to statutory authority. The issue arises in the context of an application to strike out the plaintiff's statement of claim as disclosing no reasonable cause of action. Because this is the context there is no evidence in the record to support the allegations made in the statement of claim but, in accordance with well-established principles, the facts as pleaded must for this limited purpose be taken as proved.

. . . .

Breach of Fiduciary Duty

[56] The final cause of action to be considered is breach of fiduciary duty. This possibility was not advanced by counsel in his original material but, since the issue before the Court was whether the statement of claim should be struck out "as disclosing no reasonable cause of action", the Court was of the view that it should be addressed. Counsel was accordingly invited to file written submissions of which we have had the benefit.

[57] In the past the question whether a particular relationship is subject to a fiduciary obligation has been approached by referring to categories of relationships in which a fiduciary obligation has already been held to be present. Some recognized examples of these categories are relationships between directors and corporations, solicitors and clients, trustees and beneficiaries, agents and principals, life tenants and remaindermen, and partners. As well, it has frequently been noted that the categories of fiduciary relationship are never closed: see, for example, *Guerin v. The Queen*, [1984] 2 S.C.R. 335, at p. 384 *per* Dickson J. (as he then was); *International Corona Resources Ltd. v. Lac Minerals Ltd.* (1986), 53 O.R. (2d) 737 (H.C.); *Standard Investments Ltd. v. Canadian Imperial Bank of Commerce* (1985), 52 O.R. (2d) 473; *English v. Dedham Vale Properties Ltd.*, [1978] 1 All E.R. 382, at p. 398; *Tufton v. Sperni*, [1952] 2 T.L.R. 516, at p. 522; R. Goff and G. Jones, *The Law of Restitution* (2nd ed. 1978), at pp. 490–91. An extension of fiduciary obligations to new "categories" of relationship presupposes the existence of an underlying principle which governs the imposition of the fiduciary obligation.

[58] However, there has been a reluctance throughout the common law world to affirm the existence of and give content to a general fiduciary principle which can be applied in appropriate circumstances. Sir Anthony Mason ("Themes and Prospects" in P. Finn, ed., *Essays in Equity* (1985), at p. 246) is probably correct when he says that "the fiduciary relationship is a concept in search of a principle". As a result there is no definition of the concept "fiduciary" apart from the contexts in which it has been held to arise and, indeed, it may be more accurate to speak of relationships as having a fiduciary component to them rather than to speak of fiduciary relationships as such: see J. C. Shepherd, *The Law of Fiduciaries* (1981), pp. 4–8. Perhaps the biggest obstacle to the development of a general fiduciary principle has been the fact that the content of the fiduciary duty varies with the type of relationship to which it is applied. It seems on its face therefore to comprise a collection of unrelated rules such as the rule against self-dealing, the misappropriation of assets rule, the conflict and profit rules and (in Canada) a special business opportunity rule: see R. P. Austin, "The Corporate Fiduciary: Standard Investments Ltd. v. Canadian Imperial Bank of Commerce" (1986–87), 12 *Can. Bus. L.J.* 96, at pp. 96–97; P. D. Finn, *Fiduciary Obligations* (1977). The failure to identify and apply a general fiduciary principle has resulted in the courts relying almost exclusively on the established list of categories of fiduciary relationships and being reluctant to grant admittance to new relationships despite their oft-repeated declaration that the category of fiduciary relationships is never closed.

[59] A few commentators have attempted to discern an underlying fiduciary principle but, given the widely divergent contexts emerging from the case law, it is understandable that they have differed in their analyses: see, for example, E. Vinter, *A Treatise on the History and Law of Fiduciary Relationships and Resulting Trusts* (3rd ed. 1955); Ernest J. Weinrib, "The Fiduciary Obligation" (1975), 25 *U.T.L.J.* 1; Gareth Jones, "Unjust Enrichment and the Fiduciary's Duty of Loyalty" (1968), 84 *L.Q.R.* 472; George W. Keeton and L. A. Sheridan, *Equity* (1969), at pp. 336–52; Shepherd, *supra*, at p. 94. Yet there are common features discernible in the contexts in which fiduciary duties have been found to exist and these common features do provide a rough and ready guide to whether or not the imposition of a fiduciary obligation on a new relationship would be appropriate and consistent.

[60] Relationships in which a fiduciary obligation have been imposed seem to possess three general characteristics:

(1) The fiduciary has scope for the exercise of some discretion or power.
(2) The fiduciary can unilaterally exercise that power or discretion so as to affect the beneficiary's legal or practical interests.
(3) The beneficiary is peculiarly vulnerable to or at the mercy of the fiduciary holding the discretion or power.

[61] Very little need be said about the first characteristic except this, that unless such a discretion or power is present there is no need for a superadded obligation to restrict the damaging use of the discretion or power: see, for example, *R. H. Deacon & Co. v. Varga* (1972), 30 D.L.R. (3d) 653 (Ont. C.A.), aff'd *sub nom. Varga v. F. H. Deacon & Co.*, [1975] 1 S.C.R. 39.

[62] With respect to the second characteristic it is, of course, the fact that the power or discretion may be used to affect the beneficiary in a damaging way that makes the imposition of a fiduciary duty necessary. Indeed, fiduciary duties are frequently imposed on those who are capable of affecting not only the legal interests of the beneficiary but also the beneficiary's vital non-legal or "practical" interests. For example, it is generally conceded that a director is in a fiduciary relationship to the corporation. But the corporation's interest which is protected by the fiduciary duty is not confined to an interest in the property of the corporation but extends to non-legal, practical interests in the financial well-being of the corporation and perhaps to even more intangible practical interests such as the corporation's public image and reputation. Another example is found in cases of undue influence where a fiduciary uses a power over the beneficiary to obtain money at the expense of the beneficiary. The beneficiary's interest in such a case is a pecuniary interest. Finally, in *Reading v. Attorney-General*, [1951] A.C. 507 (H.L.), a British soldier who was able to smuggle items past Egyptian guards because these guards excused uniformed soldiers from their inspections was held to be a fiduciary. The Crown's interest was a "practical" or even a "moral" one, namely that its uniform should not be used in corrupt ways. The soldier-fiduciary had no power to change the legal position of the British Crown, so how could the Crown's legal interests have been affected by the soldier's action? The same can be said of the Crown's interest in *Attorney-General v. Goddard* (1929), 98 L.J. (K.B.) 743, where the Crown was able to recover bribes which had been paid to its employee, a sergeant in the Metropolitan Police. In my view, what was protected in that case was not a "legal" interest but a vital and substantial "practical" interest.

[63] The third characteristic of relationships in which a fiduciary duty has been imposed is the element of vulnerability. This vulnerability arises from the inability of the beneficiary (despite his or her best efforts) to prevent the injurious exercise of the power or discretion combined with the grave inadequacy or absence of other legal or practical remedies to redress the wrongful exercise of the discretion or power. Because of the requirement of vulnerability of the beneficiary at the hands of the fiduciary, fiduciary obligations are seldom present in the dealings of experienced businessmen of similar bargaining strength acting at arm's length: see, for example, *Jirna Ltd. v. Mister Donut of Canada Ltd.* (1971), 22 D.L.R. (3d) 639 (Ont. C.A.), aff'd [1975] 1 S.C.R. 2. The law takes the position that such individuals are perfectly capable of agreeing as to the scope of the discretion or power to be exercised, i.e., any "vulnerability" could have been prevented through the more prudent exercise of their bargaining power and the remedies for the wrongful exercise or abuse of that discretion or power, namely damages, are adequate in such a case.

· · · ·

[65] In my view, the relationship between the custodial parent and the non-custodial parent fits within the fiduciary principle I have described. There is no doubt that prior to the custody and access order the parent who will become the non-custodial parent has a very substantial interest in his or her relationship with the child. The granting of the access order confirms that the relationship between the non-custodial parent and the child is of benefit to the child and therefore worth preserving. That relationship predated the access order and it continues to subsist after the access order is made. It is not itself created by the access order. But the custody and access order, by splitting access from custody, puts the custodial parent in a position of power and authority which enables him or her, if so motivated, to affect the non-custodial parent's relationship with his or her child in an injurious way. The selfish exercise of custody over a long period of time without regard to the access order can utterly destroy the non-custodial parent's relationship with his child. The non-custodial parent (and, of course, the child also) is completely

vulnerable to this. Yet the underlying premise in a grant of custody to one parent and access to the other is that the custodial parent will facilitate the exercise of the other's access rights for the sake of the child.

[66] It seems to me that the three underlying characteristics of relationships in which fiduciary duties are imposed are present in the relationship under review. The custodial parent has been placed as a result of the court's order in a position of power and authority over the children with the potential to prejudicially affect and indeed utterly destroy their relationship with their non-custodial parent through improper exercise of the power. There can be no doubt also that the requisite vulnerability is present and that in practical terms there is little that the non-custodial parent can do to restrain the custodial parent's improper exercise of authority or to obtain redress for it. The options open to an aggrieved non-custodial parent in the face of a campaign by a custodial parent to cut the non-custodial parent off from the child are exceedingly limited. As mentioned above, s. 37 of the *Children's Law Reform Act* gives courts the authority to direct a sheriff or police force, or both, to locate, apprehend and deliver back a child who is being unlawfully withheld from a person entitled to custody or access. This does not appear to be an appropriate means of compelling a custodial parent to permit access and it seems unlikely that any parent sensitive to his or her child's feelings would resort to it. The option of refusing payment of child maintenance in order to secure a right of access is not available to a non-custodial spouse: *Wright v. Wright* (1973), 1 O.R. (2d) 337 (C.A.) The powers of the court to order a custodial parent to post a bond or other security, to have support payments made to a specified trustee who holds them subject to certain conditions, and to have the custodial parent give up his or her passport are usually ineffective. The forfeiture of the bond or other security and the withholding of support payments by a trustee may not be in the child's best interests (it may affect the custodial parent's ability to meet the expenses of raising the child) and the giving up of the passport only prevents the child from being removed from the country. Section 39 of the *Children's Law Reform Act* allows a Provincial Court (Family Division) to impose fines of up to $1,000 and/or imprisonment of up to ninety days for contempt. But imprisoning and fining the custodial parent will usually not be in the child's best interests and will therefore seldom be available to the non-custodial parent. As James G. McLeod has written

("Annotation" to *O'Byrne v. Koresec* (1986), 2 R.F.L. (3d) 104, at pp. 105):

> Where they [access orders] are wilfully ignored, proper sanctions must be imposed. Such actions may be a fine ... or imprisonment.... Neither of these sanctions however, is entirely appropriate. In many cases, the custodial spouse may not have the resources to pay the fine without resort to funds required for day-to-day living expenses, in which event the child will suffer.... Where imprisonment is ordered, one approach would be to imprison the custodial parent over weekends when access by the other parent could be enjoyed, so as to minimize disruption to the children. Even then, the children may suffer from the knowledge (which they will surely gain!) that one parent has put the other parent in jail.

[67] It is sometimes suggested that transferring custody is an appropriate means of punishing the custodial parent for an ongoing denial of access: see, for example, the suggestions made in *Woodburn v. Woodburn* (1975), 11 N.S.R. (2d) 528, 21 R.F.L. 179 (S.C.), at pp. 182–183; *Jones v. Jones* (1970), 1 R.F.L. 295 (Ont. C.A.), at pp. 295–96; *Currie v. Currie* (1975), 18 R.F.L. 47 (Alta. S.C.), at p. 55; *Donald v. Donald* (1973), 6 N.B.R. (2d) 665, at p. 668. And indeed this is being done: see *Nayar v. Nayar* (1981), 24 R.F.L. (2d) 400 (B.C.C.A.), and *Fast v. Fast* (1983), 33 R.F.L. (2d) 337 (Sask. C.A.) But again, because of the bonding that takes place between the custodial parent and his or her child over a period of time, such a step may not be in the child's best interests. In *Racine v. Woods*, [1983] 2 S.C.R. 173, a case involving a custody dispute between an Indian child's natural parents and the child's adopted parents, this Court stressed the need for children to have continuity of relationships. It held that, while an Indian child's cultural heritage and background were important factors to be considered by the court in applying the best interests doctrine, these factors had declined in importance in light of the degree of psychological bonding which had developed with the foster parents. Because of this psychological bonding a transfer of custody may not be a suitable remedy. Finally, as has been indicated above, there are good reasons for not extending common law causes of action in tort in order to permit the non-custodial parent to obtain redress for the custodial parent's denial of access.

[68] I have already indicated that substantial non-legal, practical interests are protected by the imposition of fiduciary duties in appropriate cases. It cannot be denied that the non-custodial parent's

interest in his or her child is as worthy of protection as some interests commonly protected by a fiduciary duty. For example, just as a corporation has a substantial interest in its relationship to corporate opportunities and customers that is worthy of protection (see, for example, *Canadian Aero Service Ltd. v. O'Malley*, [1974] S.C.R. 592) it can be said that a non-custodial parent has a substantial interest in his or her relationship with his or her child that is worthy of protection. However, one salient distinction between the non-custodial parent-child relationship and the corporation-customer relationship is that the former involves a substantial non-economic interest of the parent while the latter normally involves a substantial economic interest of the corporation. But I believe that this distinction should not be determinative. The non-custodial parent's interest in the relationship with his or her child is without doubt of tremendous importance to him or her. To deny relief because of the nature of the interest involved, to afford protection to material interests but not to human and personal interests would, it seems to me, be arbitrary in the extreme. In contract law equity recognizes interests beyond the purely economic when, instead of awarding damages in the market value of real estate against a vendor who has wrongfully refused to close, it grants specific performance. Other non-economic interests should also be capable of protection in equity through the imposition of a fiduciary duty. I would hold, therefore, that the appellant's interest in a continuing relationship with his or her child is capable of protection by the imposition of such a duty.

[69] Before a cause of action for breach of fiduciary duty can be said to exist in this limited area within the field of family law, it is necessary to ask the same question as was asked in the context of the various torts proposed by the appellant, namely should existing fiduciary principles be extended? In examining this question it will again be necessary to consider the possibility that this cause of action might be used as a weapon by vindictive spouses and, more important still, it is necessary to consider whether or not the extension of fiduciary principles to this particular relationship would be in the best interests of children.

[70] This cause of action has, in my view, a number of significant advantages over the others. First, it arises only in one particular circumstance, the circumstance of vulnerability created by the splitting of the custody and access of children by the issuance of a court order. Unlike some of the torts examined, this action would not be available in any other fam-

ily law context. This is a very important consideration in light of the possible detrimental impact on children of recurring lawsuits by one parent against the other.

[71] Second, the cause of action for breach of fiduciary duty creates a very strong incentive to custodial parents to exercise their custodial rights so as to further the best interests of their children, to recognize that their children are entitled to an ongoing relationship with their other parent and that it is a serious matter to use the authority confided in them by an order of the court to deprive their children of this other dimension in their lives. I believe that this cause of action will help to promote a healthy and beneficial relationship between a child and both parents and is, in this respect, much more conducive to the best interests of the child than the tort actions previously considered.

[72] Finally, unlike the causes of action in tort, the cause of action for breach of fiduciary duty allows the court to take into account conduct of a non-custodial parent (whether related to custody and access issues or not) which might be contrary to the best interests of children. When considering breaches of equitable duty and awarding equitable remedies the court has a wide scope for the exercise of discretion which does not exist in respect of common law causes of action. In the context of breach of fiduciary duty this discretion would allow the court to deny relief to an aggrieved party or grant relief on certain terms if that party's conduct has disabled him or her from full relief, e.g., non-payment of spousal support or previous abuse of access rights. There is neither precedent nor historical basis for the exercise of such a discretion in the case of a common law tort action. The tort would be actionable regardless of the inequitable conduct of the plaintiff.

[73] It may be objected that despite these advantages which the action for breach of fiduciary duty possesses over the tort actions I have examined, the availability of any action would be contrary to the best interests of children because of the unavoidable deleterious effects of litigation on children. To some extent, this objection is well-founded. Inter-spousal litigation may create a conflict of loyalties in the children and may also have the effect of impairing child support. But it is within the jurisdiction of the courts, particularly courts of equity, to prevent a cause of action from proceeding if there is any risk of injury to the children's interests. The interests of the children are the paramount concern. I would hold, therefore, that the cause of action for breach

of fiduciary duty can proceed only if there is no risk that the support of the children will be impaired and no risk of a harmful conflict of loyalties arising in the children. The former condition may be satisfied when the children are fully grown and self-supporting or where the custodial parent has substantial assets. The latter condition may be satisfied where the relationship between the non-custodial parent and the children has been so severely damaged by the custodial parent's conduct that it is unlikely that a conflict of loyalties would occur. Accordingly, it will not be every denial of access rights that will give rise to a cause of action for breach of fiduciary duty but only where a sustained course of conduct has caused severe damage to the non-custodial parent-child relationship to the detriment of both the non-custodial parent and the child.

[74] The legislature has provided a series of remedies for the violation of the court order by the denial of access rights on specific occasions. As I have indicated earlier in the context of a common law cause of action enforcing a parental right of access, it is not open to this Court to introduce common law causes of action which the legislature did not see fit to provide in order to redress the violation of a court order. The ability of the court to introduce common law actions into areas where the legislature has intervened was recently addressed by this Court in *Seneca College of Applied Arts and Technology v. Bhadauria*, [1981] 2 S.C.R. 181. In that case the plaintiff sought recognition of a new common law tort against unjustified invasion of one's interest not to be discriminated against in respect of an employment opportunity on grounds of race or national origin. The plaintiff urged that this common law right of action arose directly from a breach of *The Ontario Human Rights Code*, R.S.O. 1970, c. 318, as amended. This Court denied the existence of such an action because of "the comprehensiveness of the Code in its administrative and adjudicative features, the latter including a wide right of appeal to the Courts on both fact and law" (at p. 183 *per* Laskin C.J.) Laskin C.J. noted, at p. 188, that there was "a narrow line between founding a civil cause of action directly upon a breach of a statute and as arising from the statute itself and founding a civil cause of action at common law by reference to policies reflected in the statute and standards fixed by the statute". In his view, the proposed action fell into the former category. Laskin C.J. at p. 189 also stated:

> It is one thing to apply a common law duty of care to standards of behaviour under a statute;

that is simply to apply the law of negligence in the recognition of so-called statutory torts. It is quite a different thing to create by judicial fiat an obligation — one in no sense analogous to a duty of care in the law of negligence — to confer an economic benefit upon certain persons, with whom the alleged obligor has no connection, and solely on the basis of a breach of statute which itself provides comprehensively for remedies for its breach.

. . . .

[77] Accordingly, it would be my view that the cause of action for breach of fiduciary duty should be extended to this narrow but extremely important area of family law where the non-custodial parent is completely at the mercy of the custodial parent by virtue of that parent's position of power and authority over the children. If this is a situation which for very good reason the common law is ill-equipped to handle, resort to equity is entirely appropriate so that no just cause shall go without a remedy. The breach will be actionable only when judgment recovery will not impair child support and when the non-custodial parent-child relationship has been so severely damaged by the custodial parent's conduct as to make it highly unlikely that the action brought by the non-custodial parent would be the cause of any conflict of loyalties in the children. Such a cause of action, properly tailored as only equity can do and has done in other contexts, will create a strong incentive to further the best interests of children while eliminating the more harmful effects commonly associated with inter-spousal litigation.

. . . .

4. CONCLUSION

[84] The facts as pleaded in the statement of claim could, if proved, give rise to a cause of action for breach of fiduciary duty. The plaintiff alleges that the defendants engaged in a course of conduct over a substantial period of time designed to defeat his access rights and destroy his relationship with his children, that they were in fact successful in so doing, and that he incurred financial loss, the loss of his relationship with his children, and damage to his psychiatric and physical health as a consequence. The action should therefore proceed to trial.

. . . .

Appeal dismissed with costs, **WILSON J.** *dissenting.*

(c)   *Lac Minerals Ltd. v. International Corona Resources Ltd.*†

Supreme Court of Canada

[SOPINKA J. (segment on facts only):]

This appeal and cross-appeal raise important issues relating to fiduciary duty and breach of confidence. In particular, they require this Court to consider whether fiduciary obligations can arise in the context of abortive arm's-length negotiations between parties to a prospective commercial transaction. Also at issue are the nature of confidential information and the appropriate remedy for its misuse.

THE FACTS

The parties to these proceedings are International Corona Resources Ltd. (which I will refer to as either "Corona" or the "respondent") and Lac Minerals Ltd. (which I will refer to as either "Lac" or the "appellant"). Corona, which was incorporated in 1979, was at material times a junior mining company listed on the Vancouver Stock Exchange. Lac is a senior mining company which owns a number of operating mines and is listed on several Stock Exchanges. This action arises out of negotiations between Corona and Lac relating to the Corona property, the Williams property and the Hughes property, all of which are located in the Hemlo area of northern Ontario.

The Corona property consists of 17 claims with an area of approximately 680 acres. The Williams property consists of 11 patented claims, covering a total of about 400 acres, and is contiguous to the Corona property and to the west. The Hughes property consists of approximately 156 claims and surrounds both the Corona and Williams properties, except to the north of the Williams property. It is now in the names of Golden Sceptre Resources Limited, Goliath Gold Mines Limited and Noranda Exploration Company, Limited.

In October 1980, Corona had retained Mr. David Bell, a geologist consultant to carry out an extensive exploration programme on its property which involved extensive diamond drilling. Bell hired Mr. John Dadds, a mining technician, to assist him. The core that was obtained from the drilling was

identified, logged and then stored inside a core shack built on the Corona property. Assay results were sent to Bell and to the Corona office in Vancouver. Some of the results were communicated to the Vancouver Stock Exchange in the form of news releases and assay results, and were published from time to time in the *George Cross News Letter*, a daily newsletter published in Vancouver.

The results of this exploratory work led Bell to an interesting theory. The trial judge describes it in some detail, at p. 744:

> Mr. Bell testified that by February, 1981, he was sufficiently encouraged by the results of the drilling programme that he decided that it was time to acquire the Williams property and the claims to the north. Mr. Bell said that within the first month of drilling his opinion of the geology changed from what he initially thought was a secondary intrusive model, from reading the literature of the area, to a syngenetic deposit. That is a deposit formed at the same time and by the same process as the enclosing rocks. He concluded that the mineralization and gold values were not tied into a vein but rather that the mineralization was in a zone, or beds, of [metasediment] that indicated a volcanic origin. In Mr. Bell's opinion, in all likelihood, the distribution of gold could be spread over quite a large area and there could be pools or puddles of ore, indicating to him that the exploration programme should be extended along the zone to adjoining properties.

This increased the interest in surrounding properties and Bell, on behalf of Corona, requested Mr. Donald McKinnon, a prospector who was familiar with the properties, to attempt to acquire the Williams property. Representatives of Lac read about these results in the March 20, 1981 *George Cross News Letter* and arranged to visit the Corona property. ... Bell said that before he left, Sheehan told him that he "wanted me to drop into Toronto when I was there and to further the discussions of their visit and talk about possible terms". A meeting was arranged for May 8 in Toronto at Lac's head office.

---

† [1989] 2 S.C.R. 574.

[The trial judge] found as a fact that there were no discussions regarding confidentiality during the May 6 property visit except in connection with an unrelated matter.

Following the site visit, Sheehan and Pegg returned quickly to Lac's exploration office in Toronto and instructed Lac personnel to gather information on the Hemlo area from the Lac library of files. They then went to the Assessment Office of the Ontario Department of Mines to obtain copies of all claim maps, reports, publications and assessment work files that were available on the area. Sheehan told a Lac geologist to ascertain what claims would be necessary to cover the favourable belt to the east of the Corona property. The geologist decided that about 600 claims should be staked and immediately thereafter, on May 8, Lac began staking what are now known as the White River claims.

On May 8, Bell and Sheehan met and discussed the geology of the area, its similarity to the Bousquet area of Quebec, at which both Pegg and Sheehan had worked, and the possible terms of an agreement between Corona and Lac. Sheehan told Bell of Lac's staking to the east. Bell said that the two men discussed the properties around the Corona property. Corona's interest in the Williams and Hughes properties was mentioned and Sheehan gave Bell advice on how to pursue a patented claim. Bell told Sheehan that Corona had somebody doing that, without mentioning McKinnon by name. A number of avenues for progress were discussed and Sheehan said that he would send a letter outlining the terms that were discussed. Again, nothing was said regarding confidentiality.

On May 19, Sheehan wrote to Bell as follows (at p. 750):

> Further to our meeting in Toronto I would like to give you this letter as further evidence of our sincerity in joining with Corona re exploration in the Hemlo area.
>
> As we discussed there are a number of avenues that could be explored regarding a working arrangement re the property and to that end I will list the various possibilities:
> a) Corona could have our Company do a financing and ultimately we would scale it forward so as to control Corona.
> b) We form a joint venture where Long Lac (a Lac subsidiary) spends say 1.5 to 2.0 times amount spent by Corona for a 60% interest. Beyond that point we spend on a 60-40 basis or use a dilution formula down to a minimum should one party decide to stop contributing. In addition Lac would have to spend a definite amount of money to reach a threshold before they would acquire any interest.
> c) A possible significant cash payment with a variation in interests as a result of the amount of cash payment. Followed by a Lac work proposal.
>
> As discussed we should entertain the possibility of Corona participate (*sic*) in the Hughes ground and that should be actively pursued. In addition we are staking ground in the area and recognizing Corona's limited ability to contribute we could work Corona into the overall picture as part of an overall exploration strategy.
>
> I believe at some point within the next few weeks we should have an understanding that Corona and Lac should seriously examine an avenue for continual work in the area. Perhaps you could give our management a presentation of results to date ie, sections, general geology, longitudinal presentation — location potential etc. Based on foregoing we could then arrive at a sound basis for structuring a working agreement.

... Bell replied by letter dated May 22 as follows:

> I am in receipt of your letter dated May 19, 1981 regarding the Hemlo Property.
>
> First may I thank you for your fine hospitality during my brief visit to Toronto.
>
> I am forwarding a copy of your proposal to Vancouver for the other directors to review. We are presently well into our Phase II, exploring and extending the previously examined parameters outlined in Phase I. Our present plans are to complete 30,000 to 35,000 feet of diamond drilling at which time a general over-all review will take place.
>
> At this point, until I hear otherwise from the directors in Vancouver, I like your idea of Corona's contribution with Long Lac Minerals Exploration Limited as part of an overall exploration programme in the area.
>
> In the meantime I do believe we should keep in touch and maintain the fine relationship presently established.

. . . .

On May 27, Corona released to the Vancouver Stock Exchange encouraging assay results of a drill hole, which the trial judge referred to as the "discovery hole". These results were published in the *George Cross News Letter* of May 29, and further results confirming an extension of the "discovery hole" were released on June 4 and published in the *George Cross News Letter* of June 8.

Subsequently, the results of further drill holes that were encouraging were published by Corona. On June 8, Mr. Murray Pezim, a stock promoter from Vancouver, became a director of Corona. Pezim arranged for Bell to make a presentation in Vancouver on behalf of Corona to a large number of brokers. Some of the information developed by Bell was imparted to those present at this meeting.

On June 15 a meeting was also arranged for June 30 at Lac's head office in Toronto, at which Bell was to make a presentation in accordance with Sheehan's letter of May 19. Following the meeting, sections, a detailed drill plan and apparently a vertically longitudinal section were left with Lac. Mr. Peter Allen, the President of Lac, advised Bell to be aggressive in his pursuit of the Williams property and Bell responded that Corona had somebody pursuing this property on their behalf. Allen told Sheehan to get a proposal out to Corona and Sheehan indicated that he would have such a proposal out within three weeks.

According to Bell, no one from Lac ever told him that they would not acquire the Williams property and Lac was never told that the information given to it was private, privileged or confidential. Although the evidence was contradictory, the trial judge found as a fact that the pursuit by Corona of the Williams property was mentioned at the meeting. This and other information revealed to Lac went beyond the information that had been made public. This finding was confirmed by the Court of Appeal. The trial judge also found that it was agreed that a proposal would be sent by Lac to Corona within three weeks, and that the purpose of the meeting was to discuss a possible deal between Corona and Lac in order to provide Corona with the financing needed to develop a mine.

Meanwhile, on June 8, McKinnon had spoken to Mrs. Williams by telephone and made an oral offer for the Williams property, which was followed by a written offer prepared by solicitors. On July 3, after some searching, Sheehan located Mrs. Williams by telephone and made an oral offer to her. She asked for a written offer and by letter dated July 6, 1981, Lac's legal counsel put it in writing.

... Lac's offer was accepted on July 28 and a formal agreement was signed on August 25, 1981.

After hearing that the Lac offer had been accepted, Pezim turned the matter over to his solicitors. On August 18, 1981, Sheehan went to Vancouver to attempt to resume negotiations with Pezim, who asked for the return of the Williams property. No agreement was reached. Later, Mr. Donald Moore, another director of Corona

attempted to revive negotiations with Sheehan, without success.

. . . .

[WILSON J.:]

... I agree with my colleague, La Forest J., as to the appropriate remedy in this case. I propose to comment briefly on the three issues before the Court on this appeal as identified by them:

(1) Fiduciary Duty

It is my view that, while no ongoing fiduciary relationship arose between the parties by virtue only of their arm's length negotiations towards a mutually beneficial commercial contract for the development of the mine, a fiduciary duty arose in Lac Minerals Ltd. ("Lac") when International Corona Resources Ltd. ("Corona") made available to Lac its confidential information concerning the Williams property, thereby placing itself in a position of vulnerability to Lac's misuse of that information. At that point Lac came under a duty not to use that information for its own exclusive benefit. Lac breached that fiduciary duty by acquiring the Williams property for itself.

It is, in other words, my view of the law that there are certain relationships which are almost *per se* fiduciary such as trustee and beneficiary, guardian and ward, principal and agent, and that where such relationships subsist they give rise to fiduciary duties. On the other hand, there are relationships which are not in their essence fiduciary, such as the relationship brought into being by the parties in the present case by virtue of their arm's length negotiations towards a joint venture agreement, but this does not preclude a fiduciary duty from arising out of specific conduct engaged in by them or either of them within the confines of the relationship. This, in my view, is what happened here when Corona disclosed to Lac confidential information concerning the Williams property. Lac became at that point subject to a fiduciary duty with respect to that information not to use it for its own use or benefit.

(2) Breach of Confidence

I agree with my colleagues that Lac's conduct may also be characterized as a breach of confidence at common law with respect to the information concerning the Williams property. The breach again consisted of Lac's acquisition of the Williams property for itself, such property being the subject of the confidence.

. . . .

[La FOREST J.:]

INTRODUCTION

The short issue in this appeal is whether this Court will uphold the Ontario Court of Appeal and trial court decisions ordering Lac Minerals Ltd. ("Lac") to deliver up to International Corona Resources Ltd. ("Corona"), land (the Williams property) on which there is a gold mine, on being compensated for the value of improvements Lac has made to the property ($153,978,000) in developing the mine.

. . . .

It is convenient to set forth my conclusions at the outset. I agree with Sopinka J. that Lac misused confidential information confided to it by Corona in breach of a duty of confidence. With respect, however, I do not agree with him about the nature and scope of that duty. Nor do I agree that in the circumstances of this case it is appropriate for this Court to substitute an award of damages for the constructive trust imposed by the courts below. Moreover, while it is not strictly necessary for the disposition of the case, I have a conception of fiduciary duties different from that of my colleague, and I would hold that a fiduciary duty, albeit of limited scope, arose in this case. In the result, I would dismiss the appeal.

THE ISSUES

Three issues must be addressed:

1. What was the nature of the duty of confidence that was breached by Lac?
2. Does the existence of the duty of confidence, alone or in conjunction with the other facts as found below, give rise to any fiduciary obligation or relationship? If so, what is the nature of that obligation or relation?
3. Is a constructive trust an available remedy for a breach of confidence as well as for breach of a fiduciary duty, and if so, should this Court interfere with the lower courts' imposition of that remedy?

BREACH OF CONFIDENCE

I can deal quite briefly with the breach of confidence issue. I have already indicated that Lac breached a duty of confidence owed to Corona. The test for whether there has been a breach of confidence is not seriously disputed by the parties. It consists in establishing three elements: that the information conveyed was confidential, that it was communicated in confidence, and that it was misused by the party to whom it was communicated. In *Coco v. A. N. Clark (Engineers) Ltd.*, [1969] R.P.C. 41 (Ch.), Megarry J. (as he then was) put it as follows at p. 47:

> In my judgment, three elements are normally required if, apart from contract, a case of breach of confidence is to succeed. First, the information itself, in the words of Lord Greene, M.R. in the *Saltman* case on page 215, must "have the necessary quality of confidence about it." Secondly, that information must have been imparted in circumstances importing an obligation of confidence. Thirdly, there must be an unauthorized use of that information to the detriment of the party communicating it . . .

This is the test applied by both the trial judge and the Court of Appeal. Neither party contends that it is the wrong test. Lac, however, forcefully argued that the courts below erred in their application of the test. Lac submitted that "The real issue is whether Corona proved that LAC received confidential information from it and [whether] it should have known such information was confidential".

Sopinka J. has set out the findings of the trial judge on these issues, ... Essentially, the trial judge found that the three elements set forth above were met: (1) Corona had communicated information that was private and had not been published; (2) while there was no mention of confidence with respect to the site visit, there was a mutual understanding between the parties that they were working towards a joint venture and that valuable information was communicated to Lac under circumstances giving rise to an obligation of confidence; and, (3) Lac made use of the information in obtaining the Williams property and was not authorized by Corona to bid on that property. I agree with my colleague that the information provided by Corona was the springboard that led to the acquisition of the Williams property. I also agree that the trial judge correctly applied the reasonable man test. The trial judge's conclusion that it was obvious to Sheehan, Lac's Vice-President Exploration, that the information was being communicated in circumstances giving rise to an obligation of confidence, following as it did directly on a finding of credibility against Sheehan, is unassailable.

In general, then, there is no difference between my colleague and me that Lac committed a breach of confidence in the present case. Where we differ — and it is a critically important difference — is in the nature and scope of the breach. The precise extent of that difference can be seen by a closer examination of the findings and evidence on the third element of the test set forth above, and I will, therefore, set forth my views on this element at greater length.

. . . .

... [The trial judge] concluded that there had been an unauthorized use since Lac had not been authorized by Corona to bid on the Williams property. In other words, Corona did not consent to the use of the information by Lac for the purpose of acquiring the Williams land for Lac's own account, or, for that matter, for any purpose other than furthering negotiations to jointly explore and develop these properties. He also found that the information had been used to the detriment of Corona. When the sole question the learned trial judge was addressing was whether Lac misused the confidential information Corona had provided to it and his sole conclusion was that "but for the actions of Lac, Corona would have acquired the Williams property and therefore Lac acted to the detriment of Corona" [emphasis added], I find the conclusion inescapable that the trial judge found as a fact that but for the underline{confidential information received and misused}, Corona would have acquired the Williams property and that Lac was not authorized to obtain it.

If, as we saw, each of the three elements of the above-cited test are made out, a claim for breach of confidence will succeed. The receipt of confidential information in circumstances of confidence establishes a duty not to use that information for any purpose other than that for which it was conveyed. If the information is used for such a purpose, and detriment to the confider results, the confider will be entitled to a remedy.

. . . .

The evidence of Lac's President, Mr. Allen, and of the experts called on behalf of Lac also support the position that Lac was not entitled to bid on the property and that Corona could expect that Lac would not do so. Allen testified as follows, in a passage to which both courts below attached central importance:

> If one geologist goes to another geologist and says, are you interested in making some sort of a deal and between the two of them, they agree that they should consider seriously the possibility of making a deal, I think for a short period of time that while they are exploring that, that any

transference of data would be — I would hope the geologists would be competent enough to identify the difference between published, unpublished, confidential and so on but in the case that they weren't, there was just some exchange of conversation or physical data, then I would say that while both of them were seriously and honestly engaged in preparing a deal, that Lac and the other party would both have a duty towards each other not to hurt each other as the result of any information that was exchanged. [Emphasis added.]

All the experts called by Lac agreed with the tenor of this statement.

. . . .

Whether these statements amount to a legally enforceable custom or whether they create a fiduciary duty are separate questions, but at the very least, they show that Lac was aware that it owed some obligation to Corona to act in good faith, and that that obligation included the industry-recognized practice not to acquire the property which was being pursued by a party with which it was negotiating.

. . . .

This entire inquiry appears, however, to be misdirected. In establishing a breach of a duty of confidence, the relevant question to be asked is, "what is the confidee entitled to do with the information?" and not, "to what use he is prohibited from putting it?" Any use other than a permitted use is prohibited and amounts to a breach of duty. When information is provided in confidence, the obligation is on the confidee to show that the use to which he put the information is not a prohibited use. In *Coco v. A. N. Clark (Engineers) Ltd.*, *supra*, at p. 48, Megarry J. said this in regard to the burden on the confidee to repel a suggestion of confidence:

> In particular, where information of commercial or industrial value is given on a business-like basis and with some avowed common object in mind, such as a joint venture or the manufacture of articles by one party for the other, I would regard the recipient as carrying a heavy burden if he seeks to repel a contention that he was bound by an obligation of confidence....

In my view, the same burden applies where it is shown that confidential information has been used and the user is called upon to show that such use was permitted. Lac has not discharged that burden in this case.

I am therefore of the view that Lac breached a duty owed to Corona by approaching Mrs. Williams with a view to acquiring her property, and by acquiring that property, whether or not Lac intended to invite Corona to participate in its subsequent exploration and development. Such a holding may mean that Lac is uniquely disabled from pursuing property in the area for a period of time, but such a result is not unacceptable. Lac had the option of either pursuing a relationship with Corona in which Corona would disclose confidential information to Lac so that Lac and Corona could negotiate a joint venture for the exploration and development of the area, or Lac could, on the basis of publicly available information, have pursued property in the area on its own behalf. Lac, however, is not entitled to the best of both worlds.

. . . .

FIDUCIARY OBLIGATION

Having established that Lac breached a duty of confidence owed to Corona, the existence of a fiduciary relationship is only relevant if the remedies for a breach of a fiduciary obligation differ from those available for a breach of confidence. In my view, the remedies available to one head of claim are available to the other, so that provided a constructive trust is an appropriate remedy for the breach of confidence in this case, finding a fiduciary duty is not strictly necessary. In my view, regardless of the basis of liability, a constructive trust is the only just remedy in this case. Nonetheless, in light of the argument, I think it appropriate to consider whether a fiduciary relationship exists in the circumstances here.

There are few legal concepts more frequently invoked but less conceptually certain than that of the fiduciary relationship. In specific circumstances and in specific relationships, courts have no difficulty in imposing fiduciary obligations, but at a more fundamental level, the principle on which that obligation is based is unclear. Indeed, the term "fiduciary" has been described as "one of the most ill-defined, if not altogether misleading terms in our law": see Finn, *Fiduciary Obligations*, at p. 1. It has been said that the fiduciary relationship is "a concept in search of a principle"; ... Some have suggested that the principles governing fiduciary obligations may indeed be undefinable (...), while others have doubted whether there can be any "universal, all-purpose definition of the fiduciary relationship" ... The challenge posed by these criticisms has been taken up by courts and academics convinced of the view that underlying the

divergent categories of fiduciary relationships and obligations lies some unifying theme; see *Frame v. Smith*, [1987] 2 S.C.R. 99, at p. 134, *per* Wilson J.... This case presents a further opportunity to consider such a principle.

In *Guerin v. The Queen*, [1984] 2 S.C.R. 335, Dickson J. (as he then was) discussed the nature of fiduciary obligations in the following passage, at pp. 383–84:

> The concept of fiduciary obligation originated long ago in the notion of breach of confidence, one of the original heads of jurisdiction in Chancery.
>
> ...

Professor Ernest Weinrib maintains in his article *The Fiduciary Obligation* (1975), 25 U.T.L.J. 1, at p. 7, that "the hallmark of a fiduciary relation is that the relative legal positions are such that one party is at the mercy of the other's discretion." Earlier, at p. 4, he puts the point in the following way:

> [Where there is a fiduciary obligation] there is a relation in which the principal's interests can be affected by, and are therefore dependent on, the manner in which the fiduciary uses the discretion which has been delegated to him. The fiduciary obligation is the law's blunt tool for the control of this discretion.
>
> <u>I make no comment upon whether this description is broad enough to embrace all fiduciary obligations</u>. I do agree, however, that where by statute, agreement, or perhaps by unilateral undertaking, one party has an obligation to act for the benefit of another, and that obligation carries with it a discretionary power, the party thus empowered becomes a fiduciary. Equity will then supervise the relationship by holding him to the fiduciary's strict standard of conduct.
>
> It is sometimes said that the nature of fiduciary relationships is both established and exhausted by the standard categories of agent, trustee, partner, director, and the like. I do not agree. It is the nature of the relationship, not the specific category of actor involved that gives rise to the fiduciary duty. The categories of fiduciary, like those of negligence, should not be considered closed. [Emphasis added.]

Wilson J. had occasion to consider the extension of fiduciary obligations to new categories of relationships in *Frame v. Smith, supra*. She found, at p. 136 that:

> ... there are common features discernible in the contexts in which fiduciary duties have been found to exist and these common features do provide a rough and ready guide to whether or

not the imposition of a fiduciary obligation on a new relationship would be appropriate and consistent.

Relationships in which a fiduciary obligation have been imposed seem to possess three general characteristics:

(1) The fiduciary has scope for the exercise of some discretion or power.
(2) The fiduciary can unilaterally exercise that power or discretion so as to affect the beneficiary's legal or practical interests.
(3) The beneficiary is peculiarly vulnerable to or at the mercy of the fiduciary holding the discretion or power. [Emphasis added.]

It will be recalled that the issue in that case, though not originally raised by the parties but argued at the request of the Court, was whether the relationship of a custodial parent to a non-custodial parent could be considered a category to which fiduciary obligations could attach. Wilson J. would have been willing to extend the categories of fiduciary relations to include such parties. While the majority in that case did not consider it necessary to address the bases on which fiduciary obligations arise (essentially because it considered the statute there to constitute a discrete code), as will be seen from my reasons below, I find Wilson J.'s approach helpful.

Much of the confusion surrounding the term "fiduciary" stems, in my view, from its undifferentiated use in at least three distinct ways. The first is as used by Wilson J. in *Frame v. Smith, supra*. There the issue was whether a certain class of relationship, custodial and non-custodial parents, were a category, analogous to directors and corporations, solicitors and clients, trustees and beneficiaries, and agents and principals, the existence of which relationship would give rise to fiduciary obligations. The focus is on the identification of relationships in which, because of their inherent purpose or their presumed factual or legal incidents, the courts will impose a fiduciary obligation on one party to act or refrain from acting in a certain way. The obligation imposed may vary in its specific substance depending on the relationship, though compendiously it can be described as the fiduciary duty of loyalty and will most often include the avoidance of a conflict of duty and interest and a duty not to profit at the expense of the beneficiary. The presumption that a fiduciary obligation will be owed in the context of such a relationship is not irrebuttable, but a strong presumption will exist that such an obligation is present. Further, not every legal claim arising out of a relationship with fiduciary incidents will give rise to a claim for breach of fiduciary duty. ...

It is only in relation to breaches of the specific obligations imposed because the relationship is one characterized as fiduciary that a claim for breach of fiduciary duty can be founded. In determining whether the categories of relationships which should be presumed to give rise to fiduciary obligations should be extended, the rough and ready guide adopted by Wilson J. is a useful tool for that evaluation. This class of fiduciary obligation need not be considered further, as Corona's contention is not that "parties negotiating towards a joint-venture" constitute a category of relationship, proof of which will give rise to a presumption of fiduciary obligation, but rather that a fiduciary relationship arises out of the particular circumstances of this case.

This brings me to the second usage of fiduciary, one I think more apt to the present case. The imposition of fiduciary obligations is not limited to those relationships in which a presumption of such an obligation arises. Rather, a fiduciary obligation can arise as a matter of fact out of the specific circumstances of a relationship. As such it can arise between parties in a relationship in which fiduciary obligations would not normally be expected. I agree with this comment of Professor Finn in "The Fiduciary Principle", *supra*, at p. 64:

What must be shown, in the writer's view, is that the actual circumstances of a relationship are such that one party is entitled to expect that the other will act in his interests in and for the purposes of the relationship. Ascendancy, influence, vulnerability, trust, confidence or dependence doubtless will be of importance in making this out. But they will be important only to the extent that they evidence a relationship suggesting that entitlement. The critical matter in the end is the role that the alleged fiduciary has, or should be taken to have, in the relationship. It must so implicate that party in the other's affairs or so align him with the protection or advancement of that other's interests that foundation exists for the "fiduciary expectation". Such a role may generate an actual expectation that that other's interests are being served. This is commonly so with lawyers and investment advisers. But equally the expectation may be a judicially prescribed one because the law itself ordains it to be that other's entitlement. And this may be so either because that party should, given the actual circumstances of the relationship, be accorded that entitlement irrespective of whether he has adverted to the matter, or because the purpose of the relationship itself is perceived to be such that to allow disloyalty in it would be to jeopardise its perceived social utility.

It is in this sense, then, that the existence of a fiduciary obligation can be said to be a question of fact to be determined by examining the specific facts and circumstances surrounding each relationship; see Waters, *Law of Trusts in Canada* (2nd ed. 1984), at p. 405. If the facts give rise to a fiduciary obligation, a breach of the duties thereby imposed will give rise to a claim for equitable relief.

The third sense in which the term "fiduciary" is used is markedly different from the two usages discussed above. It requires examination here because, as I will endeavour to explain, it gives a misleading colouration to the fiduciary concept. This third usage of "fiduciary" stems, it seems, from a perception of remedial inflexibility in equity. Courts have resorted to fiduciary language because of the view that certain remedies, deemed appropriate in the circumstances, would not be available unless a fiduciary relationship was present. In this sense, the label fiduciary imposes no obligations, but rather is merely instrumental or facilitative in achieving what appears to be the appropriate result. ...

. . . .

To recapitulate, the first class of fiduciary is not in issue in this appeal. It is not contended that all parties negotiating towards a joint venture are a class to which fiduciary obligations should presumptively attach. As will be clear from my discussion of the third usage of the term fiduciary, I am not prepared to hold that because a constructive trust is the appropriate remedy a fiduciary label therefore attaches, though I will deal later with why, even if the relationship is not fiduciary in any sense, a constructive trust may nonetheless be appropriate. The issue that remains for immediate discussion is whether the facts in this case, as found by the courts below, support the imposition of a fiduciary obligation within the second category discussed above, and whether, acting as it did, Lac was in breach of the obligations thereby imposed.

. . . .

While it is almost trite to say that a fiduciary relationship does not normally arise between arm's length commercial parties, I am of the view that the courts below correctly found a fiduciary obligation in the circumstances of this case and correctly found Lac to be in breach of it. I turn then to a consideration of the factors which in this case support the imposition of that duty. These can conveniently be grouped under three headings, (1) trust and confidence, (2) industry practice and (3) vulnerability. As

will be seen these factors overlap to some extent, but considered as a whole they support the proposition that Corona could reasonably expect Lac to not act to Corona's detriment by acquiring the Williams land, and that Corona's expectation should be legally protected.

TRUST AND CONFIDENCE

The relationship of trust and confidence that developed between Corona and Lac is a factor worthy of significant weight in determining if a fiduciary obligation existed between the parties. The existence of such a bond plays an important role in determining whether one party could reasonably expect the other to act or refrain from acting against the interests of the former. That said, the law of confidence and the law relating to fiduciary obligations are not co-extensive. They are not, however, completely distinct. Indeed, while there may be some dispute as to the jurisdictional basis of the law of confidence, it is clear that equity is one source of jurisdiction: see *Saltman Engineering Co. v. Campbell Engineering Co.* (1948), 65 R.P.C. 203 (C.A.) In *Guerin v. The Queen, supra*, Dickson J. noted that the law of fiduciary obligations had its origin in the law of confidence. Professor Finn thought it was settled that confidential information, whether classified as property or not, will attract fiduciary law's protection provided the circumstances are such as to attract a duty of confidence: "The Fiduciary Principle", *supra*, at p. 50. I agree with the view of both courts below that the law of confidence and the law of fiduciary obligations, while distinct, are intertwined.

In a claim for breach of confidence, Gurry tells us (*Breach of Confidence*, at pp. 161–62):

> ... the court's concern is for the protection of a confidence which *has been created* by the disclosure of confidential information by the confider to the confidant. The court's attention is thus focused on the protection of the confidential information because it has been the medium for the creation of a relationship of confidence; its attention is *not* focused on the information as a medium by which a *pre-existing* duty is breached.

However, the facts giving rise to an obligation of confidence are also of considerable importance in the creation of a fiduciary obligation. If information is imparted in circumstances of confidence, and if the information is known to be confidential, it cannot be denied that the expectations of the parties may be affected so that one party reasonably anticipates that the other will act or refrain from acting in a certain way. A claim for breach of confidence will only be made out, however, when it is shown that the confidee has misused the information to the detriment of the confidor. Fiduciary law, being concerned with the exaction of a duty of loyalty, does not require that harm in the particular case be shown to have resulted.

. . . .

... In all these circumstances, I am of the view that both parties would reasonably expect that a legal obligation would be imposed on Lac not to act in a manner contrary to Corona's interest with respect to the Williams property.

INDUSTRY PRACTICE

Both courts below placed considerable weight on the evidence of Allen to the effect that there was a "duty" not to act to the other party's detriment when in serious negotiations through the misuse of confidential information. For ease of reference, I set out his testimony here again:

> If one geologist goes to another geologist and says, are you interested in making some sort of a deal and between the two of them, they agree that they should consider seriously the possibility of making a deal, I think for a short period of time that while they are exploring that, that any transference of data would be — I would hope the geologists would be competent enough to identify the difference between published, unpublished, confidential and so on but in the case that they weren't, there was just some exchange of conversation or physical data, then I would say that while both of them were seriously and honestly engaged in preparing a deal, that Lac and the other party would both have a duty towards each other not to hurt each other as the result of any information that was exchanged.

All of Lac's experts agreed with this statement.

. . . .

Undoubtedly experts on mining practice are not qualified to give evidence on whether fiduciary obligations arose between the parties, as the existence of fiduciary obligations is a question of law to be answered by the court after a consideration of all the facts and circumstances. Thus, while the term "fiduciary" was not properly used by the trial judge in this passage, the evidence of the experts is of considerable importance in establishing standard practice in the industry from which one can determine the nature of the obligations which will be imposed by law.

It will be clear then, that in my view Lac's submissions relating to custom and usage were largely misdirected. The issue is not, as Lac submitted, what is "the legal effect of custom in the industry". Rather, it is what is the importance of the existence of a practice in the industry, established out of the mouth of the defendant and all its experts, in determining whether Corona could reasonably expect that Lac would act or refrain from acting against the interests of Corona. Framed thus, the evidence is of significant importance.

. . . .

VULNERABILITY

As I indicated above, vulnerability is not, in my view a necessary ingredient in every fiduciary relationship. It will of course often be present, and when it is found it is an additional circumstance that must be considered in determining if the facts give rise to a fiduciary obligation. I agree with the proposition put forward by Wilson J. that when determining if new classes of relationship should be taken to give rise to fiduciary obligations then the vulnerability of the class of beneficiaries of the obligation is a relevant consideration. Wilson J. put it as follows in *Frame v. Smith, supra,* at pp. 137–38:

> The third characteristic of relationships in which a fiduciary duty has been imposed is the element of vulnerability. This vulnerability arises from the inability of the beneficiary (despite his or her best efforts) to prevent the injurious exercise of the power or discretion combined with the grave inadequacy or absence of other legal or practical remedies to redress the wrongful exercise of the discretion or power. Because of the requirement of vulnerability of the beneficiary at the hands of the fiduciary, fiduciary obligations are seldom present in the dealings of experienced businessmen of similar bargaining strength acting at arm's length: see, for example, *Jirna Ltd. v. Mister Donut of Canada Ltd.* (1971), 22 D.L.R. (3d) 639 (Ont. C.A.), aff'd [1975] 1 S.C.R. 2. The law takes the position that such individuals are perfectly capable of agreeing as to the scope of the discretion or power to be exercised, i.e., any "vulnerability" could have been prevented through the more prudent exercise of their bargaining power and the remedies for the wrongful exercise or abuse of that discretion or power, namely damages, are adequate in such a case.

However, as I indicated, this case does not require a new class of relationships to be identified, but requires instead an examination of the specific facts of this case.

The Oxford English Dictionary, vol. 19, 2nd ed., at p. 786, defines "vulnerable" as follows:

> ... That may be wounded; susceptible of receiving wounds or physical injury.
> ... Open to attack or injury of a non-physical nature; *esp.*, offering an opening to the attacks of raillery, criticism, calumny, etc.

Persons are vulnerable if they are susceptible to harm, or open to injury. They are vulnerable at the hands of a fiduciary if the fiduciary is the one who can inflict that harm. It is clear, however, that fiduciary obligations can be breached without harm being inflicted on the beneficiary. *Keech v. Sandford* (1726), Sel. Cas. T. King 61, 25 E.R. 223, is the clearest example. In that case a fiduciary duty was breached even though the beneficiary suffered no harm and indeed could not have benefitted from the opportunity the fiduciary pursued. Beneficiaries of trusts, however, are a class that is susceptible to harm, and are therefore protected by the fiduciary regime. Not only is actual harm not necessary, susceptibility to harm will not be present in many cases. Each director of General Motors owes a fiduciary duty to that company, but one can seriously question whether General Motors is vulnerable to the actions of each and every director. Nonetheless, the fiduciary obligation is owed because, as a class, corporations are susceptible to harm from the actions of their directors.

I cannot therefore agree with my colleague, Sopinka J., that vulnerability or its absence will conclude the question of fiduciary obligation. As I indicated above, the issue should be whether, having regard to all the facts and circumstances, one party stands in relation to another such that it could reasonably be expected that that other would act or refrain from acting in a way contrary to the interests of that other. In any event, I would have thought it beyond argument that on the facts of this case Corona was vulnerable to Lac.

. . . .

The present litigation is, according to the evidence of Corona's witness Dr. Bragg, one of the reasons that confidentiality agreements are being used with increasing frequency. Where it is not established that the entering of confidentiality agreements is a common, usual or expected course of action, this Court should not presume such a procedure, particularly when the law of fiduciary obligations can operate to protect the reasonable expectations of the parties. There is no reason to clutter normal business practice by requiring a contract.

In this case the vulnerability of Corona at Lac's hand is clearly demonstrated by the circumstances in which Lac acquired the Williams property. Even though the offer from Corona would have paid to Mrs. Williams $250,000 within three years plus a 3 percent net smelter return, Mrs. Williams accepted the offer from Lac which paid only half that return. It is nothing short of fiction to suggest that *vis-à-vis* third parties or each other Lac and Corona stood on an equal footing. Corona was a junior mining company which needed to raise funds in order to finance the development of its property. This is why Corona welcomed the overture of Lac in the first place. Lac was a senior mining company that had the ability to provide those funds. Indeed Lac used this as a selling point to Mrs. Williams when it advised her that it was "an exploration and development company with four gold mines in production and had been in the mining and exploration business for decades".

I conclude therefore that Corona was vulnerable to Lac. The fact that these are commercial parties may be a factor in determining what the reasonable expectations of the parties are, and thus it may be a rare occasion that vulnerability is found between such parties. It is, however, shown to exist in this case and is a factor deserving of considerable weight in the identification of a fiduciary obligation.

CONCLUSION ON FIDUCIARY OBLIGATIONS

Taking these factors together, I am of the view that the courts below did not err in finding that a fiduciary obligation existed and that it was breached. Lac urged this Court not to accept this finding, warning that imposing a fiduciary relationship in a case such as this would give rise to the greatest uncertainty in commercial law, and result in the determination of the rules of commercial conduct on the basis of *ad hoc* moral judgments rather than on the basis of established principles of commercial law.

I cannot accept either of these submissions. Certainty in commercial law is, no doubt, an important value, but it is not the only value. As Grange J. has noted ("Good Faith in Commercial Transactions," *Commercial Law: Recent Developments and Emerging Trends*, Special Lectures of the Law Society of Upper Canada, 1985, at p. 70):

> There are many limitations on the freedom of contract both in the common law and by statute. Every one of them carries within itself the seeds of debate as to its meaning or at least its applicability to a particular set of facts.

In any event, it is difficult to see how giving legal recognition to the parties' expectations will throw commercial law into turmoil.

Commercial relationships will more rarely involve fiduciary obligations. That is not because they are immune from them, but because in most cases, they would not be appropriately imposed. I agree with this comment of Mason J. in *Hospital Products Ltd. v. United States Surgical Corp., supra*, at pp. 456–57:

> There has been an understandable reluctance to subject commercial transactions to the equitable doctrine of constructive trust and constructive notice. But it is altogether too simplistic, if not superficial, to suggest that commercial transactions stand outside the fiduciary regime as though in some way commercial transactions do not lend themselves to the creation of a relationship in which one person comes under an obligation to act in the interests of another. The fact that in the great majority of commercial transactions the parties stand at arms' length does not enable us to make a generalization that is universally true in relation to every commercial transaction. In truth, every such transaction must be examined on its merits with a view to ascertaining whether it manifests the characteristics of a fiduciary relationship.

. . . .

The argument on morality is similarly misplaced. It is simply not the case that business and accepted morality are mutually exclusive domains. Indeed, the Court of Appeal, after holding that to find a fiduciary relationship here made no broad addition to the law, a view I take to be correct, noted that the practice established by the evidence to support the obligation was consistent with "business morality and with encouraging and enabling joint development of the natural resources of the country". This is not new. Texts from as early as 1903 refer to the obligation of "good faith by partners in their dealings with each other extend[ing] to negotiations culminating in the partnership, although in advance of its actual creation" (Lindley, *A Treatise on the American Law Relating to Mines and Mineral Lands* (reprint of 2nd ed. 1903). In my view, no distinction should be drawn here between negotiations culminating in a partnership or a joint venture.

REMEDY

The appropriate remedy in this case cannot be divorced from the findings of fact made by the courts below. As I indicated earlier, there is no doubt in my mind that but for the actions of Lac in misusing confidential information and thereby acquiring the Williams property, that property would have been acquired by Corona. That finding is fundamental to the determination of the appropriate remedy. Both courts below awarded the Williams property to Corona on payment to Lac of the value to Corona of the improvements Lac had made to the property. The trial judge dealt only with the remedy available for a breach of a fiduciary duty, but the Court of Appeal would have awarded the same remedy on the claim for breach of confidence, even though it was of the view that it was artificial and difficult to consider the relief available for that claim on the hypothesis that there was no fiduciary obligation.

The issue then is this. If it is established that one party, (here Lac), has been enriched by the acquisition of an asset, the Williams property, that would have, but for the actions of that party been acquired by the plaintiff, (here Corona), and if the acquisition of that asset amounts to a breach of duty to the plaintiff, here either a breach of fiduciary obligation or a breach of a duty of confidence, what remedy is available to the party deprived of the benefit? In my view the constructive trust is one available remedy, and in this case it is the only appropriate remedy.

In my view the facts present in this case make out a restitutionary claim, or what is the same thing, a claim for unjust enrichment. When one talks of restitution, one normally talks of giving back to someone something that has been taken from them (a restitutionary proprietary award), or its equivalent value (a personal restitutionary award). As the Court of Appeal noted in this case, Corona never in fact owned the Williams property, and so it cannot be "given back" to them. However, there are concurrent findings below that but for its interception by Lac, Corona would have acquired the property. In *Air Canada v. British Columbia*, [1989] 1 S.C.R. 1161, at pp. 1202–03, I said that the function of the law of restitution "is to ensure that where a plaintiff has been deprived of wealth that is either in his possession <u>or would have accrued for his benefit</u>, it is restored to him. The measure of restitutionary recovery is the gain the [defendant] made at the [plaintiff's] expense." [Emphasis added.] In my view the fact that Corona never owned the property should not preclude it from the pursuing a restitutionary claim: see Birks, *An Introduction to the Law of Restitution*, at pp. 133–39. Lac has therefore been enriched at the expense of Corona.

That enrichment is also unjust, or unjustified, so that the plaintiff is entitled to a remedy. There is, in the words of Dickson J. in *Pettkus v. Becker*, [1980] 2 S.C.R. 834, at p. 848, an "absence of any juristic reason for the enrichment". The determination that the enrichment is "unjust" does not refer to abstract notions of morality and justice, but flows directly from the finding that there was a breach of a legally recognized duty for which the courts will grant relief. Restitution is a distinct body of law governed by its own developing system of rules. Breaches of fiduciary duties and breaches of confidence are both wrongs for which restitutionary relief is often appropriate. It is not every case of such a breach of duty, however, that will attract recovery based on the gain of the defendant at the plaintiff's expense. Indeed this has long been recognized by the courts. In *In re Coomber*, [1911] 1 Ch. 723, at pp. 728–29, Fletcher Moulton L.J. said:

> Fiduciary relations are of many different types; they extend from the relation of myself to an errand boy who is bound to bring me back my change up to the most intimate and confidential relations which can possibly exist between one party and another where the one is wholly in the hands of the other because of his infinite trust in him. All these are cases of fiduciary relations, and the Courts have again and again, in cases where there has been a fiduciary relation, interfered and set aside acts which, between persons in a wholly independent position, would have been perfectly valid. Thereupon in some minds there arises the idea that if there is any fiduciary relation whatever any of these types of interference is warranted by it. They conclude that every kind of fiduciary relation justifies every kind of interference. Of course that is absurd. The nature of the fiduciary relation must be such that it justifies the interference. <u>There is no class of case in which one ought more carefully to bear in mind the facts of the case, when one reads the judgment of the Court on those facts, than cases which relate to fiduciary and confidential relations and the action of the Court with regard to them.</u> [Emphasis added.]

In breach of confidence cases as well, there is considerable flexibility in remedy. Injunctions preventing the continued use of the confidential information are commonly awarded. Obviously that remedy would be of no use in this case where the total benefit accrues to the defendant through a single misuse of information. An account of profits is also often available. Indeed in both courts below an account of profits to the date of transfer of the mine was awarded. Usually an accounting is not a restitutionary measure of damages. Thus, while it is measured according to the defendant's gain, it is not measured by the defendant's gain at the plaintiff's expense. Occasionally, as in this case, the measures coincide. In a case quite relevant here, this Court unanimously imposed a constructive trust over property obtained from the misuse of confidential information: *Pre-Cam Exploration & Development Ltd. v. McTavish*, [1966] S.C.R. 551. More recently, a compensatory remedy has been introduced into the law of confidential relations. Thus in *Seager v. Copydex, Ltd. (No. 2)*, [1969] 2 All E.R. 718 (C.A.), an inquiry was directed concerning the market value of the information between a willing buyer and a willing seller. The defendant had unconsciously plagiarized the plaintiff's design. In those circumstances it would obviously have been unjust to exclude the defendant from the market when there was room for more than one participant.

. . . .

The essence of the imposition of fiduciary obligations is its utility in the promotion and preservation of desired social behaviour and institutions. Likewise with the protection of confidences. In the modern world the exchange of confidential information is both necessary and expected. Evidence of an accepted business morality in the mining industry was given by the defendant, and the Court of Appeal found that the practice was not only reasonable, but that it would foster the exploration and development of our natural resources. The institution of bargaining in good faith is one that is worthy of legal protection in those circumstances where that protection accords with the expectations of the parties. The approach taken by my colleague, Sopinka J., would, in my view, have the effect not of encouraging bargaining in good faith, but of encouraging the contrary. If by breaching an obligation of confidence one party is able to acquire an asset entirely for itself, at a risk of only having to compensate the other for what the other would have received if a formal relationship between them were concluded, the former would be given a strong incentive to breach the obligation and acquire the asset. In the present case, it is true that had negotiations been concluded, Lac could also have acquired an interest in the Corona land, but that is only an expectation and not a certainty. Had Corona acquired the Williams property, as they would have but for Lac's breach, it seems probable that negotiations with Lac would have resulted in a concluded agreement. However, if Lac, during the negotiations, breached a duty of confidence owed to Corona, it seems certain that Corona would have broken off negotiations and Lac would be left with nothing. In such circumstances, many business people, weighing the risks, would breach the obligation and acquire the asset. This does nothing for the preservation of the institution of good faith bargaining or relationships of trust and confidence. The imposition of a remedy which restores an asset to the party who would have acquired it but for a breach of fiduciary duties or duties of confidence acts as a deterrent to the breach of duty and strengthens the social fabric those duties are imposed to protect. The elements of a claim in unjust enrichment having been made out, I have found no reason why the imposition of a restitutionary remedy should not be granted.

. . . .

In the case at hand, the restitutionary claim has been made out. The Court can award either a proprietary remedy, namely that Lac hand over the Williams property, or award a personal remedy, namely a monetary award. While, as the Chief Justice observed, "The principle of unjust enrichment lies at the heart of the constructive trust": see *Pettkus v. Becker*, at p. 847, the converse is not true. The constructive trust does not lie at the heart of the law of restitution. It is but one remedy, and will only be imposed in appropriate circumstances. Where it could be more appropriate than in the present case, however, it is difficult to imagine.

The trial judge assessed damages in this case at $700,000,000 in the event that the order that Lac deliver up the property was not upheld on appeal. In doing so he had to assess the damages in the face of evidence that the Williams property would be valued by the market at up to 1.95 billion dollars. Before us there is a cross-appeal that damages be reassessed at $1.5 billion. The trial judge found that no one could predict future gold prices, exchange rates or inflation with any certainty, or even on the balance of probabilities. Likewise he noted that the property had not been fully explored and that further reserves may be found. The Court of Appeal made the following comment, at p. 59, with which I am in entire agreement:

> ... there is no question but that gold properties of significance are unique and rare. There are almost insurmountable difficulties in assessing the value of such a property in the open market. The actual damage which has been sustained by Corona is virtually impossible to determine with any degree of accuracy. The profitability of

the mine, and accordingly its value, will depend on the ore reserves of the mine, the future price of gold from time to time, which in turn depends on the rate of exchange between the U.S. dollar and Canadian dollar, inflationary trends, together with myriad other matters, all of which are virtually impossible to predict.

To award only a monetary remedy in such circumstances when an alternative remedy is both available and appropriate would in my view be unfair and unjust.

There is no unanimous agreement on the circumstances in which a constructive trust will be imposed. Some guidelines can, however, be suggested. First, no special relationship between the parties is necessary. I agree with this comment of Wilson J. in *Hunter Engineering Co. v. Syncrude Canada Ltd.*, *supra*, at p. 519:

> Although both *Pettkus v. Becker* and *Sorochan v. Sorochan* were "family" cases, unjust enrichment giving rise to a constructive trust is by no means confined to such cases: see *Deglman v. Guaranty Trust Co.*, [1954] S.C.R. 725. Indeed, to do so would be to impede the growth and impair the flexibility crucial to the development of equitable principles.

. . . .

Secondly, it is not the case that a constructive trust should be reserved for situations where a right of property is recognized. That would limit the constructive trust to its institutional function, and deny to it the status of a remedy, its more important role. Thus, it is not in all cases that a pre-existing right of property will exist when a constructive trust is ordered. The imposition of a constructive trust can both recognize and create a right of property. When a constructive trust is imposed as a result of successfully tracing a plaintiff's asset into another asset, it is indeed debatable which the Court is doing. ...

In the [view of Goff and Jones] a proprietary claim should be granted when it is just to grant the plaintiff the additional benefits that flow from the recognition of a right of property. It is not the recognition of a right of property that leads to a constructive trust. It is not necessary, therefore, to determine whether confidential information is property, though a finding that it was would only strengthen the conclusion that a constructive trust is appropriate. This is the view of Fridman and McLeod, *Restitution*, at p. 539, where they say:

> ... there appears to be no doubt that a fiduciary who has consciously made use of confidential

information for private gain will be forced to account for the entire profits by holding such profits made from the use of the confidential information on a constructive trust for the beneficiary-estate. The proprietary remedy flows naturally from the conclusion that the information itself belonged to the beneficiary and there has been no transaction effective to divest his rights over the property.

I do not countenance the view that a proprietary remedy can be imposed whenever it is "just" to do so, unless further guidance can be given as to what those situations may be. To allow such a result would be to leave the determination of proprietary rights to "some mix of judicial discretion ... subjective views about which party 'ought to win'..., and 'the formless void of individual moral opinion'" ...

. . . .

Much of the difficulty disappears if it is recognized that in this context the issue of the appropriate remedy only arises once a valid restitutionary claim has been made out. The constructive trust awards a right in property, but that right can only arise once a right to relief has been established. In the vast majority of cases a constructive trust will not be the appropriate remedy. ... [A] constructive trust should only be awarded if there is reason to grant to the plaintiff the additional rights that flow from recognition of a right of property. Among the most important of these will be that it is appropriate that the plaintiff receive the priority accorded to

the holder of a right of property in a bankruptcy. More important in this case is the right of the property holder to have changes in value accrue to his account rather than to the account of the wrongdoer. Here as well it is justified to grant a right of property since the concurrent findings below are that the defendant intercepted the plaintiff and thereby frustrated its efforts to obtain a specific and unique property that the courts below held would otherwise have been acquired. The recognition of a constructive trust simply redirects the title of the Williams property to its original course. The moral quality of the defendants' act may also be another consideration in determining whether a proprietary remedy is appropriate. Allowing the defendant to retain a specific asset when it was obtained through conscious wrongdoing may so offend a court that it would deny to the defendant the right to retain the property. This situation will be more rare, since the focus of the inquiry should be upon the reasons for recognizing a right of property in the plaintiff, not on the reasons for denying it to the defendant.

Having specific regard to the uniqueness of the Williams property, to the fact that but for Lac's breaches of duty Corona would have acquired it, and recognizing the virtual impossibility of accurately valuing the property, I am of the view that it is appropriate to award Corona a constructive trust over that land.

Appeal and cross-appeal dismissed with costs, McINTYRE *and* SOPINKA JJ. *dissenting in part.*

(d) *Hodgkinson v. Simms*[†]

Supreme Court of Canada

[La FOREST J.:]

I. INTRODUCTION

This is a case of material non-disclosure in which the appellant alleges breach of fiduciary duty and breach of contract against the respondent in the performance of a contract for investment advice and

other tax-related financial services. The respondent, Mr. Simms, was a Chartered Accountant and partner in the respondent firm Simms & Waldman. Though the firm and Mr. Waldman are parties to these proceedings, I shall, because of Mr. Simms' central role, generally be referring to him when I speak of "the respondent". Mr. Simms had developed a special expertise in relation to multi-unit residen-

---

† [1994] 3 S.C.R. 377.

tial buildings (MURBs). In 1980 the appellant Mr. Hodgkinson retained Mr. Simms' services in the areas of tax planning and preparation, and in finding stable, tax-sheltering investments. Mr. Hodgkinson was a "neophyte" in the field of tax planning and tax-related investments. He approached Mr. Simms as an independent professional who would give him the impartial service and advice he was looking for. Mr. Hodgkinson decided to put himself in Mr. Simms' hands with respect to his tax planning and tax sheltering needs. In the course of their relationship, Mr. Simms recommended four MURB projects to Mr. Hodgkinson as meeting his investment criteria. Mr. Hodgkinson duly invested in these projects. What Mr. Hodgkinson did not know, however, was that at the time Mr. Simms was making these recommendations, he was in a financial relationship with the developers of the projects. The more MURBs Mr. Simms sold to Simms & Waldman clients, the larger the fees he reaped from the developers. While Mr. Simms attempted to deny the non-disclosure by arguing at discovery that his relationship with the developers was in fact disclosed to Mr. Hodgkinson, and then stating at trial that his business relationship with the developers did not commence until after Mr. Hodgkinson had invested in the projects, this line of defence was rejected by the trial judge and was not pursued on appeal. Rather, this appeal concerns the proper characterization of the relationship between the parties and determining the nature and extent of the civil liability, if any, flowing from the non-disclosure.

. . . .

II.   FACTS

The appellant, Mr. Hodgkinson, was in January 1980 a 30-year-old stockbroker working for Canarim Investments Ltd. He had joined Canarim in 1979, after a 7 year stint with A. E. Ames & Co., which he described as a conservative, blue-chip securities firm. By contrast, Mr. Hodgkinson described Canarim as an aggressive firm which dealt in speculative underwritings in the oil and gas and mining trades. At Canarim Mr. Hodgkinson's gross income increased from between $50,000 to $70,000 per year which he had been earning at A. E. Ames & Co. to $650,000 in 1980 and $1.2 million in 1981. Prior to retaining the services of Simms & Waldman, Mr. Hodgkinson had always prepared his own tax returns. His investment experience was quite limited. He had an interest in a ski chalet at Mt. Baker, two units in a MURB townhouse development in White

Rock, and some flow-through shares in a mineral exploration tax shelter. In addition, he had bought and sold a small house in West Vancouver. However, with the 10 to 20-fold increase in his gross income, Mr. Hodgkinson decided to seek professional assistance in both accounting for his money and sheltering it from taxation.

The respondent Simms was in 1980 a Chartered Accountant and a partner in the firm of Simms & Waldman. He is a member of the Canadian and British Columbia Institutes of Chartered Accountants. While Mr. Simms specialized in providing general tax and business advice to small businessmen and professionals, beginning in 1979 he developed a practice of evaluating real estate "tax shelter" investments, or MURBs, on behalf of clients. According to his evidence at trial, he and Mr. Russ Long, another accountant associated with Simms & Waldman, had analyzed approximately 70 tax shelters in 1979.

. . . .

Mr. Hodgkinson first consulted Mr. Simms in early January 1980. He was planning to marry in a few months and wanted to protect a portion of his earnings from the risks associated with the securities markets. In entrusting Mr. Simms with his financial matters, Mr. Hodgkinson placed a premium on the fact that Mr. Simms was not part of the high risk world of "promoters" in which he normally operated in his job at Canarim. He looked to Mr. Simms as someone who could be relied on for independent analysis in the complex area of tax shelter investments. While Mr. Hodgkinson desired assistance in preparing tax returns, his most important objective was to minimize his exposure to income tax while at the same time acquiring some stable long-term investments. Mr. Simms suggested MURBs as an ideal instrument for Mr. Hodgkinson in realizing his investment goals. He and Mr. Hodgkinson shared the view, common at the time, that real estate provided a stable long-term investment. In addition, investment in MURBs generated the potential for significant tax savings. MURBs were a product of a 1974 change in taxation policy made by the Minister of Finance to stimulate investment in rental real estate. Pursuant to regulation 1100(1) and Schedule B to the *Income Tax Act*, S.C. 1970-71-72, c. 63, individual taxpayers could shelter their income by claiming capital cost allowances from qualifying investments in real estate. As such, real estate developers, rather than selling apartment units on a "turn-key" basis, sold an undivided interest in the vacant land to each investor. The investors then entered into a construction contract with the developer, who would in turn construct the building on behalf of the investors. In this way investors became "mini-developers", and as such could deduct certain related costs (typically financing costs) incurred during the construction period. These deductions were known as "soft costs".

The relationship between the parties, and in particular Mr. Hodgkinson's confidence in Mr. Simms, was such that Mr. Hodgkinson did not ask many questions regarding the investments. He trusted Mr. Simms to do the necessary analysis, and believed if he recommended a project it was a good investment. By turns, Mr. Hodgkinson made substantial investments in four MURBs recommended by Mr. Simms. These investments were, in chronological order: (1) "Duncana", a mixed residential-commercial project in Penticton, B.C., (2) "Bella Vista", a 41-unit MURB apartment block also in Penticton, (3) "Oliver Place", a shopping centre in Oliver, B.C., and (4) "Enterprise Way", a warehouse project in Surrey, B.C. ...

As these proceedings attest, Mr. Hodgkinson's investments lost virtually all their value. When the real estate market crashed in 1981, Mr. Hodgkinson lost substantially on all of them. Each of the MURB units he purchased on the advice of Mr. Simms was either sold at a loss to avoid cash calls, or was the subject of foreclosures when they could not be sold or rented.

This is not a case of fraud or deceit. Mr. Hodgkinson did not pay any more than fair market value for any of the MURB units he purchased. He does not complain about this. Rather, the gravamen of Mr. Hodgkinson's complaint lies in the fact that, unknown to him, Mr. Simms was during the relevant period acting for the developers in the "structuring" of each of these MURB projects. Specifically, Mr. Simms advised and assisted the developers in the analysis and maximization of tax deductible expenses that could be incorporated into the real estate investments offered for sale. ...

Thus, while Mr. Hodgkinson got what he paid for from the developers, the same cannot be said of his relationship with Mr. Simms. Mr. Hodgkinson looked to Mr. Simms as an independent professional advisor, not a promoter. In short, Mr. Hodgkinson would not have invested in the impugned projects had he known the true nature and extent of Mr. Simms' relationship with the developers.

Mr. Hodgkinson brought an action in the Supreme Court of British Columbia for breach of fiduciary duty, breach of contract and negligence to recover all his losses on the four investments recommended by the respondent Simms. The claim in neg-

ligence was dismissed at trial and was not pursued before the Court of Appeal. The trial judge, Prowse J., however, allowed Mr. Hodgkinson's action for breach of fiduciary duty and breach of contract and awarded him damages in the amount of $350,507.62. The British Columbia Court of Appeal upheld the trial judge on the breach of contract issue, but reversed on the issue of fiduciary duties. As well, the Court of Appeal varied the damages award, setting damages at an amount equal to the fees received by Mr. Simms from the developers on account of the four projects, prorated as between the various investors in those projects.

. . . .

IV. ANALYSIS

Recovery for Breach of Fiduciary Obligation

The Legal Concept

Before turning to the particular facts of this case, it is useful to review the principles underlying the notion of fiduciary duties, for, in my view, liability in this case inexorably flows from these principles. In the famous case of *Lloyds Bank Ltd. v. Bundy*, [1975] Q.B. 326, Sir Eric Sachs of the English Court of Appeal stated the fiduciary principle as follows, at p. 341:

> Such cases tend to arise where someone relies on the guidance or advice of another, where the other is aware of that reliance and where the person upon whom reliance is placed obtains, or may well obtain, a benefit from the transaction or has some other interest in it being concluded. In addition, there must, of course, be shown to exist a vital element which in this judgment will for convenience be referred to as confidentiality. It is this element which is so impossible to define and which is a matter for the judgment of the court on the facts of any particular case.

From a conceptual standpoint, the fiduciary duty may properly be understood as but one of a species of a more generalized duty by which the law seeks to protect vulnerable people in transactions with others. I wish to emphasize from the outset, then, that the concept of vulnerability is not the hallmark of fiduciary relationship though it is an important *indicium* of its existence. Vulnerability is common to many relationships in which the law will intervene to protect one of the parties. It is, in fact, the "golden thread" that unites such related causes of action as breach of fiduciary duty, undue influence, unconscionability and negligent misrepresentation.

. . . .

The concepts of unequal bargaining power and undue influence are also often linked to discussions of the fiduciary principle. Claims based on these causes of action, it is true, will often arise in the context of a professional relationship side by side with claims related to duty of care and fiduciary duty; see Horace Krever and Marion Randall Lewis, "Fiduciary Obligations and the Professions" in *Special Lectures of the Law Society of Upper Canada, 1990, Fiduciary Duties*, at pp. 291–93. Indeed, all three equitable doctrines are designed to protect vulnerable parties in transactions with others. However, whereas undue influence focuses on the sufficiency of consent and unconscionability looks at the reasonableness of a given transaction, the fiduciary principle monitors the abuse of a loyalty reposed; see G. H. L. Fridman, *The Law of Contract in Canada* (2nd ed. 1986), at pp. 301–11. Thus, while the existence of a fiduciary relationship will often give rise to an opportunity for the fiduciary to gain an advantage through undue influence, it is possible for a fiduciary to gain an advantage for him- or herself without having to resort to coercion; see *Hospital Products, supra*; and *Canadian Aero Service Ltd. v. O'Malley*, [1974] S.C.R. 592. Similarly, while the doctrine of unconscionability is triggered by abuse of a pre-existing inequality in bargaining power between the parties, such an inequality is no more a necessary element in a fiduciary relationship than factors such as trust and loyalty are necessary conditions for a claim of unconscionability ...

. . . .

Having distinguished the fiduciary principle from other related equitable and common law doctrines, it is now possible to examine the nature of the fiduciary duty itself with a surer hand. While the legal concept of a fiduciary duty reaches back to the famous English case of *Keech v. Sandford* (1726), Sel. Cas. T. King 61, 25 E.R. 223, until recently the fiduciary duty could be described as a legal obligation in search of a principle. Indeed, commentators busied themselves in an effort to sort out this area of the law; see Ernest J. Weinrib, "The Fiduciary Obligation", *supra*; P. D. Finn, *Fiduciary Obligations* (1977); J. C. Shepherd, *The Law of Fiduciaries* (1981); Tamar Frankel, "Fiduciary Law" (1983), 71 *Calif. L. Rev.* 795; and P. D. Finn, "The Fiduciary Principle", *supra*. As I stated in *M. (K.) v. M. (H.)*, [1992] 3 S.C.R. 6, at p. 62, over the past ten years or so this Court has had occasion to consider and

enforce fiduciary obligations in a wide variety of contexts, and this has led to the development of a "fiduciary principle" which can be defined and applied with some measure of precision. ...

This conceptual approach to fiduciary duties was given analytical structure in the dissenting reasons of Wilson J. in *Frame v. Smith*, [1987] 2 S.C.R. 99, at p. 136, who there proposed a three-step analysis to guide the courts in identifying new fiduciary relationships. She stated that relationships in which a fiduciary obligation has been imposed are marked by the following three characteristics: (1) scope for the exercise of some discretion or power; (2) that power or discretion can be exercised unilaterally so as to effect the beneficiary's legal or practical interests; and, (3) a peculiar vulnerability to the exercise of that discretion or power. Although the majority held on the facts that there was no fiduciary obligation, Wilson J.'s mode of analysis has been followed as a "rough and ready guide" in identifying new categories of fiduciary relationships; see *Lac Minerals, supra, per* Sopinka J., at p. 599, and *per* La Forest J., at p. 646; *Canson, supra*, at p. 543; and *M. (K.) v. M. (H.), supra*, at pp. 63–64. Wilson J.'s guidelines constitute *indicia* that help recognize a fiduciary relationship rather than ingredients that define it.

In *Lac Minerals* I elaborated further on the approach proposed by Wilson J. in *Frame v. Smith*. I there identified three uses of the term fiduciary, only two of which I thought were truly fiduciary. The first is in describing certain relationships that have as their essence discretion, influence over interests, and an <u>inherent</u> vulnerability. In these types of relationships, there is a rebuttable presumption, arising out of the inherent purpose of the relationship, that one party has a duty to act in the best interests of the other party. Two obvious examples of this type of fiduciary relationship are trustee-beneficiary and agent-principal. In seeking to determine whether new classes of relationships are *per se* fiduciary, Wilson J.'s three-step analysis is a useful guide.

As I noted in *Lac Minerals*, however, the three-step analysis proposed by Wilson J. encounters difficulties in identifying relationships described by a slightly different use of the term "fiduciary", viz., situations in which fiduciary obligations, though not innate to a given relationship, arise as a matter of fact out of the specific circumstances of that particular relationship; see at p. 648. In these cases, the question to ask is whether, given all the surrounding circumstances, one party could reasonably have expected that the other party would act in the former's best interests with respect to the subject matter at issue. Discretion, influence, vulnerability and trust were mentioned as non-exhaustive examples of evidential factors to be considered in making this determination.

Thus, outside the established categories, what is required is evidence of a mutual understanding that one party has relinquished its own self-interest and agreed to act solely on behalf of the other party. ... In relation to the advisory context, then, there must be something more than a simple undertaking by one party to provide information and execute orders for the other for a relationship to be enforced as fiduciary. ...

More generally, relationships characterized by a unilateral discretion, such as the trustee-beneficiary relationship, are properly understood as simply a species of a broader family of relationships that may be termed "power-dependency" relationships. I employed this notion, developed in an article by Professor Coleman, to capture the dynamic of abuse in *Norberg v. Wynrib*, *supra*, at p. 255. *Norberg* concerned an aging physician who extorted sexual favours from a young female patient in exchange for feeding an addiction she had previously developed to the pain-killer Fiorinal. The difficulty in *Norberg* was that the sexual contact between the doctor and patient had the appearance of consent. However, when the pernicious effects of the situational power imbalance were considered, it was clear that true consent was absent. While the concept of a "power-dependency" relationship was there applied to an instance of sexual assault, in my view the concept accurately describes any situation where one party, by statute, agreement, a particular course of conduct, or by unilateral undertaking, gains a position of overriding power or influence over another party. Because of the particular context in which the relationship between the plaintiff and the doctor arose in that case, I found it preferable to deal with the case without regard to whether or not a fiduciary relationship arose. However, my colleague Justice McLachlin did dispose of the claim on the basis of the fiduciary duty, and whatever may be said of the peculiar situation in *Norberg*, I have no doubt that had the situation there arisen in the ordinary doctor-patient relationship, it would have given rise to fiduciary obligations; see, for example, *McInerney v. MacDonald*, [1992] 2 S.C.R. 138.

As is evident from the different approaches taken in *Norberg*, the law's response to the plight of vulnerable people in power-dependency relationships gives rise to a variety of often overlapping duties. Concepts such as the fiduciary duty, undue influence, unconscionability, unjust enrichment, and even the duty of care are all responsive to abuses of vulnerable people in transactions with others. The existence of a fiduciary duty in a given case will depend upon the reasonable expectations of the parties, and these in turn depend on factors such as trust, confidence, complexity of subject matter, and community or industry standards. For instance in *Norberg*, *supra*, the Hippocratic Oath was evidence that the sexual relationship diverged significantly from the standards reasonably expected from physicians by the community. This inference was confirmed by expert evidence to the effect that any reasonable practitioner in the defendant's position would have taken steps to help the addicted patient, in stark contrast to the deplorable exploitation which in fact took place; see also *Harry v. Kreutziger* (1978), 95 D.L.R. (3d) 231 (B.C.C.A.), at p. 241 *per* Lambert J.A.

In seeking to identify the various civil duties that flow from a particular power-dependency relationship, it is simply wrong to focus only on the degree to which a power or discretion to harm another is somehow "unilateral". In my view, this concept has neither descriptive nor analytical relevance to many fact-based fiduciary relationships. *Ipso facto*, persons in a "power-dependency relationship" are vulnerable to harm. Further, the relative "degree of vulnerability", if it can be put that way, does not depend on some hypothetical ability to protect one's self from harm, but rather on the nature of the parties' reasonable expectations. Obviously, a party who expects the other party to a relationship to act in the former's best interests is more vulnerable to an abuse of power than a party who should be expected to know that he or she should take protective measures. J. C. Shepherd, *supra*, puts the matter in the following way, at p. 102:

> Where a weaker or reliant party trusts the stronger party not to use his power and influence against the weaker party, and the stronger party, if acting *reasonably*, would have known or ought to have known of this reliance, we can say that the stronger party had notice of the encumbrance, and therefore in using the power has accepted the duty. [Emphasis in original.]

Thus in *Lac Minerals*, *supra*, I felt it perverse to fault Corona for failing to negotiate a confidentiality agreement with Lac in a situation where the well-established practice in the mining industry was such that Corona would have had no reasonable expectation that Lac would use the information to its detriment. To imply that one is not vulnerable to an abuse of power because one could have protected, but did not protect one's self is to focus on one narrow class of "power-dependency relationship" at the expense of the general principle that transcends it. I recognize, of course, that the majority holding in that case was that "the evidence does not establish in this case the existence of a fiduciary relationship" (*per* Lamer J. (as he then was), at p. 630). But as I will indicate presently, there is a basic difference between the type of situation that arises here and that which arose in *Lac Minerals*.

In summary, the precise legal or equitable duties the law will enforce in any given relationship are tailored to the legal and practical incidents of a particular relationship. To repeat a phrase used by Lord Scarman, "[t]here is no substitute in this branch of the law for a meticulous examination of the facts"; see *National Westminster Bank plc v. Morgan*, [1985] 1 All E.R. 821 (H.L.), at p. 831.

The Authorities

. . . .

More importantly for present purposes, courts have consistently shown a willingness to enforce a fiduciary duty in the investment advice aspect of many kinds of financial service relationships ... In all of these cases, as here, the ultimate discretion or power in the disposition of funds remained with the beneficiary. In addition, where reliance on the investment advice is found, a fiduciary duty has been affirmed without regard to the level of sophistication of the client, or the client's ultimate discretion to accept or reject the professional's advice; see *Elderkin, supra*; *Laskin v. Bache & Co.*, [1972] 1 O.R. 465 (C.A.); *Wakeford, supra*, at p. 8. Rather, the common thread that unites this body of law is the measure of the confidential and trust-like nature of the particular advisory relationship, and the ability of the plaintiff to establish reliance in fact.

Much of this caselaw was recently canvassed by Keenan J. in *Varcoe v. Sterling* (1992), 7 O.R. (3d) 204 (Gen. Div.), in an effort to demarcate the boundaries of the fiduciary principle in the broker-client relationship. Keenan J. stated, at pp. 234–36:

> The relationship of broker and client is not *per se* a fiduciary relationship.... Where the elements of trust and confidence and reliance on skill and knowledge and advice are present, the relationship is fiduciary and the obligations that attach are fiduciary. On the other hand, if those elements are not present, the fiduciary relationship does not exist.... The circumstances can cover the whole spectrum from total reliance to total independence.
>
> ...

> The relationship of the broker and client is elevated to a fiduciary level when the client reposes trust and confidence in the broker and relies on the broker's advice in making business decisions. When the broker seeks or accepts the client's trust and confidence and undertakes to advise, the broker must do so fully, honestly and in good faith.... It is the trust and reliance placed by the client which gives to the broker the power and in some cases, discretion, to make a business decision for the client. Because the client has reposed that trust and confidence and has given over that power to the broker, the law imposes a duty on the broker to honour that trust and respond accordingly.

In my view, this passage represents an accurate statement of fiduciary law in the context of independent professional advisory relationships, whether the advisers be accountants, stockbrokers, bankers, or investment counsellors. Moreover, it states a principled and workable doctrinal approach. Thus, where a fiduciary duty is claimed in the context of a financial advisory relationship, it is at all events a question of fact as to whether the parties' relationship was such as to give rise to a fiduciary duty on the part of the advisor.

Policy Considerations

Apart from the idea that a person has breached a trust, there is a wider reason to support fiduciary relationships in the case of financial advisors. These are occupations where advisors to whom a person gives trust has power over a vast sum of money, yet the nature of their position is such that specific regulation might frustrate the very function they have to perform. By enforcing a duty of honesty and good faith, the courts are able to regulate an activity that is of great value to commerce and society generally.

This feature of fiduciary law has been remarked upon by several prominent academics in the area; see Ernest J. Weinrib, "The Fiduciary Obligation", *supra*, at p. 15; Shepherd, *supra*, at pp. 78–83; Tamar Frankel, "Fiduciary Law", *supra*, at pp. 802–4; Tamar Frankel, "Fiduciary Law: The Judicial Process and the Duty of Care" in *The 1993 Isaac Pitblado Lectures, supra*, pp. 143–62, at p. 145; P. D. Finn, "The Fiduciary Principle", *supra*, at pp. 27, 50–51; P. D. Finn, "Contract and the Fiduciary Principle", *supra*, at p. 82; P. D. Finn, "Conflicts of Interest and Professionals", paper presented at Professional responsibility Seminar, University of Auckland, May 29, 1987, pp. 4–48, at pp. 14–15. For example, Professor Frankel states, at pp. 144–45:

Fiduciary law regulates the providers of very special services. These services can be divided into two groups. The first group consists of services that require entrustment of property or power to the fiduciary. Without such entrustment the services cannot be rendered at all, or they can be rendered with less than maximum efficiency. The second group consists of services requiring skills that are very costly to master; for example, lawyering, and some kinds of investment management.

Because the relationship poses for one party ("the entrustor") substantial risks of misappropriation and monitoring costs and because public policy strongly supports both groups of services, fiduciary law interferes to reduce these risks and costs. The law aims at deterring fiduciaries from misappropriating the powers vested in them solely for the purpose of enabling them to perform their functions....

Professor Finn puts the matter this way in "Conflicts of Interest and Professionals", *supra*, at p. 15:

> In some spheres conduct regulation would appear to be becoming an end in itself and this because there can be a public interest in reassuring the community — not merely beneficiaries — that even the appearance of improper behaviour will not be tolerated. The emphasis here seems, in part at least, to be the maintenance of the public's acceptance of, and of the credibility of, important institutions in society which render "fiduciary services" to the public.

Finally, Professor Weinrib speaks in terms of "maintaining the integrity of the marketplace", *supra*, at p. 15.

The social importance of the fiduciary principle is embedded in the very genesis of the legal concept, as it was developed in *Keech v. Sandford*, *supra*. In *Keech* the defendant trustee held a lease of a market in trust for an infant beneficiary. Prior to the expiration of the lease the lessor stated he would not renew the lease to the infant, upon which the trustee took the lease for himself. The court, however, ordered the renewed lease to be held on a constructive trust for the infant beneficiary, and held the defendant to account for the profits. The Lord Chancellor stated the following at p. 223 (E.R.) and at p. 62 (Sel. Cas. T. King):

> ... I very well see, if a trustee, on the refusal to renew, might have a lease to himself, few trust-estates would be renewed to *cestui que* use.... This may seem hard, that the trustee is the only person of all mankind who might not have the lease: but it is very proper that rule should be strictly pursued, and not in the least

relaxed; for it is very obvious what would be the consequence of letting trustees have the lease, on refusal to renew to *cestui que* use. [Emphasis added.]

The desire to protect and reinforce the integrity of social institutions and enterprises is prevalent throughout fiduciary law. The reason for this desire is that the law has recognized the importance of instilling in our social institutions and enterprises some recognition that not all relationships are characterized by a dynamic of mutual autonomy, and that the marketplace cannot always set the rules. By instilling this kind of flexibility into our regulation of social institutions and enterprises, the law therefore helps to strengthen them.

I earlier referred to the coincidence of business and accepted morality in *Lac Minerals*, *supra*, at p. 668. The concern there was with reinforcing the established norms by which the development of the natural resources of this country could be most efficiently accomplished. ...

Further, in many advisory relationships norms of loyalty and good faith are often indicated by the various codes of professional responsibility and behaviour set out by the relevant self-regulatory body. The *raison d'être* of such codes is the protection of parties in situations where they cannot, despite their best efforts, protect themselves, because of the nature of the relationship. These codes exist to impose regulation on an activity that cannot be left entirely open to free market forces. I have already referred to the function of the professional standards expected of doctors in *Norberg*, *supra*. The professional rules of conduct governing lawyers was considered in *Granville Savings and Mortgage Corp. v. Slevin* (1990), 68 Man. R. (2d) 241 (Q.B.), rev'd [1992] 5 W.W.R. 1 (Man. C.A.), trial judgment restored [1993] 4 S.C.R. 279. There, the defendant law firm undertook to prepare certain mortgage documents in connection with a mortgage transaction between their client (the mortgagor) and the plaintiff mortgagee. As it turned out, the lawyers negligently represented to the plaintiffs that their mortgage constituted a first charge on the property. The plaintiffs sued in tort, contract, and fiduciary duty. The trial judge allowed the claim on all three heads of liability. This was reversed by the Court of Appeal, but on a further appeal to this Court, the trial judge's judgment was restored. The finding of a fiduciary duty was consistent with Commentary 8, Chapter 19 of the Canadian Bar Association's *Code of Professional Conduct*, which instructs lawyers to urge unrepresented parties to seek representation, and, failing that, to ensure that the party "is not proceeding under the impression that the lawyer is protecting such person's interests". The code goes on to warn lawyers that they may have an obligation to a person whom the lawyer does not represent.

In the present case, the trial judge found as a fact that the standards set by the accounting profession at the relevant time compelled full disclosure by the respondent of his interest with the developers. ...

In sum, the rules set by the relevant professional body are of guiding importance in determining the nature of the duties flowing from a particular professional relationship; see *MacDonald Estate v. Martin*, [1990] 3 S.C.R. 1235. With respect to the accounting profession, the relevant rules and standards evinced a clear instruction that all real and apparent conflicts of interest be fully disclosed to clients, particularly in the area of tax-related investment advice. The basis of this requirement is the maintenance of the independence and honesty which is the linchpin of the profession's credibility with the public. It would be surprising indeed if the courts held the professional advisor to a lower standard of responsibility than that deemed necessary by the self-regulating body of the profession itself.

Application to the Case at Bar

. . . .

THE NATURE OF THE RELATIONSHIP

The trial judge's findings on this point are virtually uncontestable. The respondent under cross-examination admitted that his relationship with the appellant was such that he was under a duty to serve the best interests of the appellant at the expense of his own self-interest. The relevant testimony is as follows:

Q. But you know that he came to trust you? He trusted you an awful lot, didn't he?
A. Yes he did.

...

Q. Now, Mr. Hodgkinson trusted you as his professional advisor, correct?
A. Correct.
Q. He was trusting you to give him independent advice, correct?
A. Correct.
Q. Advice which was not directed towards protecting your personal interests but was directed exclusively to protecting his interests as your client, correct?
A. Correct.
Q. And he was trusting you not to protect the interests of someone on the other side of a transaction on which you were advising but to protect exclusively his interests, correct?

A. Correct.
Q. And you assumed that responsibility to provide him with independent advice?
A. Yes, I did. [Emphasis added.]

In my view this testimony, taken by itself, vindicates the appellant's fiduciary expectation. Concepts like "trust", independence from outside interests, disregard for self-interest, are all hallmarks of the fiduciary principle. It lies ill in the mouth of the respondent to argue that the appellant was not vulnerable to a breach of loyalty when he himself concedes that loyalty was the central feature of the parties' business relationship. As it turned out, of course, the respondent used the position of ascendency granted him by the appellant to line his own pockets and the pockets of his developer clients.

The frequency with which courts have enforced fiduciary duties in professional advisory relationships is not surprising. The very existence of many professional advisory relationships, particularly in specialized areas such as law, taxation and investments, is premised upon full disclosure by the client of vital personal and financial information that inevitably results in a "power-dependency" dynamic. The case at bar is typical. ... I would have thought it self-evident that the type of disclosure that routinely occurs in these kinds of relationships results in the advisor's acquiring influence which is equivalent to a discretion or power to affect the client's legal or practical interests. As I stated in *Lac Minerals*, at p. 664, power and discretion in this context mean only the ability to cause harm. Vulnerability is nothing more than the corollary of the ability to cause harm, viz., the susceptibility to harm. For this reason, it is undesirable to overemphasize vulnerability in assessing the existence of a fiduciary relationship. ... In the advisory context, the advisor's ability to cause harm and the client's susceptibility to be harmed arise from the simple but unassailable fact that the advice given by an independent advisor is not likely to be viewed with suspicion; rather, it is likely to be followed. Shepherd observes that transfers of power can inform our analysis of the underlying power dependence dynamic. He describes the power dynamic in these types of situations as follows, at p. 100:

> Powers are not only transferred formally. There are many ways of transferring powers either consciously but informally, or totally unconsciously. When an individual relies on another, for example a professional adviser, there is a quite conscious transfer of power, but rarely is there a document in which the beneficiary writes "I hereby grant you the power to influence my decision-making".

A retainer, when combined with the disclosure of confidential information or the vesting of discretion or power, is strong evidence of the existence of an underlying dynamic of power dependency in relation to certain duties. The appellant's testimony confirms the overt, if not explicit, power transfer which in fact occurred. He stated, "I was paying him for his advice. If I didn't want to take it, why would I pay him? I did not disagree with any of his advice." This remark cannot help but strike one as intuitively reasonable, particularly given the appellant's relative inexperience in MURB investing. As I noted earlier, the refusal to protect this reliance on the grounds that the appellant somehow had the means to protect his own interests is to take an impoverished view of the law in this area.

RELIANCE

I have already noted the importance of reliance in relation to fiduciary duties; see *Varga v. F. H. Deacon & Co.*, [1975] 1 S.C.R. 39; *Hospital Products Ltd. v. United States Surgical Corp.*, *supra*, at p. 488 (*per* Dawson J.). It is important, however, to add further precision about the nature of reliance, particularly as it applies in the advisory context. Reliance in this context does not require a wholesale substitution of decision-making power from the investor to the advisor. This is simply too restrictive. It completely ignores the peculiar potential for overriding influence in the professional advisor and the strong policy reasons, to which I have previously referred, favouring the law's intervention by means of its jurisdiction over fiduciary duties to foster the fair and proper functioning of the investment market, an important social and economic activity that cannot really be regulated in other ways. As I see it, the reality of the situation must be looked at to see if the decision is effectively that of the advisor, an exercise that involves a close examination of facts. Here, as I see it, the trust and reliance the appellant placed in the respondent (a trust and reliance assiduously fostered by the respondent) was such that the respondent's advice was in substance an exercise of a power or discretion reposed in him by the appellant. This was the view taken by the trial judge respecting the appellant's investment in the four MURB projects, and her decision is amply supported by the evidence.

In this respect, the appellant stated the following during the course of his testimony:

> I was relying on him [the respondent]. It was his recommendation. He was the guy with all the expertise about, number one, analysing real estate ventures, particularly tax shelters, and he

was certainly the one that had expertise about the economics of investing — and the economics. He was the one that knew these people that were going to be involved in it, and based on our discussions I took his opinion.

. . . .

Moreover, in finding that the appellant relied on the respondent's recommendations, the trial judge did not simply prefer the appellant's evidence over that of the respondent. On the contrary, she thoroughly examined all the circumstances of the relationship. Consider the following. The appellant approached the respondent as a "neophyte" taxpayer, with no experience in dealing with large real estate tax shelters. The parties developed a relationship that involved frequent telephone and personal contact. The respondent identified the appellant as one of his "special" clients. While the respondent did not hold himself out as an investment counsellor *per se*, he did not qualify his experience as a tax shelter or investment advisor in any way. He did not refer the appellant to any other professionals for investment advice. In sum, the parties' relationship was such that the trial judge was able to conclude, at p. 168, "[i]n effect, Mr. Simms assumed the responsibility for Mr. Hodgkinson's choice. He analyzed the investments, he recommended the investments, and he effectively chose the investments for Mr. Hodgkinson" (emphasis added).

The respondent, for his part, actively cultivated this high degree of reliance. He was fully aware of the appellant's lack of experience with MURBs, and he held himself out as an expert in the assessment of MURB-type investments. The respondent's influence over the appellant was built upon the latter's confidence that the respondent was independent from the developers. During the course of the appellant's examination-in-chief, the following exchange took place:

> Q. Mr. Hodgkinson, would you have followed Mr. Simms' advice had you known that he was acting for and getting paid by the vendors of these projects when he was advising you on the question of whether you should invest or not?
>
> A. No, I would not have.... Had I known and particularly the size of the funds that transferred between Simms and the developers, I wouldn't have gone close to these investments. It would have been an obvious conflict and I wouldn't have been getting the independent professional advice I was looking for.

The trial judge was satisfied, at p. 127, that it was the appellant's intention to, "drop his tax and financial-planning problems into Mr. Simms' lap and to go about his business as a stockbroker". All the while, the respondent was fully aware that the appellant's lack of expertise meant that he wielded considerable influence over the appellant's investment decisions.

The case put against the trial judge's findings of fact seems to turn on four points. First, the respondent's letters to his investor clients included various disclaimers to the effect that each individual investor should study the enclosed data to his or her own satisfaction before following the recommendation of Simms & Waldman. Second, with respect to the final two investments a considerable amount of time elapsed between the appellant's being made aware of the opportunity and recommendations and his decision to invest. Third, the appellant had a chance to meet personally with the developers. Fourth, during the relevant period the appellant made several investments outside of his relationship with the respondent, some of which might be considered "risky". Based on these facts, the Court of Appeal concluded, at p. 277, "[t]he plaintiff [the appellant] was not relying solely upon the defendant for financial advice. He was fully acquainted with questions of risk and he was in many respects a free agent".

At the outset, it should be noted that the trial judge did not overlook any of these points in her assessment of the facts; on the contrary, each point was examined and eventually rationalized within the overall factual mix of the case. Turning, then, to the disclaimers. The letter sent out by Mr. Simms to his investor clients regarding Bella Vista stated, in part, "it is your money and you must place your expectations on what you anticipate will happen in the future ...". The disclaimers attaching to the Oliver Place and Enterprise Way projects were even stronger:

> These analyses are based on revenues and expenses estimated by the promoters and not by us. It would be necessary, before investing in these projects, to satisfy yourself that these figures are realistic and reflect current conditions in the rental market place.
>
> ...
>
> We are in no way recommending that you buy one of these investments. We are saying that if you are investing and will be considering a tax shelter this year, that these two projects appear to merit your serious consideration.

The trial judge considered this evidence, but concluded that the appellant did not believe that the disclaimers applied to him based on his "special" relationship with the respondent. She found the letters were reasonably interpreted by Mr. Hodgkinson as endorsements, particularly given the surrounding circumstances of the parties' relationship. It must be kept in mind that throughout the period these investments were made the parties were in frequent contact, by letter, telephone, and in person. The appellant testified:

> At all times he [the respondent] had recommended these investments highly to me and so I didn't think that much of his sentence when he says, "I in no way recommend this investment to you." I felt it was a natural disclaimer that would be there for those that weren't used to dealing with him on the intimate level that I felt I was.

The appellant described the respondent as very enthusiastic about the projects. He even went so far as to fabricate a false sense of scarcity in relation to the Oliver Place project, stating in a September 26, 1980 letter that the high demand for the units required they be allocated on a first-come, first-serve basis. The respondent's enthusiasm was apparently infectious. All but four of the purchasers involved in Oliver Place were Simms & Waldman clients, while the Enterprise Way project, save for two units taken by the developer, was completely sold out to Simms & Waldman investors. In short, I see no reason to disturb the trial judge's dismissal of the effect of the disclaimers. ...

. . . .

Turning to the third point, it is true that the appellant's meetings with the various developers could conceivably give rise to an inference of independence. When considered in light of all the evidence, however, it is clear that it was the respondent's stamp of approval that was decisive for the appellant. In this context the appellant's decision not to invest in the Ladner Downs project, discussed above, is of particular significance. More generally, the appellant stated: "If I had been approached directly by Jerry Olma, I would have considered him too much the promoter type of individual and I wouldn't have invested in his projects." With respect to the April 11 meeting with the developers concerning Duncana, the appellant testified: "He [the respondent] felt it was important that I know the developers on a firsthand basis." In fact, the appellant had already made up his mind to invest in

Duncana based on the respondent's recommendation. As he put it, he approached the meeting with "chequebook in hand". This was in fact the only formal meeting the appellant attended with any of the developers to discuss the MURB projects. While the appellant did happen to meet Mr. Dale-Johnson once as they crossed paths at the Simms & Waldman offices, and he also made one informal stop at Mr. Olma's residence in relation to the Ladner Downs project, these meetings have almost no probative value and I will not comment on them except to acknowledge that they occurred.

. . . .

CONCLUSION ON FIDUCIARY DUTY ISSUE

To conclude, I am of the view that the trial judge did not err in finding that a fiduciary obligation existed between the parties, and that this duty was breached by the respondent's decision not to disclose pecuniary interest with the developers.

DAMAGES

[The award of damages by the trial court judge in the amount of $350,507.62 was upheld.] The trial judge assessed damages flowing from both breach of fiduciary duty and breach of contract. She found the quantum of damages to be the same under either claim, namely the return of capital (adjusted to take into consideration the tax benefits received as a result of the investments), plus all consequential losses, including legal and accounting fees. As I stated at the outset, I cannot find fault with the trial judge's disposition of the damages question.

It is useful to review some key findings of fact that bear on the issue of damages. The trial judge found the appellant paid fair market price for each of the four investments. However, she found that throughout the period during which the appellant was induced by the respondent's recommendations into making the investments, the respondent was in a financial relationship with the developers of the projects. In short, the trial judge found the respondent stood to gain financially if the appellant invested according to his recommendations. She further found that if the appellant had known of the true relationship between the respondent and the developers, he would not have invested. She also found that had the parties turned their minds to the potential consequences of the respondent's relationship with the

developers it would have been reasonably foreseeable that the appellant would not have invested.

I turn now to the principles that bear on the calculation of damages in this case. It is well established that the proper approach to damages for breach of a fiduciary duty is restitutionary. On this approach, the appellant is entitled to be put in as good a position as he would have been in had the breach not occurred. On the facts here, this means that the appellant is entitled to be restored to the position he was in before the transaction. The trial judge adopted this restitutionary approach and fixed damages at an amount equal to the return of capital, as well as all consequential losses, minus the amount the appellant saved on income tax due to the investments.

The respondent advanced two arguments against the trial judge's assessment of damages for breach of fiduciary duty. Both raise the issue of causation, and I will address these submissions as they were argued.

The respondent first submitted that given the appellant's stated desire to shelter as much of his income as possible from taxation, and his practice of buying a wide variety of tax shelters, the appellant would still have invested in real-estate tax shelters had he known the true facts. The main difficulty with this submission is that it flies in the face of the facts found by the trial judge. The materiality of the non-disclosure in inducing the appellant to change his position was a live issue at trial which the judge resolved in the appellant's favour, a finding accepted by the Court of Appeal. For reasons given earlier, I agree with this finding.

What is more, the submission runs up against the long-standing equitable principle that where the plaintiff has made out a case of non-disclosure and the loss occasioned thereby is established, the onus is on the defendant to prove that the innocent victim would have suffered the same loss regardless of the breach; see *London Loan & Savings Co. v. Brickenden*, [1934] 2 W.W.R. 545 (P.C.), at pp. 550–51; see also *Huff v. Price, supra*, at pp. 319–20; *Commerce Capital Trust Co. v. Berk* (1989), 57 D.L.R. (4th) 759 (Ont. C.A.), at pp. 763–64. This Court recently affirmed the same principle with respect to damages at common law in the context of negligent misrepresentation; see *Rainbow Industrial Caterers Ltd. v. Canadian National Railway Co.*, [1991] 3 S.C.R. 3, at pp. 14–17. I will return to the common law cases in greater detail later; it suffices now to say that courts exercising both common law and equitable jurisdiction have approached this issue in the same manner. In *Rainbow*, Sopinka J., on behalf of a 6–1 majority of this Court, had this to say, at pp. 15–16:

> The plaintiff is the innocent victim of a misrepresentation which has induced a change of position. It is just that the plaintiff should be entitled to say "but for the tortious conduct of the defendant, I would not have changed my position". A tortfeasor who says, "Yes, but you would have assumed a position other than the *status quo ante*", and thereby asks a court to find a transaction whose terms are hypothetical and speculative, should bear the burden of displacing the plaintiff's assertion of the *status quo ante*.

Further, mere "speculation" on the part of the defendant will not suffice; see *ibid.*, at p. 15; *Commerce Capital, supra*, at p. 764. In the present case the respondent has adduced no concrete evidence to "displac[e] the plaintiff's assertion of the *status quo ante*", and this submission must, therefore, be dismissed.

The respondent also argued that even assuming the appellant would not have invested had proper disclosure been made, the non-disclosure was not the proximate cause of the appellant's loss. Rather, he continued, the appellant's loss was caused by the general economic recession that hit the British Columbia real estate market in the early 1980s. The respondent submits that it is grossly unjust to hold him accountable for losses that, he maintains, have no causal relation to the breach of fiduciary duty he perpetrated on the appellant.

. . . .

Put another way, equity is not so rigid as to be susceptible to being used as a vehicle for punishing defendants with harsh damage awards out of all proportion to their actual behaviour. On the contrary, where the common law has developed a measured and just principle in response to a particular kind of wrong, equity is flexible enough to borrow from the common law. As I noted in *Canson*, at pp. 587–88, this approach is in accordance with the fusion of law and equity that occurred near the turn of the century under the auspices of the old *Judicature Acts*; see also *M. (K.) v. M. (H.), supra*, at p. 61. Thus, properly understood *Canson* stands for the proposition that courts should strive to treat similar wrongs similarly, regardless of the particular cause or causes of action that may have been pleaded. As I stated in *Canson*, at p. 581:

> ... barring different policy considerations underlying one action or the other, I see no reason why

the same basic claim, whether framed in terms of a common law action or an equitable remedy, should give rise to different levels of redress.

In other words, the courts should look to the harm suffered from the breach of the given duty, and apply the appropriate remedy.

. . . .

From a policy perspective it is simply unjust to place the risk of market fluctuations on a plaintiff who would not have entered into a given transaction but for the defendant's wrongful conduct. I observe that in *Waddell, supra*, Bramwell L.J. conceded, at p. 680, that if *restitutio in integrum* had been possible, the plaintiff could probably have recovered in full. Indeed counsel for the appellant argued that the proper approach to damages in this case was the monetary equivalent of a rescisionary remedy. I agree. In my view the appellant should not suffer from the fact that he did not discover the breach until such time as the market had already taken its toll on his investments. This principle, which I take to be a basic principle of fairness, is in fact reflected in the common law of mitigation, itself rooted in causation; see S. M. Waddams, *The Law of Contracts* (3rd ed. 1993), at p. 515. In *Asamera Oil Corp. v. Sea Oil & General Corp.*, [1979] 1 S.C.R. 633, this Court held that in an action for breach of the duty to return shares under a contract of bailment, the obligation imposed on the plaintiff to mitigate by purchasing like shares on the open market did not commence until such time as the plaintiff learned of the breach or within a reasonable time thereafter.

There is a broader justification for upholding the trial judge's award of damages in cases such as the present, namely the need to put special pressure on those in positions of trust and power over others in situations of vulnerability. This justification is evident in American caselaw, which makes a distinction between simple fraud related to the price of a security and fraudulent inducements by brokers and others in the investment business in positions of influence. In the case at bar, as in *Kelly Peters* and the American cases cited by the appellant, the wrong complained of goes to the heart of the duty of loyalty that lies at the core of the fiduciary principle. In redressing a wrong of this nature, I have no difficulty in resorting to a measure of damages that places the exigencies of the market-place on the respondent. Such a result is in accordance with the principle that a defaulting fiduciary has an obligation to effect restitution *in specie* or its monetary equivalent; see *Re Dawson; Union Fidelity Trustee Co. v. Perpetual Trustee Co.*, [1966] 2 N.S.W.R. 211; *Island Realty Investments Ltd. v. Douglas* (1985), 19 E.T.R. 56 (B.C.S.C.), at pp. 64–65; *Rothko v. Reis*, 372 N.E.2d 291 (C.A.N.Y. 1977). I see no reason to derogate from this principle; on the contrary, the behaviour of the respondent seems to be precisely the type of behaviour that calls for strict legal censure. Mark Ellis puts the matter in the following way in *Fiduciary Duties in Canada, supra*, at p. 20–2:

> ... the relief seeks primarily to protect a party owed a duty of utmost good faith from deleterious actions by the party owing the fiduciary duty. The vehicles by which the Court may enforce that duty are diverse and powerful, but are premised upon the same desire: to strictly and jealously guard against breach and to redress that breach by maintenance of the pre-default status quo, where possible.

The remedy of disgorgement, adopted in effect if not in name by the Court of Appeal, is simply insufficient to guard against the type of abusive behaviour engaged in by the respondent in this case. The law of fiduciary duties has always contained within it an element of deterrence. This can be seen as early as *Keech* in the passage cited *supra*; see also *Canadian Aero, supra*, at pp. 607 and 610; *Canson, supra*, at p. 547, *per* McLachlin J. In this way the law is able to monitor a given relationship society views as socially useful while avoiding the necessity of formal regulation that may tend to hamper its social utility. Like-minded fiduciaries in the position of the respondent would not be deterred from abusing their power by a remedy that simply requires them, if discovered, to disgorge their secret profit, with the beneficiary bearing all the market risk. If anything, this would encourage people in his position to in effect gamble with other people's money, knowing that if they are discovered they will be no worse off than when they started. As a result, the social benefits of fiduciary relationships, particularly in the field of independent professional advisors, would be greatly diminished.

In view of my finding that there existed a fiduciary duty between the parties, it is not in strictness necessary to consider damages for breach of contract. However, in my view, on the facts of this case, damages in contract follow the principles stated in connection with the equitable breach. The contract between the parties was for independent professional advice. While it is true that the appellant got what he paid for from the developers, he did not get the services he paid for from the respondent. The relevant contractual duty breached by the respondent is of precisely the same nature as the equitable duty considered in the fiduciary analysis, namely the duty to make full disclosure of any material conflict of interest. This was, in short, a contract which provided for the performance of obligations characterized in equity as fiduciary.

Further, it remains the case under the contractual analysis that but for the non-disclosure, the contract with the developers for the MURBs would not have been entered into. The trial judge found as a fact that it was reasonably foreseeable that if the appellant had known of the respondent's affiliation with the developers, he would not have invested. This finding is fully reflected in the evidence I have earlier set forth. Put another way, it was foreseeable that if the contract was breached the appellant would be exposed to market risks (i.e., in connection with the four MURBs) to which he would not otherwise have been exposed. Further, it is well established that damages must be foreseeable as to kind, but not extent; as such any distinction based on the unforeseeability of the extent of the market fluctuations must be dismissed; see *H. Parsons (Livestock) Ltd. v. Uttley Ingham & Co.*, [1978] Q.B. 791, at p. 813; *Asamera, supra*, at p. 655. See also S. M. Waddams, *The Law of Damages* (2nd ed. 1991), at paras. 14.280 and 14.290.

· · · ·

DISPOSITION

I would allow the appeal, set aside the order of the British Columbia Court of Appeal and restore the order of the trial judge, with costs throughout, including letter of credit costs to avoid a stay and allow recovery on the trial judgment pending appeal to the Court of Appeal.

(e) Reliance (Re-visited)[†]

Stephen Waddams

Trust, confidence, and reliance are closely related concepts, and where common law courts have failed to protect reliance the law has often been supplemented by the equitable concept of fiduciary duty. An example previously mentioned is *Nocton* v. *Ashburton*[73] (1914) where a solicitor was held liable for negligent misrepresentation fifty years before a general duty in such circumstances was recognized in English law. The concept of fiduciary duty, though of pervasive and fundamental importance in Anglo-American private law, has usually, with notable exceptions,[74] been omitted from conceptual maps and diagrams. Fiduciary relations cannot be allocated to the law of property to the exclusion of obligations, or vice versa; nor can they be subordinated to contracts, wrongdoing, or unjust enrichment; nor can they be visualized as parallel to but separate from these concepts, for they have close affinities with all of them. As with other equitable concepts,[75] their very function has been, in a sense, to subvert the categories established by the common law. The concepts of wrongdoing, contracts, unjust enrichment, property, and public policy have operated with cumulative effect. Breach of fiduciary duty, though not a common law tort, is a wrong. But it depends not on a duty 'towards persons generally'[76] but on a fiduciary relationship between claimant and defendant, which usually, though not always,[77] springs from a contract between them. ...

Benefits derived from breach of fiduciary duty must be restored. This aspect of fiduciary duties has been treated by many writers as part of the law of unjust enrichment.[78] Other writers have objected, however, that restitution of profits depends on proof of wrongdoing and therefore belongs to the law of wrongs.[79] From a historical perspective both views are correct: unjust enrichment is an important reason for requiring profits to be restored; but it is true also that the result cannot be attributed to unjust enrichment considered in isolation from other legal concepts. An important feature of fiduciary duties is that the claimant can often assert, in addition to a personal obligation, a property interest in such benefits and in their proceeds. This has crucial consequences where the recipient is insolvent,[80] and has caused a sharp division of opinion among courts and commentators.[81]

Considerations of public policy have played a prominent role in the establishment of fiduciary relationships and in the extension of the consequences of breach of them. Justice Cardozo called the fiduciary concept 'part of a pervasive policy of the law to protect the integrity of commercial organizations'.[82] Paul Finn has said that 'it originates, self-evidently, in public policy'.[83] In *Norberg* v. *Wynrib*,[84] a physician who had taken advantage of a patient's dependence on drugs for his own sexual gratification was held by two members of the Supreme Court to be a fiduciary, and to be liable for aggravated and punitive damages. The judgments have strong moral and public policy overtones. Again, in *Hodgkinson* v. *Simms*,[85] an accountant on whom an investor had relied for advice was held to be a fiduciary, and to be liable for loss caused by a general decline in market values, in addition to an obligation to restore profit derived from the transaction. La Forest J said that 'the remedy of disgorgement ... is simply insufficient to guard against the type of abusive behaviour engaged in ... in this case. The law of fiduciary duties has always contained within it an element of deterrence.'[86]

The fluidity of the concept of fiduciary duty, its proprietary implications, its interaction with concepts of contract, wrongdoing, and unjust enrichment, and its response to changing views of public policy all militate against the easy inclusion of fiduciary duties on any map or diagrammatic scheme of private law.

Cases involving the misuse of confidential information, often described as 'sui generis',[87] have also been said to be 'distinct' from but 'intertwined' with the law of fiduciary duty.[88] Francis Gurry has written that 'attempts to confine it exclusively within one conventional jurisdictional category should be resisted'.[89] In the notorious case of *Prince Albert* v. *Strange* (1849), a bookseller and publisher, William Strange, had come into possession of copies of private etchings and engravings made personally by Queen Victoria and Prince Albert, the copies

---

† From Stephen Waddams, *Dimensions of Private Law* (Cambridge: Cambridge University Press, 2003) at 73–79. [Notes/references omitted.] Reprinted with the permission of Cambridge University Press.

having been obtained surreptitiously by another person. Strange was restrained not only from publishing copies of the engravings themselves,[90] but from publishing a descriptive catalogue of them. Strange's conduct was, no doubt, perceived at the time as a disgraceful invasion of royal privacy, but it was not obvious that it fell into any known category of legal wrong. The Queen and the Prince had no property in the catalogue, and Strange was in breach of no personal obligation, and had committed no wrong previously recognized by the common law.[91] Counsel for the defendant, though expressly disavowing any 'sympathy with the defendant privately',[92] opposed the injunction precisely on this ground:

> A confusion seems to be created by mixing up the several distinct matters which compose the whole. First there is a right of property in the canvas of a painting; and, secondly, there is a right of property in the form of the idea which adorns the canvas .... And, further, if a party is bound by any contract, he may be restrained from using the knowledge he has obtained respecting the painting .... But the possessor, independently of contract, has no right or property in the idea which is acquired by another party from a knowledge of that particular chattel....[93]

Counsel argued that 'in all cases the jurisdiction is founded on property or upon breach of contract or of confidence'.[94] But the Lord Chancellor (Cottenham) rejected the dichotomy, and put his decision on both grounds:

> It was argued by one of the defendant's counsel that the case for injunction must rest on *one either* of two grounds — of property in the plaintiff, or breach of contract or of trust by the defendant. It is my opinion that *both* these grounds exist in this case[95] ... Upon the first question, ... that of property, I am clearly of opinion, that, the exclusive right and interest of the plaintiff in the composition and works in question being established ... the plaintiff is entitled to the injunction .... But this case by no means depends solely on the question of property; for a breach of trust, confidence, or contract itself would entitle the plaintiff to the injunction .... The possession of the defendant ... must have originated in a breach of trust, confidence, or contract in Brown, or some person in his employ, taking more impressions than were ordered .... I am bound to assume that the possession of the etchings or engravings, on the part of the defendant ... has its foundation in a breach of trust, confidence or contract.[96]

This takes the concept of property beyond anything recognized at common law;[97] considerations of

wrongdoing,[98] breach of contract, and breach of fiduciary obligation were also in play, and all interrelated with each other and with the concept of property. The concept of unjust enrichment,[99] though not by that name, also had appeared strongly in the court below:

> That the object of printing and publishing the catalogue was money, was gain, no man, of course, can doubt: and that it would be very saleable ... is highly probable. What, however, can be the defendant's right, or that of any person but the owners of the plates, to this benefit? It is for them to use, or bestow or withhold, nor can a stranger be allowed to say that they do not want it. They alone are entitled to decide whether, and when, and how, and for whose advantage, their property shall be made use of.[100]

Considerations of public policy were also plainly influential. The Vice-Chancellor who heard the case at first instance described the defendant's conduct as

> An intrusion not only in breach of conventional rules, but offensive to that inbred sense of propriety natural to every man — if intrusion, indeed, fitly describes a sordid spying into the privacy of domestic life — into the home (a word hitherto sacred among us), the home of a family whose life and conduct form an acknowledged title ... to the most marked respect in this country.[101]

Two years later, in *Morison* v. *Moat* (1851), a case involving a secret medical formula, another Vice-Chancellor also stressed the interrelation of concepts:

> Different grounds have indeed been assigned for the exercise of that jurisdiction. In some cases it has been referred to property, in others to contract, and in others, again, it has been treated as founded upon trust or confidence, meaning, as I conceive, that the Court fastens the obligation on the conscience of the party, and enforces it against him in the same manner as it enforces against a party to whom a benefit is given the obligation of performing a promise on the faith of which the benefit has been conferred: but upon whatever grounds the jurisdiction is founded, the authorities leave no doubt as to the exercise of it.[102]

Later cases have stressed considerations of public policy. In *Argyll* v. *Argyll* (1967) the Duke of Argyll was restrained at the suit of his former wife from publishing confidential details about their marriage. The court said of confidential communications between husband and wife that 'preservation of those communications inviolate is an objective of public policy', referring later to the policy of the law as 'the basis of the court's jurisdiction'.[103] The possibility of countervailing public policy interests has also been recognized. In *Norwich Pharmacal Co.* v. *Customs and Excise Commissioners*,[104] Lord Denning said:

> The cases show that the public interest has two sides to it. On the one hand it is usually in the public interest that when information is received in confidence ... it should not be used for other purposes .... On the other hand, confidences will sometimes be overcome by a higher public interest, such as the interest of justice itself, the prevention of wrongdoing, or the security of the State .... So in every case it is a question of weighing the public interest. The courts must consider the relationship and rule upon it as and when it comes before them.

In the modern Canadian case of *LAC Minerals Ltd* v. *International Corona Resources Ltd*[105] (1989) the plaintiff revealed valuable information in anticipation of a joint venture with the defendant. No joint venture resulted, but the defendant took advantage of the information to acquire land for its own benefit. Three of the five judges in the Supreme Court of Canada held the defendant liable for breach of confidence, and two for breach of fiduciary duty. A differently constituted majority held that the plaintiff was entitled to a proprietary interest in the land acquired by the defendant. Considerations of reliance, unjust enrichment, property, contract, wrongdoing, and public policy were all clearly influential. As Sopinka J said, 'the foundation of [the] action for breach of confidence does not rest solely on one of the traditional jurisdictional bases for action of contract, equity, or property. The action is *sui generis* relying on all three to enforce the policy of the law that confidences be respected.'[106]

Very similar (though not involving a misuse of confidential information in the usual sense) is the situation where the defendant acquires property on the understanding that it will be shared with the plaintiff, and the plaintiff in reliance on the understanding refrains from attempting to acquire the property independently. In these cases the understanding is too uncertain or too preliminary to constitute a contract. The defendant's conduct is not, in the ordinary sense, wrongful. The usual requirements of unjust enrichment are not satisfied, for the plaintiff may not have suffered any loss corresponding to the defendant's gain. Nor does the plaintiff lose any preexisting property interest. But considerations of contract, enrichment,[107] wrongdoing, and property, together with the concept of fiduciary relationship and general considerations of public policy have combined to support the imposition in these circumstances of a constructive trust:[108]

> Equity will intervene by way of constructive trust, not only to compel a defendant to restore the plaintiffs property to him, but also to require a defendant to disgorge property which should have been acquired, if at all, for the plaintiff. In the latter category of case, the defendant's wrong lies not in the acquisition of the property, which may or may not have been lawful, but in his subsequent denial of the plaintiff's beneficial interest ... [The defendant's] possession of the property is coloured from the start by the trust and confidence by means of which he obtained it, and his subsequent appropriation of the property to his own use is a breach of that trust.[109]

A map or diagram that supposes a separation between property and obligations, and the whole field of obligations occupied by contract, wrongs, and unjust enrichment, cannot accommodate the cases discussed in this chapter. They cannot be assimilated with contracts because there is no requirement of bargain, consideration, or promise, and because the remedy does not always correspond to the plaintiff's expectation; nor can contracts be subordinated to reliance, or vice versa. The cases cannot be assimilated with wrongdoing, because the obligation arises without any wrongful conduct; although it is possible to say that the defendant acts wrongly, once having induced the plaintiff's reliance, in failing to protect it, this 'wrong' is the failure to satisfy the obligation that the law *has imposed* (to protect the reliance), and cannot itself constitute the reason for the obligation. Failure to acknowledge an obligation cannot be the reason for imposing it. Nor can the cases be assimilated with unjust enrichment because in many of them the defendant is not enriched, and the amount awarded has not usually been measured by enrichment. The concepts of obligation and property cannot be disentangled: in the proprietary estoppel cases, for example, as in other kinds of equitable case, the consequence of the court's judgment has undoubtedly been to create property interests, but the primary reason for the intervention of equity has not been in any real sense to vindicate prior property rights, but rather to afford a protection to reliance that the ordinary law of obligations had failed to give. The establishment of a fourth category of obligations, or consignment of the reliance cases to a separate 'miscellaneous' category, would scarcely resolve the difficulties, because reliance has not been so much *separate* from the concepts of property, contract, tort, and unjust enrichment, as intimately linked with all of them.

405

(f)   The Fiduciary Concept, Contract Law, and Unjust Enrichment: A Functional Comparison[†]

Leonard I. Rotman

INTRODUCTION

The fiduciary concept has a peculiar status in Canadian law. While the Canadian law of fiduciaries traces its origins to the same foundation as fiduciary jurisprudence emanating from other common law jurisdictions, the fiduciary concept has been applied more aggressively (*i.e.*, to a wider range of circumstances and in more unique ways) in Canada than elsewhere. Sir Anthony Mason, former chief justice of the Australian High Court, once made the colourful extra-curial suggestion that Canadian fiduciary jurisprudence is divided into three parts: '[t]hose who owe fiduciary duties, those to whom fiduciary duties are owed and judges who keep creating new fiduciary duties.'[1]

Despite the growth of the fiduciary concept in Canada and elsewhere, a significant *sense* of uncertainty still plagues the fiduciary concept.[2] Even a cursory glance at existing fiduciary jurisprudence and commentary indicates this phenomenon. Curiously, this state of affairs has not impeded the fiduciary concept's continued use. This is not an exclusively modern development. Nor, for that matter, is it peculiarly Canadian.[3] There has long been a greater interest in the ends to be achieved through the application of the fiduciary concept than in infusing it with greater certainty to guide its use.[4] This is a problematic development, because, as former Chief Justice Bora Laskin of the Supreme Court of Canada once said:

> ... important as it is to know what the law is, it is at least equally important to know what the law is for. The distinction that I draw is between a purely formal, mechanical view of the law, antiseptic and detached, and a view of the law that sees it as purposive, related to our social and economic conditions, and serving ends that express the character of our organized society.[5]

The growth in use of the fiduciary concept in the face of questions over its application and implications has created what I call the 'fiduciary paradox'.[6]

As Justice La Forest bluntly states in *LAC Minerals Ltd. v. International Corona Resources Ltd.*, '[t]here are few legal concepts more frequently invoked but less conceptually certain than that of the fiduciary relationship.'[7] While there is international confusion over the appropriate scope and application of the fiduciary concept, a solution to this situation does not necessitate throwing the baby out with the bath water.

To retain its status as an important legal tool, the fiduciary concept must be used judiciously and only where it is warranted by the circumstances rather than in any situation it may be squeezed into given the right amount of persuasion. As Sir Robert Megarry once warned, '[t]he traditional beauty of a land flowing with milk and honey is marred by the realisation that it would be very sticky. What of a land awash with fiduciary relationships?'[8] Indeed, overly broad applications of the fiduciary concept both lessen its impact and lend credence to criticism that it may annex fields traditionally belonging to areas of law such as contract or tort.[9]

Birks has cogently observed that '[t]hings are ... not understood unless they are articulately differentiated from others which they closely resemble.'[10] This paper articulates a vision of the fiduciary concept that distinguishes it functionally from the contiguous areas of contract and unjust enrichment. It suggests that the fiduciary concept's broad social and economic goals are far more ambitious than those of either contract or unjust enrichment, which are primarily designed to facilitate individual justice between parties.[11] Thus, the very purpose of the fiduciary concept will be shown to justify its doctrinal separation from contract, unjust enrichment and, indeed, other areas of law.

The fiduciary vision articulated herein differs from much of contemporary fiduciary orthodoxy.[12] It suggests that the fiduciary concept is a tool that facilitates the construction and preservation of social and economic interdependency.[13] Specifically, the fiduciary concept maintains the viability of inter-

[†]   From Paula Giliker, ed., *Re-examining Contract and Unjust Enrichment* (Boston: Martinus Nijhoff, 2007) at 87–93, 99–108. [Notes/references omitted.] Reproduced with permission of Koninklijke BRILL NV.

dependent societies by preserving the integrity of important social and economic interactions of high trust and confidence that facilitate specialization and lead to fiscal and informational wealth. The interdependency that allows for this broad form of wealth creation is constructed upon the trust of its participants. Yet, where one party holds power over another's interests, the latter may become vulnerable to the use, misuse, or abuse of that power. Thus, this process of interdependency and specialization runs the risk of creating what Anderson calls 'distorted incentives,' which arise when specialists realize the personal benefits from taking advantage of others' trust.[14]

Where trust is abused, the interdependency premised upon it is jeopardized. Protecting the trust that underscores this interdependency is no small task. The common law is largely ill-equipped for this purpose; its goals are, for the most part, relatively modest and direct, focussing on individual rights and their enforcement.[15] The fiduciary concept's prescription of other-regarding behaviour looks beyond the limitations and immediacy of self-interest and allows individuals to trust that their interests will be cared for by others in particular forms of association. Thus, the policy underlying the fiduciary concept and the interests it protects are rather distinct from what exists under the common law. This is reflective of the distinction between the approaches of the common law and Equity, of which the fiduciary concept is arguably its most doctrinally-pure expression.[16]

The distinction between the common law and Equity, to paraphrase Keeton, is not just one of history, but one of attitude.[17] As he explains:

> [t]he common law was concerned with the establishment and enforcement of rights. Equity looked farther, and sought to make the parties conform to a standard of social conduct prescribed by itself. It operated upon the 'conscience of the wrongdoer.' The Chancery is a Court of Conscience, and to purge a guilty conscience it was first necessary that the wrongdoer should redress the harm done, so far as that was possible and compellable.[18]

The common law's proscriptive focus, which generally dictates what individuals are not to do, is profoundly illustrated by Oliver Wendell Holmes' 'bad man' approach to law described in 'The Path of the Law': '[i]f you want to know the law and nothing else, you must look at it as a bad man, who cares only for the material consequences which such knowledge enables him to predict, not as a good one, who finds his rea-

son for conduct, whether inside the law or outside of it, in the vaguer sanctions of conscience.'[19]

Holmes' 'bad man' approach contrasts sharply with the prescriptivism of Equity, which stresses modes of behaviour that are to be aspired to because of Equity's focus on conscience and its emphasis on substance rather than form. Equity's emphasis renders it more ideologically suited to the task of maintaining the trust needed for the type of interdependency described above than the common law's narrower focus on individual justice. The fiduciary concept accentuates the unique aspects of individual relations, thereby facilitating an expansive understanding of the nature of obligations existing between parties — or what is sometimes referred to as their 'spirit and intent'— that transcends their strict, common law characterization. Thus, its focus is rather distinct from that of the common law.[20]

As a creature of Equity, the fiduciary concept presupposes the goodness of conscience and seeks to maintain or restore that goodness. Where individuals stray from their otherwise intrinsically good nature, Equity intervenes to purge their consciences of the effects of their bad behaviour.[21] The fiduciary concept, as with Equity generally, looks to law as a good person does,[22] with an emphasis upon the larger social or economic benefits that may be enjoyed by society as a whole by following certain prescriptions designed to foster and enhance interdependency.

Not all interactions where one party has power over the interests of another are properly described as fiduciary, though. The fiduciary concept is applied only where there are compelling policy reasons, rooted in Equity or statute, to preserve and reinforce the integrity, vitality, and value of important social and economic relationships.[23] Relations that are appropriately subject to fiduciary scrutiny may be identified by their substance (*i.e.*, their more-than-fleeting nature), important social or economic character, and the high trust and confidence that exists within them. They are also conspicuous by the power held by one party over the interests of another that results in the latter's implicit dependency upon and peculiar vulnerability to the former within the fiduciary element(s) of their interaction.[24]

Where the fiduciary concept is appropriately invoked, strict duties are imposed upon the fiduciaries who hold the seat of power within the fiduciary element(s) of an interaction.[25] These duties include, *inter alia*, duties of utmost good faith, full and complete disclosure, the avoidance of conflicts, and the inability to profit. Fiduciaries must serve those beneficiary interests that are tangibly related to their fiduciary interactions and eschew any correlative personal or third party interests. Whether the fiduciaries' personal interests or the interests of third parties are complementary or antagonistic to the beneficiaries' interests is immaterial.[26] Fiduciaries may only act in self-interest or in the interests of parties other than their beneficiaries with the express and fully-informed consent of their beneficiaries.[27] In matters outside the fiduciary nature of their associations, fiduciaries may do whatever they wish.[28]

As will be seen in the sections below, these characteristics evidence the fiduciary concept's functional distinction from contract law or unjust enrichment.

. . . .

One would be rather hard pressed to find much discussion of the fiduciary concept and unjust enrichment,[50] notwithstanding the important connections of the fiduciary concept and unjust enrichment to restitution,[51] the fact that the frontiers of fiduciary interaction and unjust enrichment are no more limited than the categories of negligence at common law,[52] and their basis in similarly broad, foundational postulates.

The leading fiduciary case of *Keech v. Sandford*[53] did by no means create a fully-fleshed out concept of fiduciary obligation. Rather, in finding that a trustee held the benefits of a profitable lease for his infant beneficiary even though the lessor had refused to renew it for the infant, Lord Chancellor King indicates both the selflessness required of fiduciaries and that, in situations of intimate and trusting relations, courts must not guard only against *actual* harm or abuse of a beneficiary's interests, but also the *potential* harm and abuse of those interests. The strictness of the principle in *Keech v. Sandford* is necessary to maintain the integrity and viability of fiduciary interactions by promoting the good faith discharge of one's duty to another and deterring those with authority over the interests of others from using their positions or their knowledge for the benefit of persons other than those individuals they are bound to serve.

The history of unjust enrichment may be traced to the ancient Roman maxim, attributed to Pomponius, which states 'For this by nature is equitable, that no one be made richer through another's loss.'[54] This sentiment is also evident in the two foundational cases establishing the concept of unjust enrichment. In *Moses v. Macferlan*, Lord Mansfield states:

If the defendant be under an obligation, from the ties of natural justice, to refund, the law implies a debt, and gives this action, founded in the equity of the plaintiff's case, as it were upon a contract (*'quasi ex contractu'* as the Roman law expresses it).... This kind of equitable action, to recover back money, which ought not in justice to be kept, is very beneficial and therefore much encouraged. It lies only for money which, *ex aequo et bono*, the defendant ought to refund ... In one word, the gist of this kind of action is that the defendant, upon the circumstances of the case, is obliged by the ties of natural justice and equity to refund the money.[55]

Meanwhile, Lord Wright indicates in *Fibrosa Spolka Akcyjna v. Fairbairn Lawson Combe Barbour Ltd.*, that 'any civilized system of law is bound to provide remedies for cases of what has been called unjust enrichment or unjust benefit, that is to prevent a man from retaining money of, or some benefit derived from, another which it is against conscience that he should keep.'[56]

Thus, like the broad notion of fiduciary obligation observed in *Keech v. Sandford*, neither *Moses v. Macferlan* nor *Fibrosa Spolka Akcyjna v. Fairbairn Lawson Combe Barbour Ltd.* distill anything resembling a fully-formed conception of unjust enrichment. Nonetheless, each of these cases establish or reiterate a foundational postulate that is the basis from which more specific governing principles are derived.[57] *Keech v. Sandford* establishes the basis for the fiduciary concept's broad postulate of protecting the integrity of important social and economic interactions of high trust and confidence. Both *Moses v. Macferlan* and *Fibrosa Spolka* illustrate unjust enrichment's similarly broad postulate that one party ought not benefit at the expense of another where retaining such benefit is improper.[58]

In this sense, both the fiduciary concept and unjust enrichment distinctly parallel the genesis of the modern law of negligence and Lord Atkin's formulation of the 'neighbour' principle in *Donoghue v. Stevenson*.[59] Rather than providing a list of 'neighbours,' Lord Atkin's judgment provides criteria for determining who is a neighbour that are fashioned out of the broad postulate that one must not injure one's neighbour. These criteria function like the principles fashioned out of the broad postulates established for the fiduciary concept and unjust enrichment.[60] They also provided a basis for the further refinement of the broad principle of negligence enunciated in *Donoghue v. Stevenson* rather than leaving individual applications to the whim of judicial discretion. Transforming foundational postulates into governing principles is no simple process; it is gradual and evolutionary. The growing pains currently being experienced by unjust enrichment are, at least in this respect, similar to those that still affect the fiduciary concept and that have also been experienced by the law of negligence.[61]

The broad, conceptual approach used by the fiduciary concept and unjust enrichment is rather distinct from that undertaken by more traditional civil obligations such as contract law that employ taxonomy to facilitate their emphasis on narrower issues. This distinctiveness in approach arose purposefully and in response to the inadequacies of the common law and the body of civil obligations that it had created. Thus, the relationship of either the fiduciary concept or unjust enrichment vis-à-vis civil obligations such as contract law and tort is much like the relationship between Equity and the common law.

The authority of law requires the elucidation of positive criteria for implementation so that its standards are clear and intelligible. Because it is not possible to foresee all potential situations in which particular legal rules or presumptions ought to apply, law must be articulated in a determinate and general manner.[62] Inevitably, situations will arise that fall outside of the garden variety of scenarios that the law in question was designed to respond to. As a result, gaps are created. As responses to the inadequacies of the basis of civil obligations seen in contract and tort, the fiduciary concept and unjust enrichment supplement them and smooth over their deficiencies much like Equity augments and corrects the common law.[63] These functions serve as the basis for the description of the fiduciary concept and unjust enrichment as gap-fillers.[64]

Although both the fiduciary concept and unjust enrichment complement the common law and fill in gaps where the common law is deficient, the gaps they fill and the manner in which they fill them are distinct. The fiduciary concept's function of preserving the integrity of important social and economic interactions of high trust and confidence fills a void left by the common law's emphasis on achieving individual justice. Unjust enrichment's foundational notion that one party ought not retain a benefit obtained at the expense of another in the absence of legal justification fills a void in the law of civil obligations by establishing liability where the law of contract or tort cannot,[65] as, for example, in the situation of mistaken payments.[66]

More fundamentally, however, unjust enrichment possesses a far more limited and much less ambitious mandate than the fiduciary concept. While the fiduciary concept seeks to maintain the integrity of the interactions that fall within its mandate for broader social and economic purposes, unjust enrichment undertakes only to reverse improper gains obtained at the expense of another in order to facilitate individual justice between parties. As indicated by Gummow, 'the concepts of unjust enrichment involving restitution for a benefit derived at the expense of a plaintiff ... cannot readily accommodate equitable doctrines which exist, not so much to adjust the rights of parties, as to protect the public at large.'[67] Thus, whereas the fiduciary concept looks beyond the immediate needs of the parties in favour of the broader purpose of maintaining the vitality of the important social and economic interactions that those parties are involved in, unjust enrichment turns its attention inward in order to fulfill the narrow and more immediate goal of providing relief for aggrieved parties.[68]

CONCLUSION

The fiduciary concept has been argued to be a tool to facilitate and maintain social and economic interdependency. Few legal principles are premised upon such grand aspirations. This makes encapsulating the fiduciary concept with the explicitness generally desired by legal actors a rather formidable, if not impossible, task.

There is always great difficulty in law in maintaining a proper balance between certainty and flexibility. Too much certainty can result in excessive rigidity and inflexibility that may leave just claims that exist outside of the garden variety of cases without remedy. Too much flexibility, however, results in insufficient knowledge and predictability about expected standards and legal outcomes. This conundrum profoundly affects the fiduciary concept, which is applauded for its inherent ability to respond to an infinite variety of circumstances, but which is also criticized for its lack of certainty.

This paper began with a quote from former Chief Justice Mason of the Australian High Court and it fittingly ends with another because of his attraction to Canadian use of the fiduciary concept. He once suggested that '[t]he fiduciary relationship is a concept in search of a principle.'[69] His sentiments were cited approvingly in La Forest J.'s minority judgment in *LAC Minerals Ltd. v. International Corona Resources Inc.*: '[i]n specific circumstances and in specific relationships, courts have no difficulty in imposing fiduciary obligations, but at a more fundamental level, the principle on which that obligation is based is unclear.'[70] While the concern underscoring these statements is valid, the characterizations themselves are inaccurate.

'Fiduciary' is not a concept in search of a principle, but a 'vibrant and exciting facet of law whose potential is only beginning to be tapped.'[71] The fiduciary concept is neither 'a wholly illusory wrong'[72] nor 'a blot on our law'[73] as Birks has characterized it; moreover, it should not be 'feared for its unpredictability' as Davies has suggested.[74] While the fiduciary concept may well be a 'taxonomic nightmare,'[75] it is, as Mitchell has observed, possible to ascertain the content of the fiduciary concept even in the absence of rigid rules:

> [i]t may be that fiduciary doctrine is not crystal clear, in the sense of a rule requiring traffic to stop at red lights. But the argument from certainty can be overblown.... For lawyers to argue that fiduciary duty creates significant uncertainty is specious. Anybody reading the cases soon develops a sense of what is and what is not allowed.[76]

The fiduciary concept is organic; thus, like the living tree analogy of Canadian constitutional law put forward in *Edwards v. AG Canada*, it is 'capable of growth and expansion within its natural limits.'[77] As suggested earlier, the difficulties that plague the fiduciary concept are not reflective of any inherent problems, but, rather, stem from the curt and unreflective manner in which the fiduciary concept has been applied as well as the continued dissatisfaction of those who seek to replace its innate and requisite flexibility with rigid rules.[78]

The fiduciary concept's emphasis on selfless behaviour, utmost good faith, and conscience distinguishes it from contract law and unjust enrichment. The fiduciary concept promotes selfless behaviour in its attempt to ensure the integrity of important social and economic interactions of high trust and confidence. Thus, its focus is on relationships rather than the parties to them.[79] Contract law, meanwhile, expects and encourages self-interested behaviour. As the principle of efficient breach indicates, contract

law allows for deviations from its general premise that promises are to be kept provided that the party in breach of contract adequately compensates for the effects of any breach. Thus, it is not terribly concerned about the integrity of interactions if the interests of the parties to them may nonetheless be satisfied. Unjust enrichment, like contract, is also primarily designed to facilitate individual justice between parties. Its concern is simply to reverse improper shifts of wealth, not to promote social or economic interdependency.

The fiduciary concept connects the narrow or rigid vision of law and what it can accomplish to a fuller conceptualization of law that integrates its rigour and fills in gaps where it is deficient, giving strength to the spirit of the law and not merely its letter. This is effected through the broad postulate underscoring the fiduciary concept. Unjust enrichment shares this vital gap-filling role with the fiduciary concept, although, in some ways, it has more in common with contract law. Thus, it may be said that unjust enrichment occupies a middle ground between contract and fiduciary law along the broad spectrum of legal obligations.[80]

This paper has attempted to foster a greater appreciation for the fiduciary concept by distinguishing it functionally from contiguous areas of law. Contracts and unjust enrichment have been the comparators for this paper, but others exist as well.[81] While the brevity of this paper has necessitated the simplification of compound ideas resting at the foundation of complex areas of law, they nonetheless reveal profoundly different functions.

By distinguishing the fiduciary concept from contract law and unjust enrichment, the former may be more effectively and appropriately used in Canadian jurisprudence and elsewhere. Certainly, further efforts to augment current understandings of the fiduciary concept would be favourably received and may go some ways to eliminating the fiduciary paradox described earlier. This would be a most welcome development for the fiduciary concept.

(a) *Lloyds Bank v. Bundy*[†]

England and Wales Court of Appeal (Civil Division)

[Lord DENNING (The Master of the Rolls):]

Broadchalke is one of the most pleasing villages in England. Old Herbert Bundy was a farmer there. His home was at Yew Tree Farm. It went back for 300 years. His family had been there for generations. It was his only asset. But he did a very foolish thing. He mortgaged it to the bank. Up to the very hilt. Not to borrow money for himself, but for the sake of his son. Now the bank have come down on him. They have foreclosed. They want to get him out of Yew Tree Farm and to sell it. They have brought this action against him for possession. Going out means ruin for him. He was granted legal aid. His lawyers put in a defence. They said that, when he executed the charge to the bank he did not know what he was doing: or at any rate [did not know that] the circumstances were such that he ought not to be bound by it. At the trial his plight was plain. The Judge was sorry for him. He said he was a "poor old gentleman". He was so obviously incapacitated that the Judge admitted his proof in evidence. He had a heart attack in the witness-box. Yet the Judge felt he could do nothing for him. There is nothing, he said, "which takes this out of the vast range of commercial transactions". He ordered Herbert Bundy to give up possession of Yew Tree Farm to the bank.

Now there is an appeal to this Court. The ground is that the circumstances were so exceptional that Herbert Bundy should not be held bound.

The events before December 1969.

Herbert Bundy had only one son, Michael Bundy. He had great faith in him. They were both customers of Lloyds Bank at the Salisbury branch. They had been customers for many years. The son formed a company called M.J.B. Plant Hire Ltd.

It hired out earth-moving machinery and so forth. The company banked at Lloyds too at the same branch.

In 1961 the son's company was in difficulties. The father on 19th September 1966 guaranteed the company's overdraft for £1300 and charged Yew Tree Farm to the bank to secure the £1500. Afterwards the son's company got further into difficulties. The overdraft ran into thousands. In May 1967 the assistant bank manager, Mr. Bennett, told the son the bank must have further security. The son said his father would give it. So Mr. Bennett and the son went together to see the father. Mr. Bennett produced the papers. He suggested that the father should sign a further guarantee for £5,000 and to execute a further charge for £6,000. The father said that he would help his son as far as he possibly could. Mr. Bennett did not ask the father to sign the papers there and then. He left them with the father so that he could consider them over night and take advice on them. [The] father showed them to his solicitor, Mr. Trethowan, who lived in the same village. The solicitor told the father the £5,000 was the utmost that he could sink in his son's affairs. The house was worth about £10,000 and this was half his assets. On that advice the father on 27th May 1969

† [1974] EWCA Civ 8, [1975] QB 326.

did execute the further guarantee and the charge, and Mr. Bennett witnessed it. So at the end of May 1967 the father had charged the house to secure £7500.

The events of December 1969.

During the next six months the affairs of the son and his company went from bad to worse. The bank had granted the son's company an overdraft up to a limit of £10,000, but this was not enough to meet the outgoings. The son's company drew cheques which the bank returned unpaid. The bank were anxious. By this time Mr. Bennett had left to go to another branch. He was succeeded by a new assistant manager, Mr. Head. In November 1969 Mr. Head saw the son and told him that the account was unsatisfactory and that he considered that the company might have to cease operations. The son suggested that the difficulty was only temporary and that his father would be prepared to provide further money if necessary.

On 17th December 1969 there came the occasion which, in the Judge's words, was important and disastrous for the father. The son took Mr. Head to see his father. Mr. Head had never met the father before. This was his first visit. He went prepared. He took with him a form of guarantee and a form of charge filled in with the father's name ready for signature. There was a family gathering. The father and mother were there. The son and the son's wife. Mr. Head said that the bank had given serious thought as to whether they could continue to support the son's company. But that the bank were prepared to do so in this way:

(i) The bank would continue to allow the company to draw money on overdraft up to the existing level of £10,000, but the bank would require the company to pay 10% of its incomings into a separate account. So that 10% would not go to reduce the overdraft. Mr. Head said that this would have the effect "of reducing the level of borrowing". In other words, the bank was cutting down the overdraft.

(ii) The bank would require the father to give a guarantee of the company's account in a sum of £11,000 and to give the bank a further charge on the house of £3,500, so as to bring the total charge to £11,000. The house was only worth about £10,000, so this charge for £11,000 would sweep up all that the father had.

On hearing the proposal, the father said that Michael was his only son and that he was 100%

behind him. Mr. Head produced the forms that had [already] been filled in. The father signed them and Mr. Head witnessed them there and then. On this occasion, Mr. Head, unlike Mr. Bennett, did not leave the forms with the father: nor did the father have any independent advice.

It is important to notice the state of mind of Mr. Head and of the father. Mr Head said in evidence:

> Defendant asked me what in my opinion the company was doing wrong and [the] company's position. I told him. I did not explain the company's affairs very fully as I had only just taken over the account.... The son said that [the] company had a number of bad debts. I was not entirely satisfied with this. I thought the trouble was more deep seated .... It did not occur to me that there was any conflict of interest. I thought there was no conflict of interest. I would think the defendant relied on me implicitly to advise him about the transaction as bank manager. I knew he had no other assets except Yew Tree Cottage.

The father said in evidence:

> I always thought Mr. Head was genuine. I have always trusted him.... No discussion how business was doing that I can remember. I simply sat back and did what they said.

The solicitor, Mr. Trethowan, said of the father: "He is straightforward. Agrees with anyone. I doubt if he understood all that Mr. Head explained to him."

So the father signed the papers. Mr. Head witnessed them and took them away. The father had charged the whole of his remaining asset, leaving himself with nothing. The son and his company gained a respite. But only for a short time. Five months later, in May 1970, a receiving order was made against the son. Thereupon the bank stopped all overdraft facilities for the company. It ceased to trade. The father's solicitor, Mr. Trethowan at once went to see Mr. Head. He said he was concerned that the father had signed the guarantee.

In due course the bank insisted on the sale of the house. In December 1971 they agreed to sell it for £7,500 with vacant possession. The family were very disappointed with this figure. It was, they said, worth much more. Estate agents were called to say so. But the Judge held it was a valid sale and that the bank can take all the proceeds. The sale has not been completed, because Herbert Bundy is still in possession. The bank have brought these proceedings to evict Herbert Bundy.

THE GENERAL RULE.

Now let me say at once that in the vast majority of cases a customer who signs a bank guarantee or a charge cannot get out of it. No bargain will be upset which is the result of the ordinary interplay of forces. There are many hard cases which are caught by this rule. Take the case of a poor man who is homeless. He agrees to pay a high rent to a landlord just to get a roof over his head. The common law will not interfere. It is left to Parliament. Next take the case of a borrower in urgent need of money. He borrows it from the bank at high interest and it is guaranteed by a friend. The guarantor gives his bond and gets nothing in return. The common law will not interfere. Parliament has intervened to prevent moneylenders charging excessive interest. But it has never interfered with banks.

Yet there are exceptions to this general rule. There are cases in our books in which the Courts will set aside a contract, or a transfer of property, when the parties have not met [on] equal terms — when the one is so strong in bargaining power and the other so weak — that, as a matter of common fairness it is not right that the strong should be allowed to push the weak to the wall. Hitherto those exceptional cases have been treated each as a separate category in itself. But I think the time has come when we should seek to find a principle to unite them.

I put on one side contracts or transactions which are voidable for fraud or misrepresentation or mistake. All those are governed by settled principles. I go only to those where there has been inequality of bargaining power, such as to merit the intervention of the Court.

III   The Categories.

The first category is that of *"duress of goods"*. A typical case is when a man is in a strong bargaining position by being in possession of the goods of another by virtue of a legal right, such as, by way of pawn or pledge or taken in distress. The owner is in a weak position because he is in urgent need of the goods. The stronger demands of the weaker more than is justly due: and he pays it in order to get the goods. Such a transaction is voidable. He can recover the excess, see *Astley v. Reynolds* (1731) 2 Stra. 915; *Green v. Duckett* (1883) 11 Q.B.D. 275. To which may be added the cases of "colore officii", where a man is in a strong bargaining position by virtue of his official position or public profession. He relies upon it so as to gain from the weaker — who is urgently in need — more than is justly due, see *Pigott's case* cited by Lord Kenyon L.J. in 2 Espinasse

at pages 723–4; *Parker v. Bristol & Exeter Railway Co.* (1851) 6 Exch. 702; *Steele v. Williams* (1853) 8 Exch. 625. In such cases the stronger may make his claim in good faith honestly believing that he is entitled to make his demand. He may not be guilty of any fraud or misrepresentation. The inequality of bargaining power — the strength of the one versus the urgent need of the other — renders the transaction voidable and the money paid to be recovered back, see *Maskell v. Horner* (1915) 3 K.B. 106.

The second category is that of the *"expectant heir."* A man is so placed as to be in need of special care and protection and yet his weakness is exploited by another far stronger than himself so as to get his property at a gross undervalue. The typical case is that of the "expectant heir". But it applies to all cases where a man comes into property, or is expected to come into it — and then being in urgent need — another gives him ready cash for it, greatly below its true worth, and so gets the property transferred to him, see *Evans v. Llewellyn* (1787) 1 Cox Eq. Cas. 333. Even though there be no evidence of fraud or misrepresentation, nevertheless the transaction will be set aside, see *Fry v. Lane* (1888) 40 Ch. D. 312., where Mr. Justice Kay said (at page 522):

> The result of the decisions is that where a purchase is made from a poor and ignorant man at a considerable undervalue, the vendor having no independent advice, a Court of Equity will set aside the transaction.

The third category is that of *"undue influence"* usually so called. These are divided into two classes as stated by Lord Justice Cotton in *Allcard v. Skinner* (1887) 36 Ch. D. at page 171. The first are those where the stronger has been guilty of some fraud or wrongful act — expressly so as to gain some gift or advantage from the weaker. The second are those where the stronger has not been guilty of any wrongful act, but has, through the relations which existed between him and the weaker, gained some gift or advantage for himself. Sometimes the relations are such as to raise a presumption of undue influence, such as parent over child, solicitor over client, doctor over patient, spiritual adviser over follower. At other times a relation of confidence must be proved to exist. But to all of them the general principle obtains which was stated by Lord Chelmsford, Lord Chancellor, in *Tate v. Williamson* (1861) L.R. 2 Ch. App 55 at page 61:

> Wherever the persons stand in such a relation [to one another that while the relationship] continues, confidence is necessarily reposed by one [in the other], and the influence which natu-

rally grows out of that confidence is possessed by the other, and this confidence is abused, or the influence is exerted, to obtain an advantage at the expense of the confiding party, the person so availing himself of his position, will not be permitted to obtain the advantage, although the transaction could not have been impeached if no such confidential relation had existed.

. . . .

The fourth category is that of *"undue" pressure*. The most apposite of that is *Williams v. Bayley* (1866) L.R. 2 H.L. 200, where a son forged his father's name to a promissory note, and, by means of it, raised money from the bank of which they were both customers. The bank said to the father, in effect:

> Take your choice — give us security for your son's debt. If you do take that on yourself, then it will all go smoothly: if you do not, we shall be bound to exercise pressure.

Thereupon the father charged his property to the bank with payment of the note. The House of Lords held that the charge was invalid because of undue pressure exerted by the bank. Lord Westbury said at page 218:

> A contract to give security for the debt of another, which is a contract without consideration. Is above all things a contract that should be based upon the free and voluntary agency of the individual who enters into it.

Other instances of undue pressure are where an employer — the stronger party — had employed a builder — the weaker party — to do work for him. When the builder asked for payment of sums properly due (so as to pay his workmen) the employer refused to pay unless he was given some added advantage. Vice-Chancellor Stuart said:

> When an agreement, hard and inequitable in itself, has been executed under pressure on the part of the party who executes it, the Court will set it aside,

see *Ormes v. Beadel* (1860) 2 Giff. 166 at page 174 (reversed on another ground, 2 de G.F. & J- 333; *D. & C. Builders Ltd. v. Rees* (1966) 2 Q.B. at page 623.

The fifth category is that of *salvage agreements*. When a vessel is in danger of sinking and seeks help, the rescuer is in a strong bargaining position. The vessel in distress is in urgent need. The parties cannot be truly said to be on equal terms. The Court of Admiralty have always recognised that fact. The fundamental rule is:

> If the parties have made an agreement, the Court will enforce it, unless it is manifestly unfair and unjust; but if it be manifestly unfair and unjust, the Court will disregard it and decide what is fair and just.

See *Akerblom v. Price* (1881) 7 Q.B.D. 129 at page 133 by Lord Justice Brett applied in a striking case *The Port Caledonia and The Anna* (1903) p. 184, when the rescuer refused to help with a rope unless he was paid £1,000.

IV. The General Principles.

Gathering all together, I would suggest that through all these instances there runs a single thread. They rest on "inequality of bargaining power". By virtue of it, the English law gives relief to one who, without independent advice, enters into a contract or transfers property for a consideration which is grossly inadequate, when his bargaining power is grievously impaired by reason of his own needs or desires, or by his own ignorance or infirmity, coupled with undue influences or pressures brought to bear on him by or for the benefit of the other. When I use the word "undue" I do not mean to suggest that the principle depends on proof of any wrongdoing. The one who stipulates for his own excessive sum may be moved solely by his own self-interest, unconscious of the distress he is bringing to the other. I have also avoided any reference to the will of the one being "dominated" or "overcome" by the other. One who is in extreme need may knowingly consent to a most improvident bargain, solely to relieve the straits in which he finds himself. Again, I do not mean to suggest that every transaction is saved by independent advice. But the absence of it may be fatal. With these explanations, I hope this principle will be found to reconcile the cases. Applying it to the present case, I would notice these points:

(1) The consideration moving from the bank was grossly inadequate. The son's company was in serious difficulty. The overdraft was at its limit of £10,000. The bank considered that its existing security was insufficient. In order to get further security, it asked the father to charge the house — his sole asset — to the uttermost. It was worth £10,000. The charge was for £11,000. That was for the benefit of the bank. But not at all for the benefit of the father, or indeed for the company. The bank did not [promise] to continue the overdraft or to increase it. On the contrary, it required the overdraft to be reduced. All that the company gained was a short respite from impending doom.

(2) The relationship between the bank and the father was one of trust and confidence. The

bank knew that the father relied on it implicitly to advise him about the transaction. The father trusted the bank. This gave the bank much influence on the father. Yet the bank failed in that trust. It allowed the father to charge the house to his ruin.

(3) The relationship between the father and the son was one where the father's natural affection had much influence on him. He would naturally desire to accede to his son's request. He trusted his son. There was a conflict of interest between the bank and the father. Yet the bank did not realise it. Nor did it suggest that the father should get independent advice. If the father had gone to his solicitor — or to any man of business — there is no doubt that any one of them would say: "You must not enter into this transaction. You are giving up your house, your sole remaining asset, for no benefit to you. The company is in such a parlous state that you must not do it."

These considerations seem to me to bring this case within the principles I have stated. But, in case that principle is wrong, I would also say that the case falls within the category of undue influence of the second class stated by Lord Justice Cotton in *Allcard v. Skinner*. I have no doubt that the assistant bank manager acted in the utmost good faith and was straightforward and genuine. Indeed the father said so. But beyond doubt he was acting in the interests of the bank — to get further security for a bad debt. There was such a relationship of trust and confidence between them that the bank ought not to have swept up his sole remaining asset into its hands — for nothing — without his having independent advice. I would therefore allow this appeal.

. . . .

[Sir ERIC SACHS:]

At trial in the County Court a number of complex defences were raised, ranging from *non est factum*, through undue influence and absence of consideration to negligence in, and improper exercise of, the bank's duty when contracting for the sale of the relevant property. It is thus at the outset appropriate to record that in this Court no challenge has been offered to any of the conclusions of the learned County Court Judge on law or on fact save as regards one aspect of one of the defences — appropriately pleaded as undue influence. As regards that defence, however, it is clear that he vitally misapprehended the law and the points to be considered and

that moreover he apparently fell into error — as his own notes disclose — on an important fact touching that issue. In the result this Court is thus faced with a task that is very far from being easy.

The first and most troublesome issue which here falls for consideration is as to whether on the particular and somewhat unusual facts of the case, the bank was, when obtaining his signatures on the 17th December 1969, in a relationship with Mr. Bundy that entailed a duty on their part of what can for convenience be called fiduciary care. (The phrase "fiduciary care" is used to avoid confusion with the common law duty of care — a different field of our jurisprudence.)

. . . .

On the other hand, whilst disclaiming any intention of seeking to catalogue the elements of such a special relationship, it is perhaps of a little assistance to note some of the elements which have in the past frequently been found to exist where the Court has been led to decide that this relationship existed as between adults of sound mind. Such cases tend to arise where someone relies on the guidance or advice of another, where the other is aware of that reliance and where the person upon whom reliance is placed obtains, or may well obtain, a benefit from the transaction or has some other interest in it being concluded. In addition, there must, of course, be shown to exist a vital element of what in this judgment will for convenience be referred to as confidentiality. It is this element which is so impossible to define and which is a matter for the judgment of the Court on the facts of any particular case.

Confidentiality, a relatively little used word, is being adopted, albeit with some hesitation, to avoid the possible confusion that can arise through referring to "confidence". Reliance on advice can in many circumstances be said to import that type of confidence which only results in a common law duty to take care — a duty which may co-exist with but is not coterminous with that of fiduciary care. "Confidentiality" is intended to convey that extra quality in the relevant confidence that is implicit in the phrase "confidential relationship" ... and may perhaps have something in common with "confiding" and also "confident", when, for instance, referring to someone's "man of affairs". It imports some quality beyond that interest in the confidence that can well exist between trustworthy persons who in business affairs deal with each other at arms length. It is one of the features of this element that once it exists, influence naturally grows out of it ...

It was inevitably conceded on behalf of the bank that the relevant relationship can arise as between banker and customer. Equally, it was inevitably conceded on behalf of Mr. Bundy that in the normal course of transactions by which a customer guarantees a third party's obligations, the relationship does not arise. The onus of proof lies on the customer who alleges that in any individual case the line has been crossed and the relationship has arisen.

. . . .

The situation was thus one which to any reasonably sensible person, who gave it but a moment's thought, cried aloud Mr. Bundy's need for careful independent advice. Over and above the need any man has for counsel when asked to risk his last penny on even an apparently reasonable project, was the need here for informed advice as to whether there was any real chance of the company's affairs becoming viable if the documents were signed. If not, there arose questions such as, what is the use of taking the risk of becoming penniless without benefiting anyone but the bank; is it not better both for you and your son that you, at any rate, should still have some money when the crash comes; and should not the bank at least bind itself to hold its hand for some given period? The answers to such questions could only be given in the light of a worthwhile appraisement of the company's affairs — without which Mr. Bundy could not come to an <u>informed judgment</u> as to the wisdom of what he was doing.

No such advice to get an independent opinion was given; on the contrary, Mr. Head chose to give his own views on the company's affairs and to take this course, though he had at trial to admit: "I did not explain the company's affairs very fully as I had only just taken over." (Another answer that escaped entry in the learned Judge's original notes.)

On the above recited facts, the breach of the duty to take fiduciary care is manifest. It is not necessary for Mr. Bundy to rely on another factor tending to show such a breach. The bank knew full well that Mr. Bundy had a well-known solicitor of standing, Mr. Trethowan, who usually advised on important matters — including the previous charge signed in May 1969, only seven months earlier. Indeed, on that occasion the bank seems very properly to have taken steps which either ensured that Mr. Trethowan's advice was obtained or at least assumed it was being obtained. It is no answer that Mr. Head, relatively a newcomer to the Bundy accounts at the Salisbury branch, may not personally have known these matters — it is the bank's knowledge that is material. Incidentally, Mr. Head had discussed the relevant accounts with his manager.

. . . .

The conclusion that Mr. Bundy has established that as between himself and the bank the relevant transaction fell within the second category of undue influence cases referred to by Lord Justice Cotton in *Allcard v. Skinner* is one reached upon the single issue pursued on behalf of the appellant in this Court. On that issue we have had the benefit of cogent and helpful submissions on [a] matter plainly raised in the pleadings. As regards the wider areas covered in masterly survey in the judgment of my Lord, the Master of the Rolls, but not raised arguendo, I do not venture to express an opinion — though having some sympathy with the views that the Courts should be able to give relief to a party who has been subject to undue pressure as defined in the concluding passage of his judgment on that point.

. . . .

The appeal should be allowed.

(b) *Harry v. Kreutziger*[†]

Court of Appeal for British Columbia

[McINTYRE J.A.:]

[1] The appellant sued to have the court set aside the sale to the respondent of his 6-ton fishing boat, the "Glenda Marion". He alleged fraudulent misrepresentation, and in the alternative sought relief from an unconscionable bargain. At trial, the action was dismissed. This appeal was taken, and before this

---

† (1978), 9 BCLR 166.

court the appellant confined his claim to that of unconscionable bargain.

[2] The appellant is an Indian who lives in Powell River, British Columbia. He is married, with six children, aged from 6 to 19. He suffers from a congenital hearing defect, but is by no means totally deaf. He has grade 5 education, and according to the trial judge is a mild, inarticulate, retiring person, and it would appear from the evidence that he is not widely experienced in business matters. He is a commercial fisherman and a logger.

[3] In 1958 the appellant purchased the "Glenda Marion", a 30-foot gas-powered fishing boat. It was registered as a 6-ton vessel and was used for gill-netting and trolling. The vessel had become largely obsolete by 1973 and had very small value as a boat. However, because of the commercial fishing licence attributable to the vessel it acquired substantial value after 1968, and particularly in 1973.

[4] Prior to 1968, any person could apply for and acquire a commercial salmon fishing licence. In 1968 the situation changed, when the government adopted the policy of reducing the size of the salmon fishing fleet in the interests of economy and conservation. Fishing boats were granted licences in one of three categories, "A", "B" and "C", depending upon quantities of salmon landed in previous years. Any new boat could be licensed for salmon fishing only if a transfer of an existing licence from an old boat could be arranged. The effect of this arrangement was to freeze the number of commercial licences, and as a result they began to acquire real value.

[5] The appellant wished to replace the "Glenda Marion", which had a licence, with a new boat. He had saved $5,200 towards a new vessel, and had made two unsuccessful applications, one in 1971 and one in 1972, to the Indian Fishermen's Assistance Programme for financial assistance for this purpose. He made a third application in 1973. This programme was administered by the Fisheries Service of the Department of the Environment, and received its funds from the Department of Indian Affairs and Northern Development. Under this plan, an Indian could obtain a grant of tonnage, that is, an entitlement to a commercial fishing licence based on the tonnage of a boat, from a "tonnage bank" operated by the programme. This tonnage had to be purchased by the acquisition of licensed boats by the scheme. It was available to needy Indians who were assisted under the programme. If the appellant's application had been accepted, the programme could have acquired the "Glenda Marion" by purchase

from the appellant. The licence or tonnage attributable to the vessel, that is, 6 tons, would have passed with the purchase to the tonnage bank. When the appellant purchased his new boat, if the events reached that stage, the tonnage in the tonnage bank would have been available to him. His new boat would have been licensed. He was also free, if he chose, to sell the boat privately. If he adopted this course, however, the licence or tonnage would follow the sale, and he would lose it and thereby virtually exclude himself from further fishing. He had been warned by an officer of the programme that the assistance fund, formed as it was to protect and assist Indian fishermen, would not look favourably upon an application for assistance if the appellant sold his boat privately, thus depriving the fund of the tonnage and making it more difficult to carry out its objectives.

[6] After making his application for aid in August 1973 the appellant spoke to one Robinson, administrator of the programme, who arranged to have one Fred Shaughnessy acquire the "Glenda Marion" for the fund. On 4th October 1973 the appellant signed a transfer of the boat to the Department of the Environment for $2,000. The department held the transfer, but the matter was never concluded. No reason for the failure to complete the sale was given in evidence. Had it been concluded, the appellant would have received $2,000 and the tonnage would have been passed to the tonnage bank. On the acquisition of his new boat, he could have applied, and he intended to apply, for the tonnage from the bank. Subject to qualifying for assistance in the first place, he would have received the tonnage and had the licence and would have acquired a new boat fully licenced. The only fair inference one can draw from these facts is that in the abortive arrangements made with the Indian Assistance Fund and described above the appellant was attempting to dispose of his boat only, and was not surrendering as well the licence or the tonnage necessary for his continued fishing.

[7] A further detail regarding the licensing of boats should be mentioned. The category of licence sought by the respondent in his purchase of the "Glenda Marion" was an "A" licence. The "Glenda Marion" had an "AI" licence. This was a form of licence available only to Indians, for which a lower licence fee was payable than upon an "A" licence. Otherwise, the licences were identical. When a boat with an "AI" licence was sold to a white man, he could convert the "AI" licence to an "A" licence, but only upon paying to the government full licence fees for

the previous years during which it had existed as an "AI" licence.

[8] In November 1973 the respondent was seeking to purchase a vessel with an "A" licence. It was clear from the evidence that, due to the restrictive licensing policy described above and due as well to the fact that 1973 yielded one of the best salmon harvests in British Columbia's history, licences had acquired great value. The evidence showed, and the trial judge found, that Class "A" licenced tonnage was worth about $2,500 per ton. This Figure was in addition to the value of the hull and machinery. The "Glenda Marion", being licensed for 6 tons, had a value for licence alone of $15,000. The respondent was well aware of this valuation. He knew the licence had value apart from the boat. The trial judge said [p. 352]:

> I am satisfied the defendant believed the 'Glenda Marion' with its licence had a value of $16,000 in November 1973 and that sales of similar vessels on the open market at that time supported this belief.

There was ample evidence to support this conclusion. It may be found in the evidence of one Mazzone, an employee of a large fishing company actively engaged in 1973 in the purchase of tonnage, and of one Bell, engaged then in the "Government Buy Back Programme", by which licensed vessels were acquired by the government and retired from fishing to assist in reducing the fleet. It should also be observed that in registering the transfer of the boat with the Regional Director of Fisheries in Vancouver the respondent was required to sign a record of transfer form covering the transaction. In completing the form in the space for purchase price which required that he show "total value including value of all other consideration", he entered the figure of $16,000.

[9] The respondent approached the appellant on 18th November 1973 in Powell River. The "Glenda Marion" had sunk a few days before (no reason was disclosed in the evidence) and had been refloated by the appellant. This fact is mentioned to indicate the boat as such was of small value at this time. After some discussion, during which the appellant told the respondent of his arrangement to sell the boat to the assistance programme, the appellant expressed doubt about the sale and said he wished to acquire a new boat and licence. The respondent, though he conceded in evidence that he knew little of the operation of the assistance programme, assured the appellant that as an Indian he would not have any

difficulty in acquiring a new licence after sale to the respondent. The respondent gave the appellant a cheque for $2,000, which had been back-dated by the respondent to 1st September 1973, obviously to give the impression that the sale had been arranged before the agreement with the assistance programme. The appellant took the cheque and said he would consider the matter and give the respondent his decision the next day.

[10] The appellant decided against the sale overnight, after discussions with his brother, and gave the cheque to his brother to return to the respondent. He said he adopted this course because he did not wish to face the respondent. The cheque was returned the next day, but after receipt the respondent went to the appellant's home and slipped the cheque under his door. A further meeting took place on 20th November 1973, when the respondent gave further assurances to the appellant that he would be able to get a licence for a new boat. The cheque was handed back and forth several times, the respondent returning it to the appellant after each refusal to sell. Finally it was agreed that the boat would be sold for $4,500. A handwritten memorandum to this effect was signed by the parties. A further cheque for the remainder of the purchase price was given to the appellant. However, when the respondent sought to transfer the licence he discovered the necessity to repay back licence fees in the amount of $570 in order to convert the licence into an "A" licence. He stopped payment of the cheque for $2,000, and issued a new one for $1,430, which was sent to the appellant. This was done without notice to or consent of the appellant.

[11] For this recital it is at once clear that the appellant made an improvident bargain. He parted with an asset worth $16,000 for $4,500, later reduced by $570. The question for decision is: Did he enter into this bargain under such circumstances that the court will exercise its equitable jurisdiction to rescind the contract and return the parties to their original positions? The trial judge held that he had not. He said, after declining to find that the appellant had been induced to enter the contract by false representations and after discussing various authorities [pp. 355–56]:

> In the present case I conclude that the principles discussed by Lord Denning M.R. in the *Bundy* case [*Lloyds Bank Ltd. v. Bundy*, [1974] 3 W.L.R. 501, [1974] 3 All E.R. 757 (C.A.)] are not applicable. To begin with, this is not a case where the plaintiff was compelled to enter into the transaction by reason of his own needs or

desires. He complains that he did not have any independent advice before entering into the transaction. But, again, this is not a situation where the agreement was reached as a result of one session of bargaining. Rather, the defendant approached the plaintiff and made a proposal to him and tendered a cheque. The plaintiff accepted that cheque but reserved his right to consider the proposal before reaching a decision. Then he went away and, after considering the matter, decided not to sell the 'Glenda Marion' to the defendant. He had his brother return the cheque the next day. Thereupon the defendant attended at the residence of the plaintiff and slipped the cheque under the door. At that point the plaintiff had made his decision known to the defendant. He could have torn up the cheque and refused to discuss the matter further with the defendant. Instead, he went the next day and bargained with the defendant. He indicated to the defendant that he had been dealing with a third party who had considered offering him $4,500 for the vessel. Apparently that transaction had fallen through. Ultimately the defendant offered to pay $4,500 for the 'Glenda Marion' and the plaintiff accepted that offer. Now the plaintiff complains that the consideration was grossly inadequate. However, over the span of the three days during which negotiations took place the plaintiff had an opportunity, if he had desired, to seek independent advice as to the current market value of a Class 'AI' commercial salmon fishing licence with a six-ton vessel. He did not seek such independent advice. In the circumstances he cannot be heard to complain that the price was inadequate.

[12] The principles upon which a court will interfere with a concluded transaction and nullify it upon the ground that it is unconscionable have found frequent expression. An early Canadian case is *Waters v. Donnelly* (1884), 9 O.R. 391. The leading pronouncement on the subject in British Columbia is to be found in *Morrison v. Coast Finance Ltd.* reflex, (1965), 54 W.W.R. 257, 55 D.L.R. (2d) 710 (C.A.), where Davey J.A., speaking for himself and Bull J.A., said at p. 259:

> The equitable principles relating to undue influence and relief against unconscionable bargains are closely related, but the doctrines are separate and distinct. The finding here against undue influence does not conclude the question whether the appellant is entitled to relief against an unconscionable transaction. A plea of undue influence attacks the sufficiency of consent; a plea that a bargain is unconscionable invokes relief against an unfair advantage gained by an unconscientious use of power by a stronger party

against a weaker. On such a claim the material ingredients are proof of inequality in the position of the parties arising out of the ignorance, need or distress of the weaker, which left him in the power of the stronger, and proof of substantial unfairness of the bargain obtained by the stronger. On proof of those circumstances, it creates a presumption of fraud which the stronger must repel by proving that the bargain was fair, just and reasonable: *Aylesford (Earl) v. Morris* (1873), 8 Ch. App. 484, 42 L.J. Ch. 546, *per* Lord Selborne at p. 491, or perhaps by showing that no advantage was taken: See *Harrison v. Guest* (1855), 6 De G.M. &G. 424 at 438, affirmed (1860), 8 H.L. Cas. 481 at 492, 493, 11 E.R. 517. ...

. . . .

[14] From these authorities, this rule emerges. Where a claim is made that a bargain is unconscionable, it must be shown for success that there was inequality in the position of the parties due to the ignorance, need or distress of the weaker, which would leave him in the power of the stronger, coupled with proof of substantial unfairness in the bargain. When this has been shown a presumption of fraud is raised, and the stronger must show, in order to preserve his bargain, that it was fair and reasonable.

[15] Like many principles of law, it is much easier to state than to apply in any given case. In the cases cited above the facts were such that the application of the remedy was clearly required. In the case at bar the facts do not speak as clearly. Nonetheless, I am of the view that this appeal should succeed and the contract be rescinded. The appellant, by education, physical infirmity and economic circumstances, was clearly not the equal of the respondent. The evidence supports the conclusion that the appellant wanted to continue fishing and wanted to retain his licence or tonnage. It shows as well that the respondent proceeded aggressively with full knowledge of the value of the licence. He expressed regret at one stage that he had not acquired three or four more licences, they were so valuable. The appellant did not wish to sell, and resisted for a time by returning the cheque and delaying a decision. The arbitrary withholding of $570 by the respondent is illustrative of his attitude to the appellant. Despite the fact that the trial judge found that the appellant had not shown that he entered the contract on the basis of representations made by the defendant, I cannot but conclude that the appellant was anxious to preserve his licence, and that he was assured falsely or reck-

lessly by the respondent that he would have no difficulty getting another licence if he sold the "Glenda
Marion" to the respondent. In this respect, he was
given assurances on a subject of prime importance
by the respondent, who admitted he knew little or
nothing of the matter. The respondent also knew
that the preservation of his licence was a vital consideration to the appellant. The respondent sought
out the appellant and in his dealings would not take
no for an answer. He persuaded the appellant to
enter a bargain after, by his own admission, making
assurances which were untrue regarding the chance
of the appellant to get a licence. He thereby pro-
cured an asset worth $16,000 for $4,500, which he
later chose to reduce by $570. The position taken by
the appellant's counsel was that the appellant's ignorance, coupled with pressures exerted upon him by
the respondent, caused the inequality of the bargaining position. In my view, the improvidence of the
bargain is shown. On the whole of the evidence, it is
also my view that the appellant was so dominated
and overborne by the respondent that he was, in the
sense of that term used by Davey J.A. in the *Morrison* case, supra, within the power of the respondent
in these dealings.

[16] Some more precise reference to the evidence
may be helpful. The first meeting between the
respondent and the appellant took place on 18th
November 1973. During the conversation that day
the licence was discussed and, while the appellant
indicated that he would be willing to sell the boat,
he did not wish to part with the licence. He was told
"there was no problem to get licences for Indians".
There was also conversation about another possible
purchaser for the boat who, it was said, might pay
$4,500. This was why the respondent raised his price.
At the close of this meeting the respondent gave the
appellant a cheque for $2,000, which, as has been
noted, he backdated to 1st September 1973 to give
the appearance that the sale had preceded the sale
to the assistance scheme. The appellant took the
cheque because, he said, the respondent kept telling
him he could easily get a licence. That evening,
after a discussion with his brother, he returned the
cheque by sending it back with his brother. He said,
"I did not want to face him". The respondent,
despite this incident, pressed on to acquire the boat.
He returned the cheque to the appellant's house.
When the appellant received it — he was absent
when it arrived — he took it back personally. He
said, "He kept phoning me all the time at night and
I thought if I went back I might as well face him,
you know."

[17] There is some confusion about how many subsequent meetings occurred. The appellant's brother
testified that two more meetings took place, and that
at both these meetings the appellant continually
reiterated his fear that he would not be able to
obtain another licence, and received repeated assurances that, being an Indian, he would get one easily.
The respondent said, however, that there was only
one more meeting. In any event, this final meeting
occurred on 20th November 1973 in the coffee shop
of the Marine Hotel; the respondent, the appellant
and the appellant's brother, James Harry, were present. At this meeting the appellant again returned the
respondent's cheque, saying, "I am not going to sell
my boat, I am scared of losing my licence." Discussion continued for some time; they left the coffee
shop and went into the bar, where the respondent
and James Harry drank beer but apparently the
appellant did not. At length the appellant apparently
decided that he would sell his boat for $4,500. He
swore that the only reason for finally agreeing to the
sale was that he had accepted the advice that he
could preserve his licence. He said in cross-examination, "I believed him, that is the only reason I let
her go." In my opinion, it is clear from the evidence
that the respondent, a man of greater business experience, greater education and with a full knowledge
of the value attributable in the autumn of 1973 to a
commercial fishing licence, took advantage of his
general superiority and prevailed upon the appellant
to enter into this bargain against his best interests.

[18] I take this view with the utmost respect to the
trial judge. I have, however, considered his reasons
for refusing to apply the principles in the *Bundy*
case, supra, and I remain of the view that I have
expressed. It is true, as he has pointed out, that the
appellant could have sought advice; he could have
torn up the cheque; he could have refused to have
any dealings with the respondent; but this will be
true of almost any case where an unconscionable
bargain is claimed. If the appellant had done these
things, no problem would have arisen. The fact
remains, however, he did not, and in my view of the
evidence it was because he was overborne by the
respondent because of the inequality in their positions, and the principles of the cases cited apply.

[19] I would allow the appeal and direct that the
contract be rescinded; that the respondent deliver
the "Glenda Marion" to the appellant upon payment
by the appellant to the respondent of the sum of
$3,930.

. . . . .

[LAMBERT J.A.:]

[23] I do not disagree that the principle, as stated by Davey J.A. and by McIntyre J.A., is appropriate to apply in this case as an aid in the determination of whether this is a case where rescission should be granted, though I am not satisfied that the principle, so stated, exhausts all cases where rescission might be ordered under the rubric of unconscionable bargain.

[24] I agree wholeheartedly with McIntyre J.A. when he says that it is easier to state the principle than to apply it in a given case. Indeed, to my mind the principle is only of the most general guidance. It is not a principle of the type which can be applied to facts to produce, by a logical process, a clear conclusion. To think of it as such a principle is to obscure the real process of consideration and judgment that leads to a decision in this kind of case.

[25] I consider that the judgment of the English Court of Appeal in *Lloyd's Bank Ltd. v. Bundy*, [1974] 3 W.L.R. 501, [1974] 3 All E.R. 757, is subject to the same limitation. In that case, Lord Denning M.R. analyzed five types of unconscionable bargain and synthesized them into one general principle. He called the five types: duress of goods, unconscionable transactions, undue influence, undue pressure and salvage agreements. He stated the general principle in these terms [p. 765]:

> Gathering all together, I would suggest that through all these instances there runs a single thread. They rest on 'inequality of bargaining power'. By virtue of it, the English law gives relief to one who, without independent advice, enters into a contract on terms which are very unfair or transfers property for a consideration which is grossly inadequate, when his bargaining power is grievously impaired by reason of his own needs or desires, or by his own ignorance or infirmity, coupled with undue influences or pressures brought to bear on him by or for the benefit of the other. When I use the word 'undue' I do not mean to suggest that the principle depends on proof of any wrongdoing. The one who stipulates for an unfair advantage may be moved solely by his own self-interest, unconscious of the distress he is bringing to the other. I have also avoided any reference to the will of the one being 'dominated' or 'overcome' by the other. One who is in extreme need may knowingly consent to a most improvident bargain, solely to relieve the straits in which he finds himself. Again, I do not mean to suggest that every transaction is saved by independent advice. But the absence may be fatal. With these explanations, I hope this principle will be found to reconcile the cases.

This statement was clearly not intended as a touchstone, since the liberal employment of adjectives makes it too flexible for that purpose, but rather as a demonstration that the categories of grounds for rescission are interrelated and based on a common foundation, so that cases of one of the five types may provide guidance on another of the types. Accordingly, again, the statement of principle has been of only the most general assistance to me in reaching my decision on the facts of this case.

[26] In my opinion, questions as to whether use of power was unconscionable, an advantage was unfair or very unfair, a consideration was grossly inadequate, or bargaining power was grievously impaired, to select words from both statements of principle, the *Morrison* case and the *Bundy* case, are really aspects of one single question. That single question is whether the transaction, seen as a whole, is sufficiently divergent from community standards of commercial morality that it should be rescinded. To my mind, the framing of the question in that way prevents the real issue from being obscured by an isolated consideration of a number of separate questions; as, for example, a consideration of whether the consideration was grossly inadequate, rather than merely inadequate, separate from the consideration of whether bargaining power was grievously impaired, or merely badly impaired. Such separate consideration of separate questions produced by the application of a synthetic rule tends to obscure rather than aid the process of decision.

[27] The single question of whether the transaction, seen as a whole, is sufficiently divergent from community standards of commercial morality that it should be rescinded must be answered by an examination of the decided cases and a consideration, from those cases, of the fact patterns that require that the bargain be rescinded and those that do not. In that examination, Canadian cases are more relevant than those from other lands, where different standards of commercial morality may apply, and recent cases are more germane than those from earlier times when standards were in some respects rougher and in other respects more fastidious. In my opinion, it is also appropriate to seek guidance as to community standards of commercial morality from legislation that embodies those standards in law. I have therefore particularly considered the facts and decisions in *Morrison v. Coast Finance Ltd.*, supra; *Knupp v. Bell* (1966), 58 D.L.R. (2d) 466, affirmed 67 D.L.R. (2d) 256 (Sask. C.A.); *Miller v. Lavoie* reflex, (1966), 63 W.W.R. 359, 60 D.L.R. (2d) 495 (B.C.); *Marshall v. Can. Permanent Trust Co.* (1968),

69 D.L.R. (2d) 260 (Alta.); *Gladu v. Edmonton Land Co.* (1914), 8 Alta. L.R. 80, 7 W.W.R. 279, 19 D.L.R. 688; and *Hnatuk v. Chretien* reflex, (1960), 31 W.W.R. 130 (B.C.); and I have considered the provisions of the Trade Practices Act, 1974 (B.C.), c. 96, and the Consumer Protection Act, 1977(B.C.), c. 6.

[28] I have applied the standards derived from those authorities to the facts in this case, which are that the respondent purchased for $4,500 a boat that he knew to be worth $16,000 from the appellant, whom he knew to be partially deaf, easily intimidated and ill-advised, by a process of harassment. In my opinion, the whole circumstances of the bargain reveal such a marked departure from community standards of commercial morality that the contract of purchase and sale should be rescinded.

. . . .

[30] I would allow the appeal and make the order proposed by McIntyre J.A.

(c)   The Synthetic Approach and Unjustifiable Enrichment[†]

R.A. Samek

2.   LEGAL CONCEPTUAL SCHEMES AS SPECIFIC LEGAL POINTS OF VIEW

... [I]t is the relevance of certain legal norms to a 'legal conceptual scheme,' and vice versa, which gives these norms the coherence and unity of a branch of law. The same legal norms may be relevant to more than one legal conceptual scheme, in which case they will figure in more than one branch of law. Although legal conceptual schemes appear to have grown up organically, they are in fact constructed and reconstructed through a process of trial and error by judges, and through a process of rationalization by legal commentators. Their adequacy should be judged mainly by their relevance to the legal norms with reference to which they are constructed, by their simplicity and elegance, and by their legal and social fruitfulness.[6]

Legal conceptual schemes fulfil three interdependent functions, namely a systematizing function, a developmental function, and a social function. Since legal norms are not static, and do not operate in a vacuum, they cannot be systematized without taking into account their future development and social purposes. They cannot be developed without systematizing them and taking into account their social purposes; and their social purposes cannot be achieved without systematizing them and taking into account their future development.[7]

In order to construct a legal conceptual scheme based on the key concept of unjustifiable enrichment,[8] we must face the question not only of where but of how we are to draw the boundary between this legal conceptual scheme and others; in short, we must face the general question of how to delimit legal conceptual schemes inter se. I suggest that we should think of a legal conceptual scheme not as conferring an exclusive jurisdiction over a certain legal territory, but rather as a specific legal point of view which has common areas of interface with many others. From this perspective, unjustifiable enrichment does not have exclusive jurisdiction over any one territory; it is a specific legal point of view which is interrelated with many others.

All specific legal points of view operate under the umbrella of the 'legal point of view.' This marks out an exclusive field of interest which distinguishes it from other general points of view, such as the 'moral point of view,' the 'political point of view,' the 'scientific point of view,' the 'aesthetic point of view,' and so on. I have suggested that the exclusive field of interest marked out by the legal point of view is 'that *mode* of institutional social control which is enforced through the effective application of a norm system by courts or tribunals acting as norm-authorities of the system. The content of the norms of this system is adapted for the purpose of that social control from a range of values drawn from different points of view, and in particular from the

---

† (1977) 27 U.T. Law Rev. 335 at 336–38, 350–55. [Notes/references omitted.] Reprinted with permission from University of Toronto Press Incorporated (www.utpjounals.com).

moral point of view which provides the foundation of values on which a legal norm-system is built.'⁹

. . . .

Specific legal points of view, ... interpenetrate each other. The object of the synthetic approach, far from seeking to delimit their precise boundaries, is the reverse, namely to reach a synthesis in the areas of their interface. For instance, if *we* adopt this approach *we* do not classify a fact situation which has elements of both contract and unjustifiable enrichment under either one or the other point of view; on the contrary, we synthesize the two in the common areas of their interface.

The synthetic approach ... spares us the unprofitable and necessarily dogmatic task of drawing precise boundaries between different legal conceptual schemes (and, *a fortiori*, between different legal categories within them). Second, it enables us to harness all the resources of the legal point of view to problems which fall within its general field of interest, instead of stretching the narrow resources of each branch of law (and of each category within it) beyond its breaking point. As long as *we* have the legal point of view, *we* are forced to translate social problems into legal problems, but we should not add a new dimension of distortion to this process by locking them into hard and fast legal conceptual schemes, (or into legal categories within them). If we adopt the legal point of view. let us at least avoid splitting it up into a wide spectrum of mutually exclusive perspectives.

I said in my previous paper that a legal conceptual scheme is not a purely theoretical construct, but one with a certain empirical content and a certain predictive power.¹⁰ What, it may be asked, is the approach of the courts in the matter of boundary delimitation? Do they in fact adopt the synthetic approach? They do not, of course, say so, nor do they say the opposite. We must infer their real attitude from their practice. This is never easy to do, and in this case it is further complicated by what may be called the cumulative approach of the common law. Under that approach, the same legal problem may be classified alternately as, for instance, an unjustifiable enrichment problem, a contract problem, a trust problem, a corporation problem, a family law problem, and so on.

. . . .

I suggest that the synthetic approach which I am advocating is congruent with that adopted by the courts in many cases. Legal conceptual schemes are

abstractions; they do not operate in any pure form. The courts are in practice aware of the legal context in which legal conceptual schemes must operate, and within the constraints of the prevailing ideology, of the social context as well. The proper disposition of a case requires a synthesis of all relevant legal conceptual schemes, and not the application of one legal conceptual scheme to the exclusion of the others.

The synthetic approach has a feedback effect on the legal conceptual schemes involved in the synthesis. Every case of synthesis not only helps us to dispose of a case in an area of interface; it helps us to clarify the interrelations of the legal conceptual schemes involved in its disposal. We must not think of legal conceptual schemes as fixed and stable; on the contrary, they are exposed to continuous interaction and to inevitable growth and decay.

. . . .

B. Lloyds Bank v. Bundy³⁷

1. The Facts and the decision

Lord Denning's recent promotion in *Lloyds Bank* of the general principle of 'inequality of bargaining power,' does not go so far as to change the common law's attitude to economic equality; but the very formulation of such a principle opens up a hidden interface between contract and unjustifiable enrichment which exemplifies well the potential of the synthetic approach. The facts of the case were briefly as follows:

The defendant was an elderly farmer who knew little about business. His only asset was an old farmhouse in which he lived. The defendant and his son were both customers at the same branch of the plaintiff bank. The son formed a company which also banked at that branch. It ran into difficulties. The defendant, who had great faith in his son, guaranteed the company's overdraft for £1,500, and charged his house to the bank to secure the loan. The company's difficulties increased. The assistant bank manager suggested that the defendant should sign a further guarantee for £5,000 and execute a further charge for £6,000. The defendant's solicitor advised him that, since the house was worth only £10,000, he should not commit more than £5,000 to his son's business. He then executed the further guarantee and charge. Thereafter the company's affairs went from bad to worse. The assistant manager's successor told the defendant in the presence of his son, that the bank would only continue to support the company if he increased both the guarantee and charge up to £11,000. The new assistant manager realised that the defendant relied on his advice, and that he had no assets other than the house. The defendant said that he was willing to back his son, and signed the documents which were handed to him. When a receiving order was made against the son, the bank sought to enforce the charge and guarantee against the defendant. It entered into an agreement to sell the defendant's house and brought an action for possession against him.

The Court of Appeal allowed the defendant's appeal from the county court's order of possession. Lord Denning MR mentioned five categories of exceptions to the general rule that a customer who signs a bank guarantee or a charge cannot get out of it, which, he claimed, were all based on inequality of bargaining power. (He left aside contracts voidable for fraud, misrepresentation, or mistake, on the ground that these were based on settled principles.)

2. Lord Denning's five categories

The first category is that of 'duress of goods.' A typical case is that of a pledgee who demands more than is justly his due, and the pledgor pays in order to get back the goods. The stronger party may make his claim in good faith, without being guilty of any fraud or misrepresentation. The inequality of bargaining power of the parties renders the transaction voidable, and the money paid can be recovered back.

The second category is that of the 'unconscionable transaction.' A man is so placed as to be in need of special care and protection. His weakness is exploited by one far stronger than himself so as to get his property at a gross undervalue. The typical case is that of the 'expectant heir.' The transaction will be set aside, even if there has been no fraud or misrepresentation. The inequality of bargaining power of the parties renders it voidable, and the money paid can be recovered back.

The third category is that of 'undue influence.' This is divided into two classes. The first comprises the cases where the stronger has been guilty of some fraud or wrongful act so as to gain some gift or advantage from the weaker. The second comprises those where the stronger has not been guilty of any wrongful act, but has, through his relationship with the weaker, gained such a gift or advantage. Sometimes the relationship raises a presumption of undue influence; at other times, a relationship of confidence must be proved to exist. In all of these cases, the stronger party will not be allowed to abuse his position of confidence to his advantage at the expense of the weaker.

The fourth category is that of 'undue pressure.' An apposite case is where a son forges his father's name to a promissory note in order to raise money from a bank of which they are both customers. Under pressure from the bank, the father charges his property with payment of the note. The charge is invalid.

The fifth category is that of salvage agreements. When a vessel is in danger of sinking, the rescuer is in a strong bargaining position. Hence, if the parties make an agreement, the courts will disregard it if it is manifestly unfair and unjust, and decree what is fair and just.

3. The principle of inequality of bargaining power

According to Lord Denning, a single thread runs through all these instances:

> They rest on 'inequality of bargaining power'. By virtue of it, the English law gives relief to one who, without independent advice, enters into a contract in terms which are very unfair or transfers property for a consideration which is grossly inadequate, when his bargaining power is grievously impaired by reason of his own needs or desires, or by his own ignorance or infirmity, coupled with undue influences or pressures brought to bear on him by or for the benefit of the other. When I use the word 'undue' I do not mean to suggest that the principle depends on proof of any wrongdoing. The one who stipulates for an unfair advantage may be moved solely by his own self-interest, unconscious of the distress he is bringing to the other. I have also avoided any reference to the will of the one being 'dominated' or 'overcome' by the other. One who is in extreme need may knowingly consent to a most improvident bargain, solely to relieve the straits in which he finds himself. Again, I do not mean to suggest that every transaction is saved by independent advice. But the absence of it may be fatal. With these explanations, I hope this principle will be found to reconcile the cases.[38]

Applying the above principle to the present case, Lord Denning noted the following points:

1. The consideration which moved from the bank in respect of the last agreement was grossly inadequate.
2. The relationship between the bank and the father was one of trust and confidence.
3. The relationship between the father and the son was one where the father's natural affection had much influence on him.
4. There was a conflict of interest between the bank and the father, yet the bank did not realize it, and did not suggest that the father should get independent advice.

In view of these considerations, Lord Denning held that the principle of inequality of bargaining power applied to the present case; he also held that if it were wrong, the case fell within the second class of undue influence stated above.

Sir Eric Sachs decided the case on this second point, and Cairns LJ agreed with him. Sir Eric was at pains to distance himself from Lord Denning's wider *ratio*: 'As regards the wider areas covered in masterly survey in the judgment of Lord Denning MR, but not raised arguendo, I do not venture to express an opinion — though having some sympathy with the views that the courts should be able to give relief to a party who has been subject to undue pressure as defined in the concluding passage of his judgment on that point.'[39]

Insofar as Lord Denning synthesized his general category of inequality of bargaining power from five categories which transcend any one legal conceptual scheme, his approach may be said to have been synthetic; on the other hand, insofar as he used this category or concept to state a common principle which covered all the cases as instances, he adopted a reductionist form of synthesis which is opposed to the synthetic approach which I am advocating. According to my approach, each case is dealt with separately by drawing on the resources of the particular area of the interface of the legal conceptual schemes, or of the internal categories, into which it falls; according to Lord Denning's, all the cases are inductively subsumed under a common principle, which may straddle different conceptual schemes and internal categories. It is true that Lord Denning's principle is composed of different elements, but it seems that they must all be present in every case if the principle is to apply. If that is so, Lord Denning's approach is essentialist — his principle has a common essence, compound though it is — while my approach is anti-essentialist; it denies the existence of a common essence in any principle, and allows for its modification in different circumstances.

The disadvantage of Lord Denning's reductionist synthetic approach is that it formulates principles which are both over-simple and over-complex; they are over-simple because they are exclusionary of other elements, and they are over-complex because they consist of certain essential elements which must always be present. The result is rigidity, and dogmatism, which increase with the mechanical application of principles to new fact situations. The following criticism by Sealy, of Lord Denning's principle of inequality of bargaining power illustrates the intuitive synthetic wisdom of the common law:

To the extent that Lord Denning is pleading that the courts ought not to continue to perpetuate the fine distinction made in the old cases between, say, duress of goods inducing the payment of money and the same duress inducing the making of an agreement to pay money in the future, his views would find support among most scholars ... But, as a general proposition of law, it is surely doubtful whether there is any advantage to be gained in mixing together a number of features which are to be found in some — but in no case all — of the old-established categories in which relief may be given, and to put them forward as an all-embracing statement of principle to replace those categories. After all, it is not certain that the next set of facts to come before a court will so conveniently combine all the features on which Lord Denning laid stress in *Bundy's* case. It is not obvious that the absence of independent advice is vital to a case of salvage, or that inadequacy of consideration should be present when undue influence is invoked. While, therefore, these remarks will without doubt serve as a valuable stimulus to thought and as an authoritative inducement to a future court to depart from points of unwarranted technicality, there is also much to be said for the retention of the old categories whenever their rules are directly in point.[40]

Slayton draws attention to the civilian nature of Lord Denning's approach:

Cases are treated not as *sui generis*, standing by themselves and supported by the doctrine of precedent, but as *examples* of the application of a great principle. Here, in some measure, are civilian tendencies at work, not in the sense of the unthinking use by a judge of a rule laid down by the legislature, but in the sense of an impetus to synthesize or codify. Dare one suggest that Lord Denning is a civilian at heart?[41]

So far I have been concerned with Lord Denning's general approach rather than with his general 'principle' of inequality of bargaining power. The first thing to observe is that inequality of bargaining power, like unjustifiable enrichment, is a category or concept, and not a legal principle.[42] Like the latter, however, it may be used elliptically to state a principle, and this is precisely what Lord Denning does. But if we look at the principle so stated it does not seem to rest on inequality of bargaining power; and if we look at the five categories which are supposed to be connected by it, we find that they are much more convincingly connected by the concept of unconscionability, notwithstanding that Lord Denning locks this concept into one of them. Even unconscionability, I suggest, is no more than an equity which may be invoked to rebut and mitigate inequitable claims, and not a key concept for developing a legal conceptual scheme of its own. The equity of unconscionability is not limited to unjustifiable enrichment, but it is never very far from its interface with other legal conceptual schemes.

I suggest that *Lloyds Bank* falls into the areas of interface between contracts, unjustifiable enrichment, mortgages, banking, and family law, and in particular into those where there are elements of unconscionability present. However, the transaction does not strike one as inherently unconscionable. The inequality of the parties was the normal one in a client-banker relationship. Presumably, if the defendant had had independent legal advice in regard to the last transaction, the decision would have gone against him; yet he had previously taken such advice which covered it. So why should its absence have been the crucial element in the case?

Looking at Lord Denning's other points in favour of invoking his principle of equality of bargaining power, they scarcely inspire greater confidence. The real pressure came from the son, not from the bank. As in the case of the legal advice, Lord Denning separates the last transaction from the others, but this cannot be done. There was nothing unconscionable on the part of the bank to insist on gradually raising its price in a deal which became more and more inauspicious. The mere fact that the family relationship motivated the father to help the son cannot be held against the bank, unless it took advantage of it, and there was no evidence of that here.

What concerns me is not so much Lord Denning's tenderness for the defendant as his unconcern for the wider implications of unjustifiable enrichment. This is what he says in introducing the common law's general rule of non-interference with bargains:

Now let me say at once that in the vast majority of cases a customer who signs a bank guarantee or a charge cannot get out of it. No bargain will be upset which is the result of the ordinary interplay of forces. There are many hard cases which are caught by this rule. Take the case of a poor man who is homeless. He agrees to pay a high rent to a landlord just to get a roof over his head. The common law will not interfere. It is left to Parliament. Next take the case of a borrower in urgent need of money. He borrows it from the bank at high interest and it is guaranteed by a friend. The guarantor gives his bond and gets nothing in return. The common law will not interfere. Parliament has intervened to prevent moneylenders charging excessive interest. But it has never interfered with banks.[43]

Codification of the law by building up a tight framework of general categories[,] or principles, cannot meet the need for finding acceptable solutions for multi-faceted problems. In these cases, any dogmatic preference for one category or principle over another is necessarily inadequate. It is the strength, and not the weakness of the common law, that it is sufficiently open-textured to allow new synthetic solutions to be reached, even if this can only be done under the cloak of cumulation or analytical reconstruction. Any crusade for a system of classification which would put the law in a better-cut straitjacket can only lead to a new and more dangerous dogmatism. What is wrong with the common law is that it is dogmatic; it is so not just in the wrong way, but over the wrong issues and in the wrong interests. Moreover, it is crippled by its institutional structure. What is the use of reforming the substance of the law, when its procedure remains cumbersome, dilatory, and expensive?

(d) Doing Theory in First Year Contracts: The Iceberg Method[†]

Richard Devlin, Anthony Duggan and Louise Langevin

1. INTRODUCTION

. . . .

... Legal analysis, among other things, requires the capacity to ask the simple question of what is the underlying rationale or purpose of a particular

---

† (2007) 1 Canadian Legal Education Annual Review 1 at 4–34. [Footnotes omitted.] Reprinted by permission of Carswell, a division of Thomson Reuters Canada Limited.

legal rule. If a lawyer is not able to locate a legal rule in this broader context, s/he is not likely to be able to give a client good advice. Legal theory provides insight into the various goals that law might seek to pursue.

Second, beyond purposiveness, legal analysis entails the skills of normative assessment. It is not sufficient to know what the rule is or what its underlying purpose might be. It is also essential that one be able to provide a rational justification for that rule or purpose. Law and legal rules are important social phenomena that have an impact on our larger political, economic and cultural lives,[11] so it is important that students be able to identify, critically interrogate, and defend or challenge the values that underpin the law. Legal theory helps to illuminate the principles, policies and norms that can be invoked to justify the deployment of law.

Third, we want our students to be more than legal automatons:[12] doctrinal proficiency and normative awareness are necessary but insufficient outputs for a system of legal education. Legally trained persons, whether they go on to practise law or not, are beneficiaries of a significant social investment. Despite the fact that the costs of legal education are being increasingly borne by the students themselves in common law faculties,[13] much of the actual expenses are still being covered by the larger community. We believe that as a quid pro quo for this investment, we law professors should do our best to help the students to become reflective citizens.[14] Law is an important social discourse that is politically polyvalent; as Arthur Leff once commented, it makes us responsible for both good and evil.[15] The capacity to engage in law talk is a capacity to engage in an act of power. This can lead to beneficial or dangerous consequences. Consequently it is important that those who are legally trained have a sense not only of the values that are "out there" underpinning law, but also the values that are "in there",[16] generating their individual preferences and choices. Legal theory, we suggest, can help identify those preferences and inform those choices and a responsible educational system should, as best it can, seek to nurture such reflective citizenship.[17]

. . . .

... [W]e favour a "top-down" or what we prefer to call "iceberg" approach to teaching legal theory in [contract law]. As is probably obvious, by this we mean that rather than focusing on the conceptual framework of a particular theoretical tradition in the abstract, it might be better to start with a precise

legal issue and actual legal text (a common law case or a provision of the Civil Code and accompanying case law) and then unpack the text to explore its theoretical implications. The process might be illustrated as follows:

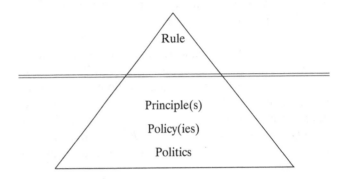

The legal rule (the *ratio* of a case at common law, or the meaning of a Civil Code provision as interpreted by the courts) is dependent upon some underlying principle(s), which is in turn dependent upon deeper policy preference(s), which in turn is premised upon a yet deeper political vision of social organization. For the purposes of this essay the rule we unpack relates to the enforceability of spousal guarantees;[22] the case is in fact two cases, *O'Brien*[23] and *Etridge*[24] and the theories deployed are Critical Legal Studies, Law and Economics and Feminism.[25]

. . . .

2. THE ISSUE AND THE CASES

Banks commonly ask for a guarantee to support a loan repayment obligation. In many cases, the guarantor and the debtor will be members of the same household, for example, parent and son or daughter or wife and husband. A commonly occurring situation is where one spouse, almost invariably the husband, or, alternatively, a company the husband controls, borrows money from the bank to finance a new project and the husband offers the family home as security for the loan. The property is jointly owned by the husband and the wife and they both sign the security documents. The project fails and the bank attempts to enforce the security. Australian feminist scholars have coined the expression "sexually transmitted debt" to describe this scenario: the husband or the husband's company contracts the debt, but the wife ends up carrying a substantial part of the risk.[27] In sexually transmitted debt cases, there is a strong probability that the husband will have obtained the wife's signature by misrepresentation or undue influence.

427

The leading United Kingdom cases in point are the two House of Lords decisions in *Barclays Bank plc v. O'Brien*[28] and *Royal Bank of Scotland v. Etridge*.[29] Canadian common law appears to be developing along the same lines: *O'Brien* and *Etridge* have been followed in a number of provincial court decisions[30] and, while the Supreme Court of Canada has yet to hear a spousal guarantee case, in *Gold v. Rosenberg*[31] both the majority and minority judgments discussed the possible application of *O'Brien's* case in other factual settings and, in doing so, appear to endorse the decision. There have been parallel developments in Quebec.[32] A leading case is *Fiducie canadienne italienne v. Rudolpho Folini*[33] and in Quebec teachers could use this case as the focus for discussion.

O'Brien and *Etridge* can be summarized in point form, as follows:

(1) There is no special equity favouring wives and spousal guarantee cases are subject to the same general principles governing undue influence as apply in other cases.

(2) Nevertheless, the general principles governing undue influence should be applied generously in favour of the wife in recognition of the facts that: (a) the transaction is on its face not to her financial advantage; and (b) there is a substantial risk of undue influence on the husband's part.

(3) If the wife establishes undue influence or misrepresentation against her husband, the bank will be fixed with constructive notice, and will be unable to enforce the guarantee, if the evidence shows that it knew about the relationship.

(4) The bank can avoid being fixed with constructive notice by taking reasonable steps to satisfy itself that the wife entered into the transaction freely and with knowledge of the true facts.

(5) Unless there are exceptional circumstances, the bank will have taken such reasonable steps if it:

   (a) warns the wife (at a meeting not attended by the husband) of the amount of her potential liability and the risks involved; and

   (b) encourages the wife to obtain independent advice.

(6) Alternatively to (5), the bank may insist that the wife obtains independent advice relating to the legal aspects and risks of the transaction.

(7) In relation to (6), the solicitor's duty will usually be to make sure the wife understands the transaction. The solicitor does not have to go

further and make sure she is free from her husband's influence.

(8) The bank must obtain written confirmation from the solicitor that the solicitor has advised the wife and that she appeared to understand the transaction. In the usual case, the bank will be entitled to rely on the solicitor's confirmation and need not enquire into the quality of the advice.

(9) The bank must provide the solicitor with all the information the solicitor will need to advise the wife properly.

(10) The foregoing rules, though developed in cases where the debtor and guarantor were husband and wife, are not limited to this context: they apply in every case where the relationship between the guarantor and the debtor is a non-commercial one.[34] The justification is that there can be "no rational cut-off point, with certain types of relationship being susceptible to the *O'Brien* principle and others not".[35]

[VIEWING THE CASES WITH DIFFERENT THEORETICAL LENSES]

3. CRITICAL LEGAL STUDIES

(a) Introduction

The central claim of Critical Legal Studies (CLS) is that all law, including contract law, is an unavoidably political and normative enterprise.[36] That is to say, law is a human artifact, constructed by mortals who inevitably bring to bear their values and thereby shape law in their own image. In other words, law is not independent of larger political moralities and ideologies, but rather a manifestation of particular political moralities and ideologies. Contract law is therefore best understood not as a system of abstract rules and principles with their own inner coherence but as a regulatory regime that constructs, channels, polices and legitimizes particular economic and social relationships. More specifically, contract is not just about the resolution of disputes between two private parties, it is also about the values and ideals that we embrace as a society. The Common Law, just like public law, tells us something about who and what we are as a community, and judges — who are the "guardians of the Common Law" — are key political actors in so far as they are the ones who determine what those values are.

The second claim advanced by CLS is that, historically, the values articulated in law, including contract law, have tended to reflect the perspectives and experiences of those who have been socially dominant. CLS argues that the conventional approach to contract analysis, a.k.a. the classical model of contracts, invokes two key ideas:

- *a preference for a formalistic judicial methodology*: the dominant view argues that the primary function of contract law is to establish a stable, coherent, scientific and rational system of rules and subrules in order to provide certainty in the marketplace. The role of the judge is passive and formalistic: (s)he is simply to discover the appropriate rules and apply them to the facts of the case. Hence the essence of contract law is often reduced to the formula $O + A + C + I = K$ (offer + acceptance + consideration + intention = contract).

- *An ideological disposition:* CLS also argues that underlying the quest for stable rules and judicial passivity there is a certain vision of the world, one that reflects the political morality of capitalism. Thus the formula of $O + A + C + I$ neatly captures the ideas and ideals of freedom of contract (people can contract with whoever they like, for whatever they like); *sanctity of contract* (once a contract is formed it is binding); and *privity of contract* (the contract, unlike torts, is binding only on those parties who agree to it; other collateral relationships are irrelevant). The high water mark of this ideological predisposition is to be found in Sir George Jessel's proposition that:

> If there is one thing more than another which public policy requires, it is that men of full age and competent understanding shall have the utmost liberty of contracting, and that their contracts entered into freely and voluntarily shall be held sacred and shall be enforced by Courts of Justice.[37]

(b) Application

This freedom of contract ideology was essentially the position adopted by Barclays Bank and accepted by the trial judge in the *O'Brien* case. First, the bank argued it had done nothing wrong; the wife freely entered into the surety contract with the bank and any issues of inappropriate conduct were between her and the husband. Second, it is vital that such contracts be held sacrosanct not only because people are bound by their word but also because to allow them to exit the contract would cause instability in the marketplace. Third, while there may be collateral damage to third parties (e.g. other family members) that is not the concern of contract law.[38]

However, the House of Lords did not accept these arguments. Why not? The answer is that the House of Lords is no longer in the thrall of a classical model of contract. Rather it is embracing a somewhat different set of values and a more activist methodology. This change has come about because the House of Lords has recognized that contract law is caught between various values that are in tension with each other: individualism v. communitarianism; liberty v. equality; public v. private; and consent v. constraint.

(i) *Individualism v. communitarianism.*

CLS argues that all societies, and thereby all legal systems, including contract law, have to locate themselves somewhere on the spectrum between individualistic values and communitarian values. The classical model of contracts, because of its commitment to freedom of contract, gravitates towards the individualistic end of the spectrum. However, in the twentieth century there was "a renaissance of equity" in which greater solicitude has been shown for the protection of vulnerable parties to a contract. Of equal importance, throughout the latter half of the twentieth century, there have been significant legislative interventions designed to enhance consumer protectionism. Both of these developments reflect the more communitarian values of the era. The equitable predisposition of some courts is perhaps best understood as simply the legalistic encoding of communitarian ideals. CLS identifies the potential of communitarian values, not just as exceptions or deviations from the classical individualistic model, but as an alternative normative vision, a set of counterprinciples to regulate social and economic relations. These are principles of good faith and fair dealing in which courts are sensitive to relationships of interdependence and trust. Undue influence is just one example of several doctrines which encode this normative ideal, others include economic duress, unconscionability, fundamental breach, promissory estoppel, and interpretive doctrines such as *contra proferentem* and reasonable expectations, and implied terms.

Mrs. O'Brien's lawyers picked up on these equitable norms and argued that because of the Bank's economic power in the marketplace it is a pressure point in the circulatory system of social and economic relations.[39] Consequently, it has a duty to act not only in its own interests, but also to inform her of the risks of the surety because it knows, or should know, that she is likely to be in a position of vulnerability. The bank cannot parasitically take advantage of her vulnerability to her husband. The House of Lords, as we have seen, reacts quite positively to this claim by endorsing the equitable doctrine of constructive notice: the Bank has a duty to ensure that Mrs. O'Brien is warned of the risks of the surety. Why? The Court does not explicitly refer to communitarian values, instead it invokes another framework of analysis: equality.[40]

(ii) The liberty principle v. the equality principle.

The previously cited quotation from Sir George Jessel is often characterized as the Liberty Principle. The classical model of contracts tended to assume that if liberty was maximized, equality would inevitably follow. The primary role of the courts was to ensure that contracts were enforced because this would maximize autonomy. CLS argues that this idea might have made sense in an era when the primary users of the courts were mostly reasonably well positioned commercial players. Hence it was logical for the law to reflect their needs, interests and aspirations.

However, as the twentieth century unfolded, a more diverse clientele began to turn to the courts in order to access justice. Of particular significance here was the emergence on the part of the judiciary of a "consumer consciousness." This consciousness identified two major concerns: significant inequality of bargaining power between sellers and buyers of goods and services and, secondly, the widespread use of standard form contracts, a.k.a. contracts of adhesion. As a result of these concerns, society in general, and judges in particular, began to realize that embracing the liberty principle did not necessarily engender equality. In fact, in some situations, the maximization of liberty would guarantee the enforcement of inequality. Contracts would be an instrument of subordination rather than autonomy. Thus in the twentieth century judges began to emphasize the importance of equality principles, peaking with Lord Denning's "inequality of bargaining power" principle in *Lloyds Bank v. Bundy*[41] or Lambert J.A.'s decision in *Harry v. Kreutziger* embracing "community standards of commercial morality."[42] The mantra of "freedom of contract" was forced to compete with the mantra "freedom from contract."[43]

O'Brien brings this tension between liberty and equality into especially sharp relief. If one is predisposed towards the liberty principle, one will tend to favour the bank's argument that Mrs O'Brien acted voluntarily; if one is predisposed towards the equality principle, one will be responsive to Mrs. O'Brien's argument, that she is a vulnerable consumer, burdened by an oppressive contract of adhesion. The

House of Lords, CLS would suggest, appears to be gravitating towards the latter. While the Court rejects a "special equity"[44] for wives, it endorses a "tenderness"[45] in the law of undue influence given the substantial risk of inappropriate conduct on the husband's part. Moreover, it is important to emphasize that the House of Lords was not compelled by precedent to adopt this solution. Indeed, as several commentators have noted, the approach it adopted, the doctrine that the bank is put on constructive notice, was an innovative if not unorthodox deployment of this doctrine.[46] CLS argues that this illustrates the indeterminacy thesis: rules of law are rarely absolute and fixed, rather rules are always in flux, sometimes expanding, sometimes contracting. The rules of contract are malleable and flexible, their [plasticity] rendering them deployable in a variety of contexts, depending upon the underlying value choices of the judges. In short, result determinism is the name of the game.

(iii) Public / private dichotomy.

In *O'Brien* the House of Lords is very sensitive to the fact that the sureties of wives is a complex and controversial issue that gives rise to "a difference of judicial view."[47] The old split between the public world of business and the private world of family is no longer a social or economic reality. Historically, the courts have been unwilling to enter into the sphere of contracts involving family relations. As Lord Atkin said in 1919 "the principles of the common law ... are such as to find no place in the domestic code ... each house is a domain into which the King's writ does not seek to run, and to which his officers do not seek to be admitted ..."[48] But now, as the House of Lords recognizes, the public world of finance is often dependent upon the private world of family finances:

> It is easy to allow sympathy for a wife who is threatened with loss of her home at the suit of a rich bank to obscure an important public interest, viz, the need to ensure that the wealth currently tied up in the matrimonial home does not become economically sterile. If the rights secured to wives by the law render vulnerable loans granted on the security of matrimonial homes, institutions will be unwilling to accept such security, thereby reducing the flow of loan capital to business enterprises.[49]

Having intervened in the private realm of the family, a critical question becomes where to stop the "tenderness" of the law? In *O'Brien* the House of Lords admitted it would be inappropriate to identify "wives" as the only potentially vulnerable sureties, so it also included others who engage in "unmarried cohabitation, whether heterosexual or homosexual ..."[50] However, in *Etridge* the Court realized that even this was too narrow, and it invoked the language of "non-commercial relationships," "relationships of trust and confidence" and "emotional pressure."[51] What started as a very particular exception to the freedom of contract rule has the potential to encompass a very large number of relationships that may go beyond the quintessentially private. Freedom of contract appears to be losing ground to freedom from contract. Once the communitarian cat is out of bag, it is very difficult to get it back in again.

(iv) Consent v. constraint.

For some the "tenderness" of *O'Brien* may be seen not just as a radical departure from the classical law of contracts, but a fundamental undermining of its core values. Traditionally, the key idea of contracts is intent: the function of the courts is to give effect to the will of the parties. A fundamental rule of contract is the principle of *L'Estrange v. Graucob*: "if you sign, you are bound."[52] Consent is the keystone of the edifice of contracts.

The surety cases raise some very tricky questions involving complex issues of gender and power consent and constraint. For years, in the criminal law context, judges have been confronted with the debate on whether "no really means no" in relation to sexual assault. Now in contract law there is the inverse problem of whether "yes really means yes." From the critical perspective this creates some very messy problems, indeed judgment calls, for judges. On the one hand, if a court finds "yes means yes" it can be accused of undervaluing the experiences of vulnerable women; if it says "yes does not necessarily mean yes" then it can be accused of paternalism, if not infantilization.

What of the House of [Lords'] solution in *O'Brien* and *Etridge*? It held that banks have two options if they want to avoid the doctrine of constructive notice: (a) they have a pre-contractual duty to warn the wife in a private meeting absent the husband of the potential liabilities and risks of the contract and encourage her to obtain independent advice, or (b) they can insist that the wife obtain independent advice relating to the legal aspects and risks of the transaction. The critical concern is that while at first blush this might seem to be a progressive, balanced and sensitive resolution, in fact it is a procedural solution to a substantive problem. The inequality of many wives is a reality, both materially and emotionally.[53] So, realistically, how effective are such warnings and/or lawyerly advice likely to be?[54] A procedural response to substantive inequality may create the appearance of a solution, thereby further obscuring the reality. In fact, the reality seems to be that banks are now choosing the second option: they insist that the vulnerable surety receive independent legal advice, and then they receive a certificate from the lawyer confirming that the surety appears to understand the agreement.

Consequently, despite all the doctrinal innovation, it seems that when the rubber hits the road, banks have very little responsibility, and the real risk is transferred to lawyers. This means, then, sureties will have to sue the lawyers for negligent advice ... which is a highly formidable, not to mention expensive, challenge! Moreover, CLS worries that the requirement that the wife bears the burden of proof of showing undue influence or misrepresentation by the husband (rather than simple lack of understanding on her part) before being able to trigger the bank's duty to warn or the lawyer's duty to advise may, in reality, make this an illusive remedy for a very large number of women. This double whammy indicates that what the House of Lords appears to be giving with one hand, it may be taking away with the other.

(c) **Conclusion**

So the critical spin on contract law, undue influence and vulnerable sureties highlights four points. First, CLS emphasizes that while doctrine and precedent are absolutely vital, they are not determinative. Judicial decision making (often covertly) always goes beyond the simplistic formalistic quest for the right rule, because there is no right rule. There is no holy grail of doctrinal purity with oracular solutions because indeterminacy and change are the very essence of the common law.

Second, and correlatively, CLS encourages us to identify the various principles and social policies that might be at stake in every case and the political moralities and ideologies that underlie such principles and policies. Often these political moralities, principles and policies will be in direct competition with each other (individualism v. communitarianism, liberty v. equality, private v. public, consent v. constraint) and difficult choices will have to be made by the judges.

Third, in choosing which principles, policies and moralities to embrace judges will necessarily be driven by larger social values. These are the macro forces. At the same time, CLS emphasizes the importance of microforces, especially the particular facts of each case.[55] It is often said that hard cases make bad law; but CLS argues hard cases reveal the true nature of law as a profoundly normative enterprise.

Fourth, and finally, despite the doctrinal and ideological developments in *O'Brien* and *Etridge*, it is not clear if much has really changed for vulnerable sureties or for banks. While banks have to jump over a few more hurdles, in the end, the House of Lords' desire to keep the family home as a valuable source of finance trumps the competing urge to protect vulnerable sureties. "Freedom of contract" continues to overwhelm "freedom from contract," the liberty principle continues to eclipse the equality principle, and the nod to communitarianism is more symbolic than substantive. The result of these judicial choices is that banks are still laughing all the way to the bank, while sureties, and their families, are still likely to find themselves homeless.

4. LAW AND ECONOMICS

(a) Introduction

Traditional legal analysis relies on an *ex post* perspective. It takes the harm resulting from a defendant's wrong as given and asks, what can the law do to make the plaintiff whole? From an *ex post* perspective, the measure of the law's effectiveness is how well it compensates the plaintiff. By contrast, economic analysis of law relies on an *ex ante* perspective. It looks at cost-justified precautions the defendant might have taken to prevent the harm and asks, how can the law encourage the defendant and others to take those precautions in future? From an *ex ante* perspective, the measure of the law's effectiveness is how well it reduces avoidable future losses.

As this last statement suggests, the economic analysis of law focuses on the costs and benefits of legal rules. The lessons it teaches are:

(1) no legal intervention is cost-free;
(2) before deciding on a legal rule, we should identify the costs and benefits and we should be confident that the benefits exceed the costs; and
(3) failure to address cost-benefit considerations may lead to "substitution effects": a substitution effect is where the new legal rule actually harms the class of persons it was meant to help.[56]

O'Brien and *Etridge* are good cases to study from a law and economics perspective because in *O'Brien*, Lord Browne-Wilkinson expressly acknowl-

edged these three points. Here is part of what he says:

> [A]lthough the concept of the ignorant wife leaving all financial decisions to the husband is outmoded, the practice does not yet coincide with the ideal ... In a substantial proportion of marriages, it is still the husband who has the business experience and the wife is willing to follow his advice without bringing a truly independent mind and will to bear on financial transactions. The number of recent cases in this field shows that in practice many wives are still subjected to, and yield to, undue influence by their husbands ...[57]

He goes on to identify, as a competing goal, "the need to make sure that the wealth tied up in the matrimonial home does not become economically sterile".[58]

In other words:

(1) the benefit of a rule protecting the wife is that future contracts are more likely to reflect the wife's real preferences;
(2) The cost of a rule protecting the wife is the potentially chilling effect on banks' willingness to lend; and
(3) Excessive protection may be counter-productive if it cuts off finance for business ventures that could make the family wealthier.

Trebilcock and Elliott expand on the economic policy considerations in spousal guarantee cases as follows:[59]

> The difficulties of intra-familial contract regulation arise out of the fact that no family is a perfect unity. The communality of family life is never absolute — even in the most harmonious households, family members have several as well as mutual ends. These differences of interest are accentuated by the possibility of family breakdown. The high incidence of divorce in most western societies and the prevalence of elder abandonment mean that the prospect of breakdown should usually weigh in the making of intra-familial financial arrangements. Prudent family members will want to protect their personal position in light of this contingency. The trust and informality that result from family communality can easily be abused by a member seeking to favour their own severable interests at the expense of their family. The purpose of regulating intra-familial arrangements is to put safeguards in place to prevent this from happening.

They go on to point out that statistics show the average standard of living for women following divorce declines, whereas for men it rises. The rea-

432

son is partly women's lack of earning power due to the time they have to spend at home and out of the work force. The risk of divorce therefore makes the conservation of family assets a relatively more important issue for women than it is for men. In many cases, the probability is that the wife will take insufficient account of this consideration in agreeing to mortgage the family home as security for the husband's debts.[60] In other cases, the husband may use the threat of divorce as a weapon to secure the wife's agreement.

The justification for invalidating the bank's security in spousal guarantee cases is not that the bank itself is guilty of exploiting the wife's dependency. Rather, it has to do with what Trebilcock and Elliott describe as a "gatekeeper function".[61] The bank is in a position to prevent the husband from exploiting the wife by refusing the husband co-operation or support. As between the wife and the bank, the bank is the party best placed to avoid the wife's loss. If the husband has coerced or misled the wife, her capacity for self-help will be limited. She may not even be aware of the need for caution. On the other hand the bank is relatively well placed, by virtue of its relationship with both the husband and the wife, to check for signs of the husband's wrongdoing and take appropriate steps. By invalidating the bank's security in the event of the husband's wrongdoing, the courts give lending institutions the incentive to take such steps in future.

The challenge for the courts is to set the bank's gatekeeping obligations at a level that minimises the sum of compliance costs and the costs of the husband's wrongdoing. Excessively stringent gatekeeping obligations may deliver a high level of protection to the wife, but at the cost of discouraging legitimate lending activity. Conversely, excessively lenient obligations may lower the bank's lending costs, but deliver a less than optimal level of protection to the wife. Efforts to strike the right balance can be seen in Points (3), (5), (6), (7) and (8) of the summary in Part 2, above. We address these points further in the next section.

(b) Striking the right balance

(i) Requirement for proof of undue influence or misrepresentation.

To succeed against the bank, the wife must show the husband was guilty of undue influence or misrepresentation (Point (3) of the summary in Part 2, above). It is not enough for her to show that she failed to understand the transaction. The plaintiff in *Etridge* failed for this reason. The law is different in

Australia. According to the second limb of the rule in *Yerkey v. Jones*,[62] if the wife fails to understand the effect of the document and the significance of giving a guarantee, she can have the transaction set aside unless the bank took steps to inform her about the transaction and reasonably supposed that she understood.

Other things being equal, there is no reason in principle for limiting the wife's protection to cases of misrepresentation or undue influence by the husband. The key question is whether the transaction reflects her true preferences. It is likely not to do so if the husband misleads or coerces her into signing. But it is just as likely not to do so if she lacks understanding of the transaction's implications.[63] To quote Trebilcock and Elliott again:

> Grounds for judicial contract regulation may exist where an actor has a stable and coherent preference structure but the choices they make in particular circumstances are inconsistent with that structure. This inconsistency may be due to either coercion or information failure. Information failure consists in problems of either availability or processing ability.[64]

On the other hand, extending the wife's protection to cases of "information failure" increases the risk to the bank of losing its security.[65] Therefore, limiting judicial intervention to cases of misrepresentation or coercion may make sense in terms of the trade-off referred to above: it delivers less protection for the wife, but it also lowers lending costs. It may be worth noting that, while the Australian rule gives more protection, the scope of the rule is narrower than it is in England: as presently stated, the rule only applies where the debtor and guarantor are husband and wife whereas in England, the rule extends to all cases where the relationship is a non-commercial one. The narrower scope of the Australian rule may offset the costs of the additional protection it offers.[66]

(ii) Alternative precautions open to bank.

The bank can avoid liability by taking one or other of two measures. It may warn the wife, at a meeting not attended by the husband, of the amount of her potential liability and the risks involved and encourage her to obtain independent advice (Point (5) of the summary in Part 2, above). Alternatively, it may insist that she obtain independent advice (Point (6)).

Again, the law in Australia is different. As a practical matter, the rule in *Yerkey v. Jones* requires proof of independent advice: it is not sufficient for the bank to give the advice itself.[67]

The greater leeway the bank has under English law reduces the level of protection for the wife but, by the same token, it may also reduce the bank's compliance costs. The trade-off reflects the tension between the policy concerns underpinning the rule.

(iii) The content of the advice.

The advisor is limited to informing the wife about the legal aspects and risks of the transaction (Point (6) of the summary in Part 2, above). In *Etridge*, Lord Nicholls described the solicitor's duty in some detail. In summary, the solicitor must explain the documents and their legal consequences, make it clear to the wife that she has a choice whether to sign and confirm that she wishes to proceed.[68]

In many cases, the husband wants the loan to finance a business venture. The solicitor's obligations do not extend to advising the wife about the commercial viability of the business venture.[69] In terms of the need for protecting the wife from contract failure, this limitation seems an arbitrary one. The wife's decision whether to sign is likely to be affected as much by her understanding of the business venture as it is by what she knows of the legal documentation. On the other hand, solicitors may not be qualified to give financial advice and if the bank had to insist on independent advice from an accountant or the like as well, compliance costs would rise substantially.[70]

(iv) The impact of the advice.

As a general rule, the solicitor's duty is to make sure the wife understands the transaction. The solicitor does not have to make sure that she is free from her husband's influence (Point (7) of the summary in Part 2, above). This is a significant limitation on the protection the rule offers: telling the wife about her choices is likely to be pointless if she is not free to exercise them. On the other hand, a requirement that the advice be both taken and followed would interfere with the wife's autonomy: "it effectively imposes a lawyer's view" of what is in the wife's best interests.[71] To minimize this effect, the rule would have to be limited to cases where undue influence was likely. However, if the transaction goes ahead, it would then be harder for the bank to know in advance whether it will withstand a subsequent court challenge. The increased uncertainty would be reflected in higher lending costs. In *Etridge*, Lord Nicholls acknowledged the problem when he said that in exceptional cases, where it is "glaringly obvious" that the wife is being "grievously wronged", the solicitor should decline to act further.[72] However, as the adverbs attest, this stops well short of a wholesale solution and so it represents yet another example of the trade-offs this area of the law involves.

(v) Reliance on certificate.

The bank is entitled to rely on the solicitor's confirmation of advice and it does not have to inquire into the quality of the advice (Point (8) of the summary in Part 2, above). This compromises the wife's protection because it means she will be held to the transaction even if the advice the solicitor gives her is inadequate. The countervailing benefit of the limitation is that it reduces the bank's compliance costs.

If the advice is inadequate, the wife may have an action against the solicitor for negligence. There are trade-offs at work here too. The heavier the solicitor's responsibilities, the greater the potential chilling effect on their willingness to provide advice to spousal guarantors at an affordable price. For example, if solicitors were required to provide financial advice in addition to advice about the legal aspects of the transaction it can be anticipated that many would react by simply refusing to undertake the task.[73] Limiting the solicitor's responsibilities means lower quality protection but, by the same token, it also means better access to legal services.

(c) Conclusion

It is sometimes said that equity has a role to play in improving business morality. This is because, unlike the common law which promotes self-interested behaviour by firms, equity promotes concern for the welfare of others.[74] The spousal guarantee cases suggest that, while this may be true, it is true only in a limited sense. *O'Brien* and *Etridge* promote "other-regarding behaviour" on the bank's part. However, they do this by appealing to the bank's self-interest, not its better nature. By transferring the risk of the husband's wrongdoing from the wife to the bank, the cases give the bank the incentive to take cost-justified precautions. The cases limit the bank's exposure, in the various ways discussed above, with a view to ensuring that "the wealth currently tied up in the matrimonial home does not become economically sterile", to use Lord Brown-Wilkinson's words in *O'Brien*. The protection the cases give to guarantors increases the bank's transactions costs and so it might be tempting to conclude that they are an impediment to business. However, the correct focus of inquiry is not on the bank's costs alone, but on the bank's and the guarantor's *combined* transactions costs. Seen in this light, the cases make economic sense.

5. FEMINISM

(a) Introduction

In her now famous speech entitled "Will Women Judges Really Make a Difference?",[75] Justice Wilson said that certain areas of law, such as contract law, would not benefit from being reconstructed according to a particularly "feminine perspective". The following discussion questions this affirmation seventeen years later, and proposes a feminist re-reading of guarantees, and more particularly the issue of the quality of the lay guarantor's consent.[76]

A feminist approach to the law of contracts aims to analyze those rules while taking into account gender, that is to say, while taking into account the subordinate position of women in society.[77] One must consider in what way women's experiences were excluded or included in the development of contractual rules. It is possible to analyze these rules from an external perspective. For instance, do women have access to the contractual mechanism? What kind of contracts do they conclude? Are some situations seen as outside the contractual relationship, which denies them legal protection? Are contracts between common law spouses enforceable just as marriage contracts are? Are surrogate motherhood contracts enforceable? Are women the victims of discrimination in the supply of public goods? Consider, for example, business women who have problems obtaining credit or single mothers who have problems finding decent housing. Contractual principles may also be analyzed from an internal perspective, once women have access to contracts. What are the effects of formation rules or of contractual remedies on women? Therefore, a feminist perspective helps determine if contracts constitute a tool of subordination, protection or empowerment for women. The ultimate goal of all feminist critiques is to reach true equality for women. Even if law has been used historically to keep women in a subordinate position, it might also be seen as a tool for social change for women.

Upon examination of Justice Wilson's affirmation, according to which a feminist approach to contracts would not be possible or necessary, it is not surprising to find that the area of contracts can benefit from a feminist re-reading. In fact, like all legal institutions, contracts constitute a masculine institution constructed and based on men's needs. Moreover, contract theory, which solidified in the nineteenth century, was developed for the business world, which was closed to women for a long time. We must not be taken in by the abstract and neutral character of legal rules, which have been very much denounced by feminist writings.[78] Other areas of law, which at first sight appear completely neutral, have been criticized by feminists.[79] Contract law is no exception, and can be deconstructed and reconstructed by feminist critics[80] because the situation of the inequality of women can also be noted in this area.

(b) Application

(i) Introduction.

From the point of view that takes women's realities into account, the objective here is to examine the requirement of free and informed consent as an essential element in the formation of the guarantee, and particularly of the guarantee signed in the context of the family. Let us first define the legal problems that "sexually transmitted debts" raise for female guarantors. Then, we will propose a feminist re-reading of *O'Brien* and *Etridge*.

(ii) "Love Money": Sexually Transmitted Debts.

As mentioned earlier, the expression "sexually transmitted debt" was coined by feminist scholars to describe the fact pattern in cases like *O'Brien* and *Etridge*.[81] In order to clearly understand the issues raised by sexually transmitted debts, it is necessary to specify the nature of the guarantee. It is a unilateral contract, in which only the guarantor assumes obligations, and obtains no consideration, contrary to businesses that specialize in construction guarantees. In addition, the guarantee in the context of sexually transmitted debt possesses all the characteristics of the adhesion contract. It is presented as a standard form contract. Therefore, the bank imposes its conditions and negotiations are rarely possible. The contract also distinguishes itself by its clauses which are very often incomprehensible to the lay guarantor, who does not always ask questions, because she does not feel at ease, because the climate does not lend itself to those kinds of questions or because the lay guarantor does not wish to appear too ignorant.

The signing of this contract carries a high number of risks for the guarantor: the risk of the principal's [husband's] future insolvency is part of the nature of the guarantee, although it may be presented or perceived as a commitment with no consequences, or like a moral obligation. Thus, the guarantor cannot request that her commitment be nullified due to an error, on the grounds that she did not know that the principal [husband] would become insolvent. In addition, the creditor may pursue the guarantor several years after she has made the commitment. It may be that the guarantor no longer has a special relationship with the principal, for example following the break-up of the spousal union. On top of that, the guarantor exercises no power over the business of the principal in order to protect her interests. Thus, she does not control the amount of the debt, as interest, penalties and expenses may be added to it.

(iii) A feminist re-reading of O'Brien and Etridge.

A feminist re-reading of the *O'Brien* and *Etridge* cases asks questions such as: in what ways do these cases take into consideration women's various experiences? Do the cases examine the social context? What are the positive and negative effects of these decisions on women? Do these decisions make the guarantee contract an instrument of subordination or of empowerment for women? Let us address three aspects of the *O'Brien* and *Etridge* cases. First, these guarantees, which might lead to sexually transmitted debts, are characterized by the existence of a privileged relationship between the surety wife and her spouse. How does the House of Lords deal with that fact? Secondly, these contracts bring to the forefront the public-private sphere dichotomy and illustrate that the "personal is political". Thirdly, in searching for the adequate solution, the equality dilemma shows up. At the end, the issue of sexually transmitted debts raises the capacity of law to protect surety wives adequately.

(iv) A privileged relationship.

These guarantees, which might lead to sexually transmitted debts, are characterized by the existence of a privileged relationship between the "well-meaning" guarantor and the principal, who is a family member. In fact, the guarantor agrees to be bound due to the particular relationship of trust or friendship that she has with the principal. That affective relationship may beguile the signatory who can no longer appreciate the risks involved in the transaction or, although she is conscious of the risks involved, does not have the choice to refuse. In addition, the guarantor or co-borrower — be it a spouse, a father or a mother — gains no direct benefit from the transaction, which is to say that she does not touch the money or directly participate in the financial venture. In fact, the transaction is very disadvantageous for her. Her interest is instead indirect. She agrees to be bound for various reasons:[82] she does not wish to harm her spousal relationship; she wants to help her spouse obtain the loan; she

desires to ensure the well-being of her family; or she even hopes to maintain a friendship.

In *O'Brien*, Lord Browne-Wilkinson well understood the nature of these contracts based on matrimonial solidarity and the doubt they cast on the quality of the consent of the vulnerable party, the female spouse.[83] How can courts detect undue pressures exerted by the husband on the wife? How can courts adequately protect her? The House of Lords does not ask the lender to check the free and informed nature of [the] surety wife's consent. Rather the bank escapes quite easily from the situation: as long as the lender gets a certificate from a solicitor confirming that the guarantor has obtained independent legal advice, it will bear no responsibility. This solution might not be the best. It might become a pure formality. Independent legal advice does not settle the power imbalance in couples or families. Isn't the bank benefiting from this "love money"? Do banks need all the guarantees they ask for? Should banks refrain from demanding security from wives? In fact, until 1969, the Civil Code of Lower Canada prohibited a married wife from acting as a guarantor for her husband.[84] Should the guarantor be transformed into a co-borrower, thus making her legal obligations clearer? Shouldn't there be an obligation imposed on the bank to inform the guarantor? Are legal solutions the only ones? Can't we think of an information campaign on the legal consequences of a guarantee?

(v) The public-private sphere dichotomy.

Apart from the question of the female spouse being under pressure to sign, Lord Browne-Wilkinson's statement also raises the issue of the private nature of the contract. Courts have usually been reluctant to interfere with private matters. Feminist scholars writing about the public-private sphere dichotomy argue that it is a false dichotomy which confines women to the private sphere and keeps them in a subordinate position.[85] Feminist academics have shown the ways in which the legal system maintains and reproduces this dichotomy.[86] In the case of white middle class women, this division has prevented them from having access to paid labour, which has kept them economically dependent. In the past, the State has also refused to intervene in domestic violence cases because they were considered family matters.

Guarantee contracts are examples of what might be described as the "private in the private." First, according to the public-private sphere dichotomy, the contract may be seen as opposed to the family. A contract represents the "free market", which distinguishes itself from the "truly" private sphere, where contractual relationships are perceived as foreign. The family setting does not need legal mechanisms to settle matters. Solidarity, trust and love are enough. Do couples think of the legal consequences of marriage when they marry?[87] Secondly, but also as a consequence of the public-private sphere division, the contract is often characterized as part of the private. The contractual relationship still represents the consent of two persons to share obligations and the contract has a binding effect. In this sense, the contract is part of the private sphere.

Finally, in cases of contracts concluded in the family setting, the contract, which is part of the private realm, rules private relationships. The private sphere is even more private. The contract concluded in the family sphere would therefore be the quintessence of the private.[88] Thus one would expect the state to refuse to interfere for that reason. But, at the same time, the contractual rules coming from the public domain that are applied to the private sphere take the contract out of that private realm and put it in the public sphere.

The guarantee contract maintains the borders between the two spheres, but also breaks through them. It maintains the two spheres because it is a contract signed in the family context, far from the business world. But it also engages the public sphere because contractual rules apply to it and because assets benefiting the family, such as the family home, are used to finance a business, which is in the public sphere. The House of Lords in *O'Brien* and *Etridge* also breaches the public-private sphere dichotomy. By addressing the issue of the quality of surety wives' consent, the court places this question in the public sphere. The solidarity relationship and the power imbalance in the couple or in the family become public matters. The court has to deal with emotions, family pressures, informed consent, freedom to contract, personal decisions between spouses, family budgets, the ways banks deal with this issue, and the role of the lender in giving information. This situation illustrates that "the personal is political", as feminists have argued.[89]

(vi) The equality dilemma.

Lord Browne-Wilkinson's statement also underlines the equality dilemma. Women have achieved equality, are able to take enlightened decisions and do not need "special tenderness" from the law. However, the reality can often be different. Some wives still rely on their spouses for all financial matters and need some protection from the law. Lord Browne-Wilkinson's judgment reflects this tension.

On the one hand, he says that the wife-husband relationship does not automatically give rise to a presumption of undue influence (it is not a "category 2A" relationship), but on the other hand, he concedes that wives need protection.

This raises the issue of how much protection surety wives need. What would be a feminist solution? Feminism is not monolithic. Various solutions that can be called feminist, and which are designed to meet women's needs, may seem contradictory. On the one hand, some feminist reform proposals claim that the courts should become more interventionist in order to ensure real protection for women who assume the role of guarantor.[90] These feminists suppose, then, that women cannot give free and informed consent due to family pressures and that they have an increased need for protection. Obviously, some may criticize that approach for being too protectionist or paternalistic, treating women like minors, stripping them of responsibilities, supposing that they cannot give free and informed consent due to their matrimonial status, reducing them to their matrimonial status, and damaging their credit history. Not all female spouse-guarantors are victims of undue pressure from their spouse or the bank. They may have deliberately assumed the risk of helping their spouse. We must not fall into the trap of essentialism and impose a single model for women.

On the other hand, an equally feminist analysis may be less interventionist. Based on the beliefs that women are equal to men (from a formal point of view), that they have made a lot of progress, that they are no longer limited to the private sphere and that they are more knowledgeable about business, this other position does not claim any special protection for female spouse-guarantors beyond those that apply to all guarantors.[91] This more liberal solution is also imperfect. It maintains the *status quo*, adopts a formal approach to equality and assumes that current legal measures are sufficient to ensure the protection of guarantors.

This dilemma of identical treatment vs. different treatment which has, for a long time, divided feminists, is false because in both cases the male remains the model and ideal to be attained. Therefore, we should reject the abstract model of the individual who is detached from her social context, and who is able to read and understand all of the documents that she signs, who makes the best decisions, and who is able to negotiate.[92] One must think about this problem in a different way. If we want contractual equality to trump formal equality, the courts must take into account the nature of the guarantee and the position of the disinterested guarantors (whether they be spouses, parents or friends), and give particular attention to sexually transmitted debts. And this is what the House of Lords does in granting protection to surety wives in the *O'Brien/Etridge* cases.

But we must pinpoint the reason why the law should demonstrate "special tenderness" with respect to these women.[93] It is not a question of doubting the validity of their consent on the grounds that they would be incapable of understanding financial concepts or the wide-reaching effects of their acts. Those grounds, which reinforce the image of the servile wife, would indeed be degrading for women. Their freedom to consent must instead be closely examined due to the pressure created in the marital relationship by emotional and sexual bonds. Despite their experiences in the working world or the business world, which under other circumstances would make them more wary, female spouses trust their male partners. They do not think that their spouses wish to drag them into a risky financial venture. They sign, among other reasons, in order to preserve a healthy relationship, or a relationship that they know to be threatened, or even simply to indicate their support for their spouses.

(c) Conclusion

Are *O'Brien* and *Etridge* positive decisions for women from a feminist point of view? Yes and no. First, it is a good thing that the issue of sexually transmitted debt was raised in the House of Lords twice in a short period of time. It makes the issue a public one. Key elements of the private realm — the effect of emotions on the quality of the consent, matrimonial solidarity that at the end of the day benefits the lender, pressures coming from the spouse looking for money, the relations between banks and women — all become public. Secondly, the fact that the two decisions take account of the real social context is positive: women's condition has improved, but not for all. Some need protection. Thirdly, *O'Brien* and *Etridge* also offer a larger vision of the family beyond the traditional heterosexual family. The rules elaborated in the two cases apply to any relationship which is a non-commercial one.

However, the proposed solution — independent legal advice — does not solve all the problems because surety wives may understand the legal implications of their transactions but have no other choice. What about women who are not victims of undue influence, but family pressures? "They say that love is blind."[94] Independent legal advice does not seek to give a full picture of the financial situation of the spouse or his business. Other solutions may be necessary. There are also problems with the fact that the House of Lords has granted a "special protection" to surety wives and other persons involved in identical situations. Is it really a special protection any more? Isn't it now the general rule that has been changed in the case of non-commercial third party guarantees?